Taking SIDES

Clashing Views on Controversial Issues in World Civilizations

Second Edition

Taking
SIDES

**Clashing Views on
Controversial Issues in
World Civilizations**

Second Edition

Edited, Selected, and with Introductions by

Joseph R. Mitchell
Howard Community College
and
Helen Buss Mitchell
Howard Community College

Dushkin/McGraw-Hill
A Division of The McGraw-Hill Companies

For Jason, our first successful collaboration

Photo Acknowledgments

Cover image: © 2000 by PhotoDisc, Inc.

Cover Art Acknowledgment

Charles Vitelli

Manufactured in the United States of America

Second Edition

3456789BAHBAH32

Library of Congress Cataloging-in-Publication Data

Main entry under title:
    Taking sides: clashing views on controversial issues in world civilizations/edited, selected,
    and with introductions by Joseph R. Mitchell and Helen Buss Mitchell.—2nd ed.
        Includes bibliographical references and index.
        1. Civilization. I. Mitchell, Joseph R., *comp.* II. Mitchell, Helen Buss, *comp.*
                                                                                            901
    0-07-303195-X   ISSN: 1094-7582

PREFACE

In *Taking Sides: Clashing Views on Controversial Issues in World Civilizations*, we identify the issues that need to be covered in the teaching of world civilizations and the scholarly and readable sources that argue these issues. We have taken care to choose issues that will make these volumes multicultural, gender-friendly, and current with historical scholarship, and we frame these issues in a manner that makes them user-friendly for both teachers and students. Students who use these volumes should come away with a greater understanding and appreciation of the value of studying history.

One of the valuable aspects of this book is its flexibility. Its primary intended use is for world civilization courses, world history courses, and other courses that pursue a global/historical perspective. However, since more than half the issues in this volume focus on Western civilizations, teachers of Western civilization will be able to use these issues within the framework of their teaching and then assign the non-Western civilization issues as comparative studies or supplements for placing the Western materials in a wider context.

Plan of the book   This book is made up of 24 issues that argue pertinent topics in the study of world civilizations. Each issue has an issue *introduction*, which sets the stage for the debate as it is argued in the pro and con selections. Each issue concludes with a *postscript* that makes some final observations and points the way to other questions related to the issue. In reading the issue and forming your own opinions, you should not feel confined to adopt one or the other of the positions presented. There are positions in between the given views or totally outside them, and the *suggestions for further reading* that appear in each issue postscript should help you to find resources to continue your study of the subject. We have also provided Internet site addresses (URLs) in the *On the Internet* page that accompanies each part opener. At the back of the book is a listing of all the *contributors to this volume*, which will give you information on the historians and commentators whose views are debated here.

Changes to this edition   The first edition of this book comprised two volumes. This second edition has combined both volumes and has been extensively revised and updated. There are 10 completely new issues: *Does Alexander the Great Merit His Exalted Historical Reputation?* (Issue 3); *Did Same-*

Sex Unions Exist in Medieval Europe? (Issue 5); *Were the Crusades Motivated Primarily by Religious Factors?* (Issue 8); *Were Christopher Columbus's New World Discoveries a Positive Force in the Development of World History?* (Issue 10); *Were the Witch-Hunts in Premodern Europe Misogynistic?* (Issue 11); *Did the Meiji Restoration Constitute a Revolution in Nineteenth-Century Japan?* (Issue 15); *Were Indigenous Sex Workers Under British Imperialism Always Powerless?* (Issue 17); *Was Stalin Responsible for the Cold War?* (Issue 20); *Were Ethnic Leaders Responsible for the Disintegration of Yugoslavia?* (Issue 23); and *Will the Oslo Peace Accords Benefit Both Israelis and Palestinians?* (Issue 24). For one of the issues retained from the previous edition, the issue question has been significantly modified to focus the debate more sharply and the NO selection has been replaced: *Was German "Eliminationist Anti-Semitism" Responsible for the Holocaust?* (Issue 19). In addition, the following selections have been replaced in issues retained from the previous edition: the YES and NO selections for Issue 1 on the origin of *Homo sapiens*; the YES selection for Issue 4 on the liberation of women by Christianity. In all, 24 of the 48 selections in this second edition are new.

A word to the instructor An *Instructor's Manual With Test Questions* (multiple-choice and essay) is available through the publisher. A general guidebook, *Using Taking Sides in the Classroom*, which discusses methods and techniques for integrating the pro-con approach into any classroom setting, is also available. An online version of *Using Taking Sides in the Classroom* and a correspondence service for Taking Sides adopters can be found at http://www.dushkin.com/usingts/. For students, we offer a field guide to analyzing argumentative essays, *Analyzing Controversy: An Introductory Guide*, with exercises and techniques to help them to decipher genuine controversies.

Taking Sides: Clashing Views on Controversial Issues in World Civilizations is only one title in the Taking Sides series. If you are interested in seeing the table of contents for any of the other titles, please visit the Taking Sides Web site at http://www.dushkin.com/takingsides/.

Acknowledgments We would like to thank Larry Madaras of Howard Community College, fellow teacher, good friend, and coeditor of *Taking Sides: Clashing Views on Controversial Issues in American History*, for encouraging us to pursue a Taking Sides volume in world civilizations, for introducing us to the editorial team at Dushkin/McGraw-Hill, and for suggesting issues for us to pursue. We are also grateful to Jean Soto, Susan Myers, and the entire staff of the Howard Community College Library for their assistance with this volume. A special debt of gratitude goes to Shannon "Shan" Tenney, our good friend, who read every word contained here, caught many errors, and offered sage advice on the presentation of its content.

Special thanks go to Ted Knight, list manager for the Taking Sides series, and Juliana Poggio, developmental editor, who guided us through the publishing side of the book and gave encouraging words and positive feedback.

Joseph R. Mitchell
Howard Community College

Helen Buss Mitchell
Howard Community College

CONTENTS IN BRIEF

CONTENTS

Science researcher Christopher Stringer and science writer Robin McKie state that modern humans first developed in Africa and then spread to other parts of the world. Paleoanthropologists Milford Wolpoff and Rachel Caspari counter that modern humans developed simultaneously in different parts of the world.

Clinton Crawford, an assistant professor who specializes in African arts and languages as communications systems, asserts that evidence from the fields of anthropology, history, linguistics, and archaeology prove that the ancient Egyptians and the culture they produced were of black African origin. Assistant professor of archaeology Kathryn A. Bard argues that although black African sources contributed to the history and culture of ancient Egypt, the country's people and culture were basically multicultural in origin.

Professor emeritus of Greek N. G. L. Hammond states that research has proven that Alexander the Great is deserving of his esteemed historical reputation. Senior research fellow and lecturer E. E. Rice maintains that, other than his conquests, Alexander the Great left few tangible legacies to merit his exalted historical reputation.

Professor of religion and associate of the Institute for Antiquity and Christianity, Karen Jo Torjesen, presents evidence of women deacons, priests, prophets, and bishops during the first millennium of Christianity—all roles that suggest both equality and liberation for women. Professor of religious studies Karen Armstrong finds in the early Christian Church examples of hostility toward women and fear of their sexual power which she contends led to the exclusion of women from full participation in a male-dominated church.

Yale University history professor John Boswell states that same-sex unions, which date back to pagan times, existed in medieval Europe until they were gradually done away with by the Christian Church. Reviewer Philip Lyndon Reynolds, while admitting that "brotherhood" ceremonies took place in medieval Europe, asserts that these ceremonies did not have the same authority as sacred unions and therefore cannot be equated with marriage rites.

Professor of history and philosophy of education Mehdi Nakosteen traces the roots of the modern university to the golden age of Islamic culture (750–

1150 C.E.). He maintains that Muslim scholars assimilated the best of classical scholarship and developed the experimental method and the university system, which they passed on to the West before declining. The late historian Charles Homer Haskins (1870–1937) traces the university of the twentieth century to its predecessors in Paris and Bologna, where, he argues, during the twelfth and thirteenth centuries the first universities in the world sprang up.

Professor of anthropology Richard E. W. Adams argues that although military factors played a role in the Mayan demise, a combination of internal factors was more responsible for that result. Professor of anthropology George L. Cowgill contends that although there is no single explanation for the Mayan collapse, military expansion played a more important role than scholars originally thought.

German historian Hans Eberhard Mayer states that although there were other factors important to the development of the Crusades, the strongest motivation was a religious one. British historian Ronald C. Finucane counters that although the religious influence on the Crusades was significant, political, social, economic, and military factors in medieval Europe also played a role in their origin, development, and outcome.

Historian Mary R. Beard contends that during the Renaissance, Italian women
of the higher classes turned to the study of Greek and Roman literature and
committed themselves alongside men to developing well-rounded personalities. Historian Joan Kelly-Gadol argues that women enjoyed greater advantages during the Middle Ages and experienced a relative loss of position and
power during the Renaissance.

Historian Felipe Fernández-Armesto states that although Columbus was far
from perfect, the overall results of his work merit consideration as one who
helped to shape the modern world. Writer Kirkpatrick Sale sees Columbus
as a product of a sick, dispirited Europe and concludes that the selfish nature
and results of his voyages prevented Europe from using the New World
discoveries as an opportunity for the continent's salvation.

History professor Anne Llewellyn Barstow asserts that the European witch-
hunt movement made women its primary victims and was used as an attempt
to control their lives and behavior. History professor Robin Briggs states that
although women were the European witch-hunts' main victims, gender was
not the only determining factor in this sociocultural movement.

Professor of history William H. McNeill states that in 1500, western Europe began to extend its influence to other parts of the world, bringing about a revolution in world relationships in which the West was the principal benefactor. History professor Steven Feierman argues that because historians have viewed modern history in a unidirectional (European) manner, the contributions of non-European civilizations to world history have gone either undiscovered or unreported.

Historian Edward Shorter argues that employment opportunities outside the home that opened up with industrialization led to a rise in the illegitimacy rate, which he attributes to the sexual emancipation of unmarried, working-class women. Historians Louise A. Tilly, Joan W. Scott, and Miriam Cohen counter that unmarried women worked to meet an economic need, not to gain personal freedom, and they attribute the rise in illegitimacy rates to broken marriage promises and the absence of traditional support from family, community, and the church.

Peter Kropotkin (1842–1921), a Russian prince, revolutionary, and anarchist, argues that the French Revolution eradicated both serfdom and absolutism and paved the way for France's future democratic growth. History professor

Simon Schama counters that not only did the French Revolution betray its own goals, but it produced few of the results that it promised.

Professor Thomas M. Huber states that the Meiji Restoration produced revolutionary changes in nineteenth-century Japan. Examples of reforms that he asserts are the direct result of the Meiji Restoration are cited. It was the Chōshū leaders' dedication to change during this period that enabled these reforms to occur. Ruth Benedict, one of the twentieth century's leading anthropologists, argues that while substantive changes were brought to Japan by the Meiji Restoration, they were based on Japanese traditions that had been present for centuries.

History professor John King Fairbank makes the case that conservative forces, rooted in the Confucian virtues, subverted attempts by some to bring China into the modern world. History professor Jonathan D. Spence offers an economic analysis that draws on the ideas of Adam Smith and Karl Marx to explain China's initial failure to modernize and the role that foreign powers played in its eventual modernization.

British historian Denis Judd finds that throughout the British Empire sexual contact with "native" women was one of the perks of the imperial system. He documents the abuse and exploitation of indigenous sex workers, or prostitutes, calling it part of a pattern of conquest wherever the British flag was raised. Historian of African history Luise White interviewed indigenous sex workers in Nairobi, Kenya, and concluded that rather than being passive victims, these women acted as historical agents, doing through prostitution what in better times they would have done through marriage—stock their fathers' herds and keep livestock values competitive.

History professor Richard Stites argues that in the early years of the Bolshevik Revolution, the Zhenotdel, or Women's Department, helped many working women take the first steps toward emancipation. Film historian Françoise Navailh contends that the Zhenotdel had limited political influence and could do little to improve the lives of Soviet women in the unstable period following the revolution.

Professor of government Daniel Jonah Goldhagen states that due to the nature of German society in the twentieth century—with its endemic, virulent anti-Semitism—thousands of ordinary German citizens became willing participants in the implementation of Holocaust horrors. Holocaust scholar Christopher R. Browning argues that Goldhagen's thesis is too simplistic and that a multicausal approach must be used to determine why ordinary German citizens willingly participated in the Holocaust.

Historian John Lewis Gaddis states that after more than a half a century of cold war scholarship, Joseph Stalin still deserves most of the responsibility for the onset of the cold war. Historian Martin J. Sherwin counters that the origins of the cold war can be found in the World War II diplomacy involving the use of the atomic bomb, and he places much of the blame for the cold war on the shoulders of Franklin D. Roosevelt, Harry S. Truman, and Winston Churchill.

Professor of Middle East studies John L. Esposito sees the Iranian Revolution against Western-inspired modernization and Egypt's "holy war" against Israel as examples of the Islamic quest for a more authentic society and culture, which challenges a stable world order. Albert Hourani, an emeritus fellow of St. Antony's College, Oxford, finds hope for a stable world order in modern Islam's moderate position, which blends the traditional religious commitment to social justice with a more secular strain of morality and law.

Economics professor George B. N. Ayittey contends that since achieving independence, many African countries' interests have been betrayed by their own incompetent, corrupt, power-hungry leaders. Political science professor

Ali A. Mazrui argues that colonialism's legacy is at the root of many of the problems facing African countries today.

Career diplomat Warren Zimmerman, the United States' last ambassador to Yugoslavia, argues that the republic's ethnic leaders, especially Slobodan Milosovic, bear primary responsibility for the nation's demise. Political science professor Steven Majstorovic contends that while manipulation by elite ethnic leaders played a role in the disintegration of Yugoslavia, the fragile ethnic divisions within the country also played an important role in the country's demise.

Journalist Mark Perry was allowed access to major participants of the Israeli and Palestinian peace process. He states that, as a result of the Oslo peace accords, Israel is returning to its borders, as well as its ideals, and that Palestine is reinvigorating the movement for national independence. Columbia University professor Edward W. Said insists that peace was not achieved by the signing of the Oslo Agreement; instead, Israel achieved all its tactical and strategic objectives at the expense of the Arab and Palestinian struggle for national independence.

INTRODUCTION

World Civilizations and the Study of History

Helen Buss Mitchell

WHAT IS A CIVILIZATION?

What do we mean by the term *civilization*? Usually it designates a large group of people, spread out over a vast geographical area. In the modern world, we typically think in terms of nations or states, but these are a relatively recent development, traceable to sixteenth-century Europe. Before the rise of national states, the land that we call Europe belonged to a civilization known as Christendom—the unity of people ruled by the spiritual and temporal power of the Christian Church. At that time, other great civilizations of the world included China, Africa, India, Mesoamerica, and the Islamic Empire.

Civilization began about 5,000 years ago, when humans reached high levels of organization and achievement. When we look at world civilizations, we are considering the ancient and the contemporary versions of human alliances. Even in this age of national states, perhaps it makes sense to think of the West (Europe and North America) as a civilization. And the movement for European unity, which includes attempts to create a common currency, suggests that Europe may be thought of as a civilization despite its division into many separate nations. Postcolonial Africa is a continent of separate countries, and yet, in some ways, it remains a unified civilization. China, once a vast and far-flung group of kingdoms, has united as a civilization under communism. And Islam, which united the warring tribes of the Arabian Peninsula in the seventh century, is again defining itself as a civilization. What would be gained and what would be lost by shifting our focus from the national state to the much larger entity civilization?

Civilizations are systems for structuring human lives, and they generally include the following components: (1) an economic system by which people produce, distribute, and exchange goods; (2) a social system that defines relationships between and among individuals and groups; (3) a political system that determines who governs, who makes the laws, and who provides services for the common good; (4) a religious and/or intellectual orientation by which people make sense of the ordinary and extraordinary events of life and history—this may appear as a formal religious system, such as Judaism, Christianity, Islam, Buddhism, or Hinduism, or as an intellectual/values system, such as communism, Confucianism, or democracy; and (5) a cultural system, which includes the arts, and symbol systems, which give expression and meaning to human experience. Some of these components stand out more clearly than others in the selections in this volume, but all of them are present to one degree or another in every civilization.

WHAT IS HISTORY?

History is a dialogue between the past and the present. As we respond to events in our own world, we bring the concerns of the present to our study of the past. What seems important to us, where we turn our attention, how we approach a study of the past—all these are rooted in the present. It has been said that where you stand determines what you see. This is especially true with history. If we stand within the Western tradition exclusively, we may be tempted to see its story as the only story, or at least the only one worth telling. And whose perspective we take is also critical. From the point of view of the rich and powerful, the events of history take one shape; through the lens of the poor and powerless, the same events can appear quite different. If we take women as our starting point, the story of the past may present us with a series of new surprises.

Revisionism

History is not a once-and-for-all enterprise. Each generation will have its own questions and will bring new tools to the study of the past, resulting in a process called *revisionism*. Much of what you will read in this book is a product of revisionism in that the featured historians have reinterpreted the past in the light of the present. You will find that whereas one generation might value revolutions, the next might focus on their terrible costs. Likewise, one generation might assume that great men shape the events of history, while the next might look to the lives of ordinary people to illuminate the past. There is no final answer, but where we stand will determine which interpretation seems more compelling to us.

As new tools of analysis become available, our ability to understand the past improves. Bringing events into clearer focus can change the meanings that we assign to them. Many of the selections in this book reflect new attitudes and new insights made possible by the tools that historians have recently borrowed from the social sciences.

Presentism

Standing in the present, we must be wary of what historians call *presentism*, that is, reading the values of the present back into the past. For example, if we live in a culture that values individualism and prizes competition, we may be tempted to see these values as good even in a culture that preferred communalism and cooperation. And we may miss a key component of an ancient civilization because it does not match what we currently consider to be worthwhile. We cannot and should not avoid our own questions and struggles; they will inform our study of the past. Yet they must not warp our vision. Ideally, historians engage in a continual dialogue in which the concerns but not the values of the present are explored through a study of the past.

HISTORIOGRAPHICAL FOCUSES

All cultures are vulnerable to the narrow-mindedness created by *ethnocentrism*—the belief that one culture is superior to all others. From inside a particular culture, certain practices may seem normative—that is, we may assume that all humans or all rational humans must behave the way that we do or hold the attitudes that we hold. When we meet a culture that sees the world differently than we do, we may be tempted to write it off as inferior or primitive. An alternative to ethnocentrism is to enter the worldview of another and see what we can learn from expanding our perspective. The issues in this book will offer you many opportunities to try this thought experiment.

Stepping outside the Western tradition has allowed historians to take a more global view of world events. Accusing their predecessors of Eurocentrism, some historians have adopted a view of world history that emphasizes Africa's seminal role in cultural evolution. Also, within the Western tradition, women have challenged the male-dominated perspective that studied war but ignored the family. Including additional perspectives complicates our interpretations of past events but permits a fuller picture to emerge. We must be wary of universalism—for example, the assumption that patriarchy has always existed or that being a woman was the same for every woman no matter what her historical circumstances. If patriarchy or the nuclear family has a historical beginning, then there must have been a time when some other pattern existed. If cultures other than the West have been dominant or influential in the past, what was the world like under those circumstances?

The New Social History

Proponents of the new social history reject what they call "history from the top down." This refers to the previous generation of historians who had sometimes acted as if only the influential—often referred to as the "great man"—had a role in shaping history. Social historians assume that all people are capable of acting as historical agents rather than being passive victims to whom history happens. With this shift in attitude, the lives of slaves, workers, all women, and children become worthy of historical investigation. Social historians call this technique of examining ordinary people's lives "history from the bottom up."

Because the poor and powerless seldom leave written records, other sources of information must be analyzed to understand their lives. Applying the methods of social scientists to their own discipline, historians have broadened and deepened their field of study. Archaeological evidence, DNA analysis, the tools of paleoanthropology, and computer analysis of demographic data have allowed the voiceless to speak across centuries. Analyzing "material culture" (the objects that the people discarded as well as the monuments and other material objects they intended to leave as markers of their civilizations), for example, reveals to historians the everyday lives of people. At certain points in human history, to own a plow made the difference between merely surviving and having some surplus food to barter or sell. What people left to their heirs can tell us how much or how little they had while they lived. Fossil evidence and the analysis of mitochondrial DNA—the structures within cells that we inherit only from our mothers—may each be employed, sometimes with strikingly different results, to trace the migrations of preliterate peoples. As we continue to dig, for instance, we find our assumptions confirmed or denied by the fossils of once-living organisms. Evidence of sea life on the top of a mountain lets us know that vast geologic changes have taken place. And, in another example, our genetic material—our DNA—has information scientists are just now learning to decode and interpret that may settle important questions of origin and migration.

The high-speed comparative functions of computers have allowed historians to analyze vast quantities of data and to look at demographic trends. Consider this question: At what age do people marry for the first time or have a child? Looking at the time between marriage and the birth of a first child can help us to calculate the percentage of pregnant brides and to gain some insight into how acceptable or unacceptable premarital sex may have been to a certain population at a certain time in the context of an expected future marriage. If we study weather patterns and learn that certain years were marked by periods of drought or that a glacier receded during a particular time period, we will know a little more about whether the lives of the people who lived during these times were relatively easier or more difficult than those of their historical neighbors in earlier or later periods.

Race, Class, and Gender

The experience of being a historical subject is never monolithic. That is, each of us has a gender, a race, a social class, an ethnic identity, a religion (even if it is atheism or agnosticism), an age, and a variety of other markers that color our experiences. At times, the most important factor may be one's gender, and what happens may be more or less the same for all members of a particular gender. Under other circumstances, however, race may be predominant. Being a member of a racial minority or of a powerful racial majority may lead to very different experiences of the same event. At other times social class may determine how an event is experienced; the rich may have one story to tell, the poor another. And other factors, such as religion, ethnic identity, or even age, can become the most significant pieces of a person's identity, especially if prejudice or favoritism is involved. Historians generally try to take into account how race, class, and gender (as well as a host of other factors) intersect in the life of a historical subject.

ISSUES INVOLVED IN HISTORICAL INTERPRETATION

Often historians will agree on what happened but disagree about why or how something occurred. Sometimes the question is whether internal or external factors were more responsible for a happening. Both may have contributed to an event but one or the other may have played the more significant role. Looking at differing evidence may lead historians to varying interpretations. A related question considers whether it was the circumstances that changed or the attitudes of those who experienced them. For example, if we find that protest against a situation has been reduced, can we conclude that things have gotten better or that people have found a way to accommodate themselves to a situation that is beyond their control?

Periodization

The student of the past must wonder whether or not the turning points that shape the chapters in history books are the same for all historical subjects. The process of marking turning points is known as *periodization*. This is the more or less artificial creation of periods that chunk history into manageable segments by identifying forks in the road that took people and events in new directions. Using an expanded perspective, we may find that the traditional turning points hold for men but not for women or reflect the experiences of one ethnic group but not another. And when periodization schemes conflict, which one should we use?

It is also important to keep in mind that people living at a particular moment in history are not aware of the labels that later historians will attach to their experiences. People who lived during the Middle Ages, for example, were surely not aware of living in the middle of something. Only long after the fact were we able to call a later age the Renaissance. To those who lived during what we call the Middle Ages or the Renaissance, marriage, childbirth, work, weather, sickness, and death were the primary concerns, just as they are for us today. Our own age will be characterized by future historians in ways that might surprise and even shock us. As we study the past, it is helpful to keep in mind that some of our assumptions are rooted in a traditional periodization that is now being challenged.

Continuity or Discontinuity?

A related question concerns the connection or lack of connection between one event or set of events and another. When we look at the historical past, we must ask ourselves whether we are seeing continuity or discontinuity. In other words, is the event we are studying part of a normal process of evolution, or does it represent a break from a traditional pattern? Did the Industrial Revolution take the lives of workers in wholly new directions, or did traditional behaviors continue, albeit in a radically different context? Questions of continuity versus discontinuity are the fundamental ones on which the larger issue of periodization rests.

Sometimes events appear continuous from the point of view of one group and discontinuous from the point of view of another. Suppose that factory owners found their world and worldview shifting dramatically, whereas the lives and perspectives of workers went on more or less as they had before. When this is the case, whose experience should we privilege? Is one group's experience more historically significant than another's? How should we decide?

Public or Private?
Another consideration for historians is whether we can draw firm lines between public and private worlds. For instance, if a person is highly respected in private but discriminated against in public, which is the more significant experience? Is it even possible to separate the two? In the postindustrial world, women were able to exercise some degree of autonomy within the sphere of home and family. This might have compensated for their exclusion from events in the wider world. On the other hand, can success in the public sphere make up for an emotionally impoverished or even painful personal life? Every person has both a public and a private life; historians are interested in the balance between the two.

Nature or Nurture?
It seems plausible that our experiences within the private sphere, especially those we have as children, may affect how we behave when we move outside the home into a more public world. However, some of what we are in both worlds may be present at birth—that is, programmed into our genes. When historians look at the past, they sometimes encounter one of the puzzles of psychology and sociology: Are we seeing evidence of nature or nurture? That is, does biology or culture offer the more credible explanation for people's behavior through history? Do women and men behave in particular ways because their genetic makeup predisposes them to certain ways of acting? Or is behavior the result of an elaborate system of socialization that permits or rewards some actions while forbidding or punishing others? If people in the past behaved differently than those in the present do, what conclusions may we draw about the relative influence of nature and nurture?

The Power of Ideas
Can ideas change the course of history? People have sometimes been willing to die for what they believe in, and revolutions have certainly been fought, at least in part, over ideas. Some historians believe that studying the clash of ideas or the predominance of one idea or set of ideas offers the key to understanding the past. What do you think? Would devotion to a political or religious cause lead you to challenge the status quo? Or would poor economic conditions be more likely to send you into the streets? Historians differ in ranking the importance of various factors in influencing the past. Do

people challenge the power structure because they feel politically powerless, or because they are hungry, or because of the power of ideas?

A related question might be, What makes a person feel free? Is it more significant to have legal and political rights, or is the everyday experience of personal autonomy more important? If laws restrict your options but you are able to live basically as you choose, are you freer than someone who has guaranteed rights but feels personally restricted? And, again, does the public sphere or the private sphere exert the greater influence? Suppose that you belong to a favored class but experience gender discrimination. Which aspect of your experience has a greater impact? On the other hand, suppose you are told that you have full political and economic rights and you are treated with great respect but are prevented from doing what you like. Will you feel freer or less free than the person who is denied formal status but acts freely? In the quest to understand the past, these questions are interconnected, and they are becoming increasingly difficult to answer.

THE TIMELINESS OF HISTORICAL ISSUES

If you read the newspaper or listen to the news, you will find that there are a confusing number of present-day political, economic, religious, and military clashes that can be understood only by looking at their historical contexts. The role of the United States in world events, the perennial conflicts in the Middle East, China's emerging role as an economic superpower, the threat posed by religious fundamentalism, Africa's political future, the question of whether revolutions are ever worth their costs—these concerns of the global village all have roots in the past. Understanding the origins of conflicts increases the possibility of envisioning their solutions. The issues in this book will help you to think through the problems that are facing our world and give you the tools to make an informed decision about what you think might be the best courses of action.

In a democracy, an informed citizenry is the bedrock on which a government stands. If we do not understand the past, the present will be a puzzle to us and the future may seem to be out of our control. Seeing how and why historians disagree can help us to determine what the critical issues are and where informed interpreters part company. This, at least, is the basis for forming our own judgments and acting upon them. Looking critically at clashing views also hones our analytic skills and makes us thoughtful readers of textbooks as well as magazines and newspapers.

WHY STUDY WORLD CIVILIZATIONS?

At times it seems that the West's power and dominance in the world make its story the only one worth studying. History, we are sometimes told, is written by the winners. For the Chinese, the Greeks, the Ottoman Turks, and many other victors of the past, the stories of other civilizations seemed irrelevant, unimportant, and not nearly as valuable as their own triumphal sagas. The Chinese considered their Middle Kingdom the center of the world; the Greeks labeled all others barbarians; and the Ottoman Turks never expected to lose their position of dominance. From our perspective in the present, these stories form a tapestry. No one thread or pattern tells the tale, and all stories seem equally necessary for a complete picture of the past to emerge.

Any single story—even that of a military and economic superpower—is insufficient to explain the scope of human history at a given moment in time. Your story is especially interesting to you. However, as we are learning, any one story achieves its fullest meaning only when it is told in concert with those of other civilizations, all of which share an increasingly interconnected planet. As communications systems shrink the Earth into a global village, we may be ignoring the rest of the world at our own peril. At the very least, the study of civilizations other than our own can alert us to events that may have worldwide implications. And, as we are beginning to learn, no story happens in isolation. The history of the West, for example, can be accurately told only within a global context that takes into account the actions and reactions of other civilizations as they share the world stage with the West. As you read the issues that concern civilizations other than those of your heritage, stay alert for what you can learn about your own civilization.

The readings in this book will enrich your understanding of how the peoples of the world have understood themselves and their relationships with others. As we become a more multicultural society, we have an additional reason for studying about other civilizations that have blended with our own through immigration. Perhaps the biggest challenge for an increasingly diverse America is to understand its own role in world affairs and its relationship with other civilizations that may have different histories, value systems, and goals.

On the Internet . . .

Human Origins and Evolution in Africa
This Web site maintains links to Web sites on Africa,
evolution, and archaeology.
http://www.indiana.edu/~origins/

Fossil Evidence for Human Evolution in China
This site introduces the fossil evidence for human evolution in China. It includes a catalog of Chinese human
fossil remains; links to other sites dealing with paleontol-
ogy, human evolution, and Chinese prehistory; and other
resources that may be useful for gaining a better understanding of China's role in the emergence of humankind.
http://www.cruzio.com/~cscp/index.htm

Duke Papyrus Archive
The Duke Papyrus Archive provides electronic access to
texts about and images of 1,373 papyri from ancient
Egypt. *http://scriptorium.lib.duke.edu/papyrus/*

The Perseus Project
This Web site is a library of study materials on ancient
Greece created and edited by classics professor Gregory
Crane of Tufts University. *http://medusa.perseus.tufts.edu/*

PART 1

The Ancient World

Beginning with the question of the origins of humankind, this section covers the development of the world's earliest civilizations, and crosses over to the classical era. It analyzes and evaluates the origin and development of civilizations; the challenges they faced; how they responded to them; and, what resulted from that process. It is during this period that written history originated, and with it began the never-ending process of historical revisionism.

■ Did *Homo Sapiens* Originate in Africa?

■ Was Egyptian Civilization African?

■ Does Alexander the Great Merit His Exalted Historical Reputation?

■ Did Christianity Liberate Women?

ISSUE 1

Did *Homo Sapiens* Originate in Africa?

YES: Christopher Stringer and Robin McKie, from *African Exodus: The Origins of Modern Humanity* (Henry Holt & Company, 1996)

NO: Milford Wolpoff and Rachel Caspari, from *Race and Human Evolution* (Simon & Schuster, 1997)

ISSUE SUMMARY

YES: Science researcher Christopher Stringer and science writer Robin McKie state that modern humans first developed in Africa and then spread to other parts of the world.

NO: Paleoanthropologists Milford Wolpoff and Rachel Caspari counter that modern humans developed simultaneously in different parts of the world.

Where did we come from? This question strikes at the heart of human existence. For each individual, its answer provides an identity that no one else can share. When it is applied universally to all humankind, it can provide answers that go back to the origin of the species: How did we get here? From whom are we descended? How old are we? To what extent are we all related?

In the twentieth century, the origin of our ancestors was determined by the most recent fossilized discovery. With each time period, the location shifted from one part of the world to another, until the last generation's pioneering work placed the origins of our ancestors firmly in East Africa. But this answers only the origins part of the human puzzle. When did these "ancestors" evolve into *Homo sapiens*, and where did this occur?

Answers to these questions have come within the domain of scientists known as *paleoanthropologists*. Relying on fossil discoveries and the latest tools and methodologies used to analyze and evaluate them, these scientists have done much to provide information regarding the origins of humankind. But, recently, they have been joined in the quest by another group of scientists —molecular biologists (or molecular geneticists)—who have used advances in the study of DNA in their search for answers to the same questions.

In 1987 the latter group published their findings, thus firing the opening shots in what would be an interdisciplinary conflict within the scientific community. By examining the mitochondrial DNA, taken from the placentas of women representing every identifiable racial and ethnic group possible, they concluded that approximately 200,000 years ago, our earliest traceable human ancestor existed in Africa. This species migrated throughout the world, thus making Africa the birthplace of *Homo sapiens*. This is known as the "out-of-Africa" theory.

The popular media has picked up on the debate: articles in *Time, Newsweek*, the *New York Times*, and many other publications have publicized the new findings, naming our common ancestor "Eve" and proclaiming her to be "the mother of us all."

For a time, the DNA proponents seemed to dominate the world's attention with "Eve." But it did not take long for some paleoanthropologists to fire back. Claiming the reasoning of the DNA disciples to be flawed, they offered evidence to support a multiregional approach to the evolution of humankind, in which prehistoric creatures originated in Africa, migrated to other parts of the world, and then separately evolved into *Homo sapiens*. This has been referred to as the "multiregional" theory in regard to the origins of humankind.

Although the media has made this seem more like a battle between the old school paleoanthropologists and the new school molecular biologists than it really is, there are fundamental differences in the arguments developed by both sides that require further research and evaluation. In the April 1992 issue of *Scientific American*, the two sides squared off for a page-by-page debate on the subject. This was followed by the publication of several books on the subject, as each side attempted to gain the upper hand in this academic dispute. The two selections in this issue are taken from such books. Christopher Stringer and Robin McKie argue for the "out-of-Africa" theory by presenting DNA evidence to support their assertions. Milford Wolpoff and Rachel Caspari contend that the "multiregional" theory is more accurate by presenting what they perceive are flaws in the "out-of-Africa" theory.

It is hoped that the publicity generated by this debate will lead to further studies into the origins of humankind. Perhaps we will then be closer to definitive answers to the questions stated in the first paragraph of this introduction.

YES

Christopher Stringer
and Robin McKie

THE MOTHER OF ALL HUMANS?

It is not the gorilla, nor the chimpanzee, nor the orangutan, that is unusual.... Each enjoys a normal spectrum of biological variability. It is the human race that is odd. We display remarkable geographical diversity, and yet astonishing genetic unity. This dichotomy is perhaps one of the greatest ironies of our evolution. Our nearest primate relations may be much more differentiated with regard to their genes but today are consigned to living in a band of land across Central Africa, and to the islands of Borneo and Sumatra. We, who are stunningly similar, have conquered the world.

This revelation has provided the unraveling of our African origins with one of its most controversial chapters. And it is not hard to see why. The realization that humans are biologically highly homogeneous has one straightforward implication: that mankind has only recently evolved from one tight little group of ancestors. We simply have not had time to evolve significantly different patterns of genes. Human beings may look dissimilar, but beneath the separate hues of our skins, our various types of hair, and our disparate physiques, our basic biological constitutions are fairly unvarying. We are all members of a very young species, and our genes betray this secret.

It is not this relative genetic conformity per se that has caused the fuss but the results of subsequent calculations which have shown that the common ancestor who gave rise to our tight mitochondrial DNA lineage must have lived about 200,000 years ago. This date, of course, perfectly accords with the idea of a separate recent evolution of *Homo sapiens* shortly before it began its African exodus about 100,000 years ago. In other words, one small group of *Homo sapiens* living 200 millennia ago must have been the source of all our present, only slightly mutated mitochondrial DNA samples—and must therefore be the fount of all humanity. Equally, the studies refute the notion that modern humans have spent the last one million years quietly evolving in different parts of the globe until reaching their present status. Our DNA is too uniform for that to be a realistic concept....

Not surprisingly, such intercessions into the hardened world of the fossil hunter, by scientists trained in the "delicate" arts of molecular biology and genetic manipulation, have not gone down well in certain paleontological circles. The old order has reacted with considerable anger to the interference of these "scientific interlopers." The idea that the living can teach us anything about the past is a reversal of their cherished view that we can best learn about ourselves from studying our prehistory. Many had spent years using fossils to establish their interpretations of human origins, and took an intense dislike to being "elbowed aside by newcomers armed with blood samples and computers," as *The Times* (London) put it. "The fossil record is the real evidence for human evolution," announced Alan Thorne and Milford Wolpoff in one riposte (in *Scientific American*) to the use of mitochondrial DNA to study our origins. "Unlike the genetic data, fossils can be matched to the predictions of theories about the past without relying on a long list of assumptions." Such a clash of forces has, predictably, generated a good many sensational headlines, and triggered some of the most misleading statements that have ever been made about our origins. Scientists have denied that these genetic analyses reveal the fledgling status of the human race. Others have even rejected the possibility of ever re-creating our past by studying our present in this way. Both views are incorrect, as we shall see. Even worse, the multiregionalists have attempted to distort the public's understanding of the Out of Africa theory by deliberately confusing its propositions with the most extreme and controversial of the geneticists' arguments. By tarnishing the latter they hope to diminish the former. This [selection] will counter such propaganda and highlight the wide-ranging support for our African Exodus provided, not just by the molecular biologists, but by others, including those who study the words we speak and who can detect signs of our recent African ancestry there. We shall show not only that the majority of leading evolutionists and biologists believe in such an idea but that their views raise such serious questions about the multiregional hypothesis that its future viability must now be very much in doubt.

Unraveling the history of human migration from our current genetic condition is not an easy business, of course. It is a bit like trying to compile a family tree with only an untitled photograph album to help you. "Our genetic portrait of humankind is necessarily based on recent samplings, [and] it is unavoidably static," says Christopher Wills of the University of San Diego. "Historical records of human migrations cover only a tiny fraction of the history of our species, and we know surprisingly little about how long most aboriginal people have occupied their present homes. We are pretty close to the position of a viewer who tries to infer the entire plot of *Queen Christina* from the final few frames showing Garbo's rapt face."

It is an intriguing image. Nevertheless, biologists are beginning to make a telling impact in unraveling this biological plot and in understanding *Homo sapiens'* African exodus. And they have done this thanks to the development of some extraordinarily powerful techniques for splitting up genes, which are made of stands of DNA (deoxyribonucleic acid) and which control the process of biological inheritance....

[T]his is exactly what Allan Wilson, Rebecca Cann, and Mark Stoneking, working at the University of California, Berkeley, did in 1987. They took specimens from placentas of 147 women from various ethnic groups and analyzed each's mitochondrial DNA. By comparing these in order of affinity, they assembled a giant tree, a vast family network, a sort of chronological chart for mankind, which linked up all the various samples, and therefore the world's races, in a grand, global genealogy.

The study produced three conclusions. First, it revealed that very few mutational differences exist between the mitochondrial DNA of human beings, be they Vietnamese, New Guineans, Scandinavians, or Tongans. Second, when the researchers put their data in a computer and asked it to produce the most likely set of linkages between the different people, graded according to the similarity of their mitochondrial DNA, it created a tree with two main branches. One consisted solely of Africans. The other contained the remaining people of African origin, and everyone else in the world. The limb that connected these two main branches must therefore have been rooted in Africa, the researchers concluded. Lastly, the study showed that African people had slightly more mitochondrial DNA mutations compared to non-Africans, implying their roots are a little older. In total, these results seemed to provide overwhelming support for the idea that mankind arose in Africa, and, according to the researchers' data, very recently. Their arithmetic placed the common ancestor as living between 142,500 and 285,000 years ago, probably about 200,000 years ago. These figures show that the appearance of "modern forms of *Homo sapiens* occurred first in Africa" around this time and "that all present day humans are descendants of that African population," stated Wilson and his team.

The Berkeley paper outlining these findings was published in the journal *Nature* in January 1987, and made headlines round the world, which is not surprising given that Wilson pushed the study's implications right to the limit. He argued that his mitochondrial tree could be traced back, not just to a small group of *Homo sapiens*, but to one woman, a single mother who gave birth to the entire human race. The notion of an alluring fertile female strolling across the grasslands of Africa nourishing our forebears was too much for newspapers and television. She was dubbed "African Eve"—though this one was found, not in scripture, but in DNA. (The honor of so naming this genetic mother figure is generally accorded to Charles Petit, the distinguished science writer of the *San Francisco Chronicle*. Wilson claimed he disliked the title, preferring instead, "Mother of us all" or "One lucky mother.")

The image of this mitochondrial matriarch may seem eccentric but it at least raises the question of how small a number of *Homo sapiens* might have existed 200,000 years ago. In fact, there must have been thousands of women alive at that time. The planet's six billion inhabitants today are descendants of many of these individuals (and their male partners), not just one single super-mother. As we have said, we humans get our main physical and mental characteristics from our nuclear genes, which are a mosaic of contributions from myriad ancestors. We appear to get our mitochondrial genes from only one woman, but that does not mean she is the only mother of all humans.

"Think of it as the female equivalent of passing on family surnames," states Sir Walter Bodmer, the British geneticist. "When women marry they usually lose their surname, and assume their husband's. Now if a man has two children, there is a 25 percent chance both will be daughters. When they marry, they too will change their name, and his surname will disappear. After twenty generations, 90 percent of surnames will vanish this way, and within 10,000 generations —which would take us from the time of 'African Eve' to the present day— there would only be one left." An observer might assume that this vast, single-named clan bore a disproportionately high level of its originator's genes. In fact, it would contain a fairly complete blend of all human genes. And the same effect is true for mitochondrial DNA (except of course it is the man who is "cut out"). The people of the world therefore seem to have basically only one mitochondrial "name." Nevertheless, they carry a mix of all the human genes that must have emanated from that original founding group of *Homo sapiens*. It is a point that Wilson tried, belatedly, to make himself. "She wasn't the literal mother of us all, just the female from whom all our mitochondrial DNA derives." ...

And there we have it. The blood that courses through our veins, the genes that lie within our cells, the DNA strands that nestle inside our mitochondrial organelles, even the words we speak —all bear testimony to the fact that 100,000 years ago a portion of our species emerged from its African homeland and began its trek to world dominion. (The other part, which stayed behind, was equally successful in diversifying across the huge African continent, of course.) It may seem an exotic, possibly unsettling, tale. Yet there is nothing strange about it. This process of rapid radiation is how species spread. The real difference is just how far we took this process—to the ends of the earth. A species normally evolves in a local

ecology that, in some cases, provides a fortuitously fertile ground for honing a capacity for survival. Armed with these newly acquired anatomies, or behavior patterns, it can then take over the niches of other creatures. This is the normal course of evolution. What is abnormal is the supposed evolution of mankind as described by the multiregionalists. They place their faith in a vast global genetic link-up and compare our evolution to individuals paddling in separate corners of a pool.... According to this scheme, each person maintains their individuality over time. Nevertheless, they influence one another with the spreading ripples they raise—which are the equivalent of genes flowing between populations.

Let us recall the words of Alan Thorne and Milford Wolpoff....

They state that:

The dramatic genetic similarities across the entire human race do not reflect a recent common ancestry for all living people. They show the consequences of linkages between people that extend to when our ancestors first populated the Old World, more than a million years ago. They are the results of an ancient history of population connections and mate exchanges that has characterised the human race since its inception. Human evolution happened everywhere because every area was always part of the whole.

Gene flow is therefore crucial to the idea that modern humans evolved separately, for lengthy periods, in different corners of the earth, converging somehow into a now highly homogeneous form. Indeed, the theory cannot survive without this concept—for a simple reason. Evolution is random in action and that means that similar environmental pressures—be they associated with climate change, or disease, or other factors—often generate different genetic responses in separate regions. Consider malaria, a relatively new disease that spread as human populations became more and more dense after the birth of agriculture. Our bodies have generated a profusion of genetic ripostes for protection in the form of a multitude of partially effective inherited blood conditions. And each is unique to the locale in which it arose. In other words, separate areas produced separate DNA reactions. There has been no global human response to malaria.

Nevertheless, multiregionalism maintains that gene flow produces just such a global response. Given enough time gene exchange from neighboring peoples will make an impact, its proponents insist. This phenomenon, they say, has ensured that the world's population has headed towards the same general evolutionary goal, *Homo sapiens;* though it is also claimed that local selective pressure would have produced some distinctive regional physical differences (such as the European's big nose). And if the new dating of early *Homo erectus* in Java is to be believed (as many scientists are prepared to), then we must accept that this web of ancient lineages has been interacting—like some ancient, creaking international telephone exchange—for almost two million years.

Now this is an interesting notion which makes several other key assumptions: that there were enough humans alive at any time in the Old World over that period to sustain interbreeding and to maintain the give and take of genes; that there were no consistent geographical barriers to this mating urge; that the different human groups or even species that existed then would have wished to

have shared their genes with one another; and that this rosy vision of different hominids evolving globally towards the same happy goal has some biological precedent.

So let us examine each supposition briefly, starting with the critical question of population density. According to the multiregionalists, genes had to be passed back and forward between the loins of ancient hominids, from South Africa to Indonesia. And this was done, not by rapacious, visiting males spreading their genotype deep into the heart of other species or peoples (a sort of backdoor man school of evolution), but by local interchange. In neighboring groups, most people would have stayed where they were, while some individuals moved back and forward, or on to the next group as they intermarried. In other words, populations essentially sat still while genes passed through them. But this exchange requires sufficient numbers of neighboring men and women to be breeding in the first place. By any standard, hominids—until very recent times—were very thin on the ground. One calculation by Alan Rogers, a geneticist at the University of Utah, in Salt Lake City, and colleagues uses mitochondrial DNA mutations to assess how many females the species possessed as it evolved. The results he produced are striking. "The multiregional model implies that modern humans evolved in a population that spanned several continents, yet the present results imply that this population contained fewer than 7,000 females," he states in *Current Anthropology.* It is therefore implausible, he adds, that a species so thinly spread could have spanned three continents and still have been connected by gene flow.

[handwritten margin note: based on their mitochondrial DNA mutate!]

Then there is the question of geography. To connect humanity throughout the Old World, genes would have had to flow ("fly" might be a better word) back and forth up the entire African continent, across Arabia, over India, and down through Malaysia; contact would therefore have had to have been made through areas of low population density such as mountains and deserts, coupled with some of the worst climatic disruptions recorded in our planet's recent geological past. Over the past 500,000 years, the world was gripped by frequent Ice Ages: giant glaciers would have straddled the Himalayas, Alps, Caucasus Mountains; meltwater would have poured off these ice caps in torrents, swelling inland lakes and seas (such as the Caspian) far beyond their present sizes; while deserts, battered by dust storms, would have spread over larger and larger areas. Vast regions would have been virtually blocked to the passage of humans. At times our planet was extremely inhospitable while these straggling hordes of humans were supposed to be keeping up the very busy business of cozy genetic interaction. "Even under ecologically identical conditions, which is rarely the case in nature, geographically isolated populations will diverge away from each other and eventually become reproductively isolated.... It is highly improbable that evolution would take identical paths in this multidimensional landscape," writes the Iranian researcher Shahin Rouhani.

[Luca] Cavalli-Sforza agrees: "What is very difficult to conceive is a parallel evolution over such a vast expanse of land, with the limited genetic exchange that there could have been in earlier times." He acknowledges that it is theoretically possible that the genes of west European humans would have

been compatible with those of east Asia despite their ancient separation. Barriers to fertility are usually slow to develop: perhaps a million years or more in mammals. However, he adds, "barriers to fertility of a cultural and social nature may be more important than biological ones." Two very different looking sets of people may have been able to interbreed physically but would have considered such action as breaking a gross taboo.

In other words, we are expected to believe that a wafer-thin population of hominids, trudging across continents gripped by Ice Ages, were supposed to be ready to mate with people they would have found extraordinarily odd-looking and who behaved in peculiar ways. Cavalli-Sforza, for one, does not buy this. "Proponents of the multiregional model simply do not understand population genetics," he states. "They use a model that requires continuous exchange of genes, but it requires enormous amounts of time to reach equilibrium. There has been insufficient time in human history to reach that equilibrium." The spread of modern humans over a large fraction of the earth's surface is more in tune with a specific expansion from a nuclear area of origin, he adds.

Now this last point is an important one, for it is frequently presented in the popular press that the Out of Africa theory represents a divergence from the natural flow of biological affairs, that its protagonists are somehow on the fringes of orthodoxy, proposing strange and radical notions. The reverse is true—the large number of scientists quoted [here] indicates the wide intellectual support now accorded the theory. It is a very new idea, admittedly. It is only a little more than a decade since it was first proposed, on the basis of fossils, by scientists like [Gunter]

Bräuer and [Chris] Stringer. Yet its precepts now affect many areas of science, and its implications are accepted by their most distinguished practitioners. We are witnessing a rare moment in science, the replacement of a redundant orthodoxy by a formerly heretical vision. Hence the words of Yoel Rak as he staggered from a multiregionalists' symposium in 1991. "I feel like I have just had to sit through a meeting of the Flat Earth Society," he moaned.

Of course, Rak became an African Exodus proselytizer many years ago. A more damning convert, if you are multiregionalist, is that of *Science*, a journal noted for its dispassion and conservatism. "The theory that all modern humans originated in Africa is looking more and more convincing," it announced in March 1995, "and the date of the first human exodus keeps creeping closer to the present . . . the evidence coming out of our genes seems to be sweeping the field."

In fact, the idea that the opposition —the multiregionalists—represent the norm in biological thinking is to present the story of human origins "ass backwards," as Stephen Jay Gould succinctly puts it.

Multi-regionalism . . . is awfully hard to fathom. Why should populations throughout the world, presumably living in different environments under varying regimes of natural selection, all be moving on the same evolutionary pathway? Besides, most large, successful, and widespread species are stable for most of their history, and do not change in any substantial directional sense at all. For non-human species, we never interpret global distribution as entailing preference for a multiregional view of origins. We have no multiregional theory for the origin of rats or pigeons, two species that match our success and geographical spread. No one envisions proto-rats on all continents evolving together toward improved ratitude. Rather we assume that *Rattus rattus* and *Columbia livia* initially arose in a single place, as an entity or isolated population, and then spread out, eventually to cover the globe. Why uniquely for humans, do we develop a multiregional theory and then even declare it orthodox, in opposition to all standard views about how evolution occurs?

The answer to that critical question has much to do with an outlook that has pervaded and bedeviled science throughout history. We have, at various times, been forced to abandon species-centric scientific notions that we live at the center of the cosmos, and that we were specially created by a supreme being. A last vestige of this urge to self-importance can be seen in multiregionalism, which holds that our brain development is an event of all-consuming global consequence towards which humanity strived in unison for nearly two million years. It argues that *Homo sapiens'* emergence was dictated by a worldwide tendency to evolve large braincases, and share genes and "progress." Humanity is the product of a predictable proclivity for smartness, in other words, so we cannot possibly be the outcome of some local biological struggle. Surely that would demean us. To believe that humanity could be the product of a small, rapidly evolving African population who struck it lucky in the evolution stakes is therefore viewed as being worse than apostasy by these people. Unfortunately for them, there is little proof to support their specialist, global promotion of mankind—as we have seen. Once again we must adopt the simplest scientific explanation (i.e., the one for which the facts best fit) as the superior one. As this [selection] has made clear, there is no good genetic evidence to sustain an argument that places humanity on a plinth of global superiority. To do so is to indulge in mysticism. *Homo sapiens* is not the child of an entire planet, but a creature, like any other, that has its roots in one place and period—in this case with a small group of Africans for whom "time and chance" has only just arrived. Nor is our species diminished in any way by such interpretations. Indeed, we are enriched through explanations that demonstrate our humble origins, for they place us in an appropriate context that, for the first time, permits proper self-evaluation and provides an understanding of the gulf we are crossing from a clever ape to a hominid that can shape a planet to its requirements— if only it could work out what these are.

NO

Milford Wolpoff and Rachel Caspari

MULTIREGIONAL EVOLUTION AND EVE: SCIENCE AND POLITICS

WHAT IS MULTIREGIONAL EVOLUTION?

The fundamental question that has been asked historically is how people all over the world could evolve in the same way, all becoming modern humans, and yet maintain some regional differentiation for long periods of time. This is an observation, and the fundamental problem is how to resolve the contradiction that seems to lie at its heart. The genic exchanges between populations that would seem critical for one would seem equally destructive of the other. Confronted with compelling similarities between Australasian specimens separated by three quarters of a million years, and somewhat different similarities across perhaps an even longer time span in China, patterns of details not shared by fossils from other regions, Milford [Wolpoff], Alan [Thorne], and Wu [Xinzhi] developed a model to explain these sets of seemingly contradictory observations that have puzzled paleoanthropologists for close to a century—evidence of long-standing regional differences between human groups in the face of evidence of important global similarities in the direction of evolution....

Multiregional evolution provides resolution of the contradictions between genetic exchanges and population differentiations in a broad-based theory that links gene flow and population movements, and natural selection, and their effects on populations both at the center and at the peripheries of the geographic range of the human species. In a nutshell, the theory is that *the recent pattern of human evolution has been strongly influenced by the internal dynamics of a single, far-flung human species, internally divided into races. Human populations developed a network of interconnections, so behavioral and genetic information was interchanged by mate exchanges and population movements. Gradients along these interconnections encouraged local adaptations. These and other sources of population variation that depended on population histories developed, and stable adaptive complexes of interrelated features evolved in different regions. But, at the same time, evolutionary changes across the species occurred as advantageous features appeared and dispersed because of the success they imparted. These changes took on different forms in different places because of the differing histories of populations reflected in their gene pools, and the consequences of population placements in terms of habitat and their relations to other populations. Some evolutionary changes happened everywhere, because of these processes and because of common aspects of selection created by the extra information exchanges allowed by the evolving cultural and communications systems. Consequently, throughout the past 2 million years humans have been a single widespread polytypic species, with multiple, constantly evolving, interlinked populations, continually dividing and merging. Because of these internal divisions and the processes that maintain them, this species has been able to encompass and maintain adaptive variations across its range without requiring the isolation of gene pools. This pattern emerged once the Old World was colonized, and there is no evidence of speciations along the human line since then that would suggest there were different evolutionary processes, such as complete replacement, at work.*

Over the past decade Multiregional evolution has itself evolved into a broad and malleable frame. It is a *general* explanation for the pattern and process of human evolution within which virtually any hypothesis about dynamics between specific populations can be entertained, from the mixture, even replacement, of some populations to the virtual isolation of others. To be valid, the model must be able to incorporate a wide range of population dynamics, from expansion to extinction, leaving paleoanthropologists room to derive more detailed understandings of specific evolutionary patterns for particular times and places. Various groups of people behave in different ways that affect their de-

mographic structure (that is, the specific attributes of their population, such as its size, mortality rates, sex ratios, age profiles). If you are trying to predict patterns of evolutionary change, this demographic information is absolutely essential, since the major evolutionary forces of natural selection and genetic drift operate differently on populations with diverse demographic structures. As with all social animals, every human population has a different evolutionary story, with its own historical, biological, and social constraints that affect its evolution. The human evolutionary pattern is even more dynamic than that of other species, because cultural and linguistic factors are added to the list of constraints, even as they expand the different ways in which populations can exchange and share information. Culturally prescribed marriage systems, trading networks, religious practices, likes and dislikes, all affect reproduction, death, and breeding group size and therefore the evolution of these populations. Consequently, *detailed* understanding of the course and processes of human evolution is unusual, and can be obtained only for small temporal and geographic windows, where many ecological, demographic, and cultural variables are known. Multiregional evolution can be thought of as the structure in which these windows sit. It is compatible with all the windows we've looked through so far, a structure that allows them all to exist together. In other words, it is a model that fits the skeletal and genetic data we have today, and we also think it works in the past, where the information is much less precise, and there is much less of it.

Using the Multiregional model for interpreting the past assumes that the modern pattern of human evolution is the best model for interpreting the human condition ever since the first colonizations of the world outside of Africa began. If this assumption is valid, the present can be used as a model for explaining the past; this is the principle of "uniformitarianism" that the geologist Charles Lyell so successfully applied during the last century to interpreting the geological and paleontological record, work that was critical to Darwin's emerging theory of evolution. We consider this the most logical approach to understanding the recent pattern of human evolution, and treat it as the null hypothesis (the hypothesis of no difference, or no change, is the hypothesis to disprove, or try to disprove, with ongoing research and discoveries) for interpreting the past. It is the simplest hypothesis, one that models the evolutionary patterns of our behaviorally complex, geographically widespread predecessors after the living species most like them: our own.

We are quite aware that people have not always been the same. The evolutionary dynamics of modern humans are far from fully understood, and there are many factors in modern human populations that cannot be applied to the past. People have changed dramatically in recent times—their cultures have become incredibly complex, their demographics have altered remarkably, populations have expanded dramatically—and there is no way that evolutionary processes at work today can be expected to be identical with those of the past, just as the evolutionary processes at work today vary from population to population. But stepping away from the details, there is a frame of conditions these processes work within, and it is here that we draw the basis for applying the uniformitarian principle. It seems to us that the bases for approaching the past this way are twofold: we recognize no biological species formation in humanity once *Homo sapiens* appeared some 2 million years ago, and the fundamental shift from a solely African scavenging/gathering species to a colonizing species taking place at *Homo sapiens* origins or early in their evolution set up the conditions of polytypism across a broad geographic range that allowed Multiregionalism to work.

Thus Multiregional evolution is a gradualist model, with the primary tenet that humans *are* a single polytypic species and *have been* for a very long time into the past. It interprets the fossil record to show that human beings—that is, our species *Homo sapiens* and its main attribute *humanity*—happened only once, and once on the scene they evolved without a series of speciations and replacements. No speciation events seem to separate us from our immediate ancestors, and cladogensis, the splitting of one species into two, last characterized our lineage at the origin of *Homo sapiens* some 2 million years ago, when members of what we once called *"Homo erectus"* first appeared in East Africa. For 2 million years, from the end of the Pliocene until now, ancient and modern *Homo sapiens* populations are members of the same species. This doesn't mean they didn't change—*au contraire*—but we think these changes neither led to nor required a speciation. The broad-based evolutionary processes proposed in Multiregional evolution are formulated to explain patterns of variation *within* a polytypic species: the same evolutionary processes shown to be important in other polytypic species have shaped our patterns of diversity in the past and do so in the present.

The ability to account for all the data it is supposed to explain is only one hurdle for a hypothesis. It also must, at least in principle, be refutable. Multiregional evolution would be wrong, a disproved and invalid hypothesis, if the evolutionary changes it accounts for and the contradiction between genic exchanges and local continuity of features it resolves were explained instead by a series of successive speciations and replacements. Multiregional evolution would also be wrong if the pattern of human evolution it describes never existed—that is, if the interpretation of long-standing polytypism in the human fossil record is incorrect, since the explanations would then be elucidating a pattern that did not exist. Evidence of multiple speciations, indicating a different *pattern* of human evolution and, in particular, a recent speciation for modern humans, could provide this refutation, and the Eve theory claimed to rest on just such evidence.

So Eve came as a wake-up call for Multiregionalism. Although not particularly aimed that way at first, it was soon correctly perceived by all as the first serious attempt at its disproof, and for "Popperian" scientists, refutation is the key way that science proceeds. Milford is a deductionist, strongly influenced by the philosopher of science Karl Popper and most concerned with refuting hypotheses. The role of deduction comes after a hypothesis is framed; what matters most is whether it is explanatory, is testable, and requires the least number of assumptions. Multiregional evolution is our null hypothesis, the simplest and most explanatory hypothesis that covers the pattern of Pleistocene human evolution. But it was just recently developed, at least in its modern form, and until the Eve theory there were no significant attempts to disprove it.

After the publication of the 1984 paper, Alan, Wu, and Milford didn't think too much about Multiregional evolution in a theoretical way. Prior to the marketing of Eve, they had each proceeded to treat Multiregional evolution as a working hypothesis. Many others accepted the hypothesis as well, and research was initiated within a Multiregional paradigm, which in itself was not the focus of the investigations. As Multiregionalists studied human evolution, they were consciously aware of geographic variation and its confounding effects in understanding human evolution as a whole; Multiregional scholars were, and are, careful to view temporal trends as potentially regional phenomena and cautious not to generalize too quickly between one region and another, often avoiding a kind of ethnocentrism applied to the fossil record.

Before Eve, the few attempts to show species change in the recent human fossil record were focused on the seemingly unending Neandertal issue and were unconvincing to most scientists. Nothing effectively challenged the explanatory value of Multiregionalism as an explanation for worldwide change. As Alan made movies all over the world, the patterns of variation in the people he visited fit the Multiregional model. He collected and bred snakes, and the patterns of their variation fit the Multiregional model. Wu struggled with the long-awaited completion of his monograph on the Dali skull. Milford returned to focused, problem-oriented research. Always interested in patterns and causes of variation, he wrote papers on allometry, on sexual dimorphism, and on biomechanics, seeking explanations for trends that extended across broad periods of human evolution. But they all returned to issues of Multiregional evolution after the 1987 publication announcing what was soon widely called the Eve theory, and several publications following in the next year cited evidence that could refute the Multiregional model and our entire understanding of the human fossil record.

The Eve theory played *the* lead role in what quickly became a confrontation between paleontological and molecular genetic interpretations of the past. The development of Multiregionalism owes a great deal to her. When the Eve publications emerged, the Multiregional camp quickly responded to them, pointing out several problems that prevented them from refuting the Multiregional hypothesis. The Eve debates made us very introspective about our proposals and their implications. We were forced to think about Multiregionalism's development and testability and the things we think make it a good hypothesis....

THE POLITICIZATION OF EVE

Eve was new. Eve was modern. Eve was glamorous and sexy. Eve was a simple theory that made science reporting easy and fun. Eve gave answers and represented 20th-century technology providing answers—telling us about our origins. Eve implied the brotherhood of all humankind and was politically correct. Eve was perfect in every way, actually too good to be true. How is it that a theory so flawed could be embraced by so many? Why was she so uncritically accepted? The answer incorporates politics, and Eve gained political favor two ways: first by the appeal of new science, new technology, and new ideas replacing old-fashioned ones. It was a demonstration that public tax dollars were not really being misspent, that the results tell us some-

thing new about ourselves and something we can all understand. Second, it underscored the genetic unity of the human species, something we all need to be reminded of in the face of so many factious elements in our world. Both factors contributed to Eve's appeal to the public, and both entered the scientific discourse because science, in the end, is a human activity.

Unlike many scientific debates, where different sides may write quiet (or not so quiet) articles back and forth in professional journals for decades, the Eve debate quickly became politicized for a variety of reasons.... As the science of human origins has always been, this debate is public. It is sometimes pitched as a battle between the paleontologists (using archaic science) and the geneticists (modern scientists, exploiting the advantages of new techniques and modern technology), although this is far from true. Much hay is made over personal differences between the investigators in the different disciplines and even more over the differences in technology used. In a sense the fuss over Eve is an appealing topic because it illustrates the advantages of the modern age. Images are fostered of bright young geneticists using modern techniques the doddering old fossil hunters, ill prepared to understand, let alone participate in real science, cannot hope to. This is actually actively promoted by a few of the Eve researchers in statements such as those of [Allan] Wilson and [Rebecca] Cann in *Scientific American*, no less, where they contrast paleoanthropologists with "biologists trained in modern evolutionary theory" who "reject the notion that fossils provide the most direct evidence of how human evolution actually proceeded." Cann then held paleoanthropology in especially low regard, once saying "it is too much to hope the trickle of bones from fossil beds would provide a clear picture of human evolution any time soon." The paleoanthropologists themselves are portrayed as poor scientists engaged in circular reasoning. For instance Wilson and Cann quipped in *Scientific American*, "fossils cannot, in principle, be interpreted objectively... [paleoanthropologists'] reasoning tends to circularity."

In fact, there is nothing particularly difficult to understand about mitochondrial genetics, or the Eve position. We find the fuss over technology something less than relevant, since quality of science is not measured by the level of technology employed, but by the design of questions asked and testing methodology (not technology). Many people seem to believe something seen with the naked eye is less valid or scientific than something seen with a microscope, and the more powerful the microscope the more valuable the observation. But microscopes "showed" scientist after scientist that humans had 48 chromosomes, when they actually have only 46.

Scientists working today do have great advantages over their historical counterparts, and some of the advantage comes from technology and its applications in research. Advances in instrumentation are extremely beneficial, but by themselves do not make "good" science. In fact, there has been a real tendency for the technologies themselves to drive the direction of scientific research, as they become techniques in search of questions to answer. Real advantages we enjoy come from our recognition of the understandings arrived at by our predecessors and their incorporation into our consciousness, our world view. As Newton said of himself, "If I see so far, it is because I stand on the shoulders of giants." Multiregional evolution was only derived now, in spite of age-old grappling with many of the same problems, not because of the advance of technology, but because our world view has changed. The triumph of Darwinian thinking and an appreciation of population dynamics are actually very recent. Whatever insights we may have into the evolution of humans as a polytypic species are due to the influence on our thinking, both conscious and unconscious, of the prior work of others.

Misconceptions about the power of technology are generated by the press, not the geneticists (with one or two notable exceptions). For the most part, there are very good feelings between geneticists and paleontologists, two groups of scientists who study different data bases, but who sometimes ask the same questions of them. Both kinds of data can give us information about evolutionary history and relationships. One kind of data, whether from genes or bones, is not "better" than the other, and if data from different, independent sources seem to bring totally conflicting evidence to bear on a single question, it is not time to choose between them, but rather to see what is wrong with our hypotheses and methods of analysis.

There are other, far more serious ways than the technology issue in which the public aspects of the debate have influenced it, the positions taken by its participants, and its perceived outcome. These evolved over the question of political correctness. It is possible, as the late Glynn Isaac reportedly said, that Multiregional evolution holds the high ground on the political correctness issue because by positing an ancient divergence between races it implies that the small racial differences humans show must have evolved slowly and therefore are insignificant. But the high ground is widely perceived to be held by the Eve theory, not Multiregional evolution, and in any event Multiregional evolution does not mean that the modern *races* are particularly ancient: groups of features, not groups of populations, are ancient according to this model.

Even as the debate was first joined, Eve theorists claimed the high moral ground for themselves. In 1987 S. J. Gould wrote: "We are close enough to our African origins to hope for the preservation of unity in both action and artifacts." In 1988 he proclaimed: "Human unity is no idle political slogan... all modern humans form an entity united by physical bonds of descent from a recent African root." Of course, if the Eve theory means the *unity* of humankind, what could Multiregional evolution mean? And why should either side be more politically correct? A paper read by Fatimah Jackson at the 1994 meetings of the American Anthropological Association tars all of the modern human origins theories with typology and racism in one form or another. As she sees the debate, it begins with the presumption that there are typologically distinct races. She believes that this assumption is a reflection of Eurocentrism: the races must be distinct for Europeans to be distinct from the others. Writing with L. Lieberman, she goes on to conclude of all the theories, "Each... relies to varying degrees on static, typological definitions of human biological variation at some point in its analysis, and this reliance limits the explanatory power and utility of each model for understanding the origins and maintenance of human diversity."

Although there is much truth in what she says, Dr. Jackson misses a fundamental point. Far from having the same view on race and human variation, different views on these topics underscore the various theories of modern human origins. The different origins theories hold very different positions on how to model human variation, or race, and therefore on evolutionary pattern. Or perhaps it is the other way around: proponents of different origins theories have different ideas about evolutionary pattern, and this influences their views on race and modern human variation. Whatever the case, the two issues (race and modern human origins) are inextricably related. Multiregional evolution is clearly tied to race: it was developed to explain regional continuity which, given our own views of race, *should not exist*. But by accepting the existence of regional continuity, we recognize morphology that has been interpreted to both elevate and rank the importance of human differences, we believe incorrectly, with horrendous consequences. In order to understand the nature of the mutual influences of race and human evolution we need to examine how these mutual influences developed.... There, we can also find clues to the origins of modern predispositions toward one theory or another.

POSTSCRIPT

Did *Homo Sapiens* Originate in Africa?

The recent debate over human origins has been clouded by the emergence of race and political correctness as factors to be included in the equation. Those with Afrocentric viewpoints resist any attempt to deny Africa its status as humankind's place of origin, and they see racism as being behind any scheme to do so. See Milford Wolpoff and Rachel Caspari, *Race and Human Evolution* (Simon & Schuster, 1996), pp. 43–47, for an analysis of this current controversy. It is hoped that this diversion will not in any way obfuscate the search for answers to the questions inherent in this debate—questions that are important to an understanding of the origins of human existence.

This issue is a classic example of the influence that technology can have on an academic discipline and its work. New tools now make it possible for scholars to produce results that were only dreamed about a generation ago. But is it possible that too much importance can be placed on the tools and that the search for humankind's origins could end up a "tail wagging the dog" situation?

For further research, the April 1992 *Scientific American* articles would provide a brief, yet concise summary. Obviously, the Stringer/McKie and Wolpoff/Caspari books are the most recent definitive works devoted to the subject. In addition, Stephen J. Gould's *Dinosaur in a Haystack: Reflections in Natural History* (Harmony Books, 1995), pp. 101–107, offers an interesting update and commentary on the multiregional/out-of-Africa debate while leaning toward support for a common ancestry (probably African). Fossil hunter Richard Leakey and Roger Lewin, in *Origins Reconsidered: In Search of What Makes Us Human* (Doubleday, 1992), provide a balanced view of the debate and what might ultimately come from it in a chapter entitled "Mitochondrial Eve and Human Violence." In addition, James Shreeve's *The Neandertal Enigma: Solving the Mystery of Modern Human Origins* (Avon Books, 1995), is important when researching this subject, since the questions it raises provide insight to the question of the origin of Homo Sapiens.

Finally, Jean M. Auel's *Clan of the Cave Bear* (Crown, 1980) presents a fictional account of the "dawn of humankind" through the eyes of a woman. A film version of this work is also available.

ISSUE 2

Was Egyptian Civilization African?

YES: Clinton Crawford, from *Recasting Ancient Egypt in the African Context: Toward a Model Curriculum Using Art and Language* (Africa World Press, 1996)

NO: Kathryn A. Bard, from "Ancient Egyptians and the Issue of Race," in Mary R. Lefkowitz and Guy MacLean Rogers, eds., *Black Athena Revisited* (University of North Carolina Press, 1996)

ISSUE SUMMARY

YES: Clinton Crawford, an assistant professor who specializes in African arts and languages as communications systems, asserts that evidence from the fields of anthropology, history, linguistics, and archaeology prove that the ancient Egyptians and the culture they produced were of black African origin.

NO: Assistant professor of archaeology Kathryn A. Bard argues that although black African sources contributed to the history and culture of ancient Egypt, the country's people and culture were basically multicultural in origin.

For a place that is considered by many to be the birthplace of humankind, Africa has not been treated kindly by its global neighbors. Exploitation of every kind—culminating with the heinous Atlantic slave trade and resultant imperialism—has marked Africa's experiences with the outside world. Westerners, in particular, developed theories to prove African inferiority in order to justify their barbaric actions. No field of academic endeavor escaped this prejudicial treatment, and by the nineteenth century Africa had been totally denied its history, and its culture had been denigrated as savage and primitive.

It is not surprising, therefore, that when most of Africa gained independence after World War II, the continent's intellectuals sought to reaffirm their continent's rich and glorious past and to eradicate the onus placed upon them by Western historians and scientists. With assistance from African American scholars such as W. E. B. Du Bois, African historians—led by the Senegalese scientist and historian Cheikh Anta Diop—sought to write history from an African perspective in order to provide the continent with a positive account of its past. The Afrocentric view of history came of age during this time.

With archaeological discoveries suggesting that humankind originated in East Africa, it was natural for Africa's historians to explore the connections between black Africa and ancient Egyptian civilization. Their findings seemed to confirm the interrelatedness of the two. Hence, these historians concluded that one of the oldest and most respected ancient civilizations was African in origin.

But is this claim totally accurate? Many scholars today maintain that ancient Egypt possessed a cosmopolitan, multicultured society, one that was influenced by all of its neighbors. While acknowledging African influences on Egyptian society, these scholars hold that the claims of the Afrocentrists are too broad and historically inaccurate. In their opinion, to deny Egypt its multicultural past does a great disservice to all concerned parties.

In recent years, history has been used by some to promote racial or ethnic pride and solidarity. Although every group has a right to seek the glories of its past, exaggerations and false claims benefit no one. Those who have seen their past distorted beyond recognition, such as Africans and African Americans, maintain that they are merely rewriting their history to give credibility to what has been denied for centuries.

In the following selections, Clinton Crawford, using evidence from a variety of academic disciplines—history, linguistics, archaeology, anthropology, and art—argues that ancient Egypt was indeed African in origin. Those who believe so, he states, "share a common ideological concern, namely that the social and political histories of the Egyptians must be told truthfully." Kathryn A. Bard analyzes the same information and comes to a different conclusion —that ancient Egyptians were "North African peoples, distinct from Sub-Saharan blacks" and that anyone who claims that Egypt was a black or white civilization is promoting "a misconception with racist undertones that appeals to those who would like to increase rather than decrease the racial tensions that exist in modern society."

Clearly, the battle lines have been drawn in a scholarly debate that is likely to last well into the twenty-first century.

YES

Clinton Crawford

ORIGIN AND DEVELOPMENT OF THE ANCIENT EGYPTIANS

This [selection] discusses the origin, development, and interrelationship of the people and the culture of ancient Egypt. When people and their culture are viewed as reciprocal, we can understand more fully the evolution of a culture.

Slowly but surely, American academia is beginning to admit the centrality of Egyptian civilization and its sub-Saharan antecedents to the history of the arts and sciences. It is impossible to reprise this debate in any detail here, but let us at least develop the outlines of the discourse. It is also imperative that ancient Egypt be understood as a Black civilization if it is to be a source of self-esteem for African-Americans.

Consider the following oft-cited remarks from Count C. F. Volney's *Ruins of Empire:*

> There [at Thebes, ancient metropolis of Upper Egypt], a people, now forgotten, discovered, while others were yet barbarians, the elements of the arts and science. A race of men now rejected for their *sable skin and frizzled hair,* founded on the study of the laws of nature, those civil and religious systems which still govern the universe. (Volney 1991: 16–17)

This eighteenth-century scholar was puzzled by characterizations of the "Negro" slaves of the western hemisphere because they looked very similar to the indigenous Africans he met in Egypt. Volney attempted to prove that the indigenous Africans in Egypt were similar to the American "Negro" slaves on the basis of his description of the Sphinx of Gizeh. He described the monument's facial characteristics—a common determinant of racial origin—as identical with all people of the Black races.

Similarly, a contemporary of Volney, Baron Denon (1798), also sought the identity of the ancient Egyptians through an examination of the Sphinx. He described the portraits he examined as having the indigenous African characteristics—broad noses, thick lips, and wooly hair. Denon argues that his drawings document an accurate appearance of the Sphinx's head before

Napoleon's troops destroyed some of the evidence of its "Negroid looks" (ben-Jochannan, 1989, p. 14).

The list of historians and artists who affirm Volney's and Dennon's work is long. Among them are the German scholar and explorer Frobenius (1910), and Egyptian art historian Cyril Aldred (1956, 1961; 1962). On numerous occasions both scholars have made reference to the racial characteristics of the ancient Egyptians. Hopefully, Reba Ashton-Crawford's faithful rendering of the head of King Aha, or Narmer-Memes, together with the photograph of the Boston Museum of Fine Arts bust of Khafre, may help convert those who have been misled by the modern falsification that the makers of ancient Egypt were not Negroid and African.

Among other scholars on the long list, Cheikh Anta Diop, who is well known in the disciplines of history, egyptology, and anthropology, has advanced well-researched arguments in support of the position that the ancient Egyptians were Africoid and undoubtedly "black" in racial origin. Supporting Diop is Yosef ben-Jochannan, a renowned scholar of ancient and contemporary history and egyptology. Other supporters are Basil Davidson, Ivan Van Sertima, John Henrik Clarke, Chancellor Williams, Leonard Jefferies, Frank Snowden, and James Brunson.

Foremost, ben-Jochannan (1989) places the controversy in its historical context. Ben-Jochannan and Chancellor Williams (1976) argue that the ancient Egyptians were always referred to by the Greeks and Romans as people whose descendants came from the interior of Africa. He cites many examples from ancient texts which validate the point.

For example, Manetho (early and third century B.C.), a high priest of mixed Egyptian and Greek parentage, who wrote the first chronology of the Egyptian dynasties, testifies to the undisputed Negroid origin of the ancient Egyptians. Ben-Jochannan, as if unsatisfied with Manetho's accounts, recalls the many works of Herodotus which referred to the Egyptian as black. Herodotus observed that the probability of encountering men with black skin, woolly hair, without any other ethnic feature common of Negroes, is scientifically nil. To term such individuals as "whites" with black skin because of their fine features is no less absurd than the appellation "blacks" with white skin. If the absurdity of the latter is applied to three-fourths of the Europeans who lack Nordic features, then what can one conclude? Looking at these two appellations and their contradictions, one can conclude that a pseudo-scientific approach has given way to inaccurate generalization (History of Herodotus, p. 115). This decree by Herodotus is but one of many such testimonies by the Greek "father of history," who made many pilgrimages to Egypt in the fifth century B.C.

Over the span of several centuries, from the fall of ancient Egypt to sometime in the 1800s, classical authors of antiquity [cited by Anta Diop (1974) and ben-Jochannan (1989)] had no difficulty classifying the physical characteristics of the ancient Egyptians. Diop commends Aristotle (389–332 B.C.), Lucan the Greek (125–190 A.D.), Aeschylus (525–456 B.C.), Strabo (58–25 A.D.), and Diodorus of Sicily (63–14 B.C.), among many others, for bearing out this evidence about the ancient Egyptians. Each of the ancient historians usually included a graphic description of the ancient Egyptians. For example, Diodorus of Sicily described the Egyptians as follows:

> The Ethiopians say that Egyptians are one of their colonies which was brought into Egypt by Osiris.... It is from them that the Egyptians have learned to honor kings and gods and bury them with such pomp; sculpture and writing were invented by the Ethiopians. (Anta Diop, 1974, pp. 1–2)

Diodorus' account supports Herodotus' statement. Diop employs Diodorus' account to illuminate at least two plausible implications: (1) that Ethiopia is an older civilization than Egypt; (2) that the Egyptians were a different race than the Ethiopians. Diodorus seriously discussed the possibility of considering the ancient Egyptians to be either close neighbors (separated by a physical barrier—a cataract) or actual descendants of Black Africans (Ethiopians). Herodotus, in Histories II (457–450 B.C.) had stated that the Colchians, Ethiopians, and Egyptians bore all of the Negroid racial characteristics of thick lips, broad nose, woolly hair, and dark complexion—a statement that parallels Diodorus' observations, documented many years later.

Despite the testimonies of the ancients, ben-Jochannan and Diop also sought new data to support their position. Ben-Jochannan uses many strategies to advance his claims. Conspicuously, some of the strategies included examining the names and terminologies which the African Egyptians used to describe themselves and their country. He also reviews the works of some of the modern-day scholars who have advanced the claim of an Indo-European/Caucasian genesis for the ancient Egyptians. Furthermore, to counter what he regards as a deliberate attempt to discredit the contributions of a great Black civilization, ben-Jochannan cites the findings from Ellio Smith's examination of mummies from the tombs of Egyptian Royalty (1912).

Ben-Jochannan argues that before the Greeks imposed the name *Egyptos* on the people of *Alke-bu-lan* (modern day Africa), the linguistic and papyrological evidence show that the Egyptians called their land *Kimit, Kham, Ham, Mizrain,* and *Ta-Merry.* It cannot be coincidental, according to ben-Jochannan, that the same words chosen to describe the empire of the ancient "Egyptians" also refer to the land and its people as "children of the sun." The fact remains, these people were of dark pigmentation. And it is no mistake that even the Greek word *Egyptos* means "land of the dark people."

In addition to his linguistic and papyrologic evidence, ben-Jochannan cites that the Nile Valley and (African) Great Lakes High Cultures, peopled by Blacks of Egypt and its close neighbor Nubia, had an organized system of education called the Mysteries System.... At the height of ancient Egyptian culture, the Grand Lodge of Alexandria was known as the world center of learning. Those foreign to ancient Egypt who did not attend the main educational center received training at the "established subordinate Lodges of the Osirica—which was centered in the Grand Lodge at Luxor, Nubia" (ben-Jochannan, 1989, p. xxv). This puts into a new perspective the well-known fact that the Greek philosophers Socrates, Aristotle, and Pythagoras all testified to the education they received from the Egyptians.

Having established the ancient Egyptian preference for how they wanted to be called and the consistent testimonies of other ancients, ben-Jochannan focuses primarily on several examples of the racist hypotheses which are still used in academic circles as authentic scholarship on Africa, especially as it relates to Egypt.

To expose some of the racist hypotheses, ben-Jochannan examines several attempts to undermine the Negroid origin of the ancient Egyptians. The most striking appeared in the January 9th, 1972 issue of the *New York Times* in a report by Donald Janson of his interview with archaeologist Ray Winfield Smith, of the Museum of the University of Pennsylvania. The article concerned a computer reconstruction of a bas-relief sculpture in which Queen Nefertiti is shown with the same pear-shaped, elongated torso used to characterize her husband, pharaoh Akhenaten, and all other persons during their reign. Their stylized portrayal represented the aesthetic choice of King Akhenaten and Queen Nefertiti's reign—a shift away from the conventional royal portrayal to a more naturalistic style. In apparent ignorance of the aesthetic shift of the eighteenth dynasty, Smith interpreted Akhenaten's "long, narrow face, hatchet chin, thick lips, thick thighs and spindly legs" as the manifestation of apparent glandular trouble associated with the syndrome of "a physical monstrosity" (p. 12), namely, "an extreme case of destructive periodontal disease—badly abscessed teeth which results in long narrow face, thick lips, and hatchet chin." Moreover, he insisted that the outstanding and intelligent achievements of Akhenaten's reign, particularly monotheism, cannot be attributed to him. Instead, Smith credited Nefertiti (who is generally perceived to be of European extraction) with the idea of monotheism, and with the change of aesthetic canons in art. Janson goes on to quote Smith's speculation that the abnormali-

ties of Akhenaten are usually accompanied by sterility, so that Nefertiti's four daughters could not have been his. In his conclusion on Akhenaten, Smith compounded the pharaoh's plight by suggesting that Queen Nefertiti generally stood in her husband's shadow, an indication she had no need to embarrass him about his ineptness.

Winfield Smith's analysis of the Akhenaten bas-relief may not necessarily be racist, but rather one isolated incident plagued with errors. Ben-Jochannan, however, uses this article to illustrate the vicious, deliberate errors and the racism still leveled at people from Africa. He invites his readers to compare the facial characteristics of Akhenaten with those of all people indigenous to Africa and their descendants living in North America, the Caribbean, Brazil, and other parts of South America, and with the descriptions of the Egyptians by ancient Greek and Roman historians. Are we to understand that all those people who seem to fit Smith's description of Akhenaten were/are actually physically deformed?

In his quest to present further convincing evidence about the origin of the ancient Egyptians, ben-Jochannan uses some of the mummies presently on display at the Egyptian Museum in Cairo. These mummies represent many of the various facial types present in Egypt before and after the Dynastic periods. Referring to Smith's illustration, ben-Jochannan observes that most "reconstructions" of the ancient Egyptians we generally see are of the "C" type, which bears the facial characteristics of Europeans. Most people, however, if shown the majority of mummies and surviving sculpture in the round, would not have great difficulty deciding the racial origin of the ancient Egyptian. If ben-Jochannan has presented forceful and cogent evidence of the negroid origin of the ancient Egyptians, the findings presented in Anta Diop's great work, *African Origin of Civilization: Myth or Reality* (1974), are utterly convincing.

Like his contemporary ben-Jochannan, Diop presents evidence from the accounts of ancient Greeks and Romans. Beyond the ancients' testimonies, Diop employs several other approaches— linguistic, totemic, physical anthropology, microscopic analysis, osteological measurements, blood-group typing, cultural data, and the papyrus documents which illustrate how the Egyptians saw themselves. From the wealth of data Diop presents, I will focus on his scientific evidence, which has received the greatest attention from people in archaeology, anthropology, egyptology, history, and linguistics.

Diop (cited, Van Sertima, 1989) prefaces his argument by citing the theory of paleontologist Louis Leakey (cited, Diop, 1974), which has received general acceptance. Central to Leakey's theory is mankind's monogenetic and African origin. His evidence shows that man of 150,000 years ago was "morphologically identical with the man of today" and was "living in the regions of the Great Lakes of Africa, at the sources of the Nile and no where else" (p. 9). Justifying the morphological identity claim, Leakey advances two important points. First, it was out of pure necessity that the earliest men were "ethnically homogeneous and negroid" (p. 9). In defense of this assumption, Leakey uses Gloger's law, which posits that living organisms most likely adapt to their environment by developing characteristics peculiar to the given circumstances. In the case of human beings, Leakey insists, "warm blooded an-

imals evolving in a warm humid climate will secrete black pigment (eumelanin)" (p. 9). Leaky implies that if mankind originated in the areas of the tropics, around the latitude of the Great Lakes of Africa, then logic would lead us to conclude that early man of this region had a dark pigmentation. Consequently, those who moved to other climatic regions must have adapted appropriately. Accordingly then, he argues that the "original stock" was split into different races, and this is one possible conclusion. To ensure that his hypothesis is taken seriously, Leakey points to the geographical constraints of early man, identifying the only two routes available to early man for migration to other continents—the Sahara and the Nile Valley.

To support his position about the African origin of the ancient Egyptians, Diop (1974) uses the historical background of the Nile Valley route and the peopling of that Valley by Negroid races. In substance, although the evidence provided by the physical anthropologists can be used to build "reliable and definitive truths, and sound scientific conclusions," the criteria used to supposedly finalize a solution of this problem are arbitrary, thus giving way to "scientific hair-splitting" (p. 129). He cites many studies which exemplify the hair splitting of the varying percentage of negroid presence in the Valley from the distant prehistoric ages to predynastic times. Diop examines one of the conclusions in Emile Massoulard's *Histoire et protohistoire d' Egypt* (1949). Massoulard states that the Negadah skulls are said to belong to a homogeneous group and therefore can provide sufficient data for a general conclusion about the racial origin. He cites that the dimensions of the skulls' total height, length, breadth of face, nasal capacity and so forth, approximate that of the present-day negro. However, he insists that "the nasal breadth, height of orbit, length of palate and nasal index," seem similar to Germanic peoples. Generally, those who argue for the caucasian origin of the early Egyptians bypass the evidence which suggests negroid characteristics of predynastic Negadian people. Instead they focus almost exclusively on the few racial characteristics akin to the white races.

The other studies Diop cites include Thomson and Randall MacIver's 1949 study of skulls from El Amrah and Abydos, and Keith Falkenburger's recent study of 1,800 male skulls from the Egyptian populations ranging from predynastic to present day. Falkenburger's conclusions report 36 percent Negroid, 33 percent Mediterranean, 11 percent Cro-Magnoid, and 20 percent are estimated to be either Cro-Magnoid or Negroid. Falkenburger's percentage of Negroid skulls during the predynastic period of Egypt is higher than Thomas and Randall MacIver's findings of 25 percent men and 28 percent women.

Consequentially, Diop's analysis considers the discrepancies among the percentages of Negroid, Mediterranean, Cro-magnoids, and cross-bred individuals. He draws our attention to what is, perhaps, the most salient of all the arguments put forth. Common to all these arguments is that all bodies of evidence converge at a point which shows that the Egyptian population in the predynastic epoch was Negroid. In view of the common and convincing evidence about the Negro origin of predynastic Egypt, those who insist on arguments that the Negro presence came later remain suspect (Diop, 1974, pp. 129–131).

To further reverse the present-day hypothesis of "White African/Egyptians," Diop employs the science of microscopic analysis of skin to accurately define ethnic affiliation. Since melanin (eumelanin), which determines color of pigmentation, is known to be virtually indestructible, and the scientific community widely agrees that the melanin in animal skin and fossils has survived for millions of years, Diop reasons that the skin of the Egyptian mummies (unparalleled specimens of embalming technique) are prime subjects for melanocyte analysis. Although melanin is mainly found in epidermis, it also penetrates the epidermis and lodges in the dermis. For example, the sample of mummies examined from the Marietta excavation in Egypt shows a higher level of melanin than in any "white skinned races" (p. 125). He assures us that if a similar analysis is done on the best preserved mummies in the Cairo Museum, the result will parallel his findings, proving that the ancient Egyptian belongs to the black races.

Osteological measurements were also a part of Diop's scientific analysis. In physical anthropology, the measurement of bones is a more accepted criterion than craniometry for accurately determining the distinctions of race. In other words, by means of osteological measurement one can differentiate the racial characteristics of a white and a black. Citing the study of the distinguished nineteenth-century German scientist Lepsius, Diop reconfirms that the ancient Egyptians belong to the black races, for, even though physical anthropology has progressed in its methodology, Lepsius' findings have not been invalidated by the new approaches. For example, his notation of some specific characteristics unique to the Egyptian skeleton still stands unchallenged. Lepsius contends that the bodily proportions, especially the short arms, are consistent with the negroid or negrito physical type.

Further, in his quest to provide more substantive evidence for the identity of the ancient Egyptians, Diop examines the etymology of the pharaonic language to see what they called themselves. Connected to the idea of self-description, Diop finds only one term that was designated for this purpose. That word was *kmt*, which literally translated means "the negroes." It is, according to Diop, the strongest term existing in pharaonic language to indicate blackness. Likewise, the character used to symbolize the word *kmt* in hieroglyph is "a length of wood charred at both ends" and not "crocodile scale" (as is commonly misinterpreted). Actually, the word *kmt* is etymologically related to the well-known word *Kamit*, which is common in modern anthropological literature. Diop cautions, however, against the manipulation of modern anthropological literature, which seeks to distort the meaning of the word *kmt* to have it imply "white." To guard against misinformation, he redirects our attention to the authenticity of the pharaonic mother tongue where the word *kmt* meant "coal black." (For an extensive discussion of the grammar of the pharaonic language see his *The African Origin of Civilization* [1974])....

In divine epithets, according to Diop, "black" or "negro" was invariably used to identify the chief beneficent gods of Egypt. Thus, for example, *kmwr* means the "great Negro" (for Osiris). More importantly, *km* always precedes the names of the revered gods of Egypt: for example, Apis, Min Thot, Isis, Hathor, and Horus.

Many other scholars besides ben-Jochannan and Anta Diop who have succeeded in re-establishing the true origin of the ancient Egyptians also point out the African influence on the development of Greco-Roman civilization. Whereas it is not possible within the scope of this work to review many of those who have argued for the Negroid origin of the ancient Egyptians, I must not neglect to mention the challenging and thought-provoking work of Martin Bernal in *Black Athena* Volumes I and II (1987 and 1991, respectively). *Black Athena Volume I* is particularly important for establishing the racial origin of the ancient Egyptians and their contributions to a great civilization. Convinced by the archaeological findings for at least 7,000 years, he asserts that the Egyptian population comprised African, South-West Asian, and Mediterranean types. Furthermore, historically speaking, the farther south one moves along the Nile Valley, where the upper Egyptian Kingdoms had influence, "the darker and more negroid the population becomes" (p. 242). In fact, the darker and more negroid population is still dominant in these regions today.

Bernal's overall view of the ancient Egyptians is summarized in his introduction. He asserts that the Egyptian population was fundamentally African/Black and that the African dominance was remarkable in the Old and Middle Kingdoms before the approximately 150 years of Hyksos reign, which notably was restricted to Lower Egypt. Supporting the claim of African dominance, Bernal joins Basil Davidson and James Brunson (cited, Van Sertima, 1989) in affirming that the most important and powerful dynasties were I–IV, VI, XI–XIII, XVII–XVIII, and XXV, and that the pharaohs of these dynasties were black (Bernal, 1987, p. 242).

Notwithstanding that Bernal devotes little time to the racial origin of the ancient Egyptians, he echoes the views of Diop, ben-Jochannan, and others with respect to what the ancients thought of the Egyptians. He professes that the ancient Greeks unanimously agreed upon the cultural supremacy of the Pharoanic civilization. Judging from how eloquently and respectfully the ancients wrote about the Egyptians, Bernal believes, if it were possible for the Greeks to review some of the modern arguments that deny the Black African origin of ancient Egypt, they would rebuke the absurdity of early nineteenth-century scholarship. Bernal enforces his position by recalling the fact that the Greeks of the Classical Age went to Egypt to learn philosophy, mathematics, history, and many more arts and sciences. In short, Egypt was the center of learning.

Closely associated with the modern distortion of the ancient Egyptian racial origin, Bernal argues, modern racism and slavery figured prominently in the modern debasement of the negroid presence in early Egyptian civilization. Bernal suggests that those people who imposed the most brutal form of human degradation upon African people through the slave trade employed a strategy which included "proving" that Blacks were biologically incapable of creating a civilization as magnificent as Egypt. By thus establishing the so-called "biological truth," the perpetrators of racism and "continental chauvinism" were able to discount the genius of Black Egyptians and replace it with an Indo-Asiatic, white model of civilization. The mission, then, of many nineteenth- and twentieth-century historians was to maintain this status quo as "truth" despite many contradictions (Bernal, 1987, pp. 240–247).

The arguments presented here are a mere sampling of the voluminous body of findings that addresses the question of the racial origin of the ancient Egyptians. Ben-Jochannan, Anta Diop, Van Sertima, Bernal, and Williams are only a few of the modern scholars who have given credence to the testimonies of the ancients about the racial composition of the ancient Egyptians. The Greeks, in particular, maintained a reverence for the genius of the African civilization, Egypt, which was responsible for so many of their own cultural advancements.

By presenting convincing scientific evidence about the racial characteristics of the ancient Egyptians, Diop in particular helps write an important chapter in human history for the benefit of all people, especially downtrodden African peoples. The findings are overwhelmingly in favor of classifying the ancient Egyptians as belonging to the negro race.

Finally, in my arguments, I have used the work of contemporary observers—Volney, Denon, Aldred, ben-Jochannan, Chandler, Anta Diop, and museums with Egyptian art collections—who have presented written and photographic documentation about the physical characteristics of the ancient Egyptians. In every case that I have cited favoring the African/Negroid origin of the Egyptians, none of the sources sought to discount or discredit the importance of European civilization. In fact, the proponents of the African origin of Egyptian civilization share a common ideological concern, namely that the social and political histories of the Egyptians must be told truthfully. Those who are interested in having this truth told understand the need to recast Egypt into its rightful historical position. Diop and ben-Jochannan warn that the re-establishing of African history should not be used as a tool of divisiveness, but rather as a unifying force on behalf of all mankind.

This [selection] has addressed the reconsideration and accurate representation of the origin of the ancient Egyptians. In the discussion I have cited the findings of Yosef ben-Jochannan, Chiekh Anta Diop, and Martin Bernal. Generally speaking, the evidence of ancient Greek and Roman accounts affirms the African influence on ancient Egypt. In addition, scientific data from osteological measurement, eumelanin analysis, and cranium measurements independently support the argument that the ancient Egyptians were Black. As further evidence, the etymology of pharaonic language was examined to find out how the ancient Egyptians referred to themselves. Finally, photographic evidence of ancient Egyptian sculpture supplies mute yet eloquent testimony about the origin of the ancient Egyptians.

NO

Kathryn A. Bard

ANCIENT EGYPTIANS AND
THE ISSUE OF RACE

Egypt straddles two major geographical regions: the continent of Africa and the Middle East. Because it was located on the African continent, ancient Egypt was an African civilization, though perhaps its African identity has been subtly minimized within the discipline of Near Eastern studies, which has its roots in European Orientalism of the nineteenth century. Many earlier European scholars working in Egypt, particularly during the days of the British empire, assumed that ancient history began with Egypt and Mesopotamia—in other words, that the earliest civilizations were Near Eastern ones, and ancient Egypt could be understood as such (and not as an African civilization). Some scholars, such as Sir Flinders Petrie (1899, 10) and Walter Emery (Emery 1967, 39), assumed that civilization was introduced into Egypt by an invading dynastic race from southwestern Asia, who replaced the prehistoric hunters and gatherers and early farmers living along the Nile —peoples much too primitive to "invent" civilization.

It is now known that as the land bridge between Asia and Africa, Egypt was the recipient of earlier technological developments in southwestern Asia, especially agriculture. The major cereal cultigens, emmer wheat and barley, as well as the domestic sheep/goat, are species not known in their wild form in Africa; they were domesticated much earlier, in southwestern Asia, and only later introduced into Egypt (Wetterstrom 1993, 200). There is no archaeological evidence, however, to suggest that a large-scale migration of peoples from southwestern Asia brought farming into Egypt, and the mechanisms by which domesticated cereals and perhaps the technology of farming were introduced into Egypt remain unclear. But recent research on the Predynastic period in Egypt (ca. 4000–3000 B.C.E.), including my excavations near Nag Hammadi in Upper Egypt, has shown that the cultural roots of Egyptian civilization are indeed indigenous (Hoffman, 1988, 47).

Less clear, however, has been the issue of race in ancient Egypt. The modern concept of race was unknown to the ancient Egyptians. Non-Egyptians were identified by their ethnic/tribal affiliations or by the region/country from which they came. Most physical anthropologists in the second half of this century do not believe that pure races ever existed, and they view the concept of "race" as a misleading one for their studies (Trigger 1978, 27). But a number of Afrocentrists have claimed that black civilization began with ancient Egypt. The very title of Martin Bernal's *Black Athena* alludes to the putative roots of Greek—and therefore Western civilization—as a black African civilization in Egypt.

Ancient Egyptians were Mediterranean peoples, neither Sub-Saharan blacks nor Caucasian whites but peoples whose skin was adapted for life in a subtropical desert environment. Ancient Egypt was a melting pot; peoples of different ethnic identities migrated into the Nile Valley at different times in its prehistory and history. The question of whether ancient Egyptians were black or white obscures their own identity as agricultural peoples of *Kmt*, as opposed to *dšrt*, the barren "Red Land" of the desert. *Kmt* means "Black Land," the fertile floodplain of the lower Nile Valley, where cereal crops grew in such abundance. It does not mean "Land of Blacks."

Egyptians were Egyptians, the people of *Kmt*. The name points to the importance of the Nile in their lives. Unlike that of other early riverine civilizations, the Egyptian floodplain required no fallow time, nor was salinization of soils a problem with irrigation agriculture (Butzer 1976, 90). The economic base of pharaonic civilization was provided by the incredibly rich potential of cereal agriculture in the Egyptian Nile Valley. Egyptians were the indigenous farmers of the lower Nile Valley, neither black nor white as races are conceived of today.

Just who the ancient Egyptians were can be addressed by several types of evidence: language, historical records, the material culture, and physical remains (usually skeletons from burials). Evidence may be used to study cultural and biological relationships between different groups as well as within groups. For the most part, analyses of the different types of evidence have to be pursued independently, using different data because of the very different variables of such data; only after that can relationships between the different data be studied—within a specific cultural context.

Looking first at the linguistic evidence, there is nothing that links Egypt to other areas in Africa except very generally. Egyptian, the language spoken by the ancient Egyptians and written on monuments in hieroglyphs, evolved over more than four thousand years, to be finally replaced by Arabic following the Arab invasion in the seventh century C.E. Egyptian is classified by linguists as one of the five main groups of what is called the Afro-Asiatic language family. The other languages in this family include the Semitic languages spoken in southwestern Asia (including modern Arabic and Hebrew); Berber, spoken by Berbers in North Africa to the west of the Nile; the Chadic languages, spoken in northern Central Africa in the vicinity of Lake Chad; and the Cushitic languages spoken in the Horn of Africa, such as Galla in eastern Ethiopia (and probably covering Omotic; cf. Greenberg 1955, 43). Egyptian is so distinctly different from these languages in its structure and vocabulary as to be classified by itself. But it is more closely related to other languages in the Afro-Asiatic family than to any Indo-European languages or to the Bantu languages spoken today in Sub-Saharan Africa. In the New Kingdom (ca. 1558–1085 B.C.E.), when Egypt had an empire in southwest Asia, more Semitic words appeared in what is called Late Egyptian, but this can be explained by increased interaction with Semitic-speaking peoples, and not with other Africans (although that too certainly occurred). The linguistic evidence, then, points to the relative isolation of speakers of Egyptian in relation to other languages spoken in Africa.

Another important type of evidence for the study of ancient populations is from the physical remains that have been preserved in Egyptian burials. D. E. Derry, who studied the physical remains of Old Kingdom elites buried at Giza (excavated in the first decade of this century by George Reisner of Harvard University), took skull measurements and concluded, like Petrie and Emery, that the pyramid builders were a dynastic race of invaders, probably from the East, "who were far removed from any negroid element" (1956, 81).

As practiced by Derry, however, craniometry is no longer considered a valid statistical means for evaluating genetic relationships of ancient populations. A more recent analysis of nonmetrical variations in skulls (Berry and Berry 1973) suggests that the Egyptian samples show genetic continuity from Predynastic times through the Old and Middle Kingdoms—over two thousand years—with a shift in the New Kingdom, when there were considerable infiltrations of new peoples into the Nile Valley. In this same study the Egyptian skulls were then analyzed with samples from the northern Sudan (the Neolithic site of Jebel Moya), West Africa (Ashanti), Palestine (the site of Lachish), and Turkey (Byzantine period). Not surprisingly, the Egyptian skulls were not very distinct from the Jebel Moya skulls but were much more distinct from all others, including those from West Africa. Such a study suggests closer genetic affinity between peoples

in Egypt and the northern Sudan, which were close geographically and are known to have had considerable cultural contact throughout prehistory and pharaonic history. But the Egyptian and the Jebel Moya samples also seemed no more related to the samples from southwestern Asia in Palestine and Turkey than to modern (black) populations of West Africa (Berry and Berry 1973, 206).

Clearly more analyses of the physical remains of ancient Egyptians need to be done using current techniques, such as those Nancy Lovell at the University of Alberta is using in her work (see A. L. Johnson and N. Lovell 1994). Two problems, however, hinder such studies. First, graves in Egypt have been robbed since prehistoric times. Intact tombs, such as Tutankhamen's, are the great exception, and even his tomb had been penetrated twice in antiquity by robbers. Second, many skeletons excavated by earlier archaeologists working in Egypt were either not kept, or have been stored so poorly that today they are in very bad condition. The prehistoric burials that I excavated in 1978 at Naqada in Upper Egypt were sent off to storage in the basement of the Cairo Museum, never to be seen again. Even for the same age/sex group within a burial sample representing one small village community (in which there probably was some or even considerable intermarriage), there can be significant skeletal variability, and large samples need to be analyzed so that statistical findings will be valid. But nonskeletal features, which are the ones most frequently used to distinguish race today, have long since disappeared in the physical remains of burial—even when they have been mummified as in pharaonic Egypt (Trigger 1968, 11).

It is disturbing to me as an archaeologist that archaeological evidence—the artifacts, art and architecture of ancient Egypt—has been identified with race and racial issues. Racial issues, which in all fairness have arisen because of racial inequalities in the United States and elsewhere, have been imposed on the material remains of a culture even though these remains do not in themselves denote race. I am reminded of the excavation report of the Wellcome expedition at the site of Jebel Moya (Addison 1949). The English archaeologists who worked there in 1911–12 were certain that the advanced stone tools they excavated had to have been made by a prehistoric people who were white. This seems like a ridiculous conclusion today: stone tools thousands of years old cannot tell us the race of their makers any more than they can tell us what language their makers spoke.

The conventions of Egyptian art, as established by the beginning of the First Dynasty (ca. 3050 B.C.E.) do not represent humans as seen in perspective by the eye, but represent them in an analytic manner that transforms reality. The head, arms, and legs are drawn in profile; the torso is depicted frontally. Art may sometimes be grossly mannered and exaggerated, as it was during the reign of Akhenaten (ca. 1363–1347 B.C.E.) because of religious and cultural reforms conceptualized by that pharaoh. The conventions of Egyptian art were those of the crown and elites associated with the crown, and what is characteristic of Egyptian style in art for the most part represents a very small segment of the population.

Who and what were depicted on the walls of temples and tombs depended on Egyptian beliefs and ideology. Art was functional, and much of what is seen today in museums was created for the mortuary cult. Ancient Egypt was a class-stratified society, and age and sex in art were differentiated by scale of figures, style of dress, and symbols of status or office, as well as by skin tone. Statues and reliefs of women were painted in lighter tones of yellow ochre-based paint; men were painted in darker tones of red ochre-based paint. This is not to suggest that all Egyptian men were darker than all Egyptian women, but rather that established artistic conventions served to convey such ideas as sex differentiation. Such conventions, however, were not hard and fast rules, and there are many known exceptions. For example, in the tomb of Queen Nefertari, Rameses II's chief wife, the queen's skin is painted a brown (red ochre) color in a scene where she is playing a board game, as a contrast to the solid background of yellow ochre paint.

Non-Egyptian Africans, as well as Asiatics, were usually depicted in representational art as distinctly different from Egyptians, especially in their clothing and hairstyles. In the well-known scenes from the Eighteenth Dynasty tomb of Rekmire, Asiatics, Cretans, and Nubians are painted in registers bringing tribute to the court of Tuthmoses III. The Nubians, from the Nile Valley south of the First Cataract at Aswan, are painted in darker skin tones than the Asiatics, and are depicted with more prognathous jaws than the Egyptians. Bringing exotic goods and pets that originated in regions south of Nubia, the Nubians also carry gold ingots shaped into large rings. Nubia had little agricultural potential compared to Egypt, but rich gold mines were located there in *wadis* to the east of the Nile. That in part explains why Egypt occupied Nubia and built forts and temple towns there in the Middle and New Kingdoms.

Nubians bearing gold ingots and exotic tribute in paintings from the tomb of Huy (Thebes, no. 40), dating to the time of Tutankhamen, wear long, pleated Egyptian robes, but their hairstyles and large earrings are distinctly non-Egyptian. They have neck markings that may represent scarification, a practice unknown in ancient Egypt, and their facial features may possibly be interpreted as prognathous. In one scene an elite Nubian woman is depicted standing in a cart drawn by oxen, something in which Egyptian women would never have ridden. The Nubian tribute-bearers are painted in two skin tones, black and dark brown. These tones do not necessarily represent actual skin tones in real life but may serve to distinguish each tribute-bearer from the next in a row in which the figures overlap. Alternatively, the brown-skinned people may be of Nubian origin, and the black-skinned ones may be from farther south (Trigger 1978, 33). The shading of skin tones in Egyptian tomb paintings, which varies considerably, may not be a certain criterion for distinguishing race. Specific symbols of ethnic identity can also vary.

Nor are black Africans depicted by standardized conventions. The scenes of Queen Hatshepsut's expedition to the land of Punt, from her Eighteenth Dynasty mortuary temple at Deir el-Bahri, show a land very different from Egypt. Punt is thought to have been located along and to the west of the Sudanese/Eritrean coast (Kitchen 1993). The houses of the Punt peoples were hemispherical and built on elevated posts, unlike the rectangular mudbrick houses of Egyptians. Punt was the source of incense, ivory, and ebony, and tribute-bearers are seen carrying these goods to the seafaring Egyptians. A grossly obese "queen" of Punt is very unlike the lithe Egyptian upper-class women shown in tombs of this period. The "king" of Punt, whom she follows, is depicted in an Egyptian loincloth, but with a long and very un-Egyptian beard.

Though some Egyptian details appear, the ethnographic details in the Punt expedition scenes portray a culture that is distinctly non-Egyptian. But what race the Punt peoples were cannot really be determined from these scenes. Egyptian artists or scribes who accompanied this expedition recorded very distinctive ethnographic details, but the Puntites' facial features look more Egyptian than "black." Identifying race in Egyptian representational art, again, is difficult to do —probably because race (as opposed to ethnic affiliation, that is, Egyptians versus all non-Egyptians) was not a criterion for differentiation used by the ancient Egyptians.

As enemies of Egypt—peoples who threatened the boundaries of Egypt's kingdom—Nubians and Asiatics were depicted generically on the walls of Egyptian temples in the New Kingdom. The enemies of Egypt were shown as bound captives, being vanquished by pharaoh. On Egyptian temples in Nubia, reliefs showing such scenes must have had as one of their purposes the intimidation of local people. It was the duty of the king to destroy Egypt's enemies, and this is what is symbolized on the handle of a cane and on a footstool from Tutankhamen's tomb, both carved with generic Asiatic and Nubian captives. The Nubians carved on these two artifacts have very different facial features from those of the bearded Asiatics, but the facial features of both types of foreigners differ from the sculpture of Tutankhamen in the tomb.

Given that conventions for differentiating ethnic identity varied, as did artistic conventions for skin tones, anomalies in Egyptian art cannot be used with any certainty for drawing inferences about the race of ancient Egyptians. A limestone female head found in Giza tomb 4440, dating to the Fourth Dynasty (ca. 2613–2494 B.C.E.), is described in the catalogue of the Museum of Fine Arts in Boston as "of negroid type with thick lips, wide nostrils, and full cheeks" (W. S. Smith 1960, 35). A limestone head representing the woman's husband, also from tomb 4440, is distinctly different in its facial features: "the aquiline type of face so characteristic of some of the members of the Cheops family" (Smith, 35). Neither of these heads is painted, so their skin tones are unknown. The genre (called "reserve heads"), known only from the Fourth Dynasty, suggests more individualistic portraits than are usual in Egyptian art, and this female head "of negroid type" is different from other known reserve heads. As the identity of the person represented is unknown, her place in Egyptian society cannot be ascertained—though she certainly was a woman of high position.

A sandstone statue of Mentuhotep II, the king who unified Egypt and founded the Middle Kingdom in the twenty-first century B.C.E., was found in a pit to the east of the king's mortuary complex at Deir el-Bahri. The king is shown wearing a white robe and the red crown of Lower Egypt—and his skin is painted black. But as with analogous cases noted above, paint applied to a statue offers no real indication of his actual skin color. Black-painted skin could be symbolic of something of which we are unaware four thousand years later.

Perhaps better known than the painted statue of Mentuhotep II are the two New Kingdom figures of Tutankhamen that Howard Carter found guarding the entrance to that king's burial chamber. The black, resin-covered skin on these two wooden figures is contrasted by their gold skirts, sandals, headdresses, and jewelry (Reeves 1990, 128). These two black renditions of the king contrast the lighter-toned paintings of him on the walls of the burial chamber, and with the colored inlay on the back of the famous golden throne. Other art in this tomb likewise depicts a young man with brown skin, in keeping with Egyptian artistic conventions. Far from suggesting that the king had black skin, the two guardian figures of Tutankhamen may appear black simply because resin was applied to the skin areas. It is possible, too, that the resin was originally lighter and became dark over time. Resin, a costly and exotic import in ancient Egypt, was a material befitting a king who was to go to the afterlife displaying all forms of worldly wealth.

The people who lived south of Egypt are also known from archaeological evidence excavated in Nubia. From the fourth millennium B.C.E., when complex society evolved in Egypt, there is evidence in Lower Nubia of what archaeologists call the A-Group culture: people who traded with the Egyptians for Egyptian craft goods found in their burials. But with the founding of the First Dynasty in Egypt, ca. 3050 B.C.E., the newly unified Egyptian state penetrated into Lower Nubia, probably by military campaigns, and the A-Group disappeared there. Who the A-Group were in terms of race cannot be ascertained from the artifacts in their graves, but their locally made grave goods demonstrate a different material culture from that of the Predynastic Egyptians (Trigger 1976, 33).

From the Old Kingdom (ca. 2686–2181 B.C.E.) there is some archaeological evidence of small-scale Egyptian settlements in Lower Nubia, but by the late Old Kingdom a group of indigenous peoples, known to archaeologists as the C-Group, moved into Nubia as Egyptian occupation ended. After Egypt was re-unified during the Middle Kingdom (ca. 2040–1786 B.C.E.), large mudbrick forts were built along the Nile in the region of the Second Cataract (near the modern-day border of Egypt and the Sudan). But evidence of the C-Group in Lower Nubia is also known to date to the Middle Kingdom, and the C-Group culture actually survived the Egyptian withdrawal from Nubia at the collapse of the Middle Kingdom.

During the Middle Kingdom a powerful African polity arose whose capital was at Kerma near the Third Cataract in the Nile, in the northern Sudan. In Egyptian texts this culture is called "Kush." The eastern cemetery at Kerma was excavated by George Reisner, and artifacts from eight very large round tumuli are now in the Museum of Fine Arts in Boston (Reisner 1923a). These tumuli are of a different architecture than Egyptian tombs. Some of them, moreover, contained human sacrifices, not found in Egyptian burials (with the possible exception of the First Dynasty royal tombs at Abydos). A Swiss archaeologist currently excavating the town and cemetery at Kerma estimates that there are 30,000 to 40,000 burials (Bonnet 1992, 613). The sway of Kerma extended into Lower Nubia until the re-unification of Egypt at the beginning of the New Kingdom.

With Egyptian control in the New Kingdom extending as far south as Gebel Barkal near the Fourth Cataract, where a temple to the god Amen was built, the Kerma kingdom came to an end. Egyptians restored the Middle Kingdom forts in Lower Nubia and built temple towns farther south. But after the collapse of the New Kingdom, ca. 1085 B.C.E., a new Kushite power eventually arose at Gebel Barkal, where the cult of Amen continued to be practiced. The earliest burials in the royal cemetery at el-Kurru near Gebel Barkal (see Dunham 1950), also excavated by George Reisner, date to around 850 B.C.E. A hundred years later the first Kushite garrisons were established in southern Egypt during the reign of the Kushite king Piye, who later established his rule over all of Egypt (Trigger 1976, 140, 145). The Twenty-fifth Dynasty (ca. 760–656 B.C.E.), whose kings were all Kushites, ruled in Egypt for about sixty years. The later kings of this dynasty were frequently at battle with the Assyrian army, which finally succeeded in ending Kushite control in Egypt. Piye built the first pyramid tomb at el-Kurru, whereas in Egypt pyramids as royal burial monuments had not been built for a thousand years. Later Kushite kings were mummified, according to Egyptian custom, and spread the cult of Amen throughout Nubia.

The archaeological evidence of African kingdoms south of Egypt, at Kerma and Gebel Barkal, suggests distinctly different cultures that came into contact with Egypt. During the Twenty-fifth Dynasty the polity centered at Gebel Barkal actually controlled Egypt for a period. Cultural connections, if any, between the earlier Kerma kingdom and the later kingdom centered farther up the Nile at Gebel Barkal are uncertain, but the well-preserved burials recently excavated at Kerma by Bonnet (1992) provide a new source of information about Nubian populations.

Presumably the Kushites buried at Kerma and later at el-Kurru were related to the Nubians depicted in New Kingdom tomb paintings, as opposed to blacks living farther south in Africa, but once again the evidence seems ambiguous. Skin color, which is considered a criterion for race, cannot be determined from skeletal remains, and the evidence of representational art is problematic. The archaeological evidence at Kerma and el-Kurru points to African cultures that were different from Egyptian culture but that were responsible nonetheless for major cultural achievements. The Kushite peoples were considered non-Egyptians by Egyptians—in other words, ethnically different—but how physically different they were has yet to be determined by physical anthropologists. In any event, they are certainly better candidates for "black" African kingdoms than is ancient Egypt.

Culturally and linguistically the ancient Egyptians were different from other peoples living outside the Nile Valley, as well as those farther south and east. From textual and representational evidence it may be shown that ancient Egyptians had a sense of ethnic identity—of being Egyptian, as opposed to non-Egyptian. Today in Africa there are many different ethnic groups speaking many different languages. With the exception of South Africa, identity in Africa today is not by race or, for the most part, by nation, but by ethnic or tribal affiliation, which often has a close association with a spoken language or dialect. Ancient Egypt was definitely the earliest African civilization and as such certainly had an influence not only on the other cultures that arose in the Near East, but also on the states that arose farther south in Africa —at Kerma, Gebel Barkal, and later at Meroë. The evidence cited here strongly suggests that the ancient Egyptians were North African peoples, distinct from Sub-Saharan blacks. But to state categorically that ancient Egypt was either a black—or a white—civilization is to promote a misconception with racist undertones that appeals to those who would like to increase rather than decrease the racial tensions that exist in modern society.

POSTSCRIPT

Was Egyptian Civilization African?

It is sad that so much of the current debate regarding the origin of Egyptian civilization is influenced by today's volatile racial climate.

Afrocentrists consider the view that ancient Egypt had multicultural origins to be another attempt by Eurocentrist scholars to "whitewash" African history. Those who oppose the Afrocentric view of the origins of Egyptian civilization maintain that they are merely supporting the facts as they have been uncovered. These scholars assert that they fail to see how anyone can benefit from a distorted historical record, regardless of reason.

Martin Bernal's *Black Athena* (Rutgers University Press, 1987) brought renewed interest to the Egyptian/African debate, even though it was not his intention to do so. But his provocative title, which indicates African roots for the Greek goddess of wisdom, certainly caught the attention of Afrocentrists, who have embraced the book as supportive of their own views on the nature and origins of ancient Egypt. In a September 23, 1991, *Newsweek* article, Bernal suggested that "African Athena" might have been a more accurate title for his work. *Black Athena* is a difficult read, but a quick perusal of the work is a most enlightening experience, especially Bernal's exposure of the pro-Aryan bias of past scholars, which is the root of the problem here.

Support for the Afrocentric view of Egyptian civilization can be found in several books by Cheikh Anta Diop: *The African Origins of Civilization: Myth or Reality?* (Lawrence Hill Books, 1974); *Civilization or Barbarism: An Authentic Anthropology* (Lawrence Hill Books, 1981); and the chapter entitled "Origin of the Ancient Egyptians" in G. Mokhtar, ed., *Ancient Civilizations of Africa*, volume 2 of UNESCO's *General History of Africa* (University of California Press, 1981). A recent work which brings a popular touch to the subject is Richard Poe, *Black Spark, White Fire: Did African Explorers Civilize Ancient Europe?* (Prima Publishing, 1997).

The multicultural side of this debate can be found in a number of articles in *Black Athena Revisited* edited by Mary R. Lefkowitz and Guy MacLean Rogers (University of North Carolina Press, 1996). Lefkowitz, in *Not Out of Africa: How Afrocentrism Became an Excuse to Teach Myth as History* (Basic Books, 1996), deals mainly with the question of the Egyptian influence on Greek civilization, but she also devotes space to the issue of Egypt's early roots.

Two excellent videotape series that cover every aspect of the African experience and touch on the issue analyzed here are Ali A. Mazrui, *The Africans: A Triple Heritage* (Program 2, "Anatomy of a Continent"), and *Africa: A Voyage of Discovery With Basil Davidson* (Program 1, "Different But Equal").

ISSUE 3

Does Alexander the Great Merit His Exalted Historical Reputation?

YES: N. G. L. Hammond, from *The Genius of Alexander the Great* (University of North Carolina Press, 1997)

NO: E. E. Rice, from *Alexander the Great* (Sutton Publishing, 1997)

ISSUE SUMMARY

YES: Professor emeritus of Greek N. G. L. Hammond states that research has proven that Alexander the Great is deserving of his esteemed historical reputation.

NO: Senior research fellow and lecturer E. E. Rice maintains that, other than his conquests, Alexander the Great left few tangible legacies to merit his exalted historical reputation.

In the fourth century B.C.E. Greek city-states (poleis) were destroying themselves in a series of wars that have become known as the Peloponnesian Wars. Chronicled by Thucydides (460–400 B.C.), an eyewitness and participant, these wars showed the Greek polei at their worst—selfish, contentious, avaricious, and power-hungry. The result was a series of conflicts in which one side, Sparta and its allies, was able to defeat its enemy, Athens and the Delian League. Both sides suffered heavy losses and learned no lessons from the conflict. In their weakened, unenlightened state, they were easy prey to a strong, united Greek kingdom from the north—the Macedonians and their powerful king Philip.

The Macedonians were considered by the Greek city-states of the south to be barbaric. However, they had unification and military prowess on their side, and soon all of Greece was under their control. Philip was deprived of his chance for a more exalted place in history when he was assassinated by a bodyguard while participating in a festival in 336 B.C.E. He was succeeded by his son Alexander, then a young man of 19 years.

Alexander seemed to be destined for greatness. At an early age he displayed strong leadership and military skills. His father hired Aristotle as a tutor to help develop his intellectual side. Aristotle exerted a strong influence on the young man. Given the devious nature of Macedonian politics, Alexander's accession to his father's crown was not guaranteed. But he succeeded and within 14 years he conquered most of the then-known world. This earned him a place in history with the sobriquet—Alexander the Great.

Alexander's place in history was created immediately after his death. There were some who spoke of him as a divinity, even while he was alive, and the process continued through the next few centuries. The Romans, who featured likenesses of him in many of their art works, saw themselves in him as they began to follow in his footsteps, conquering much of the known world. The apex of his Roman reputation occurred when Plutarch (42–102 C.E.) wrote glowingly of him in his book *Lives*, claiming that Alexander was descended from Hercules. A few of the historical figures who engaged in Alexandrine-worship included Julius Caesar and Napoleon Bonaparte. Alexander has been featured in countless literary works from ancient to modern times.

What is the basis of Alexander's glowing historical reputation? Obviously, his conquests form its essence—but it is based on more than territorial accumulation. It is the story of the "philosopher-king," the cultured leader who attempted to create a cultural synthesis by fusing the best of the East and the West. It is the saga of an attempt by a man to create a "one world" ideal, a man trying to achieve the "impossible dream" and coming close to it.

For most of recorded history, humankind's story has been told through the words and deeds of its great men, and occasionally, great women. This is the "heroic" approach to the study of history. In the first part of the twentieth century, this version of history dominated. Historical figures such as Alexander still received favorable press. But with new tools of the trade, recently discovered materials and manuscripts, and perhaps a need to interpret history in a different vein, books about historically famous people have tended to be more critically inclined. How will Alexander fare in this new era? We will have to wait and see.

N. G. L. Hammond, who has written three books about Alexander, still finds much to admire in him, and deems him worthy of his historical appellation. On the other hand, E. E. Rice counters that Alexander's historical reputation may be undeserved due to the death and suffering caused by his military campaigns, and because he left little of permanent value as his legacy to the world.

YES

N. G. L. Hammond

THE PLANS AND PERSONALITY
OF ALEXANDER

ARRANGEMENTS AFFECTING THE
MACEDONIANS AND MACEDONIA

After the reconciliation in late summer 324 Alexander [the Great] offered his terms for any Macedonians who might volunteer to go home. They would be paid the normal wage up to their arrival in Macedonia, and each man would receive a gratuity of one talent. They were ordered to leave their Asian wives and children in Asia, where Alexander undertook to bring up the boys 'in the Macedonian manner in other respects and in military training'; and he said he would send them thereafter to their fathers in Macedonia. He made provision also for orphans of Macedonian soldiers in Asia. Some 10,000 Macedonians accepted these terms. 'He embraced them all, with tears in his eyes and tears in theirs, and they parted company.' They were being released from the campaign in Asia, not from military service. In summer 323 they reached Cilicia, where Alexander intended that they should winter. In spring 322 they were to be transported to Macedonia by his newly built fleet. By then Alexander expected to have completed his Arabian campaign and to be in Egypt or Cilicia. He was to be joined there by 10,000 Macedonians 'in their prime', who would be replaced in Macedonia by the returning veterans....

ARRANGEMENTS AFFECTING THE CITY-STATES

Alexander respected the sovereignty of the Greek Community in the settlement of affairs after the defeat of Agis and his allies, and he continued to do so, for instance by sending captured works of art to the states in the Greek Community. His conduct in these years indicates that the allegations of exceeding his powers as *Hegemon,* which were made in a speech 'On the Treaty with Alexander' in 331, were groundless. Within the Greek Community only one breach of the charter was reported in our sources, the expulsion of the people of Oeniadae from their city by the Aetolians. It happened perhaps in 325; for Alexander said that he himself would punish the Aetolians, presumably on his return to the West. In the years of peace a large number of Greek allies went east to serve in Alexander's army, and no doubt others emigrated to trade or settle in Asia. At Athens Phocion was re-elected general repeatedly as the advocate of compliance with the Charter, and Lycurgus used the prosperity which Athens enjoyed under the peace to complete the construction in stone of the auditorium of the theatre of Dionysus and to improve the naval shipyards.

In June 324, when Alexander was at Susa, one of his financial officers, Harpalus, fled to Greece in order to escape punishment for misconduct. He came to Cape Sunium with 5,000 talents, 6,000 mercenaries and 30 ships, and as an Athenian citizen (for he had been honoured earlier by a grant of citizenship) he proceeded to Athens and asked for asylum and in effect alliance against Alexander. The Assembly rejected his request. He and his forces went on to Taenarum in the Peloponnese, but he returned as a suppliant with a single ship and a large amount of money. The Assembly then granted him asylum as an Athenian citizen. Although he gave bribes freely in Athens, he did not win over the leading politicians. Meanwhile Antipater [general "with full powers"] and Olympias [handler of religious and financial affairs] made the demand that Athens as Macedonia's ally should extradite Harpalus; and envoys from Alexander came from Asia with a similar demand. On the proposal of Demosthenes the Assembly voted to arrest Harpalus, confiscate his money, and hold him and his money 'for Alexander'....

When his forces were assembled at Susa, Alexander announced to them that all exiles, except those under a curse and those exiled from Thebes, were to be recalled and reinstated.... The wording was as follows: 'Alexander to the exiles from the Greek cities... we shall be responsible for your return... we have written to Antipater about this, in order that he may compel any states which are unwilling to restore you.'... The purpose of Alexander was twofold: to resettle the floating population of exiles (we may call them refugees today), which caused instability and often led to mercenary service; and to reconcile the parties which had fought one another and caused the vicious circle of revolutionary faction.

Such an act of statesmanship was and is unparalleled. It affected almost all Greek city-states to varying degrees, and it hit Athens and Aetolia hardest. For Athens had expelled the population of Samos in 365 and occupied the island herself; and now, forty years later, she would have to restore the island to its proper owners. And Aetolia had to hand back Oeniadae to the Acarnanians she had expelled. At the time Alexander could not be accused of restoring his own partisans; for the bulk of the exiles had been opponents of the pro-Macedonian regimes in power. According to Hieronymus, an objective historian born around 364, 'people in general accepted the restoration of the exiles as being made for a good purpose'. In many states the restoration had taken place at the time of Alexander's death, but Athens and Aetolia were still making objections....

ALEXANDER'S BELIEFS AND PERSONAL QUALITIES

Alexander grew up in a kingdom which was continually at war, and he saw it as his duty to lead the Macedonians in war not from a distance but in the forefront of the fighting. He saw the destiny of Macedonia as victory in war, and he and his men made military glory the object of their ambitions. Thus he spoke of the victorious career of Philip [king of Macedonia (359–336 B.C.) and father of Alexander] as conferring 'glory' both on him and on 'the community of Macedonians'. His own pursuit of glory was boundless. As he declared to his Commanders at the Hyphasis, 'I myself consider that there is no limit for a man of spirit to his labours, except that those labours should lead to fine achievements.' He made the same demand on his Commanders and his men. They had committed themselves to following him when they had sworn the oath of allegiance (*sacramentum pietatis*), to be loyal and have the same friend and enemy as their king. If a man should be killed in his service, Alexander assured them that his death would bring him glory for ever and his place of burial would be famous.

Life was competitive for boys in the School of Pages and for boys being trained for the militia in the cities, and thereafter in civilian affairs and in the services. No Macedonian festival was complete without contests in such arts as dramatic performance, recitation of poetry, proclamation as a herald, and musicianship, and in athletic events which on occasion included armed combat. Alexander was intensely competitive throughout his life. He would be the first to tame Bucephalus [a wild horse], to attack the Theban Sacred Band [an army of the boldest Theban warriors, organized to fight the Spartans in 371 B.C.], to mount a city wall or climb an impregnable rock. He was the inspirer and often the judge of competition in others. He alone promoted soldiers and officers, awarded gifts for acts

of courage, bestowed gold crowns on successful Commanders, and decided the order in the hierarchy of military rank up to the position of Senior Friend and Leading Bodyguard. Competitions between military units and between naval crews were a part of training and of battle. Alexander himself believed that he must compete with Philip, Cyrus the Great, Heracles and Dionysus and surpass them all, and as Arrian remarked, 'if he had added Europe to Asia, he would have competed with himself in default of any rival.'

His belief in the superiority of Greek civilisation was absolute. His most treasured possession was the *Iliad* of Homer, and he had the plays of the three great tragedians sent to him in Asia, together with dithyrambic poems and the history of Philistus. They were his favourite reading. He admired Aristotle as the leading exponent of Greek intellectual enquiry, and he had a natural yearning (*pothos*) for philosophical discussion and understanding. His mind was to some extent cast in the Aristotelian mould; for he too combined a wide-ranging curiosity with close observation and acute reasoning. His belief in the validity of the Greek outlook of his time was not modified by his acquaintance with Egyptian, Babylonian and Indian ideas. One mark of Greek civilisation was the vitality of the city, both in Europe and in Asia, and Alexander believed that the best way to spread Greek culture and civilisation was by founding cities throughout Asia. At the outset the leaders in these cities were the Macedonians and the Greek mercenary soldiers, who conducted the democratic form of self-government to which they were accustomed. At the same time the future leaders were being educated 'in Greek letters and in Macedonian weaponry' in the schools which

Alexander established. The process was already well under way before Alexander died, as we see from a passage in Plutarch's *Moralia*: 'When Alexander was civilising Asia, the reading was Homer and the boys (*paides*) of the Persians, Susianians and Gedrosians used to chant the tragedies of Euripides and Sophocles... and thanks to him Bactria and Caucasus revered the Greek gods'. Egypt has yielded a teaching manual of the late third century, which was designed to teach Greek as a foreign language and included selections from Homer and the tragedians. The excavations at Ai Khanoum in Afghanistan have revealed Greek temples, theatre and odeum (for music) alongside a very large Asian temple in the late fourth century. Alexander was the standard-bearer of Greek civilisation. His influence in education and so in civilisation has been profound, extending even into our own age.

Faith in the orthodox religion of Macedonia was deeply implanted in Alexander's mind. He sacrificed daily, even in his last illness, on behalf of himself and the Macedonians and on innumerable other occasions. He organised traditional festivals in honour of the gods in the most lavish fashion. He believed as literally as Pindar had done in the presence in our world of the Olympian gods, in the labours of heroes such as Heracles and the exploits of Achilles, both being his ancestors. The deities made their wishes or their warnings manifest to men through natural phenomena and through omens and oracles, which were interpreted and delivered by inspired men and women. It was an advantage of polytheism that the number of gods was not limited, and Alexander could see Zeus in the Libyan Ammon and in the Babylonian Belus, and Heracles in the Tyrian Melkart or the Indian Krishna. His special regard for Ammon was probably due to the prophetic oracles which he received at Siwah and which were evidently fulfilled *in toto* when Alexander reached the outer Ocean. He gave thanks time and again to 'the usual gods' (the twelve Olympians) for the salvation of himself and his army, and he must have thought that he owed his charmed life to them. Even in his last illness he believed that his prayers in the course of sacrifices would be heard and that he would live. For he died without arranging for the transition of power.

Of the personal qualities of Alexander the brilliance, the range and the quickness of his intellect are remarkable, especially in his conduct of warfare. At Gaugamela and at the Hydaspes he foresaw precisely the sequence of moves by his own units and the compulsion they would place on his enemies. As Ptolemy, himself a most able commander, observed of the first campaign, 'the result was as Alexander inferred that it would be', and after the last campaign 'not a one of the operations of war which Alexander undertook was beyond his capability'(*aporon*). In generalship no one has surpassed him. Arrian wrote that Alexander had 'the most wonderful power of grasping the right course when the situation was still in obscurity'. Thus he knew on his landing in Asia that he must set up his own Kingdom of Asia and obtain the willing cooperation of his subjects. Already at Sardis he began the training of boys who would become soldiers of that kingdom. The orginality of his intellect was apparent in his development of the Indus, the Tigris and the Euphrates as waterways of commerce and his reorganisation of the irrigation of Mesopotamia. The boldness of his calculations was rewarded with success in many engagements and especially in the opening of navigation between the Indus Delta and the Persian Gulf.

His emotions were very strong. His love for his mother was such that one tear of hers would outweigh all the complaints of Antipater. He sent letters and gifts to her constantly, and he said that he would take her alone into his confidence on his return to Macedonia. His loyalty to the friends of his own generation was carried sometimes to a fault, and his passionate grief for Hephaestion [his closest friend from childhood days] was almost beyond reason. He loved his soldiers and they loved him; he and his veterans wept when they parted company; and he and they acknowledged that love in his last moments. When he killed Cleitus [an old-fashioned noble in a drunken brawl], his remorse was desperate. His compassion for the Theban Timoclea and for the family of [Persian ruler] Darius and his love for [wife] Roxane were deeply felt and led to actions which were probably unique in contemporary warfare.

As King of the Macedonians and as King of Asia he had different roles to fill. His way of life was on the same level as that of the Macedonians on campaigns and in leisure. As he said at Opis, his rations were the same as theirs and he shared all their dangers and hardships; and he enjoyed the same festivals and drinking parties as they did. He led them not by fiat but by persuasion, and a crucial element in that persuasion was that he should always tell them the truth, and they should know that he was telling them the truth. Thus he respected the constitutional rights of the Macedonians, and his reward was that he was generally able to convince them in their Assemblies that they should accept his policies. His role as King of Asia was almost the opposite. His court, like that of the Persian King of Kings, was the acme of luxury and extravagance. He gave audience in a huge pavilion which rested on fifty golden columns, and he himself sat on a golden chair, surrounded by so many richly-dressed guardsmen that 'no one dared approach him, such was the majesty associated with his person'. He accepted obeisance, and he ruled by fiat. The wealth at his command was beyond belief; for he had taken over the accumulated treasure of the Persian monarchy, and he received the fixed tribute which was paid by his subjects over a huge area. His expenditure was extraordinary by Greek standards, for instance on memorials commemorating Hephaestion, but it was in proportion to his wealth as King of Asia. The strength of his personality was such that he was able to keep the two roles separate in his mind and in his behaviour, and Ptolemy and Aristobulus were correct in seeing the real Alexander as Alexander the Macedonian.

Alexander combined his extraordinary practicality with a visionary, spiritual dimension which stemmed from his religious beliefs. As a member of the Temenid house he had a special affinity with his ancestors Heracles and Zeus, and he inherited the obligation to rule in a manner worthy of them and to benefit mankind. His vision went beyond Macedonia and the Greek Community. When he landed on Asian soil, his declaration, 'I accept Asia from the gods', and his prayer, that the Asians would accept him willingly as their king, were expressions of a mystical belief that the gods had set him a special task and would enable him to fulfil it. This spiritual dimension in his personality created in him the supreme confidence and the strength of will which overrode the resistance of the Macedonians to his concept of the Kingdom of Asia, and which convinced the Asians of the sincerity of his claim to treat them as equals and partners in the establishment of peace and prosperity. The power of his personality was all-pervading. It engaged the loyalty of Persian commanders and Indian rulers after defeat in battle and the loyalty of Asian troops at all levels in his service. It inspired *The Alexander Romance* in which Asian peoples adopted Alexander as their own king and incorporated his exploits into their own folk-lore. We owe to Plutarch [Greek writer and historian (45 A.D.–125 A.D.)], drawing probably on the words of Aristobulus, an insight into this spiritual dimension in Alexander.

Believing that he had come from the gods to be a governor and reconciler of the universe, and using force of arms against those whom he did not bring together by the light of reason, he harnessed all resources to one and the same end, mixing as it were in a loving-cup the lives, manners, marriages and customs of men. He ordered them all to regard the inhabited earth (*oikoumene*) as their fatherland and his armed forces as their stronghold and defence.

E. E. Rice

ALEXANDER THE GREAT

RETURN AND DEATH

The Departure from India

In the end, Alexander's schemes of further conquest were defeated by his army's refusal to go further, and he was forced to retreat and return to the west. The army retraced its steps back across the tributaries of the Indus to the Hydaspes, where a fleet of transport ships had been readied. The return journey took the troops south down the Indus to the sea. Arrian [a Greek historian] recounts the details of the trip in his *Indika*, based on the account of Nearchus, the admiral of the fleet. The flotilla suffered considerable damage in the fierce currents of the river. A sizeable force accompanied it by land along the banks of the Indus, receiving the submission of the local peoples or subduing them by force.

A particularly fierce campaign was waged in 326/5 BC against the Mallian people, a self-governing Indian tribe living on the east bank of the Indus between the Hydraotes and Hydaspes rivers. Numerous cities of the Malli were captured with great savagery, until their remaining combined forces, numbering some 50,000, converged upon a strongly defended city. Alexander encircled the city and mounted a siege against it. When the Macedonians had penetrated the city as far as the citadel, they mounted an attack scaling the walls by means of ladders. Alexander, leading from the front as always, mounted the wall but was isolated upon it in full view of the enemy when the ladder beneath him broke. Here occurred one of the most foolhardy acts of Alexander's career. So that he would not be such a visible target, the king leapt from the wall down into the city and engaged in hand-to-hand combat with the Indians within. A few Macedonians managed to come to his aid, but Alexander received a severe chest wound and finally became unconscious from loss of blood. The sources paint a vivid picture, with many variations, of his comrades fighting while standing over his body, one allegedly protecting him with the sacred shield from the Temple of Athena at Ilion (Troy).

In the end the attacking Macedonians broke through the wall of the citadel, and massacred every inhabitant they could find, including women and children. Alexander's unconscious body was retrieved and carried off to safety on his shield. This was not the first time that Alexander had been wounded during the course of the campaigns, but he somehow managed to survive this wound, which was by far the most serious he had received. Rumours of the king's death circulated the camp, which caused great lamentation, but in due course he was reunited with the main body of troops. Their joy was unbounded when they saw their king get up from a litter, walk, and mount his horse. Arrian records that Alexander was angry when some of his friends blamed him for taking risks, because he knew it to be true. The Malli surrendered unconditionally, and a Macedonian was appointed satrap over them. This campaign marked a new level in the savagery displayed by Alexander and his troops.

Throughout the remainder of 325 BC, the army proceeded south along the Indus river. Some of the forces travelled by ship, and others marched along the banks. More new cities and ship-stations were fortified, and Alexander received the surrender of several more Indian kings. Finally they reached Patala in the Indus delta, fortifying its citadel and constructing shipyards and docks to make it into a permanent port. The journey through this complex delta was not all smooth: on occasions the ships were damaged by storms, stranded by tides, and the captains were totally reliant on native pilots. Time was spent exploring the various mouths of the delta to find the most navigable branches for the fleet.

Alexander planned to send his fleet back west along the coast and up into the Persian Gulf to the mouths of the Tigris and Euphrates rivers. Some troops were sent back along a northern route through Afghanistan, but Alexander himself led a large detachment of troops overland in order to dig wells and stockpile provisions for the fleet as they put into land. They advanced through the Makran, ancient Gedrosia, attacking the Oritai and Gedrosian peoples and receiving their surrender as they went on.

The sixty-day march through this Gedrosian desert nearly spelled disaster for the expedition. The terrain is inhospitable in the extreme. The sources present a vivid picture of the suffering of the troops, who had little food and hardly any water. In order to stay alive they were forced to take a more inland route and send supplies to the coast for the fleet. The troops were reduced to pilfering sealed rations destined for the coast. It is reported that they feared imminent death from starvation more than punishment from their king. They endured unbearable heat and ceaseless thirst, and killed and ate their pack animals, pretending that the beasts had already died or had collapsed from fatigue. Many men were left behind to die since the wheeled vehicles could not traverse the terrain and had, in any case, few animals left to draw them. A disastrous flash flood in a dry gulley killed most of the women and children and the surviving animals. Alexander reputedly underwent the same torments as his men and was seen to pour on to the ground a helmet full of water since not all of his men could drink from it.

Many have argued that this ill-fated journey across the desert was one of Alexander's few major tactical mistakes, although others hold that the conditions were not really as dire as the sources paint them. The opinions of the ancient writers on Alexander's motives are intriguing.

Nearchus the admiral alone claimed that Alexander decided on this route through ignorance of its difficulty, but most writers claim that Alexander had heard that this desert had been crossed with an army only by Cyrus the Great (the founder of the Persian Empire) and the Assyrian Queen Semiramis, and that he aspired to emulate the achievements of these legendary figures. I would argue that either ignorance of conditions or a romantic whim points to a serious lapse of judgement. In any event, Alexander was lucky that some of his troops survived.

The army rested at the end of their desert crossing, and went on through the region of Carmania (between Gedrosia and Iran). Most sources record a celebratory revel of colossal scale, with musical and athletic events witnessed by drunken troops drawn along on carts adorned as Dionysiac bowers. Arrian states clearly that he does not believe such reports, but the comparisons between Alexander's expedition to India and that of Dionysus have already been noted (elsewhere). Nor should we underestimate the relief expressed by men who had nearly died in the desert and who were given the chance to celebrate freely after months of deprivation.

Alexander and his troops returned to the heartland of Persia during 324. This journey is described briefly in the sources, but it is marked by Alexander's harsh punishment of both Macedonian and Persian satraps who were accused of disobedience or corruption as he passed through. Many no doubt had never expected Alexander to return, and had taken upon themselves extreme powers amounting to royal prerogatives. Alexander could not tolerate this, and executed several officials in what has

been likened to a 'reign of terror' (the phrase used by the eminent historian Ernst Badian). Regardless of what these actions reveal about Alexander's increasingly autocratic behaviour and deteriorating temperament, they clearly demonstrate the fragility of the administrative arrangements he had put into place on his outward journey.

Alexander reached the royal Persian city of Pasargadae, where he was enraged to see the defilement of the tomb of Cyrus the Great. He appointed Aristoboulos, one of Arrian's two main historical sources, as overseer of its restoration. This is a further indication of the regard in which he held King Cyrus, who was exempt from the stigma of the later Persian Wars in Greece. He returned to Persepolis, which his troops had already looted and burnt, hanging the acting satrap and punishing others on his way.

In 324 BC they reached the royal city of Susa, and here Alexander staged a mass wedding of his highest-ranking officers to native ladies of noble birth. Alexander (who was already married to the Bactrian Rhoxane) also married Statira, the eldest daughter of Darius, and another Persian lady as well. We are told specifically that the ceremonies were in the Persian style. In addition, some 10,000 Macedonians who had already 'married' Asian women registered them and were given generous wedding gifts. It would appear that Alexander was urging a policy of racial fusion between Persians and Macedonians and the creation of a mixed-race ruling class to govern his empire. It is noteworthy that after Alexander's death we only hear of one of the noblewomen still married to a Macedonian general. This was Apama, daughter of the Sogdian Spitamenes, who married a general named Seleucus and became his queen when he declared himself king of the Syrian (Seleucid) Empire. Alexander continued his beneficence by discharging the debts of all his soldiers and by presenting honours and decorations to officers and men distinguished for their bravery and deeds. At this point the 30,000 Epigoni from the Upper Satrapies joined Alexander, dressed in Macedonian fashion and trained in the Macedonian art of war.

The Macedonian rank and file disapproved very much of Alexander's policy of fusion between Macedonians and Persians. It is recorded that even the bridegrooms did not like the Persian-style weddings, and that no one liked to see Alexander in Persian dress or promoting those who espoused Persian customs. They thought that the arrival of the Epigoni and the incorporation of native units into the infantry and cavalry signalled the end of his reliance upon the Macedonian troops who had endured so many adventures and hardships with their king.

These grievances exploded into mutiny again at the city of Opis on the Tigris, after Alexander had explored the delta of the Tigris which flows into the Persian Gulf. When the king proposed to discharge the time-expired and unfit veterans and send them home, keeping only those who wished to stay, the troops interpreted this as an insult to them and reacted in fury. The ringleaders said that they would all go home and leave him to fight along with his father—by whom they meant Ammon. Alexander was incandescent with rage, had the ringleaders arrested, and delivered a long speech justifying his career and the campaign (much of the preserved speech in Arrian is probably his own rhetorical elaboration of what he thought Alexander said). Again the king withdrew to his

tent for three days, but, when he began to install Persians in military commands, the Macedonians flocked to his tent and begged forgiveness. At a banquet of reconciliation, Alexander proclaimed both Persians and Macedonians as his kinsmen.

Alexander's special friend Hephaistion died at Ecbatana in 324 BC, after an illness lasting a week. Alexander was prostrate with grief, and the sources vie with each other in detailing the extravagant things he did in his despair (ordering the manes and tails of all the cavalry animals to be shorn in mourning, to give but one example). Diodorus describes in detail the elaborate funeral monument he planned for Hephaistion in Babylon, and Alexander sent to the oracle at Ammon enquiring what honours it would be appropriate to pay his friend. Yet the king was not to survive Hephaistion for long. The army proceeded to Babylon, and he entered the city in 323 BC despite dire warnings from seers, and several other portents that danger would befall him there.

The account of Alexander's last days are derived in part from a source called the 'Royal Journals' by Arrian and Plutarch. The form and content of these journals have been widely debated without universal agreement, since they do not seem to be official documents such as might have been compiled by Alexander's secretariat, but an account mainly of the excesses of Alexander's last days on earth. They are generally regarded as a bogus document forged at some stage for some reason by some unknown person to cast a gloss on the events of that turbulent period, but there is no consensus of scholarly opinion beyond that. However we are to interpret these journals, they record serious drinking sessions between Alexander and a man called Medius, after which the king contracted a fever. The fever did not abate even though Alexander rested and was carried several times to bathe in the river, offering sacrifices each time. For days he ate little, became extremely ill, and finally was unable to talk although he could still recognize his officers. We are told that the army insisted on filing past his bed, and his last actions were to greet each one by raising his head and making a sign with his eyes. He died shortly afterwards.

Many have tried to make posthumous diagnoses of Alexander's illness, but we will never know for certain what it was. Clearly the years of hardship and the various wounds he sustained took their toll and probably made his system less able to resist the fever. Perhaps the final drinking bouts exacerbated his condition. Poison was of course alleged, and the sources tell us various stories about possible motives and culprits, but, on the whole, dismiss these tales as malicious rumours. In the end, Alexander was only a mortal like all men.

It adds to the mystery of Alexander the Great that so much uncertainty still surrounds his last days and death, but with his passing the dream was shattered, and it was left to lesser men to pick up the pieces.

ALEXANDER'S PERSONALITY

I do not believe that it is possible to attempt a reconstruction of Alexander's personality without attributing to him motives which are not found in the ancient sources—our best, but ultimately unsatisfactory, evidence about him. I have therefore tried … to stay close to our sources, although it is a problem

that the recorded opinions of Arrian, Diodorus and Plutarch (all of whom lived hundreds of years after Alexander) on the king's behaviour may not be preferable to those of any modern scholar who thinks that he understands Alexander and what motivated him to act as he did in any given instance. The historiography of Alexander the Great (by which I mean the study of the histories written about him) is in itself a fascinating overview of trends in historical writing and the personalities of their authors. I hope that I have not 'identified' myself with Alexander and written an account based on what would have led me to act as he did, but perhaps this is what all biographers do despite their protestations to the contrary. What follows is not a full assessment of the man, but a short discussion of aspects of his character which I think are illuminated in the sources.

There is no doubt that Alexander was a brilliant military tactician. His battle plans are still studied in military colleges in Europe and America. Elements of his genuis were speed of movement, an appreciation of terrain, the use of his troops in the most advantageous way, and a charismatic and inspiring quality of leadership. Obviously, he was lucky to have the highly trained and experienced Macedonian army and skilled officers behind him, and he must have had a superb intelligence corps and commissariat. Because our sources focus on the king himself, these unsung heroes tend to be ignored, but without a highly developed infrastructure the huge army would have starved to death before getting far into Asia. His notions of invincibility were reinforced by spectacular military successes in set battles, siege warfare, and guerrilla tactics. Alexander led from the front and, although this was undoubtedly an inspiration to his troops, he took foolhardly risks. On more than one occasion he was lucky not to have been killed. The successive wounds which he endured must have contributed to his demise by increasing his susceptibility to the fever which killed him.

What about Alexander the man? We have no reason to suppose that he did not love his wife Rhoxane, nor that he did not take his pleasures with other women when he wished. His close friendship with Hephaistion may indicate that he was bisexual, but this was a common trait among men in ancient Greece. He rewarded loyalty, punished suspected treachery, and became increasingly autocratic in his treatment of people. Many scholars have claimed that he became a virtual tyrant by the end of his life. He had a court sculptor, portrait painter, and gem engraver to ensure that he was depicted in the correct image. Clearly it was important that an identifiable likeness of him was recognisable by the many peoples of his far-flung empire, but such a conscious manipulation of his image indicates considerable vanity. It is not a coincidence that the extant ancient portraits of Alexander are easily recognisable. They all feature an upturned gaze with consequent wrinkled forehead, eyes deep-set apparently to show fixed determination, and thick leonine locks falling from a peak in the centre of his forehead.

Much has been made of Alexander's drinking habits. Certainly the consumption of wine played a large role at court banquets, festivals, victory celebrations, and around the campfire, and it must have been a considerable consolation during long winters spent in unspeakable conditions far from home. Drinking was an accepted part of Macedonian aristocratic society and army life, and we should not see it as something out of the ordinary. It appears that Alexander drank more as he got older, and that his personality deteriorated during the years of the campaign, whatever may be the reason for this. Nor do we have any reason to doubt the various monumental drinking binges which are recorded in the sources, most famously the one which exacerbated his final illness. Clearly the influence of alcohol had occasional catastrophically detrimental effects on Alexander—his inebriated murder of Cleitus is the most striking example—but I find it hard to believe that he was an alcoholic by the modern clinical definition of the term. His military achievements alone argue that he was in control of his faculties, and more, when he needed to be.

Finally, what were Alexander's views about a divine ancestry, rivalry of the exploits of the gods, and deification? Yet again, these are impossible questions to answer because of our complete lack of evidence about what Alexander himself thought. We have seen that he repeatedly compared himself with the gods Heracles and Dionysus and with Persian heroes such as Cyrus the Great and the legendary Queen Semiramis. He also evidently saw himself in a special relationship with Zeus Ammon after his visit to the oracle at Siwah. His unsuccessful attempt to introduce proskynesis [respect or awe] among his Macedonians, and his unclear motives for so doing, have already been discussed. It is certain that Alexander was worshipped as a god after his death (he was worshipped as the 'Founder' god in Egyptian Alexandria, for example), but what is still disputed is whether Alexander demanded divine honours during his lifetime, and, if so, whether he was the first living mortal in the Greek world to do so. We cannot know whether he was intentionally deluding others to increase his stature in their eyes, or whether, in a spectacular case of *folie de grandeur,* he was ultimately deluding himself.

EPILOGUE: ALEXANDER'S LEGACY

On 10 June 323 BC, Alexander the Great died of fever in Babylon at the age of thirty-three. According to some accounts, he is alleged to have said on his deathbed, when asked to whom he was leaving his kingdom, 'to the best man'. Some sources add that he gave his signet ring to the general Perdiccas, who was virtually his second-in-command at the time. Most sources relate the further story that Alexander said that there would be a great 'funeral game' over him. This comment—whether real or invented— drips with considerable irony. Equestrian and athletic funeral games (in Greek 'epitaphia') were indeed staged as a way of commemorating the dead in ancient Greece, but here of course Alexander is referring proleptically to the bloody contest over his succession. (Diodorus describes the elaborate funeral carriage constructed for Alexander's body.)

This prophecy proved all too true. A vast conquered empire, the focus of which had been the personality of Alexander himself, and which was governed only by interim, *ad hoc* administrative arrangements, was unexpectedly left leaderless. The generals in Babylon—self-made men who had become powerful by virtue of their connection with Alexander and who by now were hardly going to be satisfied by the thought of a quiet life back in Macedonia—immediately fell out over the succession. The main party

declared Alexander's posthumous half-Bactrian son by Rhoxane as King Alexander IV, while the rank and file of the army proclaimed Alexander's half-witted half-brother Philip Arrhidaeus as King Philip III (Arrhidaeus was the son of Philip II by one of his minor wives). The infant and the simpleton were placed under the control of a regent. The turmoil which followed in the next two decades presents difficulties of nightmarish complexity, with continually shifting alliances among the leading protagonists who struggled for power even as they pretended to protect the rights of the two kings. The fight was between those who thought that they could take Alexander's place and keep his empire intact, and those who were content with control of self-contained segments of that empire. Constant warfare and the violent deaths of various contenders ensued before three separate kingdoms emerged which form the focus of the history of the next three centuries. Ultimately, the impact of Rome's increasing domination of the Greek East by the first century BC put an end to the independent existence of these empires and what is known as the 'Hellenistic' period of Greek history. Alexander's empire, by which I mean the personal empire he created in these years and not the Macedonian state, did not survive his death. In terms of the attempt to control the whole of Greece and Asia, and to create an empire based on his personality alone, Alexander's achievement was ephemeral.

Nor did he leave the legacy of a bloodline. Within thirty years of his death every member of his immediate family had been brutally murdered: his mother, his wife, his child (the teenage Alexander IV is probably the occupant of Tomb III at Vergina), an alleged illegitimate son, his half-brother Arrhidaeus, his two half-sisters and the daughter of one of them, and his full sister. This is comment enough upon those troubled years which saw the extinction of the royal Argead family to which Alexander belonged. Most of the surviving generals (the so-called 'Diadochi' or 'Successors') were killed in battles against each other, so no Macedonian dynasty of kings over the whole of Asia was created. It was only after fifty years of chaos that Antigonus Gonatas, the grandson of one of Alexander's generals, securely established himself upon the throne of Macedonia itself, thereby beginning what is known as the Antigonid dynasty in that kingdom. No descendant of Alexander had previously lived to occupy this throne for more than a few years.

Finally, what was the significance of Alexander's expedition in the history of the ancient world? On the one hand, it is undeniable that his exploits brought him everlasting fame and made him a yardstick against which many later conquerors measured themselves —Julius Caesar, the Roman emperor Trajan, and even Napoleon, to name but three. Alexander died at the pinnacle of his fame, and thereby became the quintessential romantic figure. Legend has immortalised him as the consummate young, brave, swashbuckling, invincible hero, but his early death means that we can never know what might have happened later. Could he have held his empire together? How would he have ruled it? Did he really intend the megalomaniac so-called 'Last Plans' recorded in some of our sources, which even included the circumnavigation of Africa? (The authenticity of these plans, which were read out to the army and rejected after Alexander's death, is still hotly debated.) Might he have gone on to conquer the whole inhabited world? Could he really have crossed China and reached the Pacific Ocean? What would Alexander have been like at the age of sixty? We will never know.

There are two legacies which Alexander the Great did bequeath to us, the value of both being dubious. The first was the subsequent condition of Macedonia, which he left as a youth of twenty and to which he never returned. This kingdom had to endure for eleven years with an absent king, far away and in only sporadic contact. It has been estimated that up to 40,000 men in their prime were taken out of Macedonia between 334 and 331 BC. Most of these never returned; many of those who had not succumbed to their wounds lived and died in Asia, populating the new cities founded by Alexander's successors in their new kingdoms. The consequences of this upon the Macedonian families— parents, wives, children—of these soldiers can hardly be imagined. Macedonia was supreme and invincible at the end of the reign of Philip II in 336 BC, but Alexander died leaving behind him bitter memories of brothers, husbands and sons who went with him, and the consequences of severe depopulation. One might argue that Alexander the Great, the greatest conqueror of the ancient Greek world, set his country on a path of decline that proved irreversible. In terms of the Macedonian heartland, the period of Macedonian greatness was the reign of King Philip II, not that of his overambitious heir.

John Keegan, the eminent military historian, has examined various styles of generalship in his magisterial book *The Mask of Command*. His definition of the 'mask of command' is the facade or persona which any general must wear, or the stage upon which any leader must act, to ensure that his troops follow him to the end. His discussion of Alexander the Great concludes that his style of leadership combined the ideals of heroism and nobility with that of the 'conquering urge', a savagery which all those who opposed him faced. Keegan's conclusion, with which I wholly concur, is that Alexander's 'dreadful legacy was to ennoble savagery in the name of glory and to leave a model of command that far too many men of ambition sought to act out in the centuries to come'. It is that legacy which we have inherited.

POSTSCRIPT

Does Alexander the Great Merit His Exalted Historical Reputation?

Someone once stated, "Pity the nation that has no heroes!" Someone else wryly replied, "Pity the nation that needs them!" To what extent have national desires created the aura of Alexander the Great? How many historical figures were so inspired by his story that they sought to emulate it? And what were the results of such actions? Military historian John Keegan, in *The Mask of Command* (Jonathan Cape, 1987), contends that the Alexandrine conquest model inspired others to emulate him, with the same disastrous results. Barbara Ehrenreich shares this assertion in *Blood Rites: Origins and History of the Passions of War* (Henry Holt, 1997). We may want to ask the question, Should Alexander the Great's historical reputation suffer due to the actions of those who followed and attempted to emulate him?

As one can imagine, the number of books about Alexander are numerous. The late Ulrich Wilcken's classic biography, *Alexander the Great*, first published in 1931, has been reissued in 1997 (W. W. Norton). It contains an insightful chapter entitled, "Introduction to Alexander Studies" by Eugene N. Borza of Pennsylvania State University. Robin M. Fox's *The Search for Alexander* (Little, Brown & Company, 1980) was written for an accompanying television series and contains some wonderful visual images, along with a highly readable and interesting text.

Other Alexander biographies that are worth reading are A.B. Bosworth, *Conquest and Empire: The Reign of Alexander The Great* (Cambridge University Press, 1993) and Peter Green, *Alexander of Macedon: A Historical Biography* (University of California Press, 1991). Michael Wood's *In The Footsteps of Alexander the Great* (University of California Press, 1997) is a book/television series that is worth recommending. Since the book contains the program narration, rent the videos and get the visual images along with the words.

ISSUE 4

Did Christianity Liberate Women?

YES: Karen Jo Torjesen, from *When Women Were Priests* (HarperSanFrancisco, 1995)

NO: Karen Armstrong, from *The Gospel According to Woman: Christianity's Creation of the Sex War in the West* (Anchor Press, 1987)

ISSUE SUMMARY

YES: Professor of religion and associate of the Institute for Antiquity and Christianity, Karen Jo Torjesen, presents evidence of women deacons, priests, prophets, and bishops during the first millennium of Christianity—all roles that suggest both equality and liberation for women.

NO: Professor of religious studies Karen Armstrong finds in the early Christian Church examples of hostility toward women and fear of their sexual power which she contends led to the exclusion of women from full participation in a male-dominated church.

Have women been excluded from leadership roles in the Christian Church from the beginning? The ordination of women as ministers and priests during the twentieth century gives the impression that new ground is being broken by women who seek to lead congregations. Some believe that these women are carrying the movement for women's liberation in civil society inappropriately into churches and defying a nearly two thousand year tradition that has properly excluded them.

It is deeply challenging to our modern notions of progress to think that, even by present standards, women may have been more "liberated" two thousand years ago than they are today. Our greatest challenge might come from trying to imagine how early Christian women regarded their own status in the newly formed religion. Did they feel liberated from the more patriarchal world of first-century Palestinian Judaism and Hellenistic paganism? And, regardless of how they felt, does our assessment of their status merit claiming that Christianity liberated them?

Before the Christian Church became institutionalized and before a theology was clearly defined, early converts acted out of intense personal conviction and met informally to share their faith. Most churches were based in people's homes and some state that it was this private dimension that made women's leadership possible. Gender conventions of the time identified the male's sphere of influence as being in the public arena and confined the women's sphere of influence to the home. Christianity remained an underground religion until the early fourth century when Constantine, the Roman Emperor, forbade government persecution and made Christianity a legal religion.

Missionaries converted many Greeks to Christianity, resulting in more Gentile, or non-Jewish, Christians than Jewish Christians by the third century. The Greek-speaking world was the first to accept Christianity in large numbers. If Christian women in both Jewish and Gentile environments during the early centuries enjoyed equality with men, what happened to create the climate of misogyny, or hatred of women, during later centuries?

In the sixth century a Christian Church Council actually debated whether or not women had souls. The question seemed to be whether women were made in the image and likeness of God, as men were, or merely in the image and not in the likeness. Women are still barred from the Roman Catholic priesthood, primarily using a theological argument introduced by Saint Thomas Aquinas in the thirteenth century. He stated that women are inferior by nature and incapable of assuming leadership positions.

Karen Jo Torjesen uses ancient texts, funerary epitaphs, papal letters and inscriptions, as well as mosaic art as evidence to support her thesis that women were accepted as equals and honored as leaders in the early Christian Church. However, this was only as long as Christianity remained a private phenomenon. Once it achieved official status during the fourth century, worship became more formalized and moved into public temples, called basilicas. Eager for credibility and legitimacy, church leaders bowed to prevailing gender conventions and restricted women's contributions.

Karen Armstrong focuses on negative cultural attitudes toward women. She begins the chapter from which the following selection is taken by quoting modern feminist Germaine Greer, "Women have very little idea of how much men hate them." She finds our modern culture uncomfortable with sex and traces the roots of hostility between men and women to the early days of Western Christianity. The Eastern (primarily Russian and Greek Orthodox) Christian Church, which split with the Western Church in an act of mutual excommunication in 1054, is judged by Armstrong as less misogynistic.

YES
Karen Jo Torjesen

WHEN WOMEN WERE PRIESTS

INTRODUCTION...

The complexity of the issue of women clergy, given its larger context of gender, can best be treated by first analyzing the connections among women's roles, female character, and sexuality in the culture of Christ's day. Women's leadership in Christianity is a dramatic and complex story, one in which the radical preaching of Jesus and deeply held beliefs about gender sometimes melded and sometimes clashed. Jesus challenged the social conventions of his day: He addressed women as equals, gave honor and recognition to children, championed the poor and the outcast, ate and mingled with people across all class and gender lines, and with bold rhetoric attacked the social bonds that held together the patriarchal family. When Jesus gathered disciples around him to carry his message to the world, women were prominent in the group. Mary Magdalene, Mary of Bethany, and Mary his mother are women whose names survived the retelling of the Christian story in the language and literary conventions of Roman patriarchal society. Paul's letters reflect an early Christian world in which women were well-known evangelists, apostles, leaders of congregations, and bearers of prophetic authority.

Because Christians distanced themselves from the polytheism of Greek and Roman religions, they avoided using the pagan term "priest" (*hieros*) for their clergy. Instead they used a variety of terms taken from secular life: *diakonos* (minister), *apostolos* (missionary), *presbyteros* (elder), *episcopos* (overseer), prophet, and teacher. Eventually the titles of bishop (*episcopos*), priest (*presbyteros*), and deacon (*diakonos*) came to be identified with the principal offices of the Christian church. Throughout this period of development, women held each of these offices. The Christian title presbyter (elder), meaning an older person entitled to respect, was borrowed from the Jewish synagogue, which was governed by a group of presbyters. After the emergence of the office of bishop as the head of the congregation, the presbyters governed under his or her guidance. Catholic historians translate *presbyter* as "priest." Protestant scholars simply retain the word *presbyter*. In either case, a fully ordained clergyperson is meant. When a woman's name is associated with a title, both Catholic and Protestant translators tend to minimize the office. Instead of translating *diakonos* as "minister" as they do for male office holders, they translate it as "deaconess."

During the first and second centuries, when Christian congregations met in homes, women were prominent as leaders. In early Christian communities women came to clerical offices by the same routes that brought their secular counterparts to public offices in Roman and Greek society. Preliminary training was provided by their assigned social roles as household managers. Women's authority in this domain was well established. Their administrative, economic, and disciplinary tasks in that role were excellent preparation for church (and public) office. In addition, women with relatively more wealth or higher status assumed the role of patron of a group. These patrons were often elected to public office, sometimes as a way of honoring them, and sometimes as a strategy for ensuring the patrons' continued generosity.

By the third century the processes of institutionalization gradually transformed the house churches, with their diversity of leadership functions, into a political body presided over by a monarchical bishop. Over the next two centuries, the legitimacy of women's leadership roles was fiercely contested. In the polemical writings of this period we encounter for the first time the arguments that Jesus appointed only male disciples and therefore women cannot be ordained; that Paul instructed women to keep silent during public discussions and thus women cannot teach; that if Jesus had wanted women to baptize, he would have been baptized by his mother, Mary. Although these arguments were rather weak in themselves, they were buttressed by the Greco-Roman world's beliefs about gender.

Opponents of women clergy appealed to a gender ideology that divided society into two domains, the *polis* (city), a male domain, and the *oikos* (household), a female domain. This system gave a great deal of power to women in the household while attempting to segregate them from public, political life. Christian polemicists insisted that public offices and public honors were a masculine affair and that women exercising such authority in the churches were usurping male prerogatives. During the first three centuries these voices represented a minority of the church's intellectuals, but as the church became increasingly institutionalized during the third and fourth centuries, these arguments carried greater weight.

The public-versus-private convention was in turn supported by a system of cultural values that associated men with honor and women with shame. The quest for honor and precedence associated with public office was viewed as an exclusively masculine enterprise. In contrast, a woman's honor was her shame, that is, her reputation for chastity. A woman exercising public authority could be accused of projecting a masculine personality; but, even worse, she could be called unchaste.

Although these notions about female shame and women's sexuality have their roots in the social order of ancient Greece, they have had a profound effect on Christian understandings of women, sexuality, and sin throughout the history of the church; they are foundational to the Western doctrine of sin, the church's theology of sexuality, and the Christian concepts of the self and even of God.

Understanding why and how women, once leaders in the Jesus movement and in the early church, were marginalized and scapegoated as Christianity became the state religion is crucial if women are to reclaim their rightful, equal place in the church today. Jesus' message and practice were radically egalitarian in their day and constituted a social revolution that likely provoked his crucifixion. It is high time that the church, which claims to embody his good news to the world, stop betraying its own essential heritage of absolute equality.

PREACHERS, PASTORS, PROPHETS, AND PATRONS

The Evidence for Women's Leadership
Under a high arch in a Roman basilica dedicated to two women saints, Prudentiana and Praxedis, is a mosaic portraying four female figures: the two saints, Mary, and a fourth woman whose hair is veiled and whose head is surrounded by a square halo—an artistic technique indicating that the person was still living at the time the mosaic was made. The four faces gaze out serenely from a glistening gold background. The faces of Mary and the two saints are easily recognizable. But the identity of the fourth is less apparent. A carefully lettered inscription identifies the face on the far left as Theodora Episcopa, which means Bishop Theodora. The masculine form for bishop in Latin is *episcopus;* the feminine form is *episcopa.* The mosaic's visual evidence and the inscription's grammatical evidence point out unmistakably that Bishop Theodora was a woman. But the *a* on Theodora has been partially effaced by scratches across the glass tiles of the mosaic, leading to the disturbing conclusion that attempts were made to deface the feminine ending, perhaps even in antiquity.

At a burial site on the Greek island Thera there is an epitaph for an Epiktas named as priest or presbyter (*presbytis*). Epiktas is a woman's name; she was a woman priest sometime in the third or fourth century.

In the opening scene of the *Gospel of Mary,* a second-century gnostic Gospel, Mary Magdalene rallies the despondent disciples after the ascension of their Lord. By exhortation, encouragement, and finally a rousing sermon on the teachings of Jesus, she revives their flagging spirits and sends them off on their mission. Because of her strong leadership role, she appears in some texts with the title Apostle to the Apostles.

Historical evidence like this, from art, inscriptions, and literature, belongs to the hidden history of women's leadership, a history that has been suppressed by the selective memory of succeeding generations of male historians.

In his book *The Ministry of Women in the Early Church,* Roger Gryson exemplifies this consensus of his and preceding generations of scholars:

> From the beginnings of Christianity, women assumed an important role and enjoyed a place of choice in the Christian community. Paul praised several women who assisted him in his apostolic works. Women also possessed the charism of prophecy. There is no evidence, however, that they exercised leadership roles in the community. Even though several women followed Jesus from the onset of his ministry in Galilee and figured among the privileged witnesses of his resurrection, no women appeared among the Twelve or even among the other apostles. As Epiphanius of Salamis

pointed out, there have never been women presbyters.

Most Christians today, including clergy and scholars, presume that women played little or no role in the Jesus movement or in the early church as it spread throughout the Mediterranean. But women did in fact play crucial roles in the Jesus movement and were prominent leaders along with men in a wide variety of roles in the early church. The Christian church, of course, did not spring up suddenly into a well-defined organization with buildings, officials, and large congregations. In its earliest stages it is best understood as a social movement like any other. It was informal, often countercultural in tone, and was marked by a fluidity and flexibility that allowed women, slaves, and artisans to assume leadership roles.

Why, then, are we so unaware of the prominence of women in the birth of Christianity? Why does this powerful misperception continue to marginalize women in even the more enlightened branches of contemporary Christianity? The answers to these questions are complex, but they begin and end in cultural views about gender.

The societies to which early Christians belonged (like our society) held definite ideas about male and female roles. According to the gender stereotypes of the ancient Mediterranean, public speaking and public places were the sole prerogatives of males; private spaces, like the household, were the proper sphere for women's activities. Furthermore, society insisted that a respectable woman be concerned about her reputation for chastity and her seclusion in the household; modesty and reticence were accepted as testimony to her sexual restraint. Public activities and public roles seemed incompatible with modesty.

But the real women of that time led lives that were not as circumscribed as we might think. As householders they directed the men and women who lived and worked under their authority and supervised the production and distribution of the wealth. As businesswomen they traveled, bought, sold, and negotiated contracts. Women with sufficient wealth and social status acted as patrons of individuals and groups of lower social standing by providing financial assistance, recommendations to officials, and political protection.

In order to understand the role of women in the early church, it is necessary to understand what functions secular leaders performed and what kind of people they were. We know that leaders arbitrated disputes between members of communities, collected and distributed money, represented the interests of their community to city and imperial governments, financed communal feasts, made gifts of places of worship, taught, and arranged marriages. We also know that social status was the most important factor in the makeup of potential leaders.

For its part the church took its cue from society's leadership models. Mindful of their precarious status in Roman society, Christian communities looked to members with social status and wealth to be patrons and to function as their protectors. On a smaller scale, heads of households, who were accustomed to wielding authority and who had the stores of the household at their disposal, often became leaders of house churches.

In the ancient world, both men and women were patrons and householders. The social authority, economic power, and political influence associated with these roles were not restricted by gender. Even religious authority in Greek and Roman worship was not limited by gender. Women as well as men functioned as prophets and priests. Each of these social positions in Roman society—patron, householder, prophet, and priest—provided an individual with the kind of status, authority, and experience that could be translated into similar leadership roles in the Christian community.

Among ancient mosaics, paintings, statuary, dedicatory inscriptions, and funerary epitaphs, scholars have found numerous pieces of evidence for women's leadership. In literary sources such as the writings of the New Testament, letters, sermons, and the theological treatises of the early church, women's leadership is also well attested. In the literary sources, however, we can see shadows cast by the conflict over women's leadership and the prevailing social conventions about gender roles. The New Testament writers generally mentioned women leaders only as a passing fact while hurrying on to address more pressing concerns. When they paused for a longer discussion of women's leadership, as Paul did in his first letter to the Corinthian church, one catches tones of ambivalence and anxiety. In New Testament passages where women leaders played prominent roles, the male authors muted their contributions by the way they wrote their stories....

Women Patrons in the Gospels and Epistles

Phoebe, the minister (*diakonos*) of the congregation at Cenchreae, carried Paul's letter to the Romans. She was a woman of some wealth and social status and traveled to Rome in connection with her business and social life and the affairs of the Christian church. She had agreed to carry Paul's letter to the Romans, which he hoped would provide him entry into the Roman Christian community on his upcoming visit. In his letter Paul also introduced Phoebe to the Roman Christians, identifying her as his patron (*prostatis*). With this title Paul acknowledged her generosity and her support of him, then he urged the Roman Christians to help her in whatever way she required in repayment of his own debt of gratitude to her.

Joanna, the wife of Chuza, a steward in Herod's household, was a woman in a position to be a patron (Luke 8:1–3). It is intriguing to find her traveling with the group of evangelists that accompanied Jesus from village to village. Certainly her connections to the ruling Herodian family would have eased the way in any conflicts with minor local officials. It seems that she was a member of a group of women—Mary of Magdala and Susanna are also mentioned—whose patronage protected and supported the Jesus movement. Women as well positioned socially and economically as these often established patron-client relationships.

Paul concluded his letter to the Roman Christians with personal greetings to the leaders of the community there; some he knew by reputation, and others he had met in the course of his ministry. Among the leadership of the Roman Christian community were many women. Prisca, Junia, Mary, Tryphaena, Tryphosa, and Persis were women whom Paul addressed as co-workers; they had established the faith of the Christian community through their work of teaching and exhortation. Other prominent women greeted by Paul were Julia, Olympas, the mother of Rufus, who Paul says was a mother to him also, and the sister of Nereus. Of the twenty-eight prominent people whom Paul considered it politic to greet, ten were women.

Among these women leaders of the Roman congregation was a woman apostle, Junia, whom Paul hailed as "foremost among the apostles" (Rom. 16:7). She and her husband, Andronicus, traveled teaching and preaching from city to city. The turmoil and riots occasionally provoked by Christian preaching landed her and her husband in prison, where they encountered Paul. She was a heroine of the fourth-century Christian church, and John Chrysostom's elegant sermons invoked the image of Junia, the apostle, for the Christian women of Constantinople to emulate.

Wherever Christianity spread, women were leaders of house churches. Mary, the mother of John Mark, presided over a house church of Hellenistic Jews in Jerusalem. It was on her door that the astonished Peter knocked to announce to the Christians assembled there that he been liberated from prison by an angel (Acts 12:12–17). Apphia presided with two others as leaders of a house church in Colossae (Philem. 2). Nympha in Laodicea, Lydia in Thyatira, and Phoebe at Cenchreae supervised the congregations that met in their homes (Col. 4:15; Acts 16:15; Rom. 16:1).

In John's Gospel Mary Magdalene, not Peter, is presented as the model for discipleship. At a time when Peter and the other male disciples had fled, Mary stood loyally at the foot of the cross. She was not only the first witness to the resurrection but was directly commissioned to carry the message that Jesus had risen from the dead. The original version of the Gospel of John ends with the resurrection appearance to Mary Magdalene and her witness to the Twelve in chapter 20. The story of the appearance to "doubting Thomas" at the end of chapter 20 teaches early Christians to believe without seeing. "Now Jesus did many other signs in the presence of the disciples, which are not written in this book; but these are written that you may believe that Jesus is the Christ, the Son of God, and that believing you may have life" (John 20:30–31). A later copyist added another ending to the Book of John, chapter 21. In this chapter Peter was made the key witness of the resurrection when Jesus appeared to Peter and the disciples while they were on a fishing expedition in Galilee and commissioned Peter to be the shepherd of the flock. New Testament scholars have long puzzled about the reasons for this Gospel's two endings, chapter 20 highlighting the role of Mary Magdalene as witness to the resurrection and chapter 21 highlighting Peter. A recent proposal suggests that chapter 21 was appended at a time when the Johannine community was seeking to integrate with the Christian community that saw Peter as its head. Thus chapter 21 was added to bring the Johannine community within the pale of Petrine orthodoxy by emphasizing Peter's leadership.

Ambivalence and Conflict Over Women's Leadership

When Paul wanted to claim that he too was an apostle because he had seen the risen Lord, he listed the appearances of Jesus: "He was raised on the third day in accordance with the scriptures.... He appeared to Cephas [Peter], then to the twelve. Then he appeared to more than five hundred brethren at one time.... Last of all ... he appeared to me" (1 Cor.

15:4–8). Paul omitted the announcement of the resurrected Christ to Mary even though it is attested in all four Gospels. Even some of the Gospel writers themselves betray signs of ambivalence over women's leadership. Matthew and Mark recount the women's witness to the resurrection, but the women's witness plays no role in the faith of the rest of the disciples. Luke reports that the women delivered their message to the rest of the disciples, "but these words seemed to them an idle tale, and they did not believe them" (Luke 24:12).

Women's leadership was a widespread phenomenon in the early Christian churches. Tensions were nevertheless generated by the disparity between the socially established fact of women's leadership and the strict Greco-Roman demarcation of gender roles. The mixed messages about Mary Magdalene's significance reflects the ambivalence about women's leadership as the Gospels were taking their final canonical form.

The second-century *Gospel of Mary*, discovered in 1945 among a collection of manuscripts at Nag Hammadi in upper Egypt, reveals a lost tradition about the leadership of Mary Magdalene and portrays Peter as her opponent. The scene described in the fragments of this Gospel took place on the Mount of Ascension after Jesus had departed into heaven. The disciples were disconsolate, depressed, and afraid until Mary stood up and addressed them all. She exhorted them to stop grieving, assured them that the grace of the Savior would be with them, and urged them to prepare for the work of preaching to which they had been called. Finally the disciples took heart and began to discuss the teachings of the Savior. After a while, at Peter's prompting, Mary began a long teaching discourse. When she had finished, she was quiet. Andrew was the first disciple to break the silence. He said, " 'Say what you [wish to] say about what she has said. I at least do not believe that the Savior said this. For certainly these teachings are strange ideas.' " Peter then broke in with a resentful challenge: " 'Did he really speak with a woman without our knowledge (and) not openly? Are we to turn about and all listen to her? Did he prefer her to us?' " Mary, hurt, turned to Peter and said, " 'My brother Peter, what do you think? Do you think I thought this up myself in my heart or that I am lying about the Savior?' " Finally Levi rebuked Peter:

> "Peter, you have always been hot-tempered. Now I see you are contending against the women like the adversaries. But if the Savior made her worthy, who are you indeed to reject her? Surely the Savior knows her very well. That is why he loved her more than us. Rather let us be ashamed and put on the perfect man and acquire him for ourselves as he commanded us, and preach the gospel, not laying down any other rule or other law beyond what the Savior said."

When Levi finished his speech, the disciples set out on their teaching mission.

The ambivalence about women's role, implied in Peter's comment "Did he prefer her [*a woman*] to us?" indicates tensions between the existing fact of women's leadership in Christian communities and traditional Greco-Roman views about gender roles. The discomfort of the writer/editor of John with Mary Magdalene's prominence as a witness to the resurrection, and the other Gospel's similar ambivalence about the importance of the women at the empty tomb, betray the deep conflict over women's place that developed as Christianity was becoming established and the canon was being set.

There seems to be no doubt that women figured prominently in Jesus' life and ministry, both during his lifetime and after his resurrection when the first communities were formed and his message began to spread. If these accounts of women's important participation hadn't been grounded in intractable fact, they would not have survived in such a male-dominated culture. But because such independence and prominence on the part of women conflicted directly with the view of women's roles that pervaded Greco-Roman society, these traditions were ignored and submerged as much as possible in order to conform Christian teaching and practice to social convention.

Yet up until the mid-third century, only occasional sparks were generated by this clash between the social strictures on women's roles and the freedom women found in Christianity. For more than two hundred years Christianity was essentially a religion of the private sphere, practiced in the private space of the household rather than the public space of a temple. Its concerns were the domestic life of its community rather than the political life of the city. But during the third century Christianity began evolving toward its eventual form as a public religion. The burgeoning numbers of adherents and the new formality and dignity of the Christian liturgies meant that Christian participation was increasingly a public event. By the fourth century Christians were worshiping in

their own public temples, called basilicas. During this period the friction between the social conventions about women's place and women's actual long-standing roles as house church leaders, prophets, evangelists, and even bishops precipitated virulent controversies. As Christianity entered the public sphere, male leaders began to demand the same subjugation of women in the churches as prevailed in Greco-Roman society at large. Their detractors reproached women leaders, often in strident rhetoric, for operating outside the domestic sphere and thus violating their nature and society's vital moral codes. How could they remain virtuous women, the critics demanded, while being active in public life?

With their survival instincts honed, Christian communities had gradually begun to assimilate themselves into Hellenistic culture. Jewish communities had done the same. In their increasing desire for credibility and legitimacy, the church leaders no longer resisted the tide of culture. Gradually they adopted Greco-Roman conventions regarding women's proper place and behavior. Both Jewish and Christian writers, like their pagan counterparts, argued that it was inappropriate for women to hold positions of authority in the public sphere. For both Jewish and Christian theologians, as for pagan philosophers, the good woman was a chaste woman. In their view, female sexual promiscuity posed the greatest threat to women's character. Every aspect of female deportment should evince a concern for shame, expressed through reticence, deference toward men, and sexual restraint.

NO   Karen Armstrong

THE RESULT: EVE

From almost the earliest days of Western Christianity, men started to see women as sexually dangerous and threatening, and in the grip of this fear they started a process which would eventually push women away from the male world into a separate world of their own. This might at first seem an odd development: neither Jesus nor Paul had pushed women away, but had worked closely with them and granted them full equality with men. However, later books of the New Testament, particularly the First Epistle to Timothy, which was probably written at the beginning of the 2nd century some sixty years after Paul's death, have a very different message. By this time Christianity is coping with the Gentile world of the late Empire and its terrors of sexual excess. A fear of sexuality had changed official Church policy toward women:

> I direct that women are to wear suitable clothes and to be dressed quietly and modestly without braided hair or gold and jewellery or expensive clothes; their adornment is to do the sort of good works that are proper for women who profess to be religious. During instruction, a woman should be quiet and respectful. I am not giving permission for a woman to teach or to tell a man what to do. A woman ought not to speak, because Adam was formed first and Eve afterwards, and it was not Adam who was led astray but the woman who was led astray and fell into sin. Nevertheless, she will be saved by childbearing, provided she lives a modest life and is constant in faith and love and holiness.
>
> —(1 Timothy 2:9–15)

When Paul had told the women in Corinth to keep quiet in Church, there was no hint of sexual disgust, nor was there any idea that women were potentially wicked (they just have to remember their place!). In 1 Timothy we have something different and sinister. Woman is not just inferior, she is wicked also, because of Eve. Eve fell into sin first and led Adam into sin. This is a theme which will recur again and again in the writings of the Early Fathers, and is also a deeply sexual idea.

The author of 1 Timothy begins his remarks about women with directions about the sort of clothes they should wear. Glancing through the works of the Fathers, it is extraordinary how much time they devoted to writing about women's dress—a concern that should have been beneath them. Diatribes about the way women load themselves with jewelry, cake their faces with makeup and douse themselves with perfume crop up with extreme frequency. One of the first was written by Tertullian in the 3rd century. In a treatise written to his "best beloved sisters" in the faith, Tertullian glides from affection and respect to an astonishing attack:

> If there dwelt upon earth a faith as great as we expect to enjoy in heaven, there wouldn't be a single one of you, best beloved sisters, who, from the time when she had first "known the Lord" and learned the truth about her own condition, would have desired too festive (not to say ostentatious) a style of dress. Rather she would have preferred to go about in humble garb, and go out of her way to affect a meanness of appearance, walking about as Eve, mourning and repentant, so that by her penitential clothes she might fully expiate what she has inherited from Eve: the shame, I mean, of the first sin, and the odium of human perdition. *In pains and anxieties dost thou bear children, woman; and toward thine husband is thy inclination and he lords it over thee.*[1] And do you not know that you are each an Eve? The sentence of God on this sex of yours lives in this age: the guilt must of necessity live too. *You* are the devil's gateway: *you* are the unsealer of that forbidden tree: *you* are the first deserter of the divine law: *you* are she who persuaded him whom the devil was not valiant enough to attack. *You* destroyed so easily God's image, man. On account of *your* desert—

that is death—even the Son of God had to die. And do you think about adorning yourself over and above your tunics of skins.

—(*On Female Dress*, I:i)

It is exactly the same complex of ideas that we find, less clearly articulated, in 1 Timothy: female appearance, Eve, childbirth. It seems at first sight strange that this enormous attack—each woman is completely responsible for destroying men and crucifying Christ—should start and finish with something as apparently unimportant as women's clothes. What prompts Tertullian's virulent attack is pure irrational fear. As the treatise goes on, we see that it is wholly about sex. Woman is as much of a temptation to man as Eve was to Adam, not because she is offering him an apple but because she is offering the forbidden fruit of sex. She can cause a man to lust after her just by walking around looking beautiful. "You must know," Tertullian insists, "that in the eye of perfect Christian modesty, having people lusting after you with carnal desire is not a desirable state of affairs but is something execrable" (II, ii). He is thinking of Jesus' words when he said that a man who looks at a woman lustfully has already committed adultery in his heart. Jesus was not making a particular issue of lust here, but was illustrating his admirable religious insight that mere external conformity to a set of rules is not enough for the truly religious man. It is the attitude in his heart that counts, not a meticulous performance of burdensome commandments. Tertullian twists this potentially liberating idea into a truly frightening view of the moral world. "For as soon as a man has lusted after your beauty, he has in his mind already committed the sin which his lust was imagining and he perished because of this, and you [women] have been made the sword that destroys him" (II, ii). A man's lustful glance may be entirely involuntary, but he still perishes. The woman is guilty of destroying him just as Eve was guilty of destroying Adam. She may have had absolutely no intention of tempting him—she may not even realize that she has caused any lustful thoughts at all, but she is still guilty. Both the man and the woman have sinned even though what happened was quite beyond their control.

Tertullian is quite clear that women are to blame: "even though you may be free of the actual crime, you are not free of the odium attaching to it" (II, ii). This means that, far from dressing up and making herself look pretty and desirable, a woman has a duty to look as unattractive as she possibly can:

> ... it is time for you to know that you must not merely reject the pageantry of fictitious and elaborate beauty, but even the grace and beauty you enjoy naturally must be obliterated by concealment and negligence, because this is just as dangerous to the people who glance at you. For even though comeliness is not to be censured exactly, because it is certainly a physical felicity and a kind of goodly garment of the soul, but it is to be feared, because of the injury and violence it inflicts on the men who admire you.

> —(II, ii)

This is an oft-repeated theme for Tertullian. In his treatise *On the Veiling of Virgins*, it surfaces in a particularly disturbed form. St. Paul had said that women had to wear veils in Church "because of the angels." Here he was referring to the legend of the "Sons of God," the "angels" who

lusted after earthly women and came down from heaven to mate with them.

> For if it is "because of the angels"—those beings of whom we read as having fallen from God and from heaven because of lusting after women—who can presume that it was bodies already defiled and relics of human lust which the angels yearned after, but that rather that they were inflamed for virgins, whose bloom pleads an excuse for human lust?... So perilous a face, then, ought to be kept shaded, when it has cast stumbling stones even so far as heaven. This face, when it stands in the presence of God, at whose bar it already stands accused of driving the angels from their heavenly home, may blush before the other angels who didn't fall as well.

> —(*On the Veiling of Virgins*, VII)

There is something extremely unpleasant here. It is not simply the view that sex always defiles a woman, so that afterward she is merely a "relic of human lust," a memory of a shameful act. There is also a horrible leering prurience about unsullied virgins being especially lustworthy, and there is a real terror in the idea that a woman's beauty is so dangerous and powerful that it can even cause angels to abandon heaven and fall irretrievably into sin. If even angels are not safe from a woman's beauty, then what hope is there for mere men? A woman must keep her "perilous" face hidden. She must disguise her beauty, or she will destroy men just as surely as Eve destroyed Adam. Already, years before Augustine would finally formulate for the West the doctrine of Original Sin, the emotional trinity which exists at the heart of that doctrine has been formed in the Christian neurosis of Tertullian: woman, sex and sin are fused together in his mind indissolubly. The only hope for man is that women hide themselves away—veil their faces from man's lustful eyes, hide their beauty by disfiguring themselves and make themselves ugly and sexless in the penitential garb that befits each woman as an Eve.

Christian men were told to inhabit a separate world from women. When Jerome wants to defend his friendship with the noble Roman lady St. Paula, who became one of his staunchest disciples, he stresses the fact that he was scrupulous about keeping away from women:

> Before I became acquainted with the household of the saintly Paula all Rome was enthusiastic about me. Almost everyone concurred in judging me worthy of the highest office in the Church. My words were always on the lips of Damasus of blessed memory. Men called me saintly: men called me humble and eloquent. Did I ever enter a house of any woman who was included to wantonness? Was I ever attracted by silk dresses, flashing jewels, painted faces, display of gold? No other matron in Rome could dominate my mind but one who mourned and fasted, who was squalid with dirt, almost blind with weeping. All night long she would beg the Lord for mercy, and often the sun found her still praying. The psalms were her music, the Gospels her conversation: continence was her luxury, her life a fast. No other could give me pleasure, but one whom I never saw munching food.

—(Letter xiv: To Asella)

For Jerome the only good woman is a sexually repulsive one. Paula has made herself "repellent." When Jerome went to visit her, he felt disgusted by her and his virtue was quite safe. He was in no sexual danger. Paula herself would have been delighted by this appalling description; she was only one of the

new breed of Roman ladies who were taking up the ascetic life and mutilating themselves physically and spiritually in this way. This pattern of mutilation is one that recurs in all sorts of psychological and physical ways among the women of Western Christianity. By telling a woman that she should not be physically attractive if she wanted to consort with men and still be virtuous, Jerome and his like were deeply damaging the women who obeyed them.

If a woman is not repulsive then she must be isolated and ostracized. In his letter to Nepotian, a young priest, Jerome tells him that he must be careful to keep himself away from women, even the most innocent and virtuous women, unless they are sexually repellent:

> A woman's foot should seldom or never cross the threshold of your humble lodging. To all maidens and to all Christ's virgins show the same disregard or the same affection. Do not remain under the same roof with them; do not trust your chastity. You cannot be a man more saintly than David, or more wise than Solomon. Remember always that a woman drove the tiller of Paradise from the garden that had been given him. If you are ill let one of the brethren attend you, or else your sister or your mother or some woman of universally approved faith. If there are no persons marked out by ties of kinship or reputation for chastity, the Church maintains many elderly women who by their services can both help you and benefit themselves, so that even your sickness may bear fruit in almsgiving.... There is a danger for you in the ministrations of one whose face you are continually watching. If in the course of your clerical duties you have to visit a widow or a virgin, never enter the house alone.... Never sit alone without witnesses with a woman in a quiet place.

If there is anything intimate she wants to say, she has a nurse or some elderly virgin at home, some widow or married woman. She cannot be so cut off from human society as to have no one but yourself to whom she can trust her secret.

—(Letter lii)

Merely sitting with a woman or letting her nurse you is to put yourself in grave danger. Women, therefore, have to be shunned, even if they are in trouble and need help. A woman is to be avoided and left alone in a world which is quite apart from men.

It becomes part of the advice that is given to your aspirants of both sexes who want to lead virtuous Christian lives. Men are to shun women, and women are urged to withdraw from the world and take themselves off into a separate and totally female existence. Inevitably that will be maiming, even without the fasting and the deliberate physical mutilation that the woman is urged to undertake in the name of physical penance. Simply by being deprived of the realities of the male world, by being deprived of education and normal activity, women were only being able to function in half the world. However, the most destructive thing of all was the sexual disgust which drove women into their separate worlds. There is a continual process of repulsion which we have already seen in Tertullian, a process which is neurotic and probably not even conscious. You begin speaking lovingly to your "best beloved sisters" and you end up castigating "Eve." Jerome has exactly the same reaction. Here he is writing to a young girl who has written asking for his advice about the Christian life. Jerome urges her to lock herself away from the world. Simply by walking around she will inspire male

lust, however virtuous she is. In fact, virtue itself can turn a man on:

What will you do, a healthy young girl, dainty, plump, rosy, all afire amid the fleshpots, amid the wines and baths, side by side with married women and with young men. Even if you refuse to give what they ask for, you may think that the asking is evidence of your beauty. A libertine is all the more ardent when he is pursuing virtue and thinks that the unlawful is especially delightful. Your very robe, coarse and sombre though it be, betrays your unexpressed desires if it be without crease, if it be trailed upon the ground to make you seem taller, if your vest be slit on purpose to let something be seen within, hiding that which is unsightly and disclosing that which is fair. As you walk along your shiny black shoes by their creaking give an invitation to young men. Your breasts are confined in strips of linen, and your chest in imprisoned by a tight girdle. Your hair comes down over your forehead or over your ears. Your shawl sometimes drops, so as to leave your white shoulders bare, and then, as though unwilling to be seen, it hastily hides what it unintentionally revealed. And when in public it hides the face in a pretence of modesty, with a harlot's skill it shows only those features which give men when shown more pleasure.

—(Letter cxvii)

It is not surprising that Jerome doesn't let himself near women, because this letter shows him to be sexually obsessed and one of the great voyeurs of all time. He has obviously studied women minutely, and is pruriently eager to pick up each and every movement, every mannerism. He is even excited by the creaking of a woman's shoe. Watching a woman walk down the street, he immediately imagines her underwear; his eyes are skinned to catch a glimpse of her white shoulders. It is taken for granted that she is teeming with lust. Every movement, intentional or unintentional, is a sign of her "unexpressed" sexual desire. What Jerome is doing is over-sexualizing women because of his own sexual repression. *He* is rampantly frustrated so he tells women that *they* are sexually insatiable. He has forgotten here that he is writing to a good little girl, who has asked him for advice. He is so lost in his fantasy that by the end of the paragraph he is comparing her to a harlot. In just the same way Tertullian begins by calling his readers "best beloved" and ends by calling them "Eve." Christian love for women easily modulates into sexual hatred.

Woman then is man's deepest enemy. She is the harlot who will lure a man to his doom because she is Eve, the eternal temptress. Just as Original Sin comes to be linked with sex, so woman is Eve because she is sexual. Jerome's pathological disgust with sex is shown in his letter to Furia, who had written to seek his advice about getting married again:

The trials of marriage you have learned in the married state: you have been surfeited to nausea as though with the flesh of quails. Your mouth has tasted the bitterest of gall, you have voided the sour unwholesome food, you have relieved a heaving stomach. Why would you put into it again something which has already proved harmful to you. *The dog is turned to his own vomit again and the sow that was washed to her wallowing in the mire.*

—(2 Peter 2:22)

What must Furia have felt like when she received this letter? Again she seems to have been a virtuous woman, a genuine and enthusiastic Christian, but because of her sexuality she would have been made to feel foul and sinful. Jerome is clear that she is sexually obsessed and voracious. As a widow she must be inflamed by the "pleasures of the past." The widow "knows the delights that she has lost and she must quench the fire of the devil's shafts with the cold streams of fast and vigil." Jerome sees a woman as having such strong sexual cravings that if she dresses attractively she is crying out for sex, her "whole body reveals incontinence." Again he sees her as luring poor unsuspecting men into sex and sin. Woman is Antichrist:

What have rouge and white lead to do on a Christian woman's face? The one simulates the natural red of cheeks and lips, the other the whiteness of the face and neck. They are fires to inflame young men, stimulants of lustful desire, plain evidence of an unchaste mind. How can a woman weep for her sins when tears lay her skin bare and make furrows on her face? Such adorning is not of the Lord, it is the mask of Antichrist.

—(Letter liv)

Reading this one might assume that Jerome is writing about prostitutes whose garish makeup advertises their availability. In fact here, as elsewhere, he was writing about ordinary Roman matrons who used frequently to wear cosmetics at this time.

This hostility and fear of women's sexual powers we see again and again. Augustine sees danger even in the virtuous women of the Old Testament, sometimes with ludicrous results. Trying to come to terms with the sex lives of the Patriarchs, he presents Abraham and Isaac copulating with their wives dutifully but with enormous distaste, in order to obey God's command to found the Chosen Race. They would far rather have abstained. Abraham, Augustine says, had to go on copulating with his wife Sarah for years before he managed with God's help to conceive his son Isaac. Abraham, who seems to have been a highly sexed man, would have read all this with considerable bewilderment. Isaac, Augustine continues, was more fortunate. The Bible only mentions his having sex once, and he was lucky enough to produce the twins, Esau and Jacob, straight off so he never had to do it again. When he came to Jacob, however, who had twelve sons, Augustine is in a bit of a quandary. This looks like zeal in excess of duty. However, he decides that Jacob would gladly have followed the example of Isaac and only had sex once in his life, but his two wives, Leah and Rachel, kept pestering him because of their excessive lust and sexual greed, forcing the holy Patriarch to abandon his high ideals. Yet Rachel and Leah are good women. For Augustine, as for his predecessors Jerome and Tertullian, all women, however virtuous, are men's enemies. "What is the difference," he wrote to a friend, "whether it is in a wife or a mother, it is still Eve the temptress that we must beware of in any woman" (Letter 243, 10).

There is no room for this enemy in the male world. Indeed, there is no room for her at all in God's plan. Augustine seems puzzled about why God made women at all. It is not possible that she was a friend and helpmate to man. After all, "if it was good company and conversation that Adam needed, it would have been much better arranged to have two men together, as friends, not a man and a woman" (*De Genesis ad Litteram* IX, v, 9).

The only reason he made women was for the purposes of childbearing. Luther shared this view. The only vocation he could see for a woman was to have as many children as possible, so that all the more people could be led to the Gospel. It didn't matter what effect this might have on women: "If they become tired or even die, that does not matter. Let them die in childbirth—that is why they are there." There was no other way that a woman could help man. Her place was "in the home" (the famous phrase was actually coined by Luther). There was no place for her in the male world of affairs. Similarly Calvin, who is virtually the first Christian theologian to speak favorably of women, might insist that woman *was* created to be a companion to man and that marriage was instituted by God precisely for that companionship, but his Geneva was entirely male dominated, and women's role as a companion was confined to the domestic female world of the home. Protestantism shared fully the misogyny that the Fathers had bequeathed to the Catholic Church. When Lutherans at Wittenberg discussed the question whether women were really human beings at all, they were not discussing anything new. Theologians had always been perplexed about women's place in God's plan. Thomas Aquinas was as puzzled as Augustine had been about why God had made her at all and decided that woman was a freak in nature:

As regards the individual nature, woman is defective and misbegotten, for the active force in the male seed tends to the production of a perfect likeness in the masculine sex; while the production of woman comes from a defect in the active force or from some material indisposition, or even from some external influence.

—(*Summa Theologica,* IV, Part I. Quaest. XCII, art 1, 2)

It does not help that Aquinas decides that womankind in *general* is human. The "individual nature" of women is a defect, an idea he picked up from Aristotle's biology. The norm is the male. Every woman is a failed man.

* * *

Women are therefore emotionally excluded from the male world, for all that Paul had originally insisted upon sexual equality. Even now that we are breaking into the male preserves we still tend to feel ill at ease in it. Recent surveys show that college women are even more afraid of success today than they were when Betty Friedan did her original survey in the early 1960s. Dons at Oxford and Cambridge have complained about the quality of women who are gaining admission to the colleges that used to be all-male. They have asked schools to stop sending them girls who are polite, efficient and well-behaved, and instead send them students who will argue with them

as aggressively as the boys do. Breaking into the male world is not simply a matter of opportunity. It is a question of attitude on the part of both men and women. Women are still ambiguous and fearful in these new male worlds that have recently been opened to them. They are still maintaining their guilty apologetic stance. For centuries they have been excluded not simply because they were supposed to be inferior but because they inspired sexual fear and disgust in men. Marilyn French's novel *The Women's Room* puts this humorously when she imagines the male world of Harvard terrified to admit women in case they drip menstrual blood all over this pure male preserve. Where Moslems have traditionally locked their women into harems inside their homes because they owned and valued them, men in the Christian West have locked their women outside their lives because they hate them, exiling women to a lonely, separate world.

NOTES

1. Genesis 3:16. Tertullian quotes God's words to Eve after the Fall.

POSTSCRIPT

Did Christianity Liberate Women?

The Bible and many other sources provide evidence of women's active roles during the early years of what would later be called Christianity. Eusebius (263–339 C.E.) was a Greek Christian and an intimate friend of the emperor Constantine who wrote the only surviving account of the first 300 years of Christian Church history. Sometimes called the Christian Herodotus, he certainly earned the title Father of Ecclesiastical (church) History. A translation of his work by G. A. Williamson, *The History of the Church* (Dorset Press, 1984), is easy to obtain.

In the early years of Christianity, different schools of what would later become theology existed side by side. One of these was Gnosticism, a mystical worldview that predominated in Greece and Rome. Remarkable for its androgynous view of God as father and mother, Gnosticism was condemned as the first heresy primarily because of its insistence that God only appeared to suffer and die in the person of Jesus. Four Gnostic gospels, part of what scholars call the Nag Hammadi library, found in Egypt in the 1940s, are available in Marvin W. Meyer's translation in *The Secret Teachings of Jesus* (Vintage Books, 1986). Elaine Pagels has also written about Gnosticism in *The Gnostic Gospels* (Vintage Books, 1989). Pagels writes about the origin of evil in *Adam and Eve and the Serpent* (Vintage Books, 1989) and *The Origin of Satan* (Vintage Books, 1996).

A documentary sampling of women in history from the ancient Greeks to the modern Victorians may be found in *Not in God's Image* edited by Julia O'Faolain and Lauro Martines (Harper & Row, 1973). Including both religious and nonreligious writings, this book places Western attitudes toward women in a broader context. The image of God is a critical element in understanding Christian attitudes toward women. If women are included in the image of God, then they are eligible for full membership within Christianity; if, however, the image of God is strictly a male one, then women must necessarily be excluded or marginal. Two books shed considerable light on this question: *God, a Biography* by Jack Miles (Alfred A. Knopf, 1995), which considers God the protagonist of the Hebrew scriptures (what Christians call the Old Testament), and Karen Armstrong's *A History of God: The 4,000-Year Quest of Judaism, Christianity and Islam* (Alfred A. Knopf, 1993), which traces the image of God through all three religions of the book.

Feminist theory points to an Eve/Mary split within Christianity. According to this thesis, women are offered only two roles—Eve, the temptress whose disobedience brought about the loss of Eden, or Mary, the mother of Jesus whose obedience to the will of God made possible human salvation. The two extremes represented by these roles seem to exclude all living women. If Mary is held up as an ideal—as she clearly has been during certain periods of Christian history—then women, if they remain pure and demure, may share in the honor accorded Mary. However, to slip even slightly from the perfection embodied by Mary is to fall all the way to the disdain accorded Eve. There is no middle ground. Film historians call this the virgin/whore split and cite numerous examples of film heroines who play out one of these two roles. Students may be interested in reading Molly Haskell's *From Reverence to Rape: The Treatment of Women in the Movies* (Penguin Books, 1974) and Marjorie Rosen's *Popcorn Venus* (Avon Books, 1973), which explore this theme.

On the Internet . . .

The WWW Virtual Library History Index: Medieval Europe
This Web site provides a list of on-line references focusing on Medieval history. The site is maintained by The Michigan State University Graduate Student Medieval and Renaissance Consortium.
http://www.msu.edu/~georgem1/history/medieval.htm

Mayan Culture
The great Mayan civilization vanished centuries ago, but comes to life on this site. First University of Guadalajara, Mexico, gives an overview of Mayan art, architecture, and culture.
http://udgftp.cencar.udg.mx/ingles/Precolombina/Maya/mayasintro.html

Civ Web from Providence College
This site is a guide to Internet resources related to the development of Western civilization. Information is available on Mesopotamia, Ancient Egypt, Ancient Palestine, Ancient Greece, Ancient Rome, the Middle Ages, and the Renaissance.
http://www.providence.edu/dwc/index.html

PART 2

The Medieval World

This section shows world civilizations building upon the world that the ancients created as they searched for a better life for themselves and their citizens. However, it also shows that some of the problems these civilizations faced early in their histories continued to plague them and that greater problems occurred for them as they began to have increased contact with other civilizations.

■ Did Same-Sex Unions Exist in Medieval Europe?

■ Does the Modern University Have Its Roots in the Islamic World?

■ Were Environmental Factors Responsible for the Mayan Collapse?

■ Were the Crusades Motivated Primarily by Religious Factors?

ISSUE 5

Did Same-Sex Unions Exist in Medieval Europe?

YES: John Boswell, from *Same-Sex Unions in Premodern Europe* (Villard Books, 1994)

NO: Philip Lyndon Reynolds, from "Same-Sex Unions: What Boswell Didn't Find," *The Christian Century* (January 18, 1995)

ISSUE SUMMARY

YES: Yale University history professor John Boswell states that same-sex unions, which date back to pagan times, existed in medieval Europe until they were gradually done away with by the Christian Church.

NO: Reviewer Philip Lyndon Reynolds, while admitting that "brotherhood" ceremonies took place in medieval Europe, asserts that these ceremonies did not have the same authority as sacred unions and therefore cannot be equated with marriage rites.

Few topics are as controversial today as homosexuality. Newspapers are filled with stories involving the discomfort that individuals—and institutions—have in dealing with the subject. In the United States, violence against gay males and lesbians seems commonplace, as are debates within states concerning the extent of gay rights. Even U.S. presidents find it difficult to enact policies under their jurisdiction (e.g., the role of gays in the military). Some accuse governmental leaders of first proposing policies and then reversing their position to gain public approval. The total acceptance of gay males and lesbians in society will likely be a question for debate for years to come.

No segment of society has had more difficulty dealing with this subject than religious communities. All denominations seem to have divisions in their ranks with regard to how homosexuality is to be considered in canons and doctrines and how gay males and lesbians are to be treated as members of congregations. News accounts abound concerning clergy members who challenge their church's stance on homosexuality and are reprimanded or censured for it. Occasionally, the debate reaches the highest orders of the sect, when bishops or other high-ranking officials express doubts about existing church beliefs and concomitant practices. There seems to be no way to satisfy all parties.

Some scholars have attempted to seek out the historical roots of this problem, to discover if there are any historical antecedents that can be useful in creating a consensus of understanding in regard to homosexuality. They have discovered that what some today would refer to as homosexual practices have been in existence throughout recorded history. But what may have been startling to discover was the level of acceptance such practices were afforded in the past; in fact, to many, the status of these practices has been questioned in the Western world only within the last millennium.

What significance do these historical antecedents have for the current debate? For one thing, they are vivid examples that societies can exist and thrive in times of open tolerance. If they could then, why not now? Also, it is important for gay males and lesbians to find reaffirmation for their beliefs and practices in the past, as almost all groups have found some solace in their historical, ethnic, and religious roots. Finally, a study of the past can inspire current interest in seeking solutions to our current problem with understanding and accepting sexual orientation.

If there was a wider acceptance of homosexuality in past religious histories, can that acceptance be recreated today? And can we not discover what factors in the last 1,000 years altered those earlier, more accepting conditions and use them as a catalyst for change? Such hope is at the heart of the late John Boswell's book, from which the following selection has been excerpted. Researching into archives and manuscripts long ignored, he discovered that not only was there a wider acceptance of what some today refer to as homosexual practices in the past but that there also existed in classical and medieval Europe religious rites and ceremonies he refers to as "same-sex unions." These practices existed for centuries until late medieval Christendom closed the door to such practices.

While Boswell's work was well received, it was not without its critics. Philip Lyndon Reynolds, in a lengthy review in *The Christian Century*, found that Boswell may have assigned a sacramental nature to these same-sex rites that did not exist. Also, Reynolds states that there has been a lack of clarity of purpose to Boswell's work. His review (and others) has inspired rejoinders and counterrejoinders. What will the outcome of this debate be in the hands of future historians and theologians?

YES

John Boswell

SAME-SEX UNIONS IN PREMODERN EUROPE

THE HISTORY OF SAME-SEX UNIONS IN MEDIEVAL EUROPE

The historical setting of the [same-sex union] ceremony is a bit harder to track than its liturgical context and development. It is, for example, impossible to know whether it represents the Christianization of an ancient same-sex rite—and if so, which one—or a Christian innovation. Since most ancient nuptial and same-sex union rites involved sharing of wine and a feast, it is easy to imagine that these ancient customs were simply arrayed in Christian garb to keep up with the prevailing ethos, just as Roman heterosexual marriage customs were reinvested with Christian meaning and persisted throughout the Middle Ages, or pagan statuary (e.g., of Venus and Cupid) was reconsecrated to Christian use (the Virgin Mary and the baby Jesus).

Saint couples—especially military pairs like Serge and Bacchus or the Theodores—continued to fascinate and preoccupy the Christian public (or at least the males who left literary and artistic records), and provided a Christian voice for the same sentiments that had produced the Roman phenomenon of sexual or institutional "brotherhood." Churches continued to be built for and dedicated to Serge and Bacchus throughout the Eastern end of the Mediterranean all during the early Middle Ages. Many Christians may have understood such couplings simply as expressions of devoted friendship, while those whose own romantic interests were chiefly directed to their own gender doubtless understood them in a more personal way. Both views were probably correct: coupled saints like Peter and Paul may have been overinterpreted as romantic pairs, while Serge and Bacchus were probably correctly so understood. The oldest church in Egypt, widely believed to occupy a spot where the Holy Family lived for some time during their exile in Egypt, is dedicated to St. Serge. Justinian himself, the instigator of laws sharply penalizing homosexual behavior, was believed to have added a structure dedicated to SS. Serge and Bacchus to one already consecrated to SS. Peter and Paul.

Nor should the fact that an area became Christian be interpreted to mean that all of its inhabitants suddenly embraced and followed the most ascetic teachings of the new religion. In many areas of Europe ancient practices persisted for centuries among a populace officially Christian. In Egypt, although Christianity was lively and often quite severe (as exemplified in the Didache, the Apostolic Canons, and the writings of Clement of Alexandria), there was also much variety, as appears in the Gnostic writings and the prominence of dissenting movements in the Egyptian church. Centuries after Christian doctrine had penetrated Egypt and long after the Theodosian Code had made the upper reaches of the Roman state a Roman Catholic theocracy, an Egyptian man wrote down a magical incantation seeking supernatural help to obtain the love of another male. The sixth-century African poet Luxorius, also living in a Christian world, nonetheless wrote a poem about a passively homosexual male who gave his property away to the men with whom he had sex.

The Roman custom of forming a union with another male by the legal expedient of declaring him a "brother" appears to have persisted into the early Middle Ages, although it became controversial for a somewhat unexpected reason related to the decline of urban culture and the range of lifestyles around the Mediterranean. Collateral adoption was declared invalid for some outlying provinces in a handbook of Roman law compiled (in Greek) in the fourth or fifth century and translated into Syriac, Armenian, and Arabic for Roman citizens living in regions of the East where Latin and Greek were not understood....

It is, in addition, clear that same-sex unions were commonplace in early medieval Byzantine society, even among the prominent and notable. Strategios, an imperial treasurer, was twice said in the ninth century to have been the same-sex partner... centuries before of the emperor Justinian. No other information about this relationship survives. Procopius in his *History* mentioned Strategios as a trusted patrician, "a man of good sense and ancestry" ..., but said nothing about this relationship, which may be apocryphal, although in Procopius, Strategios does seem to have been close to Justinian. In another text Severus, a patrician, is casually mentioned as the same-sex partner of another emperor, but no further details are given.

By contrast, details survive about some Byzantine cases of the early Middle Ages. St. Theodore of Sykeon, for example, a contemporary of Justinian (d. 613), was born in Galatia. He was the illegitimate son of a prostitute and an imperial messenger, Kosmas, who had been an acrobat and performed in the imperial circus on camels. Theodore became a hermit, lived for two years in a cave, and then for a time inhabited an iron cage. (This sort of flamboyant asceticism was common in the Christian East.) He became bishop of Anastasioupolis, but ultimately resigned to return to monastic life.

Theodore traveled widely (e.g., to Jerusalem and Constantinople), and was always under the special protection of St. George, whose intervention when he was a child appears to have been largely responsible for his holy life. (The Eastern St. George was invoked in the ceremony of same-sex union....) While he was visiting Constantinople the patriarch Thomas became "so attached to him and had such confidence in him that he begged him to enter into ceremonial union with him and to ask God that he would be together with him in the next life."

Although it is hardly credible that such an energetically ascetic man would enter into *any* sort of carnal relationship, it is nonetheless possible that the union was based on passionate feelings, at least on Thomas' part. Indeed, it is difficult to interpret otherwise the latter's desire for them to be together in heaven, since traditionally the chief joy of paradise consisted in the beatific vision of God. This whole incident strongly recalls the story of Serge and Bacchus, one of very few other places in early Christian literature where a personal union in heaven was emphasized. Theodore might have consented to a relationship that ordinarily had sexual possibilities without any intention of partaking in them himself: his near-contemporary St. John the Almsgiver agreed to a heterosexual marriage even though he intended to remain a virgin, and had to be forced by his father-in-law to consummate the relationship.

A few centuries later Basil I (867–886), the founder of the Macedonian dynasty that ruled the Byzantine Empire from 867 to 1156, was reported to have been twice involved in ceremonial unions with other men. Although the most important sources for his life—composed under the rule of his descendants within a century of the events in question—are contradictory on some points and occasionally unreliable, their take on this matter is largely consistent. His biographers (including Western sources . . .) all agreed that when Basil arrived in Constantinople with nothing but a staff and a knapsack—a young man from the provinces with no connections in the capital—he was befriended by a certain Nicholas of the church of St. Diomede, who rescued him from sleeping in the streets, brought him into the church, bathed and clothed him, and supported him for some time, until the ambitious Basil was able to attract the attention of a well-placed courtier related to the imperial family.

In most accounts of their relationship Nicholas and Basil are united in a church ceremony. According to one tradition, on the morning after finding him Nicholas "bathed and dressed Basil and was ceremonially united to him, and kept him as his housemate and companion." Another version is more explicit about the ceremony: "and on the next day he went with him to the baths and changed [his clothes] and going into the church established a formal union with him, and they rejoiced in each other." The odd final phrase would probably recall to a Christian Greek reader the biblical "Rejoice with the wife of thy youth."

Given the wording in the chronicles . . . and the fact that the union is accomplished in a church, there can be little doubt that the writers have in mind some form of the ceremony published and translated in this text. There is no suggestion of any tribal or family aspect to the relationship, nor of the exchange of blood; it has no military or strategic aspect, nor are any circumstances adduced as requiring or occasioning it (e.g., rescue from danger, a serious illness, which would all be occasions in later Slavic relationships modeled on it). It is clearly a personal relation, undertaken for personal reasons. Both Basil and Nicholas had living biological brothers with whom they were in regular and close contact, so it could hardly have been inspired by a need for a sibling. Indeed, it was Nicholas' own natal brother, a physician, who was responsible for Basil's introduction at court, a fact adduced immediately after the union in all versions. Nor does the mention of rejoicing suggest a coldly calculated relationship. Taken with the statement by Hamartolos that the union led to a sharing of home and hearth, it strongly evokes a wedding, followed by jubilation and a shared life.

It is striking that in a tradition about this relationship in which Nicholas is identified as a monastic, the ceremonial union is not mentioned. By contrast, the chroniclers who do discuss the union characterize Nicholas as a parish cleric in minor orders—hence, not prohibited by ecclesiastical law from entering into same-sex union....

From the perspective of Basil, who would otherwise have been sleeping on the streets, formalizing Nicholas' benevolent interest in him could only have been advantageous, at least until he found a means of advancing his career more rapidly with someone more powerful and better connected. It is less clear what Nicholas gained from the impetuous union. Taking the story—including Nicholas' supernatural information about Basil's future greatness—at face value, one could conclude that Nicholas imagined he would ultimately profit from entering into a formal relationship with someone who would one day become emperor....

While Basil was still in the service of Theophilos, they made a trip together to Greece. A wealthy widow in Achaia showered him with gifts of gold and dozens of slaves. In return for her generosity she asked nothing but that Basil should enter into ceremonial union with her son, John. At first he refused, because he thought it would make him look "cheap," but at length she prevailed and he agreed. "I seek and ask nothing from you," she assured him, "except that you love and deal kindly with us." A surviving medieval illustration of this incident shows Basil and John being united before a cleric in church, with the Gospel open before them and John's mother looking on. An accompanying frame depicts Basil, John, and Danelis (John's mother...) at a table—doubtless the artist's conception of the feast that would usually follow such a ceremony.

When he subsequently became emperor Basil immediately "sent for the son of the widow Danelis, honored him with the title *protospatarius*, and granted him intimacy with him on account of their earlier shared life in ceremonial union." The widow herself—now too elderly to ride—came to the emperor on a litter, but rather than requesting any munificence from him, she brought more extravagant gifts "than nearly any other foreign ruler had up to that time ever bestowed on a Roman emperor." In addition, she "who was worthy to be called the emperor's mother" made a large gift of her patrimony in the Peloponnese to her son and the emperor *together*....

Were it not for the genders involved, this incident would seem quite a familiar feature of the premodern political landscape: a wealthy widow offers her marriageable child to a powerful young man on the rise, along with a substantial dowry, hoping to ally her fortunes to his. Basil's own father had been married to the daughter of a wealthy widow in a striking parallel. The previous Byzantine dynasty, the Amorian, had been established under similar, though apparently heterosexual circumstances: born of humble parents, uneducated and unconnected, its founder Michael II advanced himself through strength of arms and military skill until he was able to marry Thekla, the daughter of a high-ranking officer, and attracted the attention of the emperor Leo V, who made him *protostratarius*—the same position Basil had held in the service of Theophilos—and became godfather to one of his sons.

When Leo attempted to have Michael executed on charges of treason, he was himself assassinated and Michael was crowned emperor.

The widow Danelis was much richer than Basil and, when he became emperor, realized no material gain from the relationship, so it can hardly be viewed as a mercenary arrangement on her part. On the contrary, every year of Basil's life she sent *him* expensive gifts, and years later, when both Basil and her son had died, the widow came again on a litter to see Basil's son Leo, now emperor, and made him her heir, although she had a grandson and other relatives.

The two stories about Basil are similar: in each there is a divine revelation, to a cleric or monk, about Basil's future greatness; in each the relationship established is to Basil's material advantage. It is possible that in imperial circles it was later known that Basil had profited substantially as a young man from a formal relationship with another male, and different chroniclers simply supplied different details. Each of the biographies written within a century of the events contains *one or the other* of the same-sex unions; none contains both. On the other hand, Nicholas does appear in *all* of the most important accounts of Basil's life as his benefactor, even those that mention the union with John, and the wealth of detail about the widow Danelis (including her subsequent relations with Leo) makes it seem unlikely that she was pure invention. Possibly Basil was united to both men. It is not clear that this would have been improper in Basil's day—or that issues of propriety would have constrained his behavior....

It is... clear that ceremonial same-sex unions were parallel to heterosexual marriage in the ninth century in a number of ways: they were relationships between individuals of a personal nature (rather than tribal, religious, or political); they entailed consequences for the immediate family (John's mother; Nicholas' brother) comparable to the obligations or rights of in-laws; they were recognized by society, and even respected by descendants.

It was most likely for this reason that monks were always and everywhere prohibited from entering into same-sex unions, just as they were forbidden to contract heterosexual marriage in both East and West, by both civil and ecclesiastical law (although in the East other members of the clergy could marry). Basil the Great (in the fourth century) had argued that no sexual relations ... of persons in orders ... could be regarded as "marriages," and that such unions ... must by all means be dissolved. Around 580, monks were also forbidden to make "leagues" or "associations." This rule was presumably based on a provision aimed at the laity in the same collection. In the case of the laity the prohibition was certainly *not* aimed at same-sex unions, but it is conceivable that in the case of monks the same canon was interpreted as a blanket condemnation of *all* relationships requiring an oath. A more or less contemporary ruling for laypeople makes perfectly evident that same-sex unions were altogether legal.

The real context of the prohibition to monks is evident in a restatement of St. Basil's rule for monks (the equivalent of the Rule of Benedict in the West) by St. Theodore of Studium (759–826), in which the monks were told, "Do not contract same-sex unions with or become spiritual kin [i.e., godparents] to the laity, you who have left behind the world and marriage. For this is not found among the fathers, or if it is, only rarely; it is not legal."

This rule was often repeated in later ages (e.g., "It is prohibited for monks to form same-sex unions or be godparents, and the church recommends, by way of admonition, the same [prohibition] for leaders or heads of monasteries. The law does not recognize so-called same-sex unions altogether"). Such blanket condemnations inspire skepticism, both because of the historical evidence treated in this [selection] and because same-sex union is coupled in such texts with godparenting, which was not only legal but a key element of liturgical life for most Christians in the Middle Ages....

The most obvious interpretation of such prohibitions is that they parallel the rule against monks marrying women. It would, however, be possible to understand them as stemming from a more general Christian antipathy to homosexuality of any sort. This ascetic tendency of Christian Rome—unknown before the advent of the new religion—was certainly plain in such Western legal compilations as the Theodosian Code and the Laws of the Visigoths, and in the great legal code of Justinian—all unprecedented efforts to make a Christian theocracy of the traditionally secular Roman state. But in fact sustained and effective oppression of those who engaged in homosexual behavior was not known in Europe until the thirteenth century, and was never common in the Byzantine East. Troianos notes somewhat loosely that in the High and later Middle Ages one finds fewer and fewer penalties for homosexual acts in civil and ecclesiastical sources from Byzantium, although "this circumstance in no way indicates that homosexual relations were not widespread in Byzantium."...

Roman law survived only fragmentarily in Europe after the collapse of the Roman state, and was usually replaced by Germanic law codes, which were not likely to take cognizance of same-sex relationships. Nonetheless, in Italy and Spain —comparatively urban societies by the standards of the times—the legal fiction of "brotherhood" was not complicated by questions of wife and children, since remaining a bachelor had long been a part of urban Roman life, and was enhanced by the social and financial rewards offered by the position of the diocesan clergy (i.e., as opposed to monks), who were pressured throughout the first millennium of Christian history to aspire to complete celibacy, but were not actually required to observe it until a bitter fight over the issue in the eleventh and twelfth century. In many communities, even where the ceremony of same-sex union was not known, informal relationships reminiscent of the Roman legal fiction of "brotherhood" between male lovers served many of the same functions as heterosexual unions—either legal marriages or long-term alternatives like concubinage—in their duration and legal ramifications.

The ambiguity of the few surviving texts precludes categorizing them unequivocally as same-sex marital contracts, but it equally rules out pretending that they were simply business contracts, as previous commentators have tried to do. It is, in fact, possible to interpret them as business documents, but it would also be possible (if utterly mistaken) to interpret most premodern heterosexual marriage agreements (especially prenuptial contracts among the wealthy) as business contracts. (Indeed, Roman law specifically spoke of heterosexual marriage as a "lifelong partnership.") Many aspects of the documents and the arrangements they prescribe argue forcefully against a simple partnership. In most of them there is no quid pro quo: it is not that one party provides capital or labor or land and in return the other invests property or expertise or time. In each case it is simply a division of one person's estate with another, apparently for purely voluntary and personal reasons....

EPILOGUE

Although many questions remain about same-sex unions in premodern Europe, much has also emerged with reasonable clarity. Such unions, in various forms, were widespread in the ancient world, where heterosexual matrimony tended to be viewed as a dynastic or business arrangement, and love in such relationships, where it occurred, arose *following* the coupling. Ordinary men and women were more likely to invest feelings the twentieth century would call "romantic" in same-sex relationships, either passionate friendships or more structured and institutional unions, as exemplified by the recognized couples of Crete or Scythia, the swearing of perpetual love among other Greeks, and the social phenomenon and legal stratagem of "brotherhood" among the Romans.

Since the advent of Christianity only exacerbated doubts about the emotional significance of matrimony, there was little pressure (other than widespread heterosexual desire) to re-evaluate such attitudes. Christianity's main innovation was to privilege and make real widespread voluntary celibacy, implicitly or explicitly suggesting that heterosexual matrimony was a mere compromise with the awful powers of sexual desire, even when it was directed exclusively to the procreation of children,

the one rationale Christians found convincing. But passionate friendships, especially among paired saints and holy virgins, continued to exercise a fascination over the early Christians—still residents of the ancient world—and in time were transformed into official relationships of union, performed in churches and blessed by priests.

In many ways from a contemporary point of view, the most pressing question addressed by this work is probably whether the Christian ceremony of same-sex union functioned in the past as a "gay marriage ceremony." It is clear that it did, although, as has been demonstrated at length, the nature and purposes of every sort of marriage have varied widely over time. In almost every age and place the ceremony fulfilled what most people today regard as the essence of marriage: a permanent romantic commitment between two people, witnessed and recognized by the community. Beyond this, it might or might not fulfill specific legal or canonical expectations predicated on the experience of the heterosexual majority (procreative purpose, transfer of property, dowry), but the extent to which particular heterosexual unions matched such niceties did not usually determine whether the neighbors regarded the couple (same-sex or heterosexual) as married. Indeed, in all times and places in its history (including the present) the official teaching of the Roman Catholic church (one of the two bodies in which the ceremony developed) has been that the two parties *marry each other*; the priest merely acts as a witness. If the couple intend to be married, they are. By contrast, in the Eastern Orthodox church the priest *does* perform the ceremony, and in all known cases priests performed the same-sex union.

NO

Philip Lyndon Reynolds

SAME-SEX UNIONS:
WHAT BOSWELL DIDN'T FIND

Few works of historical scholarship are treated in *Time* and *Newsweek,* much less summarized in a syndicated cartoon strip. According to the digest of [Same-Sex Unions in Premodern Europe] that appeared in Gary Trudeau's *Doonesbury,* John Boswell reveals that the Catholic Church recognized gay marriages for a thousand years. The church even provided liturgies for such marriages, liturgies that included communion and in which kissing signified union, and that were in crucial respects "just like heterosexual marriages." Later in church history, a persecuting and homophobic culture suppressed this tradition of gay marriage.

One can readily understand why a book that seems to be saying something like this would attract attention. The issue of homosexuality is extremely vexed in most Christian denominations in North America. If gay marriage used to be a regular part of Christian tradition, then the official Roman Catholic prohibition of homosexual acts must be unfounded, for the prohibition rests chiefly on the argument from tradition. Tradition still counts for a great deal in the minds of most thoughtful Protestants as well. Because they usually regard homosexual unions as something novel and experimental, Christians tend to regard them as artificial and false. If they were to be convinced that, on the contrary, homosexual union was an ancient tradition within the church that was later suppressed, they should not only have to abandon the former view but should tend to regard homosexual union as something natural and authentic. Its suppression or marginalization in the churches today would appear baseless and contrived. Is this the conclusion toward which Boswell—who died ... at age 47—directs us?

Boswell's argument consists of pointing to certain liturgical forms, some written in Greek and some in Slavonic, from the tenth to the 16th centuries. These texts record an ecclesiastical ritual for the formation of a "brotherhood" of some kind between two men. The ritual belongs to the churches of the eastern Mediterranean and represents the Christianization of a custom much older than Christianity. The liturgical forms have been unfamiliar until now, although a few classical historians have studied and written about the custom

From Philip Lyndon Reynolds, "Same-Sex Unions: What Boswell Didn't Find," *The Christian Century,* vol. 112, no. 2 (January 18, 1995). Copyright © 1995 by The Christian Century Foundation. Reprinted by permission of *The Christian Century.*

of brotherhoods in Greek society (and have come to conclusions different from Boswell's).

Boswell provides the original texts and English translations for several of these liturgical forms. Let us consider the first text in his appendix of English translations, which comes from the manuscript Grottaferrata... VII. This form, which was written in Greek in the tenth century, consists of three prayers. In the first the minister, having invoked God as the one who made humankind in his image and likeness, calls to mind two exemplary male pairs who had God's blessing: the apostles Philip and Bartholomew and the martyrs Serge and Bacchus. The text then asks for God's blessing upon the two men, N. and N., who are the subject of the ritual, asking God to enable them "to love each other and to remain unhated and without scandal all the days of their lives." In the second, briefer prayer, the minister beseeches God to bless N. and N. so that they should know the Holy Spirit and "become united more in the spirit than in the flesh." The third and longest prayer is densely rhetorical and difficult to summarize. Suffice it to say that the minister beseeches God to grant that there should be between N. and N. the brotherly love and peace known to the Apostles.

Other examples indicate (chiefly in the rubrics) what ritual acts and non-verbal symbols were used. For example, Grottaferrata... II (in Greek from the 11th century) begins with the rubric: "The priest shall place the holy Gospel on the Gospel stand and they that are to be joined together place their (right) hands on it, holding lighted candles in their left hands. Then shall the priest cense them and say..." The rubric for the conclusion of this ceremony directs the two men to "kiss the holy Gospel and the priest and one another."

One should emphasize that these ceremonies were peculiar to the liturgical traditions of Greece and the Balkans. Boswell says that the ceremony "disappeared from most of Western (as opposed to Central and Eastern) Europe," and that "no Latin versions of the ceremony survive at all, although it must have been performed in Latin in Ireland, and probably sometimes in Italy." The heterogeneous bits of evidence (some of them colorful and anecdotal) that he presents do not convince me that there was ever anything akin to the Eastern ceremony in the Latin West.

The liturgical texts that Boswell brings to our attention are certainly very interesting, and their similarities to nuptial liturgies (though not as great as Boswell suggests) call for careful consideration and comment. Nevertheless, I have some profound problems with Boswell's treatment....

Boswell does not bring the ceremonies into focus until roughly half-way through the book, by which point a judgment has already been made as to what the ceremonies were. Prior to this, Boswell discusses the vocabulary of love and marriage; "heterosexual matrimony"; various forms of same-sex and homosexual relationships in the Greco-Roman world; the Christian understanding of marriage; and nuptial liturgies. All of this material seems to be provided by way of background, not marshaled on behalf of a thesis. Scholarly opinions on the alliances in question appear piecemeal in the course of the book, so that Boswell does not give us any clear impression of the interpretations that he rejects.

... What is Boswell trying to prove? What does he suppose the ceremonies in question to have been? The texts themselves use names such as *adelphopoiêsis* ("brother-making") to denote the ritual. What kind of "brotherhood" was really involved?

* * *

Boswell recounts discovering in Italy "many versions of the ceremony that were obviously the same-sex *equivalent* of a medieval heterosexual marriage ceremony" (my italics). A stronger form of the thesis would be the claim that the ceremony was a celebration of homosexual marriage. Actually, Boswell himself never claims this much. Indeed, when he at last raises the question, "Was it a marriage?" he replies that the "answer to this question depends to a considerable extent on one's conception of marriage." The discussion that follows is inconclusive. Moreover, Boswell adds that "the concept of someone innately and exclusively 'homosexual' was largely unknown to the postclassical world," and that "relationships of this sort were not understood in a sense comparable to modern 'gay marriage.' "

Nevertheless, Boswell implies in an indirect way that these were gay marriages. For example, he speaks of those (i.e., scholars who do not share his point of view) who are "reluctant to contemplate a *nuptial rite* for same-sex union." But elsewhere he observes: "The ambiguity of the few surviving texts precludes categorizing them unequivocally as *same-sex marital contracts*." (Italics are mine in these two quotations.) This implies that there were same-sex marital contracts in the East. Crucially, Boswell consistently refers to "heterosexual matrimony," which implies that there is a generic matrimony of which there are hetero- and homosexual species. The same implication is present

(although less apparent) in the phrase "comparison of same-sex and heterosexual ceremonies of union" (which is the subtitle of chapter six). Thus Boswell declares the stronger form of his thesis only by innuendo.

Much of his argument depends upon ambiguity and equivocation. Perhaps the most serious case of conceptual slipperiness arises in the phrase "same-sex union," which Boswell uses to translate (even in the appendix of translations) terms such as *adelphopoiêsis*. Boswell argues that terms involving the word "brother" would have been confusing to English readers because of what "brother" connotes in our usage. But it is arguable that the term "same-sex union" is just as confusing for similar reasons. To any modern reader (such as Gary Trudeau, apparently), it suggests "gay marriage." Inasmuch as one assumes this, the translation of the term begs the entire question of the book.

Boswell claims that "union" is a neutral term:

> To retain this rich multiplicity of connotations [of the Greek and Slavonic words equivalent to "brother," "brotherhood," etc.]—sexual, asexual; transcending and incorporating sex—I have employed the most neutral terms I could devise in translating the original concepts, such as "union" for *adelphotês* (which could be rendered "brotherhood"), or "be united" instead of "become siblings," which would be overtly and distinctly misleading to most English speakers, since it would evoke notions of adoption.

But "union" is by no means a neutral term; it is a very strong term. Readers will inevitably assume that "union" means "marriage," and in this context the word seems to connote sexual union and the joining of "two in one flesh."

To buttress his case Boswell observes that prejudiced scholars will find the idea that the alliances in question are same-sex unions to be repellent. For example, he says that anthropologists and others are anxious to "explain away the ceremony of same-sex union" as a form of blood brotherhood. But if "same-sex union" is a neutral term, what is there to explain away? Likewise, Boswell speaks of "the native and profound disinclination of most people brought up in modern Christian societies to believe that there could have been a Christian ceremony solemnizing same-sex unions." Again, regarding a curious Irish ceremony recorded by Gerald of Wales (from the late 12th or early 13th century), Boswell writes: "Its nature has long been obscured both by artful mistranslation and a general unwillingness to recognize something *as ostensibly improbable as a same-sex union*" (italics mine). But inasmuch as "same-sex union" is a neutral term, no one can find anything ostensibly improbable in the existence of such a union.

It seems to me, therefore, that "same-sex union" is an ill-chosen and dangerously slippery term. Nevertheless, let us stipulate that it is a neutral expression that means exactly what *adelphotēs* or *adelphopoiēsis* means, whatever that may be. The existence of liturgies for same-sex unions is then incontrovertible. The question is: Were these ceremonies the "equivalent" of heterosexual marriages (to use the weaker form of Boswell's thesis)? What kind and what degree of equivalence are we looking for? Equivalence in what respect?

Boswell claims that the relation is evident (to those not blinded by their prejudices and preconceptions) in the liturgies themselves. He notes that the texts for brother-making ceremonies are often contiguous to nuptial liturgies in the manuscripts. When one compares the brother-making liturgies with nuptial liturgies, however, the similarities one finds, while interesting, are not enough to imply equivalence or to suggest that the brother-making ceremonies were in any sense nuptial.

* * *

To exemplify the "heterosexual" nuptial liturgy, Boswell provides a translation of a Western rite: that of the Gelasian Sacramentary. (Why this choice? One would have supposed that an Eastern rite would have been more pertinent.) Conspicuous in this rite are references to procreation. Thus the minister invokes God as the one who instituted matrimony "so that in the multiplication of children of adoption the fecund chastity of the holy married may persist" (Boswell's translation). Again, the rite beseeches God that husband and wife "may see the children of their children unto the third and fourth generation." And as in all Western nuptial liturgies (and, indeed, as in the more elaborate early medieval dotal contracts), the rite commemorates how God fashioned Eve from Adam's side so that all humankind should descend from them. Petition for the "fruit of the womb" is equally conspicuous in the Eastern liturgies. Needless to say, there is nothing like this in the rites for "same-sex union."

Boswell notes that there are "interesting differences" in the choice of scriptural texts. These differences are not very surprising. Among the texts commonly used in marriage were Genesis 1:28 (on fecundity), Genesis 2:18 (on the formation of Eve from Adam's side), Matthew 19:1–6 (where Jesus deduces from marriage "in the beginning" and in particular from Genesis 2:23 that divorce is contrary to God's will), and John 2:1–11 (on the marriage at Cana). In same-sex unions, Boswell tells us, the most common texts were John 15:17, 17:1 and 18–26 (on love and harmony), 1 Corinthians 13:4–8 (on love), and Psalm 133 ("Behold, how good and how pleasant it is for brethren to dwell together in unity"). There is nothing to suggest equivalence here, and no hint of anything nuptial.

Boswell writes that "the most striking parallels have to do with visual symbolism," and that the "principal structural similarities between the ceremony of same-sex union and heterosexual nuptial offices were binding with a stole or veil, the imposition of crowns, the holding of a feast after the ceremony for the families and friends, the making of circles around the altar, the use of a cross, occasionally the use of swords, and—virtually always—the joining of right hands."

If it is true that crowning was regularly involved, this would indeed be very remarkable, for the ceremony of crowning was and is central to the Eastern nuptial rite, where it took on immense and specifically nuptial significance. Boswell provides just two pieces of evidence for this. One is an obscure Crook text that prohibits monks from receiving boys from baptism, "laying hold of the crowns of marriage," and forming brotherhoods with them. Since this is a set of things *prohibited* to monks, it is not clear which elements might be permissible to non-monks. Perhaps what is in question is an abuse of the traditional brotherhood.

The other piece of evidence offered seems to me to be a serious error. "An eleventh-century exemplar [for a ceremony of same-sex union] does not mention the *removal* of crowns, which

necessarily implies their previous imposition." The exemplar in question is Grottaferrata ... II, which is in two parts. The first part, which is explicitly a ceremony for brother-making, appears to end with the rubric: "Then shall they kiss the holy Gospel and the priest and one another, and conclude..." At this point, Boswell notes, a scribe has drawn a line across the manuscript. There follows a prayer beginning with the title "Ecclesiastical canon of marriage of the Patriarch Methodius." This prayer, which is very clearly from a nuptial rite, ends with a rubric that refers to the removal of crowns.

It should be obvious that the second prayer is from a different rite, and that this text mentions only the removal, not the imposition, of crowns because the early part of it is missing. It is likely that a scribe grafted on the second text by mistake, and that he or someone else noticed this and drew the line to alert the reader's attention to the error. In a long and difficult footnote, Boswell tries to show that the line does not have this significance, but the final, manifestly nuptial prayer is different from Boswell's other examples of brother-making prayers in crucial respects: its title refers to marriage; the prayer itself refers to the "bond of marriage" and to making "two into one"; and the concluding rubric refers to the crowns. Even without the scribe's warning line, we should know that this does not belong to the brother-making ceremony.

* * *

The genuine common elements are very interesting, but what may one deduce from them? None of them is specifically nuptial. The kiss, for example, acquired a specifically nuptial meaning in marriage ceremonies (where some regarded it as a kind of premonition of sexual consummation), but in itself it was a universal and asexual symbol of greeting and concord. Similarly, the joining of right hands was a token (then as now) of any kind of agreement. To make much of this evidence, one would need carefully to analyze the history and meaning of each element, which Boswell does not do.

Moreover, the similarities between the brother-making ceremonies and nuptial ceremonies are striking and even a little shocking to us *because* we have a concept of homosexual orientation and gay marriage. A culture that possessed no such notion would not have been struck in this way by the similarities. Lacking surface evidence, one needs to know what same-sex union was and what marriage was, so that one can compare the two or at least make sense of Boswell's claim. But Boswell does not even make clear what *he* takes same-sex union to have been.

Setting out his policies of translation at the outset, Boswell explains that where the Greek and Slavonic texts for the ceremonies use terms that might be literally translated "brother" or "become brothers," it would be misleading to translate them thus. This is because, on the one hand, "the meanings of the nouns to contemporaries were 'lover,' and 'form an erotic union,' " while on the other hand English readers will "relate such concepts more to feelings of goodwill and fraternal concern than to intimacy or romantic attachment."

Should we assume, then, that in Boswell's view same-sex unions were homoerotic? Not necessarily. Later in the book Boswell modestly claims that sexual relations between men "joined in some sort of ecclesiastical union ... *probably* did not seem even mildly sinful" (my italics). (This is mere guesswork.) On the next page, he raises the question of whether same-sex unions were homosexual. Obviously (he points out), they were homosexual in the literal sense of the word, since the partners were of the same sex. But was the ceremony erotic? Boswell replies: "This is hard to answer for societies without a comparable nomenclature or taxonomy." Was the relationship intended to become erotic: "Probably, sometimes, but this is obviously a difficult question to answer about the past, since participants cannot be interrogated." Boswell then points out that "a sexual component is not generally what constitutes the definitive test of 'marriage,' particularly in premodern societies, where few people married for erotic fulfillment."

Just as Boswell fails to explain what same-sex unions were, he also fails to provide any clear account of what (heterosexual) marriage was. Statements like the one just quoted, as well as his frequent observation that in premodern societies, romantic love was (ideally) a consequence of marriage rather than its motive and origin, seem intended in part to loosen our sense of what marriage was. But this merely negative approach, while very proper in itself, does not help Boswell's case. If one aims to prove that some new virus is a variety of influenza, one can do so only to the extent that one knows what influenza is.

To grasp the sense of Boswell's claim that the brotherhoods were equivalent to (heterosexual) marriage, one needs to have some account of what the latter was. In Christian Europe during the patristic and medieval periods, numerous exigencies—cultural, legal, theological, ascetic—caused the notion of marriage to be modified, analogically transposed, extended, stretched and delimited. Nevertheless, certain basic ideas remain visible beneath the surface.

First, marriage was by definition "the union of a man and a woman" (as the Roman jurist Ulpian said). If Boswell's implied notion of generic (homo- or heterosexual) matrimony ever existed in premodern European culture, there was never a name for it. Matrimony was a union of opposites (see Colossians 3:18–19). Second, marriage was a stable joining of a man and a woman for the sake of procreating and raising children. Hence the phrase *liberorum procreandorum causa* ("for the sake of procreating children"), which appeared on Roman nuptial documents as a way of distinguishing marriage from other relationships. The difference between marriage and concubinage, in Roman law, was that only a man's children by marriage were his own children: that is, his heirs, members of his family, and (in the case of males) the continuation of his paternal power.

More basic yet in the Judaic and Christian traditions was the notion of marriage as a union of two in one flesh. As it appears in Genesis 2:24, this is probably a complex notion, but 1 Corinthians 6:16 (where Paul, by a curious irony, applies the text to prostitution) suggests that sexual union is part of the idea. Despite the efforts of some medieval theologians, the notion of sexual consummation remained integral to the church's notion of marriage. Sex is integral to marriage in other ways—for example, in the Pauline conjugal debt (see 1 Cor. 7:2–5), which was hugely important in both Eastern and Western thinking about marriage, and in the impediments of relationship (since even an unconsummated marriage is invalid when its sexual consummation would be incestuous).

Subsuming all these elements was the nuptial symbolism that entered the Bible in the Book of Hosea and culminated in Ephesians 5:31–32, a text that compares the union of "two in one flesh" to the union between Christ and the church. This text and its theology did not appear much in the nuptial liturgies, but they were central to the theology of marriage. Moreover, the symbolism was manifest in the quasi-nuptial rite in which a woman took the veil to become a religious (a bride of Christ).

To claim that there were same-sex equivalents of marriage in this historical context is to claim that same-sex unions were supposed in some way to embody this model or something analogous to it. This does not seem possible, and in any case, I see no evidence for it. One should note that Boswell does not claim or offer any evidence to suggest that the brotherhoods were in any sense an alternative to (heterosexual) marriage or exclusive of marriage.

* * *

Buried in this very muddled book is an interesting and plausible thesis, which goes like this: On the one hand, premodern Christian culture knew nothing of gay marriage, had no concept of the homosexual person and condemned homosexual acts. On the other hand, institutionalized or otherwise socially recognized same-sex relationships, such as the brotherhoods studied here, provided scope for the expression of what we would now regard as homosexual inclinations—much more scope than was possible, for example, in the cultures of the late Middle Ages and the Reformation. They may even have occasionally provided cover for homosexual acts. (If this is what Boswell had been judged to be saying, however, the book would not have captured the media's attention.)

This book has very little bearing on the issue of gay union and gay marriage in churches today. A Christian proponent of gay marriage or even of tolerated gay unions must face the fact that such acts are a radical departure from traditional norms. One can make this departure either by honestly abandoning some or all of the tradition, or (much more tenuously) by using an historical, relativist hermeneutic to locate some deeper stream within the tradition. Both of these lines of argument have appeared in the discussion of women's ordination, which also represents a radical departure from traditional norms but which is now widely accepted. But one cannot find support either for the licitness of homosexuality or for the validity of gay marriage within the tradition of the premodern church.

POSTSCRIPT

Did Same-Sex Unions Exist in Medieval Europe?

There is little dispute that the same-sex unions that Boswell describes actually existed and were used as ritualistic ceremonies. A crucial factor in this issue is what these ceremonies represented. Were they considered the equivalent of heterosexual marriages? Or, were they merely "brotherhood" agreements, which had little religious sanction? The linguistic and textual difficulties involving the sources of these ceremonies make this a difficult choice for scholars.

Another problem to consider is to what extent have current conditions and exigencies powered this issue? Have present views of same-sex unions influenced the issue's historical construction?

Boswell's *Christianity, Social Tolerance, and Homosexuality: Gay People in Western Europe from the Beginning of the Christian Era to the Fourteenth Century* (University of Chicago Press, 1980) is a useful general introduction to this issue. Volume I and II of the series *A History of Private Life*, Philippe Aries and Georges Duby, eds.; Paul Veyne, ed., *From Pagan Rome to Byzantium* (Harvard University Press, 1987); and Georges Duby, ed., *Revelations of the Medieval World* (Harvard University Press, 1988) provide general information on sexuality and sexual relations during the times covered.

Scholarly journals from the 1994–1996 years might have reviews of Boswell's books and rejoinders to them. There is an interesting review and response to it in *The New Republic*. Brent D. Shaw's review in the July 18, 1994, edition prompted a response from Ralph Hexter and a reply by Shaw in the October 3, 1994, edition of the magazine. A perusal of these pieces provides an interesting view of the workings of the historical profession.

ISSUE 6

Does the Modern University Have Its Roots in the Islamic World?

YES: Mehdi Nakosteen, from *History of Islamic Origins of Western Education* A.D. *800–1350* (University of Colorado Press, 1964)

NO: Charles Homer Haskins, from *The Rise of Universities* (Great Seal Books, 1957)

ISSUE SUMMARY

YES: Professor of history and philosophy of education Mehdi Nakosteen traces the roots of the modern university to the golden age of Islamic culture (750–1150 C.E.). He maintains that Muslim scholars assimilated the best of classical scholarship and developed the experimental method and the university system, which they passed on to the West before declining.

NO: The late historian Charles Homer Haskins (1870–1937) traces the university of the twentieth century to its predecessors in Paris and Bologna, where, he argues, during the twelfth and thirteenth centuries the first universities in the world sprang up.

In the seventh century A.D. the prophet Muhammad united the Arab world under the banner of a new monotheistic religion, Islam, which means "surrender" to Allah or God. In 622 Muhammad left the city of Mecca for the city of Medina. Since he was fleeing persecution, this flight is known as *Hijra*, or "breaking of former ties." Muslims, the followers of Islam, use that date as the first year in their calendar. Using that calendar, the year 2000 according to the Christian calendar will be 1378 A.H. (*anno Hegirae*). Christians began their calendar with the birth of Jesus, calling everything after that date A.D. for *anno Domini* (in the year of our Lord) and everything before that date B.C. (before Christ). Taking into account that much of the world is not Christian, Western scholars have begun to use the designations C.E. (for common era) to replace A.D. and B.C.E. (for before the common era) to replace B.C. You will find the A.H. and A.D. designations used in the following selections.

United under Islam, Arab warriors conquered the Persian Empire, took some Byzantine cities, crossed North Africa, and invaded Europe. Stopped at 732 in Tours, France, the Islamic conquest ushered in a "golden age" of learning centered in Cordoba, the capital of Muslim Spain. At that time the largest monastery library in Europe contained fewer than 100 books, while the library in Cordoba contained over 500,000 volumes. At a time when

Europe had lost much of its Greco-Roman intellectual heritage and learning was at a low point, Muslim scholars were translating Greek works from the Persian and Byzantine cultures into Arabic and commenting on them. This learning, along with their original contributions in mathematics, medicine, science, and philosophy, was passed on to the West when Islamic culture was conquered first by the Seljuk Turks and later by Genghis Khan and the Mongols of Central Asia.

The Western intellectual debt to Islamic scholars is undisputed. However, what about the college or university as an institution of higher learning? Were Western scholars able to take the world's heritage of learning and use it to fashion the modern world because they invented the university or because it, too, was borrowed from the Islamic world?

In the following selections, Mehdi Nakosteen argues that the language barrier and general inaccessibility of historical material to Western scholars, along with religious prejudice and the decline of Islamic culture, have made it easy for Europeans and Americans to assume credit for the modern university. In actuality, he maintains, the university is rooted in the Islamic world. Charles Homer Haskins, however, sees the medieval European universities in Paris, France, and Bologna, Italy, arising spontaneously in response to an influx of new knowledge. Although he credits the Arab scholars of Spain with much of that new knowledge, he does not trace the roots of the university as an institution to the Arab world.

Haskins delivered the lectures on which his selection is based in 1923. The challenge put forth by Nakosteen is part of the revisionist process that has been going on in history for the last 30 or so years. Part of that process is challenging assumptions that have gone unchallenged for centuries. In 1937, the year Haskins died, Western historians often credited Europe and America with all that was worthwhile in modern life. Our heritage was Greek, and the line was assumed to be unbroken. Modern scholars, however, are examining the influence of Africa on the Greeks and considering the contributions from Asia and the Arab world with a new openness. This is all part of the ongoing refinement of historical knowledge and may be expected to continue as long as there are scholars.

YES   Mehdi Nakosteen

THE NATURE AND SCOPE OF MUSLIM EDUCATION, 750–1350

All dates refer to A.D. unless otherwise specified.

Europe was in its medieval period when the Muslims wrote a colorful chapter in the history of education. Many of their greatest contributions, particularly to Western education, have gone unnoticed because of religious prejudice, language barriers, the decline of Islamic culture, and inaccessibility of historic materials for Western historians of education. The Muslims assimilated through their educational system the best of classical cultures and improved them. Among the assimilated fields were philosophy and Hellenistic medical, mathematical, and technological sciences; Hindu mathematics, medicine, and literature; Persian religions, literature, and sciences; and Syrian commentaries on Hellenistic science and philosophy. By applying the classical sciences to practical pursuits, the Muslims developed the empirical-experimental method, although they failed to take full advantage of it. Later the method was adopted in Europe. They encouraged free inquiry and made available to the public the instruments of research and scholarship. They opened their public and even private libraries to public use, not only regionally but internationally. At a time when books were "published" only through the tedious labor of copyists, they made hundreds, even thousands, of copies of reference materials and made them available to all caring to learn from them. Often they allowed scores of books—sometimes more than a hundred per person—to be borrowed for an almost indefinite time for special studies and prolonged research. They provided food, lodging, and even incidental money for scholars from far away; they made their great teachers internationally accessible by encouraging the concept of the travelling scholar.

In the golden age (750–1150) of their cultural-educational activities they did not permit theology and dogma to limit their scholarship. They searched into every branch of human knowledge, be it philology, history, historiography, law, sociology, literature, ethics, philosophy, theology, medicine, mathematics, logic, jurisprudence, art, architecture, or ceramics. They respected learn-

From Mehdi Nakosteen, *History of Islamic Origins of Western Education* A.D. *800–1350* (University of Colorado Press, 1964), pp. 37–42, 52–53, 61–63. Copyright © 1964 by University of Colorado Press. Reprinted by permission. Some notes omitted.

ing; they honored the scholar. They introduced the science and philosophy of the Greeks, Persians, and Hindus to Western Christian schoolmen. But the story of Western education's debt to Islam is still to be written with fullness of knowledge and without prejudice and predetermination of results. What kind of education was responsible for so much in so short a time?

Muslim education went through two distinct periods. First was the period covering the ninth and tenth centuries, when schools developed spontaneously with private endowments interested in public enlightenment; and second the period beginning in the eleventh century and developing through the twelfth and thirteenth centuries, when education became the function of the state, and schools were institutionalized for purposes of sectarian education and political indoctrination.

MADRASAHS AND NIZAMIYYAS

A new type of school was conceived as a state institution to promote religious indoctrination of the Sunnite Islamic faith and political indoctrination of a Turkish-Persian style, aside from general learning and particular training. Nizam-al-Mulk (d. 1092; 485 A.H.), the founder and popularizer of these *madrasahs* (schools of public instruction), was a famous vizier (prime minister) in the administration of the Seljuq sultans in the eleventh century. He established the madrasah about the middle of that century, which, though not the first school in Islam, was the first system of special schools geared to that state and Sunnite Islam. The madrasahs had, aside from their zest for learning, both political and religious purposes— the moulding of public opinion in Sun-

nite orthodox Islam against the Shi'ah branch. Large sums of money were allotted for the establishment and maintenance of these schools with generous scholarships, pensions, and rations granted to all worthy students. In fact, Nizam arranged for regular stipends to all students. The schools were institutionalized under state control and support, and standardized madrasahs were established in all large cities within Islam, with the exception of Spain and Sicily. The greatest of these academies was the one established by Nizam in Baghdad, the famous *Nizamiyyah,* which opened for teaching in 1066–67 (459 A.H.) and continued as a center of learning for several centuries, motivated primarily by religious and literary pursuits. Altogether, Nizam-al-Mulk made the greatest single contribution to education in founding and extending an almost universal system of schools (madrasahs) throughout Eastern Islam.[1] He was one of the most learned men of his time, greatly versed in Muslim hadith, or tradition, and one of the great political theorists of Islam, as shown in his famous *Siyasat-Namah.* His passion for universal education was limited only by the means at his disposal. The schools he founded all over the empire were endowed generously. He supplied them with libraries, the best professors he could find, and a system of scholarships to aid all the students. Let us look into his educational enterprise in some detail.

NIZAM-AL-MULK AND MUSLIM EDUCATION

The opening of the first school carrying the name of the Persian statesman, Nizam-al-Mulk, took place in 1066 (459 A.H.). It marks the transition from the mosque schools and the beginning of a system of public schools, or madrasahs, throughout the vast area of the Muslim world, which was under strong Persian cultural and administrative influence. This influence continued, first under Arab political supremacy under the Abbassides from the middle of the eighth century to the ninth, and again during the long period of Turkish (Ottoman) politico-religious supremacy, to the early decades of the sixteenth century (1517). It is true that the earlier Turks had a simple culture and were given to warfare and conquest. But settling down to administer their empire, they learned from the superior cultures of the Persians and the Arabs, adopted the Arabic alphabet, and accepted Islam. In time they adapted the foreign cultures to their own needs and tastes, and encouraged the establishment throughout their empire of schools to perpetuate Sunnite Islam and Turkish politics and policies. Tarikh Zaidan, in his *Al-Tamaddun al-Islami (History of Islamic Civilization),* states that the Turkish princes encouraged learning and increased the number of schools in their empire, guided by three motives: The type of heavenly reward; the fear of losing their fortunes to more greedy superiors or antagonists, so that they utilized their wealth in establishing schools; finally, but most important of all, the desire to indoctrinate religious beliefs of the founder and to combat opposing religious views.

It was the employment of the school for sectarian indoctrination and political influence and propaganda that led the famous Seljuk Sultan Saladin to found madrasahs and also to close the college of Dar al-Ilm (The House of Learning) in Cairo in order to eliminate its Shi'ite influence. In fact it was not uncommon to dismiss professors during this period

from the madrasahs because of their religious beliefs, particularly Shi'ite. Muslim scholasticism (*Ilm al-Kalam*) developed in these sectarian colleges of Sunnite or Shi'ite beliefs.

The Sunnite belief received its most sweeping expression under Nizam-al-Mulk. Before his day, there were several institutions of learning in the Islamic world which resembled a college, such as Al-Azhar in Cairo, Egypt, in the last quarter of the tenth century; Dar al-Ilm and Dar al-Hikmah, also in Cairo, in the early decades of the eleventh; Bait-al-Hikmah in Baghdad during the reign of al-Ma'mun; and Baihaqiyyah at Nishapur in Khrasan, Persia. But to Nizam-al-Mulk goes the distinct credit for having founded an institution for instruction and indoctrination under government and religious control, for political and religious ends—a sectarian system of public education with secular emphasis and political motivation.

With these objectives in mind, Nizam-al-Mulk established schools in every city and village of Iraq and Khorassan. Even a small place, such as "Kharn al-Jabal near Tus ... had its teacher and school." These schools were well distributed from Khorassan in the east to Mesopotamia in the west. These so-called madrasahs soon became standardized, and many of them were built after the example of the one in Baghdad, which was built by Nizam-al-Mulk himself, and named Nizamiyyah (or Nidhamiyyah) in his honor.

Nizamiyyahs ... were founded not only in Baghdad, but in Nisabur, Balkh, Herat, Isfahan, Marw, Basrah and Mosul. Not only did Nizam-al-Mulk establish these academies or colleges, but he endowed them. It is estimated that $1,500,000 was spent annually on educational, semi-educational and religious institutions.

Nizamiyyah University, the most famous of the chain of madrasahs, was built in Baghdad in 1065 under the educator's personal supervision. The earliest account of this university is given by ibn Khaldun, the great Arab philosopher-historian, who says:

> Nizam-al-Mulk ordered that Abu Is'haq al-Shirazi should be its professor, but when the people were assembled to hear him he did not appear. He was searched for, but was not to be found; so Abu Nasir ibn-al-Sabbagh was appointed to the post. Later Abu Is'haq met his classes in his mosque, but his students showed their dissatisfaction with his action and threatened to go over to ibn al-Sabbagh unless he accepted the professorship at the Nizamiyyah. Finally he acceded to their wishes, and ibn al-Sabbagh was dismissed after having lectured for only twenty days.

The chief reason for Abu Is'haq's refusal to teach at the Nizamiyyah was, according to ibn Khallikan, that he was "informed that the greater part of the materials employed in the construction of the college have been procured illegally." But the foregoing quotation is of extreme interest for the information it gives us that the mosques were the chief places of learning before the foundation of universities. There were over one hundred such mosques in Baghdad alone.

The principal motive in founding the Nizamiyyah was religious. Its objective was the teaching of "The Shafi'ite (Sunni) school of law," its sole emphasis being upon the teaching of theology and Islamic law, and it stood as a university of Islamic theological learning for several centuries. The great mystic al-Ghazzali taught there twenty-five years after its founding. Al-Abiwardi (d. 1104;

498 A.H.) and ibn Mubarak (d. 1184; 580 A.H.) were associated with it. Ibn Jubair who visited the school about the middle of the fourteenth century, said of it: "And in the midst of Suq al-Thalatha (Tuesday market) is the wonderful madrasah Al-Nizamiyyah, whose beauty has become proverbial."

AIMS OF MUSLIM EDUCATION

The aims of Muslim education in "medieval" times may be defined as follows:

1. Religious aims, based on (a) *Qur'an* as source of knowledge, (b) spiritual foundation of education, (c) dependence upon God, (d) sectarian morals, (e) subordination of secular subjects to religion, (f) equality of all men before God and man, (g) supremacy of Muhammad over all other prophets, (h) belief in the six articles of Imam or Creed (God, angels, scripture, prophets, judgment, decrees) and (i) belief (and application) in A'amal or religious duties, including confession of faith (There is no God but God), prayers, alms, fasting, and pilgrimage.

2. Secular aims, the importance of which is well suggested by a Muslim tradition, attributed to Muhammad, which says, "The best among you are not those who neglect this world for the other, or the other world for this. He is the one who works for both together." Among these aims were pursuit of all knowledge, as the revelation of the nature of God; education open to all on equal terms, limited only by ability and interest; and guidance and teaching as essential to promote (initiate) knowledge and education.

The *Mutakallimun (Loquentes)*, the Muslim scholastic teachers (speakers of truths), stressed the importance of teachers whose knowledge may be traced back to relevation or may have been made manifest directly by intuition. This was the view of the theologian-philosopher-educator al-Ghazzali, who believed in three degrees of knowledge: (a) Common-sense knowledge, restricted by undisciplined sense-experience and dependent upon external authority; (b) scientific knowledge; (c) intuitive knowledge.

It is of interest to note that al-Ghazzali's concept of scientific knowledge includes seven basic principles or conditions: Stimulation of the search for scientific knowledge; application of scientific arts; advancement of applied sciences and extensive application of them; development of laboratory and experimental pursuits; encouragement of arts and crafts (It was Aristotle in particular, from among the Greeks, who appealed to Islam. This was because of the Greek master's application of philosophy and science to the arts and needs of everyday living and because of the adaptability of his philosophic and scientific concepts to the art of living and the necessities of individual and civic life); encouragement of individual initiative and academic freedom for both teachers and pupils (in the college of Baghdad an inquiring student, who greeted the great teacher with devoted *salams* [bows], often ended the day with an intellectual fist fight with his master in defense of some principles, refutation of others, or hairsplitting argument over insignificant details); attainment of excellence, to produce great men of learning and leaders in public affairs. The pragmatic spirit of their education is indicated by development of textile fabrics, of irrigation systems, of iron and steel products, of earthenwares, and leather products, by architectural innovations, weaving of rugs and carpets, manufacture of paper and gunpowder, maintenance of a merchant marine of a thousand ships, and advancement of commercial activity.

Although Muslim education aimed at practical training, such training was a rule based upon instruction in fundamental sciences. Thus, in the system, practice was sustained by theory; theory verified in practice. Even in commercial training, economics as a science was a foundational training.

It is of interest to note that as Islam began to decline after the end of the eleventh century, the number of its schools of higher learning increased and flourished. These colleges were, however, almost all denominational schools opened and supported by leaders of various Islamic religious factions. Each denominational college was open, with few exceptions, only to followers of a given sect. Religious and literary studies and Arabic language and grammar dominated the subject matter at the expense of philosophy, science, and social studies. The very abundance of these religious schools indicated the gradual decline which was under way. These colleges were intolerant of innovations, suspicious of secular studies, and aloof from creative scholars. Some of these colleges survived destruction by the Mongols in the thirteenth century and remained centers of dogmatic theological instruction to the fourteenth and fifteenth centuries.

There was competition among these denominational schools, particularly between the Shi'ite and Sunnite (Hanafite) religious factions. This competition proved healthy in the increase of these colleges and in their facilities, endowments, and the like, and would have been a tremendous educational power except for their limitations because of their religious nature.

It is of interest also to note that during this same period new universities were beginning to develop in western Europe, particularly in Italy, Germany, France, and England. But unlike the Islamic denominational schools, the Western universities were preserving the best intellectual elements that Islamic research and scholarship had developed during its creative centuries, from the ninth to the twelfth centuries. Islamic works were reaching Europe at about the same period (twelfth and thirteenth centuries) when secular learning was declining in Islam. The works of hundreds of translators not only enriched and created or enlarged many Western universities but brought about the Western Renaissance of the fourteenth and fifteenth centuries. One reason for this, of course, was the revival of secular interest and research in the West, which, though curtailed by religious passion until the seventeenth and eighteenth centuries, was left relatively free from then on to discover new knowledges and usher in the modern world. . . .

THE CURRICULUM OF MUSLIM SCHOOLS

The curriculum of Muslim education at that time reminds us in its extensive and intensive nature of curricular programs of modern advanced systems of education, particularly on higher levels of education. It was not unusual to find instruction in mathematics (algebra, trigonometry, and geometry), science (chemistry, physics, and astronomy), medicine (anatomy, surgery, pharmacy, and specialized medical branches), philosophy (logic, ethics, and metaphysics), literature (philology, grammar, poetry, and prosody), social sciences, history, geography, political disciplines, law, sociology, psychology, and jurisprudence, theology (comparative religions, history of religions, study of the Qur'an, religious tradition [hadith], and other religious topics). They offered advanced studies in the professions, for example, law and medicine.

Their vocational curriculum was varied and founded on the more general studies; in fact, it appears generally to have been as comprehensive as their education was universal. The extent and depth of Muslim curriculum can be detected by references to a number of encyclopedias of general knowledge and specific disciplines, among them the celebrated Encyclopedia of the Ikhwan al-Safa (the Brethren of Purity or Sincerity), which was known to and respected by European schoolmen.

Another indication of the extent of Muslim curriculum is manifested in the fact that one Arabic dictionary contained sixty volumes, with an illustration for each definition. Again, its richness may be determined by its practical and useful consequences, leading to such ventures as calculating the angle of the ecliptic, measuring the size of the earth, calculating the procession of the equinoxes, inventing the pendulum clock, explaining in the field of optics and physics such phenomena as "refraction of light, gravity, capillary attraction and twilight," using the globe in teaching the geography of a round earth, developing observatories for the empirical study of heavenly bodies, making advances in the uses of drugs, herbs, and foods for medication, establishing hospitals with a system of interns and externs, improving upon the science of navigation, introducing new concepts of irrigation, fertilization, and soil cultivation, discovering causes of certain diseases and developing correct diagnoses of them, proposing new concepts of hygiene, making use of anesthetics in surgery with newly innovated surgical tools, introducing the science of dissection in anatomy, furthering the scientific breeding of horses and cattle, and finding new ways of grafting to produce new types of flowers and fruits. In the area of chemistry, the curriculum led to the discovery of such substances as potash, alcohol, nitrate of silver, nitric acid, sulphuric acid, and corrosive sublimate. It also developed to a high degree of perfection the arts of textiles, ceramics, and metallurgy....

SOME MUSLIM CONTRIBUTIONS TO EDUCATION

Before concluding this brief summary of "medieval" Muslim education, it may be well to point out some of its basic contributions to educational theory and practice, and state also its basic shortcomings.

1. Throughout the twelfth and part of the thirteenth centuries, Muslim works on science, philosophy, and other fields were translated into Latin, particularly from Spain, and enriched the curriculum of the West, especially in northwestern Europe.
2. The Muslims passed on the experimental method of science, however imperfect, to the West.
3. The system of Arabic notation and decimals was introduced to the West.
4. Their translated works, particularly those of men such as Avicenna in medicine, were used as texts in classes of higher education far into the middle of the seventeenth century.
5. They stimulated European thought, reacquainted it with the Greek and other classical cultures and thus helped bring about the Renaissance.
6. They were the forerunners of European universities, having established hundreds of colleges in advance of Europe.
7. They preserved Greco-Persian thought when Europe was intolerant of pagan cultures.
8. European students in Muslim universities carried back new methods of teaching.
9. They contributed knowledge of hospitals, sanitation, and food to Europe.

The strength of the Muslim educational system lay in the following areas: It produced great scholars in almost every field. It developed literacy on a universal scale when illiteracy was the rule in Europe. It transmitted the best features of classical cultures to the West. It led the way in the development of libraries and universities. Its higher education in its creative centuries was open to rich and poor alike, the only requirements being ability and ambition. It held teachers and books in reverence, particularly on higher levels of instruction. The teacher, the book, the lecture, the debate—these were the nerve centers of its educational system.

The curriculum, which was in the early centuries balanced between sectarian and secular studies, became in the later centuries scholastic, making all or practically all secular studies subject to religious and theological approval. The curriculum became formal, fixed, traditional, religious, dogmatic, backward-looking. It encouraged static minds and conformity. It became authoritarian and essentialist.

Whereas in its early centuries Muslim education encouraged debates, experimentation, and individualism, in its later stages it encouraged formal methods, memorization, and recitation. A system which was in its early stages rather spontaneous and free, encouraging individuals to pursue learning and inspire others to enlightenment, lost in the later stages this sense of intellectual adventure and its direction became superimposed from the top (the state and church) rather than inspired by the people. This led in time to an elite and aristocratic concept of education, replacing its early democratic educational spirit. Muslim education did not, and with its scholastic disciplines could not, take advantage of the tools of science and experimentation which it had inherited and improved upon. Rather, it passed on these tools to European men of science, who utilized them effectively after the Renaissance and thus initiated and developed the modern world of science.

NOTES

1. Among the leading founders of schools in Islam should also be mentioned al Ma'mun (d. 833; 218 A.H.), who supported and endowed the first great Muslim educational center in Baghdad, the famous *Bait-al-Hikmah*, and was instrumental in having Greek, Persian, and Hindu translations made into Arabic by the greatest scholars of the time; Nur-al-Din (d. 1173; 569 A.H.), the Sultan of the kingdom of Syria who, after the dissolution of the Seljuq Empire, founded schools in Damascus and throughout his kingdom, including Egypt; Saladin (d. 1193; 589 A.H.), who extended the school systems in Syria and Egypt.

NO   Charles Homer Haskins

THE EARLIEST UNIVERSITIES

Universities, like cathedrals and parliaments, are a product of the Middle Ages. The Greeks and the Romans, strange as it may seem, had no universities in the sense in which the word has been used for the past seven or eight centuries. They had higher education, but the terms are not synonymous. Much of their instruction in law, rhetoric, and philosophy it would be hard to surpass, but it was not organized into the form of permanent institutions of learning. A great teacher like Socrates gave no diplomas; if a modern student sat at his feet for three months, he would demand a certificate, something tangible and external to show for it—an excellent theme, by the way, for a Socratic dialogue. Only in the twelfth and thirteenth centuries do there emerge in the world those features of organized education with which we are most familiar, all that machinery of instruction represented by faculties and colleges and courses of study, examinations and commencements and academic degrees. In all these matters we are the heirs and successors, not of Athens and Alexandria, but of Paris and Bologna.

The contrast between these earliest universities and those of today is of course broad and striking. Throughout the period of its origins the mediaeval university had no libraries, laboratories, or museums, no endowment or buildings of its own; it could not possibly have met the requirements of the Carnegie Foundation! As an historical text-book from one of the youngest of American universities tells us, with an unconscious touch of local color, it had "none of the attributes of the material existence which with us are so self-evident." The mediaeval university was, in the fine old phrase of Pasquier, "built of men"—*bâtie en hommes.* Such a university had no board of trustees and published no catalogue; it had no student societies—except so far as the university itself was fundamentally a society of students— no college journalism, no dramatics, no athletics, none of those "outside activities" which are the chief excuse for inside inactivity in the American college.

And yet, great as these differences are, the fact remains that the university of the twentieth century is the lineal descendant of mediaeval Paris and Bologna. They are the rock whence we were hewn; the hole of the pit whence we were

From Charles Homer Haskins, *The Rise of Universities* (Great Seal Books, 1957). Copyright © 1923 by Brown University; renewed 1957 by Cornell University. Reprinted by permission of Cornell University Press.

digged. The fundamental organization is the same, the historic continuity is unbroken. They created the university tradition of the modern world, that common tradition which belongs to all our institutions of higher learning, the newest as well as the oldest, and which all college and university men should know and cherish....

* * *

In recent years the early history of universities has begun to attract the serious attention of historical scholars, and mediaeval institutions of learning have at last been lifted out of the region of myth and fable where they long lay obscured. We now know that the foundation of the University of Oxford was not one of the many virtues which the millennial celebration could properly ascribe to King Alfred; that Bologna did not go back to the Emperor Theodosius; that the University of Paris did not exist in the time of Charlemagne, or for nearly four centuries afterward. It is hard, even for the modern world, to realize that many things had no founder or fixed date of beginning but instead "just grew," arising slowly and silently without definite record. This explains why, in spite of all the researches of Father Denifle[1] and Hastings Rashdall[2] and the local antiquaries, the beginnings of the oldest universities are obscure and often uncertain, so that we must content ourselves sometimes with very general statements.

The occasion for the rise of universities was a great revival of learning, not that revival of the fourteenth and fifteenth centuries to which the term is usually applied, but an earlier revival, less known though in its way quite as significant, which historians now call the renaissance of the twelfth century. So long as knowledge was limited to the seven liberal arts of the early Middle Ages, there could be no universities, for there was nothing to teach beyond the bare elements of grammar, rhetoric, logic, and the still barer notions of arithmetic, astronomy, geometry, and music, which did duty for an academic curriculum. Between 1100 and 1200, however, there came a great influx of new knowledge into western Europe, partly through Italy and Sicily, but chiefly through the Arab scholars of Spain—the works of Aristotle, Euclid, Ptolemy, and the Greek physicians, the new arithmetic, and those texts of the Roman law which had lain hidden through the Dark Ages. In addition to the elementary propositions of triangle and circle, Europe now had those books of plane and solid geometry which have done duty in schools and colleges ever since; instead of the painful operations with Roman numerals—how painful one can readily see by trying a simple problem of multiplication or division with these characters—it was now possible to work readily with Arabic figures; in the place of Boethius, the "Master of them that know" became the teacher of Europe in logic, metaphysics, and ethics. In law and medicine men now possessed the fulness of ancient learning. This new knowledge burst the bonds of the cathedral and monastery schools and created the learned professions; it drew over mountains and across the narrow seas eager youths who, like Chaucer's Oxford clerk of a later day, "would gladly learn and gladly teach," to form in Paris and Bologna those academic gilds which have given us our first and our best definition of a university, a society of masters and scholars.

To this general statement concerning the twelfth century there is one partial exception, the medical university of Salerno. Here, a day's journey to the south of Naples, in territory at first Lombard and later Norman, but still in close contact with the Greek East, a school of medicine had existed as early as the middle of the eleventh century, and for perhaps two hundred years thereafter it was the most renowned medical centre in Europe. In this "city of Hippocrates" the medical writings of the ancient Greeks were expounded and even developed on the side of anatomy and surgery, while its teachings were condensed into pithy maxims of hygiene which have not yet lost their vogue—"after dinner walk a mile," etc. Of the academic organization of Salerno we know nothing before 1231, and when in this year the standardizing hand of Frederick II regulated its degrees Salerno had already been distanced by newer universities farther north. Important in the history of medicine, it had no influence on the growth of university institutions.

If the University of Salerno is older in time, that of Bologna has a much larger place in the development of higher education. And while Salerno was known only as a school of medicine, Bologna was a many-sided institution, though most noteworthy as the centre of the revival of the Roman law. Contrary to a common impression, the Roman law did not disappear from the West in the early Middle Ages, but its influence was greatly diminished as a result of the Germanic invasions. Side by side with the Germanic codes, Roman law survived as the customary law of the Roman population, known no longer through the great law books of Justinian but in elementary manuals and form-books which grew thinner and more jejune as time went on. The *Digest*, the most important part of the *Corpus Juris Civilis*, disappears from view between 603 and 1076; only two manuscripts survived; in Maitland's phrase, it "barely escaped with its life." Legal study persisted, if at all, merely as an apprenticeship in the drafting of documents, a form of applied rhetoric. Then, late in the eleventh century, and closely connected with the revival of trade and town life, came a revival of law, foreshadowing the renaissance of the century which followed. This revival can be traced at more than one point in Italy, perhaps not first at Bologna, but here it soon found its centre for the geographical reasons which, then as now, made this city the meeting-point of the chief routes of communication in northern Italy. Some time before 1100 we hear of a professor named Pepo, "the bright and shining light of Bologna"; by 1119 we meet with the phrase *Bononia docta*. At Bologna, as at Paris, a great teacher stands at the beginning of university development. The teacher who gave Bologna its reputation was one Irnerius, perhaps the most famous of the many great professors of law in the Middle Ages. Just what he wrote and what he taught are still subjects of dispute among scholars, but he seems to have fixed the method of "glossing" the law texts upon the basis of a comprehensive use of the whole *Corpus Juris*, as contrasted with the meagre epitomes of the preceding centuries, fully and finally separating the Roman law from rhetoric and establishing it firmly as a subject of professional study. Then, about 1140, Gratian, a monk of San Felice, composed the *Decretum* which became the standard text in canon law, thus marked off from theology as a distinct subject of higher study; and the pre-eminence of Bologna as a law school was fully assured.

A student class had now appeared, expressing itself in correspondence and in poetry, and by 1158 it was sufficiently important in Italy to receive a formal grant of rights and privileges from Emperor Frederick Barbarossa, though no particular town or university is mentioned. By this time Bologna had become the resort of some hundreds of students, not only from Italy but from beyond the Alps. Far from home and undefended, they united for mutual protection and assistance, and this organization of foreign, or Transmontane, students was the beginning of the university. In this union they seem to have followed the example of the gilds already common in Italian cities. Indeed, the word university means originally such a group or corporation in general, and only in time did it come to be limited to gilds of masters and students, *universitas societas magistrorum discipulorumque*. Historically, the word university has no connection with the universe or the universality of learning; it denotes only the totality of a group, whether of barbers, carpenters, or students did not matter. The students of Bologna organized such a university first as a means of protection against the townspeople, for the price of rooms and necessaries rose rapidly with the crowd of new tenants and consumers, and the individual student was helpless against such profiteering. United, the students could bring the town to terms by the threat of departure as a body, secession, for the university, having no buildings, was free to move, and there are many historic examples of such migrations. Better rent one's rooms for less than not rent them at all, and so the student organizations secured the

power to fix the prices of lodgings and books through their representatives.

Victorious over the townsmen, the students turned on "their other enemies, the professors." Here the threat was a collective boycott, and as the masters lived at first wholly from the fees of their pupils, this threat was equally effective. The professor was put under bond to live up to a minute set of regulations which guaranteed his students the worth of the money paid by each. We read in the earliest statutes (1317) that a professor might not be absent without leave, even a single day, and if he desired to leave town he had to make a deposit to ensure his return. If he failed to secure an audience of five for a regular lecture, he was fined as if absent —a poor lecture indeed which could not secure five hearers! He must begin with the bell and quit within one minute after the next bell. He was not allowed to skip a chapter in his commentary, or postpone a difficulty to the end of the hour, and he was obliged to cover ground systematically, so much in each specific term of the year. No one might spend the whole year on introduction and bibliography! Coercion of this sort presupposes an effective organization of the student body, and we hear of two and even four universities of students, each composed of "nations" and presided over by a rector. Emphatically Bologna was a student university, and Italian students are still quite apt to demand a voice in university affairs. When I first visited the University of Palermo I found it just recovering from a riot in which the students had broken the front windows in a demand for more frequent, and thus less comprehensive, examinations. At Padua's seventh centenary in May 1922 the students practically took over the town, with a programme of processions and ceremonies quite their own and an amount of noise and tumult which almost broke up the most solemn occasions and did break the windows of the greatest hall in the city.

Excluded from the "universities" of students, the professors also formed a gild or "college," requiring for admission thereto certain qualifications which were ascertained by examination, so that no student could enter save by the gild's consent. And, inasmuch as ability to teach a subject is a good test of knowing it, the student came to seek the professor's license as a certificate of attainment, regardless of his future career. This certificate, the license to teach (*licentia docendi*), thus became the earliest form of academic degree. Our higher degrees still preserve this tradition in the words master (*magister*) and doctor, originally synonymous, while the French even have a *licence*. A Master of Arts was one qualified to teach the liberal arts; a Doctor of Laws, a certified teacher of law. And the ambitious student sought the degree and gave an inaugural lecture, even when he expressly disclaimed all intention of continuing in the teaching profession. Already we recognize at Bologna the standard academic degrees as well as the university organization and well-known officials like the rector.

Other subjects of study appeared in course of time, arts, medicine, and theology, but Bologna was preeminently a school of civil law, and as such it became the model of university organization for Italy, Spain, and southern France, countries where the study of law has always had political and social as well as merely academic significance. Some of these universities became Bologna's competitors, like Montpellier and Orleans as well as the Italian schools nearer home. Frederick II founded the University of Naples in 1224 so that the students of his Sicilian kingdom could go to a Ghibelline school at home instead of the Guelfic centre in the North. Rival Padua was founded two years earlier as a secession from Bologna, and only in 1922, on the occasion of Padua's seven-hundredth anniversary, I saw the ancient feud healed by the kiss of peace bestowed on Bologna's rector amid the encores of ten thousand spectators. Padua, however, scarcely equalled Bologna in our period, even though at a later age Portia sent thither for legal authority, and though the university still shines with the glory of Galileo.

* * *

In northern Europe the origin of universities must be sought at Paris, in the cathedral school of Notre-Dame. By the beginning of the twelfth century in France and the Low Countries learning was no longer confined to monasteries but had its most active centres in the schools attached to cathedrals, of which the most famous were those of Liège, Rheims, Laon, Paris, Orleans, and Chartres. The most notable of these schools of the liberal arts was probably Chartres, distinguished by a canonist like St. Ives and by famous teachers of classics and philosophy like Bernard and Thierry. As early as 991 a monk of Rheims, Richer, describes the hardships of his journey to Chartres in order to study the *Aphorisms* of Hippocrates of Cos; while from the twelfth century John of Salisbury, the leading northern humanist of the age, has left us an account of the masters.... Nowhere else today can we drop back more easily into a cathedral city of the twelfth century, the peaceful town still dominated by its church and sharing, now as then,

> the minister's vast repose.
> Silent and gray as forest-leaguered cliff
> Left inland by the ocean's slow retreat,
> .... patiently remote
> From the great tides of life it breasted once,
> Hearing the noise of men as in a dream.

By the time the cathedral stood complete, with its "dedicated shapes of saints and kings," it had ceased to be an intellectual centre of the first importance, overshadowed by Paris fifty-odd miles away, so that Chartres never became a university.

The advantages of Paris were partly geographical, partly political as the capital of the new French monarchy, but something must be set down to the influence of a great teacher in the person of Abelard. This brilliant young radical, with his persistent questioning and his scant respect for titled authority, drew students in large numbers wherever he taught, whether at Paris or in the wilderness. At Paris he was connected with the church of Mont-Sainte-Geneviève longer than with the cathedral school, but resort to Paris became a habit in his time, and in this way he had a significant influence on the rise of the university. In an institutional sense the university was a direct outgrowth of the school of Notre-Dame, whose chancellor alone had authority to license teaching in the diocese and thus kept his control over the granting of university degrees, which here as at Bologna were originally teachers' certificates. The early schools were within the cathedral precincts on the Ile de la Cité, that tangled quarter about Notre-Dame pictured by Victor Hugo which has long since been demolished. A little later we find masters and scholars living on the Little Bridge (Petit-Pont) which connected the island with the Left Bank of the Seine —this bridge gave its name to a whole school of philosophers, the Parvipontani —but by the thirteenth century they have overrun the Left Bank, thenceforth, the Latin Quarter of Paris.

At what date Paris ceased to be a cathedral school and became a university, no one can say, though it was certainly before the end of the twelfth century. Universities, however, like to have precise dates to celebrate, and the University of Paris has chosen 1200, the year of its first royal charter. In that year, after certain students had been killed in a town and gown altercation, King Philip Augustus issued a formal privilege which punished his prévôt and recognized the exemption of the students and their servants from lay jurisdiction, thus creating that special position of students before the courts which has not yet wholly disappeared from the world's practice, though generally from its law. More specific was the first papal privilege, the bull *Parens scientiarum* of 1231,[3] issued after a two years' cessation of lectures growing out of a riot in which a band of students, having found "wine that was good and sweet to drink," beat up the tavern keeper and his friends till they in turn suffered from the prévôt and his men, a dissension in which the thirteenth century clearly saw the hand of the devil. Confirming the existing exemptions, the Pope goes on to regulate the discretion of the chancellor in conferring the license, at the same time that he recognizes the right of the masters and students "to make constitutions and ordinances regulating the manner and time of lectures and disputations, the costume to be worn," attendance at masters' funerals, the lectures of bachelors, necessarily more limited than those of fully fledged masters, the price of lodgings, and the coercion of members. Students must not carry arms, and only those who frequent the schools regularly are to enjoy the exemptions of students, the interpretation in practice being attendance at not less than two lectures a week.

While the word university does not appear in these documents, it is taken for granted. A university in the sense of an organized body of masters existed already in the twelfth century; by 1231 it had developed into a corporation, for Paris, in contrast to Bologna, was a university of masters. There were now four faculties, each under a dean: arts, canon law (civil law was forbidden at Paris after 1219), medicine, and theology. The masters of arts, much more numerous than the others, were grouped into four "nations": the French, including the Latin peoples; the Normans; the Picard, including also the Low Countries; and the English, comprising England, Germany, and the North and East of Europe. These four nations chose the head of the university, the rector, as he is still generally styled on the Continent, whose term, however, was short, being later only three months. . . .

It is, then, in institutions that the university tradition is most direct. First, the very name university, as an association of masters and scholars leading the common life of learning. Characteristic of the Middle Ages as such a corporation is, the individualistic modern world has found nothing to take its place. Next, the notion of a curriculum of study, definitely laid down as regards time and subjects, tested by an examination and leading to a degree, as well as many of the degrees themselves—bachelor, as a stage toward the mastership, master, doctor, in arts, law, medicine, and theology. Then the faculties, four or more, with their deans, and the higher officers such as chancellors and rectors, not to mention the college, wherever the residential college still survives. The essentials of university organization are clear and unmistakable, and they have been handed down in unbroken continuity. They have lasted more than seven hundred years—what form of government has lasted so long?

NOTES

1. H. Denifle, *Die Enstehung der Universitäten des Mittelalters bis 1400*, vol. I (Berlin, 1880).

2. H. Rashdall, *The Universities of Europe in the Middle Ages*, 2 vols. in 3 (Oxford, 1895); rev. ed., 3 vols. (Oxford, 1936). . . .

3. Trans. by L. Thorndike, *University Records and Life in the Middle Ages* (New York, 1944), pp. 35–39.

POSTSCRIPT

Does the Modern University Have Its Roots in the Islamic World?

It is tempting to think that all modern institutions, especially those that we find admirable, have come down to us in a direct line from our intellectual forebears, the Greeks. To take the university as a case in point, however, we cannot trace its origins to Greece. As Haskins points out, the Greeks and Romans had no universities. Higher education was a much less organized enterprise of student-teacher interaction. There were no diplomas, courses of study, examinations, or commencements—at least not as we understand these terms today. Agreeing that we cannot trace the Western university to the Greeks, Haskins and Nakosteen part company on where its roots actually lie. Haskins finds universities springing up in Bologna, Paris, Salerno, and Oxford in response to an infusion of new knowledge brought about by the restoration of trade routes after the Crusades. Nakosteen finds an unbroken line from the eighth-century Arab world to the late European Middle Ages. The university system, he argues, was formed in an Arab context and made its way unchanged into a European one.

If we begin a history of education from within the Islamic world, new patterns will emerge. For an introduction to Islam as a cultural system, *Islam and the Cultural Accommodation of Social Change* by Bassam Tibi (Westview Press, 1991) offers a clear introduction to the Sunni/Shi'a split in Islam, which persists today, and a discussion of language (in this case Arabic) as the medium in which cultural symbols are articulated. Students may also be interested in Francis Robinson, ed., *The Cambridge Illustrated History of the Islamic World* (Cambridge University Press, 1996), especially chapter 7, "Knowledge, Its Transmission, and the Making of Muslim Societies." In chapter 9, "The Iranian Diaspora: The Edge Creates a Center," of *Islam. A View from the Edge* (Columbia University Press, 1994), Richard W. Bulliet describes the role of Iranian scholars in the spread of *madrasa*, or Islamic colleges.

For additional background on European universities of the Middle Ages, see *The Medieval University* by Helene Wieruszowski (Van Nostrand Reinhold, 1966) and *The Scholastic Culture of the Middle Ages: 1000–1300* by John W. Baldwin (D. C. Heath, 1971). The movie *Stealing Heaven* tells the story of Heloise and Abelard. Set in twelfth-century France, it also offers a very realistic portrayal of the emerging European university system of disputation between professors and students. Finally, Norman F. Cantor's *The Civilization of the Middle Ages* (HarperCollins, 1993) has a chapter entitled "Moslem and Jewish Thought: The Aristotelian Challenge," which summarizes the influence of Islamic thought on Europe.

ISSUE 7

Were Environmental Factors Responsible for the Mayan Collapse?

YES: Richard E. W. Adams, from *Prehistoric Mesoamerica*, rev. ed. (University of Oklahoma Press, 1991)

NO: George L. Cowgill, from "Teotihuacan, Internal Militaristic Competition, and the Fall of the Classic Maya," in Norman Hammond and Gordon R. Willey, eds., *Maya Archaeology and Ethnohistory* (University of Texas Press, 1979)

ISSUE SUMMARY

YES: Professor of anthropology Richard E. W. Adams argues that although military factors played a role in the Mayan demise, a combination of internal factors was more responsible for that result.

NO: Professor of anthropology George L. Cowgill contends that although there is no single explanation for the Mayan collapse, military expansion played a more important role than scholars originally thought.

A notable civilization from long ago wrote in hieroglyphs, developed an accurate calendar, built pyramid-like structures to honor its gods, practiced polytheism with gods represented by animal imagery, and advanced in areas such as mathematics and astronomy. These characteristics could describe the ancient Egyptians. But here they are used to describe the Mayas of Mesoamerica, who established a New World civilization a millennium before the arrival of Europeans. Before this invasion, this Amerindian civilization was in a state of decline. The Spanish conquistadors completely destroyed what remained, causing it to disappear until it was uncovered in the nineteenth century by explorers seeking to find the lost civilization of the Mayas.

Within the last 100 years, work by archaeologists, linguists, and scientists of all sorts have not only exposed what remains of Mayan grandeur but, by deciphering their language, have uncovered the secrets of their advanced civilization. The continuing discoveries have inspired regular reassessments of earlier theories. It was once thought, for example, that Mayas were peaceful people, with little interest in war as a means to achieving ends. We now know that this was not true. As far as the Mayas are concerned, today's theory is only as good as the latest archaeological discovery or linguistic decipherment.

In spite of the wealth of information that scholars have on the Mayas, there are still questions about them that have not been definitively answered. One of the most important questions is, What caused the decline of the Mayan civilization? Scholars and scientists who have spent their lives studying the Mayas have developed theories about the decline of that civilization using the best evidence that is presently available. In spite of this, a definitive answer seems to be lacking.

This issue seeks to explore the two major theories involving Mayan decline: (1) It occurred because of internal factors that the Mayas could not or would not control; and (2) the demise was brought about by excessive militarism.

Both of these theories are considered by Richard E. W. Adams and George L. Cowgill, two noted Mayan scholars, in the selections that follow. Adams considers internal stresses—overpopulation, agricultural scarcities, disease, and natural disasters—to be the major factors responsible for the collapse of the city-states of the Southern Maya Lowlands. Cowgill uses the Teotihuacan civilization, centered in the Mexican Highlands, as a "contrastive example" as to what may have happened to the civilization of the Southern Maya Lowlands. He asserts that because the two histories "exhibit a similar developmental trajectory," the military factors that caused the collapse of the former may have also been responsible for the demise of the latter.

Future archaeological work in Central America is likely to shed more light on the fate of the Mayan civilization.

YES

Richard E. W. Adams

TRANSFORMATIONS

THE CLASSIC MAYA COLLAPSE

According to what we now know, Maya civilization began to reach a series of regional peaks about A.D. 650. By A.D. 830, there is evidence of disintegration of the old patterns, and by A.D. 900, all of the southern lowland centers had collapsed. An understanding of the Maya apocalypse must be based in large part on an understanding of the nature of Maya civilization. During the Terminal Classic period, A.D. 750 to 900, cultural patterns of the lowlands can be briefly characterized as follows. Demographically, a high peak had been reached at least as early as A.D. 600 and perhaps earlier. This population density and size in turn led to intensive forms of agriculture and the establishment of permanent farmsteads in the countryside. Hills were terraced, swamps were drained and modified, water impoundments were made by the hundreds, and land became so scarce that walls of rock were built both as boundaries and simply as the results of field clearance. These masses of people were also highly organized for political purposes into region-state units, which fluctuated in size. These states were more than simple aggregations of cities and were characterized by hierarchical and other complex relationships among them.

Society was organized on an increasingly aristocratic principle by A.D. 650. Dynasties and royal lineages were at the top of the various Maya states and commanded most of the resources of Maya economic life. Most of the large architecture of the cities was for their use. Groups of craft specialists and civil servants supported the elite, with the mass of the population engaged in either part-time or full-time farming. Trade was well organized among and within the states. Military competition was present but was controlled by the fact that it had become mainly an elite-class and prestige activity which did not greatly disturb the economic basis of life. Thus, Maya culture at the ninth century A.D. seems to have been well-ordered, adjusted, and definitely a success. Yet a devastating catastrophe brought it down.

Characteristics of the Collapse

It sometimes seems that the accumulation of weighty theoretical formulations purporting to explain the collapse of Maya civilization will eventually, instead, cause the collapse of Maya archaeology. A refreshingly skeptical and clear-sighted book by John Lowe reviews the major theories and tests them as well. We will not be as thorough in the following section but, it is to be hoped, just as convincing. A brief characterization of the collapse includes the following features:

1. It occurred over a relatively short period of time: 75 to 150 years.
2. During it the elite-class culture failed, as reflected in the abandonment of palaces and temples and the cessation of manufacture of luxury goods and erection of stelae.
3. Also during the period there was a rapid and nearly complete depopulation of the countryside and the urban centers.
4. The geographical focus of the first collapse was in the oldest and most developed zones, the southern lowlands and the intermediate area. The northern plains and Puuc areas survived for a while longer.

In other words, the Maya collapse was a demographic, cultural, and social catastrophe in which elite and commoner went down together. Drawing on all available information about the ancient Maya and comparable situations, the 1970 Santa Fe Conference developed a comprehensive explanation of the collapse. This explanation depends on the relatively new picture of the Maya summarized above. That is, we must discard any notion of the Maya as the "noble savage" living in harmony with nature. Certainly, the Maya lived more in tune with nature than do modern industrial peoples, but probably not much more so than did our nineteenth-century pioneer ancestors. As we shall see, some dissonance with na-

ture was at least partly responsible for its failure. More than this, however, data have been further developed since the conference which strengthen some assumptions and weaken others. Therefore, the explanation which follows is a modified version of that which appears in the report of the Santa Fe Conference.

Stresses

Maya society had a number of built-in stresses, many of which had to do with high populations in the central and southern areas. Turner's and other studies indicate that from about A.D. 600 to 900 there were about 168 people per square kilometer (435 per square mile) in the Río Bec zone. The intensive agricultural constructions associated with this population density are also found farther south, within 30 kilometers (19 miles) of Tikal. They are also to be found to the east in the Belize Valley, and there are indications elsewhere to the south that high populations were present. According to Saul's studies of Maya bones from the period, the population carried a heavy load of endemic disease, including malaria, yellow fever, syphilis, and Chagas's disease, the latter a chronic infection which leads to cardiac insufficiency in young adulthood. Chronic malnutrition is also indicated by Saul's and Steele's studies. Taken altogether, these factors indicate the precarious status of health even for the elite. Average lifespan in the southern lowlands was about thirty-nine years. Infant mortality was high; perhaps as many as 78 percent of Maya children never reached the age of twenty. Endemic disease can go epidemic with just a rise in malnutrition. In other words, the Maya populace carried within itself a biological time bomb which needed only a triggering event such as a crop failure to go off.

With population pressing the limits of subsistence, management of land and other resources was a problem, and one which would have fallen mainly on the elite. If food were to be imported, or if marginal lands were to be brought into cultivation, by extensive drainage projects, for example, then the elite had to arrange for it to be done. There were certain disadvantages to this arrangement. Aristocratic or inherited leadership of any kind is a poor means to approach matters that require rational decisions. One need only consider the disastrous manner in which seventeenth-century European armies were mishandled by officers whose major qualifications were their lineages. There is a kind of built-in variation of the Peter Principle in such leadership: one is born to his level of incompetence. Maya aristocracy apparently was no better equipped to handle the complex problems of increasing populations than were European aristocrats. There were no doubt capable and brilliant nobles, but there was apparently no way in which talent could quickly be taken to the top of society from its lower ranks. Lowe's model of the collapse of Maya civilization emphasizes the management-administrative aspects of the problem and essentially considers the collapse as an administrative breakdown.

There are also signs in the Terminal Classic period of a widening social gulf between elite and commoners. At the same time, problems were increasing in frequency and severity. The elite class increased in size and made greater demands on the rest of Maya society for its support. This created further tensions. Intensive agriculture led to greater crop yields, but also put Maya food production increasingly at hostage to the vagaries of weather, crop disease, insects, birds, and other hazards. Marginal and complex cultivation systems require large investments of time and labor and necessitate that things go right more often than not. A run of bad weather or a long-term shift in climate might trigger a food crisis. Recent work on tree rings and weather history from other sources indicates that a Mesoamerica-wide drought may have begun about A.D. 850. In addition, there are periodic outbreaks of locusts in the Maya Lowlands.

These stresses were pan–Maya and occurred to a greater or lesser degree in every region. No matter whether one opts for the city-state or the regional state model, competition over scarce resources among the political units of the Maya resulted from these stressful situations. The large southern center of Seibal was apparently taken by a northern Maya elite group about A.D. 830. Evidence is now in hand of military intrusions from north to south at Rio Azul, at the Belize sites of Nohmul, Colha, and Barton Ramie, and at Quirigua in the Motagua Valley. At least at Rio Azul and Colha a period of trade preceded the raids, presaging the later Aztec *pochteca* pattern. The patterns and nature of the intrusions indicate that the raids were probably from the Puuc zone and that a part of the motivation, as suggested by Cowgill, was to capture populations. Warfare increased markedly along the Usumacinta River during the ninth century A.D., according to hieroglyphic texts and carved pictures from that area.

There are also hints that the nature of Maya warfare may have changed during this last period. A lintel from Piedras Negras appears to show numerous soldiers in standard uniforms kneeling in ranks before an officer. In other words, organized violence may have come to involve many more people and much more effort and therefore may have become much more disruptive. Certainly competition over scarce resources would have led to an increasingly unstable situation. Further, the resultant disorganization would have led to vulnerability to outside military intervention, and that seems to have been the case as well.

There were also external pressures on the Maya. Some were intangible and in the form of new ideas about the nature of human society as well as new ideologies from the Gulf Coast and Central Mexico. The northern Maya elites seem to have absorbed a number of these new ideas. For example, they included the depiction of Mexican Gulf Coast deities on their stelae as well as some Mexican-style hieroglyphs. Altar de Sacrificios was invaded by still another foreign group from the Gulf Coast about A.D. 910. These people may have been either a truly Mexican Gulf Coast group or Chontal Maya, who were non-Classic in their culture.

A progressive pattern of abandonment and disaster in the western lowlands is suggestive. Palenque, on the southwestern edges of the lowlands, was one of the first major centers to go under; it was abandoned about A.D. 810. The major Usumacinta cities of Piedras Negras and Yaxchilan (Bird-Jaguar's City) were the next to go. They put up their last monuments about A.D. 825. Finally, it was Altar de Sacrificios's turn about A.D. 910. Clearly, there was a progressive disintegration from west to east, and it seems likely that it was caused by pressures from militaristic non–Maya groups. These peoples, in turn, were probably being jostled in the competitive situation set up after the fall of Teotihuacan and may

have been pushed ahead of peoples such as the Toltecs and their allies. Perhaps the Epi-Classic states discussed above were involved, as well as some mercenary groups. In any case, it appears certain that these groups were opportunists. They came into an area already disorganized and disturbed and were not the triggering mechanism for the catastrophe but part of the following process.

At any one Maya city or in any one region, the "mix" of circumstances was probably unique. At Piedras Negras there is evidence that the elite may have been violently overthrown from within. Faces of rulers on that site's stelae are smashed, and there are other signs of violence. Invasion finished off Altar de Sacrificios. Rio Azul was overrun by Maya groups from the north, perhaps including Toltec allies, as were a number of Maya centers along the Belize coast and down to Quirigua. At other centers, such as the regional capital of Tikal, the elite were apparently abandoned to their fate. Without the supporting populations, remnants of the Maya upper classes lingered on after the catastrophe. At Colha and Seibal, northern Maya acting as new elites attempted to continue the southern economic and political systems, but they abandoned these attempts after a relatively short time. The general demographic catastrophe and disruption of the agricultural systems were apparently too great to cope with.

In short, ecological abuse, disease, mismanagement, overpopulation, militarism, famines, epidemics, and bad weather overtook the Maya in various combinations. But several questions remain. What led to the high levels of populations which were the basis of much of the disaster?

The Maya were much more loosely organized politically during the Late Formative than during the Classic period. The episodes of interstate competition and of Teotihuacan's intervention seem to have led them to try new, more centralized political arrangements. These seem to have worked well for a time, in the case of the Early Classic expansion of Tikal. After the suggested civil wars of the sixth century there seems to have been a renewed and still stronger development of centralized states, which were probably monarchical.

Using general historical and anthropological experience, Demitri Shimkin observed that village-level societies approach population control very differently than do state-level societies. Relatively independent villages are oriented plainly and simply toward survival. There are many traditional ways of population control, female infanticide being a favorite practiced widely even in eighteenth-century England. Use of herbal abortion, late marriage, ritual ascetisicism, and other means keep population within bounds for a village. A state-level society, on the other hand, is likely to encourage population growth for the benefit of the directing elite. The more manpower to manipulate, the better. In the case of the Maya, we have noted a certain megalomania in their huge Late Classic buildings. Unfinished large construction projects at Tikal and Uaxactun were overtaken by the collapse. Such efforts required immense manpower reserves and a simultaneous disregard for the welfare of that workforce. The Maya appear to have shifted gears into a more sophisticated and ultimately maladaptive state organization.

Another question to be considered is, Why did the Maya not adjust to cope with the crises? The answer may lie in the nature of religiously sanctioned aristocracies. Given a crop failure, a Maya leadership group might have attempted to propitiate the ancestors and gods with more ritual and more monuments. This response would have exacerbated the crisis by taking manpower out of food production. Inappropriate responses of this sort could easily have been made, given the ideology and worldview that the Maya seem to have held. On the other hand, if the crisis were a long-term drought, with populations dangerously high and predatory warfare disrupting matters even more, perhaps any response would have been ineffectual.

The rapid biological destruction of the Maya is an important aspect of the collapse. From a guessed-at high of 12 million, the population was reduced within 150 years to an estimated remnant of about 1.8 million. The disease load and the stress of malnutritional factors indicate that a steady diminishment of Maya population probably started by A.D. 830 and rapidly reached a point of no recovery. An average increase of 10 to 15 percent in the annual mortality rate will statistically reduce 12 million to 1.8 million in 75 years. Obviously there was not anything like a steady decline, but the smoothed-out average over the period had to have been something of that order, or perhaps the decline began earlier, at A.D. 750, when Maya civilization reached its peak.

The disruptive nature of population declines can be easily understood if one considers the usual effects of epidemics. In such catastrophic outbreaks of disease, those first and most fatally affected are the young and the old. Even if the main working population survives relatively untouched, the social loss is only postponed. The old take with them much of the accumulated experience and knowledge needed to meet future crises. The young will not be there to mature and replace the adult working population, and a severe manpower shortage will result within fifteen to twenty years. Needless to say, much more work on population estimates and studies of the bones and the general health environment of the ancient Maya needs to be done to produce a really convincing statement on this aspect of the collapse.

A last, although not by any means final, question concerns the failure to recover. This feature may involve climatic factors. If shifts of rainfall belts were responsible for triggering the collapse, then the answer might be the persistence of drought conditions until there were too few people left to sustain the Classic cultural systems. As now seems probable, the Maya were confronted with the situation of having overcultivated their soils and having lost too much surface water. Temporary abandonment of fields would have led to their being rapidly overrun by thick, thorny, second-growth jungle, which is harder to clear than primary forest. Thus, a diminished population may have been faced with the problem of clearing heavily overgrown, worn-out soils, of which vast amounts were needed to sustain even small populations. Second-growth forest springs up overnight and is even today a major problem in maintaining archaeological sites for tourists.

Another possible answer to the question of recovery is that the Maya may have been loathe to attempt the sort of brilliant effort that had ultimately broken them. Just as they preferred to revert to swidden agriculture rather than main-

tain intensive techniques, they probably found it a relief to live on a village level instead of in their former splendid but stressful state of existence.

The above is an integrated model of the Maya collapse. It explains all the features of the collapse and all the data now in hand, but it is not proved by any means, and in some respects is more of a guide to future research than a firm explanation. If the model is more or less correct, however, it should be largely confirmed within the next ten years of research. Indeed, this process of confirmation has already begun. The 1970 conference which developed the model could explain certain features of the archaeological record only by assuming much higher levels of ancient population than were otherwise plausible at the time. The 1973 Rio Bec work of Turner and Eaton turned up a vast amount of data which indicate that higher levels of ancient populations indeed had been present. Recent work at Colha and Rio Azul has indicated the importance of militarism in the process. All of these findings lend credibility to the model.

Delayed Collapse in the North

The vast and very densely distributed centers of the Puuc area survived for a time. These Puuc cities, possibly a regional state with a capital at Uxmal, appear to have turned into predators on the southern cities. As noted before, part of the motivation may have been for the capture and enslavement of southern populations. Even so, it seems that large centers such as Uxmal, Kabah, Sayil, and Labna lasted only a century longer than the southern cities. Northern Maya chronology is much more disputed than that in the south, but it now seems likely that outsiders, including Toltec, were in

Yucatan by A.D. 900 and perhaps earlier, and there are clear indications that Uxmal was absorbing Mexican ideas much earlier. Certain motifs, such as eagles or vultures, appear on Puuc building facades late in the Classic period.

We are now faced with at least three possible explanations of the Puuc collapse: they may have succumbed to the same combination of factors that brought down the southern Maya centers; the Toltec may have conquered them; or a combination of these factors may have been at work. At this time, it appears that the northern florescence was partly at the expense of the southern area.... [E]vidence for Toltec conquest now appears even stronger, and this is presently the favored explanation for the Puuc collapse.

Chichen Itza, in north central Yucatan, is a center which was culturally allied with the Puuc cities in architecture and probably politically as well. Puuc centers have been found even in the far northeast of the peninsula. At Chichen Itza, Puuc architecture is overlaid and succeeded by Toltec architecture. Unmapped defensive walls surround both Chichen and Uxmal. The data available now make it likely that the Toltec and other groups may have appeared in Yucatan by A.D. 800 and thereafter, perhaps brought in as mercenaries, as so often happened later in Maya history. In whatever capacity they arrived, they appear to have established themselves at Chichen Itza by A.D. 950 as the controlling power. As has happened in history elsewhere, the mercenaries became the controlling forces. Toltec raids, battles, and sieges, combined with the internal weaknesses of Classic Maya culture and perhaps with changing environmental factors, brought about a swift collapse in the Puuc.

The aftermath of the collapse was also devastating. Most of the southern Maya Lowlands have not been repopulated until the last fifty years. Eleven hundred years of abandonment have rejuvenated the soils, the forests, and their resources, but modern man is now making inroads on them. Kekchi Maya Indians have been migrating into the lowlands from the northern Guatemalan highlands as pioneer farmers for the past century, and the Mexican government has colonized the Yucatan, Campeche, and Quintana Roo area with dissatisfied agriculturists from overpopulated highland areas. The forests are being logged and cut down. Agricultural colonies have failed in both Guatemala and Mexico, and some zones are already abandoned. In other areas, the inhabitants have turned to marijuana cultivation. Vast areas have been reduced to low scrub jungle, and large amounts of land are now being converted to intensive agriculture. One looks at the modern scene and wonders. Fortunately, in 1988 a movement began to set aside the remnants of the once immense monsoon forests, and it may be that a series of protected zones in the form of contiguous national parks will soon be in existence in Guatamala, Mexico, and Belize.

NO
George L. Cowgill

TEOTIHUACAN, INTERNAL MILITARISTIC COMPETITION, AND THE FALL OF THE CLASSIC MAYA

In very broad terms, the Teotihuacan civilization, centered in the Mexican Highlands, and the Classic civilization of the Southern Maya Lowlands exhibit a similar developmental trajectory. That is, both enjoyed a period of development, flourished for a time, and then collapsed. But as soon as one looks beyond these gross generalities, the evidence from each region shows striking differences in the pace and timing of events. These differences are of interest in their own right, and one of my objectives is to call attention to them. In addition, however, they help to direct our attention to some of the distinctive features of the Maya trajectory which are relevant for understanding the functioning of Late Classic Maya society and for explaining its collapse. My main concern is to point out difficulties in some recently proposed explanations ... and to suggest that escalating internal warfare may have been more a cause than a consequence of serious trouble for the Maya. I do not suggest warfare as a mono-causal explanation for the Maya collapse, but I do think it may have been an important contributing factor, and old evidence should be re-examined and new evidence sought with this possibility in mind.

Emphasis on Maya warfare is part of a widespread recognition that the Maya were not the gentle pacifists that some archaeologists would have them be. But there is a difference between sporadic raiding, with occasional enslavement or sacrifice or captives, and what David Webster calls *militarism*: institutionalized warfare intended for territorial aggrandizement and acquisition of other capital resources, with military decisions part of the conscious political policy of small elite, semiprofessional warriors, and lethal combat on a large scale. Webster and I both argue that the Late Classic Maya may have become militaristic in this sense, but we differ about the probable dynamics and consequences of Maya militarism.

Although it is clear that there were important contacts between the Highlands and the Southern Maya Lowlands, I should stress that I am *not* arguing that either Teotihuacan intervention or the withdrawal of Teotihuacan

From George L. Cowgill, "Teotihuacan, Internal Militaristic Competition, and the Fall of the Classic Maya," in Norman Hammond and Gordon R. Willey, eds., *Maya Archaeology and Ethnohistory* (University of Texas Press, 1979). Copyright © 1979 by University of Texas Press. Reprinted by permission. References omitted.

contacts played a decisive role in the Maya collapse. Direct or indirect contacts with Teotihuacan are important and extremely interesting, but I doubt if they explain much about either the rise or the fall of the Lowland Maya. In any case, my use of the Teotihuacan data here is purely as a contrastive example.

It is often assumed that Teotihuacan developed rather steadily up to a distinct peak somewhere around A.D. 500 to 600, after which it soon began a fairly rapid decline.... [L]argely through the data obtained by the comprehensive surface survey and limited test excavations completed by the Teotihuacan Mapping Project, under the direction of René Millon, evidence for a very different pattern has emerged....

Briefly, it appears that the city of Teotihuacan enjoyed an early surge of extremely rapid growth, followed by a four-to-five-century "plateau" during which growth was very much slower or may even have ceased altogether. Then, probably not before the eighth century A.D., the city collapsed, apparently rather rapidly. This pattern is most clearly suggested by the dates of major monumental construction in the city, but it is also suggested by the demographic implications of quantities and areal spreads of ceramics of various periods, both in the city itself and in all parts of the Basin of Mexico which have been systematically surveyed. Further support comes from data on Teotihuacan obsidian industry.

In contrast, the Maya site of Tikal was settled at least as early as Teotihuacan but developed more irregularly to a modest Late Preclassic climax, followed apparently by something of a pause. There seems to have been a second peak in Early Classic times, and then a distinct recession for a century or so.

Then there was a relatively brief burst of glory in the seventh and eighth centuries, immediately followed by rapid decline and very drastic population loss. Tikal population may have been relatively stable from about A.D. 550 until after A.D. 800, or it may have shot up rapidly during the 600's to a short-lived maximum in the 700's. In either case, however, it seems clear that the Late Classic population of Tikal was larger than that at any previous time. Other major sites in the Southern Maya Lowlands had rather different trajectories, but they also generally peaked during the Late Classic and collapsed during the ninth or tenth centuries.

There are also striking contrasts in spatial patterns. The early growth of Teotihuacan is concomitant with rapid and marked decline in the number and size of other settlements in the Basin of Mexico. Teotihuacan quickly achieved, and for several centuries maintained, a size probably twenty or more times larger than any other known Basin of Mexico settlement. Even Cholula, in the Valley of Puebla some ninety kilometers away; does not seem to have covered more than a sixth of the area of Teotihuacan, and other settlements in the Tlaxcala–Northern Puebla area were much smaller. In the Southern Maya Lowlands there were other major centers comparable in size to Tikal, and below these there was a hierarchy of other sites ranging from fairly large secondary centers to small hamlets and individual households. (In contrast to Marcus, Hammond argues that present evidence is insufficient for assigning specific sites to specific hierarchical levels, although hierarchies probably existed. The very fact of the controversy points up the contrast with Teotihuacan, where there is no dispute at all about its primacy in the settlement hierarchy.) There is no suggestion that Tikal or other major centers ever drew people away from other sites or monopolized power to anywhere near the extent that Teotihuacan did in central Mexico....

IMPLICATIONS OF THE TEOTIHUACAN EVIDENCE

Several implications of the Teotihuacan pattern suggest themselves. The long duration of Teotihuacan seems unreasonable unless economic and political power were quite strong and quite effectively centralized in the city, and much other evidence also suggest this. In contrast, both the more or less concomitant development of many Lowland Maya centers and the dynastic evidence so far gleaned from inscriptions indicate that no single Southern Lowland Maya center ever gained long-term firm political or economic control of any very large region, although there is plenty of evidence for brief domination of one center by another, and of political alliances often bolstered by dynastic marriages.

The obvious next step is to suggest that Teotihuacan was long-lived and highly centralized because it was a "hydraulic" state, based on intensive irrigation agriculture in a semiarid environment, while the Southern Maya Lowlands was politically less centralized and enjoyed a much briefer climax because of critical deficiencies in its tropical forest environment. I do not think that environmental considerations are unimportant, but I do feel that there are extremely serious difficulties with these explanations.

Discussions of Teotihuacan irrigation usually do not deal adequately with its *scale*. Evidence for pre-Toltec irrigation in the Teotihuacan Valley remains circum-

stantial rather than direct, but it seems quite likely that canal irrigation there does date back to Patlachique or Cuanalan times. But the maximum area available for permanent canal irrigation is less than four thousand hectares. This is not a very large area, nor does it call for large or complex canals, dikes, or flood-control facilities. Assuming a peak population of 125,000, there would have been about one irrigated hectare for 30 people. It is clear that the city grew well beyond any population limits set by irrigation agriculture, and a substantial fraction of its subsistence must have come from other sources, including riskier and much less productive alternative forms of agriculture, and collecting and hunting wild plants and animals. Faunal analyses and paleoethnobotanical studies provide evidence that Teotihuacanos ate a wide variety of wild as well as domesticated plants and wild animals.

It seems unlikely that there were any environmental or purely technical factors which would have made it impossible for the Teotihuacanos to have practiced intensive chinampa agriculture in the southern part of the Basin of Mexico. Chinampas were an important subsistence source for the Aztec population, which was much larger than the Teotihuacan population. Yet there is no evidence for extensive use of chinampas in Teotihuacan times. It is tempting to speculate that technical difficulties in assembling food for more people in one place may be at least part of the reason that Teotihuacan grew so little after Tzacualli times (a point also made by J. R. Parsons). If indeed there were environmental reasons, such as a change in lake levels, which prevented extensive chinampa exploitation in Teotihuacan times, then Teotihuacan is an instance of a population which expanded until it approached a perceived subsistence limit and then stabilized, rather than disastrously exceed that limit. If, as seems more likely, there was no environmental reason why the Teotihuacanos could not have fed more people by simply moving part of the population down to the chinampa area and investing in chinampa developments, their apparent failure to do so must have been for social or political reasons. If so, Teotihuacan population growth in the Basin of Mexico halted at a level well below the number of people it would have been technically possible to feed.

Teotihuacan's behavior has particular significance for the Maya because Culbert suggests that the Maya collapsed because they were unable to control runaway expansion which caused them to "overshoot" disastrously the productive limits of their environment.

Whether or not I am right in suspecting that Teotihuacan population growth leveled off before environmental limits were approached, it is logically inescapable that it was biologically possible for Teotihuacan population to have continued to expand until it "overshot" all technically feasible subsistence possibilities. If it were simply the case that rapid development tends to acquire a sort of momentum which carries it beyond environmental limits and into disaster before it can be stopped, then the ability of the Teotihuacanos to slow down and stop short of disaster would be puzzling.

An extended discussion of Teotihuacan's eventual collapse is not possible here, but I should add that I do not know of any convincing evidence that even the end of Teotihuacan was primarily due to climatic deterioration or other environmentally generated subsistence difficulties. Growing competition from other Highland centers was probably important, and I suspect that Teotihuacan may have collapsed for political, economic, and military reasons, rather than purely ecological reasons.

Proponents of either "population pressure" or "hydraulic" explanations for early states may perhaps argue that Teotihuacan "plateaued" instead of overshooting because the power of the state was very much stronger and more centralized than in the Maya cities, so that when the disastrous consequences of further expansion of the city became evident, the state had the power to intervene effectively and halt further population growth. Possibly this may be part of the explanation, but I do not think this explanation is required. The main reason may have been that there was simply no advantage in further expansion that would have offset attendant inconveniences. There is much evidence that population growth rates are very responsive to shifts in other variables. Assuming the Southern Lowland Maya did indeed "overshoot" their environment, even in the face of growing subsistence difficulties, it is the Maya behavior which is puzzling—far more puzzling than Culbert assumes—and it is the Maya "overshoot" rather than the Teotihuacan "plateau" which is most in need of explanation.

Culbert's "overshoot" explanation of the Maya collapse is one of the least unsatisfactory suggestions made so far. Culbert himself cogently disposes of most previous explanations. And archaeological evidence for the Southern Maya Lowlands in the eighth century does suggest a population so large that, in spite of evidence for terraces, ridged fields, and tree and root crops in addition to swidden, a subsistence crisis seems a real possibility. Nevertheless, there are serious problems with Culbert's explanation. He speaks of many causal factors, but inspection shows that excessive population growth plays a central role in his model. And, in his 1974 book, he offers no particular explanation for the population growth itself. More recently he has attributed population growth to economic development. But the question remains: what would have driven the Maya to expand population and/or environmental exploitation to the point where a subsistence crisis was produced? And if, instead, there was little population growth after about A.D. 550, as Haviland (1970 and personal communication) argues, then the postponement of collapse for some 250 years seems even more puzzling.

A different explanation for the Maya collapse suggests that the eighth-century Maya "florescence" was not, in fact, a time of Maya prosperity at all, but instead an attempt to cope with already serious troubles. This theory, if I understand it correctly, suggests that ability to obtain foreign goods by trade was critical for elite Maya prestige, for the power that derived from that prestige, and as a means of providing incentives for local production. Exclusion of central Peten elites from developing Mesoamerican trade networks supposedly precipitated a crisis for these elites, in which they attempted to offset their sagging prestige by even more ambitious monumental construction projects. But clearly nothing indispensable for subsistence was lacking, and prestige games can be played with whatever one defines as status markers, as Sanders points out. Goods need not be obtained by long-distance trade in order to be scarce and valuable. Furthermore my guess is that

the decline of Teotihuacan, if anything, expanded the possibilities for profitable trade by Southern Lowland Maya elites. Webb's postulated development of new Mesoamerican trading networks following the decline of Teotihuacan seems, in very broad outline, a reasonable possibility. But I am much less persuaded than either Webb or Rathje that, at least at first, the Southern Lowland Maya were unable to participate in these new developments. The scale and substance of Late Classic Maya material civilization argues that they *were* able to profit from the situation, at least for a time. To be sure, there is some evidence for poor nutritional status for some Lowland Maya, but the same was probably true for much of the English and Western European population at the height of rapid economic growth in the early decades of the Industrial Revolution. It may well be that Late Classic Maya wealth was very unevenly distributed, and it also may be that the Late Classic Maya of the Southern Lowlands were increasingly "living off ecological capital," but this does not mean that the elites were already badly off, or were doing what they did in order to cope with resource pressures or an unfavorable balance of trade. The argument that the Late Classic Maya were already in serious trouble in the seventh or eighth centuries is unconvincing. Exclusion from trade networks does seem a good explanation for nonrecovery after the collapse, but not for the collapse itself....

It seems likely that in Late Classic times there was general economic development in a number of regional centers in the Southern Maya Lowlands, perhaps at least in part because of the weakening of Highland states such as Teotihuacan and Monte Alban. More speculatively, the elites of the individual centers may have increasingly seen it as both feasible and desirable to extend strong control over a relatively large surrounding area —a control based more on conquest and annexation than on political alliance and elite intermarriage. Population growth may well have been a concomitant of this economic and political development. My argument here and previously is not that population growth rarely occurs, nor that population growth does not have important reciprocal effects on other variables. My objections, instead, are to the idea that population can be counted on to increase for no reason except human procreative proclivities, and to the idea that competition and militaristic warfare would intensify mainly as a response to subsistence shortages. Instead, I suggest that if population was increasing, it was because it was useful either to elites, to peasant households, or to both. And I suggest that intensified militaristic competition is a normal extension of intensified economic competition.

Mayanists are accustomed to assuming that the political institutions of the Classic Maya Lowlands were marginally statelike. I suggest that we should seriously consider the possibility that by the seventh and eighth centuries the combination of economic development, population growth, and social changes was leading to the emergence of more highly developed and more centralized governmental structures—the kinds of structures which would make the incorporation of many small states into a single reasonably stable empire seem a realistic possibility. I would not venture to make further conjectures about the specific forms of these new political and economic developments. However, archaeological and epigraphical evidence promises not only to test the general proposition, but also to shed a great deal of further light on the precise forms of Maya political and economic organization.

What I suggest, then, is that eventually the major Maya centers may have begun to compete for effective political mastery of the whole Southern Lowlands. This postulated "heating up" of military conflict, for which there is some support in Late Classic art and inscriptions, may have played a major role in the Maya collapse. If, indeed, population growth and/or utilization of the environment expanded beyond prudent limits, the spur may have been provided by militaristic competition. And even if population and production did not expand beyond feasible steady-state values (under peaceful conditions), intensified warfare may have precipitated disaster through destruction of crops and agricultural facilities and through disruption of agricultural labor cycles. Clearly, internal warfare is not "the" single cause of the Maya collapse, but I believe it deserves renewed consideration as a contributing factor.

Webster also places new stress on the role of warfare in Maya history, but our views and emphases differ in several important ways. First, he is mainly concerned with Preclassic and Early Classic warfare as one of the causes of the *rise* of Maya civilization. This is a topic I have not discussed here. My feeling is that Webster makes some good points— there is certainly clear evidence for some Maya warfare quite early—but he probably overestimates the explanatory importance of early warfare. Second, Webster tends to see warfare largely as a response to shortages in land or other subsistence resources. I believe that this underestimates other incentives for warfare, especially for large-scale militaristic warfare.

Third, Webster places much less stress than I do on Late Classic economic development, and he differs sharply on the matter of political integration. He feels that even the largest autonomous political units were never more than forty to sixty thousand people and that incorporation of further large increments of population, especially at considerable distances, proved unworkable. Presumably, although Webster does not explicitly discuss the matter, he would assume that serious attempts to incorporate many more people and more land and other resources within single states did not play a significant role in Maya history. He does feel that warfare may have contributed to the Maya collapse, but he explains intensified warfare mainly as a consequence of the manipulation of militarism by the Maya elite for bolstering their control of their own subject populations, rather than for any extensive conquests of other states. He says that conflicts may also have intensified over strategic resources, especially capital improvements for intensified agriculture, in the intermediate zones between major centers, but he does not suggest that there may have been major attempts to expand beyond the intermediate zones to gain control of the other centers as well. He does not suggest, as I do, that an important contributory element in the Maya collapse may have been a struggle—violent, protracted, and unsuccessful—to bring into being something like the kind of polity Teotihuacan had succeeded in creating several centuries earlier.

POSTSCRIPT

Were Environmental Factors Responsible for the Mayan Collapse?

In studying the decline of civilizations, it is generally easy to see that, in most instances, both internal and external factors were responsible for their demise. This is certainly true for the Mayas. Both Adams and Cowgill would agree that there is no single explanation for the Mayan collapse; the question seems to be, Which set of factors was more responsible for the demise? Complicating the search for answers to the Mayan collapse are the regional and individual differences that existed within the myriad of city-states that provided the civilization with its political base. It should be noted that the reasons for their collapse could differ due to regional or local conditions. Today's research seems to bear out the existence of this dichotomy.

Simon Martin and Nikolai Grube, in "Maya Superstates," *Archaeology* (November/December 1995), lean toward militarism as a cause of Mayan decline. Another article from the same source, "Life and Death in Maya War Zone," (May/June, 1998) by Charles Suhler and Davis Friedel, affirms that conclusion. Others have speculated that the Mayas may have simply lost their will to rule. It is unlikely that this issue's question will ever receive a definitive answer. But future discoveries will keep the interest alive and generate more interest in this civilization, which has captured historians' imaginations at the end of the twentieth century just as the Egyptian civilization did at the beginning.

There are many highly recommendable books on the Mayas. A good starting point is *The Classic Maya Collapse* edited by T. Patrick Culbert (University of New Mexico Press, 1983), which contains a series of essays by Mayan scholars, each covering an aspect of the civilization's demise. Charles Gallenkamp's *Maya: The Riddle and Rediscovery of a Lost Civilization* (Penguin Books, 1987) offers a short, readable account of the civilization's history. The second edition of John Henderson's *The World of the Ancient Maya* (Cornell University Press, 1997) presents a handsome, up-to-date account of Maya civilization as does the fifth edition of Robert J. Sharer's *The Ancient Maya* (Stanford University Press, 1994). The contributions of the late Linda Schele have contributed enormously to our knowledge of the Mayas. *A Forest of Kings: The Untold Story of the Ancient Maya* (William Morrow, 1990) written with David Friedel and *The Code of Kings: The Language of Seven Sacred Maya Temples and Tombs* (Scribner, 1998) written with Peter Mathews, are two of her important books.

A videotape on the Mayas entitled *Central America: The Burden of Time,* from Michael Wood's *Legacy* series, gives thorough coverage to the Mayas and sets them in the context of their Mesoamerindian neighbors.

ISSUE 8

Were the Crusades Motivated Primarily by Religious Factors?

YES: Hans Eberhard Mayer, from *The Crusades*, 2d ed., trans. John Gillingham (Oxford University Press, 1988)

NO: Ronald C. Finucane, from *Soldiers of the Faith: Crusaders and Moslems at War* (St. Martin's Press, 1983)

ISSUE SUMMARY

YES: German historian Hans Eberhard Mayer states that although there were other factors important to the development of the Crusades, the strongest motivation was a religious one.

NO: British historian Ronald C. Finucane counters that although the religious influence on the Crusades was significant, political, social, economic, and military factors in medieval Europe also played a role in their origin, development, and outcome.

One of western European history's defining moments occurred in Clermont, France, in 1095 C.E. when Pope Urban II delivered an address in which he urged Christian Europe to support a movement to wrest the Holy Land from Moslem forces, which had been in control for almost 500 years. This speech set in motion a series of events, which were to span more than two centuries, and caused results that would dramatically shape the future not only of Western Europe but of the Muslim world as well. The name given to this movement was the Crusades.

From the onset, the Crusades were shrouded in myth and mystery. For example, although there are four known versions of Urban's speech, none of them has a real claim on authenticity. So the exact words Urban used to stir the crowd are not known. It has been up to historians to discern the pope's intentions from the accounts of his speech as well as his subsequent writings and actions. Even 1,000 years later there are more questions about the Crusades than answers. And, as historian Ronald C. Finucane has stated, many of the questions raised are perhaps unanswerable.

There are many important questions about the Crusades for historians to ponder: What was the physical composition of the Crusades? What social classes were represented? To what extent did women participate? How good was the leadership? How organized were those who participated in the Crusades? What immediate and long-range effects did the Crusades have on Western Europe and the Muslim world?

In spite of the significance of these questions, the one that seems to be of paramount importance to historians is the question of motivation. What caused thousands of people from all countries in Europe, representing a cross section of the continent's class structure, to leave their lives behind and make a perilous journey from which they might not return? What did they hope to gain?

At first glance, the answer seemed simple: the Crusaders embarked on their quest for religious reasons, to wrest the Holy Land from the Muslim world, thus allowing Christians to participate in the ultimate pilgrimage. Stories abounded of Muslim desecration of Christian holy sites and Muslim mistreatment of Christians. And with Western Christendom's primary leader urging the Crusaders on—even offering indulgences (full or partial remission of one's sins) as an incentive—the question seemed to have a logical answer.

But historical questions seldom have simple answers, and further study brought several other possibilities. Could the feudal system with its insistence on primogeniture (the inheritance of family lands by the oldest son, leaving younger sons with few opportunities, and possibly encouraging the younger sons to seek fame and fortune elsewhere) have been a factor? Were economic factors involving trade and commerce important? And how much was the militaristic nature of medieval society responsible for the Crusades?

In a millennium of Crusade historiography, motivation seems to revolve around two different interpretations—the religious and the secular. The former seeks the answers to Crusader incentive in sacred dimensions, pilgrimages, indulgences, and participation in a just war against despised infidels. The latter discovers interpretations in the economic, social, political, and military worlds of Western Europe, with impetus coming from potential upward mobility, the possible revival of trade and commerce, the search for new kingdoms in the East, and the martial spirit that characterized the Middle Ages.

From all of this, one certainty can be deduced: it is impossible to separate the two factors—the sacred and the profane—with regard to Crusader motivation. Thus, most historians consider both motivations as important to our understanding of the Crusades. For example, in the following selections, Hans Eberhard Mayer stresses the role of the "other-worldly," while Ronald C. Finucane spotlights the influence of secular motivations.

YES

Hans Eberhard Mayer

THE ORIGINS OF THE CRUSADES

Pope Urban II opened the Council of Clermont on 18 November 1095—the moment that has gone down in history as the starting point of the crusades. . . .

The success of the Clermont appeal has still not been fully explained and probably never can be. Nor will any definitive interpretation be offered here; after all, the reasons for taking the cross varied considerably from one individual to another. All one can do is to examine a whole range of spiritual and worldly motives of different kinds which coalesced not only to produce the spark of that unique and spontaneous success at Clermont but also to light a fire which burned for two hundred years.

Originally the object of the crusade was to help the Christian Churches in the East. However unnecessary such help may, in fact, have been, it was in these terms that Urban is supposed to have spoken at Clermont. But very soon men had a more definite object in mind: to free the Holy Land and, above all, Jerusalem, the Sepulchre of Christ, from the yoke of heathen dominion. . . . Jerusalem cannot have been used merely as a lure; the name was too potent and would inevitably have pulled the whole enterprise in this one direction. It is rather more likely in view of the evident lack of over-all planning that Urban had not in fact made much of Jerusalem while at Clermont but that during the course of the next year he gave in to public opinion which needed and created a concrete goal. . . .

Even the mere sound of the name Jerusalem must have had a glittering and magical splendour for the men of the eleventh century which we are no longer capable of feeling. It was a keyword which produced particular psychological reactions and conjured up particular eschatological notions. Men thought, of course, of the town in Palestine where Jesus Christ had suffered, died, been buried, and then had risen again. But, more than this, they saw in their minds' eye the heavenly city of Jerusalem with its gates of sapphire, its walls and squares bright with precious stones—as it had been described in the Book of Revelation and Tobias. It was the centre of a spiritual world just as the earthly Jerusalem was, in the words of Ezekiel 'in the midst of the nations and countries'. It was a meeting place for those who had been scattered, the goal of the great pilgrimage of peoples where God resides among his people;

the place at the end of time to which the elect ascend; the resting place of the righteous; city of paradise and of the tree of life which heals all men....

Counting for just as much as the images conjured up by a child-like, mystical faith was the long tradition of pilgrimage to Jerusalem. As early as 333 a pilgrim from Bordeaux reached Palestine; and not much later a Gallic noblewoman named Egeria visited the Holy Places leaving to posterity a report which is as important a monument of a Latin changing from ancient to medieval as it is for the topography of the *loca sancta*. In 386 Saint Jerome settled in Bethlehem; half a century later the Empress Eudocia went into retreat at Jerusalem. Monasteries and hospices were built to receive the travellers who, following the new fashion—as it can fairly be called—came to Palestine. The stream of pilgrims never dried up, not even after the Arab conquest of the Holy Land in the seventh century. The growing east–west trade in relics played some part in awakening and sustaining interest in the Holy Places, but more important was the gradual development of the penitential pilgrimage. This was imposed as a canonical punishment and for capital crimes like fratricide it could be for a period of up to seven years and to all the great centres: Rome, San Michele at Monte Gargano, Santiago di Compostella and, above all, Jerusalem and Bethlehem. With the belief that they were effective ways to salvation the popularity of pilgrimages grew rapidly from the tenth century onwards. Saint John of Parma journeyed no less than six times to the Holy Land—given the conditions of travel at the time an astonishing achievement. Men of violent passions like Fulk Nerra, Count of Anjou, or Robert the Devil, Count of Normandy, went on pilgrimages to Jerusalem when their consciences plagued them on account of the crimes they had committed against church and monastery, so sometimes they had to go more than once. Returning from one of these pilgrimages Fulk founded the abbey of Beaulieu near Loches and gave it as its chief relic a piece of stone which he was said to have bitten off the Holy Sepulchre while kneeling before it in ecstatic prayer. The new Cluniac order, gaining all the time in prestige and influence, used its far-flung net of contacts and its genius for organization both to urge men to go on pilgrimages and to improve facilities for those who did. For many pilgrims in the eleventh century the journey to Jerusalem took on a still deeper religious meaning; according to Ralph Glaber, himself a Cluniac monk, it was looked upon as the climax of a man's religious life, as his final journey. Once he had reached the Holy Places he would remain there until he died.

It is clear that in the middle of the eleventh century the difficulties facing pilgrims began to increase. In part this was a result of the Seldjuk invasions which made things harder for travellers on the road through Anatolia —a popular route because it permitted a visit to Constantinople. But it was also a consequence of the growing number of pilgrims, for this worried the Muslim authorities in Asia Minor and Palestine, just as the Greeks in south Italy looked sceptically upon the groups of Norman 'pilgrims' who were all too easily persuaded to settle there for good. It has been suggested that the Muslims may have had a commercial interest in promoting pilgrimages but, except perhaps in Jerusalem itself, the income from this source cannot have been very significant—poverty was, after all, one of the ideals of the pilgrim. So there was little or no incentive for them to make the journey any easier. Conditions were, of course, nothing like as bad as they had been during the persecution of the Christians under the mad caliph, Hakim, who, in 1009, had had the Church of the Holy Sepulchre in Jerusalem destroyed; but neither were they as favourable as they had been during the great days of the Byzantine Empire or in the time of Charlemagne who had himself taken a keen interest in the pilgrimage to Palestine. Yet despite the occasional trouble the number of pilgrims grew steadily. In 1064–5 Bishop Gunther of Bamberg led a party over 7,000 strong into the Holy Land. Near Ramleh in Palestine they were suddenly attacked by Muslims and for several days they had to fight a defensive battle. It is not easy to explain how they managed this since pilgrims were always unarmed.

Here we have reached the critical point of difference between crusader and pilgrim. The crusader carried weapons. A crusade was a pilgrimage, but an armed pilgrimage which was granted special privileges by the Church and which was held to be specially meritorious. The crusade was a logical extension of the pilgrimage. It would never have occurred to anyone to march out to conquer the Holy Land if men had not made pilgrimages there for century after century. The constant stream of pilgrims inevitably nourished the idea that the Sepulchre of Christ ought to be in Christian hands, not in order to solve the practical difficulties which faced pilgrims, but because gradually the knowledge that the Holy Places, the patrimony of Christ, were possessed by heathens became more and more un-

bearable. If the link between pilgrimage and crusade is obvious, the credit for bringing it about belongs to Urban II. Although historians today are less inclined to argue that the crusades were caused by increasing difficulties in the way of pilgrims, it still remains true that pilgrimages were of decisive importance in the rise of the crusading movement. In Erdmann's words, Urban 'took the popular but, in practical terms, unfruitful idea of pilgrimage and used it to fertilize the war upon the heathen'. It is significant that contemporaries were at first unable to distinguish clearly between the two things. Not until the mid-thirteenth century was there a Latin word for 'crusade' and even then it was seldom used. (The English word crusade, like the German word *Kreuzzug*, was only invented in the eighteenth century.) In the Middle Ages men almost always used circumlocutions like *expeditio, iter in terram sanctam* (journey into the Holy Land) and—especially early in the crusading period—*peregrinatio*, the technical term for pilgrimage. The line between crusade and pilgrimage was obviously a blurred one....

One more motive for taking the cross remains to be considered; and this one was to put all the others in the shade. It was the concept of a reward in the form of the crusading indulgence. In modern Roman Catholic doctrine the indulgence comes at the end of a clear process of remission of sins. First the penitent sinner must confess and receive absolution so that the guilt of the sin is remitted and instead of suffering eternal punishment he will have to suffer only the temporal penalties due to sin. (It is important to note that these penalties may take place either in this world or the next and will include purgatory.) Then in return for indulgence-earning works the Church may grant him remission of all or part of the penalty due to sin, depending on whether the indulgence is a plenary one or not. This is a judicial act of grace based on the authority of the Church's power of the keys and is entirely separate from the sacrament of penance. The indulgence would affect both the canonical punishment imposed by the Church—the penitential punishment— and the temporal punishment imposed by God, since the Church could offer God a substitute penance from the 'Treasury of Merits'—an inexhaustible reservoir of merits accumulated by Christ and added to by the saints on a scale far in excess of what they themselves needed. Undoubtedly then the indulgence has a transcendental effect before God (*in foro Dei*). Where the theologians disagree with one another is on the question of whether one can absolutely guarantee that this judicial act will have a positive result *in foro Dei* or whether it runs up against the problem of God's freedom. In this case the positive result is only indirectly and morally assured in as much as the Church guarantees that the offer of a substitute penance is sufficient to discharge the whole of the punishment due, i.e. the sinner could not have achieved any better result even if he had himself done full penance. But when considering early indulgences, especially the first crusading indulgences, it is vital to remember that this logical doctrine was a later construction designed to give theological authority to customs which, in practice, already existed.

Not until after the First Crusade did the theologians of the twelfth century, first among them Hugh of St. Victor, work out—in practical, if not yet in formal terms—the distinction between the guilt of sin and the punishment due to sin which is crucial to the theory of indulgences. And not until *c*.1230 was the important doctrine of the 'Treasury of Merits', which provided the equivalent substitute necessary if punishment were to be remitted, formulated by Hugh of St. Cher. The detailed problems of the precise nature of an indulgence and the justification for it were hotly disputed in the twelfth and thirteenth centuries. Even St. Thomas Aquinas was clearly hard put to it to explain the indulgence because he began his proof of it by producing a classic logical fallacy (*petitio principii*): 'Everyone agrees that indulgences are effective because it would be godless to say that the Church does anything in vain.' Where even theologians found much obscure, there was little chance of popular opinion being well-informed. Any discussion of the crusades must take this point more fully into consideration than has hitherto been customary. In assessing the effect of the crusading indulgence what matters is what people understood or believed they understood by it, not what it actually was. And it is worth noting that the debate about indulgences which started *c*.1130 was sparked off by the fact that they were being abused. As long as the abuses were not too blatant, people looked upon the indulgence as an acceptable innovation without bothering too much about the theology of the matter. We must always remember that the publicizing of the first crusading indulgence took place in an atmosphere which was free of the limitations imposed either by an official Church pronouncement or by a proper theological debate. The only way the new elements could be defined was by comparing them with earlier penitential practices.

The indulgence must, in fact, be seen as a development of the Church's earlier penitential discipline. This was originally divided into three stages: confession, satisfaction, and reconciliation (i.e. being readmitted to communion). Satisfaction was looked upon as the element which earned extinction of sins and thus made the reconciliation possible. At this time no distinction would have been made between remission of guilt and remission of punishment. In principle, the penance had to be equivalent to the sin committed. One had to pay, as it were, pound for pound. But obviously it was only a matter of chance whether or not a precisely equivalent penance was found; thus in addition there had to be the temporal penalties due to sin which, being imposed by God, could measure exactly any guilt that was still remaining. Since God's temporal punishment was feared far more than any earthly penance, a penitential system of draconic severity was developed on the theory that the harsher the penance in this world, the smaller would be the settlement in the next. The fact that up until the sixth century only serious offences were subject to the penance of the Church helped to establish the severity of penitential practice. Yet when, for reasons which cannot be gone into here, this changed so that penance had to be done for venial sins as well, the old system at first remained in force. But now harsh tasks and long penances during which the sinner remained excluded from the sacraments were no longer always appropriate, so inevitably there developed a trend towards a milder and a more differentiated system of punishment. At first this was done by the use of commutation and redemption, i.e. one form of punishment was exchanged for another which theoretically was still equivalent to the sin committed. Thus if it were shorter, it was also supposed to be harder; but in practice it tended to be more lenient. Lists of the penalties due to various sins were drawn up tariff-fashion in the 'Penitentials', together with the appropriate redemptions. In these redemptions we have one of the main roots of the crusading indulgence. In the eleventh century the system became still milder when it became customary to allow reconciliation to take place as soon as a man had begun his penance, though of course he still had to complete it. Thus long-term excommunication—one of the most feared consequences of sin—was in effect abolished. This change also meant the end of the old custom of total reconciliation. Its place was taken by an absolution granted immediately after confession. This involved reconciliation with God and the Church, i.e. forgiveness of the guilt of sin, but it did not mean full remission of the punishment due to sin. Nevertheless absolution went further than redemption and thus came closer to the indulgence in that the Church made a powerful plea for pardon; so a transcendental effect was at least intended. This was still not a judicial act, however, nor was it a remission of punishment granted independently of the sacrament of penance. But from here it was only a short step to the indulgence, i.e. to a more clearly defined and more certainly effective remission of the penance imposed by the Church. By an act of grace allowance was made for the transcendental effect *in foro Dei* of the Church's plea. This then made it possible to curtail the penance imposed by the Church. According to Poschmann, one of the leading Catholic experts on the subject, 'the indulgence was no longer just a part-payment on the time after death, it was also a most welcome relief during this earthly life'. The special feature of the indulgence was that the ideal of equivalence was no longer adhered to in practice. Later on the doctrine of the 'Treasury of Merits' was developed in order to justify this practice.

It is revealing that the idea of indulgence only became really effective when it was linked with the pilgrimage to Jerusalem. Papal pronouncements rather similar to indulgences were occasionally made before the crusades, but these were, in fact, usually absolutions. Alexander II, for example, promised a remission of penance to the soldiers who had joined the Barbastro expedition of 1063. In addition he also offered them the *remissio peccatorum*, the remission of the temporal penalties due to sin. It has been argued that the pope's letter is a forgery, but in fact it is a perfectly genuine plenary indulgence. Yet for various reasons it had very little effect. For one thing, it was addressed to a much smaller group than was the crusading indulgence of 1095. Alexander's offer applied only to those who had already decided to take part in the Spanish campaign; and he left it open whether he would extend the terms of the indulgence to include those who joined later. Furthermore normal penitential practice was adhered to in that a penance had first to be imposed, at least formally, before it could be considered as cancelled by the indulgence. Finally a campaign in Spain did not have the same mass-appeal as an expedition to the Holy Land. This example shows clearly why the full effects of the indulgence were felt only when it became linked with the pilgrimage to Jerusalem.

In this context it was important that the penitential journey to Jerusalem was thought to be especially meritorious and salutary. In theory the Church had always taken the view that movement from one place to another did not bring a man any nearer to God; but it was impossible to extinguish the popular belief in the value of a pilgrimage to Jerusalem. Its popularity was assured from the moment when the reconciliation with the Church was moved forward to the beginning of the work of penance, in this case the pilgrimage. This applied, of course, to any penitential pilgrimage; what gave Jerusalem its special significance was the tradition of the Holy Places. There is evidence from as early as the eighth century for the belief that remission of sins could be earned by a visit to the Church of the Holy Sepulchre. But those who shared this belief in the value of pilgrimages were denounced at the Council of Chalons in 813. The Council was relying on the authority of Jerome who had said that it was not seeing Jerusalem that was praiseworthy, but living a good life there. Indeed, in Jerome's eyes, even this had no special purifying value. He wrote that he had gone to Palestine in order to understand the Bible better, not to obtain spiritual advantages. But since the Council quoted only Jerome's first statement and not his commentary on it, it was possible to believe that both Jerome and the Council were prepared to concede an indirect purifying value to the journey to Jerusalem—i.e. when it led to a long period of residence there. Later on the Church quite patently failed to combat the belief that the pilgrimage to Jerusalem was worth an indulgence. Indeed it formally granted partial indulgences for it, like the year's indulgence allowed by Alexander III. This was during the heyday of the crusades, when the crusader was granted an unlimited plenary indulgence; understandably the peaceful pilgrim obtained just a partial indulgence....

It would, of course, be wrong to assert that the crusade propagandists avoided a more spiritual approach and worked only in... blatantly commercial terms. Nevertheless a great deal was done by such methods; we should remember that it was an age which witnessed a tremendous boom in long-distance trade. St. Bernard, though he used the vocabulary of merchants, did, of course, also say very different things, but he too did not want to renounce this effective propaganda theme.

It is perhaps better to put aside the question of whether or not the Church gave the impression that a complete remission of sin, both guilt and punishment, was possible through the indulgence and therefore through a procedure outside the Church's sacrament of penance. It is certainly possible that sometimes contemporaries did so interpret the Church's ambiguous terminology. But in any case the difference between remission of penance and remission of the temporal punishment due to sin, a difference which existed in the Church's traditional doctrine of indulgences, was of itself quite enough to explain the success of Clermont. There had been nothing new about being able to obtain remission of penance by going to fight the heathen. But that the penalties due to sin could be remitted simply as a result of taking the cross—as the crusade propagandists suggested—this was an unheard of innovation. Previously both the reconciliation granted at the start of the penance and the redeeming commutation had affected only the penances and had had no transcen-

dental effect upon the penalties due to sin. It was indeed hoped that absolution would have such an effect, but it could certainly not be guaranteed. The indulgence on the other hand availed before God in a certain and in a quantitatively measurable fashion so that both the temporal penalties due to sin and the earthly penances were remitted and, in the case of a plenary indulgence, fully cancelled. Only Alexander II had promised as much as this for the war against the heathen and his promise, being addressed only to a small group, had met with little response. It was when linked with the universally popular idea of pilgrimage to Jerusalem that the explosive force of the crusading indulgence was revealed. Ekkehard of Aura spoke of 'a new way of penance' now being opened up. Here lies the secret of the astonishing success of Urban's summons, a success which astonished the Church as much as anyone else. Imagine a knight in the south of France, living with his kinsmen in the socially and economically unsatisfactory institution of the *frérèche*. His feuds and the 'upper class' form of highway robbery which often enough went with them, were prohibited by the Peace of God. Suddenly he was offered the chance of going on a pilgrimage—in any event the wish of many men. This pilgrimage was supervised by the Church; it was moreover an armed pilgrimage during which he could fulfil his knightly function by taking part in battle. There would be opportunities for winning plunder. Above all there was the entirely new offer of a full remission of all the temporal penalties due to sin, especially of those to be suffered in purgatory. The absolution given in the sacrament of penance took from him the guilt; taking the cross meant the cancellation of all the punishment even before he set out to perform the task imposed. Not to accept such an offer, not—at the very least—to take it seriously, would indeed have been mad. The 'shrewd businessman' seized his chance. And who did not want to be numbered among the shrewd?

Taking the cross in these circumstances was, of course, an act of faith just as much as an act of naive trust in the promises made by Church publicists. Naturally not all crusaders were moved by piety. In the Middle Ages too there were sceptics and the motives for going on crusade were many, various, and tangled, often social and economic in character. But the offer of indulgence must have had an irresistible attraction for those who did not doubt the Church's teaching, who believed in the reality of the penalties due to sin, or at least accepted the possibility of their existence. Such believers must have made up a great part of those who went on the First Crusade—whatever proportion of the total population of Europe they may have been. And, of course, the crusaders of 1095 could not have guessed that the offer which they were accepting was in reality much more limited than the one promised them by the 'fishers of men'.

NO

Ronald C. Finucane

SOLDIERS OF THE FAITH: CRUSADERS AND MOSLEMS AT WAR

THE CRUSADES: AN OVERVIEW

'He who fights so the word of God may prevail is on the path of God.' The sentiments embodied in this saying attributed to Mohammad do much to explain the amazing success of Islam, which, through the zeal for *jihad* or holy war, extended from the borders of France to those of India by the early eighth century. Religious enthusiasm also lies behind the equally amazing accomplishments of the Christian warriors of the First Crusade. In both Moslem expansion and Christian conquest, however, luck was just as important as zeal. The Moslems were able to profit from the weaknesses of early seventh-century Christendom just as the crusaders, when they entered Jerusalem in bloody triumphs four and a half centuries later, were able to attribute their victory in part to dissension and weakness among the Moslems.

Because of assassinations and rivalry which could be traced back to the period following Mohammad's death, by the tenth century the Moslem world had fallen into two major (and several minor) rival camps. One of these, the Shi'ite faction, was supported by the successors of Ali, Mohammad's cousin and son-in-law. By the later tenth century, they had gained control in Egypt as the Fatimids; a fanatical offshoot, the Assassins, would spill the blood both of Christians and other rival Moslem groups. The other faction, the Sunnites, originally supported the succession of Abu Bakr, one of Mohammad's closest allies. On both sides the picture is further confused by the establishment of semi-independent emirates and caliphates of varying political and religious allegiances. Moslem Spain, for example, began to go its own way as early as the eighth century. Not only was there internal rivalry, but also, from the tenth and early eleventh centuries, the Moslem world was shaken by progressive incursions of the Seljuk Turks. These people, having become Sunnites, brought to the Near East a vitality and fervour that were reminiscent of the earliest stages in the rise of Islam. They were proud, warlike, zealous and —more to the point—very successful: in the 1050s, they captured Baghdad; by the 1070s, Asia Minor (with the defeat of the Byzantines at Manzikert in

1071), Palestine and Damascus; and by the 1080s, Antioch and Edessa. After one of their strongest leaders, Sultan Malik Shah, died in 1092, Turkish unity was dissipated by the establishment of several rival emirates, particularly in Asia Minor and Syria. This was why, during the 1090s, even as crusader swarms were moving from western Europe, the Holy Land was the scene of internal conflict and rivalry; why the crusaders often found themselves, from practical considerations, willing to accept or ask for the assistance of one or other of the Moslem parties in the ever-shifting sands of near-eastern politics. The fact that Greek Constantinople was to many westerners suspect as a perfumed den of vice and treachery, only complicated matters....

The crusaders, then, were aided not only by their own religious zeal, cupidity, curiosity and many other motives that pushed them eastwards, but also by the turmoil and rivalries among the Moslems themselves. Though this may help to explain how they succeeded in their extraordinary venture, an even more interesting problem involves timing: why, since Jerusalem had been continuously occupied by Moslems since the seventh century, did the Christian West only attempt recovery at the end of the eleventh century? What had changed in European society and thought? One way to approach this question is through an examination of earlier military relations between the Moslem and Christian worlds, beginning, for convenience, with Spain. Visigothic Spain was attacked in 711 by Tarik and his converted Berbers in a campaign which, according to legend, was brought on when the daughter of Julian, a local lord, was abducted and impregnated by King Rodrigo of Toledo.

In revenge, Julian is supposed to have invited the Moslems from North Africa to overthrow Rodrigo. Finding the job so easily accomplished, they went on to take over Spain itself, though there was resistance; by tradition the first important battle launched against the invaders by the Christians occurred in 718. Though they were eventually pushed into a narrow coastal lair behind the northern mountains, by the ninth century the Christians had begun their *Reconquista*. They had also provided themselves with a supernatural champion in St. James, at Compostella, which would become one of Europe's premier pilgrimage centres, as Jerusalem was at the other end of the Mediterranean. By the middle of the eleventh century, determined Christian kings had extended their hegemony southwards, bringing many Moslem princelings under their control. This success at last united the Moors and persuaded them to invite more ruthless co-religionists from north Africa, who reversed many of the Christian conquests. This was the confusing milieu for El Cid's sometimes unchristian adventures. In any case, on the eve of the First Crusade, Spain had already witnessed more than three centuries of warfare with the Moslems.

It was from Spain, about 720, that the Moslems moved on into southwest France. Historians still debate the extent of this threat and its potentialities, though in the short term many cities and towns undoubtedly suffered its harmful effects. Charles Martel, the 'hammer', earned his epithet by turning back in 732 or 733 near Poitiers this Moslem advance, the start of a long tradition of Frankish resistance to the Saracens. By about 770, most of the enemy had been pushed from Gaul, though they continued to harass Charlemagne and his successors. The Frankish *Annals* report that around 799 Moslem insignia captured while defending the Balearics were sent to Charlemagne, and, in 801, at the fall of Barcelona, it is said that many Saracen prisoners were taken. Heroic deeds in the Spanish March or borderlands gave rise to one of the seminal works of medieval literature, the *Chanson de Roland;* though nominally-Christian Basques seem to have attacked the proud Roland, the ultimate enemy was the Moslem. Charlemagne's son, Pepin, King of Italy (d. 810), sent a fleet against Moslems pillaging Corsica in 806, but this did not stop their overrunning both Sardinia and Corsica in 810. Even before Charlemagne's death, the *Annals* compiler mentions the ravaging of Nice —a hint of unpleasant things to come, for later in the ninth century enterprising Moslems set up a bandits' nest some fifty miles along the coast from Nice, near Fréjus, from which they terrorized the neighbourhood, the Alpine passes and the north Italian seaports. There were other robbers' dens, but Fréjus was particularly troublesome. The stronghold was destroyed in the later tenth century when a league of aggrieved parties finally captured it.

It is not surprising that Moslem pirates should show an interest in Italian ports, since the peninsula and Sicily jutted out so invitingly into what the Moslems could call, with almost as much justification as the Romans, *Mare Nostrum.* Mohammad had been dead a mere twenty years, for example, when the first (recorded) attack on Sicily occurred. Things became serious during the ninth century, and, by 902, Sicily belonged to the Moslems. Southern Italian cities also suffered during the ninth century, and

Naples often found it more expedient to ally itself with the Moslems than to fight them. Even the Eternal City itself was lusted after by the infidel, though they had to content themselves with a rampage through the suburbs, including St Peter's basilica. Pope Leo IV, in consequence, threw a wall around the saint's church and thereby laid the foundations—in the figurative sense only, considering the extensive resisting and rebuilding of later centuries—of the Vatican mini-city. Another casualty of ninth-century Moslem activities in Italy was Monte Cassino, the venerable home of Benedictine monasticism. At last the Italians began to organize resistance, and by the early tenth century managed to expel the Moslems from Italy proper. Pope John X himself took the field in 915, successfully adding spiritual to martial forces. From this point on, Italian cities turned to offensive tactics: Pisa and Genoa in particular began launching aggressive raids against Moslem ports and, by the early eleventh century, were attacking the enemy in north Africa itself. These two cities were interested in protecting their western Mediterranean trade. On the other side of the peninsula, Venice was equally concerned about maintaining commercial ties with rich Byzantium to the east.

The Byzantines were just as anxious about the Moslem threat; when Pope John X defeated the Moslems at the Garigliano in 915, it was with the help of Byzantine military power, whose encounters with the Moslems stretched back to the seventh century, with Emperor Heraclius. In fact, Roman emperors were sending troops out to skewer Saracens long before Mohammad's birth....

Among the more successful of mercenary troops hired by the Byzantines were the Varangian Guard of Scandinavians, who were established in service in Constantinople about AD 1000. After the conquest of England in 1066, many displaced or dispossessed Anglo-Saxon warriors joined them. One of the key figures and victims of that 1066 conflict, Harald Hardradi, had taken service with the Varangians for a short time in the 1030s. According to his *Saga*, on this tour he attacked the lands of the Saracens and captured eighty towns, some of which surrendered, the rest being taken by assault. Even as Harald was spilling Moslem blood, however, the Seljuk Turks were moving westward, thus creating a new, formidable enemy whose incursions would compel Emperor Alexius Comnenus to call upon the West for help and set the scene for the First Crusade.

Long before this, western Christians had acquired centuries of experience battling Moslems in Spain, France and Italy. This aggression had been encouraged by the Church in its articulation of a doctrine of holy war. Warfare presented early Christians with yet another problem through the continuous process of accommodating their ideals to the 'real' world.... By the early fifth century, that giant who helped to shape medieval thought, St Augustine, had formulated a doctrine of just war in Christian terms. Provided that a war were declared by legitimate authority, for a just cause, and fought with the right intention, Christians should have no qualms about participating. In addition to this, even during Augustine's lifetime Europe was being transformed by incoming peoples whose leaders held prowess and *virtus* in battle of great importance and needed no excuses for rushing into battle. These Germanic tribes were eventually converted, thereby bringing to Christianity their own sublimation of the warlike virtues. With the rise of the Moslems, these new Europeans, and especially the Franks, stood out as defenders not only of their kingdoms, but also of Christianity itself. And yet, this was not holy war—though it may have been just—for the rewards of victory or valour were not yet envisaged as essentially spiritual....

The Church helped to prepare the ground for... holy wars in yet another way,... through the application of a sacramental mystique to knighthood. By the early eleventh century, religious ceremonial sometimes accompanied bestowal of the sword. At the same time, knights were encouraged to observe the growing Peace and Truce of God movements. The Church, and papacy, thereby (in theory) turned this potentially dangerous lynchpin of feudalism into an ally, a knight of St Peter. Before the First Crusade, these free-ranging fighters, trained to battle but exposed (at least) to religious exhortation, formed a corps which the Church was on occasion able to direct against her enemies....

Besides these spiritual and theoretical predispositions, eleventh-century men and women were also being 'prepared' for the first great crusading outburst of 1095–99 by changing conditions within their society and economy. Decades ago Henri Pirenne used words like 'optimism', 'native strength', 'fecundity' and 'revival' to describe eleventh-century Europe, while another equally famous medievalist (Marc Bloch) spoke of a new feudal age beginning about 1050. In general, this is still the fashion among most historians, who date the inception of the 'High Middle Ages' —the flowering of medieval society— to the eleventh century. Obviously the crusades cannot be understood without reference to this general awakening of western Europe, any more than they can be 'explained' only by the factors mentioned above. Perhaps the most important and correlated developments, in a strictly material sense, were the economic as well as the demographic expansion that affected all social levels. After the external invasions of western Europe had come to an end by about AD 1000, life was less precarious, food production rose, families increased in size, new arable fields were created in forest and waste land, and more and more merchants plied their trades in and between the growing towns. About 1080, the monks of St Aubin of Angers issued the following regulation, among others, for their peasants at Meron:

> If several men have loaded an ass with different kinds of merchandise, they shall owe toll for the ass, save if it is foreign or costly merchandise.
>
> For [these] other things, the toll shall be paid according to its value...

The good monks were not about to ignore possible profits from these small-time business ventures by their villeins. Something similar was happening to more and villagers throughout western Europe. An obvious motive was the desire for immediate personal gain from new and growing markets; another, especially for peasants, was the wish to escape the sometimes crushing obligations of manorial regimes. Many others would take up the generous offers of their lords—medieval land developers—and, especially in the twelfth century, pack up their families and rude furnishings and move off as colonists to take advantage of the lighter rents and work-loads. In the eleventh century, then, social and geographical mobility were distinct possibilities.

But larger families, especially among the middle-range nobility (of feudal Normandy for instance), created problems. As the medieval tradition of primogeniture spread, hunger for land and lordship drove many frustrated younger sons far from their home territories. Even where primogeniture was not the rule, many sought escape from the limitations of too many siblings and too little land by venturing into Spain, Italy and the Balkans. The enthusiastic knights of the First Crusade were aware of the practical opportunities, as well as spiritual advantages, awaiting them in the Holy Land. These conditions may also have complicated relations between neighbouring aristocratic families, who now would have to guard constantly against trespass (while, of course, encroaching against neighbours whenever possible). Often, the Church and peasantry suffered more than anyone else in these petty feudal wrangles. It was in the interests of both that the middling nobility should curb their appetites for contention, or at least satisfy them elsewhere. This was the background to another set of conditions, which led to the crusades—the part played by the Church not only in controlling the behaviour of the laity, but in imposing its own ideals upon ordinary men and women of high and low estate....

As the foregoing suggests, the crusading movement developed out of different sets of conditions laid down before and during the eleventh century. At least this seems to be the consensus today, when the political-colonial motives and immediate papal stimulus tend to be played down, while the socio-psychological background to the movement is emphasized. [Pope] Urban II is no longer thought of as the 'founder' of the crusading surge, but as a catalyst acting upon preformed sentiments and social circumstances. Yet there is no doubt that his sermon of 1095 was crucial. Also, in the decades leading up to 1095, military conflicts with the Moslems accelerated and thereby intensified pre-existing attitudes. In Spain, for example, the army of King Alfonso VI suffered overwhelming defeat in 1086 at the hands of the north African Murabits (or Almoravids, the Veiled Ones). Christian knights from France and elsewhere in western Europe were encouraged to attempt to regain lost Spanish territory. 'My Cid plies his lance until it breaks and then takes his sword and slays Moors without number, blood dripping from his elbow down.' In Italy at about the same time—1087— several cities collaborated in launching attacks against a north African Moslem base; the successful foray was led by a papal legate. In southern Italy, the ambitious Roger and his brother Robert Guiscard —products of a large, ambitious Norman family—were active as early as mid-century. By 1072, the two had successfully blockaded, besieged and conquered Sicily's Moslem capital, Palermo. The job was completed by Roger in 1091, when the island, as well as Malta and southern Italy, came under Norman control, a southern pendant to the Norman conquest of England a generation earlier. . . .

By [October 1097] rivalries had split the crusader armies. Some of the leaders detached their contingents and went off on their own, like Baldwin of Boulogne, who travelled east to establish himself as ruler of the Armenian Christians at Edessa by March 1098. Meanwhile, the bulk of the crusader army besieged Antioch, captured in June 1098. Bohemond

of Taranto (southern Italy) took over as Prince of Antioch, with the backing of Genoese merchant-shippers who gained concessions in the city. Raymond, Count of Toulouse and *soi-disant* leader of the crusade, after bickering with Bohemond about Antioch, finally gave in to pressure from the rank-and-file and pushed on in January 1099. Jerusalem was reached and taken in mid-July 1099; Godfrey, Duke of Lower Lorraine, became 'advocate' of the Holy Sepulchre, claiming to be unworthy of any higher honour in Christ's city. On his death in 1100, his less fastidious brother, Baldwin of Edessa, took the title King of Jerusalem. Thus, on the eve of the twelfth century, the crusaders had taken the Holy Land and had established the Kingdom of Jerusalem, Principality of Antioch, County of Edessa and (by 1109) County of Tripoli, held by Bertrand, son of Raymond, Count of Toulouse. These were the so-called Crusader States. The capture of Jerusalem renewed interest in the West and resulted in three crusades in 1101, which ended in victories for the Turks and worsening Western-Byzantine relations. In fact, by 1105, Bohemond of Antioch, fearing Byzantine pressure, convinced Pope Paschal II to preach a crusade against Byzantium itself. Nothing came of this, but it was an ominous foretaste of things to come. Meanwhile, King Baldwin of Jerusalem managed to extend crusader control by taking Acre in 1103 with Genoese help and Sidon in 1110 with Norwegian and Venetian assistance. But his attack on Tyre failed, and a raid into Egypt accomplished little. Yet by 1118 when he died, most of Palestine and much of Syria were under Christian control, the crusaders now assisted by the sometimes mutually antagonistic military orders, the Templars and Hospitallers. . . .

CONCLUSION

Though it is difficult to summarize and draw conclusions about such a varied and long-lasting movement as the crusades, certain generalizations are unavoidable. For instance, it is apparent that the expression 'the crusades' must be qualified, for the First Crusade differed in many ways from those which followed. Thousands of Europeans, affected by the emotional and social upheavals of the eleventh century, undertook a long, dangerous trek towards a mystical goal which was, for them, both a place and a state of salvation. During the next two centuries, crusades became increasingly structured, moving from general to specific aims and means; the idealism of the First Crusade was superseded by sometimes incompatible ideologies imposed from above by the papacy, by the noble and royal leaders of later expeditions, and by the secular rulers of *Outremer*.

Concurrently, Christendom itself was changing: the crusades exemplified these changes, revealing much about the dynamics of religious, economic and political realignments and alterations in western Europe. To take the religious aspect as an example, the crusades encouraged a growing concern about gaining indulgences, first by service abroad, then eventually by purchase of exemption from such service; the papacy attracted more and more criticism—from thirteenth-century poets who castigated Roman greed, for instance—because of what appeared to be diversions from the crusading impulse. By the sixteenth century, such matters would become important issues in the breakdown of European religious unity. Certainly this is not to suggest that the crusades led to the Reformation, but merely that the later crusades disclosed ominous stresses within a Europe that would ultimately undergo a Reformation. In the same way, conflict between French and English crusaders during the Third Crusade was a harbinger of that later confrontation known as the Hundred Years' War. Crusader activities and interrelationships in the Holy Land, then, as well as European responses to calls for crusades, provide models of wider, more deeply rooted attitudes, ambiguities and animosities within western Europe; in this sense, each crusade was a microcosm, a diminished image of Christendom.

Another inevitable conclusion to any general study of the crusades is the fact that many questions remain unanswered, perhaps unanswerable. The sorting out of motivations, for instance, still engages the interest of scholars, as does the very composition of the groups called 'crusaders': for each knightly or noble participant, for each foot-soldier or archer, how many unarmed pilgrims, women, clergymen, went along as 'crusaders'? Did the lower classes, as [Benjamin] Kedar suggested, continue to participate as avidly in the thirteenth century as they did in the twelfth century? How many women were actively, and how many passively, 'crusaders'? Such problems, considered individually, may seem to be mere froth that floats on the surface, puzzles propounded for the delectation of scholars. Yet every clue that can be found is meaningful, every attempt to answer such questions is worth considering because, as suggested above, each crusader band that detached itself from Europe reveals to the historian varying aspects of contemporary society.

Another conclusion to be drawn from a study of the crusades is that Moslem reactions to and interactions with the crusaders, who were intrusive elements, is a topic that is usually relegated to secondary status by western historians. Yet the Islamic viewpoint is as deserving of study as the Christian; fortunately, some western scholars (who are not primarily Orientalists) are forcefully and convincingly presenting the crusades in an Islamic context, pushing us away from the Christian-centered world into a wider universe, instigating a long-overdue Copernican revolution in Christian-Moslem studies. There is a practical side to this as well: the need to understand Islam and the various peoples who call themselves Moslems is as pressing today as it ever was; and yet modern western European Christians seem in general to be as ignorant of the fundamentals of Islam as their twelfth-century predecessors. The words of a thirteenth-century Jew, Ibn Kammūna of Baghdad, concerning the lack of comprehension between Jews and Moslems of his day, apply equally well to modern Christians and Moslems:

> (D)espite numerous contacts of the bulk of the Jews with the Muslims, many Jews still do not know the basic Islamic tenets known by the rank and file Muslims, let alone the elite. It is even more natural that a similar situation should obtain on the Muslim side ...

The question of Christian-Moslem interaction naturally includes the problem of the Christian attitude towards war. An examination of the course of the crusades has led some historians to suggest that Church doctrine was deliberately manipulated to suit specific ends: though committed to condemning bloodshed, the Church itself promoted it. Keith Haines even goes so far as to remark that in Europe

> It is impossible to discern a totally pacifist ideology amongst virtually any of the leading moral, theological or political philosophers of the twelfth and thirteenth centuries ...

Another leading crusade historian has also recently emphasized how the fundamental message of Christian charity was reinterpreted to suit crusade exigencies. Crusade preachers, for instance, must have deliberately presented Christian *caritas* to their audiences in such a way as to play upon the xenophobia of the masses.

One final conclusion to be drawn from the crusading experience is the futility—in practical terms—of the Christian attempt to co-exist with Moslems peacefully in the Holy Land, while trying to maintain political control of the area. Permanent peace between Moslems and Christians, in Moslem territory, was not feasible: caught between an Islam newly dedicated to *jihad* (from Saladin's time) on the one side, and mistrusting, uncomprehending westerners on the other, the Christian Europeans of *Outremer* were, as [Jonathan] Riley-Smith points out, in an untenable position. Christian residents in the Holy Land, then, were surrounded by hostile forces, harassed by problems of logistics and military support and by divisions of opinion in Europe about crusader policy; difficulties of a similar nature would confront many modern European states in their own colonial enterprises. Eventually expelled from positions of political and military power in the Levant, Christians were allowed to return to the Holy City only as pilgrims and suppliants at the Tomb of Christ, as they had been for centuries before that fateful sermon preached by Urban II in 1095.

POSTSCRIPT

Were the Crusades Motivated Primarily by Religious Factors?

With the emergence of Islamic revivalism in the modern world, the historical relationships between the West and the Muslim world have attained a renewed level of interest. The relevance of the Crusades to this contemporary situation provides some interesting food for thought. The Islamic world has always viewed the Crusades as an invasion of its territory by a foreign power; it appears the West has not viewed them in the same light. An interesting question with contemporary applicability is to what extent can the Crusades be viewed as a Christian jihad (holy war)? As the West responds to Islamic-inspired terrorism today with shock and outrage, is it not possible that a millennium ago, Middle Eastern Muslims responded in the same manner to the European Crusaders?

Another example of the ties between past and present is the religious motivation found in both the Crusades and current Islamic revivalism. The former were at least partially motivated by several religious factors: fighting a just war in the service of God; gaining indulgences for services rendered; and the ultimate prize, gaining the right to eternal salvation. The latter is motivated by fighting a war against the infidels in the name of Allah; participating in a fierce struggle between the forces of good and evil; and ultimately acquiring a special place in heaven as martyrs of the faith. Is this an example of repeating the past without learning any lessons from it?

As far as sources on the Crusades are concerned, start with Steven Runciman's three-volume work *A History of the Crusades*, 4th ed. (Cambridge University Press, 1954). Karen Armstrong's *Holy War* (Macmillan, 1988) is a Western source, which speaks of the Crusades in an objective and critical manner, especially as they relate to contemporary problems between Muslims, Christians, and Jews in the Middle East. Jonathan Riley-Smith's *The First Crusaders, 1095–1131* (Cambridge University Press, 1997) represents current scholarship. Smith states that the Crusades "drew on the tradition of Pilgrimage to Jerusalem," and pious violence was a motivating force. He also points out that many of the Crusaders from the times he researched came from the same families and clans and concludes that the sustenance they received from these ties helped make the Crusades possible. For an Arab perspective on the Crusades, see Amin Maalouf, *The Crusades Through Arab Eyes* (Schocken Books, 1985), which finds them partially responsible for the beginning of the disintegration of the Islamic world.

On the Internet . . .

http://www.dushkin.com

Eliot Elisofon Photographic Archives at the National Museum of African Art
This is a research and reference center for visual material. It is devoted to the collection, preservation, and dissemination of visual resources that encourage and support the study of the arts, peoples, and history of Africa.
http://www.si.edu/organiza/museums/africart/resource/archives.htm

Archaeology Magazine
This is the home page of the Archaeological Institute of America's *Archaeology* magazine. It contains full texts of news briefs and abstracts of feature articles.
http://www.he.net/~archaeol/index.html

HyperHistory Online
HyperHistory presents three thousand years of world history via a combination of colorful graphics, life lines, time lines, and maps. Its main purpose is to convey a perspective of world historical events and to enable the reader to keep in mind what was happening in widely separated parts of the world simultaneously.
http://www.hyperhistory.com/online_n2/History_n2/a.html

PART 3

The Premodern World

Using the Renaissance and Age of Exploration as a starting point, this part shows how and why one civilization, the West, began to change, expand, and influence the development of its continent and the rest of the world, and what resulted from this process.

■ Did Women and Men Benefit Equally from the Renaissance?

■ Were Christopher Columbus's New World Discoveries a Positive Force in the Development of World History?

■ Were the Witch-Hunts in Premodern Europe Misogynistic?

■ Did the West Define the Modern World?

ISSUE 9

Did Women and Men Benefit Equally from the Renaissance?

YES: Mary R. Beard, from *Woman as Force in History: A Study in Traditions and Realities* (Collier Books, 1946)

NO: Joan Kelly-Gadol, from "Did Women Have a Renaissance?" in Renate Bridenthal, Claudia Koonz, and Susan Stuard, eds., *Becoming Visible: Women in European History*, 2d ed. (Houghton Mifflin, 1987)

ISSUE SUMMARY

YES: Historian Mary R. Beard contends that during the Renaissance, Italian women of the higher classes turned to the study of Greek and Roman literature and committed themselves alongside men to developing well-rounded personalities.

NO: Historian Joan Kelly-Gadol argues that women enjoyed greater advantages during the Middle Ages and experienced a relative loss of position and power during the Renaissance.

In 1974 Joan Kelly-Gadol published a pathbreaking essay that challenged traditional periodization. Before that, virtually every publication on the Renaissance proclaimed it to be a great leap forward for everyone, a time when new ideas were everywhere discussed and the old strictures of the Middle Ages were thrown off. The difficulty for Kelly-Gadol was that her own work on women during the medieval and Renaissance periods told a different story. She was one of the first to raise this troubling question: Are the turning points in history the same for women as they are for men? Kelly-Gadol found that well-born women lived in a relatively free environment during the Middle Ages. The courtly love tradition allowed powerful, property-owning women to satisfy their own sexual and emotional needs. With the arrival of the Renaissance, however, the courtly love tradition was defined by powerful male princes who found it desirable for women to be passive and chaste in order to serve the needs of the rising bourgeoisie.

Mary R. Beard is considered the original pathfinder. Her stunning 1946 book *Woman as Force in History* was written, she said, to "destroy the myth that women have done and are suited for little else than bearing and rearing children." Beard, like Kelly-Gadol, studied women of the upper classes. She was eager to find a place for women in history to counter the prevailing view of male historians that by studying the "great man" we could understand the age he created. Beard began looking for the "great woman" and found traces of her throughout human history. After Beard's book was published, it became much more difficult for historians to treat women as passive victims of history.

The field of women's history has a history of its own. Beginning with the pioneering work of historians such as Beard, scholars first engaged in what Gerda Lerner has called "compensatory history"—compensating for past omissions by researching and writing about the great women of history. In a second phase, women's history moved to "contributory history." Looking past the great women, historians took all the traditional categories of standard male history and found women who filled them—women who spent their lives as intellectuals, soldiers, politicians, and scientists. The current phase of women's history parallels more general trends in social history, concentrating on the ordinary people who lived during historical epochs. In this more fully mature phase, the emphasis is on women's culture—how women saw the world from within their own systems and ways of doing things. If Beard was doing compensatory history, Kelly-Gadol might be said to be engaging in contributory history. The women she writes about led lives similar to those of men in their class during the Middle Ages, but Kelly-Gadol contends that they had a different experience during the Renaissance.

One caution to keep in mind is that people are not aware of the times in which they live in terms of the historical periods that scholars later use for identification. People of the past, like people today, are more concerned with their personal lives and fortunes than with historical trends. Periodization, or the marking of turning points in the past, can be useful. It can help to identify broad trends and forks in the road as we explore the past. What women's history has taught us, however, is that looking at the experiences of men may or may not tell us what the experiences of women were like during the same time periods.

Mary Beard collaborated with her husband Charles Beard on many widely read history books. When she wrote *Woman as Force in History*, which is excerpted in the following selection, her aim was to demonstrate that women "have been a force in making all the history that has been made." Her book and the field of women's history that it inspired made possible the work of later scholars such as Kelly-Gadol. Mary Beard challenged traditional notions about the role of women in history; Kelly-Gadol challenged history itself. If what has been said about certain turning points in human history is true only for men or much more true for men than for women, then the whole field of history must be reconceptualized. Although both of the selections that follow were written some time ago, the questions they raise remain lively today.

YES   Mary R. Beard

EVIDENCES IN MEDIAEVAL EDUCATIONAL AND INTELLECTUAL INTERESTS

HUMANIZING EDUCATION—INDIVIDUAL, CIVIC, AND PHILOSOPHIC

Many things conspired to give leadership and acclaim in education and letters to the women of Italy, earlier than to women of other countries. Italy was the original home of the revival of the Latin classics and it was to Italy that the choicest of Greek classics were brought from Byzantium, before and after the fall of Constantinople to the Turks in 1453. To Italy came able scholars and tutors straight from the Near East; and at their hands, or under their influence, Greek and Latin grammars and texts of the classics were issued in profusion.

With the revival of classical learning came the humanizing of intellectual interest, knowledge, and public measures; that is, thought and action were directed by this learning to human concerns, as distinguished from the divine, and to the human race in general, as distinguished from individual salvation and particular peoples. Now educated men and women in Italy had at their command, for example, the great histories written by Greek and Roman authorities in antiquity and were attracted by the difference between these human and secular works and the monkish chronicles which, besides being fragmentary, twisted the story of the past to fit theological conceptions of the universe. Now Italian men and women were in possession of literary and philosophic works dealing entirely with the great human and nature subjects, without regard for those "ultimate causes" with which theologians occupied themselves on the basis of theories and convictions respecting the nature and designs of God. Moreover, instead of the degraded Latin so often employed by monkish chroniclers, Italian men and women now had models of writing by Greek and Roman thinkers and stylists, inviting them to lofty aspirations and lucid expressions whether in poetry, letters, the arts, history, philosophy, or politics.

In the promotion of the new learning, two tasks had to be carried out. The first included the recovery of additional classical works, the preparation of critical editions, the reissue of the best in manuscript form and, after the invention of printing, in book form, and critical study of the new texts. The second was the dissemination of the knowledge derived from the critical study.

The number of women who devoted themselves to scholarship was by no means as large as the number of men, for reasons other than the lack of talents; but in the fifteenth century and early sixteenth century many Italian women displayed the highest technical competence in the study, interpretation, and exposition of the revived humanist learning. Some of them, for example Isotta Nogarola, we are told by Dr. G. R. Potter in *The Cambridge Mediaeval History* (Volume VIII, Chapter XXIII), "could hold their own in matters of scholarship with the best of their male contemporaries and... were accepted and even acclaimed everywhere."

According to Dr. H. J. Mozans' *Women in Science,* women took "an active part in the great educational movement inaugurated by the revival of learning" and won "the highest honors for their sex in every department of science, art, and learning.... The universities, which had been opened to them at the close of the middle ages, gladly conferred upon them the doctorate, and eagerly welcomed them to the chairs of some of their most important faculties.... Cecelia Gonzaga, pupil of the celebrated humanist, Vittorino da Feltre, read the gospels in Greek when she was only

seven years old. Isotta and Ginevra Nogarola, pupils of the humanist, Guarino Verronese, likewise distinguished themselves at an early age by their rare knowledge of Latin and Greek.... Livia Chiavello, of Fabriano, was celebrated as one of the most brilliant representatives of the Petrarchian school.... Cassandra Fidele, of Venice, deserved, according to Poliziano, the noted Florentine humanist to be ranked with that famous universal genius, Pico de la Mirandola. So extensive were her attainments that in addition to being a thorough mistress of Latin and Greek, she was likewise distinguished in music, eloquence, philosophy, and even theology.... But for the extent and variety of her attainments, Tarquinia Molza seems to have eclipsed all her contemporaries. Not only did she excel in poetry and the fine arts, she also had a rare knowledge of astronomy and mathematics, Latin, Greek and Hebrew. So great was the esteem in which she was held that the senate of Rome conferred upon her the singular honor of Roman citizenship, transmissible in perpetuity to her descendants."

In nearly every great intellectual center of Italy women were lecturing on literature and philosophy, and religious faith could not escape impacts of the new knowledge. They were studying medicine and natural science in the light of pagan learning in these subjects. Great Italian women teachers of the awakening "sent forth such students as Moritz von Spiegelberg and Rudolph Agricola to reform the instruction of Deventer and Zwoll and prepare the way for Erasmus and Reuchlin."

Some of the women crossed the Alps themselves, as the ancient learning was said to do when Erasmus and other returning students bore back to outlying countries the knowledge gleaned in Italy. One of the most distinguished classical scholars of the age, Olympia Morata, for example, meeting difficulties as Renée's court where the duchess and all her friends were persecuted by the Duke for their religious independence, fled to Germany, with a young Bavarian student of medicine and philosophy, and was planning to continue her teaching of the classics in Heidelberg, to which she had been invited, when an untimely death closed her career.

In the dissemination of the new learning among the Italian people, especially among the rich but including some not as well off in this world's goods, five methods were widely and intensively employed: tutoring and self-directed study in families, education in schools, humanist lecturing, conversations in small private groups and larger coteries, and correspondence.

As soon as the Renaissance had got under way, Italian women in the rich commercial cities and at ducal or princely courts, such as Ferrara and Urbino, turned with avidity to the study and discussion of Greek and Roman literature.

While men of the governing class were away from their castles fighting in wars, women and girls of their families thus "improved their minds" and displayed their accomplishments to the warriors when they came home on furloughs. French officers and Spanish ambassadors who were guests in the great houses from time to time were so impressed that they let their own women relatives and friends know how backward they were and how advisable it would be for them to catch up with Italian women. When Erasmus, Grocyn, and Colet joined in the student pilgrimage to

Italy early in the sixteenth century, they found women immersed in the ancient languages and lore, surrounded by poets, artists, scholars, and writers from near and distant places as companions in the new intellectual movement.

This linguistic and literary development was not confined to the ruling circles, however. Classical schools for girls and boys were opened in Italian cities, giving to the business and professional circles, as well as to patricians, opportunities to acquire knowledge of the ancient languages and the natural, or secular, philosophies embodied in Greek and Latin literature. Here entered the insurgent bourgeois influence which Henry Adams, looking back from the twentieth century and his vantage point within it, concluded was an invincible menace to the throne of Mary, Queen of Heaven.

Among the outstanding Italians of the fifteenth century who promoted education, letters, and arts were Gian Francesco Gonzaga II and his wife, Paola Malatesta, who brought to Mantua in 1425 the exceptional humanist, Vittorino da Feltre, and established him there as the teacher of their sons and daughters. The Gonzagas took it as a matter of course that their daughters should have the same kind of instruction as their sons —in an age when women, according to a tradition of our time, were supposed to have no education at all. It was with the full support of both patrons that Vittorino was to devise and execute a program of education that made his school one of the most creative in the Italy of the Renaissance.

In Chapter XVI, Volume I, of *The Cambridge Modern History*, Sir R. C. Jebb describes the new type of civic education created by Vittorino at his school in Mantua under the patronage of Gian and

Paola Gonzaga in 1425 and carried on until his death in 1446: "His aim was to develop the whole nature of his pupils, intellectual, moral, and physical; not with a view to any special calling, but so as to form good citizens and useful members of society, capable of bearing their part with credit in public and private life. For intellectual training he took the Latin classics as a basis; teaching them, however, not in the dry and meagre fashion generally prevalent in the mediaeval schools ... but in the large and generous spirit of Renaissance humanism. Poetry, oratory, Roman history, and the ethics of Roman Stoicism, were studied in the best Latin writers.... By degrees Vittorino introduced some Greek also.... He provided for some teaching of mathematics, including geometry ... arithmetic, and the elements of astronomy. Nor did he neglect the rudiments of such knowledge as then passed for natural philosophy and natural history. Music and singing also found a place.... With great insight and tact, Vittorino saw how far social education could be given in a school with advantage to morals and without loss to manliness; he inculcated a good tone of manners, and encouraged the acquirement of such social accomplishments as the age demanded in well-educated men."

It was not only as scholars, tutors, lecturers, members of coteries, participants in the work of academies, and patrons of schools that Italian women led and cooperated in the dissemination of the humanist learning. They carried on extensive correspondence with men and other women engaged in spreading humanist knowledge and doctrines in Italy and throughout Western Europe. Of Olympia Morata, we are told that she "corresponded on equal terms with the most learned men of the day."

All these free, wide-reaching, and influential activities of Italian women in the promotion of humanist learning were in keeping with the very spirit of the Renaissance. In the third chapter of *Die Kultur der Renaissance,* Jacob Burckhardt, a renowned authority, says: "In order to understand the higher forms of social intercourse during the Renaissance, it is necessary to know that woman was regarded as in a position of perfect equality with man. One should not allow one's self to be deceived by the cunning and in part malicious researches respecting the presumptive inferiority of the beautiful sex.... Above all, the education of the woman among the higher classes is essentially the same as that of the man. There was not the slightest hesitation among the Italians of the Renaissance in according the same literary and even philological instruction to sons and daughters; for as they saw in this new classical culture the highest possession of life, so they assumed gladly that girls were welcome to it.... There was no question of a conscious 'emancipation' of woman or anything so out of the ordinary, for the situation was understood to be a matter of course. The education of the woman of rank, just as well as that of the man, sought the development of a well-rounded personality in every respect. The same development of mind and heart that perfected the man was necessary for perfecting woman."

Men of the Renaissance not only accepted as a matter of course this free and easy association with women in the advancement of learning and the civic spirit. Many writers of the period made a point of paying special tributes to women, if frequently in exaggerated form. Take, for example, Boccaccio (1313–1375), the fervent humanist, poet, story-teller, and friend of Petrarch. Besides writing *De Casibus Virorum Illustrium*, dealing with the troubles and vanities of illustrious men from the time of Adam to the fourteenth century, he wrote illustrious women, *De Claris Mulieribus*, starting with Eve and coming down to Giovanna, queen of Naples; included were Cleopatra, Lucretia, Portia, Semiramis, and Sappho. This work passed through many editions and is esteemed as among the important texts of the Renaissance. It was translated into Italian by Joseph Betussi who "in the ardor of his zeal enriched it by fifty new articles."

About a hundred years later, Henry C. Agrippa (1486–1525), German writer, soldier, physician, architect, historiographer, doctor of law, and traveler in many lands, outdid Boccaccio. In 1509 Agrippa published a work on the nobility and superexcellence of women (*De nobilitate et praecellentia feminei sexus*), dedicated to Margaret of Burgundy. In this volume of thirty chapters, Agrippa employed the writings of fable-makers, poets, historians, and the canon law in efforts to prove the case, and resorted to theological, physical, historical, moral, and even magical evidences to support his argument. He declared that he was moved to write the book by his sense of duty and obligations to duty.

Many men wrote paeans to women, as Lucian the Roman had done and as men were to continue to do in the mood of the Renaissance, in many countries, for centuries. Finally, in 1774, just two years before the Declaration of Independence at Philadelphia, an account of such hymning of women was published at Philadelphia. This was a work in two volumes: *Essay on the Character, Manners, and Genius of Women in Different Ages* —enlarged from a French work of M. Thomas by Mr. Russell, an Englishman. It included a section on the "Revival of Letters and the Learning of Women, Of the Books written in Honour of Women, and on the Superiority of the Sexes, and the subject continued."

After giving an account of the work by Boccaccio and Betussi, the author of the *Essay* continued: "Philip de Bergamo, an Augustine monk, published a volume in Latin OF ILLUSTRIOUS WOMEN. Another performance on the same subject was published by Julius Caesar Capacio, secretary to the city of Naples; one by Charles Pinto, in Latin, and in verse; one by Ludovico Domenichi; one by James Philip Tomassini, bishop of Venice; and one by Bernard Scardioni, a canon by Padua, OF THE ILLUSTRIOUS WOMEN OF PADUA.

"Francis Augustine della Chiesa, bishop of Saluca, wrote a treatise on THE WOMEN FAMOUS IN LITERATURE; Lewis Jacob de St. Charles, a Carmelite, wrote another on THE WOMEN ILLUSTRIOUS BY THEIR WRITINGS; and Alexander Van Denbushce, of the Low Countries, wrote one on THE LEARNED WOMEN.

"The celebrated Father le Moine published a volume under the title of GALERIE DE FEMMES FORTES; and Brantome wrote THE LIVES OF ILLUSTRIOUS WOMEN. But it is to be observed that Brantome, a French knight and a courtier, speaks only of queens and princesses....

"After Brantome, Hilario da Costa, a Minim, published two volumes in quarto, each volume consisting of eight hundred pages, containing, as he tells us, the panegyrics of ALL the women of the fifteenth and sixteenth centuries, distinguished by their valour, their talents, or their virtues.

But the pious ecclesiastic has, in fact, only given us the panegyrics of the CATHOLIC women of that period. He does not say a word, for example, of queen Elizabeth. . . .

"But all must yield to the indefatigable Italian, Peter Paul de Ribera, who published in his own language, a work entitled 'The Immortal Triumphs and heroic Enterprises of Eight hundred and forty-five women.' . . .

"Besides these large compilations dedicated to the honour of the whole sex, many of the writers of those times, men of taste and gallantry, addressed panegyrics to individuals, to women who were the living ornaments of their age. This practice was most common in Italy, where every thing conspired to favour it. . . . The courts of Naples, of Milan, of Mantua, of Parma, of Florence, and several others, formed so many schools of taste, between which reigned an emulation of glory and of talents. The men distinguished themselves by their address in war, or in love; the women, by their knowledge and accomplishments."

From Italy zeal for classical learning fanned out like rays from a sun. Queen Isabella of Spain became interested in it through her acquaintance with Vittoria Colonna and brought Italian men and women to Spain to instruct her courtiers and students in the universities. She studied the classics herself. She established a school of the classics in her palace. She attended examinations of students and watched with eagle eyes and sharp ears the progress of this education among her retinue. She collected texts for the courtiers to read and for students to use in the universities. One woman was commissioned to lecture on the classics at Salamanca; another on rhetoric at Alcalá. Later Philip II enriched this Spanish Renaissance by his patronage of Italian

artists. He encouraged Spanish women to paint portraits as well as write letters, by inviting the Italian women portrait painter, Sophonisba Anguisciola, to his court. Of this portrait painter Van Dyck long afterward was to say that he learned more from her, even in her blind old age, than he had learned from many seeing men.

In France enthusiasm for classical learning was stimulated by Christine de Pisan—Italian in background—who grew up at the court of Charles V, in the late fourteenth century, where her father was installed as an astrologer. After the visit of Petrarch to France in quest of Greek and Latin texts possibly among the monastic treasures, monarchs began to accumulate a library for the French court. But Christine de Pisan did more than read texts there. She studied Plato and also Arab scientific learning in some books in the library. She shared Dante's interest in the State and urged the French to come to grips with their problem of national survival so seriously menaced by the invading armies of the English King. By coming to grips she meant more than war; she meant coming to realize the necessity of granting privileges to the middle class without which, she contended, France could not get up on its feet. Before Christine died, Jeanne d'Arc took the field as commander of French troops—her actual leadership financed by the great capitalist, Jacques Coeur, her will to lead inspired by her "voices," her acceptance as leader facilitated by French adoration of the Virgin.

Christine de Pisan tried to offset the influence of Jean de Meung's stereotype of the perfect lady in his *Roman de la Rose* by her *Le Livre des trois Vertus (The Book of the Three Virtues)* addressed especially to women. She hoped to arouse and develop political consciousness among French women. To this end she defended the spirit of the freer-thinking Italian women of her day in her *Cité des Dames* and awakened such interest that she was invited to the English court. She did not accept the invitation on the ground that her supreme duty lay in France, but this book was translated into English as *The City of Women.*

NO

Joan Kelly-Gadol

DID WOMEN HAVE A RENAISSANCE?

One of the tasks of women's history is to call into question accepted schemes of periodization. To take the emancipation of women as a vantage point is to discover that events that further the historical development of men, liberating them from natural, social, or ideological constraints, have quite different, even opposite, effects upon women. The Renaissance is a good case in point. Italy was well in advance of the rest of Europe from roughly 1350 to 1530 because of its early consolidation of genuine states, the mercantile and manufacturing economy that supported them, and its working out of postfeudal and even postguild social relations. These developments reorganized Italian society along modern lines and opened the possibilities for the social and cultural expression for which the age is known. Yet precisely these developments affected women adversely, so much so that there was no renaissance for women—at least, not during the Renaissance. The state, early capitalism, and the social relations formed by them impinged on the lives of Renaissance women in different ways according to their different positions in society. But the startling fact is that women as a group, especially among the classes that dominated Italian urban life, experienced a contradiction of social and personal options that men of their classes either did not, as was the case with the bourgeoisie, or did not experience as markedly, as was the case with the nobility.

Before demonstrating this point, which contradicts the widely held notion of the equality of Renaissance women with men, we need to consider how to establish, let alone measure, loss or gain with respect to the liberty of women. I found the following criteria most useful for gauging the relative contraction (or expansion) of the powers of Renaissance women and for determining the quality of their historical experience: 1) the regulation of *female sexuality* as compared with male sexuality; 2) women's *economic* and *political roles,* that is, the kind of work they performed as compared with men, and their access to property, political power, and the education or training necessary for work, property, and power; 3) the *cultural roles* of women in shaping the outlook of their society, and access to the education and/or institutions necessary

From Joan Kelly-Gadol, "Did Women Have a Renaissance?" in Renate Bridenthal, Claudia Koonz, and Susan Stuard, eds., *Becoming Visible: Women in European History,* 2d ed. (Houghton Mifflin, 1987). Copyright © 1987 by Houghton Mifflin Company. Reprinted by permission. Notes omitted.

for this; 4) *ideology* about women, in particular the sex-role system displayed or advocated in the symbolic products of the society, its art, literature, and philosophy. Two points should be made about this ideological index. One is its rich inferential value. The literature, art, and philosophy of a society, which give us direct knowledge of the attitudes of the dominant sector of that society toward women, also yield indirect knowledge about our other criteria: namely, the sexual, economic, political, and cultural activities of women. Insofar as images of women relate to what really goes on, we can infer from them something about that social reality. But, second, the relations between the ideology of sex roles and the reality we want to get at are complex and difficult to establish. Such views may be prescriptive rather than descriptive; they may describe a situation that no longer prevails; or they may use the relation of the sexes symbolically and not refer primarily to women and sex roles at all. Hence, to assess the historical significance of changes in sex-role conception, we must bring such changes into connection with all we know about general developments in the society at large.

This essay examines changes in sex-role conception, particularly with respect to sexuality, for what they tell us about Renaissance society and women's place in it. At first glance, Renaissance thought presents a problem in this regard because it cannot be simply categorized. Ideas about the relation of the sexes range from a relatively complementary sense of sex roles in literature dealing with courtly manners, love, and education, to patriarchal conceptions in writings on marriage and the family, to a fairly equal presentation of sex roles in early Utopian

social theory. Such diversity need not baffle the attempt to reconstruct a history of sex-role conceptions, however, and to relate its course to the actual situation of women. Toward this end, one needs to sort out this material in terms of the social groups to which it responds: to courtly society in the first case, the nobility of the petty despotic states of Italy; to the patrician bourgeoisie in the second, particularly of republics such as Florence. In the third case, the relatively equal position accorded women in Utopian thought (and in those lower-class movements of the radical Reformation analogous to it) results from a larger critique of early modern society and all the relations of domination that flow from private ownership and control of property. Once distinguished, each of these groups of sources tells the same story. Each discloses in its own way certain new constraints suffered by Renaissance women as the family and political life were restructured in the great transition from medieval feudal society to the early modern state. The sources that represent the interests of the nobility and the bourgeoisie point to this fact by a telling, double index. Almost all such works—with certain notable exceptions, such as Boccaccio and Ariosto —establish chastity as the female norm and restructure the relation of the sexes to one of female dependency and male domination.

The bourgeois writings on education, domestic life, and society constitute the extreme in this denial of women's independence. Suffice it to say that they sharply distinguish an inferior domestic realm of women from the superior public realm of men, achieving a veritable "renaissance" of the outlook and practices of classical Athens, with its domestic im-

NO Joan Kelly-Gadol / 167

prisonment of citizen wives. The courtly Renaissance literature we will consider was more gracious. But even here, by analyzing a few of the representative works of this genre, we find a new repression of the noblewoman's affective experience, in contrast to the latitude afforded her by medieval literature, and some of the social and cultural reasons for it. Dante and Castiglione, who continued a literary tradition that began with the courtly love literature of eleventh- and twelfth-century Provence, transformed medieval conceptions of love and nobility. In the love ideal they formed, we can discern the inferior position the Renaissance noblewoman held in the relation of the sexes by comparison with her male counterpart and with her medieval predecessor as well.

LOVE AND THE MEDIEVAL LADY

Medieval courtly love, closely bound to the dominant values of feudalism and the Church, allowed in a special way for the expression of sexual love by women. Of course, only aristocratic women gained their sexual and affective rights thereby. If a knight wanted a peasant girl, the twelfth-century theorist of *The Art of Courtly Love*, Andreas Capellanus, encouraged him "not [to] hesitate to take what you seek and to embrace her by force." Toward the lady, however, "a true lover considers nothing good except what he thinks will please his beloved"; for if courtly love were to define itself as a noble phenomenon, it had to attribute an essential freedom to the relation between lovers. Hence, it metaphorically extended the social relation of vassalage to the love relationship, a "conceit" that Maurice Valency rightly called "the

shaping principle of the whole design" of courtly love.

Of the two dominant sets of dependent social relations formed by feudalism—*les liens de dépendance,* as Marc Bloch called them—vassalage, the military relation of knight to lord, distinguished itself (in its early days) by being freely entered into. At a time when everyone was somebody's "man," the right to freely enter a relation of service characterized aristocratic bonds, whereas hereditability marked the servile work relation of serf to lord. Thus, in medieval romances, a parley typically followed a declaration of love until love freely proffered was freely returned. A kiss (like the kiss of homage) sealed the pledge, rings were exchanged, and the knight entered the love service of his lady. Representing love along the lines of vassalage had several liberating implications for aristocratic women. Most fundamental, ideas of homage and mutuality entered the notion of heterosexual relations along with the idea of freedom. As symbolized on shields and other illustrations that place the knight in the ritual attitude of commendation, kneeling before his lady with his hands folded between hers, homage signified male service, not domination or subordination of the lady, and it signified fidelity, constancy in that service. "A lady must honor her lover as a friend, not as a master," wrote Marie de Ventadour, a female troubadour or *trobairitz.* At the same time, homage entailed a reciprocity of rights and obligations, a service on the lady's part as well. In one of Marie de France's romances, a knight is about to be judged by the barons of King Arthur's court when his lady rides to the castle to give him "succor" and pleads successfully for him, as any overlord might. Mutuality, or complementarity, marks the relation the lady entered into with her *ami* (the favored name for "lover" and, significantly, a synonym for "vassal").

This relation between knight and lady was very much at variance with the patriarchal family relations obtaining in that same level of society. Aware of its incompatibility with prevailing family and marital relations, the celebrants of courtly love kept love detached from marriage. "We dare not oppose the opinion of the Countess of Champagne who rules that love can exert no power between husband and wife," Andreas Capellanus wrote (p. 175). But in opting for a free and reciprocal heterosexual relation outside marriage, the poets and theorists of courtly love ignored the almost universal demand of patriarchal society for female chastity, in the sense of the woman's strict bondage to the marital bed. The reasons why they did so, and even the fact that they did so, have long been disputed, but the ideas and values that justify this kind of adulterous love are plain. Marriage, as a relation arranged by others, carried the taint of social necessity for the aristocracy. And if the feudality denigrated marriage by disdaining obligatory service, the Church did so by regarding it not as a "religious" state, but an inferior one that responded to natural necessity. Moreover, Christianity positively fostered the ideal of courtly love at a deep level of feeling. The courtly relation between lovers took vassalage as its structural model, but its passion was nourished by Christianity's exaltation of love.

Christianity had accomplished its elevation of love by purging it of sexuality, and in this respect, by recombining the two, courtly love clearly departed from Christian teaching. The toleration of adultery it fostered thereby was in itself not so grievous. The feudality disregarded any number of church rulings that affected their interests, such as prohibitions of tournaments and repudiation of spouses (divorce) and remarriage. Moreover, adultery hardly needed the sanction of courtly love, which, if anything, acted rather as a restraining force by binding sexuality (except in marriage) to love. Lancelot, in Chrétien de Troyes's twelfth-century romance, lies in bed with a lovely woman because of a promise he has made, but "not once does he look at her, nor show her any courtesy. Why not? Because his heart does not go out to her.... The knight has only one heart, and this one is no longer really his, but has been entrusted to someone else, so that he cannot bestow it elsewhere." Actually, Lancelot's chastity represented more of a threat to Christian doctrine than the fact that his passion (for Guinevere) was adulterous, because his attitudes justified sexual love. Sexuality could only be "mere sexuality" for the medieval Church, to be consecrated and directed toward procreation by Christian marriage. Love, on the other hand, defined as passion for the good, perfects the individual; hence love, according to Thomas Aquinas, properly directs itself toward God. Like the churchman, Lancelot spurned mere sexuality—but for the sake of sexual love. He defied Christian *teaching* by reattaching love to sex; and experiencing his love as a devout vocation, as a passion, he found himself in utter accord with Christian *feeling*....

THE RENAISSANCE LADY: POLITICS AND CULTURE

In his handbook for the nobility, Baldassare Castiglione's description of the lady of the court makes [the] difference in sex roles quite clear. On the one hand, the Renaissance lady appears as the equivalent of the courtier. She has the same virtues of mind as he, and her education is symmetrical with his. She learns everything—well, almost everything—he does: "knowledge of letters, of music, of painting, and . . . how to dance and how to be festive." Culture is an accomplishment for noblewoman and man alike, used to charm others as much as to develop the self. But for the woman, charm had become the primary occupation and aim. Whereas the courtier's chief task is defined as the profession of arms, "in a Lady who lives at court a certain pleasing affability is becoming above all else, whereby she will be able to entertain graciously every kind of man" (p. 207).

. . . The Renaissance lady is not desired, not loved for herself. Rendered passive and chaste, she merely mediates the courtier's safe transcendence of an otherwise demeaning necessity. On the plane of symbolism, Castiglione thus had the courtier dominate both her and the prince; and on the plane of reality, he indirectly acknowledged the courtier's actual domination of the lady by having him adopt "woman's ways" in his relations to the prince. Castiglione had to defend against effeminacy in the courtier, both the charge of it (p. 92) and the actuality of faces "soft and feminine as many attempt to have who not only curl their hair and pluck their eyebrows, but preen themselves . . . and appear so tender and languid . . . and utter their words so limply" (p. 36). Yet the close-fitting costume of the Renaissance nobleman displayed the courtier exactly as Castiglione would have him, "well built and shapely of limb" (p. 36). His clothes set off his grace, as did his nonchalant ease, the new manner of those "who seem in words, laughter, in posture not to care" (p. 44). To be attractive, accomplished, and seem not to care; to charm and do so coolly —how concerned with impression, how masked the true self. And how manipulative: petitioning his lord, the courtier knows to be "discreet in choosing the occasion, and will ask things that are proper and reasonable; and he will so frame his request, omitting those parts that he knows can cause displeasure, and will skillfully make easy the difficult points so that his lord will always grant it" (p. 111). In short, how like a woman—or a dependent, for that is the root of the simile.

The accommodation of the sixteenth- and seventeenth-century courtier to the ways and dress of women in no way bespeaks a greater parity between them. It reflects, rather, that general restructuring of social relations that entailed for the Renaissance noblewoman a greater dependency upon men as feudal independence and reciprocity yielded to the state. In this new situation, the entire nobility suffered a loss. Hence, the courtier's posture of dependency, his concern with the pleasing impression, his resolve "to perceive what his prince likes, and . . . to bend himself to this" (pp. 110–111). But as the state overrode aristocratic power, the lady suffered a double loss. Deprived of the possibility of independent power that the combined interests of kinship and feudalism guaranteed some women in the Middle Ages, and that the states of early modern Europe would preserve in part, the Italian noblewoman in particular entered a relation of almost universal dependence upon her family and her husband. And she experienced this dependency at the same time as she lost her commanding position with respect to the secular culture of her society.

Hence, the love theory of the Italian courts developed in ways as indifferent to the interests of women as the courtier, in his self-sufficiency, was indifferent as a lover. It accepted, as medieval courtly love did not, the double standard. It bound the lady to chastity, to the merely procreative sex of political marriage, just as her weighty and costly costume came to conceal and constrain her body while it displayed her husband's noble rank. Indeed, the person of the woman became so inconsequential to this love relation that one doubted whether she could love at all. The question that emerges at the end of *The Courtier* as to "whether or not women are as capable of divine love as men" (p. 350) belongs to a love theory structured by mediation rather than mutuality. Woman's beauty inspired love but the lover, the agent, was man. And the question stands unresolved at the end of *The Courtier*—because at heart the spokesmen for Renaissance love were not really concerned about women or love at all.

Where courtly love had used the social relation of vassalage to work out a genuine concern with sexual love, Castiglione's thought moved in exactly the opposite direction. He allegorized love as fully as Dante did, using the relation of the sexes to symbolize the new political order. In this, his love theory reflects the social realities of the Renaissance. The denial of the right and power of women to love, the transformation of women into passive "others" who serve, fits the self-image of the courtier, the one Castiglione sought to remedy. The symbolic relation of the sexes thus mirrors the new social relations of the state, much as courtly love displayed the feudal relations of reciprocal personal dependence. But Renaissance love reflects,

as well, the actual condition of dependency suffered by noblewomen as the state arose. If the courtier who charms the prince bears the same relation to him as the lady bears to the courtier, it is because Castiglione understood the relation of the sexes in the same terms that he used to describe the political relation: that is, as a relation between servant and lord. The nobleman suffered this relation in the public domain only. The lady, denied access to a freely chosen, mutually satisfying love relation, suffered it in the personal domain as well. Moreover, Castiglione's theory, unlike the courtly love it superseded, subordinated love itself to the public concerns of the Renaissance nobleman. He set forth the relation of the sexes as one of dependency and domination, but he did so in order to express and deal with the political relation and its problems. The personal values of love, which the entire feudality once prized, were henceforth increasingly left to the lady. The courtier formed his primary bond with the modern prince.

In sum, a new division between personal and public life made itself felt as the state came to organize Renaissance society, and with that division the modern relation of the sexes made its appearance, even among the Renaissance nobility. Noblewomen, too, were increasingly removed from public concerns—economic, political, and cultural—and although they did not disappear into a private realm of family and domestic concerns as fully as their sisters in the patrician bourgeoisie, their loss of public power made itself felt in new constraints placed upon their personal as well as their social lives. Renaissance ideas on love and manners, more classical than medieval, and almost exclusively a male product, expressed this new subordination of women to the interests of husbands and male-dominated kin groups and served to justify the removal of women from an "unladylike" position of power and erotic independence. All the advances of Renaissance Italy, its protocapitalist economy, its states, and its humanistic culture, worked to mold the noblewoman into an aesthetic object: decorous, chaste, and doubly dependent —on her husband as well as the prince.

POSTSCRIPT

Did Women and Men Benefit Equally from the Renaissance?

Once we begin to consider the experiences of women in history as separate from those of men, we meet a new set of challenges. Women are not a universal category, and their experiences throughout history are as varied as their race, social class, ethnicity, religion, sexual orientation, and a host of other categories make them. In recent years historians have begun to consider both the ways in which women's historical experiences are more or less the same and the ways in which one woman's experience differs radically from another's. There are instances in which being a woman is the most important variable (with regard to childbirth, access to birth control or lack of it, and female sexuality, for example), times when race is what matters most and women feel more attuned to men of their own race than to women of different races, and times when social class is the key factor and both racial and gender differences seem less significant than a common class experience or approach to life.

The periodization question remains a fascinating one. Following Kelly-Gadol, other scholars began to look at historical periods with which they were familiar with an eye to using women's experiences as a starting point. For example, in *Becoming Visible* (from which Kelly-Gadol's selection was excerpted), William Monter poses this question: Was there a Reformation for women? Beginning with women's experience, this anthology offers a number of good points of departure for exploring the issue of periodization. For a fuller explanation of the differences among compensatory, contributory, and women's culture approaches, see Gerda Lerner's essay "Placing Women in History," in *Major Problems in Women's History*, 2d ed., edited by Mary Beth Norton and Ruth Alexander (D. C. Heath, 1996). This book also contains Gisela Bock's "Challenging Dichotomies in Women's History"—which explores nature versus culture, work versus family, public versus private, sex versus gender, equality versus difference, and integration versus autonomy—and "Afro-American Women in History," by Evelyn Brooks Higginbotham, which questions the concept of a universal womanhood by exploring the varying experiences of African American women.

For a Marxist analysis of women in history, see the chapter entitled "Four Structures in a Complex Unity" in Juliet Mitchell's *Woman's Estate* (Pantheon Books, 1972). In it, Mitchell argues that production, reproduction, sexuality, and the socialization of children must all be transformed together if the liberation of women is to be achieved; otherwise, progress in one area can be offset by reinforcement in another. This links the question of women's roles in history to economic forces such as production and social forces such as sexuality and childrearing.

Another good way to start is to explore our understanding of gender—what it has meant to be a woman (or a man) at a specific time in human history. Historian Joan W. Scott considers how gender and power designators construct one another in "Gender: A Useful Category of Historical Analysis," *American Historical Review* (December 1986). She sees in the categories "man" and "woman" a primary way in which social relationships are defined and power is signified. Linda Nicholson, in "Interpreting Gender," *Signs: Journal of Women in Culture and Society* (Autumn 1994), explores the question of biological foundationalism—the extent to which physicality influences gender construction. In this analysis, the body becomes a historically specific variable whose meaning changes or is capable of changing over time.

ISSUE 10

Were Christopher Columbus's New World Discoveries a Positive Force in the Development of World History?

YES: Felipe Fernández-Armesto, from *Columbus* (Oxford University Press, 1991)

NO: Kirkpatrick Sale, from *The Conquest of Paradise: Christopher Columbus and the Columbian Legacy* (Plume, 1991)

ISSUE SUMMARY

YES: Historian Felipe Fernández-Armesto states that although Columbus was far from perfect, the overall results of his work merit consideration as one who helped to shape the modern world.

NO: Writer Kirkpatrick Sale sees Columbus as a product of a sick, dispirited Europe and concludes that the selfish nature and results of his voyages prevented Europe from using the New World discoveries as an opportunity for the continent's salvation.

In October 1998, a *New York Times* article covered a dispute between Hispanic-Americans and Italian-Americans with regard to which ethnic group should play the more important role in the organization of New York's Columbus Day Parade. While both groups had legitimate claims to the Columbus legacy (after all, Columbus was an Italian, but he did his most important work for the Spanish nation), the dispute must have drawn an ironic response from those who witnessed the revisionist bashing that the "Admiral of the Ocean Sea" had received in recent years.

In the five centuries since Columbus "sailed the ocean blue," his historical reputation and the significance of his accomplishments have undergone a series of metamorphoses. In the distant past, an unusual collection of Columbus critics would number French essayist Michel Montaigne, English writer Samuel Johnson, philosopher Jean-Jacques Rousseau, and French historian and philosopher Abbé Guillaume Raynal, some of whom believed that the world would have been better off without the admiral's discoveries.

It has only been in the last two centuries that Columbus's stock has risen in the theater of public opinion and historical significance. The United States becoming a beacon of democratic hope for an autocratic world and later an ally of Western Europe, helping to save the continent from the specter of fascism, played an important role in the reversal of Columbus's reputation. Samuel Eliot Morison's 1942 book, *Admiral of the Ocean Sea, A Life of Christopher Columbus*, marked the apex of this laudatory view of Columbus and his accomplishments.

Historians and publishers love anniversaries and the publicity such occasions generate, and, next to a millennial celebration, none may be more significant than a quincentennial one. Thus, on the 500th anniversary of Columbus's first voyage, the requisite number of tomes on Columbus and his accomplishments were made ready for an eager market. But the world of 1992 was different than the world of Morison's "Admiral of the Ocean Sea," and the historical profession had changed along with it.

The end-of-the-millennium generation of historians treated Columbus differently than had their immediate predecessors. Operating from a different worldview, Columbus became to many of them a flawed figure responsible for the horrors of the transatlantic slave trade, the annihilation of Native American civilizations through cruelty and disease, and the ecological destruction of a continental paradise.

The recently published books about Christopher Columbus opened a national dialogue on the subject. A national Columbus exhibition in Washington, D.C., was received with skepticism by some and quiet reverence by others. While some participated in the national Columbus Day celebration on October 12, 1992, others declared it a day of mourning in honor of those who lost their lives as a result of Columbus's enterprises. A cultural hornet's nest was broken open, and any who entered into the Columbus fray had to have the thickest of skin.

Fortunately, as is usually the case, time has a soothing effect, and we will probably have to wait until the year 2092 for the next major Columbus debate. For now, we have the opportunity—with cooler heads and calmer temperaments—to examine the Columbus legacy.

Felipe Fernández-Armesto presents an account of Columbus and his accomplishments that leans toward a favorable interpretation of the admiral. Kirkpatrick Sale evaluates Columbus as a representative of the forces that missed out on using the New World discoveries as a regenerative catalyst in the development of European and world civilizations.

YES

Felipe Fernández-Armesto

COLUMBUS

PREFACE

Considered from one point of view, Columbus was a crank. Even in his own lifetime he had a cranky reputation. His patrons smiled at his scheme for a crusade and courtiers treated it as a joke. On his first crossing of the Atlantic, mutineers plotted to pitch him overboard during his abstracted machinations with new-fangled and unwieldy navigational instruments. He claimed to hear celestial voices. He embarrassed the court of the Spanish monarchs by appearing provocatively attired in public, once in chains and regularly in a Franciscan habit.

These eccentricities are easy to excuse or even to applaud as such imps as often attend genius. They have had, however, one regrettable effect. Columbus has attracted cranks, as crag calls forth to crag; and if one of the many committees convened to honour the fifth centenary of the discovery of America were to offer a prize for the silliest theory about him, the competition would be keenly contested. Readers wanting to know about Columbus might be almost as badly misled by the many well-meaning amateurs who have been induced by his presumed importance to write up his life: most books about Columbus have been biographies, which even at their best can seem to abstract their protagonist from his proper context. Overwhelmingly the effect has been to project, into popular books, versions of a Columbus who was 'ahead of his time'—a Columbus inaccessible to an imagination disciplined by respect for the sources and by knowledge of the period. If scholarly biographies so far, with few exceptions, have not yielded any more convincing general impression of Columbus, misleading influence from sixteenth-century writers, loosely treated as primary sources, is probably to blame. For five hundred years, Columbus historiography has been afloat without heeding the need for a good long spell in dry dock. Like a well-barnacled bottom, it needs a vigorous scrape to get rid of the glutinous concretion of errors and false impressions. When restored to deep water, it has to be steered cautiously to elude the cranky theories and undisciplined speculations alike. In the Sea of Darkness, Siren voices rise on every side....

The Columbus who emerges may not be much more objective than any other, as his image bounces flickeringly between the reader's retina and my own. The Columbus I detect—the socially ambitious, socially awkward parvenu; the autodidact, intellectually aggressive but easily cowed; the embittered escapee from distressing realities; the adventurer inhibited by fear of failure—is, I believe, consistent with the evidence; but it would no doubt be possible to reconstruct the image, from the same evidence, in other ways. Other students have imagined him essentially as a practical tarpaulin, or a ruthless materialist, or a mystic seer, or an embodiment of bourgeois capitalism; the springs of his motivation have been perceived in an evangelical impulse, or in some more generalized religious conviction, or in crusading zeal, or in scientific curiosity, or in esoteric or even 'secret' knowledge, or in greed. I find these versions unconvincing, but I have not written in order to advance my view at their expense—only to satisfy readers who want to make their own choices from within the range of genuine possibilities.

There are, however, three traditions of Columbus historiography which I actively defy. The first is the mystifying tradition, concerned to reveal allegedly cryptic truths which the evidence cannot disclose. Works of this type argue either that Columbus was not what he seemed, or that his plan for an Atlantic crossing concealed some secret objective. For instance, the rationally unchallengeable evidence of Columbus's Genoese provenance has not prevented mystifiers from concocting a Portuguese, Castilian, Catalan, Majorcan, Galician, or Ibizan Columbus, sometimes with the aid of forged documents. At a further level of mystification, a persistent tradition has in-sisted on a Jewish Columbus. His own attitude to Jews was not free of ambivalence: at one level he treated them with respect and professed, for instance, that, like Moors and pagans, they could be accessible to the operations of the Holy Spirit; at another level he shared the typical prejudices of his day, condemning the Jews as a 'reprobate' source of heretical depravity and accusing his enemies of the taint of Jewish provenance. The theory that he was of Jewish faith or origins himself can only be advocated *ex silentio*, in default—and sometimes defiance—of evidence.

Believers in Columbus's 'secrets' thrive on lack of evidence, because, like every irrational faith, theirs is fed on indifference to proof. Thus otherwise creditable scholars have argued, for instance, that all the evidence which proves that Columbus sailed in 1492 on a mission to Asia should be 'decoded' to demonstrate the opposite; or that his plan can be explained only by access to secret foreknowledge, transmitted by an 'unknown pilot', or by means of a fortuitous pre-discovery of America by Columbus himself, or even as the result of a chance encounter with American Indians. Readers of this [selection] can rely on being spared any such rash speculations.

The second objectionable tradition treats paucity of evidence as a pretext for intuitive guesswork. Imaginative reconstructions of what Columbus 'must' have been thinking or doing at moments when the sources are silent or ignored are made the basis for vacuous conclusions. On the strength of such musings, in highly popular books, Columbus has been credited with a strenuous love-life, with visionary glimpses of America from Iceland or Porto Santo, with undocumented visitations by his 'voices', and with a plan to conceal his presumed Hebraic ancestry. Sometimes the method is defended by frank contempt for the essential resources of historical enquiry, by an appeal to 'leave the dusty documents on the shelf and come back to the flesh and the spirit' or to speculation licensed on the grounds that 'there are no documents, only the real lives of these men and women, whose blood coursed through their veins as does ours through our own'. Yet, even if one were disposed to admit this obviously fallacious reasoning, the premiss on which it is based is false. We are extremely well informed about Columbus. No contemporary of humble origins or maritime vocation has left so many traces in the records, or so much writing of his own.

The last hazard I have tried to avoid is that of subscribing to a legend of the explorer's own making. The picture transmitted by the historical tradition of a uniquely single-minded figure is false, I am sure. Though Columbus could be obsessively pig-headed, his self-image, as I try to show in this [selection], was dappled by doubts. His sense of divine purpose grew gradually and fitfully and was born and nourished in adversity. His geographical ideas took shape slowly and were highly volatile in the early stages. His mental development proceeded by fits and starts and led at different times in different directions. The contrary view —that his ideas came suddenly, as if by revelation or 'secret' disclosure, or were sustained consistently, in defiance of contemporary derision, with an inflexible sense of purpose—goes back to a 'promotional' image which Columbus projected in his own writings in the latter part of his life. His aim was not only to dramatize his story and to emphasize the unique basis of his claims to material rewards but also to support a broader picture of himself as a providen-

tial agent. He was, he professed, divinely elected to execute a part of God's plan for mankind, by making the gospel audible in unevangelized parts of the earth. That tendentious reading of his own life was adopted by the authors of the detailed sixteenth-century narratives that have influenced all subsequent writers. Bartolomé de Las Casas, whose work has been fundamental to all modern studies of Columbus, accepted Columbus's self-evaluation as a divine messenger because he shared a providential vision of history and wrote to justify and celebrate an apostolate among the Indians in which he personally played no mean part; the next most influential narrative, the *Historie dell'Ammiraglio*, reflects much of the same view, either because it was derived from Las Casas's work, or perhaps because it was genuinely the work of Columbus's son, to whom it is attributed. Although few modern historians admit to a providential conception of history, almost all have accepted a secularized version of the legend, generally with misleading results. Some wild conclusions have been based, for instance, on the myth of Columbus's 'certainty', which goes back to Las Casas's vivid image: 'so sure was he of what he would discover, that it was as if he kept it in a chamber locked with his own key.' ...

'THE MESSENGER OF A NEW HEAVEN'

Decline, Death and Reputation ...
That a weaver's son had died titular Admiral, Viceroy, and Governor; that he should have become the founder of an aristocratic dynasty and have established a claim to fame which has made and kept his name familiar to every educated

person in the western world: these are achievements which command the attention of any observer and the respect of most. But it can fairly be objected that Columbus's merits should be judged by his contribution to mankind, not his accomplishments for himself. His contemporaries had mixed views of that contribution. The New World did not shine for all beholders with the glow reflected in Columbus's gaze. For anyone who really wanted to get to Asia, it was a Stone-Age obstacle course. After its discovery in the sixteenth century, the New World tended to drift away again from the Old, developing internal economic systems, 'creole' identities, and finally independent states. When Rousseau totted up the advantages and disadvantages that accrued to mankind from the discovery of America, he concluded that it would have been better if Columbus had shown more restraint. Contemporaries as various as Abbé Raynal and Dr Johnson agreed. The fate of America has remained ever since, in a particular tradition, a paradigm of the despoliation of nature and the corruption of natural man. And if the influence of the Old World on the New was pejorative, that of the New upon the Old was slow to take full effect. Only with the improved communications and mass migrations of the nineteenth century, perhaps only with the transatlantic partnerships of the world wars in the twentieth, did the weight of America wrench the centre of gravity of western civilization away from its European heartlands. The potential of most of the continent is unrealized even today. Five hundred years after the discovery, America's hour has still not come.

Still, the sheer extent of the new lands across the Atlantic, and the large numbers of new peoples brought within the hearing of God's world, left the generation of Las Casas and Fernando Colón in little doubt of the potential importance of the events connected with Columbus's life. By 1552 the historian Francisco López de Gómara could characterize the discovery of the New World as the greatest happening since the incarnation of Christ. Yet the same writer denied that Columbus was truly the discoverer of those lands. This was a representative sentiment. Columbus had complained even in his own lifetime of being 'despoiled of the honour of his discovery' and though he was referring to the stintedness of his acclaim rather than to the elevation of the claims of rivals, it is true that his reputation has since suffered repeatedly from attempts to attribute the discovery of the New World to someone else.

The early history of the controversy was dominated by the legal wrangle between Columbus's heirs and the monarchs of Spain over the non-fulfilment of the royal promises of 1492. Any source of doubt that could be cast on Columbus's claim to have performed his side of the bargain was welcome in the prejudicial atmosphere of the first half of the sixteenth century. It was said, for instance, that the New World had formed part of the domains of King Hesperus or that the credit for the discovery belonged to Martín Pinzón, or that it rested with an 'unknown pilot' who had preceded Columbus to the New World by chance and confided his knowledge to the Genoese when on the point of death. It was this last story which López de Gómara repeated; Las Casas heard it treated as common knowledge when he was a young man in Hispaniola before 1516; in 1535 Gonzalo Fernández de Oviedo dismissed it as a vulgar rumour; and it has been echoed ever since. Testimony was even procured—almost certainly not without deliberate perjury—to deny the amply verified fact that Columbus had visited the American mainland on his third voyage in 1498. The discoverer's sons, Diego and Fernando, strenuously resisted these allegations. Diego had the testimony of numerous favourable witnesses recorded on his father's side and Fernando wrote extensively in defence of his claims. It must be said that whatever Martín Pinzón's role on the first transatlantic voyage, of which we shall never know the whole truth, he joined the enterprise only at a late stage, when Columbus's plans were already well advanced. Though Columbus was familiar with many mariners' tales of unknown lands in the west, and recorded some of them along with other evidence in support of his theories, the story of the unknown pilot is unacceptable as it stands: it proceeds from biased sources; it is unwarranted by any contemporary authority; and it relies on the hypothesis of a freak crossing such as is otherwise unrecorded in the latitude on which Columbus sailed (although accidental crossings have happened further south, on routes not known to have been frequented before Columbus's time). The argument that the unknown pilot must have existed because Columbus would not otherwise have known where to go reminds one of Voltaire's ironic case in favour of God: if He did not exist, it would be necessary to invent Him. The unknown pilot is not required, even as a comforting fiction. Columbus had assembled sufficient indicators of lands in the west, according to his own standards, by his own researches, without recourse to secret sources. By his own admission, the materials he collected included seamen's yarns about Atlantic lands, which formed only one flimsy strand in the web of evidence. The 'certainty' he is supposed to have evinced, and which can alone be explained, it is said, by some pre-discovery of America, is, as we have seen, another myth. The presumed mariner cannot have helped very much, since his information was insufficient to preclude Columbus's belief that he had found Asia. The Admiral's doubts on that score, when they arose, were clearly attributable to his own observations....

An alternative argument, still connected with the Vikings, but voiced more often by admirers of Vespucci, is that Columbus's discovery of America was no better than that of the Icelanders, since he came upon the New World quite haphazardly and failed to recognize it correctly; one cannot be said to 'discover' something unless one recognizes it for what it is. It has also been said that neither Columbus nor anyone else up to his time anticipated the existence of a second world landmass and that it is therefore imprecise to speak of the 'discovery' of something which the European mind was not conceptually equipped to comprehend. Rather, the discovery of America happened gradually and cumulatively, as, under the influence of further explorations, men's presuppositions became adapted to the facts. Now it is agreed that one cannot be said to have 'discovered' a thing without recognizing it for what it is. Otherwise the event is a mere accident, which will pass unnoticed unless someone else happens to suggest the identification which the finder failed to make. The penicillin will stay in the crucible until it is washed up; the comet will shoot out of sight. Such was not the case, however, when Columbus stumbled on America.

In the first place, the possibilities of just such a discovery as Columbus made —that of a continent separate from the Eurasian landmass—were seriously debated, actively canvassed, and, in some cases, excitedly anticipated among scholars prior to Columbus's departure. As soon as he returned to report, a considerable number of learned commentators jumped to the conclusion that he had found just such an antipodal world. Columbus himself on his third voyage correctly identified the mainland, which he then discovered for the first time, with this rumoured continent. During the virtual derangement brought on by his subsequent sufferings, he forsook the idea, and even while he still embraced it his opinion of the proximity of his discoveries to Asia was grossly exaggerated, but America did not have to be 'invented'; the discourse of the day included suitable terms for describing it and classifying it, and Columbus himself was among the first people to make use of them.

Of course the discovery of America was a process, which began with Columbus but unfolded bit by bit after his time, fitfully, without being fully complete until our own time. There has, after all, been a lot of America to discover. The outline of the coasts of South America was not fully complete until about 1540, and although the Atlantic and Pacific coasts of North America were roughly known by that time, the northern coast remained concealed beneath ice until Amundsen cut his way through it in 1905. On the main point at issue between Columbus and posterity—the relationship of America to Asia—Fernández de Oviedo pointed out in the 1530s that the whole truth was still unknown, and so it remained until the early eighteenth century, when the Bering Strait was explored. Many of the impor-

tant physical features of the interior were still unknown late in the eighteenth century and unmapped until the early nineteenth; only the advent of aerial mapping in the present century—which did not encompass the last secrets of South America until the 1970s—penetrated the final areas to defy exploration. Long as the process has been, Columbus retains a primordial place as its initiator; and the extent to which he advanced it in the span of his own short career is all the more startling against the backdrop of the process as a whole: after alighting on some islands of the Bahamas, he explored much of the coast of Cuba, Hispaniola, Jamaica, Puerto Rico, the Lesser Antilles as far as Dominica, Trinidad, and the coast of the mainland from the mouth of the Orinoco to the Bay of Honduras.

The last argument against ascribing the discovery to Columbus also raises a conceptual problem. Only from the most crassly Eurocentric perspective, it is said, could one speak of the 'discovery' of land which had been well known to its native peoples for thousands of years. It has even been argued, by a highly creditable scholar, with only the faintest trace of detectable irony, that an American discovery of Europe preceded the European discovery of America, when a Caribbean canoe was misdirected across the Atlantic, and that the knowledge of this was Columbus's 'secret'. Whatever one thinks of this prank, it is hard to deny priority to the American discovery of America. This respectable argument would make 'discovery' an almost useless term, by limiting it to uninhabited lands. It misses the point that discovery is not a matter of being in a place, but of getting to it, of establishing routes of access from somewhere else. The peopling of the New World, which was followed by isolation, was conspicuously not a discovery in that sense. So vast a hemisphere naturally afforded scope for much internal exploration: it is proper to speak of exploration, recorded in maps, by some Eskimo, North American Indian, and Mesoamerican peoples, and by the Incas, recorded in the latter case with mnemonic devices which we now barely understand. The reliance of early Spanish and Portuguese explorers on native guides, even in some cases over long distances, suggests that other histories of exploration happened in the New World, which we can only guess at. None of this makes the creation of routes which no one knew about before, such as Columbus's across the Atlantic, any less of a discovery.

Despite nearly five hundred years of assiduous detraction, his prior role in the discovery of America remains the strongest part of Columbus's credentials as an explorer. But we should recall some of the supporting evidence too: his decoding of the Atlantic wind system; his discovery of magnetic variation in the Western hemisphere; his contributions to the mapping of the Atlantic and the New World; his epic crossings of the Caribbean; his demonstration of the continental nature of parts of South and Central America; his *aperçu* about the imperfect sphericity of the globe; his uncanny intuitive skill in navigation. Any of these would qualify an explorer for enduring fame; together they constitute an unequalled record of achievement.

Columbus was a self-avowed ignoramus who challenged the received wisdom of his day. His servility before old texts, combined with his paradoxical delight whenever he was able to correct them from experience, mark him at once as one of the last torchbearers of medieval cosmography, who carried their lights on the shoulders of their predecessors, and one of the first beacons of the Scientific Revolution, whose glow was kindled from within by their preference for experiment over authority. The same sort of paradox enlivened every aspect of his character. His attraction towards fantasy and wishful thinking was ill accommodated in that hard head, half-full already with a sense of trade and profit. In his dealings with the Crown and his concern for his posterity, his mysticism was tempered by a materialism only slightly less intense—like the rich gurus who are equally familiar nowadays in spiritual retreats and business circles. Though religion was a powerful influence in his life, its effects were strangely limited; his devotional bequests were few; his charity began and almost ended at home. The Indians he discovered he contemplated with evangelical zeal and treated with callous disregard. He was an inveterate practitioner of deception, a perennial victim of self-delusion, but he was rarely consciously mendacious. In dealing with subordinates, he was calculating and ingenuous by turns. He craved admirers, but could not keep friends. His anxiety for ennoblement, his self-confessed ambition for 'status and wealth', did not prevent him from taking a certain pride in his modest origins and comparing the weaver-Admiral with the shepherd-King. He loved adventure, but could not bear adversity. Most paradoxically of all, beyond the islands and mainlands of the Ocean, Columbus explored involuntarily the marchlands between genius and insanity. Times of stress unhinged—sometimes, perhaps, actually deranged—him; in his last such sickness, he obsessively discarded his own most luminous ideas, and never recovered them.

It probably helped to be a visionary, with a flair for the fantastic, to achieve what he achieved. The task he set himself—to cross the Ocean Sea directly from Europe to Asia—was literally beyond the capacity of any vessel of his day. The task he performed—to cross from Europe to a New World—was beyond the conception of many of his contemporaries. To have accomplished the highly improbable was insufficient for Columbus—he had wanted 'the conquest of what appeared impossible'. He died a magnificent failure: he had not reached the Orient. His failure enshrined what, in the long term, came to seem a greater success: the discovery of America.

One cannot do him justice without making allowances for the weakness that incapacitated him for ill fortune. He was too fearful of failure to face adverse reality—perhaps because he had too much riding on success: not only his personal pride, but also the claims to the material rewards on which his hopes for himself and his heirs rested. It is hard to believe, for instance, that his insistence on the continental nature of Cuba was other than perversely sustained in the face of inner conviction; or that he can really have felt, in his wild and self-contradictory calculations of the longitude of his discoveries, the confidence he claimed. The ambition that drove him was fatal to personal happiness. Almost anyone, it might be thought, would rest content with so much fame, so much wealth, so many discoveries, so dramatic a social rise. But not Columbus. His sights were always fixed on unmade discoveries, unfinished initiatives, imperfect gains, and frustrated crusades. Instead of being satisfied with his achievements he was outraged by his wrongs. Unassuaged by acclaim, he was embittered by calumnies. This implacable character made him live strenuously and die miserably. Without it, he might have accomplished nothing; because of it, he could never rest on his laurels or enjoy his success. It was typical of him to abjure his achievement in discovering a new continent because he could not face failure in the attempt to reach an old one. He wanted to repeat his boast, 'When I set out upon this enterprise, they all said it was impossible', without having to admit that 'they' were right.

The Oxford Union Society once invited an American ambassador to debate the motion, 'This House Believes that Columbus Went Too Far'. The eighteenth-century debate on the moral benefits of the discovery of America no longer commands much interest, but we can still ask the less solemn question, 'What difference did it make?' The brouhaha of the fifth centenary celebrations creates the impression of a generalized and unthinking acceptance that Columbus was the protagonist of an important event; yet it may still be worth asking what exactly makes it important and what, if any, is the justification for the fuss.

One of the most conspicuous changes to have overtaken the civilization in which we live—we usually call it 'Western civilization' or 'Western society'—in the course of its history has been the westward displacement of its centre of gravity, as its main axis of communication, the Mediterranean 'frog-pond' of Socrates has been replaced by an Atlantic 'lake' across which we traffic in goods and ideas and around which we huddle for our defence. The career of Columbus, which began in the Mediterranean and took Mediterranean mariners and colonists across the Atlantic for the first time, seems to encapsulate the very change which it can be said to have initiated. At present—and for as long as quincentennial euphoria lasts—the Admiral of the Ocean Sea is bound to seem significant for us. Historians and journalists will even acknowledge, without embarrassment, that he made the sort of personal contribution to history which, in our awareness of the determining influence of the long and grinding 'structures' of economic change, we have become loath to concede to individuals. On the other hand, the judgements of history are notoriously fickle, and depend on the perspective of the time in which they are made. It may not be long now before 'Western civilization' is regarded as definitively wound up—not cataclysmically exploded, as some of our doom-fraught oracles have foretold, but merely blended into the new 'global civilization' which, with a heavy debt to the Western world but a genuinely distinct identity, seems to be taking shape around us. At the same time, the motors of the world economy are moving or have moved to Japan and California. The Pacific is likely to play in the history of 'global civilization' the same sort of unifying role which the Atlantic has played in that of the West. By 2020, when we come to celebrate the five hundredth anniversary of Magellan's crossing of the Pacific, those of us who are still alive may look back wistfully to 1992 with a feeling of *déjà vu,* and irresistible misgivings about the fuss.

NO

Kirkpatrick Sale

THE CONQUEST OF PARADISE: CHRISTOPHER COLUMBUS AND THE COLUMBIAN LEGACY

PROLOGUE

Surprising as it may seem from the present perspective, the man we know as Christopher Columbus died in relative obscurity, his passing not even recorded at the time on the subcontinent whose history he so decisively changed. But the true importance of his Discovery became clearer with every passing decade as the New World yielded up its considerable treasure to the Old, and as the historical significance became appreciated in scholarly, and then in popular, opinion. A half-century after his death it was certainly esteemed in the land that was its most obvious beneficiary—"the greatest event since the creation of the world," the Spanish historian Francisco López de Gómara called it in 1552, "excluding the incarnation and death of Him who created it"—and by the end of the sixteenth century even the French, notoriously stingy with praise for non-Gallic achievements, were ready to admit, in the words of one Louis Le Roy, that there was nothing "more honorable to our or the preceding age than the invention of the printing press and the discovery of the new world; two things which I always thought could be compared, not only to Antiquity, but to immortality." By the time two more centuries had passed, and the full incredible panoramas of the two new continents had become known (and in great measure exploited) by the nations of Europe, there were few who would have disagreed with the blunt assessment of the Scottish economist Adam Smith: "The discovery of America, and that of a passage to the East Indies by the Cape of Good Hope, are the two greatest and most important events recorded in the history of mankind."

Replete as those judgments are, however, it really has not been until the present century—indeed, until the retrospective provided by the quincentennial of the First Voyage—that a fully comprehensive measure of the Columbian achievement could be taken. Only now can we see how completely the Discovery and its legacy over the last five centuries have altered the cultures of the globe and the life-processes upon which they depend:

- It enabled the society of the European subcontinent to expand beyond its borders in a fashion unprecedented in the history of the world, and to come today to dominate virtually every other society it touches, Westernizing the great bulk of humanity, imposing its institutions and ideas, its languages and culture, its technologies and economy, around the earth.

- It enabled Europe to accumulate wealth and power previously unimaginable, the means by which it created and developed the most successful synergy of systems ever known, a mixture of humanism and secularism, rationalism and science, materialism and capitalism, nationalism and militarism—in short, the very structures of what we know as modern civilization.

- It enabled the vast redistribution of life-forms, purposely and accidentally, that has changed the biota of the earth more thoroughly than at any time since the end of the Permian Period, in effect rejoining the continents of the earth that were separated so many geological eons ago and thereby causing the extinction, alternation, and even creation of species at a speed and on a scale never before experienced.

- And most significant, it enabled humanity to achieve, and sanctify, the transformation of nature with unprecedented proficiency and thoroughness, to multiply, thrive, and dominate the earth as no single species ever has, altering the products and processes of the environment, modifying systems of soils and water and air, altering sta-

ble atmospheric and climatic balances, and now threatening, it is not too much to say, the existence of the earth as we have known it and the greater proportion of its species, including the human.

After five centuries, then, we have come to a unique position from which to judge the consequences of the Columbian discovery in their fullest dimensions. We can now appreciate especially what it means that it was the particular culture of one small promontory of the Asian landmass, with its particular historical attributes and at that historical moment, that was the cause of this event and its opulent beneficiary, and what has been the effect of the implantation of that culture throughout the world. We can now perhaps even bring ourselves to look with new eyes at the Discovery itself and the processes it unfolded, to reassess, with the wisdom of hindsight, the values and attitudes inherent in that culture and in the industrial civilization it has fostered.

In that spirit of reassessment this inquiry was undertaken. Columbus is above all the figure with whom the Modern Age—the age by which we may delineate these past five hundred years —properly begins, and in his character as in his exploits we are given an extraordinary insight into the patterns that shaped the age at its start and still for the most part shape it today. He is the figure as well who was primarily responsible for the ways in which the culture of Europe was implanted in the Americas, under not only Spanish flags but subsequent banners too, and his extraordinary career, very like his sailing routes, was the model for all those that came after. And he is the figure who, more than any other, provided the legacy by which European civilization came to dominate the American world for five centuries with consequences, we now realize, involving nothing less than issues of life and death.

This reassessment is particularly pertinent to the nation that not only is the foremost exemplar of the success of the transplanted culture but has lived out the Columbian legacy to its fullest, even taking as its greatest hero, as its very symbol, the Discoverer himself. For as Columbia, the personification invented for the newly formed United States at the end of the eighteenth century, he represents the soul and spirit of that nation and embodies what it takes to be its sense of courage and adventure, of perseverance and triumph, of brash indomitability. And thus it is in the United States that he is honored with more place names of all kinds—cities, counties, towns, rivers, colleges, parks, streets, and all the rest—than any other figure of American history save Washington, with more monuments and statues than have been erected to any other secular hero in the world. More than any other nation, the United States bears the honor, and the weight, of the Columbian achievement. More than any other nation, it is in a position to appreciate in the fullest its multiple, its quite consequential, meanings....

1625–1992...

That the Quincentennial that ends this latest century will be celebrated with more commotion and ceremony than ever before there is no question, though whether it will have much to do with the man it is supposed to commemorate there is real reason to doubt.

The official events, carefully planned, expensively mounted, and much bally-hooed, will involve every nation on both sides of the Atlantic and some few on the Pacific as well. As of 1989, thirty-two nations and twenty U.S. states and colonies had established official Quincentennial commissions, and they had authorized a bewildering array of celebrations, parades, pageants, fireworks displays, conferences, symposiums, exhibitions, projects, monuments, museum shows, contests, scholarships, grants, books, newsletters, magazines, scholarly compendiums, television programs, commemorative coins and stamps, memorabilia, sailing races, cruises, guided tours, and myriad other forms of observance, a great many hewing to the same spirit of gain that characterized the original voyage, though some of them guided by its sense of discovery and learning as well....

Obviously this foofaraw will exceed, in length, money, fervor, technology, publicity, self-congratulation, and bathos, any previous commemoration; Father Charles Polzer of the U.S. Quincentenary Jubilee Commission has described the attention drawn to it as "widespread and monumental," an understatement.

It is not, however, without its dissenters. Many of those who know well the cultures that once existed in the New World have reason to be less than enthusiastic about celebrating the event that led to the destruction of much of that heritage and the greater part of the people who produced it; some have insisted on labeling the events of 1492 an "encounter" rather than a "discovery" and having it so billed for 1992, some others have chosen to make it an occasion to direct attention to native American arts and achievements, and others still are planning to protest the entire goings-on as a wrongful commemoration of an act steeped in bloodshed, slavery, and genocide. The United Nations General Assembly, given several opportunities to endorse the Quincentennial, has been diplomatically stymied—by disputes about whether Colón was the first discoverer (Iceland and Ireland have both insisted on precedence), whether a commemoration that glorifies a colonialism from which many nations still suffer is apt, and whether West European world hegemony is a fit phenomenon for other continents to honor—and has taken no official action at all. And some of those who have sought to draw attention to the environmental destruction wrought in the aftermath of the Discovery, particularly members of various Green movements in the industrialized world, have decided to use the occasion to draw into question the nature of a civilization that could take the earth so close to ecocide.

In all of this, it seems certain, Cristóbal Colón will be quite lost, even Christopher Columbus quite hard to find, as his accomplishments are made the malleable and serviceable clay into which the breath of one cause or other, one patriotic mission or other, one testimonial to modernism or other, is blown. But that is in keeping, of course, for it is as the source of just such symbols that Colón has functioned through the five centuries of his life-after-death: from the time that he was made into a super-Hercules by Oviedo and Martyr to the time he became the early modern hero for the English who needed instigation and the Italians who needed inspiration; in the epics by which he became the personification of America as in the biographies that made him stand for wealth and progress; by the pageants that turned him into the image of this nation's skill or that one's genius and the celebrations that made him the agent of capitalist ingenuity and persistence... and beyond. It may be fitting, or only richly ironic, that, having seen the world as utilitarian, so has the world seen him.

Walt Whitman imagines Columbus on his deathbed, in Valladolid, in that May 1506, knowing the end is near, staring into the future:

> *What do I know of life? what of myself?*
>
> *I know not even my own work, past or present;*
>
> *Dim, ever-shifting guesses of it spread before me,*
>
> *Of newer, better worlds, their mighty parturition*
>
> *Mocking, perplexing me.*

Ah, but no, Colón, they do not mock and should not perplex: indeed, they live out your legacy, your destiny, more successfully and more grandly, if more terribly, than you ever could have dreamed.

* * *

1992 Worldwide population is estimated at more than 5.6 billion.

Rainforest area in the Western Hemisphere, originally 3.4 billion acres, is down to 1.6 billion, and going fast, at the rate of 25 million acres a year, or 166 square miles a day; U.S. forestland, originally more than a billion acres, is down to 500 million commercially designated acres, some 260 million having gone for beef production alone.

Topsoil depletion and runoff in the United States reaches a rate of 80 million feet per day, nearly 30 billion tons a year.

Twenty-five years after the U.S. Endangered Species Act went into effect, listing 500 of the several thousand threatened species in the country, twelve of the protected species have become extinct and 150 more are los-ing population at a rate that will lead to extinction within a decade. Two hundred threatened plants native to the United States have become extinct in the last five years. At least 140 major animal and bird species have become extinct since 1492, including four species of whales, seventeen varieties of grizzly bears, seven forms of bats, Eastern and Oregon buffalo, great auks, sea otters, sea minks, Eastern elks, long-eared kit foxes, Newfoundland and Florida wolves, Eastern cougars, Arizona and Eastern wapiti, Bad-lands bighorn sheep, heath hens, passen-ger pigeons, Jamaica wood rails, spectacled cormorants, Puerto Rico blue pigeons, Es-kimo curlews, Puerto Rican conures, Carolina parakeets, Antigua and Guadeloupe burrow-ing owls, Guadeloupe red-shafted flickers, ivory-billed woodpeckers, Berwicks wrens, Tecopa pupfish, harelip suckers, longjaw cis-cos, and blue pike.

Wilderness areas, officially designated at 90 million protected and 50 million unprotected acres, have been reduced from about 2.2 billion acres in pre-Columbian times—a decrease of roughly 96 percent.

The population of the native people of North America is about 20 million, only 1.5 million outside of Mesoamerica.

EPILOGUE

By the 1780s, the question of the im-portance of the Discovery and its im-pact on the world had become a topic of some debate in the intellectual circles of France and in the writings of the reign-ing philosophes, an extension of the old sauvage noble–bête sauvage debates earlier in the century. It was so provocative a subject, in fact, that Abbé Guillaume Rey-nal, the author of a highly popular four-volume study, A Philosophical and Political History of the Settlements and Trade of Eu-ropeans in the Two Indies, decided to see if the matter could be set to rest, in appro-priate philosophe tradition, by asking the learned men of the Academy of Lyons to hold an essay contest, invite entrants on all sides, and award a prize, which he would himself contribute, to the one they judged had made the best case. The topic of debate: "Was the discovery of America a blessing or a curse to humankind?"

Unfortunately the precise workings-out of that contest have not survived the ebb and flow of history, which was turbulent indeed in France, we may remember, at that time. It is known, however, that entries were submitted in 1787 and 1788, that the Lyons savants were unable to declare an outright winner, and that only eight essays, with a fair mixture of opinion on the several sides of the issue, survive. Of those survivors the one that is easily the most learned and lucid, as well as the most persuasive, is the one by the abbé himself.

Reynal was willing to concede some positive effects of the Discovery. "This great event hath improved the construc-tion of ships, navigation, geography, as-tronomy, medicine, natural history, and some other branches of knowledge; and these advantages have not been attended with any known inconvenience." More-over, the domains of the Indies "have given splendor, power, and wealth, to the states which have founded them," al-though it was true that great expenses had been lavished "to clear, to govern, [and] to defend them," and that eventu-ally they would all inevitably assert their independence and be lost to the "coun-try which has founded its splendor upon their prosperity." As well, "Europe is in-debted to the New World for a few con-veniences, and a few luxuries," but those were "so cruelly obtained, so unequally distributed, and so obstinately disputed" that they could not really be said to be worth the price in human lives and disruption—and "before these enjoyments were obtained, were we less healthy, less robust, less intelligent, or less happy?" And finally, although "the New World has multiplied specie amongst us," the cost was high for the peoples of the Americas, who still "languish in ignorance, superstition, and pride" and have lost "their agriculture and their manufactures" to boot, and even for Europe, where the benefits were largely overwhelmed by a concomitant inflation.

On the negative side, the effects loomed larger. For one, "the bold attempts of Columbus and of Gama" created "a spirit of fanaticism" for "making discoveries" in search of "some continents to invade, some islands to ravage, and some people to spoil, to subdue, and to massacre." Those who succumbed to such adventures became "a new species of anomalous savages" who "traverse so many countries and who in the end belong to none... who quit their country without regret [and] never return to it without being impatient of going out again," all so that they might "acquire riches in exchange for their virtue and their health." "This insatiable thirst of gold," moreover, had "given birth to the most infamous and the most atrocious of all traffics, that of slaves," the "most execrable" of crimes against nature. And with all that "the machine of government," overextended in resources both at home and in the Americas, had "fallen into confusion," with the poorest states being forced to languish "under the yoke of oppression, and endless wars," while those who were "incessantly renewed" by Indies treasure "harassed the globe and stained it with blood."

Such was the indictment from the learned philosopher. And here, in full, was his conclusion:

> Let us stop here, and consider ourselves as existing at the time when America and India were unknown. Let me suppose that I address myself to the most cruel of the Europeans in the following terms. There exist regions which will furnish you with rich metals, agreeable clothing, and delicious food. But read this history, and behold at what price the discovery is promised to you. Do you wish or not that it should be made? Is it to be imagined that there exists a being infernal enough to answer this question in the affirmative! Let it be remembered that there will not be a single instant in futurity when my question will not have the same force.

Let it be remembered.

Reynal was not alone in his condemnation. The thought had haunted some few right from the start—Montaigne, for example, in the expansionary sixteenth century, who said he was afraid "that we shall have greatly hastened the decline and ruin of this new world by our contagion"—and was not absent even from some, such as Henry Harrisse, in the ebullient nineteenth century: "As to the sum of happiness which has accrued to humanity from Columbus' discovery, philosophers may deem it light and dearly purchased" ... It is even a mortal question whether the two worlds would not have been far happier had they remained forever unknown to each other." The vantage point of five hundred years allows us to appreciate the wisdom of such few far more acutely than their contemporaries ever could.

It may be that all such judgments, including Abbé Reynal's, are in the end fruitless: history is what happened, not what should have happened. Certainly there are those who argue, with some merit, that it is foolish to think that Europe could have been anything but what it was, done anything but what it did. Why should one suppose that a culture like Europe's, steeped as it was in the ardor of wealth, the habit of violence, and the pride of intolerance, dispirited and adrift after a century and more of disease and famine and death beyond experience, would be able to come upon new societies in a fertile world, innocent and defenseless, and not displace and subdue, if necessary destroy, them? Why should one suppose such a culture would pause there to observe, to learn, to borrow the wisdom and the ways of a foreign, heathen people, half naked and befeathered, ignorant of cities and kings and metal and laws, and unschooled in all that the Ancients held virtuous? That, according to J. H. Elliott, who had wrestled with just this question, would be asking "a great deal of any society," but certainly more than the society represented by Europe in the fifteenth or even the sixteenth century.

Of course one may still wonder, and wonder long, about what that says about this society, the one now dominant in America, and the West, and the world. And one may even legitimately wonder, if it is not too painful, about what might have been. Was not Europe in its groping era of discovery in the fifteenth century in fact in search of salvation, as its morbid sonnets said, or of that regeneration which new lands and new peoples—and of course new riches—would be presumed to provide? Was that not essentially the arrangement Colón sold to the Sovereigns, confirmed in the Capitulations?

And there *was* salvation there, in the New World, though it was not of a kind the Europeans then understood. They thought first that exploitation was salvation, and they went at that with a vengeance, and found new foods and medicines and treasures, but that proved not to be; that colonization and settlement was salvation, and they peopled both continents with conquerors, and it was not that either; that progress and power and technics wrested from the new lands was salvation, and they made mighty nations and towering cities in its service, but it was not even that.

The salvation there, had the Europeans known where and how to look for it, was obviously in the integrative tribal ways, the nurturant communitarian values, the rich interplay with nature that made up the Indian cultures—as it made up, for that matter, the cultures of ancient peoples everywhere, not excluding Europe. It was there especially in the Indian consciousness, in what Calvin Martin has termed *"the biological outlook on life,"* in which patterns and concepts and the large teleological constructs of culture are not human-centered but come from the sense of being at one with nature, biocentric, ecocentric, and where there was myth but not history, circular rather than linear time, renewal and restoration but not progress, imaginative apperception far more subtle than science, understanding without words or even ideation, sacred rather than material interpretation of things, and an interpenetration into earth and its life-forms that superceded an identification with self or species.

It was there then, when Colón first encountered what he intuited, correctly, to be "in all the world . . . no better people nor better country," and it is there even now, despite the centuries of batterment, for those who stop and bend and open to hear it. It was salvation then, it might possibly be salvation now. Certainly there is no other.

An Irokwa woman in New York City, Doris Melliadis, said fifteen years ago:

> Now they come to gather for the coming disaster and destruction of the white man *by his own hands*, with his own progressive, advanced, technological devices, that only the American Indian can avert. Now the time is near. And it is only the Indian who knows the cure. It is only the Indian who can stop this plague. And this time the invisible will be visible. And the unheard will be heard. And we will be seen and we will be remembered.

So we may hope. There is only one way to live in America, and there can be only one way, and that is as Americans—the original Americans—for that is what the earth of America demands. We have tried for five centuries to resist that simple truth. We resist it further only at risk of the imperilment—worse, the likely destruction—of the earth.

There exists a nineteenth-century "bible" with the title *Oahspe*, said to have been influential among the Irokwa of the last century, which purports to be the words of "Jehovih" transmitted through a Dr. John Ballou Newbrough in 1881, in which Christopher "Columbo" is mentioned as playing a special part in the Design of God. In "one of the plans of God for redeeming the world"—a world which He acknowledged had fallen upon sinful times—Columbo was visited by the heavenly hosts and inspired by them "to go with ships to the westward, across the ocean," there to find for Europe "a new mortal anchorage," "a new country, where only the Great Spirit, Jehovih, is worshipped." He makes the momentous voyage, but the news of it is discovered by the agents of Satan, "the false Kriste," and his angels "did set the rulers of Spain against Columbo, and had him cast in prison, thus breaking the chain of inspiration betwixt Columbo and the throne of God"—and it is these evil spirits that instead lead the people of Europe across the ocean "to the countries Columbo had discovered" and there, to the consternation of Heaven, did "evil take its course."

So it may have been. However one may cast it, an opportunity there certainly was once, a chance for the people of Europe to find a new anchorage in a new country, in what they dimly realized was the land of Paradise, and thus find finally the way to redeem the world. But all they ever found was half a world of nature's treasures and nature's peoples that could be taken, and they took them, never knowing, never learning the true regenerative power there, and that opportunity was lost. Theirs was indeed a conquest of Paradise, but as is inevitable with any war against the world of nature, those who win will have lost—once again lost, and this time perhaps forever.

POSTSCRIPT

Were Christopher Columbus's New World Discoveries a Positive Force in the Development of World History?

Poring over the many Columbus-oriented works that were products of the quincentennial anniversary is likely to leave one bewildered and perplexed. One wonders how many writers can take the same information and come to diametrically opposed conclusions concerning Columbus and his place in history. Of course, as is usual in historical matters, one's experiences and the perspective derived from them are important determinants in drawing conclusions from the historical process.

It is worth noting that when the Columbus "iconography" was established in the West, civilization was a Eurocentric one, and many of its voices were muted or silent. As Western history became more "inclusionary," different voices began to appear, and a different historical view of Columbus began to take shape. What the future will hold for the subject remains to be seen.

When participating in the Columbus debate it is important to determine those things for which Columbus may be held accountable. We cannot hold him responsible for all of the evils that followed his discoveries if we do not have proof of such evil-doing. It is part of history's burden to seek the truth regardless of the consequences.

To list the major works on Columbus and his place in history is daunting. But there are a few significant works, which provide a variety of perspectives. Basil Davidson's *The Search for Africa: History, Culture, Politics* (Random House, 1994) contains a chapter entitled "The Curse of Columbus," which accuses him of playing an important role in the development of the slave trade. Paolo Emilio Taviani's *Columbus: The Great Adventure* (Orion Books, 1991) is a newer example of the iconographic Columbus viewpoint. Of course, Samuel Eliot Morison's *Admiral of the Ocean Sea* (Little, Brown & Company, 1991) has relevance and interest. Historian David E. Stannard even goes so far as to raise the specter of a "holocaust" in his book *American Holocaust: Columbus and the Conquest of the New World* (Oxford University Press, 1992). This book represents the extreme in negative viewpoints of Columbus and what resulted from his accomplishments. Finally, *Seeds of Change*, Herman Viola and Carolyn Margolis, eds. (Smithsonian Institute Press, 1991), is the book that emanated from the Smithsonian Museum of Natural History's 1992 Columbus Exposition. It is as balanced (and handsome) a treatment as one can receive about this controversial topic.

ISSUE 11

Were the Witch-Hunts in Premodern Europe Misogynistic?

YES: Anne Llewellyn Barstow, from *Witchcraze: A New History of the European Witch Hunts* (HarperCollins, 1994)

NO: Robin Briggs, from *Witches and Neighbors: The Social and Cultural Context of European Witchcraft* (Penguin Books, 1998)

ISSUE SUMMARY

YES: History professor Anne Llewellyn Barstow asserts that the European witch-hunt movement made women its primary victims and was used as an attempt to control their lives and behavior.

NO: History professor Robin Briggs states that although women were the European witch-hunts' main victims, gender was not the only determining factor in this sociocultural movement.

Virgins and whores, goddesses and devils, mystics and conjurers—historically, women have been perceived as "troublesome creatures." Their very existence has often been considered a threat to human society, especially with regard to their sexuality. This has resulted in constant attempts on the part of the patriarchal system, which has so dominated the course of history, to control women's lives. Sometimes this system resulted in second-class status, shattered dreams, and crushed spirits for women; other times the treatment of women was downright hostile. The witch-hunt craze of early modern Europe was one such example.

Although belief in witches and witchcraft dates back to recorded history's earliest days, the persecution of those accused reached its apex in Europe's early modern period, especially the sixteenth and seventeenth centuries. In the northern, western, and central parts of the continent, witch trials became a frightening reality, as thousands were tried and many were executed for their evil doings and "pacts with the devil." Although exact figures are not known, a moderate estimate of 200,000 people tried with half of those executed has been offered by Anne Llewellyn Barstow. And certainly germane to this issue is the fact that 80 percent of both groups, those brought to trial and those executed, were women.

What factors caused such a wave of witch hysteria? First, the Protestant Reformation created a religious uncertainty, which gave the witch-hunts a *raison d'être*. Protestants and Catholics battled for the hearts, minds, and souls of Europe's populace, and religious wars became the order of the day. The witch crazes were a predictable outcome given this atmosphere. Furthermore, with the concomitant growth of national states in Europe and the resultant divine-right monarchs, orthodoxy of all sorts had to be enforced to keep the dynastic ship afloat. Those who deviated had to pay the price.

Social factors also entered into the witch-craze fray. Tensions between and amongst classes led to aberrant behavior usually geared toward keeping people of the lower classes down. The trials and resultant executions served as brutal reminders to women of the power of the status quo and the lengths to which those in power would go to maintain societal control.

Of course, one cannot escape the one constant of the multicentury witch-hunts: most of the victims were women. But was gender the only factor in determining the outcome of the witch-hunts? Were women singled out for prosecution solely on the basis of their sex? Or, were there other factors—political, economic, social, legal, or local—that influenced the witch-hunts? This question had been raised in the historical debates of previous generations, but interest was renewed in the 1960s, presumably due to the increased interest in women's studies. This interest includes the study of violence against women, which has reached epic proportions in the contemporary world. Were there signs of such actions against women in the past? Was the witch craze just one extreme example of violence against women?

A seminal article by Hugh Trevor-Roper entitled "The European Witch-craze of the Sixteenth and Seventeenth Centuries," *Encounter* (May/June 1967), later republished in *The European Witch-Craze of the Sixteenth and Seventeenth Centuries, and Other Essays* (Harper Torchbooks, 1969), got the historical ball rolling. Still, it was not until recent times that the idea of witchcraft as misogyny or hatred of women reached center stage. Since that time, it has been nearly impossible to remove the gender factor from any witchcraft studies.

The two selections represent the best in recent witchcraft scholarship. Barstow makes a persuasive case for gender as the key factor in determining witch-hunt outcomes. She sees this as part of a long struggle to "keep women down." Robin Briggs admits that the large preponderance of the witch-hunts' victims were women and that gender certainly was a factor in the genesis of the craze. But he favors the presence of socioeconomic, political, religious, and legal factors as better means to understanding the witch craze; after all, misogyny has been present since the beginning of time.

YES   Anne Llewellyn Barstow

WHY WOMEN?
GENDER, NUMBERS, CLASS

Joan Peterson, a healer, "was searched again in a most unnatural and bar-
barous manner by four women" supplied by her accusers, who found "a teat
of flesh in her secret parts more than other women usually had." After bribed
witnesses testified against her, she was executed.

Searching an accused woman's body for the devil's teat was one of the
chief proofs of witchcraft. Though the investigation was normally done by
women (and not done gently, as Joan Peterson's case demonstrates), the
sessions were often witnessed by male court officials. When the constable
of Salisbury, New Hampshire, undressed Eunice Cole to be whipped for
witchcraft, he saw "under one of her brests.... A blew thing like unto a
teate hanging downeward about three quarters of an inche longe not very
thick." Men standing by saw him "rip her shift down"; moving in closer,
they affirmed that Eunice "violently scratched it away," implying that she
tried to remove the evidence from her body. When women were appointed
to examine her further, they found instead "a place in her leg which was
proveable wher she Had bin sucktt by Imps."

This lewd scene can set the tone for much of what will be investigated in
this [selection]. An analysis of violence such as this exposes the sexual terror
and brutality at the heart of the witch hunts, a topic too little discussed. The
American historian Lois Banner has observed that two of the cultural norms
specific to patriarchal society—war and rape—have been little studied by
feminist scholars, and a third, pornography, studied only by feminists and
not enough by them. In matters pertaining to the abuse of bodies, especially
women's bodies, we have been strangely silent. To her comment I would add
that writers on witchcraft also, feminist or otherwise, have tended to avoid
the specifics of what happened to the bodies of the victims and have not asked
aloud what difference it made that most of them were female. That historians
to date, following traditional interests in legal and intellectual history, have
concentrated more on the judges and theoreticians of the witchcraft trials
than on the witches may explain this omission. But one must ask if revulsion

From Anne Llewellyn Barstow, *Witchcraze: A New History of the European Witch Hunts*
(HarperCollins, 1994). Copyright © 1994 by Anne Llewellyn Barstow. Reprinted by permission
of HarperCollins Publishers, Inc. Notes omitted.

at the public exploration as well as the torture of female bodies may also have caused them to make that choice.

Having a female body was the factor most likely to render one vulnerable to being called a witch. The sexual connotations and the explicit sexual violence utilized in many of the trials make this fact clear. Just which women were targeted and under what circumstances reveals much about the status of women in early modern Europe....

NUMBERS...

This study of European society's persecutions of the people perceived to be witches will use the term in the sense that it was used at the time. Since long before the sixteenth century, people had believed that some persons had supernatural power, the ability to perform good or harmful magic (or both). A good witch, or cunning woman, as these magic workers were often called, might, for example, heal persons or animals by incantations or potions; she might just as readily kill with a curse or the evil eye. In either case, she possessed a power to be reckoned with. By the sixteenth century, many—especially among the elite—began to hold a new belief, namely, that such supernatural power came from the devil, who bestowed it chiefly on women in return for their absolute obedience to him.

Numbers are essential to this investigation. It is through an analysis of the percentage of women and men accused and of the percentage condemned that the gender bias of this persecution emerges. But first we must look at the overall size of the witchcraze. Contemporary accounts are of limited use.... [C]ontemporaries twisted the facts of a suspect's life, so they showed no more accuracy in estimating

the number of witches: Henri Boguet, the French witch hunter active around 1600, claimed there were 1,800,000 witches in Europe. Because by "witch" Boguet meant persons dedicated to serving Satan, he therefore believed there was a terrifying and widespread conspiracy of witches against Christian society. Joseph Glanvill, holding out against the rising tide of skepticism in the 1670s, maintained that England was still home to thousands of witches, but the doubter Bishop Hutchinson concluded in 1718 that there had been only "above 140 [witches]" put to death in England since the Reformation.

Somewhere between these wildly differing claims we must find a sound compromise, but many modern commentators have not used caution either. Unless speculations are based on court records and other contemporary accounts and adjusted only by educated estimates, they are useless. This limitation, however, has not stopped some modern writers from claiming numbers ranging from two hundred thousand into the millions, and this not referring to witches in general but specifically to persons executed, thus implying a far larger pool of suspects among the population.

Working on the statistics of witchcraft is like working with quicksand. Because many of the records have been lost or are defective, in most areas we cannot even speculate about what the totals may have been. Of the surviving records, many have not yet been carefully analyzed, a problem especially for Polish accounts. Even the records that have been analyzed raise more questions than they answer, for many are lacking names (hence, gender), ages, and sentences; almost all are silent about class, occupation, and marital status. Worse still is the scattered evidence that many witch accusations and executions never made it into the records. How many persons were driven out of their villages or lynched by mobs, we have no idea. One may well then ask why the historian would attempt an essay on the statistics of witchcraft, and in fact many have eschewed it. Yet despite the hazards, it is well worthwhile to speculate.

One reason for the necessity to grapple with numbers is the unrealistic totals that have been circulated. The current trend among some feminist groups to claim three million, six million, or even ten million female victims is mistaken. A statistically based figure, though lower, still makes the same point: that this was an organized mass murder of women that cannot be dismissed by historians.

Among the feminist writers claiming millions of deaths is Andrea Dworkin. Working from the only estimates available in the early 1970s, Dworkin made the claim, "In Europe, women were persecuted as witches for nearly four hundred years, burned at the stake, perhaps as many as nine million of them...." The "nearly four hundred years" almost doubles the years of actual major persecution (1560–1760), and the "nine million of them" is off by about 8,900,000. Even further off the mark is the claim by certain German feminists that ten million women were killed. Faced with such exaggerations, the historian is forced to make an estimate based on the records, no matter how incomplete they may be.

An immediate corrective to these modern inaccuracies can be found in surveying the estimates made by contemporaries, which, although lacking a statistical base, are in the realm of the possible. Looking back over the recently ended holocaust, Voltaire claimed that one hundred thousand witches had been put to death. [Jean] Bodin believed that "many thousands" had died in France. Boguet wrote that there were "thousands and thousands of stakes" in Lorraine and that "there are witches by the thousand everywhere, multiplied upon the earth even as worms in a garden." Whatever one makes of these figures, one must note that they deal not in millions but in thousands.

An even more pressing reason for working on numbers, however, is the simple need to know how many persons shared this fate. Given the chaotic state of the records, the temptation to round off the numbers is strong. Yet I found myself carefully retaining each awkward figure, even though this added hours of work for each region I studied. As Joan Ringelheim, researcher of women in the Nazi holocaust, stated of her work, to drop numbers now is to kill these persons twice. Wanting to record every known victim, to ensure that the historical record finally acknowledges her death, I offer the most complete record available at this time....

Though one cannot add up estimates like these and expect any meaningful results, still, in order to settle on a reasonable total of victims, in contrast to figures such as ten million, it is imperative to reach a sum. The most careful totals made so far are those of Brian Levack, who estimates 110,000 accusations and 60,000 deaths. I believe that though his are reasonable figures, they are almost certainly too low.

There are two pressing arguments for raising Levack's estimate of 110,000 accusations. In addition to the fact that many cases were never recorded, and of those that were, many records have been lost or destroyed, many trial entries are for unknown numbers of victims. Furthermore, additional cases are steadily turning up. Especially in view of the rate at which we are learning of new victims, I believe that Levack's estimate should be doubled, bringing us to a figure of about two hundred thousand accused.

Death estimates are even harder to deal with. Many records do not list the verdict of the trial, a strange omission given the severity of the penalties for a verdict of guilty (death or banishment in most cases). Most records do not include those who died in prison, like Issobel Pain of Scotland, who "dyed the last winter through cold hunger and other inconveniences of the prison." The three women who survived Issobel complained in 1672 that they were kept "in a dark dungeon in a most miserable conditione being always at the point of starving ... and are in such ... miserie that it ware better for them to be dead than alyve."

Others, driven to despair by torture, or, like Didier Finance of Lorraine, by fear of being burned alive, killed themselves in prison. As an alleged witch and parricide, Didier faced being burned by red-hot tongs and incinerated alive at the stake. Many accused witches were murdered in prison: for example, when the wife of a cobbler in Constance was found strangled to death in her cell, her murder was blamed on a demon. Others died in prison from the torture inflicted on them, like two female witches accused of spreading the plague in the French Jura. A widow in Alsace, after being tortured, managed to struggle home, where she was found dead lying on her bed, her neck twisted, bruised, and disjointed.

To these deaths must be added lynchings and posse-style murders of alleged witches (three hundred killed in the Ardennes, for example) that because of their extralegal nature can only be estimated. Given all these factors, one must enlarge Levack's estimate of deaths. Claiming two hundred thousand accusations (a conservative estimate, I believe) and using a death rate of 50 percent of those arraigned, one reaches a figure of one hundred thousand dead—exactly what Voltaire estimated.

But the convicted were not the only ones harmed. Once accused of being witches, few women ever returned to a normal life. So great was the fear of witchcraft that suspicion and ill will followed them to their graves, even when they moved to other areas. Those who were let go often struggled with themselves over having been associated with the hated proceedings. An old Basque woman, Mariquita de Atauri, had, under pressure, named names. She confessed to her own witchcraft and was reconciled at Logroño, but she believed she was damned anyway because she had accused others who were innocent. When she tried to cross their names off the list of the accused and spoke to the inquisitor about her guilt, he called her a liar and a hussy and drove her away. In a desperate struggle with her conscience, Mariquita drowned herself.

Those whose lives were thus ruined must in some way be taken into account in the total number of victims; the number of accused, therefore, is as important to our story as the number executed. Yet estimates are the best that one can offer.

GENDER

Almost everywhere more women than men were accused and killed. The figures show that in fact women were overwhelmingly victimized: on average, 80 percent of those accused and 85 percent of those killed were female. Some areas, however, hunted down women more ferociously than others. Among the accused in Essex, 92 percent were female, true also for the English Home Counties. The same percentage applied to the witch hunt in Namur County (in today's Belgium), and an even higher figure (95 percent) to the bishopric of Basel. I suggest that a restudy of the Essex materials, stressing women's declining economic roles and the increasingly patriarchal nature of England's society, will explain why 92 percent of those accused were women. As for Basel, the prominence there of hail-making accusations, a crime traditionally ascribed more often to women than men, may have contributed to the high number of female victims there but does not fully explain it.

What these numbers meant for women can be seen in the following facts. Not only were over 80 percent of the accused in some areas women, but even more frightening statistics emerge from local hunts: for example, all but two of the female inhabitants of Langendorf in the Rhineland were arrested. In twelfth-century Kiev, when periodic fears of witchcraft arose, all the old women of the area were seized and subjected to the ordeal by cold water (thrown, bound hand and foot, into the Dnieper). Christina Larner, the chronicler of Scottish witchcraft, observed that there were periods "when no mature woman in Fife or East Lothian can have felt free from the fear of accusation." Given these cases, we see that some notorious examples are not unbelievable: the two German villages left with only one female inhabitant apiece, and the Rhenish village where one person, most often female, out of every two families was put to death.

Though almost every area of Europe hunted women more than men, three countries reversed this ratio: in Finland, Estonia, and apparently Russia, the majority of accused witches were men.... Some other regions had relatively lower percentages of women. In the Swiss Pays de Vaud, for instance, the accused were "only" 58 percent female. The rate for men was high there because the Vaudois thought of witchcraft as heresy, and heretics were chiefly male. The Aragonese Inquisition (1600–1650) prosecuted the lowest percentage of women in any witch trials, 28 percent, but secular courts in Aragon restored the usual balance by accusing sixty-six women to only two men, raising the rate for women in Aragon to 58 percent.

The fact that overall about 20 percent of the accused were male is less an indication that men were associated with witchcraft than it appears. Most of these men were related to women already convicted of sorcery—as husbands, sons, or grandsons—and thus were not perceived as *originators* of witchcraft. Of the few who were not related, most had criminal records for other felonies, such as theft, highway robbery, murder, the theological crime of heresy, or sexual crimes such as rape, incest, fornication, adultery, or sodomy. For them, witchcraft was not the original charge but was added on to make the initial accusation more heinous. Witchcraft thus was perceived primarily as a female offense.

When brought into court on a sorcery charge, men were often let off with lighter sentences than women (hence the even smaller number executed, 15 percent, out of all persons put to death, whereas

20 percent of all accused were male). Laws favored men: for example, when the rulers of Flanders decreed no more death penalty for prepubescent witches, boys benefited more because they were seen as minors until twenty-one, whereas girls became adults at eighteen. Also, women, unable by law to give legal testimony, did not traditionally know how to use the courts, either for initial defense or for appeal. Therefore, appeals to the Parlement at Paris, which greatly moderated the force of the witchcraze in France, helped fewer women.

Legal bias led to a notorious French case in which a priest and his mistress were both accused: through money and the influence of friends, he was let go without punishment, whereas she was burned at the stake. In Lorraine, when Claudine Simonette and her son Antoine were imprisoned, she was convicted, but his fate was not mentioned in the record. When a gentleman hired Jeanette Neuve to poison his wife, she was burned at the stake, but there is no record that he received any punishment. Of the fifteen married couples convicted in England's Home Counties, more wives were executed than husbands. A combination of factors, including the greater value placed on men as workers in the increasingly wage-oriented economy and a greater fear of women as inherently evil, loaded the scales against women, even when the charges against them were identical to those against men.

The effect on the image of sixteenth-century women was dramatic: although women committed far fewer crimes than men, the chief criminal stereotype of the period, that of the witch, was female.

For all these reasons, the basic fact remains that throughout Europe during the period of major witch hunts (1560–1760), on average 80 percent of the accused and 85 percent of those executed were women. These lopsided figures are sufficiently telling when one thinks of them as individual burnings or hangings, especially considering that many of the victims were not guilty of this or any other crime. There is no need to inflate the numbers into millions; these statistics are sufficient to document an intentional mass murder of women. By documenting a persecution by gender, these numbers form the basis for this [selection]. To ignore them or acknowledge them and then put them aside is to deny the most persistent fact about the persecutions.

CLASS

[Reginald] Scot [an Englishman who was skeptical about witchcraft] describe[d] [witches] as "poore, sullen.... These go from house to house, and from doore to doore for a pot full of milk, yeast, drinke, pottage, or some such releefe; without the which they could hardlie live." In most areas of Europe the accused were very poor, and their accusers were better off than they. Even though most accusers were neighbors who also lived in poverty, still they possessed more goods than their victims. The witch in many cases was the poorest of the poor, dependent on her neighbors to stave off starvation. In the sixteenth century,... the poor were becoming poorer; more peasants were forced to beg or steal in order to survive. Old, single women, especially vulnerable in this economic crunch, came to be seen as nuisances. When they turned them down, people felt guilty, an uncomfortable state often exacerbated when the beggar cursed them for their refusal. Then when misfortune occurred, people turned on the beggars, a classic example of "blaming the victim."

Those who had a little—and the rising expectations that go with "a little"—took out their frustrations over crop failure and the high death rate of infants on those who were least able to fight back. They also used witch accusations to establish their social position. In northern France, for instance, accusers were often those villagers who could read and write, who may have identified with the new reforms of the Catholic Reformation and the central government and may have seen cooperation with the authorities as the way up in the world. They strengthened their power in the village by attacking the most vulnerable group. As John Webster remarked (in 1677) of women having a bodily mark that could be taken for the devil's mark, "few would go free, especially those that are of the poorer sort."

In some instances, wealthy women were attacked. Late in a witch hunt, after the pool of typical women victims had been depleted, bourgeois and even upper-class women and men might be accused. In some cases poor women sought revenge by naming well-to-do women. Powerful men sometimes attempted to destroy other successful men through their wives—some even used their own wives and daughters in order to effect this.

TEMPERAMENT AND AGE

Scot's description furnishes some further clues as to just which women would be singled out for accusation: "They are doting, scolds, mad, divelish; ... so firme and steadfast in their opinions, as whosoever shall onelie have respect to the constancie of their words uttered, would easilie beleeve they were true indeed." In other words, uppity women —women given to speaking out, to a bold tongue and independent spirit, women who had what Scottish people called "smeddum": spirit, quarrelsomeness, a refusal to be put down. They talked back to their neighbors, their ministers, even to their judges and executioners.

Consider, for example, the case of a woman in the Spanish Netherlands known as the village curser. A poor but proud and outspoken woman, Marguerite Carlier, married with three children, voluntarily presented herself to be cleared of charges of killing animals. When she appealed to the privy council of the Hapsburg archduke, a number of well-off men from her village testified against her, revealing the real reason for their hatred of her—their fear that she had harmed them personally, that she was obsessed with causing them misery. But they had no proof, and under torture she confessed nothing; when released, she defended herself to one and all. Her defiance and open hostility made them fear her all the more, however, and she was banished, sent away from her family. After seven years in exile, she appealed again and was pardoned. Marguerite's case illustrates the price that an independent, outspoken woman might have to pay when she was up against the big men of the village, even when there was no proof against her....

Still another way in which women were vulnerable to charges of sorcery was because of their age. Though the majority of alleged witches in New England were middle-aged, most European victims were older, over fifty. Older women were frequently notorious as scolds; those no longer beholden to father, husband, or children felt freer to express themselves and often said just what they thought. John Metcalf of Leeds, England, complained in court that Anne Dixon had cursed him, calling him, "Whoremaster, whoremonger and harlott and did sit her downe upon her knees and cursed and banned him, and his wife, and badd a vengeance light upon the wife of the said John Metcalf and upon that whoremaster and whoremonger harlott her husband . . . and prayed God that they might never thryve." The ability of early modern women to attack with words was fearsome. Curses like Anne Dixon's were the basis for many witchcraft accusations.

The typical scold and the typical witch were older females, and both were criminalized during the same period. Each had their own kind of power. By laying curses and giving "lip," old women used what power they had to make others fear them, give them "space," and maybe respect them. The fact that people feared their curse was proof that their words carried numinous power. This trait can be interpreted in two ways, as sheer bad nature or as a defensive strategy. John Demos believes that the "uppity" quality of middle-aged and older women in New England was the chief reason they "attracted" witch accusations. Seeing them as quarrelsome and intractable, especially in their relations with their husbands, and as offering unwanted advice to their neighbors, he explains their persecution by their behavior. He omits from discussion the way women were subordinated to men, especially to husbands, in Puritan New England, and thus does not include the observation that they might well turn to nagging to protect their space in their homes.

Another way of looking at this trait is as a sign of being independent-minded.

Traditionally, peasant women in bad marriages had complained of how they were treated, but increasingly now when they did so they were branded as "traitors" to their husbands. The family, not only in New England but across Europe, was becoming more patriarchal in the sixteenth century, causing women's roles within the family to shrink. Outspoken wives were called shrews and suspected of witchcraft; when they spoke out against neighbors who had been unfair or ungenerous to them, they were hauled into court for being a nuisance and a witch.

Scolding done by a female was considered a crime and was punished in Britain by the scold's bridle, which locked the victim's head inside an iron cage that drove spikes through her tongue, and by the ducking stool, used for witches as well, by which they were ducked under water in stagnant ponds or cesspools. Sixteenth-century females, especially the older ones, *were* often scolds—and the punishment they received for scolding and witchcraft was so harsh that women kept a lower profile for several centuries afterward.

Another complaint against women, especially old women, was what was seen as their overassertive sexuality. Men fancied that old women still desired them and found the idea grotesque, hence Reginald Scot's saying that "to enforce a man, how proper so ever he be, to love an old hag, she giveth unto him to eate (among other meates) his owne doong." Likewise the Kent assize reported that Goodwife Swane "vehemently suspected by church authorities [as a witch]," boasted "that she can make a drink, which she saith if she give it to any young man that she liketh well of, he shall be in love with her."

One aspect of the witchcraze, undeniably, was an uneasiness with and hostility toward dependent older women. Witch charges may have been used to get rid of indigent elderly women, past childbearing and too enfeebled to do productive work. As Barbara Walker has put it, these women "could be called witches and destroyed, like domestic animals past their usefulness.... The old woman was an ideal scapegoat: too expendable to be missed, too weak to fight back, too poor to matter."

A final important lead from Scot, one seldom followed up on by historians of witchcraft, somewhat balanced out these female handicaps: these women were "so firme and steadfast in their opinions" that people listened to them. The alleged witch may have been sliding down into economic dependency, but she still had a certain authority, some standing in her community. As a healer, midwife, advice-giver, fortune-teller, spell-lifter, she was sought after; she could therefore boast "that she (as a goddes) hath brought such things to pass." People turned *to* witches as well as turned *on* them. Like female shamans in Korea today, they were both scorned *and* considered essential to the community, were both outcasts and authority figures. That their day as folk healers and cunning women was passing was part of the tragedy in which they were caught.

NO

Robin Briggs

MEN AGAINST WOMEN: THE GENDERING OF WITCHCRAFT

THEORIES AND REALITIES

Familial problems lead inevitably into the fascinating, difficult and higher controversial question of gender. The one thing everyone 'knows' about witches is that they were women. Although every serious historical account recognizes that large numbers of men were accused and executed on similar charges, this fact has never really penetrated to become part of the general knowledge on the subject. The *Malleus Maleficarum* is routinely quoted to establish that witch-hunters were woman-haters, and one can hardly deny that its principal author, the Dominican Henry Institoris (Heinrich Krämer), blamed witchcraft largely on unbridled feminine sexuality. It is not often recognized, however, just how far this was a peculiarly misogynistic text, many of whose assertions are very misleading as a guide to what happened in typical trials. Later writers were often content to repeat such material un-critically, while their statements about gender are usually both sketchy and inadequate. Pierre de Lancre stated that the Devil 'wins over more women than men, because they are naturally more imbecile. And we see that among those brought before the *parlements* on charges of witchcraft, there are ten times more women than men'. Jean Bodin went further still: 'When we read the books of those who have written about witches, it is to find fifty female witches, or even demoniacs, for every man.' He did concede that women often endured torture with more resolution than men, only to continue with the assertion 'that it is the power of bestial desire which has reduced women to extremities to indulge these appetites, or to avenge themselves ... For the internal organs are seen to be larger in women than in men, whose desires are not so violent: by contrast, the heads of men are much larger, and in consequence they have more brains and prudence than women.' The identi-fication of witches with women was already standard form, it would appear, in the decades when trials were at their height. The demonologists would have been shocked to find their confident assertions turned against them by modern writers who use the persecution as prime evidence for men's inhumanity to women, often seeming to assume that the sex ratio was not de Lancre's 90 per cent, or even Bodin's 98 per cent, but a stark 100 per cent. When this misconception has been coupled with vast exaggerations of the numbers executed it has proved all too tempting to create the image of an earlier holocaust, in which millions of women perished.

The best-informed recent estimates place the total number of executions for witchcraft in Europe somewhere between 40,000 and 50,000, figures which allow for a reasonable level of lost documentation. Men actually made up around 25 per cent of this total, although there were large variations from one area to another and between different types of trials. Bodin and de Lancre were simply wrong about the facts, before they proceeded to offer explanations which merely repeated the conventional wisdom of the day, and now appear remarkably feeble. Their inability to observe the reality around them is significant. It suggests that received opinions were blinding them to the obvious; in this they were actually typical of most traditional thinking, much more concerned with concept affirmation than with referential accuracy. What made their error so egregious was that their own country, France, was in fact a fascinating exception to the wider pattern, for over much of the country witchcraft seems to have had no obvious link with gender at all. Of nearly 1,300 witches whose cases went to the *parlement* of Paris on appeal, just over half were men. The appeal system may have been invoked more often by men in the years before it became automatic, yet there are many reasons to doubt that this has more than a modest effect on the figures. In around 500 known cases which did not reach the *parlement*,

although there is a small majority of women, men still make up 42 per cent of the accused. Some local studies also show a predominance of men, as do the court decisions which de Lancre himself collected and printed in one of his works. There are variations within the *parlement*'s jurisdiction (covering nearly half the country), for towards the east the proportion of women rises towards 70 per cent, which fits very well with the picture just across the border, and suggests that the figures are trustworthy, while the central and western regions had a clear majority of male witches. The great majority of the men accused were poor peasants and artisans, a fairly representative sample of the ordinary population.

Relatively high proportions of male witches were common elsewhere, as the overall statistics would lead us to expect. In south-west Germany, the figures were typically rising towards 25 per cent by the 1620s, while in another sample of well over a thousand cases from the Jura and the Alps the proportion of men was 22.5 per cent. For the modern French department of the Nord, then mostly in the Spanish Netherlands, men comprised 18 per cent of a much smaller group of 294. The Saarland and Lorraine correspond closely with eastern France, around 28 per cent of those tried being men; for a sample of 547 in the neighbouring duchy of Luxembourg it was 31 per cent. There are some extreme cases in peripheral regions of Europe, with men accounting for 90 per cent of the accused in Iceland, 60 per cent in Estonia and nearly 50 per cent in Finland. On the other hand, there are regions where 90 per cent or more of known witches were women; these include Hungary, Denmark and

England. The fact that many recent writers on the subject have relied on English and north American evidence has probably encouraged an error of perspective here, with the overwhelming predominance of female suspects in these areas (also characterized by low rates of persecution) being assumed to be typical. Nor is it the case that the courts treated male suspects more favourably; the conviction rates are usually much the same for both sexes. These data create as many problems as they solve, not least because of the 'dark figure' familiar to criminologists. Formally accused witches were predominantly women, but was this also true of those suspected and never charged? Might men typically have found themselves better placed to stave off their accusers? How do we account for accusations being gender-biased, yet far from gender-specific? Is there any rational explanation for the massive variations between different regions? This last question is perhaps the most baffling of all, particularly in a case like the French one, where large differences are found within a single jurisdiction and there are no obvious cultural or social differences to invoke. Recent work on contemporary witchcraft beliefs in western France strongly suggests that the pattern has endured to the present day, without providing many clues to its rationale. It is possible that there may have been a particular tendency in these areas to see the cunning folk in very ambivalent terms, so that a high proportion of the men accused were 'good' witches reclassified as bad, but this only pushes the problem of explanation back another stage.

It remains true that most accused witches were women. Careful reading of the trial documents suggests that this was an accurate reflection of local opinion, in the sense that those tried were fairly typical of the wider group of suspects. Confessions include lists of those allegedly present at the sabbat, which obviously reflect local rumours about witchcraft, and some general statements about the attendance. Both of these usually (though not always) specify a majority of women, in line with the proportions found in the trials. Witchcraft was not a specifically feminine crime in the sense that infanticide and prostitution were, almost by definition; these offences, and domestic theft (the other crime often linked to women), were of course different in that there was something much more real to get a hold on. Infanticide and prostitution actually exemplify the double standard far better than witchcraft, since almost all those punished can fairly be depicted as the victims of male oppression, although this hardly exonerates them totally. Their seducers or clients, often from higher up the social scale, almost invariably escaped unscathed. A new punitive attitude towards these 'social' crimes, whose only direct victims were the new-born babies, was a striking feature of the sixteenth century; more women were probably executed for infanticide than for witchcraft. With very few exceptions they were denounced by other women, without whose participation the legislation would have remained a dead letter. The whole process is best seen not as the deliberate criminalization of women, but as part of a much broader drive to exercise greater moral and social control by labelling and punishing many kinds of deviant behaviour. This process was often deeply unfair and hypocritical, but patriarchy in this sense meant first and foremost the tyranny of the rich and powerful over the poor and weak. Social and gender hierarchies were naturally interlinked, so it comes as no surprise that harsher repressive policies had unfortunate consequences for women, as they did for vagrants, beggars and many others.

Historians who emphasize the social and psychological aspects of witchcraft beliefs are nevertheless bound to reject the idea that witchcraft persecution can be satisfactorily explained as the product of a great conglomerate of patriarchalism, absolutism and moral rigour. The point is not to deny all relevance to such factors, but rather to insist that witchcraft is much more than an elaborate delusion manufactured by outsiders, then misapplied to popular beliefs. It does rather seem that many interpretations imply, indeed require, such an underlying structure. At its crudest this can be seen in suggestions that clerics and judges diabolized feminine medical practice, or that women were the scapegoats for a variety of natural disasters. At a more respectable intellectual level, we have had attempts to show how a range of intellectual and symbolic devices (ranging from the equation of virtue with masculinity, through claims that women were biologically just incomplete men, to images of women as temptresses) were united by a persistent denigration of women. In its own terms there is much to be said for this view, provided we recognize the peculiar character and limited application of this kind of misogynistic language. What it cannot do is to provide a convincing explanation for persecutions which were largely initiated at village level, and whose motivation was quite clearly fear of witchcraft in the most direct sense. It is also very important not to confuse the rhetoric of justifications with the real motives for action.

Another result of the tendency to see persecution as inspired from above is to give vastly exaggerated significance to the theories of the demonologists, attributing to them a causal role they simply did not possess. These approaches end up with the idea that witch-hunting was thinly disguised women-hunting, the diabolization of the feminine. In other words, here is the war between the sexes in a peculiarly violent form. Even if this were true, we would still have to account for change over time, since variables cannot be explained in terms of constants. The problem with these crude views goes deeper, for such generalized notions are too remote from the real world our ancestors inhabited. Gender did play a crucial role in witchcraft, but we will only understand this properly as part of the whole system, within which many other forces operated. What we need to explain is why women were particularly vulnerable to witchcraft accusations, not why witchcraft was used as an excuse to attack women. To achieve this, we must be constantly aware of gender as one of the crucial polarities within the vital frontier zone where beliefs and accusations interacted. Then we must tease out the ways in which it helped to structure the various operations which turned theory into action. In the process the information from the trials can tell us a great deal about gender, establishing a rewarding dialogue.

Counting heads is a useful way of shaking our ready assumptions, and of bringing a degree of rigour into the discussion. The figures can be broken down into numerous categories, to show distribution by age as well as gender, social and economic status, marital situation, childlessness and so forth. There has been no systematic work of this kind across Europe, and one would expect to find considerable variations by region. My own findings for Lorraine cannot therefore be regarded as a safer guide to general patterns, yet they do seem to conform to general impressions from several other regions. In this area of steady but very local persecution accused witches were on average much older and slightly poorer than their neighbours. Around half the women accused were widows, of whom a fair number appear to have had no surviving children. Some men seem to have been tainted by association with a suspected wife, but they were a minority; overall the masculine group formed a diverse cross-section of the peasant community. Although this evidence might seem to offer limited support to the stereotype of elderly women as witches, a more careful look at the material tells a different story. Age at the time of the trial is an artefact of the whole process by which reputations were built up. Since it took fifteen or twenty years for the typical witch to get to court, most were first suspected when still in the prime of life. There are signs that for women this transfer into the pool of suspects had a modest tendency to coincide with the menopause or the end of childbearing; while it would be rash to build too much on this flimsy basis, there may prove to be an important relationship here. This was an important watershed for everyone, physically, emotionally and socially, and, if the change of roles were not successfully accomplished, might prove an alienating experience. Those who missed out in some sense were likely to resent this, something their neighbours were all too likely to perceive. John Demos has suggested that midlife—roughly between the ages of forty and sixty—was the time when the exercise of power usu-

ally became central to personal experience. Wealth, prestige and responsibility all typically reached their highest point in these decades; while this was most obviously true for men, it was bound to affect women as well. Many themes could be related to this one; if illegitimate and misused power was a key meaning of witchcraft, then it is not surprising to find this age group notably suspect....

PSYCHOLOGY, MISOGYNY AND WITCHCRAFT PERSECUTION

These cases also provide a particularly rich context for investigating witchcraft from a psychological standpoint. As Lyndal Roper [a professor at the University of London whose research interests include witchcraft and gender history] states, 'witchcraft confessions and accusations are not products of realism, and they cannot be analysed with the methods of historical realism'. She draws out how individuals borrowed the language and stereotypical images of witchcraft to express their own psychic conflicts, which centred on the earliest stages of the mother-child relationship.... [However,] we need to question why, as witchcraft has receded almost entirely into the sphere of fantasy in the modern world, it has come to be completely sex-specific. The witch is the bad mother, a being who subverts the basic duties of her sex by direct hostility to fertility and nurture. She also embodies the envy which originates in early mother-child relations. Again and again the details of cases can be assimilated to these underlying patterns; they are not 'caused' by them so much as structured through them. Every individual carries around a permanent legacy from the formative period of life that includes negative elements capable of being activated under stress. Such reactions are very likely to employ the processes known to psychoanalysts as splitting and projective identification, both of which first take shape in relation to the mother. Every individual's fundamental experience of love and hate is with a woman, in the mother-child relationship, or whatever surrogate takes its place. How far this creates a predisposition, perhaps independent of gender, to make women the target for murderous hostility, it is impossible to say with certainty. Nevertheless, the historical record suggests that both men and women found it easiest to fix these fantasies, and turn them into horrible reality, when they were attached to women. It is really crucial to understand that misogyny in this sense was not reserved to men alone, but could be just as intense among women. Behind it lay the position of mothers as primary objects who were felt to possess magically formidable qualities, and whose very intentionality (independent will) was perceived as dangerous.

Such analyses have severe limitations, above all because they are too general to offer useful explanations for change and local variations. We cannot suppose that child-rearing practices changed dramatically in ways which would even begin to account for the rise and fall of persecutions; no independent evidence suggests this, while only exceptional shifts would be likely to affect relations between mothers and babies significantly. Wet-nursing might seem to be a candidate here, but it simply does not correlate in any plausible way; it was characteristic of those urban and elite groups which seem to have been least involved in persecution. It is more helpful to think of numerous distinct factors meeting around a central

void filled only by fantasy, a structure which related to the essential nature of witchcraft as a crime which never happened. Some people tried to practise it, although they were a minimal fraction among the accused; many more probably died of it, but in both cases the effects were only because of what people believed. The most enduring structures still persist in modern peasant societies, including some regions of Europe. They are to be found in parts of France, for example, as earlier variants of them doubtless were in Merovingian or pre-Roman Gaul. These include both social and psychological determinants, the elements which make all witchcraft beliefs fundamentally similar across great expanses of time and space. More ephemeral factors include the religious, legal and economic shifts which help to explain why persecution occurred when and where it did. It appears that certain combinations of the latter have been sufficiently powerful to deflect a normal tendency for witchcraft to be heavily—but not exclusively—attributed to women. We are unlikely to get much further on this last point until there has been a meticulous study of a region where men comprised the majority of the accused. A great deal might also be gained from a comparison between northern and southern Europe, with their strongly contrasted marriage systems. Mediterranean culture appears to have combined powerful witchcraft beliefs with very low rates of persecution, perhaps because older women were protected by their families, and enjoyed more power and esteem. This derived from a marriage pattern in which brides were much younger than their husbands, then commonly took over as effective heads of the household when they were widowed. Such women had to expect less power during their childbearing years, frequently dominated by mothers-in-law as well as husbands; it was only in mid-life that they acquired a new authority and status that was widely regarded as legitimate. By contrast, the theoretically more equal marriages of north-western Europe actually left older women at a grave disadvantage, unless they had the good fortune to find a caring, long-lived and forceful husband. Although it would be absurd to claim that one marriage system is more 'natural' than another, one of the most obvious biological differences between the sexes lies in the ages at which they cease to be fertile. The pattern of very late marriages for women, which was an essential condition for the closely-matched ages of spouses in the north-west, has long been regarded as an exception by historical demographers, and a puzzling one at that. It is at least possible that it may have made its own contribution to 'fixing' witchcraft accusations.

There are still reasons for linking witchcraft persecution to the assertion of patriarchal values, which can be seen as one aspect of a search for order in a period when many established patterns underwent severe disruption. Temporal coincidence does not establish causal relationships, however, and it is only by adopting a quite implausible picture of persecution imposed from above that patriarchalism can be made to carry direct blame. It is much more a case of underlying causes producing parallel effects, which were only mildly self-reinforcing. In a period when all tensions were being magnified by extremely harsh and painful social and economic pressures, those between the sexes were bound to be among them. The idea of the female sex as scapegoat misdescribes a situation of this kind, in which anxieties might be displaced into the area

of gender. It is also dangerous to put too much weight on the kind of discourse employed by the demonologists. Their referential system was self-confirming, with the positive and negative polarities used for rhetorical purposes. As Stuart Clark has pointed out, they took the link between women and witchcraft as a given, rather than spending much time debating it. Even the overt misogyny of the *Malleus Maleficarum* really falls into this category. Within the confines of an agrarian society and early modern intellectual styles, it was virtually impossible for anyone to rethink gender relations, because everything was referred to ideal types. Polarized binary classification was the dominant style of early modern thought, so that demonologists had no choice but to associate women with evil and inferiority. For them gender took the form of polarity, rather than a range of overlapping possibilities, because this was how it was always conceptualized. This was such a powerful 'mind-set' that it could override empirical observation, as it often did in the medical theory of the time. At the popular level such views were expressed in the form of proverbial wisdom, later reinforced by chapbooks and almanacs. The result was an unfortunate mixture of fear and aggression towards women, whose passions were seen as a grave threat to husbands and society alike. Deficiency in capacity to reason supposedly left women unable to control the baser part of their nature, while their mysterious cycles were evidence for the way they were dominated by the womb. Eve had been responsible for original sin, and women's attraction for men led to corruption and death; women's inconstancy and self-love made them natural allies of the Devil, an eternal danger of betrayal for the men they lured on. The commonplace idea that women were more sexually voracious than men was just one expression of these attitudes, part of an association between women, original sin and sexual pollution.

Despite the pervasiveness of these grotesque misogynistic doctrines, it is not easy to find evidence that they functioned as a direct cause of action. They may indeed be evidence of a mixture of fear and ignorance which dominated gender relations, and whose roots are better sought in general psychological structures. Early modern Europe was a society in which women got a raw deal in many respects, but this did not often take the form of direct persecution; rather it operated through indirect pressures that frequently led to women accusing one another. It was of course inevitable that the courts which heard these charges would be male, but among the judges it was often those elite jurists most strongly linked to formal patriarchal theories who treated witches leniently. Ultimately witchcraft was a theory of power; it attributed secret and unnatural power to those who were formally powerless. In this way it allowed men to project their own aggression into women, notably those with whom they or their wives quarrelled. This tendency must have been strengthened because women typically responded with threats and curses, which then became part of the evidence for their malevolence. The evidence of the trials, however, suggests that quarrels between women followed much the same course as those between men and women, and often underlay subsequent direct accusations made by men as well as women. In this sense women too could use accusations as a vehicle to assert themselves and claim power against their enemies; seen

in this light witchcraft did nothing to reinforce gender solidarities. The highly stressful circumstances experienced by early modern communities produced at least as much friction between those who were closest to one another as they did between those at opposite ends of the grids of wealth and gender. We do find peasant oligarchs accusing poor women, but only in a small minority of cases, compared to the significantly larger groups in which poor peasant households directed their suspicions against tiresome neighbours or persistent beggars.

It is all too easy to fall into anachronism when writing about witchcraft and gender. This is one reason why explanations should always be firmly bedded in the surrounding social realities. It should also warn us against the kind of knee-jerk reactions and facile assumptions which have too often resulted from failure to recognize the otherness of the past. We need to ask whether explanations that invoke gender as a motive could possibly apply in this period. It seems highly unlikely that any contemporary could have seen matters in this light. One must beware of false analogies between the past and the present. Gender is now an issue everyone has to confront, whereas at the time of witchcraft persecution it was a bundle of shared assumptions. Although there was a Renaissance debate about the status of women, it took place within strict limits, and hardly touched on the central questions as we might see them. In other words, modern views tend to be held consciously, whereas earlier ones were almost wholly unconscious. This did not necessarily make them less powerful, but it did mean that they were unlikely to motivate action directly. Gender differences are bound to remain a permanent and overt issue in our world, since the clock of consciousness cannot be put back. This also applies in reverse, however, and we must not project modern ideas and feelings back on to our ancestors, nor make them fight our battles. In the specific case of witchcraft we have a phenomenon which was permeated by gender, yet in much more subtle ways than any simple argument can convey. Hostility to women did play a crucial part at several levels; no general interpretation of the subject can or should obfuscate this basic truth. At the same time, this can only ever be part of a much more complex set of causes and connections. As so often, witchcraft tells us as much about the context from which it sprang—in this case gender relations—as that context helps us to understand witchcraft.

POSTSCRIPT

Were the Witch-Hunts in Premodern Europe Misogynistic?

Violence against women, which is considered by many to be epidemic in this generation, has caused a reassessment of the history of violence against women. Domestic violence, spousal abuse, sexual assault, rape, and sexual harassment have occupied recent headlines and created an acute awareness of woman-as-victim issues. In seeking the roots of such violent behavior, a search for historical antecedents is a logical place to start. Renewed interest in the witch-hunt phenomenon has enlivened the interest in the subject of violence against women, a unique synthesis of two subjects with far-reaching results.

Despite a plethora of available information and data, we are no closer today to definitive answers to some of the major questions involving premodern Europe's witchcraft experiences. For example, were the witch-hunts a centralized movement initiated from society's "power elite," or did local variables play a more important role in their development and outcomes? If women's sexuality was a major force in the witch craze phenomenon, who introduced it into the public record, and why? If socioeconomic factors were important to the movement, why did it last through more than three centuries of societal change? And if women were viewed as "creatures of God," how could the executions of witches be accompanied by such violent tortures? Was there another lesson being taught here?

On the generation-long historiography of the European witch craze, Hugh Trevor-Roper's essay, mentioned in the Introduction to this issue, is a good place to start. William Monter's *Witchcraft in France and Switzerland: The Borderlands* (Cornell University Press, 1969) and *Ritual, Myth, and Magic in Early Modern Europe* (Ohio University Press, 1984), along with his many articles, are important contributions to the study of witchcraft. It will be provocative and enlightening to read the two books on which the selections found in this issue are based.

Finally, an excellent primary sourcebook is Alan C. Kors and Edward Peters, eds., *Witchcraft in Europe, 1100–1700: A Documentary Issue* (University of Pennsylvania Press, 1995). See also Jonathan Barry, Marianne Hester, and Gareth Roberts, eds., *Witchcraft in Early Modern Europe: Studies in Culture and Belief* (Cambridge University Press, 1998), which contains many articles on the subject written by leading European scholars.

ISSUE 12

Did the West Define the Modern World?

YES: William H. McNeill, from *The Rise of the West: A History of the Human Community* (University of Chicago Press, 1991)

NO: Steven Feierman, from "African Histories and the Dissolution of World History," in Robert H. Bates, V. Y. Mudimbe, and Jean O'Barr, eds., *Africa and the Disciplines: The Contributions of Research in Africa to the Social Sciences and Humanities* (University of Chicago Press, 1993)

ISSUE SUMMARY

YES: Professor of history William H. McNeill states that in 1500, western Europe began to extend its influence to other parts of the world, bringing about a revolution in world relationships in which the West was the principal benefactor.

NO: History professor Steven Feierman argues that because historians have viewed modern history in a unidirectional (European) manner, the contributions of non-European civilizations to world history have gone either undiscovered or unreported.

It seems to be widely accepted that beginning in 1500, western Europe embarked on a course of world domination, the effects of which are still with us today. Due to factors such as superior military technology, immunity to diseases that ravaged others, and a strong will to succeed, Europeans were able to extend their influence over peoples in other parts of the world. The trans-Atlantic slave trade and the age of European imperialism were two major results of this cataclysmic movement.

Many have assumed that the capitalism and democracy that are so prominent among the world's nations today are part of a legacy that non-Western nations inherited from their contact with the West. In this view, the Western way was the wave of the future. Also, the West's technological and military superiority over the past 500 years have naturally led generations of Western historians to look at the last half-millennium through the eyes of their world. When the civilizations of the non-Western world were considered at all, they were simply included in a secondary and ancillary manner.

All of this changed with the end of colonialism, an important result of World War II. The former colonies, mandated territories, and Western-controlled areas were now free and independent nations, ready to determine their own destinies—and interpret their own histories. In this process, they were joined by a generation of new Western historians, who did not see the world through Eurocentric-colored glasses. Together, they are forcing the historical profession to reevaluate the Eurocentric interpretation of the last 500 years.

William H. McNeill's book *The Rise of the West*, first published in 1962, has achieved classic status among world history books. In the following selection from that book, McNeill operates from the thesis that from the earliest historical times, world civilizations have had contact with one another. He argues that this has profoundly shaped the history of humankind, although it is the West—as the title of his book implies—that has had the most profound influence on our world today. McNeill concludes that this superiority began during the Age of Exploration of the sixteenth century and continues to the present.

Steven Feierman represents the new generation of historians, who are not wedded to a Western analysis of the world's history. He utilizes African social and intellectual history (his area of expertise) to argue for the need to explain the past through non-Western eyes. This will require not only a more inclusionary approach to the study of the world's past, Feierman asserts, but also new tools and attitudes to be used in analyzing and evaluating non-Western sources, many of which might be considered nontraditional from a Western perspective. But it will mainly require work on the part of future historians to move away from the unidirectional view of the past that has dominated the historical profession for so long.

YES

William H. McNeill

THE FAR WEST'S CHALLENGE TO THE WORLD, 1500–1700 A.D.

The year 1500 A.D. aptly symbolizes the advent of the modern era, in world as well as in European history. Shortly before that date, technical improvements in navigation pioneered by the Portuguese under Prince Henry the Navigator (d. 1460) reduced to tolerable proportions the perils of the stormy and tide-beset North Atlantic. Once they had mastered these dangerous waters, European sailors found no seas impenetrable, nor any ice-free coast too formidable for their daring. In rapid succession, bold captains sailed into distant and hitherto unknown seas: Columbus (1492), Vasco da Gama (1498), and Magellan (1519–22) were only the most famous.

The result was to link the Atlantic face of Europe with the shores of most of the earth. What had always before been the extreme fringe of Eurasia became, within little more than a generation, a focus of the world's sea lanes, influencing and being influenced by every human society within easy reach of the sea. Thereby the millennial land-centered balance among the Eurasian civilizations was abruptly challenged and, within three centuries, reversed. The sheltering ocean barrier between the Americas and the rest of the world was suddenly shattered, and the slave trade brought most of Africa into the penumbra of civilization. Only Australia and the smaller islands of the Pacific remained for a while immune; yet by the close of the eighteenth century, they too began to feel the force of European seamanship and civilization.

Western Europe, of course, was the principal gainer from this extraordinary revolution in world relationships, both materially and in a larger sense, for it now became the pre-eminent meeting place for novelties of every kind. This allowed Europeans to adopt whatever pleased them in the tool kits of other peoples and stimulated them to reconsider, recombine, and invent anew within their own enlarged cultural heritage. The Amerindian civilizations of Mexico and Peru were the most conspicuous victims of the new world balance, being suddenly reduced to a comparatively simple village level after the directing classes had been destroyed or demoralized by the Spaniards. Within the Old World, the Moslem peoples lost their central position in the ecumene as ocean routes supplanted overland portage. Only in the Far East were the effects of the new constellation of world relationships at first unimportant. From a Chinese viewpoint it made little difference whether foreign trade, regulated within traditional forms, passed to Moslem or European merchants' hands. As soon as European expansive energy seemed to threaten their political integrity, first Japan and then China evicted the disturbers and closed their borders against further encroachment. Yet by the middle of the nineteenth century, even this deliberate isolation could no longer be maintained; and the civilizations of the Far East—simultaneously with the primitive cultures of central Africa—began to stagger under the impact of the newly industrialized European (and extra-European) West.

The key to world history from 1500 is the growing political dominance first of western Europe, then of an enlarged European-type society planted astride the north Atlantic and extending eastward into Siberia. Yet until about 1700, the ancient landward frontiers of the Asian civilizations retained much of their old significance. Both India (from 1526) and China (by 1644) suffered yet another conquest from across these frontiers; and the Ottoman empire did not exhaust its expansive power until near the close of the seventeenth century. Only in Central America and western South America did Europeans succeed in establishing extensive land empires overseas during this period. Hence the years 1500–1700 may be regarded as transitional between the old land-centered and the new ocean-centered pattern of ecumenical relationships—a time when European enterprise had modified, but not yet upset the fourfold balance of the Old World.

The next major period, 1700–1850, saw a decisive alteration of the balance in favor of Europe, except in the Far East. Two great outliers were added to the Western world by the Petrine conversion of Russia and by the colonization of North America. Less massive offshoots of European society were simultaneously established in southernmost Africa, in the South American pampas, and in Australia. India was subjected to European rule; the Moslem Middle East escaped a similar fate only because of intra-European rivalries; and the barbarian reservoir of the Eurasian steppes lost its last shreds of military and cultural significance with the progress of Russian and Chinese conquest and colonization.

After 1850, the rapid development of mechanically powered industry enormously enhanced the political and cultural primacy of the West. At the beginning of this period, the Far Eastern citadel fell before Western gunboats; and a few of the European nations extended and consolidated colonial empires in Asia and Africa. Although European empires have decayed since 1945, and the separate nation-states of Europe have been eclipsed as centers of political power by the melding of peoples and nations occurring under the aegis of both the American and Russian governments, it remains true that, since the end of World War II, the scramble to imitate and appropriate science, technology, and other aspects of Western culture has accelerated enormously all round the world. Thus the dethronement of western Europe from its brief mastery of the globe coincided with (and was caused by) an unprecedented, rapid Westernization of all the peoples of the earth. The rise of the West seems today still far from its apogee; nor is it obvious, even in the narrower political sense, that the era of Western dominance is past. The American and

Russian outliers of European civilization remain militarily far stronger than the other states of the world, while the power of a federally reorganized western Europe is potentially superior to both and remains inferior only because of difficulties in articulating common policies among nations still clinging to the trappings of their decaying sovereignties.

* * *

From the perspective of the mid-twentieth century, the career of Western civilization since 1500 appears as a vast explosion, far greater than any comparable phenomenon of the past both in geographic range and in social depth. Incessant and accelerating self-transformation, compounded from a welter of conflicting ideas, institutions, aspirations, and inventions, has characterized modern European history; and with the recent institutionalization of deliberate innovation in the form of industrial research laboratories, universities, military general staffs, and planning commissions of every sort, an accelerating pace of technical and social change bids fair to remain a persistent feature of Western civilization.

This changeability gives the European and Western history of recent centuries both a fascinating and a confusing character. The fact that we are heirs but also prisoners of the Western past, caught in the very midst of an unpredictable and incredibly fast-moving flux, does not make it easier to discern critical landmarks, as we can, with equanimity if not without error, for ages long past and civilizations alien to our own.

... Fortunately, a noble array of historians has traversed the ground already, so that it is not difficult to divide Western history into periods, nor to charac-terize such periods with some degree of plausibility. A greater embarrassment arises from the fact that suitable periods of Western history do not coincide with the benchmarks of modern world history. This is not surprising, for Europe had first to reorganize itself at a new level before the effects of its increased power could show themselves significantly abroad. One should therefore expect to find a lag between the successive self-transformations of European society and their manifestations in the larger theater of world history. . . .

THE GREAT EUROPEAN EXPLORATIONS AND THEIR WORLD-WIDE CONSEQUENCES

Europeans of the Atlantic seaboard possessed three talismans of power by 1500 which conferred upon them the command of all the oceans of the world within half a century and permitted the subjugation of the most highly developed regions of the Americas within a single generation. These were: (1) a deep-rooted pugnacity and recklessness operating by means of (2) a complex military technology, most notably in naval matters; and (3) a population inured to a variety of diseases which had long been endemic throughout the Old World ecumene.

The Bronze Age barbarian roots of European pugnacity and the medieval survival of military habits among the merchant classes of western Europe, as well as among aristocrats and territorial lords of less exalted degree, [are worth emphasizing.] Yet only when one remembers the all but incredible courage, daring, and brutality of Cortez and Pizarro in the Americas, reflects upon the ruthless aggression of Almeida and Albuquerque in the Indian Ocean, and discovers the disdain of even so cultivated a European as Father Matteo Ricci for the civility of the Chinese, does the full force of European warlikeness, when compared with the attitudes and aptitudes of other major civilizations of the earth, become apparent. The Moslems and the Japanese could alone compare in the honor they paid to the military virtues. But Moslem merchants usually cringed before the violence held in high repute by their rulers and seldom dared or perhaps cared to emulate it. Hence Moslem commercial enterprise lacked the cutting edge of naked, well-organized, large-scale force which constituted the chief stock-in-trade of European overseas merchants in the sixteenth century. The Japanese could, indeed, match broadswords with any European; but the chivalric stylization of their warfare, together with their narrowly restricted supply of iron, meant that neither *samurai* nor a sea pirate could reply in kind to a European broadside.

Supremacy at sea gave a vastly enlarged scope to European warlikeness after 1500. But Europe's maritime superiority was itself the product of a deliberate combination of science and practice, beginning in the commercial cities of Italy and coming to fruition in Portugal through the efforts of Prince Henry the Navigator and his successors. With the introduction of the compass (thirteenth century), navigation beyond sight of land had become a regular practice in the Mediterranean; and the navigators' charts, or *portolans*, needed for such voyaging showed coasts, harbors, landmarks, and compass bearings between major ports. Although they were drawn freehand, without any definite mathematical projection, *portolans* nevertheless maintained fairly accurate scales of distances. But similar mapping could be applied to the larger distances of Atlantic navigation only if means could be found to locate key points along the coast accurately. To solve this problem, Prince Henry brought to Portugal some of the best mathematicians and astronomers of Europe, who constructed simple astronomical instruments and trigonometrical tables by which ship captains could measure the latitude of newly discovered places along the African coast. The calculation of longitude was more difficult; and, until a satisfactory marine chronometer was invented in the eighteenth century, longitude could be approximated only be dead reckoning. Nevertheless, the new methods worked out at Prince Henry's court allowed the Portuguese to make usable charts of the Atlantic coasts. Such charts gave Portuguese sea captains courage to sail beyond sight of land for weeks and presently for months, confident of being able to steer their ships to within a few miles of the desired landfall.

The Portuguese court also accumulated systematic information about oceanic winds and currents; but this data was kept secret as a matter of high policy, so that modern scholars are uncertain how much the early Portuguese navigators knew. At the same time, Portuguese naval experts attacked the problem of improving ship construction. They proceeded by rule of thumb; but deliberate experiment, systematically pursued, rapidly increased the seaworthiness, maneuverability, and speed of Portuguese and presently (since improvements in naval architecture could not be kept secret) of other European ships. The most important changes were: a reduction of hull width in proportion to length; the introduction of multiple masts (usually three or four); and the substitution of several smaller, more manageable sails for the single sail per mast from which the evolution started. These innovations allowed a crew to trim the sails to suit varying conditions of wind and sea, thus greatly facilitating steering and protecting the vessel from disaster in sudden gales.

With these improvements, larger ships could be built; and increasing size and sturdiness of construction made it possible to transform seagoing vessels into gun platforms for heavy cannon. Thus by 1509, when the Portuguese fought the decisive battle for control of the Arabian Sea off the Indian port of Diu, their ships could deliver a heavy broadside at a range their Moslem enemies could not begin to match. Under such circumstances, the superior numbers of the opposing fleet simply provided the Portuguese with additional targets for their gunnery. The old tactics of sea fighting —ramming, grappling, and boarding— were almost useless against cannon fire effective at as much as 200 yards distance.

The third weapon in the European armory—disease—was quite as important as stark pugnacity and weight of metal. Endemic European diseases like smallpox and measles became lethal epidemics among Amerindian populations, who had no inherited or acquired immunities to such infections. Literally millions died of these and other European diseases; and the smallpox epidemic raging in Tenochtitlan when Cortez and his men were expelled from the citadel in 1520 had far more to do with the collapse of Aztec power than merely military operations. The Inca empire, too, may have been ravaged and weakened by a similar epidemic before Pizarro ever reached Peru.

On the other hand, diseases like yellow fever and malaria took a heavy toll of Europeans in Africa and India. But climatic conditions generally prevented new tropical diseases from penetrating Europe itself in any very serious fashion. Those which could flourish in temperate climates, like typhus, cholera, and bubonic plague, had long been known throughout the ecumene; and European populations had presumably acquired some degree of resistance to them. Certainly the new frequency of sea contact with distant regions had important medical consequences for Europeans, as the plagues for which Lisbon and London became famous prove. But gradually the infections which in earlier centuries had appeared sporadically as epidemics became merely endemic, as the exposed populations developed a satisfactory level of resistance. Before 1700, European populations had therefore successfully absorbed the shocks that came with the intensified circulation of diseases initiated by their own sea voyaging. Epidemics consequently ceased to be demographically significant. The result was that from about 1650 (or before), population growth in Europe assumed a new velocity. Moreover, so far as imperfect data allow one to judge, between 1550 and 1650 population also began to spurt upward in China, India, and the Middle East. Such an acceleration of population growth within each of the great civilizations of the Old World can scarcely be a mere coincidence. Presumably the same ecological processes worked themselves out in all parts of the ecumene, as age-old epidemic checks upon population faded into merely endemic attrition.

The formidable combination of European warlikeness, naval technique, and comparatively high levels of resistance to disease transformed the cultural balance of the world within an amazingly brief period of time. Columbus linked the Americas with Europe in 1492; and the Spaniards proceeded to explore, conquer, and colonize the New World with extraordinary energy, utter ruthlessness, and an intense missionary idealism. Cortez destroyed the Aztec state in 1519–21; Pizarro became master of the Inca empire between 1531 and 1535. Within the following generation, less famous but no less hardy conquistadores founded Spanish settlements along the coasts of Chile and Argentina, penetrated the highlands of Ecuador, Colombia, Venezuela, and Central America, and explored the Amazon basin and the southern United States. As early as 1571, Spanish power leaped across the Pacific to the Philippines, where it collided with the sea empire which their Iberian neighbors, the Portuguese, had meanwhile flung around Africa and across the southern seas of the Eastern Hemisphere.

Portuguese expansion into the Indian Ocean proceeded with even greater rapidity. Exactly a decade elapsed between the completion of Vasco da Gama's first voyage to India (1497–99) and the decisive Portuguese naval victory off Diu (1509). The Portuguese quickly exploited this success by capturing Goa (1510) and Malacca (1511), which together with Ormuz on the Persian Gulf (occupied permanently from 1515) gave them the necessary bases from which to dominate the trade of the entire Indian Ocean. Nor did they rest content with these successes. Portuguese ships followed the precious spices to their farthest source in the Moluccas without delay (1511–12); and a Portuguese merchant-explorer traveling on a Malay vessel visited Canton as early as 1513–14. By 1557, a permanent Portuguese settlement was founded at Macao on the south China coast; and trade and missionary activity in Japan started in the 1540's. On the other side of the world, the Portuguese discovered Brazil in 1500 and began to settle the country after 1530. Coastal stations in both west and east Africa, established between 1471 and 1507, completed the chain of ports of call which held the Portuguese empire together.

No other European nations approached the early success of Spain and Portugal overseas. Nevertheless, the two Iberian nations did not long enjoy undisturbed the new wealth their enterprise had won. From the beginning, the Spaniards found it difficult to protect their shipping against French and Portuguese sea raiders. English pirates offered an additional and formidable threat after 1568, when the first open clash between English interlopers and the Spanish authorities in the Caribbean took place. Between 1516 and 1568 the other great maritime people of the age, the Dutch, were subjects of the same Hapsburg monarchs who ruled in Spain and, consequently, enjoyed a favored status as middlemen between Spanish and north European ports. Initially, therefore, Dutch shipping had no incentive to harass Iberian sea power.

This naval balance shifted sharply in the second half of the sixteenth century, when the Dutch revolt against Spain (1568), followed by the English victory over the Spanish armada (1588), signaled the waning of Iberian sea power before that of the northern European nations. Harassment of Dutch ships in Spanish ports simply accelerated the shift; for the Dutch responded by despatching their vessels directly to the Orient (1594), and the English soon followed suit. Thereafter, Dutch naval and commercial power rapidly supplanted that of Portugal in the southern seas. The establishment of a base in Java (1618), the capture of Malacca from the Portuguese (1641), and the seizure of the most important trading posts of Ceylon (by 1644) secured Dutch hegemony in the Indian Ocean; and during the same decades, English traders gained a foothold in western India. Simultaneously, English (1607), French (1608), and Dutch (1613) colonization of mainland North America, and the seizure of most of the smaller Caribbean islands by the same three nations, infringed upon Spanish claims to monopoly in the New World, but failed to dislodge Spanish power from any important area where it was already established.

* * *

The truly extraordinary *élan* of the first Iberian conquests and the no less remarkable missionary enterprise that followed closely in its wake surely mark a new era in the history of the human community. Yet older landmarks of that history did not crumble all at once. Movement from the Eurasian steppes continued to make political history—for example, the Uzbek conquest of Transoxiana (1507–12) with its sequel, the Mogul conquest of India (1526–1688); and the Manchu conquest of China (1621–83).

Chinese civilization was indeed only slightly affected by the new regime of the seas; and Moslem expansion, which had been a dominating feature of world history during the centuries before 1500, did not cease or even slacken very noticeably until the late seventeenth century. Through their conquest of the high seas, western Europeans did indeed outflank the Moslem world in India and southeast Asia, while Russian penetration of Siberian forests soon outflanked the Moslem lands on the north also. Yet these probing extensions of European (or para-European) power remained tenuous and comparatively weak in the seventeenth century. Far from being crushed in the jaws of a vast European pincer, the Moslems continued to win important victories and to penetrate new territories in southeast Europe, India, Africa, and southeast Asia. Only in the western and central steppe did Islam suffer significant territorial setbacks before 1700.

Thus only two large areas of the world were fundamentally transformed during the first two centuries of European overseas expansion: the regions of Amerindian high culture and western Europe itself. European naval enterprise certainly widened the range and increased the intimacy of contacts among the various peoples of the ecumene and brought new peoples into touch with the disruptive social influences of high civilization. Yet the Chinese, Moslem, and Hindu worlds were not yet really deflected from their earlier paths of development; and substantial portions of the land surface of the globe—Australia and Oceania, the rain forests of South America, and most of North America and northeastern Asia—remained almost unaffected by Europe's achievement.

Nevertheless, a new dimension had been added to world history. An ocean frontier, where European seamen and soldiers, merchants, missionaries, and settlers came into contact with the various peoples of the world, civilized and uncivilized, began to challenge the ancient pre-eminence of the Eurasian land frontier, where steppe nomads had for centuries probed, tested, and disturbed civilized agricultural populations. Very ancient social gradients began to shift when the coasts of Europe, Asia, and

America became the scene of more and more important social interactions and innovation. Diseases, gold and silver, and certain valuable crops were the first items to flow freely through the new transoceanic channels of communication. Each of these had important and far-reaching consequences for Asians as well as for Europeans and Amerindians. But prior to 1700, only a few isolated borrowings of more recondite techniques or ideas passed through the sea lanes that now connected the four great civilization of the Old World. In such exchanges, Europe was more often the receiver than the giver, for its people were inspired by a lively curiosity, insatiable greed, and a reckless spirit of adventure that contrasted sharply with the smug conservatism of Chinese, Moslem, and Hindu cultural leaders.

Partly by reason of the stimuli that flowed into Europe from overseas, but primarily because of internal tensions arising from its own heterogeneous cultural inheritance, Europe entered upon a veritable social explosion in the period 1500–1650—an experience painful in itself but which nonetheless raised European power to a new level of effectiveness and for the first time gave Europeans a clear margin of superiority over the other great civilizations of the world....

CONCLUSION

Between 1500 and 1700, the Eurasian ecumene expanded to include parts of the Americas, much of sub-Saharan Africa, and all of northern Asia. Moreover, within the Old World itself, western Europe began to forge ahead of all rivals as the most active center of geographical expansion and of cultural innovation. Indeed, Europe's self-revolution transformed the medieval frame of Western civilization into a new and vastly more powerful organization of society. Yet the Moslem, Hindu, and Chinese lands were not yet seriously affected by the new energies emanating from Europe. Until after 1700, the history of these regions continued to turn around old traditions and familiar problems.

Most of the rest of the world, lacking the massive self-sufficiency of Moslem, Hindu, and Chinese civilization, was more acutely affected by contact with Europeans. In the New World, these contacts first decapitated and then decimated the Amerindian societies; but in other regions, where local powers of resistance were greater, a strikingly consistent pattern of reaction manifested itself. In such diverse areas as Japan, Burma, Siam, Russia, and parts of Africa, an initial interest in and occasional eagerness to accept European techniques, ideas, religion, or fashions of dress was supplanted in the course of the seventeenth century by a policy of withdrawal and deliberate insulation from European pressures. The Hindu revival in India and the reform of Lamaism in Tibet and Mongolia manifested a similar spirit; for both served to protect local cultural values against alien pressures, though in these cases the pressures were primarily Moslem and Chinese rather than European.

A few fringe areas of the earth still remained unaffected by the disturbing forces of civilization. But by 1700 the only large habitable regions remaining outside the ecumene were Australia, the Amazon rain forest, and northwestern North America; and even these latter two had largely felt tremors of social disturbance generated by the approaching onset of civilization.

At no previous time in world history had the pace of social transformation been so rapid. The new density and intimacy of contacts across the oceans of the earth assured a continuance of cross-stimulation among the major cultures of mankind. The efforts to restrict foreign contacts and to withdraw from disturbing relationships with outsiders—especially with the restless and ruthless Westerners—were doomed to ultimate failure by the fact that successive self-transformations of western European civilization, and especially of Western technology, rapidly increased the pressures Westerners were able to bring against the other peoples of the earth. Indeed, world history since 1500 may be thought of as a race between the West's growing power to molest the rest of the world and the increasingly desperate efforts of other peoples to stave Westerners off, either by clinging more strenuously than before to their peculiar cultural inheritance or, when that failed, by appropriating aspects of Western civilization—especially technology—in the hope of thereby finding means to preserve their local autonomy.

NO   Steven Feierman

AFRICAN HISTORIES AND THE DISSOLUTION OF WORLD HISTORY

Once upon a time historians used to know that certain civilizations (Western ones) were their natural subject matter, that some political leaders (Thomas Jefferson, Napoleon, Charlemagne) were worth knowing about, and that particular periods and developments (the Renaissance, the Age of Enlightenment, the rise of the nation-state) were worthy of our attention. Other places, other people, other cultural developments less central to the course of Western civilization did not count. Now all of that has come into question. Historians no longer agree on the subjects about which they ought to write....

The loss of agreement on history's subject is only one part of the change that provokes scholars to write about fragmentation and chaos. The debate on history's subject emerged at the same time that increasing numbers of historians began to doubt their own methods. Many now find it impossible to sustain the claims they might once have made that their choices of subject and method are based on objective knowledge. These historians have become acutely aware that their own writings, their ways of constructing a narrative, conceal some kinds of historical knowledge even while they reveal others, and that their choice of subject and method is a product of their own time and circumstances, not an inevitable outcome of the impersonal progress of historical science. This change, which has roots within contemporary philosophy, also emerges from the evolution of the historian's craft itself.

It is a profound paradox of history-writing in the most recent era that our faith in objective historical knowledge has been shaken precisely because of the advance of "knowledge" in its objective sense. The authoritative version of historical knowledge has been undermined because historians, in recent decades, have built bodies of knowledge about which their predecessors could only have dreamed. By carrying assumptions about historical knowledge through to their conclusions, historians have discovered some of the limits of those assumptions....

One obvious consequence of the expansion of historical research in the years since 1960 has been to show just how limited were our earlier understandings. Much of the new specialized research focuses on people previously excluded from the general history of humanity. The history of Africa is not alone in this respect. Alongside it are new bodies of knowledge on the history of medieval peasants, of barbarians in ancient Europe, of slaves on American plantations, and of women as the previously silent majority (silent, at least, in historians' accounts) in every time and place.

The very substantial dimensions of the gains in our knowledge have led to a sense of doubt rather than triumph. Historians now understand the dubious criteria according to which women and Africans, peasants and slaves were excluded from the histories of earlier generations. They therefore cannot help but wonder which populations, and which domains of human experience, they themselves are excluding today.

The previously excluded histories do not only present new data to be integrated into the larger narrative; they raise questions about the validity of that narrative itself. University historians integrate African history into the history of the eighteenth century, or the nineteenth, and yet many histories written or recited in Africa do not measure historical time in centuries. Academic historians appropriate bits of the African past and place them within a larger framework of historical knowledge which has European roots —the history of commodity exchange, for example. They rarely think of using bits of European history to amplify African narratives, about the succession of Akan shrines or the origin and segmentation of Tiv lineages.

Even before these more difficult issues began to trouble historians, the growth of knowledge about non-European societies began to undermine earlier histories, to bring into question narratives of academic history which, in the 1960s, seemed to be beyond reproach. The new knowledge showed that what was once thought to be universal history was in fact very partial and very selective. The narrative of human history which Western historians held at that time could no longer stand. Its destruction contributed to the sense of fragmentation and lost coherence....

In the early 1960s it was still possible to describe human history in terms of a story with a single narrative thread, from the earliest periods until modern times. Now that possibility is gone. It is difficult for us to remember how profoundly our historical vision has changed unless we return to examine important works of that time. For example, William McNeill's *The Rise of the West*, published in 1963 when African history was just beginning to emerge, presented a unicentric and unidirectional narrative, of a kind that would not be acceptable today.

The Rise of the West divided the ancient world between "civilizations" and the land of "barbarians." The book focused on the diffusion of the techniques of civilization, originally from Mesopotamia, and then within the area McNeill calls the *ecumene*, as opposed to the land of the barbarians. *Oikoumenê* (one of Arnold Toynbee's terms) had been used also by the great anthropologist A. L. Kroeber to mean "the range of man's most developed cultures" and therefore "the millennially interrelated civilizations in the connected main land masses of the Eastern Hemisphere." This was an intercommunicating zone within which the basic techniques of civilization were created, and within which they spread. The zone's boundaries shifted with time, but its early core was in the ancient Near East.

The origin of civilization, in McNeill's narrative, grows out of the introduction of agriculture. On this subject he takes contradictory positions but tries to maintain a single narrative thread. Even though the introduction explains that agriculture was introduced more than once, the book's narrative focuses on the central role of Mesopotamia, making a partial exception only for the introduction of agriculture in China. About the Americas, McNeill wrote, "Seeds or cuttings must have been carried across the ocean by human agency at a very early time." Then a bit later he explained that "contacts were far too limited and sporadic to allow the Amerindians to borrow extensively from the more advanced cultures of the Old World. As a result, the Andean and Mexican civilizations developed belatedly and never attained a mastery of their environment that could rival the levels attained by their contemporaries in Eurasia." He saw no possibility that domestication had independent beginnings in Africa and wrote that agriculture came to eastern and southern Africa only within the past five centuries. Until then, "primitive hunters roamed as their forefathers had done for untold millennia."

This statement is itself incorrect by millennia. We now know, as scholars of that generation did not, that animal domestication came very early to Africa (possibly earlier than to Southwest Asia), and that there were autonomous centers of crop domestication in Africa south of the Sahara.

Historians of McNeill's generation knew that great empires had grown up in sub-Saharan Africa by the first half of the present millennium—Ghana, Mali, Songhay, and other kingdoms in West Africa, and a great many kingdoms in eastern, central, and southern Africa, of which Zimbabwe was famous because of its great stone ruins. McNeill saw all of these as borrowings. The more advanced of Africa's societies, he wrote, "were never independent of the main civilizations of Eurasia." Islam, in his view, played a central role in bringing Eurasia's civilization to Africa. Even the southward migration of Bantu-speaking agriculturalists "may have been reinforced by the migration of tribes fleeing from Moslem pressures in the northwest."

Recent archaeological research in West Africa has shown that urbanism based on commerce came to West Africa before the birth of Islam. By about A.D. 500, Jenne, on the Niger River, emerged as a town built on local trade in agricultural surpluses drawn from lands flooded by the river. In this case, West Africans built their own town, which then grew further when Islam became important.

In central and southern Africa, also, kingdoms grew out of local roots. Zimbabwe is only one among the region's many stone ruins built in similar styles. These were sited so as to make farming and transhumant cattle-keeping possible as well as long-distance trade. As in West Africa, the evidence points to the growth of locally rooted centers which came ultimately to participate in long-distance trade. History can no longer be written as a single clear narrative of the spread of civilization's arts from the *ecumene*, the historical heartland, to Africa and other parts of the world.

Accounting for the new patterns challenged historians to find new ways of defining the spatial boundaries of important processes in world history. In this, as in so much else, the development of the *Annales* school of history writing in France interacted in creative ways with the development of African history. The creators of *Annales* history had a fresh historical vision; they challenged the orthodoxies of a style of history (associated with the legacy of Leopold von Ranke) that focused on the critical study of archival documents, especially as they related to the minutiae of political events. The early *Annalistes* reacted against the narrowly political definition of the historian's subject matter. Marc Bloch, in his early work, wrote about collectively held understandings of the world, in what seems to us now like an anthropological approach. Bloch, Lucien Febvre, and others were concerned with the history of society more generally, and not only with that narrow stratum to which the main political documents referred.

Fernand Braudel, the great leader of second-generation *Annales* historians, opened up the boundaries of historical space in a way that made it easier for us to understand Africa in world history. Many earlier scholars had limited themselves to national histories, of France, or of Italy, or of Spain. Others moved beyond national boundaries to continental ones. Braudel in his masterpiece saw the Mediterranean, with its palms and olive trees, as a significant historical unit, even though it took in parts of Europe and parts of Africa and Asia. It was tied together by its sea routes, but then extended wherever human communication took it: "We should imagine a hundred frontiers, not one," he wrote, "some political, some economic, and some cultural."

A flexible approach to spatial boundaries gives us a tool with which to break out of narrow definitions of core and periphery in world history. We do not need to see West African Muslims in a narrow framework which casts them only as bearers of culture from the center of civilization to the periphery. We can see them as West Africans, in economy, in language, and in many elements of discursive practice, and yet at the same time Muslims. We do not read from a single historical map that inevitably separates Africans from Middle Easterners. We read many maps side by side, some for language, some for economy, some for religion. Similarly, when we define the boundaries of African healing practices we do not need to stop at the continent's edge; our history can extend to the Americas. If we adopt a flexible and situationally specific understanding of historical space, the plantation complex, which is often seen as narrowly American, as a phenomenon of the Caribbean, Brazil, and the southern United States, can now be understood as extending to the East Coast of Africa and to northern Nigeria.

Braudel, along with the other *Annales* historians, insisted on asking how representative our historical knowledge is in relation to the totality of the universe that might be described, if only we knew the full story. He saw the economy as studied by economists, for example, as only one small part of a much larger and more shadowy sphere of economic activity. He observed that "The market economy still controls the great mass of transactions *that show up in the statistics,*" as a way of arguing that the historian ought to be concerned also with what does not show up in the statistics. A concern with the representativeness of historical knowledge was at the heart of African history's growth, which in this sense can be seen as Braudelian in its inspiration. African historians were saying that even if conventional sources were silent on Africa, this could not be taken as evidence that nothing had happened in Africa. If the contours of world history were determined by the silence of our sources, and not by the shape of history's subject matter, then we needed to find new sources.

Yet Braudel himself could not break out of a unidirectional history of the world with Europe at its center. *Civilisation matérielle, économie et capitalisme,* his three-volume history of the world between the fifteenth and eighteenth centuries, is driven by a tension between Braudel's disciplined attempt to find the correct spatial frame for each phenomenon (to explain the eighteenth-century rise of population on a worldwide basis, for example), and his definition of modern world history as the rise of a dominant Europe.

Civilisation matérielle, as a world history, touches on Africa's place in comparative context. The first volume is concerned with the history of everyday material life: food, clothing, crops, housing, furniture, and so on. Braudel's weakness in understanding sub-Saharan Africa does not undermine his more general analysis, except as it shapes his most general reflections on the full range of human experience. The same is true of the second volume, on the techniques by which people exchanged goods in various parts of the world. In the third volume, however, the question of Africa's place in history (and Latin America's) comes closer to the center of the analysis. This volume, which draws heavily on the thought of Immanuel Wallerstein, asks about the process by which a dominant capitalist world economy emerged, with its core in the West. In 1750, he says, the countries which were later to become industrialized produced 22.5 percent of the world's gross product. In 1976 the same countries produced 75 percent of that product. What were the origins of this movement from the relative eco-nomic parity of the world's parts to the dominance of the capitalist core? ...

Braudel adopted this framework, with its concern for the systematic character of inequality between the people he called "les *have* et les *have not.*" He was interested in how the dominance of the capitalist center grew out of developments within Europe, and out of relations among local world-economies. These latter were the spatial units which achieved a certain organic integration because of the density of exchange relations within them. The Mediterranean of the sixteenth century was a world-economy in this sense.

Braudel tried to make a serious assessment of the degree to which wealth drawn from outside Europe contributed to the rise of capitalism, but he treated Africans, and to a lesser extent people of the Americas, as historical actors only to the extent that they met European needs:

> While we might have preferred to see this "Non-Europe" on its own terms, it cannot properly be understood, even before the eighteenth century, except in terms of the mighty shadow cast over it by western Europe.... It was from all over the world... that Europe was now drawing a substantial part of her strength and substance. And it was this extra share which enabled Europeans to reach superhuman heights in tackling the tasks encountered on the path to progress.

This is a rather strange statement, lumping together much of the world simply on the basis that it is not Europe and proposing to ignore non-Europe on its own terms.

Braudel describes African developments, in particular, in terms of racial essences. In his view all civilization originated from the north, radiating southwards. He writes, "I should like now to concentrate on the heartland of Black Africa, leaving aside the countries of the Maghreb—a 'White Africa' contained within the orbit of Islam." Braudel's understanding of historical space is usually a subtle one in which each spatial frame is carefully differentiated. Here, however, he merges several frames in an inflexible and inaccurate way. Firstly, he merges race ("White" or "Black") with religion (Islamic or non-Islamic), even though many of the Muslims were people he would otherwise have described as "Black."

Secondly, he characterizes "Black Africa" as passive and inert. He writes that European ships on the West Coast met "neither resistance nor surveillance" and that the same thing happened on the shores of the desert: "Islam's camel-trains were as free to choose their entry-points as Europe's ships." This is demonstrably incorrect. A very large body of historical literature explores the complex interactions between West African kings or traders and those who came across the desert from the north. The spread of Islam and of the trans-Saharan trade was shared by initiatives taken on both sides of the desert.

According to Braudel, all movement was in a single direction. "Curiously, no black explorers ever undertook any of the voyages across either the desert or the ocean which lay on their doorstep.... To the African, the Atlantic was, like the Sahara, an impenetrable obstacle." He writes this despite the knowledge (with which he was certainly acquainted) that many Muslims who traded across the desert, or who went on the pilgrimage to Mecca from the West African Sudan, were Africans he would describe as black,

carrying the cultural heritage of West Africa with them. Black African rulers are reported as having made the pilgrimage to Mecca as early as the eleventh century. Mansa Musa of Mali traveled from West Africa to Cairo and then to Mecca in the fourteenth century with a retinue reported to number 60,000. Even though the correct number is likely to be smaller, there is no question that thousands of Africans crossed the desert to visit the world of the Mediterranean and the Red Sea, and others (from the East Coast) crossed the Indian Ocean to reach the Persian Gulf and India.

Finally, it appears to be the case that Braudel's characterization of the difference between "Black Africa" and "White Africa" is based on his understanding of race. In *Grammaire des civilisations* he acknowledges that Ethiopia (in this case Christian) was a civilization, explaining that it "undeniably possess white ethnic elements, and is founded on a *métisse* population, very different, however, from those of the true Melano-Africans." At times he denies the existence of facts in order to preserve the clear distinction between a Black Africa that is uncivilized and a White Africa that is civilized. In a 1963 book he acknowledges that the region near the Gulf of Guinea was urbanized very early. But then in a later book which argues that towns were one of the distinguishing marks of civilization, he writes that there were no towns on the fringes of the Gulf of Guinea....

Because historians have come to a fuller understanding of African urbanization, and of African initiatives in intercontinental exchange, it is now easy to see the weakness of this small part of Braudel's work. A central question remains, however: whether his unidirectional interpretation of Africa is merely an unfortunate idiosyncracy of an otherwise great historian, or whether it is a sign of deeper problems in the way many historians construct their narratives....

A reading of McNeill, Braudel, Bennassar and Chaunu, Wolf, Curtin, and others points to a larger and more general development: that the emergence of African history (and of Asian and Latin American history) has changed our understanding of general history, and of Europe's place in the world, in profound ways. It is no longer possible to defend the position that historical processes among non-European peoples can be seen as the consequence of all-encompassing influences emerging from a dominant European center. This shift in our understanding is uncomfortable for those who see history as the spread of civilization from a European center, and it is equally uncomfortable for those who sketch history in terms of an all-determining system of capitalist exploitation.

The shift away from historical narratives that originate in Europe has been both accompanied and enabled by innovations in methods for constructing knowledge about people who had previously been left out of academic histories. These renovated methods, some of which achieved their fullest early development among historians of Africa, include oral history, historical archaeology, and historical linguistics, as well as anthropologically informed historical analysis. The new methods and modes of interpretation made it possible for scholars to approach the history of non-literate people, and in many cases powerless ones, without departing from the accepted critical canons of historical research. Scholars were able to know histories they had never known before. The consequences were, once again, paradoxical. These significant advances in the range and quality of historical knowledge helped to shake historians' faith in the quality of their knowledge. To glimpse whole regions of history previously unknown, to see the dark side of the moon, inevitably shook scholars' faith in their own omniscience.

The methodological advances were not narrowly African ones. They had an impact in a number of historical fields, but many of them emerged with particular clarity and power amongst historians of Africa. The impact of oral history was bound to be great in studies of sub-Saharan Africa, where many societies were ideally suited for this form of research: their people transmitted substantial bodies of knowledge from one generation to the next and sustained complex political and economic hierarchies, all without practicing writing. Oral traditions were still alive (in many cases *are* still alive) when the historians of the 1960s and 1970s went about their work. Unlike Latin America, where the colonial period had begun several centuries earlier, it was only in the late nineteenth century that most of sub-Saharan Africa experienced conquest. Before this Europeans did not, in most cases, intervene directly in the transmission of knowledge....

The amplified range of methods employed by African historians has proven useful not only in societies that lack writing, but also for studying the underclasses of societies with a considerable range of literacy. Historians have used these amplified methods to construct rich accounts of the African majority in colonial society and especially to bring us magnificent accounts of peasant resistance to colonial domination....

The sense that we can no longer tell history as a single story, from a single consistent point of view or from a unified perspective, strikes deep resonances in recent social and cultural thought. Michel Foucault wrote, in *Language, Countermemory, Practice*, that the idea of the whole society "arose in the Western world, in this highly individualized historical development that culminates in capitalism. To speak of the 'whole of society' apart from the only form it has ever taken is to transform our past into a dream." The very categories by which we understand universal experience originate in the particular experience of the core of the capitalist world.

This is the same lesson taught by an examination of African history: the categories which are ostensibly universal are in fact particular, and they refer to the experience of modern Europe. That we have learned this lesson in two different ways—through philosophically based writings on Europe and through histories of non-Europeans—forces us to ask about the relationship between the two sets of developments. A central question which has not yet been fully addressed is the relationship between the crisis of historical representation that came about when historians began to hear the voices of those who had been voiceless, and the more general epistemological crisis affecting all the social sciences and humanities....

We are left, then, with an enormously expanded subject matter, with historical narratives originating in Africa that must be given full weight alongside those originating in Europe. We have seen, however, that this is not a simple process of adding one more body of knowledge to our fund, of increasing the balance in the account. The need for historians to hear African voices originates with the same impulse as the need to hear the voices that had been silent within European history. Since that is so, it hardly feels satisfying to listen to a single authoritative African voice, leaving others silent, or to read African texts without seeking marks of power, or without asking about the authority of the historian (African or American, European or Asian) who presumes to represent history. Historians have no choice but to open up world history to African history, but having done so, they find that the problems have just begun.

POSTSCRIPT

Did the West Define the Modern World?

Changes in the historical profession in the last quarter-century can be seen clearly in the 25th anniversary edition of McNeill's *Rise of the West*. In a retrospective essay entitled "The Rise of the West After Twenty-Five Years," McNeill states that the first edition of his book was influenced by the postwar imperial mood in the United States, which was then at the apex of its power and ability to influence world affairs. He now urges historians to "construct a clear and elegant discourse with which to present the different facets and interacting flows of human history as we now understand them." McNeill expands the focus of the world's history in two published lecture series: *The Human Condition: An Ecological and Historical View* (Princeton University Press, 1979) and *Polyethnicity and National Unity in World History* (University of Toronto Press, 1985). The rise in the number of world civilization courses in college curricula (replacing the traditional Western civilization ones) is a notable part of the fruits of new historical labors.

The work of the Annales School of historical writing, with its effect of broadening the scope of historical research by encouraging the use of unorthodox and unconventional sources, played a major role in the creation of the multidirectional view of world history. Fernand Braudel's *Civilization and Capitalism, Fifteenth–Eighteenth Centuries, vol.3, The Perspective of the World* (University of California Press, 1992) has been instrumental in making these changes possible. In *Europe and the People Without History* (University of California Press, 1982), Eric Wolf seeks to present a history of the modern world from the perspective of "the people without history"—those whose stories have not yet received adequate historical coverage.

The future is likely to see a rapid increase in the number of works relating to the creation of a new world history—a history that is suited to the needs of a new multicultural, civilizational world.

On the Internet ...

http://www.dushkin.com

France During the French Revolution and Under Napoleon Bonaparte

A chronology of events and battles centered around the life of Napoleon Bonaparte can be found on this Web site, which includes information on the Egypt campaign. A bibliography list is provided for further reference.
http://www.txdirect.net/users/rrichard/napoleo1.htm

Military History

This is a good place to start exploring military history. This Web site includes a time line of major wars and links to military history by period.
http://www.cfcsc.dnd.ca/links/milhist/

PART 4

The Modern World

This section traces the development of capitalism and democracy and the influence that they had on the modern world. It also covers the rise of nationalism, and how countries were affected in both positive and negative ways. Change brought about by various types of revolutions and their effects on countries in particular as well as in the world in general is also explored.

■ Did The Industrial Revolution Lead to a Sexual Revolution?

■ Was the French Revolution Worth Its Human Costs?

■ Did the Meiji Restoration Constitute a Revolution in Nineteenth-Century Japan?

■ Were Confucian Values Responsible for China's Failure to Modernize?

ISSUE 13

Did the Industrial Revolution Lead to a Sexual Revolution?

YES: Edward Shorter, from "Female Emancipation, Birth Control, and Fertility in European History," *The American Historical Review* (June 1973)

NO: Louise A. Tilly, Joan W. Scott, and Miriam Cohen, from "Women's Work and European Fertility Patterns," *Journal of Interdisciplinary History* (Winter 1976)

ISSUE SUMMARY

YES: Historian Edward Shorter argues that employment opportunities outside the home that opened up with industrialization led to a rise in the illegitimacy rate, which he attributes to the sexual emancipation of unmarried, working-class women.

NO: Historians Louise A. Tilly, Joan W. Scott, and Miriam Cohen counter that unmarried women worked to meet an economic need, not to gain personal freedom, and they attribute the rise in illegitimacy rates to broken marriage promises and the absence of traditional support from family, community, and the church.

Historians agree that between 1750 and 1850, the illegitimacy rate rose across Europe. In many of the European countries this time period coincides with industrialization. Did the arrival of capitalism change the living and working habits of unmarried women and introduce new attitudes that made them more interested in sex? When the result is agreed upon, what matters most is the evidence offered to explain the cause.

In the selection that follows, Edward Shorter asserts that a nineteenth-century sexual revolution that had its roots in industrial capitalism occurred. In his view the market economy, with its values of self-interest and competitiveness, changed the value system of the proletarian subculture—the young men and women working for wages in industrializing countries. Earning their own money, says Shorter, gave these workers the means to live independently. Young women in particular, he argues, declared their independence from family control, struck out in pursuit of personal freedom, and began to enjoy sex as a way of finding individual self-fulfillment. The predictable result was a rise in illegitimacy rates.

Louise A. Tilly, Joan W. Scott, and Miriam Cohen, in reply, fault Shorter for offering little or no hard evidence for his hypothesis. Citing the work of other historians, they assert that family interest rather than self-interest led women to work. Women moved very slowly into industrial work, and, even by the end of the period (1850), most women who were employed were doing domestic service, dressmaking, laundering, and tailoring, not factory work. Many women earned far too little to permit them to live independently. Those who did probably kept the traditional assumption that premarital intercourse with an intended bridegroom would be followed by marriage. Tilly, Scott, and Cohen argue that what changed was not the attitudes but the external context. In the absence of traditional pressures, young men moved on to other work or better opportunities, leaving the women they had impregnated behind.

As you read these two conflicting interpretations, look for the explanation offered by each essay and, most important, at what evidence is offered to support the interpretation. It may seem logical to assume that an increase in rates of illegitimacy must be due to a sexual revolution. But is that the only or the best explanation that existing information can support? There is a real temptation to use our "common sense" to fill in the gaps, but the historian insists on evidence.

For centuries history was written exclusively from the point of view of the rich, the powerful, and the literate. For some, understanding the "great man" —Alexander the Great, Julius Caesar, and Napoleon, for example—was the key to understanding the age in which he lived. This is often called history "from the top down." Many scholars, however, have begun to uncover the lives of the poor, the powerless, and the illiterate—what some call history "from the bottom up." Borrowing the methods of the social sciences, such as archaeology, anthropology, sociology, and psychology, and using quantitative analyses of economic and demographic data, historians are trying to fill in the missing pieces of the past. The essays in this issue take on the challenge of assessing the motives of people who left few, if any, written records. Since we cannot read their diaries and letters, we must use the evidence that we do have about the lives these women led and attempt to imagine how they might have seen the world.

In this issue, the chief question concerns continuity versus discontinuity. What changed? What remained the same? Did the attitudes of working women change as they entered the capitalist labor force, as Shorter states? And did these attitudes lead them to pursue personal pleasures such as sex, which, in the absence of birth control, resulted in higher rates of illegitimacy? Or, as Tilly, Scott, and Cohen argue, did the attitudes stay the same (premarital sex, as usual, in the context of courtship and with the expectation of marriage), while the context changed, leaving women pregnant and with no expectation of marriage?

YES

Edward Shorter

FEMALE EMANCIPATION, BIRTH CONTROL, AND FERTILITY IN EUROPEAN HISTORY

The conventional wisdom about female emancipation is that it originated among upper-class women in the mid-nineteenth century, surfacing first in tandem with the movement for emancipation of the slaves, then moving forward independently as the suffrage movement. While this account may be substantially correct as involves women's participation in national political life, it is, in my opinion, inapplicable to family history. I suggest that the position of women within the family underwent a radical shift starting late in the eighteenth century; furthermore, the change progressed from young and lowly women to older women of higher status. The logic of this chronology sees involvement in the economy of the market place as the principal motor of emancipation.

What exactly is meant by "female emancipation"? General statements about the position of women within early modern European families are uncertain in the extreme because, at the same time, so many impressions of individual famous women are to be found in the literature and so little is known in a systematic, quantitative way about the cultural rules and norms of women in the popular classes. Yet one might fairly characterize the situation of most women as one of subordination. In the first place, both young men and women were subordinated to the authority of their parents, so that parental intervention in the mating market customarily replaced romantic love in bringing young couples together. In the second place, both social ideology and the force of events conspired to make the husband supreme over the woman in the household, his obligation being merely to respect her, hers, however, to serve and obey him. In most matters of sex, economics, or family authority the woman was expected to do the husband's bidding. Clearly individual exceptions existed, yet the rule seems to have been powerlessness and dependency for the woman.

Thus female emancipation involves, quite simply, the replacement of this subordination with independence. In the nineteenth and twentieth centuries

From Edward Shorter, "Female Emancipation, Birth Control, and Fertility in European History," *The American Historical Review*, vol. 78, no. 3 (June 1973). Copyright © 1973 by The American Historical Association. Reprinted by permission. Notes omitted.

married women acquired for themselves first, practical leverage on household political power, and second, a family ideology stressing their own rights to sexual gratification and emotional autonomy. And unmarried women became increasingly convinced of the impropriety of family and community restraints upon social and sexual relations, so that they came to ignore the strictures of both parents and community in order to gratify their own personal needs. Therefore women's emancipation at the popular level means disregarding outside controls upon personal freedom of action and sexuality for the sake of individual self-fulfillment.

What evidence exists that the years 1750–1850 saw a movement toward female emancipation among the popular classes? We are, alas, at the beginning of the investigation rather than the end, and so I can merely anticipate the findings of future research. Yet even within the existing literature strong hints may be found that crucial changes in the status and authority of women were under way after 1750 and that these changes were linked in some way to economic modernization. The search for evidence may be aided by considering the nature of the change in the relationship between married woman and husband as well as that between the young, unmarried woman and parental and communal authority. To demonstrate that there is in fact an *explicandum*, let us briefly review some previous findings on these questions.

Least studied to date has been the family life and authority relationships of lower-class women in the years before 1900. Save for tiny pinpricks of information here and there the subject is uncharted, yet those studies that exist converge to demonstrate a radical upheaval in popular family life in the wake of capitalism. Neil Smelser, in a classic study of the British cotton industry, describes "the reversal of traditional age and sex roles as wives and children went to the factory." Industrial growth fragmented the customary "family economy" by making individual producers of its separate members. And, for the children at least, independence accompanied wage labor. Peter Stearns has recently reviewed the German literature, finding toward the end of the nineteenth century (a period inconveniently late for the case I wish to present here) "recognition of greater independence for the woman.... There is suggested here a new sentiment within the family, the possibility of greater affection for the children, who were not underfoot all the time, and greater sensuality and equality in the relationship between man and wife." And Rudolf Braun, in his sensitive reconstruction of life among cottage and factory workers in the Zurich highlands, notes massive shifts in family patterns, starting with the eighteenth century. While Braun is silent on specific changes in the relationships between married men and women, he pulls back the canvas for a brief instant to reveal, for example, women forgetting how to cook. Why, Braun asks, were ready-made foods in such great demand in factory towns?

> It was not merely the pressure to eat at the workplace that accelerated the demand for prepared dishes, nor the lack of time at home, but also the woman factory worker's lack of skill in cooking. Bound to the machine and the factory since earliest childhood, she inadequately learned the arts of cooking and homemaking. We have seen these complaints since the woman cottage workers of the *ancien régime*, but with

factory workers they become even more urgent.

One can imagine that the authority patterns among traditional petit-bourgeois families were as different from those of worker couples out on the frontier of economic advance as night is from day.

Evidence is more abundant that young unmarried women were rebelling against parental and social authority in the period from 1750 to 1850. To draw upon my own research, I noted in early nineteenth-century Bavaria an absolute squall of outrage from middle-class observers of popular life, seated for the most part in lower levels of the governmental bureaucracy, about a new spirit of independence among young women in agricultural labor and domestic service. Through this chorus of complaints ran the themes of escape and experimentation, of throwing off old superordinates and codes, and of, in general, what a much later generation of emancipators was to call "liberation."

There was the theme of escape from old jobs. Young women wanted, when possible, to forsake domestic service for employment that would safeguard personal independence. The unpopularity of service may be seen in the cries about a shortage of rural labor *(Dienstbotenmangel)* that became a constant theme in social criticism from the mid-eighteenth century onward. Or, to take another sort of example, Munich's police chief noted in 1815:

> It is sad, and most difficult for the police to prevent, that so many young girls leave service when they grow tired of waiting on people and under one pretext or another take a room somewhere, living from their own industry. But they do little real work and let themselves be supported by boyfriends; they become pregnant and then are abandoned.

And there was the theme of escape from old residences. Young women wanted to live alone, in their own quarters and away from the oppressive supervision of either parents or employers. In the late 1830s the indignant provincial government of Würzburg observed:

> In our province the so-called practice of *Eigenzimmern* is quite customary, according to which the deflorated daughter leaves the parental house and rents a room elsewhere, not necessarily to avoid the reproaches of the parents for her misdeeds, but in order to move more freely, to accommodate the visit of the boyfriend [*Zuhälter*] and with him to live in concubinage [*wilde Ehe*].

On the matter of escape from old personal styles, let Joseph Maria Johann Nepomuck Freiherr von Frauenberg, archbishop of Bamberg, speak:

> A most detrimental alteration in the character of the female gender [has taken place]. Earlier, women distinguished themselves through their soft, withdrawn, modest, and chaste being, while nowadays they take part in all public entertainments, indeed providing some, set the tone [*den Ton angeben*], and so have entirely departed from their natural situation. Thus has female morality disappeared.

The archbishop noted this development had occurred principally in the cities. There were other complaints about how female servants and hired hands would squander their entire wages in buying expeditions to the cities, returning to the farm with clothes alien to native folkways. Still other laments were voiced about feminine indifference to pastoral authority and about newly grasping, calculating female attitudes to wage matters. All these threads led back in the opinion of contemporaries—and rightly so I think—to sexuality and thus ultimately to fertility: "In the countryside a young girl who has preserved her virgin purity until age twenty is exceptional, and moreover encounters even among her girlfriends no recognition."

Perhaps Bavaria was not typical of the rest of Europe, though I believe that it was, for within its frontiers the kingdom harbored a remarkable diversity of social and economic arrangements. Perhaps, even more serious for the case I wish to make, male complaints about "moral breakdown" among young women reflected sooner the beholder's own libidinal preoccupations than a change in objective social conditions. Perhaps, too, nostalgia is close to being a historical constant, so that most men who search their own memories invariably see behind the outlines of a gray, disorganized present the golden harmony of an idealized past. Yet in this case I doubt it. And I suspect that future research will verify that this particular set of social critics at this particular point in time—the years 1800–40 —were onto something. The objective order of the real world was in fact changing, and a shift in the position of women was moving the ground directly from under the feet of these "patriarchs."

* * *

These changes in the mentalities and sexual comportment of women may ultimately be linked to a variety of changes in economic structure that one might summarize under the label "capitalism." Three salients of industrial advance mattered to fertility, and two of the three made more of a difference to women than to men....

First, capitalism meant the formation of a proletarian subculture. Large numbers of people who had in common the fact that they were wage laborers found themselves living together in the same communities. Because the material conditions of their lives differentiated them clearly from the surrounding social order of small proprietors, these newly aggregated workers in both agriculture and industry began to develop their own rules for doing cultural business, which is, after all, the essence of a subculture. A way of life specific to the working classes began to elaborate itself within the large farm areas of modernizing agriculture, upon the upland slopes where the putting out of textiles and nail manufacture was thriving, and within the newly blossoming industrial cities themselves.

The subculture would sooner or later matter to fertility by providing alternative sets of rules for sexual comportment, target family sizes, and new techniques for contraception and abortion. But subcultures are especially important in the area of legitimation of behavior about which the individual might otherwise feel uneasy. It is now common knowledge that the charter culture of traditional Europe had internalized within young people a host of restraints against intercourse. So that if before 1750 there was relatively little premarital intercourse, it was not necessarily because external supervision was totalitarian in its strictness but because most people within the culture shared the belief that premarital sex was wrong. When in later years sex before marriage became commonplace, it was because a new generation of sexually active young men and women felt their behavior was socially accepted, at least by their peers. The point is that if an individual is going to bend the operating rules of the dominant culture, he must feel that members of his own group, whose good opinion he treasures, will support his venturesomeness.

The proletarian subculture was, of course, indulgent of eroticism. Yet this particular indulgence must not be attributed without further argument to the industrial origins of the subculture. The fact that a subculture exists does not automatically mean that its specific operating rules must be libertine. Indeed many subcultures with quite repressive sexual values have flourished in the past, such as the colonies of nineteenth-century pietists in the United States. Some additional aspect of industrialism must therefore be adduced to explain the expressly permissive sexual content of the European proletarian subculture.

The second important dimension of capitalism lay in the mentality of the market place. In the eighteenth and early nineteenth centuries the market economy encroached steadily at the cost of the moral economy, and the values of individual self-interest and competitiveness that people learned in the market were soon transferred to other areas of life. It was this process of the transfer of values that gave the proletarian subculture its libertine moral caste.

The years after 1750 saw the intrusion of the principles of the market place into popular life. In early modern Europe trade in foodstuffs and in most non-agricultural products was tightly regulated by communal and corporate bodies, so that the Continent was fragmented into countless tiny local markets, kept through a complot of regulation and poor transportation as hermetically sealed compartments. Of course long-distance trade existed, yet most of the labor force was involved in local production along noncapitalistic lines. German political economists made a classic distinction between *Export-* and *Lokalgewerbe,* and most of the population lived from the latter. Then late in the eighteenth century these locally administered economies began to be engulfed by free markets of vast territorial scope. The struggle over free trade in grain in France has been often told; the losing battle of German guilds against pack pedlars, retail merchandise shops, unlicensed competitors, and the Customs Union is similarly familiar. Everywhere the moral economy regulated by the village fathers lost out to free competition regulated only by the invisible hand of the price mechanism.

Contact with these new labor markets was the most direct source of personal autonomy. As women became immersed in the market, they learned its values. I have elsewhere suggested that capitalism's mental habits of maximizing one's self-interest and sacrificing community goals to individual profit transfer easily to other thought processes. It seems a plausible proposition that people assimilate in the market place an integrated, coherent set of values about social behavior and personal independence and that these values quickly inform the noneconomic realms of individual mentalities. If this logic holds true, we may identify exposure to the market place as a prime source of female emancipation, for women who learned autonomy and maximization of self-interest in the economy would quickly stumble upon these concepts within the family as well. Men would also have learned these values, but then it was men who had traditionally been the dominant sex; a more sensitive attunement to questions of individuality left men, if anything, less able to defend themselves against the demands for autonomy of their wives and daughters.

The moral authority of traditional society was of a piece; the same communitarian principles that held together the moral economy also maintained the authoritarian family. And they crumbled together as well.

Thus a second crucial consequence of capitalism for women came in the area of personal values: an unwillingness to accept the dictates of superordinates and a new readiness to experiment with personal freedom and gratification. The reader should at this point bear in mind that we have to juggle simultaneously three different effects of capitalism: the first dimension of subculture weakened traditional moral taboos and destroyed internalized antisexual values; the second dimension, which we have just considered, quickened interest in intercourse as an aspect of personality development; and the third dimension of capitalism, to which we now turn, removed many of the external controls upon female sexual emancipation.

This last principal salient of industrial advance worked in the interest of women by modifying with wage labor the balance of power in the family. Paid employment meant that women would bring a distinct, quantifiable contribution to the family's resources, and accordingly would probably be entitled to a greater voice in the disposal of these resources. As many sociologists of the family have noted, the wife's (or daughter's) influence within the conjugal unit is a direct function of the status she enjoys in the outside world and of the resources she is able to import from that world into the family circle. Richard F. Tomasson has convincingly explained the historical development and the present-day international singularity of the Swedish family with such an approach, arguing also

that, "Where females have greater equality and are subject to less occupational and social differentiation, the premarital sex codes will be more permissive than where the female's status is completely or primarily dependent on the status of her husband." Altogether, capitalism entailed a quite material source of female independence and autonomy, increasing vastly the leverage formerly obtained from customary, dependent, unpaid, "women's work."

Popular involvement in the market economy started with the young and the poor and ended with the older and more prosperous. It was the most marginal whom capitalism could first detach from their traditional economic moorings, and so in the eighteenth century the young members of the proletarian classes that population growth had been creating went first to the cottage looms and spinning wheels. Thereafter ever more prosperous groups of the traditional economy found themselves pulled into the flux of the market, so that by the late nineteenth century even the most isolated sectors of the old middle class had been plunged into price competition and profit rationality. Immersion in the market progressed by stages.

Early in the eighteenth century the putting-out system began its conquest of the countryside, drawing in the landless poor. Then, in the course of the century agricultural capitalism began to encroach upon traditional subsistence and manorial farming, recruiting from among the landless and especially from the youth, for often unmarried laborers would live in the farmer's house, or newly married couples in nearby cottages. Next came migration to the newly rising factories and mills. The timing varied from one region to another, but normally it was the youth whom the fresh modern sector pulled from small farms and craft shops into factories.

In the nineteenth century industrial growth created a prosperous new middle class of administrators and clerks, of technicians and professionals. Because these people had often to endure long delays before marriage, women entered their childbearing periods at relatively advanced ages and largely abstained from intercourse beforehand. Finally, in the nineteenth century capitalism tore at the heart of the traditional old middle class itself, rather than merely at the supernumary poor. Across the Continent the masters of craft shops had to accommodate themselves to industrial capitalism, either by servicing the new factories or by going to work in them. And the depopulation of the countryside on the threshold of the twentieth century is an oft-told tale. It was frequently as mature men and women that these families were forced out of the traditional sector, of which they had constituted the backbone.

Thus the market started with the youngest and lowliest on the age-status spectrum and concluded with the most established and mature. It was also in this order that, I suggest, the spirit of female emancipation spread, from young and poor to well to do and middle-aged.

* * *

How, precisely, did these massive shifts in economic structure, culture, and individual mentalities affect either marital or nonmarital fertility? The linkages between emancipation and the increase in illegitimacy seem crisp and strong; those between capitalism and marital fertility are largely artifacts.

For the unmarried woman capitalism meant personal freedom, which meant in turn sexual freedom. The young woman could withstand parental sanctions against her sexual and emotional independence because the modern sector promised employment, economic self-sufficiency, and if need be, migration from home to another town. Such independence meant often, as we have seen, a paramour and therewith, in the absence of birth control, illegitimacy.

NO

Louise A. Tilly, Joan W. Scott, and Miriam Cohen

WOMEN'S WORK AND EUROPEAN FERTILITY PATTERNS

According to [Edward] Shorter, a change in fertility rates can only mean a change in sexual practices, which has to mean a change in attitudes, particularly of women. The sequence must be linear and direct. As Shorter argues:

> It seems a plausible proposition that people assimilate in the market place an integrated, coherent set of values about social behavior and personal independence and that these values quickly inform the noneconomic realm of individual mentalities. If this logic holds true, we may identify exposure to the market place as a prime source of female emancipation.

This statement, as its language clearly reveals, is based on a claim of reasoning, not on evidence. Shorter offers nothing to prove that more women worked in the capitalist marketplace in this period. He merely assumes that they did. Similarly, he assumes that women at the end of the eighteenth century had different family roles and attitudes from their predecessors. And he assumes as well that changes in work opportunities immediately changed values. Ideas, in his opinion, instantly reflect one's current economic experience. Shorter employs a mechanistic notion of "value transfer" to explain the influence of changes in occupational structure on changes in collective mentalities: "In the eighteenth and early nineteenth centuries the market economy encroached steadily at the cost of the moral economy, and the values of individual self-interest and competitiveness that people learned in the market were soon transferred to other areas of life."

For Shorter, sexual behavior echoes market behavior at every point. "Emancipated" women gained a sense of autonomy at work that the subordinate and powerless women of pre-industrial society had lacked. That work, created by capitalist economic development, necessarily fostered values of individualism in those who participated in it, and individualism was expressed in part by a new desire for sexual gratification. Young women working outside the home, Shorter insists, were by definition rebelling against parental authority. Indeed, they sought work in order to gain the independence and individual

Excerpted from Louise A. Tilly, Joan W. Scott, and Miriam Cohen, "Women's Work and European Fertility Patterns," *Journal of Interdisciplinary History*, vol. 6, no. 3 (Winter 1976), pp. 447–476. Copyright © 1976 by The Massachusetts Institute of Technology and the editors of the *Journal of Interdisciplinary History*. Reprinted by permission of MIT Press Journals. Notes omitted.

fulfillment that could not be attained at home. It follows, in Shorter's logic, that sexual behavior, too, must have been defiant of parental restraint. As the market economy spread there arose a new, libertine, proletarian subculture "indulgent of eroticism." Once married, the independent young working women engaged in frequent intercourse because they and their husbands took greater pleasure in sex. Female "emancipation" thus began among the young and poor. In the absence of birth control, the sexual gratification of single working girls increased the illegitimate birthrate; that of married women (who worked or had worked) inflated the legitimate birthrate. In this fashion Shorter answers a central question of European historical demography. The fertility increase in the late eighteenth century was simply the result of the "emancipation," occupational and sexual, of working-class women....

It is now time to examine the historical evidence that Shorter neglected on women's role in pre-industrial society; on the effects of industrialization on women's work and on their attitudes; and on the motives which sent young girls out into the "marketplace" at the end of the eighteenth and beginning of the nineteenth century. None of the evidence that we have found supports Shorter's argument in any way. Women were not powerless in "traditional" families; they played important economic roles which gave them a good deal of power within the family. Industrialization did not significantly modernize women's work in the period when fertility rates rose; in fact, the vast majority of working women did not work in factories, but at customary women's jobs. Women usually became wage earners during the early phases of industrialization not to rebel against their parents or declare independence from their husbands, but to augment family finances. Indeed, women in this period must be studied in their family settings, for the constraints of family membership greatly affected their opportunities for individual autonomy. No change in attitude, then, increased the numbers of children whom working women bore. Rather, old attitudes and customary behavior interacted with greatly changed circumstances—particularly in the composition of populations—and led to increased illegitimate fertility.

Women eventually shed many outdated priorities, and by the end of the nineteenth century some working women had clearly adopted "modern" life styles. But these changes involved a more gradual and complex adaptation than Shorter implies. The important point, however, is that the years around 1790 were not a watershed in the history of women's economic emancipation—despite the fact that the locus of women's work began to move outside the home. These *were* the crucial years for the increases in fertility in Europe. All of the evidence is not in, by any means; what we offer, however, indicates that in this period, women of the popular classes simply were not searching for freedom or experiencing emancipation. The explanation for changed fertility patterns lies elsewhere.

WOMEN'S PLACE IN "TRADITIONAL" FAMILIES

In the pre-industrial family, the household was organized as a family or domestic economy. Men, women, and children worked at tasks which were differentiated by age and sex, but the work of all was necessary for survival. Artisans' wives assisted their husbands in their work as weavers, bakers, shoemakers, or tailors. Certain work, like weaving, whether carried on in the city or the country, needed the cooperation of all family members. Children and women did the spinning and carding; men ran the looms. Wives also managed many aspects of the household, including family finances. In less prosperous urban families, women did paid work which was often an extension of their household chores: They sewed and made lace; they also took odd jobs as carters, laundresses, and street cleaners.

Unmarried women also became servants. Resourcefulness was characteristic of poor women: When they could not find work which would enable them to contribute to the family income, they begged, stole, or became prostitutes. Hufton's work on the Parisian poor in the eighteenth century and Forrest's work on Bordeaux both describe the crucial economic contribution of urban working-class women and the consequent central role which these women played in their families.

In the country, the landowning peasant's family was also the unit of productive activity. The members of the family worked together, again at sex-differentiated tasks. Children—boys and girls—were sent to other farms as servants when their help was not needed at home. Their activity, nonetheless, contributed to the well-being of the family. They sent their earnings home, or, if they were not paid wages, their absence at least relieved the family of the burden of feeding and boarding them. Women's responsibilities included care of the house, barnyard, and dairy. They managed to bring in small net profits from marketing of poultry and dairy products and from work in rural domestic industry. Management of the household and, particularly, of finances led to a central role for women in these families. An observer in rural Brittany during the nineteenth century reported that the wife and mother of the family made "the important decisions, buying a field, selling a cow, a lawsuit against a neighbor, choice of future son-in-law." For rural families who did not own land, women's work was even more vital: From agricultural work, spinning, or petty trading, they contributed their share to the family wage—the only economic resource of the landless family.

In city and country, among propertied and propertyless, women of the popular classes had a vital economic role which gave them a recognized and powerful position within the household. It is impossible to guess what sort of sexual relations were practiced under these circumstances. We *can* say, however, that women in these families were neither dependent nor powerless. Hence, it is impossible to accept Shorter's attempt to derive women's supposed sexual subordination from their place in the preindustrial household.

WHY WOMEN WORKED

Shorter attributes the work of women outside the home after 1750, particularly that of young, single women, to a change in outlook: a new desire for independence from parental restraints. He argues that since seeking work was an individualistic rebellion against traditionalism, sexual behavior, too, reflected a defiance of parental authority. The facts are that daughters of the popular classes were most often sent into service or to work in the city by their families. Their work represented a continuation of practices customary in the family economy. When resources were scarce or mouths at home too numerous, children customarily sought work outside, generally with family approval.

Industrialization and urbanization created new problems for rural families but generated new opportunities as well. In most cases, families strategically adapted their established practices to the new context. Thus, daughters sent out to work went farther away from home than had been customary. Most still defined their work in the family interest. Sometimes arrangements for direct payment in money or foodstuffs were made between a girl's parents and her employer. In other cases, the girls themselves regularly sent money home. Commentators observed that the girls considered this a normal arrangement—part of their obligation to the family.

In some cases the conditions of migration for young working girls emphasized their ties to family in many ways limited their independence. In Italy and France, factory dormitories housed female workers, and nuns regulated their behavior and social lives. In the needle trades in British cities, enterprising women with a little capital turned their homes into lodging houses for piece-workers in their employ. Of course, these institutions permitted employers to control their employees by limiting their mobility and regulating their behavior. The point is not that they were beneficient practices, but that young girls lived in households which permitted them limited autonomy. Domestic service, the largest single occupation for women, was also the most traditional and most protective of young girls. They would be sent from one household to another and thus be given security.

Châtelain argues that domestic service was a safe form of migration in France for young girls from the country. They had places to live, families, food, and lodgings and had no need to fend for themselves in the unknown big city as soon as they arrived. It is true that servants often longed to leave their places, and that they resented the exploitation of their mistresses (and the advances of their masters). But that does not change the fact that, initially, their migration was sponsored by a set of traditional institutions which limited their individual freedom.

In fact, individual freedom did not seem to be at issue for the daughters of either the landed or the landless, although clearly their experiences differed. It seems likely that peasant families maintained closer ties with their daughters, even when the girls worked in distant cities. The family interest in the farm (the property that was the birthright of the lineage and not of any individual) was a powerful influence on individual behavior. Thus, farm girls working as domestics continued to send money home. Married daughters working as domestics in Norwegian cities sent their children home to be raised on the farm by grandparents. But even when ties of this sort were not maintained, it was seldom from rebellious motives. Braun describes the late eighteenth-century situation of peasants in the hinterland of Zurich. These peasants were willing to divide their holdings for their children because of new work opportunities in cottage industry. These young people married earlier than they would have if the farm had been held undivided, and they quickly established their own families. Braun suggests that the young workers soon lost touch with their parents. The process, as he describes it, however, was not rebellion; rather, the young people went into cottage industry to lessen the burden that they represented for the family. These motives were welcomed and encouraged by the parents. Family bonds were stretched and broken, but that was a consequence, not a cause, of the new opportunities for work.

Similarly, among urban artisans, older values informed the adaptation to a new organization of work and to technological change. Initially, artisans as well as their political spokesmen insisted that the old values of association and cooperation could continue to characterize their work relationships in the new industrial society. Artisan subculture in cities during the early stages of industrialization was not characterized by an individualistic, self-seeking ideology, as Thompson, Hufton, Forrest, Soboul, Gossez, and others have clearly shown. With no evidence that urban artisans adopted the values of the marketplace at work, Shorter's deduction about a "libertine proletarian subculture" has neither factual nor logical validity. It seems more likely that artisan families, like peasant families, sent their wives and daughters to work to help bolster their shaky economic situation. These women undoubtedly joined the ranks of the unskilled who had always constituted the urban female work force. Wives and daughters of the unskilled and propertyless had worked for centuries at service and manufacturing jobs in cities. In the nineteenth century there were more of them because the proportions of unskilled propertyless workers increased.

Eighteenth- and early nineteenth-century cities grew primarily by migration. The urban working class was thus constantly renewed and enlarged by a stream of rural migrants. Agricultural change drove rural laborers and peasants cityward at the end of the eighteenth century, and technological change drove many artisans and their families into the ranks of the unskilled. Women worked outside the home because they had to. Changed attitudes did not propel them into the labor force. Family interest and not self-interest was the underlying motive for their work.

WOMEN'S WORK

What happened in the mid-eighteenth century with the spread of capitalism, the growth of markets, and industrialization? Did these economic changes bring new work experiences for women, with the consequences which Shorter describes? Did women, earning money in the capitalist marketplace, find a new sense of self that expressed itself in increased sexual activity? In examining the historical evidence for the effects on women's work of industrialization and urbanization, we find that the location of women's work did change—more young women worked outside the home and in large cities than ever before. But they were recruited from the same groups which had always sent women to work.

The female labor force of nineteenth-century Europe, like that of seventeenth- and eighteenth-century Europe, consisted primarily of the daughters of the popular classes and, secondarily of their wives. The present state of our knowledge makes it difficult to specify precisely the groups within the working classes from which nineteenth-century women wage earners came. It is clear, however, that changes in the organization of work must have driven the daughters and wives of craftsmen out of the family shop. Similarly, population growth (a result of declining mortality and younger age at marriage due to opportunities for work in cottage industry) created a surplus of hands within the urban household and on the family farm. Women in these families always had been expected to work. Increasingly, they were sent away from home to earn their portion of the family wage.

Shorter's notion that the development of modern capitalism brought new kinds of opportunities to working-class women as early as the middle of the eighteenth century is wrong. There was a very important change in the location of work from rural homes to cities, but this did not revolutionize the nature of the work that most women did. Throughout the nineteenth century, most women worked at traditional occupations. By the end of the century, factory employment was still minimal....

Shorter is also incorrect in his assumption that the working woman was able to live independently of her family because she had the economic means to do so. Evidence for British working women indicates that this was not the case. Throughout the nineteenth century, British working women's wages were considered supplementary incomes —supplementary, that is, to the wages of other family members. It was assumed by employers that women, unlike men, were not responsible for earning their own living. Female wages were always far lower than male. In the Lancashire cotton mills in 1833, where female wages were the highest in the country, females aged 16–21 earned 7/3.5 weekly, while males earned 10/3. Even larger differentials obtained among older workers. In London in the 1880s, there was a similar differential between the average earnings of the sexes: 72 percent of the males

in the bookbinding industry earned over 30/— weekly; 42.5 percent of women made less than 12/—. In precious metals, clocks, and watch manufacturing, 83.5 percent of the males earned 30/— or more weekly; females earned 9–12/—. Women in small clothing workshops earned 10–12/— weekly, while women engaged in outwork in the clothing trades made only 4/— a week. In Birmingham, in 1900, the average weekly wage for working women less than age 21 was 10/—, for men 18/—. Women's work throughout this period, as in the eighteenth century, was for the most part unskilled. Occupations were often seasonal and irregular, leaving women without work for many months during the year. Is it possible that there were many single women who could enjoy a life of independence when the majority could not even afford to live adequately on their personal wages? ...

Women's work from 1750 to 1850 (and much later) did not provide an experience of emancipation. Work was hard and poorly paid and, for the most part, it did not represent a change from traditional female occupations. Those women who traveled to cities did find themselves free of some traditional village and family restraints. But, as we shall see, the absence of these restraints was more often burdensome than liberating. Young women with inadequate wages and unstable jobs found themselves caught in a cycle of poverty which increased their vulnerability. Having lost one family, many sought to create another.

THE ORIGINS OF INCREASED ILLEGITIMACY

The compositional change which increased the numbers of unskilled, propertyless workers in both rural and urban areas and raised their proportion in urban populations also contributed to an increase in rates of illegitimacy. Women in this group of the population always had contributed the most illegitimate births. An increase in the number of women in this group, therefore, meant a greater incidence of illegitimacy.

A recent article by Laslett and Oosterveen speaks directly to Shorter's speculations: "The assumption that illegitimacy figures directly reflect the prevalence of sexual intercourse outside marriage, which seems to be made whenever such figures are used to show that beliefs, attitudes and interests have changed in some particular way, can be shown to be very shaky in its foundations." Using data from Colyton, collected and analyzed by E. A. Wrigley, they argue that one important component in the incidence of illegitimacy is the existence of illegitimacy-prone families, which bring forth bastards generation after generation. Nevertheless, they warn, "this projected sub-society never produced all the bastards, all the bastard-bearers."

The women who bore illegitimate children were not pursuing sexual pleasure, as Shorter would have us believe. Most expected to get married, but the circumstances of their lives—propertylessness, poverty, large-scale geographic mobility, occupational instability, and the absence of traditional social protection—prevented the fulfillment of this expectation. A number of pressures impelled young working girls to find mates. One was the loneliness and isolation of work in the city. Another was economic need: Wages were low and employment for women, unstable. The logical move for a single girl far from her family would be to find a husband with whom she might re-establish a family

economy. Yet another pressure was the desire to escape the confines of domestic service, an occupation which more and more young women were entering.

Could not this desire to establish a family be what the domestic servants, described by the Munich police chief in 1815, sought? No quest for pleasure is inherent in the fact that "so many young girls leave service.... But they do little real work and let themselves be supported by boyfriends; they become pregnant and then are abandoned." It seems a sad and distorted version of an older family form, but an attempt at it, nevertheless. Recent work has shown, in fact, that for many French servants in the nineteenth century, this kind of transfer to urban life and an urban husband was often successful.

Was it a search for sexual fulfillment that prompted young women to become "engaged" to young men and then sleep with them in the expectation that marriage would follow? Not at all. In rural and urban areas premarital sexual relationships were common. What Shorter interprets as sexual libertinism, as evidence of an individualistic desire for sexual pleasure, is more likely an expression of the traditional wish to marry. The attempt to reconstitute the family economy in the context of economic deprivation and geographic mobility produced unstable and stable "free unions."

... The central point here is that no major change in values or mentality was necessary to create these cases of illegitimacy. Rather, older expectations operating in a changed context yielded unanticipated (and often unhappy) results.... Women's work in the late eighteenth and early nineteenth centuries was not "liberating" in any sense. Most women stayed in established occupations. They were so poorly paid that economic independence was precluded. Furthermore, whether married or single, most women often entered the labor force in the service of the family interest. The evidence available points to several causes for illegitimacy, none related to the "emancipation" of women: economic need, causing women to seek work far from the protection of their families; occupational instability of men which led to *mariages manqués* (sexual intercourse following a promise of marriage which was never fulfilled). Finally, analysis of the effects of population growth on propertied peasants and artisans seems to show that the bifurcation of marriage and property arrangements began to change the nature of marriage arrangements for propertyless people.

POSTSCRIPT

Did the Industrial Revolution Lead to a Sexual Revolution?

In the world of the "great man," women, racial and ethnic minorities, and the poor are nearly invisible. They appear as passive participants in the historical drama; it is as if history happens to them. Revisionist historians, however, insist that even the apparently powerless have the potential to act as agents of historical change rather than as passive victims. Both Shorter and Tilley et al. assume that working-class, European women in the years between 1750 and 1850 made decisions and acted upon them. For reasons that may never be completely clear, there was a rise in illegitimacy rates, evidence that more babies than in the past were being born outside of marriage. What changed? A higher illegitimacy rate can mean that more sexual activity is taking place, but it can also mean that fewer unmarried, pregnant women are marrying.

To help you to make your own decision, you may wish to consider the evidence offered in the following books and essays. For a Marxist interpretation, see Friedrich Engels, *The Origin of the Family, Private Property and the State* (International Publishers, 1972). Ivy Pinchbeck, in *Women Workers and the Industrial Revolution, 1750–1850* (F. Cass, 1969), argues that occupational changes played a significant role in women's legal and political emancipation. Rudolf Braun, in "The Impact of Cottage Industry on an Agricultural Population," in David Landes, ed., *The Rise of Capitalism* (Macmillan, 1966), describes an economic system in rural Switzerland in which the daughters in a family learned to spin and weave, contributing their earnings to the family economic unit as a matter of course. Olwen Hufton makes a similar point about the Parisian poor in the eighteenth century in "Women in Revolution, 1789–1796," *Past and Present* (vol. 53, 1971) and about a broader segment of the population in "Women and the Family Economy in Eighteenth-Century France," *French Historical Studies* (vol. 9, 1975). Whether or not young working women kept their own wages and had enough money to support an independent lifestyle is a key historiographic question. For more work by this issue's authors, students may wish to read "Women's Work and the Family in Nineteenth Century Europe," *Comparative Studies in Society and History* (vol. 17, 1975) and *Women, Work, and Family* (Holt, Rinehart & Winston, 1978) by Joan W. Scott and Louise A. Tilly. Essays by Edward Shorter include "Illegitimacy, Sexual Revolution and Social Change in Modern Europe," *Journal of Interdisciplinary History* (vol. 2, 1971) and "Sexual Change and Illegitimacy: The European Experience," in Robert J. Bezucha, ed., *Modern European Social History* (D. C. Heath, 1972).

ISSUE 14

Was the French Revolution Worth Its Human Costs?

YES: Peter Kropotkin, from *The Great French Revolution, 1789–1793* (Schocken Books, 1971)

NO: Simon Schama, from *Citizens: A Chronicle of the French Revolution* (Alfred A. Knopf, 1989)

ISSUE SUMMARY

YES: Peter Kropotkin (1842–1921), a Russian prince, revolutionary, and anarchist, argues that the French Revolution eradicated both serfdom and absolutism and paved the way for France's future democratic growth.

NO: History professor Simon Schama counters that not only did the French Revolution betray its own goals, but it produced few of the results that it promised.

Few historical eras have created the emotional responses and concomitant debates as has the French Revolution. Taking advantage of one of the largest bodies of historical data ever gathered, historians of the past two centuries have analyzed, synthesized, and evaluated every facet of this seminal event in the history of the Western world.

From this scholarship has come a myriad of important questions regarding the political, economic, social, religious, cultural, and intellectual aspects of the Revolution—questions involving causation, behavior, outcomes, and assessments. Each generation of historians has taken the work of its predecessors and used it to shape an understanding of the Revolution that emanates from the uncovering of new sources of information, the creation of new tools to assist in the process, and the development of new schools of thought that attempt to give a more contemporary, relevant slant to this important event. To list the major questions raised by this debate could well cover most of the pages in a work devoted to the subject.

But of all the questions that the French Revolution has raised, a double-edged one that is both elemental and significant is, What were its outcomes, and were they worth the price that was paid to achieve them?

The debate began before anyone knew what course the Revolution would take. In a 1790 treatise entitled *Reflections on the Revolution in France*, English statesman Edmund Burke (1729–1797) uncannily predicted the future course of the Revolution and its catastrophic consequences for both France and

Europe. He also argued in favor of the slow, evolutionary style of change that was taking place in his own country, rather than the sudden, spasmodic one that was beginning to envelop France. Burke's message was simple: the revolution in France will be costly and counterproductive.

A year later, the French Revolution gained its first articulate defender, an English-born American citizen named Thomas Paine (1737–1809). In *Common Sense* (1776), a stirring call-to-arms for American colonists to throw off the yoke of English oppression, Paine acquired a reputation as a foe of tyrannical government and as a strong supporter of human freedom and equality. In Part 1 of his political pamphlet *The Rights of Man*, published in 1791, Paine argued that revolution was necessary to purge civilization of those elements that stood in the way of societal reform. According to Paine, no price was too high to pay for the realization of these cherished goals.

As generations passed, the basic question debated by Burke and Paine faded into the background as historians began to explore other fertile areas of historical research. There was either a general acceptance of the French Revolution's value in changing the course of human history or a quiet acquiescence in its outcomes, regardless of the consequences.

The following selection is by Peter Kropotkin, an early historical defender of the French Revolution. Obviously influenced by his radical, anarchistic background and his desire to see all people freed from the yoke of oppression, his view of the Revolution was somewhat simplistic and uncritical. Coming from a ninteenth-century environment, in which revolutions were common and seen by many as an inevitable part of political evolution, his opinions on the French Revolution are representative for his time—and for generations to come.

Of all the books written about the French Revolution in recent years, none have been as popular as Simon Schama's *Citizens: A Chronicle of the French Revolution*, which is excerpted in the second selection of this issue. Published in the midst of the Revolution's bicentennial celebration, the book aroused much controversy for many reasons; among them was his view that the French Revolution was not worth its human costs. Seeing violence as an endemic part of the revolutionary process, Schama states that the French Revolution produced few of the results that it had promised.

YES
Peter Kropotkin

THE GREAT FRENCH REVOLUTION, 1789–1793

When one sees that terrible and powerful Convention wrecking itself in 1794–1795, that proud and strong Republic disappearing, and France, after the demoralising *régime* of the Directory, falling under the military yoke of a Bonaparte, one is impelled to ask: "What was the good of the Revolution if the nation had to fall back again under despotism?" In the course of the nineteenth century, this question has been constantly put, and the timid and conservative have worn it threadbare as an argument against revolutions in general.

... Those who have seen in the Revolution only a change in the Government, those who are ignorant of its economic as well as its educational work, those alone could put such a question.

The France we see during the last days of the eighteenth century, at the moment of the *coup d'état* on the 18th Brumaire, is not the France that existed before 1789. Would it have been possible for the old France, wretchedly poor and with a third of her population suffering yearly from dearth, to have maintained the Napoleonic Wars, coming so soon after the terrible wars of the Republic between 1792 and 1799, when all Europe was attacking her?

The fact is, that a new France had been constituted since 1792–1793. Scarcity still prevailed in many of the departments, and its full horrors were felt especially after the *coup d'état* of Thermidor, when the maximum price for all foodstuffs was abolished. There were still some departments which did not produce enough wheat to feed themselves, and as the war went on, and all means of transport were requisitioned for its supplies, there was scarcity in those departments. But everything tends to prove that France was even then producing much more of the necessaries of life of every kind than in 1789.

Never was there in France such energetic ploughing, Michelet tells us, as in 1792, when the peasant was ploughing the lands he had taken back from the lords, the convents, the churches, and was goading his oxen to the cry of *"Allons Prusse! Allons Autriche!"* Never had there been so much clearing of lands—even royalist writers admit this—as during those years of revolution. The first good harvest, in 1794, brought relief to two-thirds of France—at least in the villages, for all this time the towns were threatened with scarcity of food. Not that it was scarce in France as a whole, or that the *sans-culotte* municipalities neglected to take measures to feed those who could not find employment, but from the fact that all beasts of burden not actually used in tillage were requisitioned to carry food and ammunition to the fourteen armies of the Republic. In those days there were no railways, and all but the main roads were in the state they are to this day in Russia—well-nigh impassable.

A new France was born during those four years of revolution. For the first time in centuries the peasant ate his fill, straightened his back and dared to speak out. Read the detailed reports concerning the return of Louis XVI. to Paris, when he was brought back a prisoner from Varennes, in June 1791, by the peasants, and say: "Could such a thing, such an interest in the public welfare, such a devotion to it, and such an independence of judgment and action have been possible before 1789?" A new nation had been born in the meantime, just as we see to-day a new nation coming into life in Russia and in Turkey.

It was owing to this new birth that France was able to maintain her wars under the Republic and Napoleon, and to carry the principles of the Great Revolution into Switzerland, Italy, Spain, Belgium, Holland, Germany, and even to the borders of Russia. And when, after all those wars, after having mentally followed the French armies as far as Egypt and Moscow, we expect to find France in 1815 reduced to an appalling misery and her lands laid waste, we find, instead, that even in its eastern portions and in the Jura, the country is much more prosperous than it was at the time when

Pétion, pointing out to Louis XVI. the luxuriant banks of the Marne, asked him if there was anywhere in the world a kingdom more beautiful than the one the King had not wished to keep.

The self-contained energy was such in villages regenerated by the Revolution, that in a few years France became a country of well-to-do peasants, and her enemies soon discovered that in spite of all the blood she had shed and the losses she had sustained, France, in respect of her *productivity*, was the richest country in Europe. Her wealth, indeed, is not drawn from the Indies or from her foreign commerce: it comes from her own soil, from her love of the soil, from her own skill and industry. She is the richest country, because of the subdivision of her wealth, and she is still richer because of the possibilities she offers for the future.

Such was the effect of the Revolution. And if the casual observer sees in Napoleonic France only a love of glory, the historian realises that even the wars France waged at that period were undertaken to secure the fruits of the Revolution—to keep the lands that had been retaken from the lords, the priests and the rich, and the liberties that had been won from despotism and the Court. If France was willing in those years to bleed herself to death, merely to prevent the Germans, the English, and the Russians from forcing a Louis XVIII. upon her, it was because she did not want the return of the emigrant nobles to mean that the *ci-devants* would take back the lands which had been watered already with the peasant's sweat, and the liberties which had been sanctified with the patriots' blood. And France fought so well for twenty-three years, that when she was compelled at last to admit the Bourbons, it was she who imposed conditions on them. The Bourbons might reign, but the lands were to be kept by those who had taken them from the feudal lords, so that even during the White Terror of the Bourbons they dared not touch those lands. The old *régime* could not be re-established.

This is what is gained by making a Revolution.

* * *

There are other things to be pointed out. In the history of all nations a time comes when fundamental changes are bound to take place in the whole of the national life. Royal despotism and feudalism were dying in 1789; it was impossible to keep them alive; they had to go.

But then, two ways were opened out before France: reform or revolution.

At such times there is always a moment when reform is still possible; but if advantage has not been taken of that moment, if an obstinate resistance has been opposed to the requirements of the new life, up to the point when blood has flowed in the streets, as it flowed on July 14, 1789, then there must be a Revolution. And once the Revolution has begun, it must necessarily develop to its conclusions—that is to say, to the highest point it is capable of attaining— were it only temporarily, being given a certain condition of the public mind at this particular moment.

If we represent the slow progress of a period of evolution by a line drawn on paper, we shall see this line gradually though slowly rising. Then there comes a Revolution, and the line makes a sudden leap upwards. In England the line would be represented as rising to the Puritan Republic of Cromwell; in France it rises to the *Sans-culotte* Republic of 1793. However, at this height progress cannot be maintained; all the hostile forces league together against it, and the Republic goes down. Our line, after having reached that height, drops. Reaction follows. For the political life of France the line drops very low indeed, but by degrees it rises again, and when peace is restored in 1815 in France, and in 1688 in England—both countries are found to have attained a level much higher than they were on prior to their Revolutions.

After that, evolution is resumed: our line again begins to rise slowly: but, besides taking place on a very much higher level, the rising of the line will in nearly every case be also much more rapid than before the period of disturbance.

This is a law of human progress, and also a law of individual progress. The more recent history of France confirms this very law by showing how it was necessary to pass through the Commune to arrive at the Third Republic.

The work of the French Revolution is not confined merely to what it obtained and what was retained of it in France. It is to be found also in the principles bequeathed by it to the succeeding century —in the line of direction it marked out for the future.

A reform is always a compromise with the past, but the progress accomplished by revolution is always a promise of future progress. If the Great French Revolution was the summing up of a century's evolution, it also marked out in its turn the programme of evolution to be accomplished in the course of the nineteenth century.

It is a law in the world's history that the period of a hundred or a hundred and thirty years, more or less, which passes between two great revolutions, receives its character from the revolution in which this period began. The nations endeavour to realise in their institutions the inheritance bequeathed to them by the last revolution. All that this last could not yet put into practice, all the great thoughts which were thrown into circulation during the turmoil, and which the revolution either could not or did not know how to apply, all the attempts at sociological reconstruction, which were born during the revolution, will go to make up the substance of evolution during the epoch that follows the revolution, with the addition of those new ideas to which this evolution will give birth, when trying to put into practice the programme marked out by the last upheaval. Then, a new revolution will be brought about in some other nation, and this nation in its turn will set the problems for the following century. Such has hitherto been the trend of history.

Two great conquests, in fact, characterise the century which has passed since 1789–1793. Both owe their origin to the French Revolution, which had carried on the work of the English Revolution while enlarging and invigorating it with all the progress that had been made since the English middle classes beheaded their King and transferred his power to the Parliament. These two great triumphs are: the abolition of serfdom and the abolition of abosolutism, by which personal liberties have been conferred upon the individual, undreamt of by the serf of the lord and the subject of the absolute king, while at the same time they have brought about the development of the middle classes and the capitalist *régime*.

These two achievements represent the principal work of the nineteenth century, begun in France in 1789 and slowly spread over Europe in the course of that century.

The work of enfranchisement, begun by the French peasants in 1789, was continued in Spain, Italy, Switzerland, Germany, and Austria by the armies of the *sans-culottes*. Unfortunately, this work hardly penetrated into Poland and did not reach Russia at all.

The abolition of serfdom in Europe would have been already completed in the first half of the nineteenth century if the French *bourgeoisie*, coming into power in 1794 over the dead bodies of Anarchists, Cordeliers, and Jacobins, had not checked the revolutionary impulse, restored monarchy, and handed over France to the imperial juggler, the first Napoleon. This ex-*sans-culotte*, now a general of the *sans-culottes*, speedily began to prop up aristocracy; but the impulsion had been given, the institution of serfdom had already received a mortal blow. It was abolished in Spain and Italy in spite of the temporary triumph of reaction. It was closely pressed in Germany after 1811, and disappeared in that country definitively in 1848. In 1861, Russia was compelled to emancipate her serfs, and the war of 1878 put an end to serfdom in the Balkan peninsula.

The cycle is now complete. The right of the lord over the person of the peasant no longer exists in Europe, even in those countries where the feudal dues have still to be redeemed.

This fact is not sufficiently appreciated by historians. Absorbed as they are in political questions, they do not perceive the importance of the abolition of serfdom, which is, however, the essential feature of the nineteenth century. The rivalries between nations and the wars resulting from them, the policies of the Great Powers which occupy so much of the historian's attention, have all sprung from that one great fact—the abolition of serfdom and the development of the wage-system which has taken its place.

The French peasant, in revolting a hundred and twenty years ago against the lord who made him beat the ponds lest croaking frogs should disturb his master's sleep, has thus freed the peasants of all Europe. In four years, by burning the documents which registered his subjection, by setting fire to the châteaux, and by executing the owners of them who refused to recognise his rights as a human being, the French peasant so stirred up all Europe that it is to-day altogether free from the degradation of serfdom.

On the other hand, the abolition of absolute power has also taken a little over a hundred years to make the tour of Europe. Attacked in England in 1648, and vanquished in France in 1789, royal authority based on divine right is no longer exercised save in Russia, but there, too, it is at its last gasp. Even the little Balkan States and Turkey have now their representative assemblies, and Russia is entering the same cycle.

In this respect the Revolution of 1789–1793 has also accomplished its work. Equality before the law and representative government have now their place in almost all the codes of Europe. In theory, at least, the law makes no distinctions between men, and every one has the right to participate, more or less, in the government.

* * *

The absolute monarch—master of his subjects—and the lord—master of the soil and the peasants, by right of birth—have both disappeared. The middle classes now govern Europe.

But at the same time the Great Revolution has bequeathed to us some other principles of an infinitely higher import; the principles of communism. We have seen how all through the Great Revolution the communist idea kept coming to the front, and how after the fall of the Girondins numerous attempts and sometimes great attempts were make in this direction. Fourierism descends in a direct line from L'Ange on one side and from Chalier on the other. Babeuf is the direct descedant of ideas which stirred the masses to enthusiasm in 1793; he, Buonarotti, and Sylvain Maréchal have only systematised them a little or even merely put them into literary form. But the secret societies organized by Babeuf and Buonarotti were the origin of the *communistes matérialistes* secret societies through which Blanqui and Barbès conspired under the *bourgeois* monarchy of Louis-Philippe. Later on, in 1866, the International Working Men's Association appeared in the direct line of descent from these societies. As to "socialism" we know now that this term came into vogue to avoid the term "communism," which at one time was dangerous because the secret communist societies became societies for action, and were rigorously suppressed by the *bourgeoisie* then in power.

There is, therefore, a direct filiation from the *Enragés* of 1793 and the Babeuf conspiracy of 1795 to the International Working Men's Association of 1866–1878.

There is also a direct descent of ideas. Up till now, modern socialism has added absolutely nothing to the ideas which were circulating among the French people between 1789 and 1794 and which it was tried to put into practice in the Year II. of the Republic. Modern socialism has only systematised those ideas and found arguments in their favour, either by turning against the middle-class economists certain of their own definitions, or by generalising certain facts noticed in the development of industrial capitalism, in the course of the nineteenth century.

But I permit myself to maintain also that, however vague it may have been, however little support it endeavoured to draw from arguments dressed in a scientific garb, and however little use it made of the pseudo-scientific slang of the middle-class economists, the popular communism of the first two years of the Republic saw clearer, and went much deeper in its analyses, than modern socialism.

First of all, it was communism in the consumption of the necessaries of life— not in production only; it was the communalisation and the nationalisation of what economists know as consumption —to which the stern republicans of 1793 turned, above all, their attention, when they tried to establish their stores of grain and provisions in every commune, when they set on foot a gigantic inquiry to find and fix the true value of the objects of prime and secondary necessity, and when they inspired Robespierre to declare that *only the superfluity of food stuffs should become articles of commerce, and that what was necessary belonged to all.*

Born out of the pressing necessities of those troublous years, the communism of 1793, with its affirmation of the right of all to sustenance and to the land for its production, its denial of the right of any one to hold more land than he and his family could cultivate—that is, more than a farm of 120 acres—and its attempt to communalise all trade and industry— this communism went straighter to the heart of things than all the minimum

programmes of our own time, and even all the maximum preambles of such programmes.

In any case, what we learn to-day from the study of the Great Revolution is, that it was the source of origin of all the present communist, anarchist, and socialist conceptions. We have but badly understood our common mother, but now we have found her again in the midst of the *sans-culottes,* and we see what we have to learn from her.

Humanity advances by stages and these stages have been marked for several hundred years by great revolutions. After the Netherlands came England with her revolution in 1648–1657, and then it was the turn of France. Each great revolution has in it, besides, something special and original. England and France both abolished royal absolutism. But in doing so England was chiefly interested in the personal rights of the individual, particularly in matters of religion, as well as the local rights of every parish and every community. As to France, she turned her chief attention to the land question, and in striking a mortal blow at the feudal system she struck also at the great fortunes, and sent forth into the world the idea of nationalising the soil, and of socialising commerce and the chief industries.

Which of the nations will take upon herself the terrible but glorious task of the next great revolution? One may have thought for a time that it would be Russia. But if she should push her revolution further than the mere limitation of the imperial power; if she touches the land question in a revolutionary spirit—how far will she do? Will she know how to avoid the mistake made by the French Assemblies, and will she socialise the land and give it only to those who want to cultivate it with their own hands? We know not: any answer to this question would belong to the domain of prophecy.

The one thing certain is, that whatsoever nation enters on the path of revolution in our own day, it will be heir to all our forefathers have done in France. The blood they shed was shed for humanity —the sufferings they endured were borne for the entire human race; their struggles, the ideas they gave to the world, the shock of those ideas, are all included in the heritage of mankind. All have borne fruit and will bear more, still finer, as we advance towards those wide horizons opening out before us, where, like some great beacon to point the way, flame the words—LIBERTY, EQUALITY, FRATERNITY.

NO

Simon Schama

CITIZENS: A CHRONICLE OF THE FRENCH REVOLUTION

Asked what he thought was the significance of the French Revolution, the Chinese Premier Zhou En-lai is reported to have answered, "It's too soon to tell." Two hundred years may still be too soon (or, possibly, too late) to tell.

Historians have been overconfident about the wisdom to be gained by distance, believing it somehow confers objectivity, one of those unattainable values in which they have placed so much faith. Perhaps there is something to be said for proximity. Lord Acton, who delivered the first, famous lectures on the French Revolution at Cambridge in the 1870s, was still able to hear firsthand, from a member of the Orléans dynasty, the man's recollection of "Dumouriez gibbering on the streets of London when hearing the news of Waterloo."

Suspicion that blind partisanship fatally damaged the great Romantic narratives of the first half of the nineteenth century dominated scholarly reaction during the second half. As historians institutionalized themselves into an academic profession, they came to believe conscientious research in the archives could confer dispassion: the prerequisite for winkling out the mysterious truths of cause and effect. The desired effect was to be scientific rather than poetic, impersonal rather than impassioned. And while, for some time, historical narratives remained preoccupied by the life cycle of the European nation-states—wars, treaties and dethronements—the magnetic pull of social science was such that "structures," both social and political, seemed to become the principal objects of inquiry.

In the case of the French Revolution this meant transferring attention away from the events and personalities that had dominated the epic chronicles of the 1830s and 1840s. De Tocqueville's luminous account, *The Old Regime and the Revolution,* the product of his own archival research, provided cool reason where before there had been the burning quarrels of partisanship. The Olympian quality of his insights reinforced (albeit from a liberal point of view) the Marxist-scientific claim that the significance of the Revolution was to be sought in some great change in the balance of social power. In both these views, the utterances of orators were little more than vaporous claptrap, unsuccessfully disguising their helplessness at the hands of impersonal historical forces. Likewise, the ebb and flow of events could only be made intelligible by being displayed to reveal the *essential*, primarily social, truths of the Revolution. At the core of those truths was an axiom, shared by liberals, socialists and for that matter nostalgic Christian royalists alike, that the Revolution had indeed been the crucible of modernity: the vessel in which all the characteristics of the modern social world, for good or ill, had been distilled.

By the same token, if the whole event was of this epochal significance, then the causes that generated it had necessarily to be of an equivalent magnitude. A phenomenon of such uncontrollable power that it apparently swept away an entire universe of traditional customs, mentalities and institutions could only have been produced by contradictions that lay embedded deep within the fabric of the "old regime." Accordingly, weighty volumes appeared, between the centennial of 1889 and the Second World War, documenting every aspect of those structural faults. Biographies of Danton and Mirabeau disappeared, at least from respectable scholarly presses, and were replaced by studies of price fluctuations in the grain market. At a later stage still, discrete social groups placed in articulated opposition to each other—the "bourgeoisie," "sans-culottes,"—were defined and anatomized and their dialectical dance routines were made the exclusive choreography of revolutionary politics.

In the fifty years since the sesquicentennial, there has been a serious loss of confidence in this approach. The drastic social changes imputed to the Revolution seem less clear-cut or actually not apparent at all. The "bourgeoisie" said in the classic Marxist accounts to have been the authors and beneficiaries of the event have become social zombies, the product of historiographical obsessions rather than historical realities. Other alterations in the modernization of French society and institutions seem to have been anticipated by the reform of the "old regime." Continuities seem as marked as discontinuities.

Nor does the Revolution seem any longer to conform to a grand historical design, preordained by inexorable forces of social change. Instead it seems a thing of contingencies and unforeseen consequences (not least the summoning of the Estates-General itself). An abundance of fine provincial studies has shown that instead of a single Revolution imposed by Paris on the rest of a homogeneous France, it was as often determined by local passions and interests. Along with the revival of place as a conditioner have come people. For as the imperatives of "structure" have weakened, those of individual agency, and especially of revolutionary utterance, have become correspondingly more important.

... I have pressed one of the essential elements in de Tocqueville's argument— his understanding of the destabilizing effects of modernization *before* the Revolution—further than his account allows it to go. Relieved of the revolutionary coinage "old regime," with its heavy semantic freight of obsolescence, it may be possible to see French culture and society in the reign of Louis XVI as troubled more by its addiction to change than by resistance to it. Conversely, it seems to me that much of the anger firing revolutionary violence arose from hostility towards that modernization, rather than from impatience with the speed of its progress.

... [I attempt] to confront directly the painful problem of revolutionary violence. Anxious lest they give way to sensationalism or be confused with counter-revolutionary prosecutors, historians have erred on the side of squeamishness in dealing with this issue. I have returned it to the center of the story since it seems to me that it was not merely an unfortunate by-product of politics, or the disagreeable instrument by which other more virtuous ends were accomplished or vicious ones were thwarted. In some depressingly unavoidable sense, violence *was* the Revolution itself. . . .

* * *

The tenth to the twelfth of March [1793] saw the first stage in the uprising, when spontaneously assembled crowds in villages and *bourgs* attacked the offices and houses of mayors, *juges de paix, procureurs* and dangerously isolated units of the National Guard. The riot at Machecoul was repeated, with less murderous consequences, in Saint-Florent-le-Veil, Sainte-Pazanne, Saint-Hilaire-de-Chaléons and Clisson. The leaders who emerged from this first wave of violence were often, like the gamekeeper and ex-soldier Stofflet, men who had long been identified in their locality with resistance to the revolutionary authorities. Once they had evicted their enemies and taken their weapons, the crowds coalesced with each other, forming processions towards larger towns and snowballing in size as they traveled along the roads.

At this stage, the riots in the Vendée seemed no different from similar antirecruitment riots taking place in many other parts of France from the Calvados in Normandy to the Côte d'Or in Burgundy and the Puy in the southern Massif Central. Some of the worst upheavals occurred north of the Loire in Brittany. But there the government had been so obsessed by the possibility of counterrevolutionary plots, it had in place sufficient force to take rapid and decisive action against the centers of resistance. The Vendée, in contrast, was dangerously depleted of troops. At Challans, for example, there were just two hundred Patriot Guards who had to face more than a thousand insurgents on the twelfth of March. By the time that reinforcements could be provided, the several riots had already fused into a general insurrection. Moreover, even of the fifty thousand republican soldiers who were eventually concentrated in the Vendée by the third week of March, only a tiny proportion—perhaps fewer than two thousand—were veterans of the "line"—the old royal army. The remainder were unseasoned volunteers, badly fed and equipped and, more critically for the situation they faced, extremely apprehensive about the rebels. None of the armies of France in the spring and summer of 1793 showed such propensity to take to panic and break ranks as the *bleus* of the Vendée. Perhaps they feared the fate of the republicans of Machecoul. As it was, many of them were dispersed in small units of fifty or some hundreds, numerous enough to provide a target for the infuriated rebels but not substantial enough to overawe them.

By the time that the Republic understood the gravity of the situation, the rebels had already taken many of the larger centers, in particular Cholet, Chemillé and Fontenay-le-Comte. On the fourteenth of March, Stofflet joined his forces with those attached to another gamekeeper, Tonnelet, and men following the wagoner-vendor Cathelineau. After failing to persuade the republican troops, commanded by the citizen-marquis de Beauveau, to lay down their arms, the rebels overwhelmed the *bleus* in a great barrage of fire, mortally wounding de Beauveau....

* * *

The second half of March brought a steady drumbeat of calamity to republican France. Within the same week, the Convention heard of the defeat at Neerwinden, a further military collapse near Louvain, Custine's abrupt retreat in the Rhineland and the Vendéan uprising. Report after report described Republican armies dissolving on contact with the enemy (especially in the Vendée); volunteers demoralized and disorderly, deserting or taking to their heels; the tricolor trampled in the mud. When Delacroix returned from the Belgian front, he brought with him a gloom as deep and as dark as the weeks before Valmy. French troops had fallen back on Valenciennes, but if that fortress fell, he warned, there was nothing between the Allied armies and Paris. To many deputies, and not just those of the Mountain, there could be only one explanation for this sorry trail of disasters: conspiracy. The commissioners with General Marcé's defeated army in the Vendée accused him of either "the most cowardly ineptness" or, worse, "the most cowardly treason." His son; his second-in-command, Verteuil; and another Verteuil presumed to be *his* son (but in fact a distant relative) were all arrested for being "in treasonable contact with the enemy." ...

Faced with this military landslide, the Convention, with very few exceptions, acknowledged that it had to strengthen the powers of the state. Without an effective executive and a coherent chain of command, centrifugal forces would pull France apart. For the first time since the beginning of the Revolution, the legislature set about creating strong organs of central authority authorized to do the Republic's work without endless reference to the "sovereign body." On March 6 it dispatched eighty of its own members (known, from April on, as "representatives on mission") to the departments to ensure compliance with the central government's will. They were, in effect, a revolutionary version of the old royal *intendants,* traveling embodiments of sovereignty. Much of their work was meant to concern itself with judicial and punitive matters. On March 11 a special Revolutionary Tribunal was established in Paris to try suspects accused of counter-revolutionary activities. On March 20, with the rebellions in the Vendée and Brittany in mind, the Convention adopted Cambacérès' proposal giving military courts jurisdiction over anyone who had been employed in public positions (including clergy and nobles) and who was found with the white royalist cockade or fomenting rebellion. If guilty, they were to be shot within twenty-four hours. A day later, every commune in the country was equipped with committees of surveillance and all citizens were encouraged to denounce anyone they suspected of uncertain loyalties. Predictably, the law rapidly became a charter for countless petty dramas of revenge.

Finally, on April 6, it was decided to replace the Committee of General Defense, set up in January as a body of twenty-five to coordinate the work of the several committees of the Convention. In its place was to be a much tighter committee of just nine members, to be known as the Committee of Public Safety....

On October 10 Saint-Just came before the Convention to issue a report in the name of the Committee of Public Safety on the "troubles affecting the state." He took the righteously self-scrutinizing line of declaring that the people had only one enemy, namely the government itself, infected as it was with all sorts of spineless, corrupt and compromised creatures of the old regime. The remedy was unremitting austerity of purpose, implacable punishment for the backsliders and the hypocrites. The charter of the Terror—the Law of Suspects, enacted on September 17, which gave the Committee and its representatives sweeping powers of arrest and punishment over extraordinarily broad categories of people defined as harboring counter-revolutionary designs—should be applied with the utmost rigor. "Between the people and their enemies there can be nothing in common but the sword; we must govern by iron those who cannot be governed by justice; we must oppress the tyrant.... It is impossible for revolutionary laws to be executed unless the government itself is truly revolutionary." ...

* * *

The Terror went into action with impressive bureaucratic efficiency. House searches, usually made at night, were extensive and unsparing. All citizens were required to attach to their front doors a notice indicating all residents who lived inside. Entertaining anyone not on that list, even for a single night, was a serious crime. Denunciations poured into the Commission. People were accused of defaming Chalier, of attacking the liberty tree, secreting priests or émigrés, making speculative fortunes and—one of the standard crimes of· the year II—writing or uttering *"merde à la république."* From early December the guillotine went into action at a much greater tempo. As in Paris, pride was taken in its mechanical efficiency. On the eleventh of Nivôse, according to the scrupulous accounts kept, thirty-two heads were severed in twenty-five minutes; a week later, twelve heads in just five minutes.

For the most eager Terrorists, though, this was still a messy and inconvenient way of disposing of the political garbage. Citizens in the Streets around the place des Terreaux, on the rue Lafont, for example, were complaining about the blood overflowing the drainage ditch that led from beneath the scaffold. A number of the condemned, then, were executed in mass shootings on the Plaine des Brotteaux—the field beside the Rhone where Montgolfier had made his ascent. Yet another ex-actor, Dorfeuille, presided over some of these *mitraillades*, in which as many as sixty prisoners were tied in a line by ropes and shot at with cannon. Those who were not killed outright by the fire were finished off with sabers, bayonets and rifles. On the fourth of December, Dorfeuille wrote to the President of the Convention that a hundred and thirteen inhabitants of "this new Sodom" had been executed on that single day and in those that followed he hoped another four to five hundred would "expiate their crimes with fire and shot." ...

By the time that the killings in "Ville-Affranchie" had finished, one thousand nine hundred and five people had met their end. ...

* * *

The violence did not stop, however, with the Terror. Richard Cobb has written eloquently of the waves of the Counter-Terror, especially brutal in the Midi and the Rhone Valley; of anarchic murder gangs picking off selected targets implicated in Jacobinism. Republican officials; army officers; members of departmental administrations; conspicuous militants of the popular societies; and, in the south, Protestant farmers and merchants—all became prey for the *sabreurs* of the year III. Corpses were dumped in front of cafés and inns in the Midi or thrown into the Rhone or Saône. In many areas, the Counter-Terrorists would gather together at an inn as if for a day's hunting, and go off in search of their quarry.

Considerable areas of the country—the Midi and Rhone Valley, Brittany and western Normandy—remained in a virtual state of civil war, though the violence now proceeded in a haphazard, hit-and-run fashion rather than by organized insurrection. The great engines of capitalist prosperity in late eighteenth-century France, the Atlantic and Mediterranean ports, had been broken by antifederalist repression and British naval blockade. When Samuel Romilly returned to Bordeaux during the peace of 1802, he was dismayed to find the docks silent and ghostly and grass growing tall between the flagstones of the quai des Chartrons. Marseille and Lyon only recovered as the Revolution receded and the reorientation of the Bonapartist state towards Italy offered new markets and trade routes.…

What had the Revolution accomplished to balance these penalties? Its two great social alterations—the end of the seigneurial regime and the abolition of the guilds—both promised more than they delivered. Though many artisans were undoubtedly happy to be free of the hierarchy of the corporations that constrained their labor and reward, they were, if anything, even more nakedly exposed to the economic inequities that persisted between masters and journeymen. Likewise the abolition of feudalism was more in the way of a legal than a social change and merely completed the evolution from lords to landlords that had been well under way in the old regime. There is no question that peasants were thankful for the end of seigneurial exactions that had imposed a crushing burden of payments on static rural incomes. Equally certainly, they were determined at all costs to oppose their reimposition. But it is hard to say whether the mass of the rural population were measurably better off in 1799 than they had been in 1789. Though the redemption tariff for feudal dues had been abolished outright in 1793, landlords often compensated themselves by various rent strategies that deepened the indebtedness of share-cropping *métayers*. Moreover, the taxes demanded by the Republic —among them the single land tax, the *impot fôncier*—were certainly no lighter than those exacted by the King. Before long the Consulate and Empire would revert to indirect taxes on at least as onerous a scale as under the old regime. All that they were spared, fiscally, were extraordinary poll taxes, including the old *capitation* and the *vingtième*, but this relief was only a consequence of the ever-expanding military frontier. Taxes lifted from the shoulders of the French were now dropped on those of the Italians, Germans and Dutch. When that frontier suddenly retreated in 1814, back to the old limits of the hexagonal *patrie*, the French were stuck with the bill, which, just as in 1789, they adamantly refused to pay, thus sealing the Empire's fate.

Was the world of the village in 1799 so very different from what it had been ten years before? In particular regions of France where there had been heavy emigration and repression, rural life had indeed been emptied of noble dominance. But this obvious rupture disguises a continuity of some importance. It was exactly those sections of the population who had been gaining economically under the old regime that profited most from the sale of noble and church lands. Those sales were declared irreversible, so there was indeed a substantial transfer of wealth. But much of that transfer was *within* the landed classes—extending from well-to-do farmers up to "patriot" nobles who had managed to stay put and actually benefited from the confiscations. Fat cats got fatter.... There were, to be sure, many regions of France where the nobility as a group lost a considerable part of their fortune. But there were also others—in the west, the center and the south—where, as Jean Tulard has shown, lands that remained unsold could be recovered by families who returned in substantial numbers after 1796. Thus, while many of the leading figures in this history ended their lives on the guillotine, many others stayed put and reemerged as the leading notables of their department....

By contrast, the rural poor gained very little at all from the Revolution. Saint-Just's Ventôse laws remained a dead letter and it became harder than ever to pasture animals on common land or gather fuel from the open woods. In all these respects the Revolution was just an interlude in the inexorable modernization of property rights that had been well under way before 1789. No government—that of the Jacobins any more than that of the King —had really answered the cries for help that echoed through the rural *cahiers de doléances* in 1789....

Had the Revolution, at least, created state institutions which resolved the problems that brought down the monar-

chy? Here, too, as de Tocqueville emphasized, it is easier to discern continuities, especially of centralization, than any overwhelming change. In public finance, the creation of a paper currency came to be recognized as a catastrophe beside which the insolvencies of the old regime looked almost picayune. Eventually the Bonapartist Consultate (whose finances were administered overwhelmingly by surviving bureaucrats of the old regime) returned to a metallic system based on Calonne's important monetary reform of 1785 fixing the ratio of silver to gold. Fiscally, too, post-Jacobin France slid inexorably back to the former mixture of loans and indirect as well as direct taxes. The Republic and Empire did no better funding a large army and navy from these domestic sources than had the monarchy and depended crucially on institutionalized extortion from occupied countries to keep the military pump primed.

The Napoleonic prefects have always been recognized as the heirs of the royal *intendants* (and the revolutionary *représentants-en-mission*), brokering administration between central government priorities and the interest of the local notability. Without any question that notability had suffered a violent shock during the height of the Jacobin Terror, especially in the great provincial cities, where, after the federalist revolt, they were virtually exterminated. The constitution of the year III, however, with its reintroduction of tax qualifications for the electoral assemblies, returned authority to those who had, in many places, exercised it continuously between the mid-1780s and 1792. As we have seen, in some small towns, such as Calais, where adroit mayors paid lip service to passing regimes, there was unbroken continuity of office from 1789 through the Restoration.... For these men and countless others like them, the Revolution had been but a brutal though mercifully ephemeral interruption of their social and institutional power....

What killed the monarchy was its inability to create representative institutions through which the state could execute its program of reform. Had the Revolution done any better? On one level, the succession of elected legislatures, from the Estates-General to the National Convention, was one of the most impressive innovations of the Revolution. They took the intensive debate on the shape of governing institutions in France, which had been going on for at least half a century, into the arena of representation itself and articulated its principles with unparalleled eloquence. But for all their virtues as theaters of debate, none of the legislatures ever managed to solve the issue that had bedeviled the old regime: how to create a viable working partnership between the executive and the legislature? Once the Constituent had rejected Mounier and Mirabeau's "British" proposal of drawing ministers from the assembly, it regarded the executive not as the administration of the country, working in good faith, but as a fifth column bent on subverting national sovereignty. With this doomed beginning, the executive and legislative branches of the constitution of 1791 simply intensified the war with each other until their mutual destruction in 1792. The Terror effectively reversed matters by putting the Convention under the thrall of the committees, but still make it impossible to change governments except by violence.

The framers of the constitution of the year III (1795) obviously learned something from this unhappy experience. A two-chamber legislature was introduced,

elected indirectly from colleges in which property was the criterion for membership. A governing council was in theory accountable to the legislature (as indeed the committees had been). In practice, however, the experiment remained darkened by the long shadow of the revolution itself, so that factions inevitably crystallized, not around specific issues of government but plans for the overthrow of the state, hatched either by royalists or neo-Jacobins. With the separate organs of the constitution in paralyzing conflict with each other, violence continued to determine the political direction of the state far more than did elections.

But the violence was, after the year III, no longer coming from the streets and *sections* but from the uniformed army. If one had to look for one indisputable story of transformation in the French Revolution, it would be the creation of the juridical entity of the citizen. But no sooner had this hypothetically free person been invented than his liberties were circumscribed by the police power of the state. This was always done in the name of republican patriotism, but the constraints were no less oppressive for that. Just as Maribeau— and the Robespierre of 1791—had feared, liberties were held hostage to the authority of the warrior state. Though this conclusion might be depressing, it should not really be all that surprising. The Revolution, after all, had begun as a response to a patriotism wounded by the humiliations of the Seven Years' War. It was Vergennes' decision to promote, at the same time, maritime imperialism and continental military power which generated the sense of fiscal panic that overcame the monarchy in its last days. A crucial element—perhaps, indeed, *the* crucial element—in the claim of the revolutionaries of 1789 was that they could better regenerate the *patrie* than could the appointees of the King. From the outset, then, the great continuing strand of militancy was patriotic. Militarized nationalism was not, in some accidental way, the unintended consequence of the French Revolution: it was its heart and soul. It was wholly logical that the multimillionaire inheritors of revolutionary power —the true "new class" of this period of French history—were not some *bourgeoisie conquérante* but *real* conquerors: the Napoleonic marshals, whose fortunes made even those of the surviving dynasts of the nobility look paltry by comparison.

For better or worse, the "modern men" who seemed poised to capture government under Louis XVI—engineers, noble industrialists, scientists, bureaucrats and generals—resumed their march to power once the irritations of revolutionary politics were brushed aside. *"La tragédie, maintenant, c'est la politique,"* claimed Napoleon, who, after the coup d'état that brought him to power in 1799, added his claim to that which had been made by so many optimistic governments before him, that "the Revolution is completed."

At other times, though, he was not so sure. For if he understood that one last achievement of the Revolution had been the creation of a military-technocratic state of immense power and emotional solidarity, he also realized that its *other* principal invention had been a political culture that perennially and directly challenged it. What occurred between 1789 and 1793 was an unprecedented explosion of politics—in speech, print, image and even music—that broke all the barriers that had traditionally circumscribed it. Initially, this had been the monarchy's own doing. For it was in the tens of thousands of little meetings convened to draft *cahiers* and elect deputies to the

Estates-General that French men (and occasionally women) found their voice. In so doing, they became part of a process that tied the satisfaction of their immediate wants into the process of redefining sovereignty.

That was both the opportunity and the problem. Suddenly, subjects were told they had become Citizens; an aggregate of subjects held in place by injustice and intimidation had become a Nation. From this new thing, this Nation of Citizens, justice, freedom and plenty could be not only expected but required. By the same token, should it not materialize, only those who had spurned their citizenship, or who were by their birth or unrepentant beliefs incapable of exercising it, could be held responsible. Before the promise of 1789 could be realized, then, it was necessary to root out Uncitizens.

Thus began the cycle of violence which ended in the smoking obelisk and the forest of guillotines. However much the historian, in the year of celebration, may be tempted to see that violence as an unpleasant "aspect" of the Revolution which ought not to distract from its accomplishments, it would be jejune to do so. From the very beginning—from the summer of 1789—violence was the motor of the Revolution. The journalist Loustalot's knowing exploitation of the punitive murder and mutilation of Foulon and Bertier de Sauvigny conceded nothing in its calculated ferocity to the most extreme harangues of Marat and Hébert. *"Il faut du sang pour cimenter la révolution"* (There must be blood to cement revolution), said Mme Roland, who would herself perish by the logical application of her enthusiasm. While it would be grotesque to implicate the generation of 1789 in the kind of hideous atrocities perpetrated under the Terror, it would be equally naive not to recognize that the former made the latter possible. All the newspapers, the revolutionary festivals, the painted plates; the songs and street theater; the regiments of little boys waving their right arms in the air swearing patriotic oaths in piping voices—all these features of what historians have come to designate the "political culture of the Revolution"—were the products of the same morbid preoccupation with the just massacre and the heroic death.

Historians are also much given to distinguishing between "verbal" violence and the real thing. The assumption seems to be that such men as Javogues and Marat, who were given to screaming at people, calling for death, gloating at the spectacle of heads on pikes or processions of men with their hands tied behind their backs climbing the steps to the *rasoir national* were indulging only in brutal rhetoric. The screamers were not to be compared with such quiet bureaucrats of death as Fouquier-Tinville who did their jobs with stolid, silent efficiency. But the history of "Ville-Affranchie," of the Vendée-Vengé, or of the September massacres suggests in fact a direct connection between all that orchestrated or spontaneous screaming for blood and its copious shedding. It contributed greatly to the complete dehumanization of those who became victims. As "brigands" or the "Austrian whore" or "fanatics" they became nonentities in the Nation of Citizens and not only could but had to be eliminated if it was to survive. Humiliation and abuse, then, were not just Jacobin fun and games; they were the prologues to killing.

Why was the French Revolution like this? Why, from the beginning, was it powered by brutality? The question might seem to be circular since if, in fact, reform had been all that had been required, there would have been no Revolution in the first place. The question nonetheless remains important if we are ever to understand why successive generations of those who tried to stabilize its course—Mirabeau, Barnave, Danton —met with such failure. Was it just that French popular culture was already brutalized before the Revolution and responded to the spectacle of terrifying public punishments handed out by royal justice with its own forms of spontaneous sanguinary retribution? That all naive revolutionaries would do, would be to give the people the chance to exact such retribution and make it part of the regular conduct of politics? This may be part of the explanation, but even a cursory look beyond French borders, and especially over the Channel to Britain, makes it difficult to see France as uniquely damaged, either by a more dangerous distance between rich and poor or indeed by higher rates of crime and popular violence, than places which avoided violent revolution.

Popular revolutionary violence was not some sort of boiling subterranean lava that finally forced its way onto the surface of French politics and then proceeded to scald all those who stepped in its way. Perhaps it would be better to think of the revolutionary elite as rash geologists, themselves gouging open great holes in the crust of polite discourse and then feeding the angry matter through the pipes of their rhetoric out into the open. Volcanoes and steam holes do not seem inappropriate metaphors here, because contemporaries were themselves constantly invoking them. Many of those who were to sponsor or become caught up in violent change were fascinated by seismic violence, by the great primordial eruptions which geologists now said were not part of a single Creation, but which happened periodically in geological time. These events were, to borrow from Burke, both sublime and terrible. And it was perhaps Romanticism, with its addiction to the Absolute and the Ideal; its fondness for the vertiginous and the macabre; its concept of political energy, as, above all, electrical; its obsession with the heart; its preference for passion over reason, for virtue over peace, that supplied a crucial ingredient in the mentality of the revolutionary elite: its association of liberty with wildness. What began with Lafayette's infatuation with the hyena of the Gévaudan surely ended in the ceremonies of the pike-stuck heads.

There was another obsession which converged with this Romanticization of violence: the neoclassical fixation with the patriotic death. The annals of Rome (and occasionally the doomed battles of Athens and Sparta) were the mirrors into which revolutionaries constantly gazed in search of self-recognition. Their France would be Rome reborn, but purified by the benison of the feeling heart. It thus followed, surely, that for such a Nation to be born, many would necessarily die. And both the birth and death would be simultaneously beautiful.

POSTSCRIPT

Was the French Revolution
Worth Its Human Costs?

In many ways, Schama's book was revolutionary and was considered so by his peers in the historical profession. Covering a subject that had been dominated by Marxists, Annalistes, and social historians, he returned to the domain of the historical narrative as his vehicle of expression, something that had lost favor with many of the French Revolution's leading scholars. Secondly, according to the preface from *Citizens*, Schama's focus was "an unfashionable 'topdown' rather than 'bottom up' approach." Finally, although a scholar of impeccable credentials, he was considered an outsider in the field of French Revolution historiography because he had not "been a lifetime toiler in the vineyards of the Revolution," according to Alan Spitzer, in "Narrative's Problems: The Case of Simon Schama," *Journal of Modern History* (March 1993).

The most controversial feature of the French Revolution was the infamous Reign of Terror, and it is a subject that all toilers in the garden of the Revolution have to explain. The horrors of this century (some committed in the name of revolution) demand that the Terror gets the fullest treatment possible. Only then can the question of whether or not the Revolution was worth its human costs be answered. As always, the present and the search for relevance in the past will be the final arbiter. If Kropotkin's work speaks to the spirit of the nineteenth century's era of democratic revolutions, Schama's does the same to the dreams deferred and lives lost to that century's failed revolutions.

To list all of sources on the French Revolution is daunting. William Doyle, *The Oxford History of the French Revolution* (Oxford University Press, 1989) and Donald M. G. Sutherland, *France, 1789–1815: Revolution and Counter-Revolution* (Oxford University Press, 1986) are two scholarly, general accounts of the era. As always, much can be learned from Alexis de Tocqueville, whose *Old Regime and the French Revolution*, first published in the 1850s, could be a useful starting point for a study of French Revolutionary historiography. *The French Revolution and the Birth of Modernity* (University of California Press, 1990), edited by Ferenc Fehar, offers a series of essays about the past, present, and future of French Revolutionary historiography. Finally, the 1984 film *Danton*, which deals with the French Revolution and especially the Terror gone mad, is worth seeing.

ISSUE 15

Did the Meiji Restoration Constitute a Revolution in Nineteenth-Century Japan?

YES: Thomas M. Huber, from *The Revolutionary Origins of Modern Japan* (Stanford University Press, 1981)

NO: Ruth Benedict, from *The Chrysanthemum and the Sword: Patterns of Japanese Culture* (Houghton Mifflin Company, 1989)

ISSUE SUMMARY

YES: Professor Thomas M. Huber states that the Meiji Restoration produced revolutionary changes in nineteenth-century Japan. Examples of reforms that he asserts are the direct result of the Meiji Restoration are cited. It was the Chōshū leaders' dedication to change during this period that enabled these reforms to occur.

NO: Ruth Benedict, one of the twentieth century's leading anthropologists, argues that while substantive changes were brought to Japan by the Meiji Restoration, they were based on Japanese traditions that had been present for centuries.

In 1603, the Japanese closed themselves off from the rest of the world. Fearful of Western economic and religious influences, which could corrupt their traditions and mores, they banned foreign contacts and meted out severe punishments (including death) to any who violated the ban. Part of this process was the outlawing of Christianity as a recognized religion in Japan. This self-imposed exile was to last for more than 250 years.

The decision to isolate was made by the Tokugawa Shogunate (1603–1868), Japan's ruling power during that period. Since the feudal period of Japanese history, the country had been ruled by shoguns, who were hereditary leaders. Like dynastic rulers anywhere, their right to rule lasted as long as their ability to maintain control, and they could always be replaced by another leader who could then establish his family's rule over the country. Thus, for most of this millennium, Japan was ruled by successive shogunates: Kamakura (1192–1333), Ashikaga (1335–1673), and Tokugawa (1603–1868). During this time civil wars were prevalent, as there was no shortage of ambitious men to test the waters of political supremacy.

The shoguns were assisted in their rule by *daimyo,* feudal lords who sometimes posed threats to their masters. The samurai, Japan's legendary warrior class, provided the power base for any shogun. Under this system, the Japanese emperor, whose office dated back to the fifth century C.E., had been reduced to a figurehead. With the modern world casting covetous eyes around the globe, many wondered how long Japan's self-imposed exile would last and whether it would end by outside force or national choice.

In 1853, United States Commodore Matthew Perry arrived in Tokyo, seeking a treaty with the Japanese government. Although the treaty's terms were not seriously detrimental to Japanese hegemony, it did start a trend that resulted in similar treaties with other foreign nations. In Japan, these actions had the dual effect of forcing the Japanese to consider what they could do to limit further Western intervention and causing the rise of nationalist sentiment against foreign elements. This resulted in an overthrow of the Tokugawa shogunate by an alliance of feudal lords in 1866, and the emperor was returned to a position of power in the new Japanese government. The new emperor took the name *Meiji* (enlightened government) and since that time, the period in Japanese history from 1868 to 1912 has been known in the West as the Meiji Restoration. Thus began Japan's modern history.

The changes brought to Japan seemed to be profound; no part of Japanese life escaped the winds of change. Although those who overthrew the Tokugawa government had no set plan—and many of the rebels had diametrically opposed goals and objectives—change was the order of the day. One of the most important outcomes of Meiji rule was the growth of Japan's industrial and military power, presumably accomplished to cope with Western power in Asia. This was completed under the aegis of a highly centralized government, which featured a "top down" power structure. Under such a system, a premium was placed on nationalism as a unifying force. Some of the Meiji-made decisions were to have a positive impact on Japan's modernization; others were to have drastic consequences for the nation and its people.

One basic historical question about the Meiji Restoration concerns the nature of the movement itself. To what extent was it revolutionary? To what extent was it an attempt to restore ancient Japanese values? Two scholars, representing different academic disciplines, come to complementary yet differing viewpoints. Thomas M. Huber states that the Meiji Restoration was led by "men dedicated to reformist principles" whose work constituted "the most dramatic event in Japan's modern history." Ruth Benedict (1887–1948) views the same period and notes the same changes taking place but sees these changes as rooted in the traditional Japanese character and its concomitant values system, which had been around for centuries.

YES

Thomas M. Huber

THE REVOLUTIONARY ORIGINS
OF MODERN JAPAN

INTRODUCTION

The creation of the Meiji Restoration government in 1868, and the sweeping reforms that followed, constitute the most dramatic event in Japan's modern history. Within a decade Japanese leaders established a system of universal education, formed a modern army and navy, and recruited an efficient administrative bureaucracy, both nationally and locally. They developed a network of telegraph and rail communications, and laid the broad fiscal and financial foundations that were needed for rapid industrialization. The Restoration transformed Japan into a modern society by the standards of the day, and rescued her alone among her Asian neighbors from the bondage of colonialism, and from the feudal encumbrances of her own past....

This [selection] will show that the Meiji transformation was accomplished only after a long and daring political insurgency, by men dedicated to reformist principles that were articulated in the 1850's and even earlier. It was over these principles, representing as they did the vision of a new society and the aspirations of a new social class, that the bitter struggles of the 1860's were waged, and for the sake of these principles that the Chōshū men and others put their lives at risk. The Chōshū leaders probably did not see themselves at first as being the foremost champions of these new values, but when fortune so decreed, they proved worthy of the task. In this [selection] the origins of the Meiji state are characterized as revolutionary. If the explanation offered here is correct, they were nothing less....

IDEALISM AND REVOLUTION

... In the decade between 1868 and 1878, the newly constituted imperial government under the Chōshū leaders and their colleagues implemented national reforms at a rapid pace. A central administrative bureaucracy recruited solely on a basis of merit was established immediately. A national university was created in 1869, as if in belated response to Yoshida Shōin's repeated

From Thomas M. Huber, *The Revolutionary Origins of Modern Japan* (Stanford University Press, 1981). Copyright © 1981 by the Board of Trustees of the Leland Stanford Junior University. Reprinted by permission of the Stanford University Press. Notes omitted.

petitioning for one ten years before. An ambitious public educational system was founded in 1872 that would soon open tens of thousands of primary and secondary schools throughout the country. All of the gratuitous privileges of the samurai class were phased out in the 1870's, and official discrimination based on the old classes was completely abolished. Hundreds of semiautonomous feudal domains were legally reconstituted as homogeneous prefectures, and a solid fiscal basis for the new government was achieved by imposing a uniform tax on land. The new tax eliminated and displaced the heavy domainal dues on land that had been the main material foundation of the old aristocratic system. A modern army and navy patterned after Western models and open to talent were equipped and readied for service by 1876. Timely and imaginative reforms were carried out in the judiciary, foreign relations, banking, communications, and many other fields as well.

These sweeping changes altered the essential quality of public life. They brought a vitality and rationality that enlivened all spheres of public action. There soon followed unprecedented growth in crop yields, commerce, and industry There arose a vigorous press and a healthy general clamor for democracy. Philosophy, literature, and the arts, nourished by foreign as well as native inspiration, flourished as never before. Famine was unknown, and modern medical knowledge spread across the land. In the end the reforms would rescue tens of millions of ordinary Japanese from ignorance, disease, and want. Their momentous impact makes the search for their origins a matter of utmost historiographical importance....

The Origins of the Meiji Reforms

The Restoration reforms were carried out swiftly after the "imperial army" entered Edo in 1868. These reforms went smoothly because the principles behind the programs, and even the programs themselves, were understood by many, long before 1868. The Meiji reforms of the 1870's grew out of reformist interests that were already being articulated by political thinkers in Chōshū in the 1850's and even earlier. This is a matter of crucial importance for any analysis of the Meiji Restoration, yet one that historians have tended to overlook.

Virtually all of the later Meiji reforms were guided by two broad principles used by Chōshū thinkers early in the 1850's to justify major departures from the institutional status quo. These were, first, the substitution of preferment by merit for preferment by birth and, second, the redirection of the realm's institutional energies to better meet the people's actual needs in the present and to eliminate lavish expenditure on the empty ritual practices of the past. These principles were developed by local reformers who were trying to overcome organizational contradictions that had long plagued the institutional life of their own domains, especially contradictions associated with university training. By the 1850's these same thinkers had come to realize that solutions that were desirable at the local level would be still more desirable if implemented nationally. [Commodore] Perry's [a United States naval officer] sudden appearance had made such a reconstruction seem not only more useful but also more likely of achievement. Moreover, as the years wore on, the reformers had reached an anguished understanding that the old society could not tolerate the kinds of changes they wanted. In order to stabilize their reforms, they would have to impose them everywhere in a manner that would change permanently the center of gravity of public life.

...Yoshida Shōin [a thinker and educator who plotted against the government] demanded rigorous merit recruitment for the Chōshū academy in 1848. Once Yoshida had developed his basic reformist concepts in the institutional microcosm of the Chōshū university, he was able to apply them rapidly to a broad spectrum of institutional practices that reached far beyond the walls of the local academy. By 1858 he was applying his reformist approaches to the larger task of reordering national institutions. Having reached this point, however, Yoshida was executed before he could take the next step, which was to apply his innovative ideas to the problem of radically reorganizing the apparatus of the central authority itself.

Kusaka Genzui converted his mentor's many discrete proposals into a plan for Restoration by taking this last step. In 1862 he recommended that the Bakufu in its national responsibilities be replaced altogether by a new merit bureaucracy centered on the court. Kusaka substantially described in 1862 the institutional pattern that would be realized by his closest friends and followers in 1868.

The Meiji reforms rested not only on twenty years of reformist articulation but also on ten years of actual experimentation within Chōshū. [Author and historian] W. G. Beasley has referred to these developments as a "Meiji Restoration in miniature." By the mid-1860's, Chōshū had already instituted a large degree of merit selection in government posts, the elimination of almost all rank considerations in favor of ability in han-sponsored education, the nucleus of a Western-style infantry and navy composed of commoners as well as samurai, and a significantly streamlined bureaucracy. This pattern of Chōshū as bellwether continued even after 1868. The abolition of autonomous han, announced in 1871, was piloted by the voluntary surrender of privileges to the Tokyo government by Chōshū and three other reformist han in 1869.

There is another instructive case of the reformers' tendency to use Chōshū as an experimental forerunner. On 12/2/68 Chōshū's activist-controlled government slashed samurai stipends of 1,000 koku or more by 90 percent, and even stipends between 100 and 1,000 koku were all reduced to 100. At the same time, stipends of less than 100 koku were left entirely untouched. Fiscally, this bold stroke was the end of the "men of large stipend" who had been the perennial target of Yoshida Shōin's complaints in the 1850's. This act was a prelude, of course, to the restorationists' abolition of these and other feudal privileges on a national scale several years later.

It is meaningful, then, to speak of the Meiji reforms of the 1870's as representing a well-developed version of the political goals sought by the Chōshū intelligentsia even before they became involved in the activism of the mid-1860's. Rationalizing reforms like those carried out in the 1870's had been the object of the Chōshū activists' study, petitioning, and experimentation for decades....

Modern Idealism and World Revolution

It has sometimes been claimed that the Meiji Restoration was sui generis, a type of revolutionary transformation unique to Japan. Although it is true that the Restoration does not resemble the familiar "bourgeois" and "proletarian" archetypes of revolutionary change, there are elements of similarity linking the Meiji experience with the "great" revolutions of the West. Consideration of such similarities may yield some interesting comparative insights. I will try to highlight some of these by applying to Western revolutions the Japanese paradigm... instead of the reverse approach that has been more common. I will sketch the paradigm, then apply it. I will argue that the utopian goals and ideal motives that distinguished the Chōshū restorationists have been present in most of the great revolutionary upheavals of recent history.

Late Tokugawa society represented a neofeudal or "absolutist" stage of development, characterized by sophisticated social organization and considerable surplus wealth. This was so especially in the vicinity of the country's national and regional metropolises. Much of this wealth went to the lavish support of a politically powerful but functionally noncontributive aristocracy. Coexisting with these privileged few was a more numerous service class, who held only minor aristocratic perquisites. These persons, literate and resourceful, actually managed and produced the growing social wealth, while absorbing little of it themselves.

This inequitable state of affairs was stable, because it was sanctioned by custom and tradition, and because confident aristocratic elements used their political power boldly to protect privilege, whereas the service strata lacked leverage, confidence, and traditional sanction.

This stable traditional pattern was shaken by the sudden intrusion of a formidable external threat: Commodore Perry. The traditional assumptions justifying aristocratic social organization

were thus critically undermined causing a shift of the center of political gravity toward the service classes. Service elements enjoyed two advantages that allowed them to parlay this security crisis into a large-scale social reconstruction: ideological competence and paramilitary opportunity. The basic conceptual tools needed to plan and legitimize a new society had been forged a generation and more before Perry, and so were readily available to many when the moment came. In addition, the reformers were fortunate in being able to mobilize an effective army, relying on a combination of service-class loyalties and various forms of sentimental nationalism.

The restorationists' determined ideological activity, combined with their military power, enabled them in time to overwhelm the old order. They then appropriated the country's large aristocratic surpluses as planned and invested them in new forms of socially creative activity, including industrialization. The result was a new regime with startling advantages. The new society was more equitable, orderly, and provident for everyone.

Absolutist society is tormented by a paradox: its means have become modern, but its ends are still feudal. Its wealth is generated by firm, modern institutions, but gathered in by a small class of aristocratic grandees and financial notables. This leads to other paradoxes, namely, a tremendous artificial disparity between rich and poor in general, and the emergence of a disciplined service intelligentsia that selflessly creates and harvests all the growing wealth, but is nonetheless excluded, like the ordinary people, from its major benefits. Two other circumstances, if added to this milieu, will produce a revolutionary reconstruction: a widespread ideological preparation for change among the public, to which is added a national security crisis (or sense that the national interest is being compromised). This is what happened in the Japanese case.

Let us consider the origins of the innovative class that brought the Restoration about. It had arisen as a consequence of the increasingly sophisticated institutional growth that characterized much of the long Tokugawa era. Its ranks included scholars, administrators, physicians, clerics, military technicians, and even a few poets. Although it had come into existence gradually over the course of the preceding two centuries, this group already represented a substantial and active minority in the society of perhaps 10 to 15 percent of the population.

The Meiji Restoration can be understood as a revolution carried out by this modern social class, which found itself oppressed by the institutional configurations of the late feudal status quo. It bears a resemblance to one of the four social classes described by Max Weber [a German sociologist and political economist]. In the middle ground between small merchants and persons "privileged through property," Weber identified a social class that consisted of "propertyless intelligentsia," "specialists," and "civil servants." The intelligentsia, Weber maintained, was a major social category, essentially distinct, in both its social attributes and its political interests, from other social groups.

In other words, the Japanese intelligentsia was a modern social class that had emerged from a long process of institutional evolution. This modernizing evolutionary process is that described by Weber as "rationalization" and "bureaucratization." (It was in this connection that Weber once asserted that the Christian monk was the first modern man.) The restorationists were a class produced by this Weberian dynamic of institutional rationalization and increasing social efficiency, and who had an interest both in carrying that process further, and in terminating the lingering neofeudal (or "patrimonial") misappropriation of its hard-won benefits.

Although this group was obviously interested in a more equitable distribution of material rewards, ideal values must nevertheless be regarded as the key to the distinctive identity and conduct of this class. Their selfless dynamism, in both service and rebellion, is hard to explain without reference to ideal interests and rewards. The realm's disciplined new intelligentsia was prepared to give much yet take little because it was motivated not by simple quid pro quo advantages, but rather by "loyalty" (chūkō), or what Weber called "vocation." They were encouraged throughout to respond to ideal values, not material values. Thus the high social cost of service functions of modern quality was borne at first in such a way as not to undermine the premises of aristocratic social organization, by the remarkable expedient of paying for it with "ideal" rewards. (This pattern also dictated the necessity of extreme thrift as a value in the private lives of much of the service class, thus imparting a "puritanical" quality to the ethos of that class.) The immense advantages for an aristocratic elite that could perpetrate such an arrangement on its ablest servants are obvious. Yet it would not be proper to assume that the servants themselves were simply exploited by this. They, after all, had the highest gratification of all: doing right (or believing that they did).

The cultivated idealism of the intelligentsia by and by came to have a momentum of its own, however. The intellectual capabilities of the service classes and their idealist values eventually combined to yield utopian goals. It occurred to philosophers of the service echelon that the selfless rationality by which they gathered the new surplus wealth might also be applied to the allocation of that wealth in such a way as to create a more dynamic society and general enrichment. The loyalties of the service class eventually shifted, from the transitional absolutist institutions that had brought them into being, toward the more modern forms that were still only imagined. A satisfying utopian program, a strong ideal interest in the well-being of all, and consequently a very high tolerance for personal risk, are the essential characteristics of modernizing intelligentsia-based revolution that distinguish it from political agitation on the part of other interest groups. Modern idealism is the hallmark of service revolution.

Recent work by the Japanese scholar Ueyama Shumpei suggests that the phenomenon of service revolution was not unique to Bakumatsu Japan, and that elements of it can be found in the French Revolution. Ueyama observed close institutional similarities between the minor royal officials and priests who made up the revolutionary majority in France's Estates General in 1789 and the "lower-class samuari" who brought about the Meiji Restoration. He found close parallels in the language of the revolutionary ideologist Abbé Sieyès and the Mito scholar Fujita Tōko regarding the unsatisfactory relationship between public service echelons and the privileged minority.

Ueyama's analysis is directly supported by the work of Alfred Cobban, John McManners, and others. In his *Myth of the French Revolution,* Cobban pointed out that the "bourgeois" revolution in 1789 is hard to find, and suggested that the essence of the revolutionary phenomenon in France may have been something very different, namely, a rebellion of "minor officials." The militant leaders and followers of the Third Estate, whether from the church, the military, or the royal administration, fell overwhelmingly into this category. In Cobban's words, "a class of officials and professional men moved up from the minor to the major posts in government and dispossessed the minions of an effete Court: this was what the bourgeois revolution meant."

There were, of course, enormous differences in the respective ideologies and forms of violence that emerged in the Meiji Restoration and in the French Revolution. Nevertheless, the French case, like the Japanese case, sprang from many decades of growing awareness among the nation's leading thinkers that a better world was possible. From the days of Montesquieu and Voltaire on, Enlightenment philosophers began with growing excitement to hammer out among themselves what liberty and equality could really mean. Ideas were everywhere for reconstructing every conceivable institutional practice.

When in 1789 only a courageous stand was needed to bring these ideas into reality, thousands stood up for revolution without looking back. In the French Revolution as in the Japanese Restoration, privileges relating solely to birth were aggressively eliminated, and in both cases, thousands of career opportunities were suddenly opened to "talent." Both cases involved sudden and conscious institutional reform in the direction of radical bureaucratization, and other structural ameliorations that would lead quickly to a phenomenal increase in general welfare and prosperity.

The European revolution most explicitly associated with intelligentsia activity is the Russian Revolution of 1917. Ideologies and forms of violence once again differed markedly from other cases. Still, the leadership role of the intelligentsia was unmistakable. Beginning with Alexander Herzen on the institutional side and [Mikhail] Bakunin and [Peter] Kropotkin on the theoretical side, Russian thinkers were embarked for much of the nineteenth century on a quest for new utopian values and needed structural reforms. Although even discussing these matters involved great risk, many proponents of a new Russia were soon going beyond this to sacrifice themselves in lone terrorist assaults on the living symbols of old regime authority. These thinkers and activists were the *raznochintsy,* and their ranks were filled primarily by "clergy" and "the minor professional and bureaucratic classes." Martin Malia has seen the Russian intelligentsia as a "class" with its own autonomous interests. The boundaries of that class, as in the French and Japanese cases, were defined institutionally, that is, by university experience and institutional condition.

The upheaval of 1917 led to a "rational" restructuring of Russian society leading among other things to large-scale industrial development. Thousands of careers were suddenly open to talent, while aristocratic privileges, material and political, were swept away. The intelligentsia itself did benefit from this, but the Russian masses were perhaps the greatest beneficiaries, and there is no doubt that many of the revolutionaries shared idealistic motives.

A few years ago, Michael Walzer published a well-received study entitled *Revolution of the Saints.* Walzer argued that England's seventeenth-century revolution against monarchical authority was carried out by a "Puritan intelligentsia." These men had the kind of Calvinist calling described by Weber, but it was not directed at economic activity. Rather it was aimed at political activity, such that in the evolutionary course of things they had as a group finally come to wield more power in the state than the prince and the peerage. Moreover, they achieved success by engaging in a disciplined form of "radical politics," leading Walzer to characterize puritanical "radicalism" as a "general historical phenomenon." He has suggested the need for a "systematic comparison of Puritans, Jacobins, and Bolsheviks."

The utopian dimension was prominent in the English Revolution. Francis Bacon in his *New Atlantis* of 1626 had described a perfect land in the Americas where philosophers in the House of Solomon would assure the health and welfare of the people. Many Puritan intellectuals in Bacon's day believed that with God's inspiration they could remake society and create a paradise on earth. (The contemporaneous rise of modern science was one consequence of this attitude.) This was an exhilarating prospect for them, and in the political upheaval and Great Migration to North America that followed, many of the institutional reforms they envisioned came true.

Service revolution deriving from a Weberian evolutionary dynamic may be more than a Japanese idiosyncrasy. Rebellion of the service intelligentsia for its own reasons may have been a powerful or even decisive factor in each of the great revolutions of Europe. In Japan as in Europe, and now in new nations as ideologically diverse as Vietnam and Israel, the Weberian, or organizational, transformation has preceded the large-scale industrial, or Marxist, transformation. In each case, the transformational upheaval has generally been carried out by service elements, often with minor aristocratic perquisites of their own, operating in the name of utopian values against a powerful aristocratic (or colonial) stratum, in circumstances of a widely perceived external threat to the national welfare.

In the typical Third World case, impoverished proletarians are nowhere to be seen. Rather, students, professors, clergymen, technicians, teachers, young officers, and the like join to demand reform in the name of transcendent social values. Despite great risk, they strive relentlessly against a small class of estateholders and financial grandees who are thought to enjoy close ties with foreign interests. The reformers' insurgency has often been focused on a monarch figure who derives lavish personal income from public functions owned by himself, and who serves as the absolutist guarantor of a larger system of social privilege. Signs of this dynamic have been apparent in recent years in Nicaragua, Ethiopia, Iran, and elsewhere. The insurgent group may seek to organize ordinary people for paramilitary activity, and always fashions a judicious combination of traditional folk belief and modern social philosophy such as will accommodate both the demands of sentimental nationalism and the insurgents' program of social rationalization. This kind of pattern conforms closely to the assumptions of service revolution.

In both European and non-European cases, the dynamics of idealist service revolution have gone largely unnoticed in the past, because so little attention has been paid to developing the theoretical paradigms against which they could be perceived. Careful scrutiny of the Meiji Restoration, where the dynamic of service revolution is so clearly present, may provide the essential contours of such a paradigm.

NO

Ruth Benedict

THE MEIJI REFORM

The battlecry that ushered in the modern era in Japan was *Sonno joi,* 'Restore the Emperor and expel the Barbarian.' It was a slogan that sought to keep Japan uncontaminated by the outside world and to restore a golden age of the tenth century before there had been a 'dual rule' of Emperor and Shogun. The Emperor's court at Kyoto was reactionary in the extreme. The victory of the Emperor's party meant to his supporters the humiliation and expulsion of foreigners. It meant reinstatement of traditional ways of life in Japan. It meant that 'reformers' would have no voice in affairs. The great Outside Lords, the daimyo [feudal barons] of Japan's strongest fiefs who spearheaded the overthrow of the Shogunate, thought of the Restoration as a way in which they, instead of the Tokugawa, could rule Japan. They wanted a mere change of personnel. The farmers wanted to keep more of the rice they raised but they hated 'reforms.' The samurai wanted to keep their pensions and be allowed to use their swords for greater glory. The merchants, who financed the Restoration forces, wanted to expand mercantilism but they never arraigned the feudal system.

When the anti-Tokugawa forces triumphed and 'dual rule' was ended in 1868 by the Restoration of the Emperor, the victors were committed, by Western standards, to a fiercely conservative isolationist policy. From the first the regime followed the opposite course. It had been in power hardly a year when it abolished the daimyo's right of taxation in all fiefs. It called in the land-registers and appropriated to itself the peasants' tax of '40 per cent to the daimyo.' This expropriation was not without compensation. The government allotted to each daimyo the equivalent of half his normal income. At the same time also the government freed the daimyo of the support of his samurai retainers and of the expenses of public works. The samurai retainers, like the daimyo, received pensions from the government. Within the next five years all legal inequality among the classes was summarily abolished, insignia and distinctive dress of caste and class were outlawed—even queues had to be cut—the outcasts were emancipated, the laws against alienation of land withdrawn, the barriers that had separated fief from fief were removed

From Ruth Benedict, *The Chrysanthemum and the Sword: Patterns of Japanese Culture* (Houghton Mifflin, 1989). Copyright © 1946 by Ruth Benedict; renewed 1974 by Donald G. Freeman. Reprinted by permission of Houghton Mifflin Company. Notes omitted.

and Buddhism was disestablished. By 1876 the daimyo and samurai pensions were commuted to lump sum payments which were to become due in five to fifteen years. These payments were either large or small according to the fixed income these individuals had drawn in Tokugawa days and the money made it possible for them to start enterprises in the new non-feudal economy. 'It was the final stage in the sealing of that peculiar union of merchants and financial princes with the feudal or landed princes which was already evident in the Tokugawa period.'

These remarkable reforms of the infant Meiji regime were not popular. There was far more general enthusiasm for an invasion of Korea from 1871 to 1873 than for any of these measures. The Meiji government not only persisted in its drastic course of reform, it killed the project of the invasion. Its program was so strongly opposed to the wishes of a great majority of those who had fought to establish it that by 1877 Saigo, their greatest leader, had organized a full-scale rebellion against the government. His army represented all the pro-feudal longings of Imperial supporters which had from the first year of the Restoration been betrayed by the Meiji regime. The government called up a nonsamurai voluntary army and defeated Saigo's samurai. But the rebellion was an indication of the extent of the dissatisfaction the regime aroused in Japan.

The farmers' dissatisfaction was equally marked. There were at least 190 agrarian revolts between 1868 and 1878, the first Meiji decade. In 1877 the new government made its first tardy moves to lessen the great tax burden upon the peasants, and they had reason to feel that the regime had failed them. The farmers

objected in addition to the establishment of schools, to conscription, to land surveys, to having to cut their queues, to legal equality of the outcasts, to the drastic restrictions on official Buddhism, to calendar reforms and to many other measures which changed their settled ways of life.

Who, then, was this 'government' which undertook such drastic and unpopular reforms? It was that 'peculiar union' in Japan of the lower samurai and the merchant class which special Japanese institutions had fostered even in feudal times. They were the samurai retainers who had learned statecraft as chamberlains and stewards for the daimyos, who had run the feudal monopolies in mines, textiles, pasteboards and the like. They were merchants who had bought samurai status and spread knowledge of productive techniques in that class. This samurai-merchant alliance rapidly put to the fore able and self-confident administrators who drew up the Meiji policies and planned their execution. The real problem, however, is not from what class they came but how it happened that they were so able and so realistic. Japan, just emerging from medievalism in the last half of the nineteenth century and as weak then as Siam is today, produced leaders able to conceive and to carry out one of the most statesmanlike and successful jobs ever attempted in any nation. The strength, and the weakness too, of these leaders was rooted in traditional Japanese character and it is the chief object of this [selection] to discuss what that character was and is. Here we can only recognize how the Meiji statesmen went about their undertaking.

They did not take their task to be an ideological revolution at all. They treated it as a job. Their goal as they conceived it was to make Japan into a country which must be reckoned with. They were not iconoclasts. They did not revile and beggar the feudal class. They tempted them with pensions large enough to lure them into eventual support of the regime. They finally ameliorated the peasants' condition; their ten-year tardiness appears to have been due rather to the pitiful condition of the early Meiji treasury than to a class rejection of peasants' claims upon the regime.

The energetic and resourceful statesmen who ran the Meiji government rejected, however, all ideas of ending hierarchy in Japan. The Restoration had simplified the hierarchal order by placing the Emperor at its apex and eliminating the Shogun. The post-Restoration statesmen, by abolishing the fiefs, eliminated the conflict between loyalty to one's own seigneur and to the State. These changes did not unseat hierarchal habits. They gave them a new locus. 'Their Excellencies,' the new leaders of Japan, even strengthened centralized rule in order to impose their own workmanlike programs upon the people. They alternated demands from above with gifts from above and in this way they managed to survive. But they did not imagine that they had to cater to a public opinion which might not want to reform the calendar or to establish public schools or to outlaw discrimination against the outcasts.

One of these gifts from above was the Constitution of Japan, which was given by the Emperor to his people in 1889. It gave the people a place in the State and established the Diet. It was drawn up with great care by Their Excellencies after critical study of the varied constitutions of the Western World. The writers of it however, took 'every possible precaution to guard against popular interference and the invasion of public opinion.' The very bureau which drafted it was a part of the Imperial Household Department and was therefore sacrosanct.

Meiji statesmen were quite conscious about their objective. During the eighteen-eighties Prince Ito, framer of the Constitution, sent the Marquis Kido to consult [evolutionary philosopher] Herbert Spencer in England on the problems lying ahead of Japan and after lengthy conversations Spencer wrote Ito his judgments. On the subject of hierarchy Spencer wrote that Japan had in her traditional arrangements an incomparable basis for national well-being which should be maintained and fostered. Traditional obligations to superiors, he said, and beyond all to the Emperor, were Japan's great opportunity. Japan could move forward solidly under its 'superiors' and defend itself against the difficulties inevitable in more individualistic nations. The great Meiji statesmen were well satisfied with this confirmation of their own convictions. They meant to retain in the modern world the advantages of observing 'proper station.' They did not intend to undermine the habit of hierarchy.

In every field of activity, whether political or religious or economic, the Meiji statesmen allocated the duties of 'proper station' between the State and the people. Their whole scheme was so alien to arrangements in the United States or England that we usually fail to recognize its basic points. There was, of course, strong rule from above which did not have to follow the lead of public opinion. This government was administered by a top hierarchy and this could never include elected persons.

At this level the people could have no voice. In 1940 the top government hierarchy consisted of those who had 'access' to the Emperor, those who constituted his immediate advisors, and those whose high appointments bore the privy seal. These last included Cabinet Ministers, prefectual governors, judges, chiefs of national bureaus and other like responsible officers. No elected official had any such status in the hierarchy and it would have been out of the question for elected members of the Diet, for instance, to have any voice in selecting or approving a Cabinet Minister or head of the Bureau of Finance or of Transportation. The elected Lower House of the Diet was a voice of the people which had the not inconsiderable privilege of interrogating and criticizing the Higher Officials, but it had no real voice in appointments or in decisions or in budgetary matters and it did not initiate legislation. The Lower House was even checked by a non-elected Upper House, half of them nobility and another quarter Imperial appointees. Since its power to approve legislation was about equal to that of the Lower House, a further hierarchal check was provided.

Japan therefore ensured that those who held high government posts remain 'Their Excellencies,' but this does not mean that there was not self-government in its 'proper place.' In all Asiatic nations, under whatever regime, authority from above always reaches down and meets in some middle ground local self-government rising from below. The differences between different countries all concern matters of how far up democratic accountability reaches, how many or few its responsibilities are and whether local leadership remains responsive to the whole community or is preempted by local magnates to the disadvantage of the people. Tokugawa Japan had, like China, tiny units of five to ten families, called in recent times the *tonari gumi*, which were the smallest responsible units of the population. The head of this group of neighboring families assumed leadership in their own affairs, was responsible for their good behavior, had to turn in reports of any doubtful acts and surrender any wanted individual to the government. Meiji statesmen at first abolished these, but they were later restored and called the *tonari gumi*. In the towns and cities the government has sometimes actively fostered them, but they seldom function today in villages. The hamlet (*buraku*) units are more important. The buraku were not abolished nor were they incorporated as units in the government. They were an area in which the State did not function. These hamlets of fifteen or so houses continue even today to function in an organized fashion through their annually rotating headmen, who 'look after hamlet property, supervise hamlet aid given to families in the event of a death or a fire, decide the proper days for co-operative work in agriculture, house-building or road repair, and announce by ringing the fire bell or beating two blocks together in a certain rhythm the local holidays and rest days.' These headmen are not responsible, as in some Asiatic nations, also for collecting the State taxes in their community and they do not therefore have to carry this onus. Their position is quite unambivalent; the function in the area of democratic responsibility.

Modern civil government in Japan officially recognizes local administration of cities, towns and villages. Elected 'elders' choose a responsible headman who serves as the representative of the community in all dealings with the State,

292 / 15. DID THE MEIJI RESTORATION CONSTITUTE A REVOLUTION?

which is represented by the prefectural and national governments. In the villages the headman is an old resident, a member of a land-owning farm family. He serves at a financial loss but the prestige is considerable. He and the elders are responsible for village finances, public health, maintenance of the schools and especially for property records and individual dossiers. The village office is a busy place; it has charge of the spending of the State's appropriation for primary school education for all children and of the raising and spending of its own much larger local share of school expenses, management and rent of village-owned property, land improvement and afforestation, and records of all property transactions, which become legal only when they are properly entered at this office. It must also keep an up-to-date record of residence, marital status, birth of children, adoption, any encounter with the law and other facts on each individual who still maintains official residence in the community, besides a family record which shows similar data about one's family. Any such information is forwarded from any part of Japan to one's official home office and is entered on one's dossier. Whenever one applies for a position or is tried before a judge or in any way is asked for identification, one writes one's home community office or visits it and obtains a copy to submit to the interested person. One does not face lightly the possibility of having a bad entry inscribed on one's own or one's family's dossier.

The city, town, and village therefore has considerable responsibility. It is a community responsibility. Even in the nineteen-twenties, when Japan had national political parties, which in any country means an alternation of tenure between 'ins' and 'outs,' local administration generally remained untouched by this development and was directed by elders acting for the whole community. In three respects, however, local administrations do not have autonomy; all judges are nationally appointed, all police and school teachers are employees of the State. Since most civil cases in Japan are still settled by arbitration or through go-betweens, the courts of law figure very little in local administration. Police are more important. Police have to be on hand at public meetings but these duties are intermittent and most of their time is devoted to keeping the personal and property records. The State may transfer policemen frequently from one post to another so that they may remain outsiders without local ties. School teachers also are transferred. The State regulates every detail of the schools, and, as in France, every school in the country is studying on the same day the same lesson from the same textbook. Every school goes through the same calisthenics to the same radio broadcast at the same hour of the morning. The community does not have local autonomy over schools or police or courts of justice....

The true difference between the Japanese form of government and such cases in Western Europe lies not in form but in functioning. The Japanese rely on old habits of deference set up in their past experience and formalized in their ethical system and in their etiquette. The State can depend upon it that, when their Excellencies function in their 'proper place,' their prerogatives will be respected, not because the policy is approved but because it is wrong in Japan to override boundaries between prerogatives. At the topmost level of policy 'popular opinion' is out of place. The government asks only 'popular support.' When the State stakes out its own official field in the area of local concern, also, its jurisdiction is accepted with deference. The State, in all its domestic functions, is not a necessary evil as it is so generally felt to be in the United States. The State comes nearer, in Japanese eyes, to being the supreme good.

The State, moreover, is meticulous in recognizing 'proper place' for the will of the people. In areas of legitimate popular jurisdiction it is not too much to say that the Japanese State has had to woo the people even for their own good. The State agricultural extension agent can act with about as little authoritarianism in improving old methods of agriculture as his counterpart can in Idaho. The State official advocating State-guaranteed farmers' credit associations or farmers' cooperatives for buying and selling must hold long-drawn-out round-tables with the local notables and then abide by their decision. Local affairs require local management. The Japanese way of life allocates proper authority and defines its proper sphere. It gives much greater deference—and therefore freedom of action —to 'superiors' than Western cultures do, but they too must keep their station. Japan's motto is: Everything in its place.

In the field of religion the Meiji statesmen made much more bizarre formal arrangements than in government. They were however carrying out the same Japanese motto. The State took as its realm a worship that specifically upholds the symbols of national unity and superiority, and in all the rest it left freedom of worship to the individual. This area of national jurisdiction was State Shinto. Since it was concerned with proper respect to national symbols, as saluting the flag is in the United States, State

Shinto was, they said, 'no religion.' Japan therefore could require it of all citizens without violating the Occidental dogma of religious freedom any more than the United States violates it in requiring a salute to the Stars and Stripes. It was a mere sign of allegiance. Because it was 'not religion,' Japan could teach it in the schools without risk of Occidental criticism. State Shinto in the schools becomes the history of Japan from the age of the gods and the veneration of the Emperor, 'ruler from ages eternal.' It was State-supported, State-regulated. All other areas of religion, even denominational or cult Shinto, to say nothing of Buddhist and Christian sects, were left to individual initiative much as in the United States. The two areas were even administratively and financially separated; State Shinto was in the charge of its own bureau in the Home Office and its priests and ceremonies and shrines were supported by the State. Cult Shinto and Buddhist and Christian sects were the concern of a Bureau of Religion in the Department of Education and were supported by voluntary contributions of members.

... [T]he Japanese people carry on the great sects and fête-days which are close to their hearts. Buddhism remains the religion of the great mass of the people and the various sects with their different teachings and founding prophets are vigorous and omnipresent. Even Shinto has its great cults which stand outside of State Shinto. Some were strongholds of pure nationalism even before the government in the nineteen-thirties took up the same position, some are faith-healing sects often compared to Christian Science, some hold by Confucian tenets, some have specialized in trance states and pilgrimages to sacred mountain shrines. Most of the popular fête-days, too, have been left outside of State Shinto. The people on such days throng to the shrines. . . .

Meiji statesmen, . . . carefully marked out the area of State functioning in government and of State Shinto in the field of religion. They left other areas to the people but they ensured to themselves as top officials of the new hierarchy dominance in matters which in their eyes directly concerned the State. In setting up the Armed Forces they had a similar problem. They rejected, as in other fields, the old caste system but in the Army they went farther than in civilian life. They outlawed in the Armed Services even the respect language of Japan, though in actual practice old usage of course persists. The Army also promoted to officer's rank on the basis of merit, not of family, to a degree which could hardly be put into effect in other fields. Its reputation among Japanese in this respect is high and apparently deservedly so. It was certainly the best means available by which to enlist popular support for the new Army. Companies and platoons, too, were formed from neighbors of the same region and peacetime military service was spent at posts close to one's home. This meant not only that local ties were conserved but that every man who went through Army training spent two years during which the relationship between officers and men, between second-year men and first-year men, superseded that between samurai and farmers or between rich and poor. The Army functioned in many ways as a democratic leveler and it was in many ways a true people's army. Whereas the Army in most other nations is depended upon as the strong arm to defend the status quo, in Japan the Army's sympathy with the small peasant has lined it up in repeated protests against the great financiers and industrialists.

Japanese statesmen may not have approved of all the consequences of building up a people's army but it was not at this level where they saw fit to ensure Army supremacy in the hierarchy. That objective they made sure of by arrangements in the very highest spheres. They did not write these arrangements into the Constitution but continued as customary procedure the already recognized independence of the High Command from the civil government. The Ministers of the Army and the Navy, in contrast for instance to the head of the Foreign Office and domestic bureaus, had direct access to the Emperor himself and could therefore use his name in forcing through their measures. They did not need to inform or consult their civilian colleagues of the Cabinet. In addition the Armed Services held a whip hand over any Cabinet. They could prevent the formation of a Cabinet they distrusted by the simple expedient of refusing to release generals and admirals to hold military portfolios in the Cabinet. Without such high officers of the active service to fill the positions of Army and Navy Ministers there could be no cabinet; no civilians or retired officers could hold these posts. Similarly, if the Armed Services were displeased at any act of the Ministry, they could cause its dissolution by recalling their Cabinet representatives. On this highest policy level the top military hierarchy made sure that it need brook no interference. If it needed any further guarantees it had one in the Constitution: 'If the Diet fails to approve the budget submitted, the budget of the previous year is automatically available to the Government for the current year.' The exploit of the Army in occupying

Manchuria when the Foreign Office had promised that the Army would not take this step was only one of the instances when the Army hierarchy successfully supported its commanders in the field in the absence of agreed Cabinet policy. As in other fields, so with the Army: where hierarchal privileges are concerned the Japanese tend to accept all the consequences, not because of agreement about the policy but because they do not countenance overriding boundaries between prerogatives.

In the field of industrial development Japan pursued a course which is unparalleled in any Western nation. Again their Excellencies arranged the game and set the rules. They not only planned, they built and financed on government money the industries they decided they needed. A State bureaucracy organized and ran them. Foreign technicians were imported and Japanese were sent to learn abroad. Then when, as they said, these industries were 'well organized and business was prosperous,' the government disposed of them to private firms. They were sold gradually at 'ridiculously low prices' to a chosen financial oligarchy, the famous Zaibatsu, chiefly the Mitsui and Mitsubishi families. Her statesmen judged that industrial development was too important to Japan to be entrusted to laws of supply and demand or to free enterprise. But this policy was in no way due to socialistic dogma; it was precisely the Zaibatsu who reaped the advantages. What Japan accomplished was that with the minimum of fumbling and wastage the industries she deemed necessary were established.

Japan was by these means able to revise 'the normal order of the starting point and succeeding stages of capitalist production.' Instead of beginning with the production of consumer goods and light industry, she first undertook key heavy industries. Arsenals, shipyards, iron works, construction of railroads had priority and were rapidly brought to a high stage of technical efficiency. Not all of these were released to private hands and vast military industries remained under government bureaucracy and were financed by special government accounts.

In this whole field of the industries to which the government gave priority, the small trader or the non-bureaucratic manager had no 'proper place.' Only the State and the great trusted and politically favored financial houses operated in this area. But as in other fields of Japanese life there was a free area in industry too. These were the 'leftover' industries which operated with minimum capitalization and maximum utilization of cheap labor. These light industries could exist without modern technology and they do. They function through what we used to call in the United States home sweat-shops. A small-time manufacturer buys the raw material, lets it out to a family or a small shop with four or five workers, takes it back again, repeats by letting it out again for another step in processing and at last sells the product to the merchant or exporter. In the nineteen-thirties no less than 53 per cent of all persons industrially employed in Japan were working in this way in shops and homes having less than five workers. Many of these workers are protected by old paternalistic customs of apprenticeship and many are mothers who in Japan's great cities sit in their own homes over their piecework with their babies strapped on their backs.

This duality of Japanese industry is quite as important in Japanese ways of life as duality in the field of government or religion. It is as if, when Japanese statesmen decided that they needed an aristocracy of finance to match their hierarchies in other fields, they built up for them the strategic industries, selected the politically favored merchant houses and affiliated them in their 'proper stations' with the other hierarchies. It was not part of their plan for government to cut loose from these great financial houses and the Zaibatsu profited by a kind of continued paternalism which gave them not only profit but high place. It was inevitable, granted old Japanese attitudes toward profit and money, that a financial aristocracy should fall under attack from the people, but the government did what it could to build it up according to accepted ideas of hierarchy. It did not entirely succeed, for the Zaibatsu has been under attack from the so-called Young Officers' groups of the Army and from rural areas. But it still remains true that the greatest bitterness of Japanese public opinion is turned not against the Zaibatsu but against the *narikin*. Narikin is often translated 'nouveau riche' but that does not do justice to the Japanese feeling.... [I]n Japan a narikin is a term taken from Japanese chess and means a pawn promoted to queen. It is a pawn rampaging about the board as a 'big shot.' It has no hierarchal right to do any such thing. The narikin is believed to have obtained his wealth by defrauding or exploiting others and the bitterness directed toward him is as far as possible from the attitude in the United States toward the 'home boy who makes good.' Japan provided a place in her hierarchy for great wealth and kept an alliance with it; when wealth is achieved in the field outside, Japanese public opinion is bitter against it.

The Japanese, therefore, order their world with constant reference to hierarchy. In the family and in personal relations, age, generation, sex, and class dictate proper behavior. In government, religion, the Army, and industry, areas are carefully separated into hierarchies where neither the higher nor the lower may without penalty overstep their prerogatives. As long as 'proper station' is maintained the Japanese carry on without protest. They feel safe. They are of course often not 'safe' in the sense that their best good is protected but they are 'safe' because they have accepted hierarchy as legitimate. It is as characteristic of their judgment on life as trust in equality and free enterprise is of the American way of life.

Japan's nemesis came when she tried to export her formula for 'safety.' In her own country hierarchy fitted popular imagination because it had moulded it. Ambitions could only be such as could take shape in that kind of a world. But it was a fatal commodity for export. Other nations resented Japan's grandiloquent claims as an impertinence and worse. Japan's officers and troops, however, in each occupied country continued to be shocked that the inhabitants did not welcome them. Was Japan not offering them a place, however lowly, in a hierarchy and was not hierarchy desirable even for those on the lower steps of it? Their War Services continued to get out series of war films which figured China's 'love' for Japan under the image of desperate and disordered Chinese girls who found happiness by falling in love with a Japanese soldier or a Japanese engineer. It was a far cry from the Nazi version of conquest yet it was no more successful in the long run. They could not exact from other nations what they had exacted of themselves. It was their mistake that they thought they could. They did not recognize that the system of Japanese morality which had fitted them to 'accept their proper station' was something they could not count on elsewhere. Other nations did not have it. It is a genuine product of Japan. Her writers take this system of ethics so much for granted that they do not describe it and a description of it is necessary before one can understand the Japanese.

POSTSCRIPT

Did the Meiji Restoration Constitute a Revolution in Nineteenth-Century Japan?

An interesting question raised by this issue is the nature and meaning of the term *revolution*. The criteria used would have a significant impact on the debate. A good place to begin this issue would be a brief exploration of the term revolution, with comparisons made with other noted world revolutions.

Sources of modern Japanese history abound. A general reference work is Marius B. Jansen, ed., *The Cambridge History of Japan, vol. 5: The Nineteenth Century,* (Cambridge University Press, 1989). W. G. Beasley's *The Rise of Modern Japan* (St. Martin's Press, 1995) is a readable volume, written by one who has contributed much to an enlightened understanding of Japan and its history. Some sources on the Meiji era include Carol Gluck, *Japan's Modern Myths: Ideology in the Late Meiji Period* (Princeton University Press, 1985); Kenneth B. Pyle, *The New Generation in Meiji Japan, 1885–1895* (Stanford University Press, 1969); and two works by Beasley, *The Meiji Restoration* (Stanford University Press, 1972) and *Japanese Imperialism, 1894–1945* (Oxford University Press, 1987), which concentrates on late Meiji diplomacy and its influence on Japan's future course in the twentieth century. A specialized study is Marius Jansen and Gilbert Rozman, eds., *Japan in Transition: From Tokugawa to Meiji* (Princeton University Press, 1986), which contains scholarly essays on related aspects of Japanese history during this important time period. Finally, those interested in exploring the Japanese character should read Benedict's book, *The Chrysanthemum and the Sword: Patterns of Japanese Culture* (Houghton Mifflin, 1989), which is excerpted in this issue.

ISSUE 16

Were Confucian Values Responsible for China's Failure to Modernize?

YES: John King Fairbank, from *The Great Chinese Revolution: 1800–1985* (Harper & Row, 1986)

NO: Jonathan D. Spence, from *The Search for Modern China* (W. W. Norton, 1990)

ISSUE SUMMARY

YES: History professor John King Fairbank makes the case that conservative forces, rooted in the Confucian virtues, subverted attempts by some to bring China into the modern world.

NO: History professor Jonathan D. Spence offers an economic analysis that draws on the ideas of Adam Smith and Karl Marx to explain China's initial failure to modernize and the role that foreign powers played in its eventual modernization.

Most China scholars would agree that China's failure to modernize may be traced to a combination of internal and external forces—the uniquely Chinese version of traditionalism rooted in classic texts attributed to the philosopher Confucius and the economic realities of a worldwide market economy. For centuries both China and Japan remained aloof from the rest of the world. China, in particular, thought of itself as the Middle Kingdom, the center of the universe, and its centuries of scholarship and high culture had convinced many that China had nothing to learn from upstarts in the "barbarian West." Whereas Japan chose to enter the modern world on its own terms in the late nineteenth century, China refused to do so. This decision has had far-reaching consequences for China and continues to puzzle historians.

To look at an internal cause thesis, we must consider the writings of Confucius, which date back to the sixth century B.C.E., and which became deeply embedded in Chinese society 2,000 years later. Focusing on proper behavior and patterns of deference, the Confucian system stressed the practice of virtue—especially the cardinal virtues of faithfulness, sincerity, earnestness, and respectfulness—as the route to a stable social order and a defense against forces of corruption. Children were schooled to obey parents, wives to submit to husbands, younger siblings to look to older siblings for guidance and ministers to be guided by rulers. The system of examinations—the path to civil service jobs that remained in effect until 1905—was based on knowledge of the Confucian classics. Some scholars hold that continuing to honor these premodern values accounts for China's failure to modernize.

However, external factors also may have played a role. When we look at China's history during the last century, we cannot fail to take into account its large land mass and growing population. Economists, beginning with Adam Smith in his influential book *The Wealth of Nations* (1776), noted that while China was not amassing further wealth, its population was continuing to expand, which cheapened both labor and the value of human life. In the nineteenth century, the German philosopher Karl Marx saw Asia as being outside the influence of what his mentor G. W. F. Hegel had called the "World Spirit" in its march through history. As European powers invaded China and exploited its economic resources, some historians blamed China's failure to modernize on capitalist imperialism, a clearly external force.

In the following selection, John King Fairbank (1901–1991) chooses to put the explanatory emphasis on conservative forces within China. He argues that ethnocentrism, the belief that one's own culture is superior to all others, made China smugly confident of its ability to keep its old ways and prosper. Confucian platitudes, combined with the conservatism of the imperial dynasty, subverted the forces of modernization and made China vulnerable to invasion by the Western powers.

In the second selection, Jonathan D. Spence summarizes the economic explanation that came into general acceptance during the first decades of the twentieth century. He notes that Marx, following the analysis of Hegel, had left Asia out of the historic development of world cultures under the guidance of the World Spirit. Left to its self-imposed isolation, China (according to Smith's analysis and Hegel's model) would never modernize. The only hope for China, Hegel and Marx agreed, would be for the Western powers to plant the seeds of their superior mode of production and more fully developed notion of freedom in Chinese soil.

YES

John King Fairbank

EFFORTS AT MODERNIZATION

The forty years beginning in 1860 form a distinct era in the buildup of the Chinese Revolution—a time when the old system seemed to work again and some Western ways were adopted, yet China's progress was so comparatively slow that she became a sitting duck for greater foreign aggression. The imperialist rivalry of the powers came to a terrifying climax in the 1898 "scramble for concessions," and the period ended with troops of eight nations occupying Peking in 1900. Obviously these were the four decades when China missed the boat. While Japan ended her seclusion, adroitly began to Westernize, got rid of her unequal treaties, and was prepared to become a world power, why did China fail to do the same?

This question has haunted Chinese patriots throughout the twentieth century. At first the explanation was found in Social Darwinism. China had simply lost out in the competition for survival among nations. Partly this was due to her tardiness in ceasing to be an ancient empire and becoming a modern nation. The fault lay within.

By 1920, however, a more satisfying explanation was offered by Marxism-Leninism. The fault lay with the capitalist imperialism of the foreign powers who invaded China, secured special privileges under the unequal treaties, exploited Chinese markets and resources, and suppressed the stirrings of Chinese capitalism. Since many foreigners announced loudly that they were going to do just that, all sides could agree. The same decades saw the triumph of colonialism all around China's periphery. Burma and Malaysia were taken over by Britain, Vietnam by France, Taiwan by Japan. Foreign aggression and exploitation were too plain to be denied.

Two generations of argument over these explanatory theories have come to rest in the 1980s on a "both . . . and" formula: internal weakness invited foreign invasion, just as Confucius said 2,500 years ago. The real argument has been over the proportions between the two and the timing of their influence. As the onward march of scholarship helps us to learn more about China within, I believe the claims of Marxism-Leninism will be watered down as time goes on but no one can deny their validity in many important respects.

From John King Fairbank, *The Great Chinese Revolution: 1800–1985* (Harper & Row, 1986). Copyright © 1986 by John King Fairbank. Reprinted by permission of HarperCollins Publishers, Inc. Notes omitted.

How does this apply to 1861–94? The era began with a joint leadership of Manchus and Chinese, at Peking and in the provinces, who agreed on a general program of appeasing the Anglo-French invaders while suppressing the Chinese rebels. There are few better examples of how to turn weakness into strength, though sometimes at the expense of the Chinese populace.

By mid-1860 a revived Taiping offensive had invaded the Yangtze delta, taking the major cities of Hangchow and Soochow and threatening Shanghai, while at the same time an Anglo-French army arrived off Tientsin in two hundred ships, and fought its way to Peking. Facing this double disaster, the Manchu leadership executed a neat double appeasement: they finally gave Tseng Kuo-fan supreme command against the Taipings, abandoning the old rule that Chinese civil officials should not control armies in the provinces, and they accepted the Anglo-French demands to open China further to foreign trade and proselytism. As they put it in the dynastic councils, the rebels were an "organic disease," the foreigners merely an "affliction of the limbs." (This of course would be the way Chiang Kai-shek phrased his problems with Japanese invasion and Communist rebellion in the 1930s and 1940s.) All the British wanted was trade; so their opium trade was legalized and inland trade on the Yangtze promised them as soon as the Taipings (who stubbornly prohibited opium) should have been destroyed.

American and British mercenaries, like F. T. Ward of Salem, Massachusetts, were hired to use steamers and artillery in amphibious warfare around Shanghai. Having got the terms they wanted at Peking, the British and French abandoned neutrality and let officers like C. G. "Chinese" Gordon fight the Taipings while, even more important, foreign merchants sold Remingtons and howitzers to the imperial armies. Anglo-French forces had returned from humbling Peking to defend Shanghai and the Yangtze delta, and so help save the dynasty.

In this way the Ch'ing restoration of the 1860s secured foreign help while still expounding the classical ideology of rule by virtue. Tseng Kuo-fan ... set the tone of the restoration by his admirable strength of character and rather simple-minded faith in the Confucian ideals of proper behavior.

"Barbarian affairs are hard to manage," he wrote his understudy Li Hung-chang in 1862, "but the basic principles are no more than the four words of Confucius: *chung, hsin, tu,* and *ching*—faithfulness, sincerity, earnestness and respectfulness.... Hsin means merely not to tell a lie, but it is very difficult to avoid doing so...

"Confucius says, 'If you can rule your own country, who dares to insult you?' If we are unified, strict and sober, and if hundreds of measures are fostered, naturally the foreigners will not insult and affront us without reason." (Obviously, a man so indoctrinated with the Confucian virtues could be entrusted with the fate of the dynasty.)

"In your association with foreigners," Tseng told Li, "your manner and deportment should not be too lofty, and you should have a slightly vague, casual appearance. Let their insults, deceitfulness, and contempt for everything appear to be understood by you and yet seem not understood, for you should look somewhat stupid."

What better prescription could one suggest for swallowing pride and appeasing an invader? The Manchus at court had quoted the ancient saying "Resort to peace and friendship when temporarily obliged to do so; use war and defense as your actual policy." The dynasty and its Chinese ruling class were in the soup together.

After Tseng Kuo-fan died in 1872 the lead in dealing with foreigners for the next thirty years was taken by Li Hung-chang, a tall (over six feet), vigorous, and extremely intelligent realist, who was eager to take responsibility and became adept at hanging on to power. He was devoted to the art of the possible and, working within that limitation, became the leading modernizer of his day. Although Li Hung-chang himself went around the world only toward the end of his career in 1896, he realized from the first moment his troops got their Remington rifles that foreign things were the key to China's defense and survival. He became the leading advocate of what Peking a century later under Deputy Premier Deng Hsiao-p'ing would call "modernization."

Li had benefited from the fact that his father had been a classmate of Tseng Kuo-fan in the top examination of 1838. After Li won his provincial degree, he studied under Tseng at Peking. He got his own top degree there in 1847, and in the early 1850s went back to his native place (Ho-fei in Anhwei) to organize militia against the rebels, much as Tseng was doing in Hunan. He assisted the provincial governor in campaigns and then in 1859 joined Tseng Kuo-fan's staff, became his chief secretary, and drafted his correspondence. When the Ch'ing court was finally obliged to give Tseng overall command in 1860, Li had his chance.

Backed by Tseng to organize his own Anhwei army on the model of Tseng's Hunan army, Li in April 1862 used seven foreign steamers hired by refugee gentry to bring his troops down the Yangtze to Shanghai. At age thirty-nine he now became governor of Kiangsu province at the fulcrum of Sino-foreign relations. Shanghai he found to be an Anglo-French military base, with foreign troops far better armed and trained than his Chinese forces. Troops so armed could take over China! Indeed, he feared "the hearts of the officials and of the people have long since gone over to the foreigners." He felt himself "treading on frost over ice." Could Shanghai be kept from a foreign takeover? Li rushed to buy Western arms and build up his Anhwei army. Within two years he had forty thousand men with ten thousand rifles and cannon using thirty-six-pound shells. He got Western cooperation against the Taipings but kept it strictly within limits.

In this way Li Hung-chang moved in on the ground floor of the late Ch'ing establishment. Having qualified first as a scholar, he won the dynasty's confidence as a general commanding troops. His Anhwei army helped surround and strangle the Taipings in the Lower Yangtze and then in the late 1860s finished off the Nien rebels, whose cavalry had been raiding all across North China. Purchasing foreign rifles, setting up arsenals, and drilling troops gave the dynasty the edge over dissident peasants from this time on. Simultaneously the British with their gunboats and troops at Hong Kong and the treaty ports and on the Yangtze became an integral part of China's power structure, helping to maintain political order in the interests of foreign trade....

Li Hung-chang's diplomatic efforts gave him high visibility, and Western journalists occasionally touted him as the

"Bismarck of the East." The comparison can be instructive. Li Hung-chang (1823–1901) no doubt had many of the abilities of his German contemporary Otto von Bismarck (1815–98). He was a big man, an astute diplomat and energetic administrator, above all a realistic practitioner of the possible, who for forty years played principal roles in China. But, while Bismarck between 1862 and 1890 engineered and won three wars to create the German empire and dominate central Europe, Li confronted rebellions at home and foreign aggression on China's borders that led the Ch'ing empire steadily downhill. While Bismarck was fashioning a new balance of power in Europe, Li had to deal with the breakup of the Ch'ing tribute system that had once provided a kind of international order in East Asia. The Iron Chancellor held central executive power among a people already leading the way in modern science, industrial technology, and military nationalism. Li Hung-chang never held central power but only represented Peking as a provincial governor-general. His influence hung by the thread of his loyalty to the regent for two boy emperors in succession, the Empress Dowager Tz'u-hsi, a clever, ignorant woman intent on preserving Manchu rule at all costs. Li's loyalty to his ruler had to be expressed in large gifts and unquestioning sycophancy, to the point where in 1888–94 Li's North China navy, racing against Japan's naval buildup, had to divert its funds to build Tz'u-hsi's new summer palace. In place of a Bleichroder, who financed Bismarck in the clinches, Li Hung-hang had to collect his own squeeze by the usual age-old filching from his official funds. After he negotiated the secret Russo-Chinese alliance in 1896 he received a personal gift of a million roubles. Some said he amassed a fortune worth $40 million. It is plain that he got some things done, but he led the late Ch'ing effort at modernization only by persistent pushing and constant manipulation of an intractable environment.

This was a two-front struggle, to find out the practical secrets of Western power and also to convince indoctrinated fellow officials that imitating the West was necessary. Tseng Kuo-fan, for example, supported the Shanghai Arsenal and it built a steamship, on which he even ventured to sail. But he opposed telegraphs, railways, and other uses of Western technology as likely to harm Chinese livelihood and give foreigners too much influence. Li had to steer a devious and indirect course. For instance, Tseng offered him the conventional Confucian wisdom (or balderdash) that "warfare depends on men, not weapons" (an old idea, but modified today by a thought of Mao Tse-tung's). Li countered by describing British and French warships he had visited. "I feel deeply ashamed," he said, at China's inferiority in weapons. "Every day I warn and instruct my officers to be humble-minded, to bear the humiliation, to learn one or two secret methods from the Westerners."

If we recall the American need in public discussions of the Cold War era to first reassure an audience that Communism, the enemy, was not for us, we can sympathize with Li Hung-chang's problem. To the court at Peking he wrote in 1863: "Everything in China's civil and military system is far superior to the West. Only in firearms it is absolutely impossible to catch up with them. Why? Because in China the way of making machines is for the scholars to understand the principles, while the artisans put them into practice.... The two do not consult each other.... But foreigners are different.... I have learned that when Western scholars make weapons, they use mathematics for reference."

Li also pointed to the Japanese success in learning to navigate steamships and make cannon. If China could stand on her own feet militarily, he prophesied, the Japanese "will attach themselves to us." But if not, "then the Japanese will imitate the Westerners and will share the Westerners' sources of profits."

By 1864 Li ventured to recommend that science and technology be added to the topics in the examination system. From today's point of view this was surely the starting point for China's adaptation to the modern world. But the idea never had a chance. Even the proposal that regular degree holders be recruited to study Western science in the interpreters' college that Hart was financing at Peking, and in similar small government schools at Shanghai and Canton, was shot down.

The imperial tutor Wo-jen, a Mongol who dominated the Peking literary bureaucracy, spoke for the orthodox majority: "The way to establish a nation is to stress propriety and righteousness, not power and plotting... the minds of people, not technology.... The barbarians are our enemies. In 1860 they rebelled against us." They invaded Peking, he continued, burned the imperial summer palace, killed our people. "How can we forget this humiliation even for a single day?" Why, he asked, was it necessary to "seek trifling arts and respect barbarians as teachers?... Since the conclusion of the peace [in 1860], Christianity has been prevalent and half our ignorant people [the Taipings] have been fooled by it.... Now if talented scholars have to change from their regular course of study to follow the barbarians... it will

drive the multitude of the Chinese people into allegiance to the barbarians.... Should we further spread their influence and fan the flame?"

These sentiments coincided with the vested interest of every scholar who taught, and every young man who studied, the classics. Modern learning was effectively kept out of the examinations until they were finally abolished in 1905.

The modernization of China thus became a game played by a few high officials who realized its necessity and tried to raise funds, find personnel, and set up projects in a generally lethargic if not unfriendly environment. Hope of personal profit and power led them on, but the Empress Dowager's court, unlike the Meiji Emperor's in Japan, gave them no firm or consistent backing. Tz'u-hsi on the contrary found it second nature to let the ideological conservatives like Wo-jen stalemate the innovators so that she could hold the balance. Since South China was as usual full of bright spirits looking for new opportunities, especially in the rapidly growing treaty-port cities, the late nineteenth century was a time of much pioneering but little basic change. Westernization was left to the efforts of a few high provincial officials partly because this suited the central-local balance of power—the court could avoid the cost and responsibility —and partly because treaty-port officials in contact with foreigners were the only ones who could see the opportunities and get foreign help.

On this piecemeal basis Li Hung-chang found allies in Cantonese entrepreneurs whose long contact with Westerners gave them new channels to climb up. For example there was a T'ang clan based ten miles from Macao who grew rich making shrimp sauce and selling it there. The clan steadily gained influence during the nineteenth century as its members passed local and provincial examinations. However, Tong King-sing (T'ang T'ing-shu, 1832–92) opened up a new channel. He learned English in a missionary school, became an interpreter in the Hong Kong police court and the Shanghai customs house, and after 1863 grew wealthy as Jardine's top comprador. From investing in pawn shops and native banks he moved on to shipping companies, insurance, and even a newspaper. Meanwhile he bought degree status and an official title, which the dynasty was now selling for revenue. From 1873 Li Hung-chang got Tong's assistance in his industrial-development projects.

Instead of battling his fellow Confucians on the intellectual front, Li found it easier to compete with foreign economic enterprise in China. China's domestic commerce in private hands was already actively expanding. Li pursued the traditional idea of enlisting Chinese merchant capital in projects that would be "supervised by officials but undertaken by merchants," something like the salt trade. After all, the proportion of China's national income that passed through the governments hands and sticky fingers was still very low.

Li in 1872 started a joint-stock steamship line, even calling it the China Merchants Steamship Company, and soon got Tong King-sing to be the manager. But merchant capital came forward only in small amounts. The crash of 1877 allowed Li to buy up the fleet of Russell and Company, the Boston firm that with Chinese merchant help had inaugurated steamboating on the Yangtze. But a majority of the funds had to come from official sources. When in 1885 Robert Hart lent one of his young customs commissioners (H. B. Morse, Harvard '74) to advise the China Merchants' managers, Morse found the company overloaded with personnel and being milked of its profits. It survived by hauling the tribute rice to Tientsin and making rate deals with the British lines of Jardine, Matheson & Company and Butterfield and Swire, who continued for the next fifty years under the unequal treaty system to dominate water transport within China.

When Li Hung-chang in 1876 started the Kaiping coal mine north of Tientsin to fuel his steamships and give them return cargo to Shanghai, he made Tong manager of the mining company. At Kaiping Tong brought in a dozen Western engineers and installed modern pumps, fans, and hoists. Soon Kaiping had a machine shop, telephones and telegraphs, and a small railway, and was producing 250,000 tons of coal a year. It was so successful that Peking could not keep its hands off. A Chinese squeeze artist from the court succeeded Tong, squeezed the company dry, and kept it going mainly on foreign loans. Finally in the Boxer crisis of 1900 a British company, represented by an up-and-coming American mining engineer named Herbert C. Hoover, got control of it. China's legal counsel in London later claimed that this takeover was almost indistinguishable from grand larceny. After 1912 the Kaiping mines were run by the Anglo-Chinese Kailan Mining Administration.

A similar spottiness marked Li's first venture in sending students abroad. This had been proposed by another Cantonese, a school classmate of Tong named Yung Wing, who had gone so far as to accept missionary support and make it to Yale. He became Yale's first

Chinese graduate, in 1854. Trying to make himself useful back in China, he was eventually sent out to buy the machinery for the Shanghai Arsenal. Finally in 1872 he was given charge of the Chinese educational mission that during the next decade brought 120 long-gowned Chinese youths to America. The first batch, selected by Tong King-sing, included seven of his relatives, and the third group, his nephew T'ang Shao-i.

On the advice of the Connecticut commissioner of education, Yung Wing set up headquarters in Hartford, but President Porter of Yale suggested the students should board with families up and down the Connecticut Valley. Soon they learned to tuck their queues under their caps and play very smart baseball, while Yung Wing himself married Mary Louise Kellogg of Avon, Connecticut. Yung Wing's co-supervisor, a proper long-gowned scholar, was horrified: the boys were becoming barbarized. They were not mastering the classics in preparation for their examinations back in China! In 1881 the project was abandoned. Chinese students came to America again only thirty years later, not as young teenagers, and without their queues and classics, after the end of the dynasty.

The 120 students from the Hartford project made their mark in China's foreign relations and industrialization after 1900. If the project had continued after 1881, China's modern history might have been different....

When China's Ch'ing dynasty restoration after thirty years confronted Japan's Meiji restoration in warfare, the two protagonists were Li Hung-chang and one of Japan's founding fathers, Itō Hirobumi. They had first met in 1885 over the Korean question and agreed that Japan and China should both stay out of Korea, where they were backing rival factions. Li noted, however, "In about ten years, the wealth and strength of Japan will be admirable... a future source of trouble for China."

Sure enough, when the Japanese intervened in 1894, ostensibly to quell Korean rebels, they routed Li's North China army and in one of the first modern naval battles, off the Yalu River, sank or routed his fleet. It was commanded by an old cavalry general who brought his ships out line abreast like a cavalry charge, while the Japanese in two columns circled around them. Today when tourists visit the marble boat which stands in the summer palace lake outside Peking, they should be able to imagine a caption on it—"In memoriam: here lies what might have been the late Ch'ing navy."

In 1895 when Li was sent to Shimonoseki to sue for peace, he and Itō had a polite dialogue, which was recorded in English. Li said: "China and Japan are the closest neighbors and moreover have the same writing system. How can we be enemies? ... We ought to establish perpetual peace and harmony between us, so that our Asiatic yellow race will not be encroached upon by the white race of Europe."

Itō said: "Ten years ago I talked with you about reform. Why is it that up to now not a single thing has been changed or reformed?"

Li could only reply, "Affairs in my country have been so confined by tradition that I could not accomplish what I desired.... I am ashamed of having excessive wishes and lacking the power to fulfill them."

From our perspective today, the startling thing is that China's first modern war should have been left on the shoulders of a provincial official as though it were simply a matter of his defending his share of the frontier. The Manchu dynasty has of course been blamed for its non-nationalistic ineptitude, but the trouble was deeper than the dynasty's being non-Chinese; the fault evidently lay in the imperial monarchy itself, the superficiality of its administration, its constitutional inability to be a modern central government.

Jonathan D. Spence

THE SEARCH FOR MODERN CHINA

WESTERN IMAGES OF CHINA

Until the middle of the eighteenth century, China generally received favorable attention in the West. In large part this stemmed from the wide dissemination of books and published correspondence by Catholics, especially the Jesuits, who saw in the huge population of China a potential harvest of souls for the Christian faith. Although mindful of some of China's problems, most Catholic observers followed the example of the Jesuit missionary Matteo Ricci, who had lived in China from 1583 to 1610 and admired the industry of China's population, the sophistication of the country's bureaucracy, the philosophical richness of its cultural traditions, and the strength of its rulers.

The French Jesuits, who dominated the China missions late in Kangxi's reign, presented an even more laudatory picture of the early Qing state, one deliberately designed to appeal to the "Sun King," Louis XIV, and to persuade him to back the missionaries with money and personnel. Central to these flattering presentations was the idea that the ethical content of the Confucian Classics proved the Chinese were a deeply moral nation and had once practiced a form of monotheism not so different from that found in the Judaeo-Christian tradition. With a little effort, therefore, the Chinese could be brought back to the true values they had once espoused, and did not have to be forced to convert.

Although the Jesuits rapidly lost influence in China during the last years of Kangxi's reign, and declined in prestige in Europe during the eighteenth century until suppressed altogether in 1773, their books on Chinese government and society remained far the most detailed available. The German philosopher Gottfried Wilhelm von Leibnitz read them and became deeply interested in the structure of the hexagrams in the *Book of Changes.* Even the anticlerical philosopher Voltaire was intrigued by what he read about the Chinese. Since Voltaire was intent on attacking the power of the Catholic church in eighteenth-century France, he cleverly used the information about

China provided by the Catholics to disprove their more extreme claims. If, argued Voltaire, the Chinese really were so moral, intelligent, ethical, and well governed, and if this was largely attributable to the influence of Confucius, it followed that since Confucius had not been a Christian it was obviously possible for a country to get along admirably without the presence of Catholic clerical power.

In a series of influential works written between 1740 and 1760, Voltaire expounded his ideas about China. In one novel he presented his views on the parallelism of moral values in different societies, European and Asian. In a play he suggested that the innate moral strength of the Chinese had been able to calm even the Mongol conquerors led by Genghis Khan. And in an unusual historiographical gesture, Voltaire *began* his review of world history—*Essai sur les moeurs et l'esprit des nations* ("An Essay on the Customs and Spirit of Nations")—with a lengthy section on China. He did this to emphasize the values of differing civilizations and to put European arrogance in perspective: "The great misunderstanding over Chinese rites sprang from our judging their practices in light of ours: for we carry the prejudices that spring from our contentious nature to the ends of the world." Unable to find a "philosopher-king" in Europe to exemplify his views of religion and government, Voltaire believed Emperor Qianlong would fill the gap, and he wrote poems in the distant emperor's honor.

Voltaire's praise for Chinese institutions appeared in a cultural context that was intensely sympathetic to China. During this same brief period in the mid-eighteenth century, Europe was swept by a fascination with China that is usually described by the French word *chinoiserie*, an enthusiasm drawn more to Chinese decor and design than to philosophy and government. In prints and descriptions of Chinese houses and gardens, and in Chinese embroidered silks, rugs, and colorful porcelains, Europeans found an alternative to the geometrical precision of their neoclassical architecture and the weight of baroque design. French rococo was a part of this mood, which tended to favor pastel colors, asymmetry, a calculated disorder, a dreamy sensuality. Its popular manifestations could be found everywhere in Europe, from the "Chinese" designs on the new wallpapers and furnishings that graced middle-class homes to the pagodas in public parks, the sedan chairs in which people were carried through the streets, and the latticework that surrounded ornamental gardens.

Yet this cult of China, whether intellectual or aesthetic, faded swiftly as angry and sarcastic accounts like George Anson's became available. Voltaire's very enthusiasms made him the object of sarcasm or mockery as other great figures among the French Enlightenment philosophers began to find his picture of China unconvincing. Jean-Jacques Rousseau and the Baron de Montesquieu worried that the Chinese did not seem to enjoy true liberty, that their laws were based on fear rather than on reason, and that their elaborate educational system might lead to the corruption of Chinese morals rather than to their improvement. Other writers declared that China did not seem to be progressing, had indeed no notion of progress; from this it was but a short step to see the Chinese as, in fact, retrogressing. In the somber words of the French historian Nicolas Boulanger, written in 1763 and translated from the French the following year by the English radical John Wilkes:

> All the remains of her ancient institutions, which China now possesses, will necessarily be lost; they will disappear in the future revolutions; as what she hath already lost of them vanished in former ones; and finally, as she acquires nothing new, she will always be on the losing side.

Reflecting on these arguments concerning China and the Chinese, some leading European thinkers labored to assess the country's prospects. One of these was the Scottish philosopher Adam Smith, who wrote on China in *The Wealth of Nations*, first published in 1776. In his analysis of the productive capacities of different countries, Smith found China useful for comparative purposes, especially with the nations of Europe and the developing societies of North America. Examining population growth as an index of development, he concluded that in Europe, where countries doubled their populations every five hundred years, growth was steady if undramatic. In North America, where the population doubled every twenty or twenty-five years, there was instant employment for the entire new work force; the New World was therefore "much more thriving, and advancing with much greater rapidity to the further acquisition of riches."

China, however, "long one of the richest, that is, one of the most fertile, best cultivated, most industrious, and most populous countries in the world," had reached that stage in the cycle of growth where it had "acquired that full complement of riches which the nature of its laws and institutions permits it to acquire." In such a situation, continued population growth brought serious economic repercussions: "If in such a country the wages of labour had ever been more than sufficient to maintain the labourer, and to enable him to bring up a family, the competition of the labourers and the interest of the masters would soon reduce them to this lowest rate which is consistent with common humanity." The result was that "the poverty of the lower ranks of people in China far surpasses that of the most beggarly nations in Europe" and infanticide became an integral social practice. As Smith acidly phrased it: "Marriage is encouraged in China, not by the profitableness of children, but by the liberty of destroying them." China was exacerbating these problems, according to Smith, by refusing to consider change. By staying aloof from the growth of the world economy, China was sealing its fate: "A country which neglects or despises foreign commerce, and which admits the vessels of foreign nations into one or two of its ports only, cannot transact the same quantity of business which it might do with different laws and institutions."

In a famous series of lectures delivered by the German philosopher Georg Wilhelm Friedrich Hegel in the early 1820s, the various critical analyses explored by Boulanger, Rousseau, Montesquieu, and Smith were synthesized in such a way that "Oriental Civilizations"—China preeminent among them—came to be seen as an early and now by-passed stage of history. The view of "Asiatic Society" synthesized by Hegel was to have a profound influence on the young Karl Marx and other later nineteenth-century thinkers. History, to Hegel, was the development of what he called the ideas and practices of freedom throughout the world. Freedom was the expression of the self-realization of the "World Spirit," and that spirit was reaching its fullest manifestations in the Christian states of Europe and North America. Optimistic about his own time, Hegel developed a theory that downplayed China's past. He described China as dominated by its emperors or despots, as typical of the "oriental nations" that saw only *one* man as free. In the West, the Greeks and Romans had come to see that *some* men were free; and, centuries later, Hegel's generation had come to see that *all* humans were free. Lacking an understanding of the march of Spirit in the world, even the Chinese emperor's "freedom" was "caprice," expressed as either "ferocity—brutal recklessness of passion—or a mildness and tameness of the desires, which is itself only an accident of Nature."

Part of China's fate, Hegel wrote, turned on geographical factors: "The extensive tract of eastern Asia is severed from the general historical development." In a powerfully worded passage, Hegel explained that China had lacked the great boldness of the Europeans in exploring the seas and instead had stayed tied to the agricultural rhythms of her great plains. The soil presented only "an infinite multitude of dependencies," whereas the sea carried people "beyond these limited circles of thought and action.... This stretching out of the sea beyond the limitations of the land, is wanting to the splendid political edifices of Asiatic States, although they themselves border on the sea—as for example, China. For them the sea is only the limit, the ceasing of the land; they have no positive relation to it." Though such a statement would have startled the wealthy ocean-going merchants of Fujian had they seen it, Hegel was basically correct that the Qing state itself was not interested in maritime exploration.

In a series of bleak conclusions, Hegel consigned the Chinese permanently to their space outside the development of the World Spirit. Although China had historians galore, they studied their country within their own limited preconceptions, not realizing that China itself lay "outside the World's History, as the mere presupposition of elements whose combination must be waited for to constitute their vital progress." Although Chinese emperors may speak words of "majesty and paternal kindness and tenderness to the people," the Chinese people "cherish the meanest opinion of themselves, and believe that men are born only to drag the car of Imperial Power." In a passage that moved beyond anything Lord Macartney had opined about the fate of the Qing dynasty, Hegel mourned for the Chinese people themselves: "The burden which presses them to the ground, seems to them to be their inevitable destiny: and it appears nothing terrible to them to sell themselves as slaves, and to eat the bitter bread of slavery."

Yet perhaps China was not caught forever in a metaphysical and geographical isolation. In one of his most ambiguous asides, Hegel added that "a relation to the rest of History could only exist in their case, through their being sought out, and their character investigated by others." The question of by whom or how that seeking out was to be done was left open by Hegel, but the Western powers, with their ships, their diplomatic missions, and their opium, were rapidly beginning to provide an answer....

FOREIGN PRESSURES AND MARX'S VIEWS

One of many factors that helped the Qing overthrow the Taiping was the assistance of foreigners in the early 1860s, whether in the form of customs dues collected through the foreign-managed Shanghai Inspectorate of Customs or in the form of the Ever-Victorious Army, led in the field by Western officers. The reasons for that support had mainly to do with international affairs, in which, once again, the primary actors were the British. Disappointed at the results of the Nanjing treaty and frustrated by continued Qing intransigence, the British reacted with scant sympathy when the Qing were threatened by the spread of the Taiping rebellion. Instead the British made the highly legalistic decision to apply the most-favored-nation clause to the American treaty of 1844, which had stipulated that that treaty be renegotiated in twelve years. By applying that renewal stipulation to their own Nanjing treaty of 1842, British authorities forced the Chinese to renegotiate in 1854.

The British foreign secretary saw the speciousness of this argument, writing to the governor of Hong Kong that "the Chinese Authorities may perhaps and with some degree of plausibility object that the circumstances of the time are unsuitable for the commencement of such a work. But he nevertheless suggested that the Qing be presented with the following formidable list of requests: access for the British to the entire interior of China or, failing that, to all of coastal Zhejiang and the lower Yangzi up to Nanjing; legalization of the opium trade; cancellation of internal transit dues on foreign imports; suppression of piracy; regulation of Chinese labor emigration; residence in Peking for a British ambassador; and reliance on the English version rather than the Chinese in all disputed interpretations of the revised treaty.

Despite some caution because of their involvement in the Crimean War against Russia, the British moved jointly with the Americans and French to press for treaty revision, which the beleaguered Qing continued to oppose. The British finally took advantage of an allegedly illegal Qing search of a ship formerly of Hong Kong registry, the *Arrow,* to recommence military actions at Canton in late 1856. After some delays in getting reinforcements—the Indian mutiny was now raging, and the idea of a war in east Asia was not popular with the British people—the British seized Canton in December 1857 and exiled the consistently hostile governor-general of the region to Calcutta. Sailing north in a near repeat of the 1840 campaign, they took the strategic Dagu forts in May 1858 and threatened to seize Tianjin. In June, with the way to Peking now open to the British forces, the Qing capitulated and agreed to sign a new treaty. By the terms of the most-favored-nation clause, all British gains would also be shared by the other major foreign powers.

This "Treaty of Tianjin" of 1858 imposed extraordinarily strict terms on China. A British ambassador was henceforth to reside in Peking, accompanied by family and staff, and housed in a fitting residence. The open preaching of Christianity was protected. Travel anywhere inside China was permitted to those with valid passports, and within thirty miles of treaty ports without passports. Once the rebellions currently raging in China were suppressed, trade was to be allowed up the Yangzi as far as Hankou, and four new Yangzi treaty ports (Hankou, Jiujiang, Nanjing, and Zhenjiang) would be opened. An additional six treaty ports were to be opened immediately: one in Manchuria, one in Shandong, two on Taiwan, one in Guangdong, and one on Hainan Island in the far south.

The Tianjin treaty also stipulated that all further interior transit taxes on foreign imports be dropped upon payment of a flat fee of 2.5 percent. Standard weights and measures would be employed at all ports and customshouses. Official communications were to be in English. The character for *barbarian*... must no longer be used in Chinese documents describing the British. And British ships hunting pirates would be free to enter any Chinese port. A supplementary clause accompanying the various commercial agreements stated explicitly: "Opium will henceforth pay thirty taels per picul [approximately 130 pounds] Import Duty. The importer will sell it only at the port. It will be carried into the interior by Chinese only, and only as Chinese property; the foreign trader will not be allowed to accompany it." This condition was imposed despite the prohibition in the Chinese penal code on the sale and consumption of opium. Virtually the only British concession was to pull back from Tianjin and return the Dagu forts to Qing control.

The British evidently expected China's rulers to abandon the struggle at this point, but the Qing would not, and showed no intention of following the treaty clause that permitted foreign ambassadors to live in Peking. In June 1859, to enforce the new treaty terms, the British once more attacked the Dagu forts, now strengthened and reinforced by Qing troops. Fighting was heavy and the British were beaten back, even though the American naval commodore Josiah Tattnall, despite his country's declared neutrality, came to the aid of wounded British Admiral Hope with the ringing cry "Blood is thicker than water." Re-pulsed from the Dagu forts, the British sent a team of negotiators to Peking by a different route in 1860, but they were arrested by the Qing and some were executed. Determined now to teach the Qing a lesson they could not ignore, Lord Elgin, Britain's chief treaty negotiator, ordered his troops to march on Peking. On October 18, 1860, following Elgin's orders, the British burnt to the ground the Yuan Ming Yuan—the exquisite summer palace in the Peking suburbs built for Qianlong's pleasure using the plans of Jesuit architects. The British, however, spared the Forbidden City palaces within Peking, calculating that destruction of those hallowed buildings would be a disgrace so profound that the Qing dynasty would inevitably fall.

The emperor had already fled the city for Manchuria and named his younger brother, Prince Gong, to act as negotiator. But there was nothing left to negotiate, and on the very day the summer palace burned, Prince Gong reaffirmed the terms of the 1858 Tianjin treaty. In an additional "Convention of Peking," the emperor was stated to express his "deep regret" at the harassment of the British queen's representatives. He also promised a further 8 million taels in indemnity, permitted Chinese emigration on British ships, made Tianjin itself a treaty port, and ceded part of the mainland Kowloon peninsula to Hong Kong. Thus did the "treaty system" reach its fruition.

With these spectacular new gains firmly embedded in treaty form, and confident that Prince Gong would see to their enforcement, the British now swung to strong support for the Qing. The logic seemed clear: if the Qing beat back the Taiping, the foreigners would keep their new gains; if the Taiping defeated the Qing, even under the semi-Westernized aegis of Hong Ren'gan, then the West would have to start the tiresome process of negotiation—and perhaps wage fresh wars—all over again. A sardonic observer of these international shifts was Karl Marx, who had been following the progress of the Taiping rebellion and of British foreign policy with great interest. Marx, born in 1818 in Germany, had written the *Manifesto of the Communist Party* in 1848 with his friend Friedrich Engels. Expelled from both Germany and France for his radical views, he settled in London in 1849 and thereafter made England his home. By 1853, the revolutionary surge for which Marx had hoped in Europe had faded in the face of sustained opposition from reactionary government forces, and he turned to China to find reassurance for his belief that revolutionary change might still be possible.

That same year, as the Taiping seized Nanjing, Marx wrote that he now believed all of China's various dissident forces were at last "gathered together in one formidable revolution." Although he could not tell what "religious, dynastic, or national shape" the Taiping would take, he was confident in ascribing the rise of the Taiping movement to the British opium trade, reinforced by British cannon. Together, these had ended China's self-imposed isolation, wrecked the myth of Manchu authority, and involved China's once venerated mandarins in a cycle of smuggling and corruption. The upshot could only be that Qing "dissolution must follow as surely as that of any mummy carefully preserved in a hermetically sealed coffin, whenever it is brought into contact with the open air."

The result of China's collapse would be spectacular, thought Marx, since the Western powers had become so strongly committed to the balance of their Chinese trade with Indian opium production, and the taxation of that trade to maintain their own domestic revenues, that they could not do without it. Accordingly, Marx wrote, "it may safely be augured that the Chinese revolution will throw the spark into the overloaded mine of the present industrial system and cause the explosion of the long-prepared general crisis, which, spreading abroad, will be closely followed by political revolutions on the continent." It was an apocalyptic version of that dragging of China into the modern world that Hegel had speculated about thirty years before.

By the later 1850s, however, events in China had not had this kind of direct impact on European society. Still, Marx found his attention drawn to the new phase of British imperialism in China, which was represented by the "*Arrow war*" and the fighting that led first to the Treaty of Tianjin, and finally to the ratification of the Convention of Peking in 1860. He compared the British actions in bombarding Canton to the filibustering activities of "General" William Walker in California, Mexico, and Nicaragua, and wondered if it were possible that "the civilized nations of the world will approve this mode of invading a peaceful country, without previous declaration of war, for an alleged infringement of the fanciful code of diplomatic etiquette." Marx was intrigued when Parliament censured Lord Palmerston in March 1857 for initiating the war, leading to a dissolution of Parliament, a general election, and what Marx saw as the end of "Palmerston's dictatorship."

When Palmerston was vindicated in the elections and England returned to the fray in China, Marx could only reiterate his sense of the injustice of the entire enterprise and the dangers that it implied for constitutional government. But Marx shrewdly added that the China trade was not going to expand as much as the ever-hopeful British merchants expected, because the Chinese could not possibly afford *both* large imports of opium and large imports of British manufacturers' goods. He observed too that the nation with the most to gain in the protracted Chinese negotiations was Russia. Despite setbacks in the Crimean War, Russia had now expanded its railway network into east Asia, was strengthening its hold over the coastline north of Korea, and had seized for itself immense areas of territory along the Amur River, where it had been excluded ever since the Treaties of Nerchinsk and Kiakhta, negotiated by Emperors Kangxi and Yongzheng.

Following up on ideas suggested by Hegel thirty years before, Marx divided world history into four stages of the "modes of production"—namely, "Asiatic, ancient, feudal, and modern bourgeois." One might observe that the sequence of ancient-feudal-bourgeois has both chronological and analytical meaning in the European world. It provides, indeed, a way of summarizing the movement from Greco-Roman slave-owning empires, through the feudal epoch of medieval Europe, to the development of merchant guilds and municipal urban governments that spelled the start of bourgeois society. But the "Asiatic" mode is a geographical one; it lies outside the time sequence of the other three. And although Marx wrote that the four modes represented "progressive epochs in the economic formation of society," in reality he followed Hegel in placing China (and India) outside the development of world history. Asiatic modes had in no way been subsumed into later development—they had merely limped on alongside them.

One of Marx's powerful formulations in the *Critique of Political Economy,* which he wrote in 1859, was this: "No social order ever perishes before all the productive forces for which there is room in it have developed; and new, higher relations of production never appear before the material conditions of their existence have matured in the womb of the old society itself." Marx might have followed Adam Smith in seeing China as having exhausted its "room" for fresh productive forces, but he was also suggesting that Westerners had the power to implant the seeds of "new, higher relations of production," since China had (as Marx wrote elsewhere) "a fossil form of social life." Thus, in a sense, the destructive march of foreign imperialism had a constructive effect: in weakening China's traditional structures, it would speed the day of successful proletarian revolution.

Here Marx's speculations on China stop. By 1862 he was growing weary and sarcastic about continuing news of Taiping horrors. Nor did he draw solace from the rapid rise of a completely new rebellion, that of the Nian, which had begun raging in north China well before the Taiping had been suppressed. As he and Engels had written so vividly in the *Communist Manifesto:* although "the 'dangerous class,' the social scum, that passively rotting mass thrown off by the lowest layers of the old society," might be briefly swept up in revolutionary movements, it would inevitably revert to its logical role as the "bribed tool of reactionary intrigue." Yet one haunting and powerful idea continued to hang over Marx's various writings on China. Sometime in the future, he reflected, as the reactionaries fled Europe in the face of an enraged proletariat, seeking shelter in what they regarded as a last bastion of conservative power, they might find to their astonishment, written in bold letters upon the Great Wall, the words "Chinese Republic: Liberty, Equality, Fraternity."

POSTSCRIPT

Were Confucian Values Responsible for China's Failure to Modernize?

China's failure to modernize in the last four decades of the nineteenth century was probably due to a combination of internal and external pressures. The tendency to gaze inward and to fear internal rebellion more than external aggression made China vulnerable to forces it did not yet understand. At the same time, the stagnation of its economy and the invasion of Western trade, especially the traffic in opium, corrupted China and opened the door to exploitative trade policies and even military intervention by the Western imperial powers. The Manchu dynasty, wanting above all to consolidate and maintain its power, failed to take into account the dangers that threatened it until it was too late.

Fairbank and Spence are among the best-known Western chroniclers of Chinese history. Fairbank's masterwork *China: A New History* (Harvard University Press, 1992) covers four millennia of Chinese history, and Spence's *God's Chinese Son* (W. W. Norton, 1996) recounts the bizarre story of Hong Xiuquan, leader of the Taiping uprising of 1845–1864. *Modernization and Revolution in China* (M. E. Sharpe, 1991) by June Grasso, Jay Corrin, and Michael Kort offers a readable survey of 4,000 years of Chinese history that is accessible to undergraduates and lay historians. Mary Clabaugh Wright's *Last Stand of Chinese Conservatism* (Stanford University Press, 1957) focuses on the T'ung-Chih Restoration of 1862–1874, which she considers the beginning of modern Chinese conservatism. For a positive analysis of the empress dowager, who some feel has been unfairly characterized as an iron-willed concubine who ruled through murder and intrigue, see Sterling Seagrave's strongly revisionist biography *Dragon Lady: The Life and Legend of the Last Empress of China* (Alfred A. Knopf, 1992). Students who wish to read something from Hegel should try *Reason in History* translated by Robert S. Hartman (Bobbs-Merrill, Inc., 1953), and those wishing to explore Marx might enjoy *Marx and Engels: Basic Writings on Politics and Philosophy* edited by Lewis S. Feuer (Doubleday, 1959). Any translation of the *Analects* provides a good introduction to Confucius.

A final recommendation is Bernardo Bertolucci's Academy Award-winning film *The Last Emperor*, which begins with the death of the empress dowager and takes us inside the Forbidden City, the official residence of the emperors of the Ming and Quing dynasties.

On the Internet . . .

http://www.dushkin.com

Russia on the Web
In addition to the many other links at this comprehensive site, click on "History" for a virtual tour of the palace where Nicholas II and Alexandra lived, Mikhail Gorbachev's home page, and Russian Studies on the Internet, which is a listing of sites related to Russian history and culture. *http://www.valley.net/~transnat/*

U.S. Holocaust Memorial Museum
From this site you can access the official trial records as well as photographs of the Nuremberg trials, along with extensive information about the Holocaust. *http://www.ushmm.org/*

World War I (1914–1918)
This page is dedicated to World War I and features links to many related subjects, including trench warfare, the Versailles Treaty, individual countries' participation, and lost poets of the war. *http://www.cfcsc.dnd.ca/links/milhist/wwi.html/*

World War II on the Web
From this page you can explore over 400 links to World War II material, including Pacific War chronology, women at war, rescuers during the Holocaust, and the rise of Adolf Hitler. *http://www.bunt.com/~mconrad/*

PART 5

The Early Twentieth Century

This section covers the first half of the creative, chaotic twentieth century, which was marked by great technological improvements and two disastrous world wars. The events of the twentieth century prove that societies in every century face the same problems. However, as the world becomes more technologically sophisticated, the stakes seem to get higher.

- Were Indigenous Sex Workers Under British Imperialism Always Powerless?

- Did the Bolshevik Revolution Improve the Lives of Soviet Women?

- Was German "Eliminationist Anti-Semitism" Responsible for the Holocaust?

- Was Stalin Responsible for the Cold War?

ISSUE 17

Were Indigenous Sex Workers Under British Imperialism Always Powerless?

YES: Denis Judd, from *Empire: The British Imperial Experience, from 1765 to the Present* (BasicBooks, 1996)

NO: Luise White, from "Prostitution, Differentiation, and the World Economy: Nairobi 1899–1939," in Marilyn J. Boxer and Jean H. Quataert, eds., *Connecting Spheres: Women in the Western World, 1500 to the Present* (Oxford University Press, 1987)

ISSUE SUMMARY

YES: British historian Denis Judd finds that throughout the British Empire sexual contact with "native" women was one of the perks of the imperial system. He documents the abuse and exploitation of indigenous sex workers, or prostitutes, calling it part of a pattern of conquest wherever the British flag was raised.

NO: Historian of African history Luise White interviewed indigenous sex workers in Nairobi, Kenya, and concluded that rather than being passive victims, these women acted as historical agents, doing through prostitution what in better times they would have done through marriage—stock their fathers' herds and keep livestock values competitive.

Sex workers, or prostitutes, have traditionally been thought of as victims who were forced to sell their bodies under unsafe and degrading conditions. They have also been viewed as passive and lacking alternatives. Typically, the transaction between male customer and female provider is thought of as signifying his power and her powerlessness. The question to consider in this issue is whether or not this assessment is valid. Focusing on the British Empire, the colonial experience should be examined from the differing perspectives of colonizing males and indigenous women.

In his selection, Denis Judd analyzes the 1903 suicide of Sir Hector Mac-Donald, the commander-in-chief of British forces in Ceylon (a location chosen to avoid facing a court-martial for homosexual activity with young boys) in the wider context of sex and the British Empire. The experience of the colonial empire provided British men with opportunities for sexual expression, which would not likely have been available at home. The men who served in the armed forces or as administrators or traders usually were not accompanied by British women (at least not at first). For sexual release and satisfaction, they turned to indigenous women, asserts Judd. As holders of status and privilege, British men made the decisions. In Judd's view they were the powerful ones; women, although sometimes appreciated and even valued, were powerless.

Using interviews with 170 women who had been sex workers in Nairobi, Kenya, and 26 men who had visited prostitutes, Luise White concluded that sexuality can be shaped by forces other than personal desire. She discovered motivations due to family considerations as well as larger forces, such as cattle disease and drought. White states that prostitution is neither a marginal nor an aberrant activity; instead, it can be seen as economically rational behavior. During the early 1900s White's subjects turned to prostitution in response to a sudden decline in fortune experienced by their wealthy agricultural families. A devastating series of cattle epidemics, accompanied by drought and smallpox, had left a generation of wealthy men in central Kenya without the means to continue their way of life. Particularly at risk were those men who had several wives and many daughters. Marriage, the traditional method of exchanging and solidifying wealth in cattle, had suddenly become inoperative.

By the early years of the twentieth century, the daughters of these men became temporary sex workers, not for personal survival but to purchase the cattle that would maintain their family's position of wealth and status. Cattle that would ordinarily have come to the family by way of a bride price (paid by the husband's family) were, instead, supplied through the resourcefulness of the daughters. After the daughters accomplished this objective, they retired from the trade and returned home. During World War I, another group of Kenyan sex workers sought out British and South African troops in pursuit of extra money. They saved the cash they earned or used it to buy urban real estate. It is important to note that pimping was not practiced; whatever money a woman earned by controlling and regulating sexual access to her body was hers to keep.

White argues that the daughters of wealthy families understood that permanent sexual access to them (through marriage) had an exchange value, by coming to Nairobi for a time and engaging in sex work, they merely controlled the exchange in such a way that repeated access to many men yielded the cattle that allowed the family to retain its status and wealth. Far from being powerless, these women understood very well how to use their power, concludes White.

YES

Denis Judd

SEX AND THE BRITISH EMPIRE

... Just as explorers, missionaries, traders, administrators, soldiers and settlers could make their fortunes, enhance their reputations or indeed, fail
miserably, as a result of their activities within the [British] Empire, so they
could follow, indulge, or even discover their sexual needs. [The] Empire provided countless men, and even some women, with the opportunity to express
their sexuality in ways which would have been difficult, if not downright impossible, at home. In a variety of ways, the British Empire acted as a liberating
agent, allowing British libidos unrestrained fulfilment overseas.

There were several obvious reasons why this should have been the case.
To begin with, over the decades, millions of British men either served in the
armed forces which conquered and controlled the Empire, pushed forward
the frontiers of settlement or became administrators and traders within the
imperial system. Far more often than not, they were not accompanied, at least
initially, by British women. As a result, sexual release and satisfaction could
be found in the arms of prostitutes or the women of indigenous cultures....

Within the Empire there were manifold opportunities to act out heterosexual inclinations in contact with indigenous societies whose attitude towards
a wide range of sexual needs and tastes was far more relaxed and compliant
than those officially upheld with such puritanical rigour at home. In addition,
the vast majority of British men living or serving within the British Empire
held positions of power and authority, whether based on their official status,
their wealth, or their positions as landowners, merchants, explorers, missionaries and the like. It has often been remarked that political power is one of
the most potent of aphrodisiacs. So, too, was the power—official, personal
and financial—wielded by plantation overseer, chain-gang leader, prosperous trader, the wearer of a military uniform, or even the possessor of a white
skin.

There is no question that sexual relations between individuals or groups of
people are frequently based on, or largely manifest themselves in, struggles

for power or financial reward. Within the Empire there was, for the most part, no doubt where power lay. This is not to say that sexual relationships between rulers and ruled were invariably exercises in power and control. The history of the British Empire is littered with examples of loving and tender contact and of fond, long-term relationships between the British and their subject peoples, as well as between countless individuals of different colour, ethnicity and national identity. Although there is considerable evidence that the British abused their power in a variety of ways within the Empire, and mostly at the expense of local women, who were raped, abducted, forced into unwelcome liaisons or simply seduced, there were also many examples of permanent or semi-permanent relationships; these included marriage or long-term concubinage (as it was rather quaintly called by contemporaries), in the negotiating of which local forms and customs were often followed scrupulously. Lonely British administrators in the African bush, or in the rainforests of South-East Asia, quite frequently went through the formalities of paying the 'bride-price' for the women with whom they formed partnerships and liaisons.

Nor is there a great deal to choose between the undoubted power exercised by British men over the women of indigenous cultures and the way in which such females were subjected to the authority and control of their own menfolk. In a material sense, and perhaps also in terms of the respect and attention paid to her, a 'native' woman might well be better treated by a European male than by a husband or partner from her own tribe or race. The wholesale subordination of women, and indeed children of both sexes, to the needs and desires of indigenous males was unmistakable throughout the history of the British Empire, and is plainly discernible today throughout much of the world. This fact does not, of course, excuse or modify the British imperial male's exploitation of power and position in regard to sexual satisfaction, but it does at least put it into some sort of perspective.

It has often been argued that within the great sweep of territories that comprised the British Empire, men—and they are overwhelmingly men, not women—were also able to find sublimation or release in a variety of activities, from the demands of military campaigning to exploration, from administrative triumphs to the founding of new colonies. On this analysis, the 'asexual' male was able to 'sublimate' his sexual feelings in the undertaking of satisfying and constructive work, or in the completion of noble, or indeed ignoble, missions. Thus men described by their contemporaries as 'misogynists' or 'women-haters'... found fulfilment and, often obliquely, the satisfaction of their erotic needs in deeds of Empire.

... What the Empire provided for those British citizens who emigrated to it, served in it, or ruled it, was a wider, more complex, more varied, and often more compliant environment in which to fulfil their sexual needs than at home. It was often waggishly remarked during the heyday of British imperialism that 'the sun never set upon the Empire' because the Almighty was unable to trust what the British would get up to in the dark. It is now clear that at least some of what the British got up to in the dark was sexual and erotic in nature.

Even when this was not the case, a variety of perverse tastes could more easily be satisfied in the Empire's service. It was, for example, almost inevitable that service overseas involved British officials and officers in the handing out of punishment to both indigenous people and British subjects in the colonies. To those with a love of blood-letting, or simply with the desire to terrify and dominate their victims, the Empire was rich in opportunity.

This temptation to indulge sadistic inclinations could be found at the highest level. The activities of Lord Curzon, Viceroy of India between 1898 and 1905, are instructive in this respect. It is evident that Curzon was easily hurt, and also enjoyed hurting others. He was cruel to his exotic mistress, Elinor Glyn—of 'tiger skin' fame; he bullied his subordinates so constantly that when he left India it was said that there was not a single administrator of any standing whom he had not personally insulted; he routinely humiliated Indians, even the princes he affected to admire; he dismissed whole nations out of hand—Greeks, Bengalis, Egyptians and Turks.

But Curzon was not just a sadistic tormentor—a trait which perhaps sprang from what he claimed was a tyrannical fathering, and perhaps from homosexual harassment at Eton—he was also a masochist. He suffered for most of his life from the agonies—as he described it—of a permanently injured back. He reacted to political and administrative frustration with self-pitying disbelief. As Balfour shrewdly told him: 'You seem to think you are injured whenever you do not get exactly your own way!' His bitter quarrel with Kitchener [of Khartoum] over whether the latter—as Commander-in Chief of the Indian Army—or the Military Member of the Viceroy's Council should have control of

military policy and spending left him so broken and humiliated that he resigned his office in a tantrum. Almost his last great reform in India was the highly controversial partition of Bengal; this can be seen as both an act of cruel viceregal butchery and a Samson-like display of self-destruction, in that it ruined at a stroke his proclaimed strategy of convincing the Indian people that British rule was benevolent and superior to the rule of their own leaders.

It should not be supposed, however, that nineteenth- or early-twentieth-century Britain was a bastion of morality, peopled either by a race of rigidly controlled puritans or by individuals with uncomplicated, unwavering heterosexual tastes. The caricature of Victorian society as one of almost universal sexual repression and restraint is exactly that —a caricature. Despite the fact that the age of marriage among men was unusually high compared with that throughout much of the African and Asian countries of the Empire—averaging twenty-nine for males at the middle of the nineteenth century; despite the fact that upper- and middle-class opinion-makers and moralists insisted that children had no interest in sex and that 'respectable' women found little or no pleasure in sexual intercourse; despite the conspiracy of silence over sexual matters that descended all too often upon the home and almost completely upon the school classroom; despite the tendency to deny—or vehemently condemn—illegitimacy, prostitution and 'fornication', the Victorians were at least as sexually active within the United Kingdom as the generations that came before and after them.

For males from the upper and middle classes, heterosexual opportunities were almost limitless. By the 1880s the servant population, which was overwhelmingly female, numbered nearly 1,500,000, many of whom 'lived in'. Chambermaids and assistant cooks often carried out the 'off-duty' work of initiating young male members of the household into sexual knowledge and techniques. Nor did exile to boarding school mean the end of sexual experience. The public school system not merely taught Greek and Latin, the games ethic and various forms of muscular Christianity to its pupils, but also provided a flourishing venue for extra-curricular activities such as buggery and bullying.

For those older public school boys who preferred it, heterosexual sex was readily and cheaply available, often only a short walk from their seats of learning. Prostitution was one of the major industries of Victorian Britain. Although, unfortunately, it could do nothing to reduce the annual deficit in commodity trading, Victorian prostitution was an established fact of life throughout the country. Naturally enough, prostitutes worked mostly in the cities and towns of Britain: by the mid-nineteenth century it has been estimated that some 80,000 operated in London, with proportional amounts scattered throughout other cities and towns. The widespread use of prostitutes—particularly by men from the middle and upper classes—at least kept the ideals of the virgin bride and the chaste wife intact. A considerable number of female prostitutes were juveniles, perhaps not surprisingly in an age when so many families lived in poverty and when the age of consent for girls remained at twelve until 1875, when it was raised to thirteen.

The age of consent did not apply to boys at all, which may well have accounted for the considerable number of youthful male prostitutes who not merely worked in brothels but also hung around the London parks and railway stations, and were to be found in other major urban areas.

To all of this must be added the widespread accessibility and prevalence of pornography. The British Vice Society confiscated over 250,000 pornographic photographs between 1868 and 1880, and London was recognised towards the end of the century as the capital, not only of the British Empire, but of a booming international trade in erotic pictures and pornographic writing.

The poverty, and the overcrowded and brutal living conditions, which far too often characterised the life of the urban poor were doubtless important contributory factors to what Victorian moralists denounced as 'vice'. A considerable number of working-class marriages—perhaps as many as a third—took place with the woman already pregnant. As if all of this was not bad enough for the moralists, the level of venereal disease, and the difficulty in curing it, gave rise to widespread concern. The embarrassing discovery at the outset of the Boer War in 1899 that a very substantial number of working-class volunteers were unfit for military service merely confirmed in a dramatic fashion the various forms of ill-health that were endemic among an alarming proportion of the population.

All of this accorded ill with the late-Victorian and Edwardian need to see Britain as a nation fit to triumph in the struggle between rival imperial systems and economies. It also coincided with, and partly provoked, the increasingly widely expressed anxieties over national degeneracy and decline, anxieties that became linked in the minds of many individuals and groups with the perils of masturbation and licentious living. Lord Rosebery asserted in 1900 that 'An Empire such as ours requires as its first condition an Imperial race—a race vigorous and industrious and intrepid. Health of mind and body exalt a nation in the competition of the universe. The survival of the fittest is an absolute truth in the conditions of the modern world.'

This rising tide of anxiety and self-criticism not merely encouraged the social reforms of the Edwardian era, but had already helped to launch a vigorous and frequently intolerant 'Purity Campaign' towards the end of the nineteenth century. Although it is difficult to estimate the impact of the Purity Campaign upon sexual activities of all kinds, there is no doubt that it led many leading figures in British society to pursue their sexual inclinations with far more prudence than before. It was in juxtaposition to this trend that the trial and prosecution of Oscar Wilde in 1895 became such a *cause célèbre*, not least because Wilde was perceived as hurling an obscene challenge at the purity campaigners through the ostentation with which he flaunted his homosexuality.

As a result of all this, by the turn of the century it had become virtually impossible to discuss sexual matters in public, and almost as difficult to speak of them in private. Rather than face condemnation, disgrace and ridicule, the overwhelming majority of British people, especially those from the upper and middle classes, refrained from mentioning sexual matters and as a consequence failed to address, either in public or in private, sexual problems and difficulties.

Within the British Empire, however, it was far easier to lead relatively uninhibited sexual lives. There is overwhelming evidence that throughout the impe-

rial system white men continued to liaise with, abuse and exploit the women of indigenous societies wherever the British flag was raised. Sexual contact with 'native' women became a perk of the imperial system, something to be anticipated and enjoyed rather than avoided and disguised. Indeed, many Victorian men glorified in the sexual opportunities thus vouchsafed them, and recorded their pleasures unashamedly:

[Native women] understand in perfection all of the arts and wiles of love, are capable of gratifying any tastes, and in face and figure they are unsurpassed by any women in the world.... It is impossible to describe the enjoyment I experience in the arms of such syrens.

The dancing girls of South India, the Chinese women of Malaya, girls from Nigeria, the exotic maidens of the South Seas, and the mixed-race females of the West Indies were all praised for their sexual skills and their passion, as well as for their availability.

The sexual services of local boys and men were also widely available throughout the Empire, nearly always on the basis of payment, or at least material reward. Despite the moral indignation that evidence of such 'free-market' sodomy provoked among the purity campaigners and many others, the economic imperatives of Empire, particularly manifested in the shipping of tens of thousands of indentured labourers to man plantations, build railways or work the mines, made homosexual activity in the workers' compounds an inevitable part of the process. The moral outcry that accompanied the campaign in Britain against the system of 'Chinese slavery' in the gold mines of the Transvaal after the Boer War owed at least part of its intensity to the belief that homosexual activity was commonplace within the mining compounds.

Indentured labourers and miners locked up in their dormitories at night could at least protest that they were being denied access to women. For their part, many British men who engaged in sexual relationships with 'native females' also tended to claim that they acted as they did chiefly because they were unable to find enough European women to meet their needs. For much of the history of the British Empire, service overseas often did indeed mean a solitary lifestyle or living within an all-male environment. Despite the disapproval of purity campaigners, it was generally recognised that sexual activity brought emotional release and some degree of private satisfaction to individual lives.

It was thus possible to construct a plausible argument that sexual relationships with African and Asian women, and, at a pinch, with local males, fulfilled an important imperial function. If the energies and activities of traders, military personnel, administrators and emigrants —among others—made the wheels of Empire turn, the complex machinery was at least partially lubricated by the sexual activities of the British overseas.

In India during the eighteenth century, British servants of the East India Company had been positively encouraged to enter into liaisons with, or even to marry, Indian females. No doubt such contacts helped to improve and consolidate the commercial and political relationships between Europeans and the indigenous people. By the end of the eighteenth century, however, official policy stamped out the hitherto cosmopolitan and inter-racial character of the British presence in the sub-continent. Not merely were Indians prohibited from holding military and civil office under the East India Company, but Anglo-Indians—the products of inter-racial marriage and intercourse —were denied office and barred from official functions. By the beginning of the nineteenth century intermarriage between British and Indians had virtually ceased.

Later, by the mid-Victorian period, the improved and speedier communications between Britain and India, as well as the need to stabilise and consolidate British control in the post-Mutiny period, had led to the arrival of large numbers of British women in the sub-continent. As the memsahibs grew in number, social contacts between British males and Indians, whether male or female, dwindled. The presence of the memsahibs also made British men more sensitive to the perceived dangers of Indian men finding British females sexually attractive. The end-product of all of this was a deepening of distrust and an increase in intolerance.

There was another price to pay for British imperial expansion. This was, quite simply, a substantial increase in overseas prostitution, and the concomitant increase in venereal disease amongst British men serving in the Empire. In order to keep some control of the situation, the British authorities in India sanctioned the introduction of regulated prostitution. During the post-Mutiny period, until the late 1880s, seventy-five cantonments were designated as centres of regulated prostitution, complete with medical examination, systematic registration, and the hospital facilities to treat prostitutes suffering from venereal disease. The introduction of the system had more to do with maintaining the good health of the troops and, as a consequence, military efficiency, than with demonstrating liberal enlightenment.

It was, nonetheless, an effective arrangement. Between 1880 and 1888, when these practical arrangements were officially suspended as a result of the objections of the moral purity campaigners, the incidence of syphilis in the army in India was running at a rate below that recorded among soldiers serving in the British Army at home. But after 1888 there was a dramatic increase in the occurrence of syphilis in the Indian Army, peaking at over 250 per thousand troops in 1895. So bad had the situation become that by 1897 new regulations were introduced which had the effect once more of dramatically reducing the incidence of syphilis in the Indian Army, which had fallen to a new low by 1908.

During the twentieth century, and particularly after the First World War, the elaborate prostitution networks which had characterised the latter part of the nineteenth century, as well as the incidence of venereal disease among British men serving overseas, diminished. Among the factors that contributed to this were the improvements in the employment prospects of women, particularly in Europe, the greater availability of the condom for the male, improved standards of personal hygiene and somewhat more open attitudes towards sexual identity and sexual problems. . . .

It would be a pointless exercise to attempt to evaluate what nearly four centuries of contact between the British and the indigenous people of their colonies amounted to. It has been argued that, on balance, 'Sexual interaction between the British and non-Europeans probably did more long-term good than harm to race relations.' Whether anybody can arrive at a more concrete and confident judgement is extremely doubtful.

As in the lives of individuals and communities throughout the world, sexual contacts within the British Empire were characterised by joyful discovery, mutual esteem, exploitation, abuse, violence, compromise and accommodation. Although whites were overwhelmingly in control of the interaction, they were not universally so, and some at least, like the suicidal Hector MacDonald [the Commander-in-Chief of British forces in Ceylon (now Sri Lanka)], paid a terrible price.

In one area, moreover, the potential for sexual interaction between the races was almost always damaging and destructive. This was when black or brown men made advances to, were perceived to desire, or even had sexual relationships with, white females. On these rare occasions, the cause of race relations was certainly not advanced, and violent and deep-seated hatreds of black or brown men, who were perceived—consciously or unconsciously—as representing the primitive, atavistic 'other', became common currency.

Finally it must be remembered that very large numbers of British men overseas refrained, for a whole variety of reasons, from sexual relationships with indigenous females. Although Empire was almost always about economic profitability and political power, it would be wrong to assume that the ruthless and unbridled sexual exploitation of the black and brown subjects of imperial rule was an inevitable part of the power structure —a perk of office like a handsome pension or a solar topee.

At the same time, it is perhaps too much to claim that 'There are, at least in the pre-AIDS era, worse sins in running an empire, as in life, than the sexual ones.' The use of one individual by another solely for the purpose of self-gratification, however, is rarely an edifying spectacle, as even the briefest assessment of late-twentieth-century prostitution, particularly of the growth of 'sexual tourism' to economically needy states like Thailand or the Philippines, will reveal. In this regard the British Empire can claim no special dispensation. The imagery of imperial control reeked of sexuality: continents were 'penetrated', tribes 'subdued', districts 'ravished', territories 'mastered', local potentates 'seduced', countries 'raped'. It was small wonder that uncountable numbers of indigenous people suffered similar fates.

NO

Luise White

PROSTITUTION, DIFFERENTIATION, AND THE WORLD ECONOMY: NAIROBI 1899–1939

THE ERA OF THE INTERVENTIONIST STATE...

We tend to think that sexual relations are personal and private matters. While we may read dozens of books advising us on how to achieve intimacy, we generally believe that decisions about who sleeps with whom, where, for how long, and under what kinds of encouragement are the results of passions so personal that they cannot be studied systematically. We believe this partly because we see matters such as sexual attraction and choosing a partner as timeless qualities, where choice is personal, so personal as to make any serious inquiry difficult, if not pointless. But how do we know what is personal and what is not? Perhaps if we look at those sexual relations that are the most furtive—conducted in alleys and doorways not because either party likes it better that way, but because those are the only spaces available for such acts —we can see people brought together by forces other than their personal desires. Perhaps we can begin to observe people who occasionally sleep together because of cattle diseases, falling food crop prices, and increased cash crop production.

In this [selection] I want to look at two forms of prostitution that developed in Nairobi, Kenya between 1899 and 1939. Both forms, or ways for women to conduct the sale of sexual access to themselves, emphasized brief sexual relations with customers rather than night-long fictions of matrimonial bliss, and both forms were known for the aggressiveness with which women sought their customers. All the labor forms, in Nairobi and presumably elsewhere, were determined by specific crises in rural society and the women's relationship to housing in the town. In Kenya there is no evidence, oral or written, of anything that could be even vaguely construed as pimping: when women prostitute themselves, they retain all their earnings. How a woman prostitutes herself—with which form—indicates the urgency with which she requires money. In Kenya the women who walked the streets (*watembezi* in

Swahili, widely spoken in Nairobi) were precisely those women who took the pennies from sex conducted in doorways back to the stunted agricultural economies of East Africa, and enabled their families to recoup some of the losses the world economy had forced upon them. It was the women who quietly waited in their rooms for men to come to them (*malaya* in Swahili), the ones who provided the widest range of domestic services, including cooked food and bath water, and had the most discreet and circumspect of relationships, who accumulated capital for themselves, and most definitely not for their families.

Nairobi was founded in 1899 at the foot of the fertile highlands that were to be taken over by white settlers. Built around a swamp where no one had lived before, everyone who came there, black or white, female or male, was a migrant of some sort. Europeans came to settle because Kenya offered more opportunities than they might otherwise inherit in their homes; African men came because their inheritance was substantially delayed (by the untimely combination of natural disaster and European conquest), and because they were forced to do so. From 1902, a tax was levied on married men, payable in coin that could most easily be obtained by working for Europeans. Young African men were observed to work to pay their fathers' taxes (polygamous men had higher tax rates), and then work to enhance their own inheritance. They left the wage labor force once they married, and to secure a still larger supply of male laborers, in 1910 a tax was introduced on all males over 16.

Why did women come to Nairobi, and why did they become prostitutes? We know that they became prostitutes because there were simply no jobs for women then or in the next forty years. Some came to set themselves up as independent heads of households. "In those days," said one widow, "I didn't get another husband; there was another way to make a living then." Another woman said, "At home, what could I do? Grow crops for my husband and my father. In Nairobi, I could earn my own money, for myself." But most women came to help their families. By the end of the nineteenth century those families were primarily agriculturalists already differentiated into rich and poor and everything in between. In almost all those families women and livestock were the traditional elements of wealth, exchange, reproduction, and, of course, status. They could be exchanged for each other and they could reproduce more like themselves. They were integral elements in the cycle of family formation and they were at the same time investments. Thus, men with many wives could produce more daughters and grain with which to exchange for livestock, and young men would work for their fathers so that they would eventually be given the livestock with which to wed. The most valuable livestock was cattle, then sheep, then goats.

In the 1890s, a devastating series of cattle epidemics swept through Eastern Africa. By 1897, central Kenya was struck by drought, famine, and smallpox. It had the effect of turning the world (and its values) inside out—with as many as 60 percent of all the local cattle dead, famine devalued the remaining cattle and, indeed, everything but foodstuffs. Agriculturalists dominated, and men with many wives could find no one to marry their daughters and thus replenish their herds. Virtually an entire generation of wealthy men faced an end to their way of life. All the available evidence points to the fact that these men's dwindling status and wealth was restored and restocked by their daughters' prostitution. These women already knew that permanent sexual access to them had an exchange value; they simply transformed the location and control of the work so that they sold repeated sexual access to themselves to many men. Thus, as early as 1899 daughters of the "loose women" in Kenya's rudimentary townships, and by 1909 some 300 Masai *watembezi* prostitutes were arrested in Nairobi.

How do we know that these women were the daughters of wealthy fathers? How do we know they were not impoverished young women who sought through prostitution to better their own lives? First of all, we know that in the years before World War I, prostitutes earned roughly between four and eight times what male wage-earners did (partly due to the low value of the currency at that time), so that any rapid gains accruing to the older generation would almost have to have come from prostitutes' earnings. Secondly, we know because these women, the *watembezi*, left prostitution once the requisite number of livestock were acquired. Those women who came from impoverished households also came to Nairobi, and the best evidence I have indicates they and they alone became *malaya* prostitutes.

The pre-World War I interaction of the colonial state, the Masai, and other pastoral peoples provides an excellent example of a sequence of destocking, prostitution, and livestock acquisition. Masai herds were decimated in the epidemics of the 1890s and their economy seriously undermined; Masai women seem to have been active in prostitution even

before Nairobi was established, and in the early years of this century they were said to dominate Nairobi prostitution. Meanwhile, pastoral peoples in western Kenya, an area largely unaffected by the cattle epidemics, raided British installations. The British led Masai soldiers in punitive expeditions against the Kipsigis and Nandi, and by 1905 it was estimated that 55 percent of Nandi cattle had been taken to Nairobi. The Masai soldiers were paid in goats that they parlayed into cattle (at rates of about fifteen goats per cow), just as prostitutes' profits were invested in livestock. In 1911, when Masai herds were said to approach their nineteenth-century levels, there was a noticeable Masai retreat from prostitution and wage labor. By 1907, however, colonial officials began to observe an increasing number of Kipsigis and Nandi women entering prostitution, replacing the Masai women and accosting men on settlers' farms and on the streets of Nairobi. These women, too, were said to buy livestock with their earnings, at rates that were at least double what the Masai had paid, as white settlements brought about a demand for meat that slowly began to raise the value of cattle. According to contemporary male authors, by 1909 Nandi women were "notorious" throughout Kenya and by 1913 "the most enlightened" Nandi were those prostitutes who had returned home after a few years in Nairobi—presumably they knew the most English and belonged to the wealthiest families.

What were these women doing? They were doing through prostitution what in better times they would have done through marriage: stock their fathers' herd and keep livestock values competitive. They had to restore their fathers' property—cattle, not daughters—to its earlier level of prestige. That they were doing this in the streets, in alleys, loudly, aggressively, testifies to the urgency with which monies were required. For despite how disrespectful the *watembezi* form looked, despite its emphasis on brief sexual encounters in less than sensual surroundings, the means of accumulation was anything but disorderly: it was aggressive and swift by design; it matched high risks with high profits. It would then seem that anything more than occasional *watembezi* prostitution was not caused by dire poverty; it was the response of relatively wealthy families to a sudden decrease in their wealth. Young women became streetwalkers not as a survival strategy, but to help their families maintain previous levels of differentiation— and most of these women did not just survive, they prospered.

During World War I prostitution in Nairobi changed. The *watembezi* form still dominated, indeed it took on a revitalized dimension in pursuit of British and South African troops during the war, but its practitioners tended to be long-term residents of Nairobi, not immigrants from newly impoverished societies. "It was extra money, we went to pick beans and had a man in secret; sometimes a woman would go... just for the men," said a teenage woman who had been born in Nairobi. World War I *watembezi* were on the whole older than the young women who had sought men on the streets and back alleys of the prewar city. Wartime *watembezi* earned large sums, but they saved their cash or bought urban real estate. They could not have bought cattle with their earnings had they wanted to, so successfully had pastoralist fathers and daughters managed to reconstruct and reestablish the value of their herds.

Unlike pastoralists, many East African cultivators prospered from the events of the 1890s and the coming of colonial rule. Not only were they able to sell grain at exceptionally high rates of exchange to other Africans, they fed the European expansion into East Africa as well. Until World War I, African agriculturalists dominated local and export markets, and many of the Kikuyu farmers in central Kenya became wealthy. Until the ravages of military conscription during World War I and the rapidly increased white settlement after the war, the Kikuyu had sent relatively few sons into wage labor and fewer daughters into prostitution. The combined weight of white farmers' land-grabbing, and legislation introduced to prevent further white farmers' labor shortages, reduced many Kikuyu farmers to resident laborer status on European farms. Nevertheless, many Kikuyu "squatters" and cultivators on their own farms were able to produce and sell surplus crops. By the mid-1920s the increased production of maize and rice in other parts of the country began to erode the profits Kikuyu farmers could get for potatoes and millet in Nairobi. The price of potatoes, for example, had increased by 57 percent between 1924 and 1928 and the prices of other Kikuyu crops had risen as well: fewer people bought them. By 1928, both Kikuyu chiefs and *malaya* prostitutes in Nairobi complained about married Kikuyu women coming to town as if they were selling vegetables, but prostituting themselves with workingmen in the alleys of the African areas, and returning to their homes before dark. It seems very likely that these Kikuyu *watembezi* were not acting out of any immorality or personal insecurities; they were engaging in prostitution so that they could maintain the standard of living that only a few years before they had obtained solely through the sale of their farm produce. This *watembezi* prostitution was not about any preference for sex conducted in doorways and bushes, but about keeping a standard of living buoyant in the face of declining food profits.

Cattle diseases and state-sponsored destocking do not qualify as an incursion of the world economy into peoples' private lives. Rising crop prices are facts of life for farmers all over the world, and are not a unique characteristic of colonized peoples. To see how the world economy influences what we think of as intimate behavior, we have to look at those crops introduced specifically by colonial powers for the specific reason of making their colonies pay off: cash crops. Coffee, tea, cotton, sugar, and tobacco are a few examples. Among critics of imperialism, cash crops have an importance almost unmatched by any other colonial introduction: they are almost never edible crops; they take up arable land that might be better used for food crops; they are often produced on plantations and concentrate local labor in such a way as to remove people from food production. They are often produced at gunpoint. This list could go on for pages, but the most significant thing about cash crops is that they draw producers into a worldwide system of supply and profit and loss that is determined by conditions far outside the country producing the coffee, tea, or sugar. Unlike mining—the wholesale extraction of a country's wealth—cash crop production pits various countries' producers against each other. Coffee growers in Kenya do not compete with each other, they compete with coffee growers in Brazil and Colombia and Sumatra. The amount they pay their workers in each of these countries has nothing to do with how hard these men

and women work; it has to do with the competitive value of their coffee crop relative to that of coffees produced thousands of miles away under different conditions. The only real influence local producers have on profit is quantity, but this can backfire when demand drops. In most colonies it was a crime for Africans to uproot their cash crops when prices were low and plant food crops instead. Some scholars have argued that cash crop production enabled Africans to resist the depredations of wage labor, but this argument fails to tell us what happens when the cash crop is not wanted, or is overproduced, or is deemed obsolete by the production of synthetics. The introduction of cash crops made African cultivators as dependent on the health and stability of world markets as they were on the rainfall.

It is this kind of dependence that determines not only who becomes a prostitute, but the duration of the services prostitutes provide. The process does not happen overnight, but it does happen with great clarity. In 1903 the German colonizers of what was to become Tanganyika (when it was handed over to the British at the end of World War I) introduced coffee to the Haya people on the western shore of Lake Victoria, a thousand kilometers (600 miles) from the sea. They did not concentrate coffee in plantations, but gave some to every large farm. Before the War, coffee did well in the fertile hills of Bukoba, but it was not until the worldwide boom of the 1920s that Haya producers began to see spectacular profits. By the mid-1920s the wealthier Haya were almost heady with success; they hired laborers from the neighboring Belgian colonies to come pick their coffee and "squat" on their land, and as Christians they ceased exchanging their daughters for livestock and requested and received a cash bride-price, which by about 1927 was the equivalent of $175 or more. Unlike many African peoples, the Haya permitted divorce, and fathers returned the bride-price in full. Thus, in 1930 when the world price of coffee dropped a staggering 90 percent, Haya producers were in trouble; it was not even worth their while to ship their produce to the coast, but they had laborers living on their farms who demanded payment nonetheless. Although the problem lay in cash crop production, the solution was found in women. Young wives were divorced and fathers repaid the bride-price, shifting the problem back on themselves—a generation of fathers now had to come up with cash to repay their own increasing debts and refurbish the foundations of a sagging cash crop economy. How the decision to solve this problem was made within individual households is not known, but within two or three years Haya women in their early twenties appeared in large numbers on the streets of Kampala (Uganda), Dar es Salaam (Tanganyika), and Nairobi.

Haya women did not walk in the streets in these towns; instead they rented rooms in the African areas and sat outside their houses and solicited men from there. This was called the *Wazi-Wazi* form, from a slang term for Haya common in Nairobi. Haya women scandalized the more sedate and circumspect prostitutes of these areas, who saw such open solicitation and aggressive behavior as a threat to their respectability and their profits. Haya women were known for shouting out their prices to men, and they took these men into the four-by-eight foot rooms they shared with other Haya immigrants for brief sexual

encounters, for which they received just about 17 percent of the world price of raw coffee beans. Between 1930 and 1935 the world price for a thirty-five-pound bag of coffee beans varied between three and seven shillings. In those same years, *Wazi-Wazi* prostitutes in Nairobi charged fifty cents—one half of one shilling—for sexual intercourse. *Malaya* women were justifiably upset since this had the overall effect of lowering the price for brief sexual relations for all prostitutes, at a time when most *malaya* prostitutes earned perhaps a third more than male laborers did. *Wazi-Wazi* prostitutes were also said to fight with the men who refused to pay them and call on their neighbors for help—practices unheard of by both *malaya* and *watembezi* women in 1930s Nairobi. An old woman born near Nairobi in about 1900 said that the biggest change she observed in her lifetime was that after the mid-1930s "women beat up men." According to a younger *malaya* woman, cash was so important to a Haya woman that she "would risk her blood to get her money." Indeed, it was so important to Haya women that they were reputed to send money home each week or month, and if a Haya woman died in Nairobi her friends would take her body and her money the hundreds of miles back to Bukoba. Why did Haya do all this? Clearly because the advantages and opportunities of being a daughter of a well-to-do coffee-growing family outweighed the disadvantages of being a prostitute in Nairobi.

How did the colonial state respond to streetwalkers and *Wazi-Wazi* women? While it was not in the interests of public order that women be allowed to call out a price to men as they returned from work, there were few arrests of *watembezi* prostitutes in colonial Nairobi, and none of Haya women. More than any other kind of political entity, colonial states do not act with one voice, let alone motivation; they mediate between different and competing interests—the government at home, the settlers it must protect, the African leaders who make ruling easier, and the Africans who must be made to work in colonial enterprises, but in ways that do not antagonize any of the groups above. Although we might think that no state encourages prostitution, these particular interest groups had nothing against it. In Nairobi and other cities, the presence of prostitutes and the amenities and cooked food they sometimes offered, made the task of getting urban Africans back to work day after day somewhat easier. It also reduced African wages just enough to keep them at work a few months longer than they otherwise would have stayed. Moreover, the colonial police were busy with the Africans the state made into criminals, those Africans who broke the law by spending more than a month looking for work in Nairobi, or leaving an employer before their labor contract had expired. The state knew about Haya and *watembezi* women, but found them more of a service than an offense. The values of accumulation and entrepreneurship subsidized solid, Christian, patriarchal households on the western shore of Lake Victoria and helped extend the laboring time of hundreds of badly needed unskilled African workers in Nairobi.

No new forms of prostitution emerged after 1939. While the *watembezi* form dominated World War II prostitution, it did so under special circumstances, only some of which could be identified as young women's family labor. That no new forms emerged after the mid-1930s is especially significant, and may well mark a point of transition in East African agricultural history. The biggest change in African colonial history has nothing to do with barbarism and civilization, nothing to do with tribe and nation. It has to do with a transition around the issue of Africans' participation in wage labor. In most of Africa in the era before World War II, wage labor was a means by which Africans could supplement their farm production. It was not something they relied on solely for their subsistence. The monies earned working enhanced farming, however unwillingly and hesitantly that labor was originally undertaken. By World War II, in those areas where most men were migrant laborers, wage labor became the means by which most people subsisted, and farming itself was dependent on the cash migrant laborers brought home. So atrophied were the agricultural systems of these parts of Africa that women farmers could not plant maize or cotton or beans unless their husbands, working on tea estates in Kenya or the docks of East Africa, sent them the money to buy seeds—even subsistence required an assist from wage labor. These areas also sent a steady stream of prostitutes to towns, but they went as independent accumulators, not as daughters bailing their families out of trouble. Elsewhere, African agriculture took off in ways that colonialists had not full expected—and in fact were to complain about—and these families did not have daughters who became prostitutes. That no new forms of prostitution emerged after 1939 testifies to the impoverishment of the poorest peasant households; they continued to have crises, but they no longer attempted to solve them—if they could be solved at all—from within the family.

POSTSCRIPT

Were Indigenous Sex Workers Under British Imperialism Always Powerless?

A good source for consideration of the subject of prostitution or sex work is Judith R. Walkowitz's *Prostitution and Victorian Society: Women, Class, and the State* (Cambridge University Press, 1980). Placed in the context of moral reform and, specifically, of the Contagious Diseases Acts of 1864, 1866, and 1869, Walkowitz's study examines the complex net of social attitudes and relationships in late-nineteenth-century Victorian England within which women became prostitutes. Prostitution still represented a choice when all other alternatives were undesirable. And, Walkowitz found, the trade was largely organized by women who established a strong female subculture; they were not victims but agents of change for their own lives.

Margaret Strobel explores the experience of British women in "Gender, Race, and Empire in Nineteenth- and Twentieth-Century Africa and Asia," in Renate Bridenthal, Susan Mosher Stuard, and Merry E. Weisner, eds., *Becoming Visible: Women in European History*, 3rd ed. (Houghton Mifflin, 1998). As wives of colonial administrators, domestic servants, missionaries, ethnographers, and anthropologists, British women were sometimes also reformers. Critical of indigenous practices, they were, however, unwilling or unable to critique imperialism itself.

Patricia W. Romero has edited *Women's Voices on Africa: A Century of Travel Writings* (Markus Wiener Publishing, 1992). Spanning the century from 1853 to 1954, this collection ranges from Nigeria and the Gold Coast in West Africa, through Capetown and Durban in southern Africa, to Kenya and Ethiopia in East Africa. The book includes the voices of missionaries, colonial wives, and travelers. Many of these women are interested in and comment on the African women they meet, sometimes critically, often maternalistically.

Ruth Rosen's *The Lost Sisterhood: Prostitution in America, 1900–1918* (Johns Hopkins University Press, 1982) examines prostitution as both a cultural symbol and a social institution that women used as a means of survival. Many reformers saw in prostitution proof of the sexual and economic exploitation of women in a patriarchal society; for sex workers, it may have been simply a form of work, better than some, worse than others. Chapter 9 of Christine Stansell's *City of Women: Sex and Class in New York, 1789–1860* (University of Illinois Press, 1987) draws a similar conclusion. Titled "Women on the Town," the chapter deals with the movement of prostitution out of the bawdy houses and into public spaces like Broadway, observing that prostitution was neither a tragic fate (as the moralists believed) nor an act of defiance, but rather it was a way of "getting by."

ISSUE 18

Did the Bolshevik Revolution Improve the Lives of Soviet Women?

YES: Richard Stites, from *The Women's Liberation Movement in Russia: Feminism, Nihilism, and Bolshevism, 1860–1930* (Princeton University Press, 1978)

NO: Françoise Navailh, from "The Soviet Model," in Françoise Thébaud, ed., *A History of Women in the West, vol. 5: Toward a Cultural Identity in the Twentieth Century* (Belknap Press, 1994)

ISSUE SUMMARY

YES: History professor Richard Stites argues that in the early years of the Bolshevik Revolution, the Zhenotdel, or Women's Department, helped many working women take the first steps toward emancipation.

NO: Film historian Françoise Navailh contends that the Zhenotdel had limited political influence and could do little to improve the lives of Soviet women in the unstable period following the revolution.

Compared with life under the czars, life for women after the Bolshevik Revolution was characterized by greater variety and freedom. The Romanov dynasty had ruled Russia for 300 years, and the Orthodox Church had ruled for a much longer period. Both had reinforced a world of patriarchal authority, class structure, and patterns of deference. Although the revolution overthrew the power of both church and monarch, the new communist state had a power and authority of its own. Between 1917 and 1920 Soviet women received equal rights in education and marriage, including the choice to change or keep their own names and the opportunity to own property; the rights to vote and to hold public office; access to no-fault divorce, common-law marriage, and maternity benefits; workplace protection; and access to unrestricted abortion. They were the first women to gain these rights—ahead of women in France, England, and the United States—but the question is whether or not these legal rights translated into improvements in their day-to-day lives.

A feminist movement had developed in urban areas as early as the 1905 workers' revolution, and women joined men in leading strikes and protest demonstrations. By the time of the Bolshevik Revolution in 1917, however, the goals of the leadership were primarily economic, and feminism was dismissed as bourgeois or middle class. In a workers' revolution, women and men were to be equal. Housework and child care were to be provided collectively, and the family, like the monarchy, was to be replaced with something new. Women gained access to economic independence by becoming workers, which was supposed to provide them with the basis for equality within marriage.

The German philosopher Karl Marx had argued that the family reflects the economic system in society. Under capitalism, the bourgeois family exists to reproduce workers and consumers; it exploits women by unfairly burdening them with full responsibility for housework and child care. If similarly exploited workers—what Marx called the proletariat—overthrew the capitalist system that allowed factory owners to grow rich from their workers' labor, Marx believed that the family would undergo an equally dramatic transformation. In this scenario, no one would be "owned" by anyone else. Prostitution would disappear, and, as the state took responsibility for childrearing and education, women would be free to work and become economically self-sufficient. People would then be free to marry for love or sexual attraction rather than for economic considerations.

V. I. Lenin, who emerged as the leader and architect of the new order, was committed to women's rights. First and foremost, however, he was committed to a socialist revolution. When the struggle to make legal changes that would be felt in women's lives came into conflict with the goals of the revolution, there was no question in Lenin's mind about which would have to be sacrificed. In this early period, a fascinating group of women briefly held highly visible leadership positions and had the chance to put their ideas into practice, at least during the first decade. Alexandra Kollontai was one of the most articulate and effective leaders of the Zhenotdel, or Women's Department of the Communist Party, whose purpose between 1919 and 1930 was to educate and mobilize the women of the Soviet state to participate fully in the revolution.

In the following selections, Richard Stites focuses on the work of the Zhenotdel in reaching out to the Jewish, Christian, Muslim, and Buddhist women of the East whose lives in the Caucasus, Volga, and Central Asia were the most severely restricted. Raising the consciousness of these women in the face of brutal male opposition contributed significantly to women's liberation and the development of the socialist state, Stites concludes.

Françoise Navailh, in contrast, maintains that although Soviet women were granted unprecedented legal rights, almost without a struggle, the real task of Zhenotdel was to translate these rights into a new way of life. Navailh judges it to have failed in significantly improving the lives of Soviet women.

YES

Richard Stites

BOLSHEVIK LIBERATION

"Don't make an issue of my womanhood."

—*Ninotchka* (1939)
C. Brackett, B. Wilder, *and* W. Reisch

THE LIMITS OF EQUALITY

"The future historian," said Kollontai after the Civil War, "will undoubtedly note that one of the characteristics of our revolution was that women workers and peasants played not—as in the French Revolution—a passive role, but an active important role." The following paragraphs may serve as a gloss on this remark. Though there was a good deal of spontaneous activity among the women of the Red side, Bolshevik women organizers—Kollontai foremost among them—did not leave much to chance. In a propaganda pamphlet of 1920 addressed to women, Kollontai directly invited working and peasant women to support the Red Front in every possible way including combat. Conscious of her own former anti-war propaganda, she was careful to point out the difference between the exploitative character of the Great War and the liberating and defensive nature of the present one, tying together the thesis of women's capacity to fight with the need to defend the equality that they had won in the Revolution. The Soviet publicist, V. Bystryansky, began his argument in *Revolution and Woman* (1920) with a reference to Fourier's statement about measuring a society's level of progress by examining the level of women's emancipation in that society, and made flattering comments about the military potential of women. Variations of these themes were the stock in trade of propagandists such as Krupskaya, Balabanova, and other Bolshevik women who held important propaganda posts during the Civil War.

What is striking about Russian women's participation in this War is the variety and novelty of the functions that they performed. As in the past, women carried out every conceivable support task on the home front, ranging from feeding and sanitary operations to building fortifications and digging trenches in beleaguered cities. As in World War I, women served in medical and combat capacities, but on a broader scale and in a much more organized context. Propaganda, psychological warfare, espionage, and police work—known previously to only a few exceptional women —now recruited large numbers of them. Women's participation was erratic and tentative during the first year of the War. In October 1919, the Zhenotdel gave greater definition to the functions of women and set up the machinery for large-scale and orderly recruitment. By the end of the war in 1920, conscription of young women for non-combatant service had begun, and high-ranking posts in Military Revolutionary Committees and Political Departments of the Red Army were occupied by women.. . .

The role of women in the political life of the country in the generation following the Revolution may be seen in two fairly distinct stages. In the first, roughly 1917–1923, a small but visible group of women held responsible positions during and immediately after the Civil War. After 1923–1925, when there were no more prominent individual Bolshevik women even close to the seats of power, a second stage began. Women were then and for the future absent both from positions of power and prestige and largely from public prominence; but at the same time, the lowest strata of women had begun to stir and to participate in a limited but real way in the political process, such as it was. And a modest number of women were permanently lodged in the middle range of political and administrative authority. The "major" women Bolsheviks as a group were clearly less eminent than the men on any reasonable list of leading Bolsheviks. There are, however, a few who, in terms of political work, public image, or both, may be set off from other Bolshevik women: Stasova, Armand, Bal-

abanova, Kollontai, and Krupskaya, all born between 1869 and 1878, and all possessing revolutionary credentials dating from the turn of the century or earlier (though only Krupskaya and Stasova could claim to be Old Bolsheviks).

Elena Stasova was at the very center of events in 1917, serving as the functioning Secretary of the Party during and immediately after the Revolution. Her reputation as storehouse of the Party's traditions had made her the logical candidate for the job. When the government moved to Moscow, however, Stasova remained behind; Lenin had found a more effective administrator in Yakov Sverdlov who had a talent for making policy as well. When Sverdlov died in 1919, Stasova resumed her work in the Secretariat under the tripartite management of Krestinsky, Preobrazhensky, and Serebryakov. But in 1920, when the staff was reorganized, Stasova resigned and requested a chancery position in one of the higher Party organizations. Krestinsky suggested instead that she go to work in Zhenotdel—a suggestion that Stasova immediately declined. Having worked at the center of political life, she perhaps resented being shunted off to what might have seemed mere auxiliary work. Stasova eventually found a congenial assignment as leader of the International Red Aid (MOPR)—a Comintern version of the old political Red Cross. From 1920 onward, she had no impact on the Soviet political scene. Here is a clear case of a woman who, in spite of certain administrative talents, was by her own admission always hazy on matters of theory and thus ultimately unsuited for top leadership in a Party which was still composed largely of intellectuals.

Inessa Armand died of cholera in 1920. She had been second only to Kollontai in energy and range of political work. In addition to founding and directing Zhenotdel, Inessa held important posts in the highest Party, Soviet, and economic agencies of Moscow Province; and she helped shape the international communist movement by organizing foreigners of Bolshevik sympathies into the Club of the Third International. Her political prominence was clearly enhanced by her exceptionally close relationship with Lenin (and Krupskaya). The notion, however, that Inessa had been Lenin's mistress—though gaining acceptance among a number of Western students—has no relevance to the question of her political importance, and the evidence is flimsy and unconvincing.

Angelica Balabanova (Balabanoff)... was an almost archetypical radical Russian woman. Brought up amid the luxury of a large Ukrainian manor house, she had felt the stirrings of revolutionary consciousness early, perceiving, as she says, the "difference between those who could *give* and those who had to *receive*." "My ardent desire," she recalled, "was to escape my conventional and egoistic milieu in order to devote myself fully to a cause from which I could live and die. This was not self-abnegation, but a wish to live a life which would make me *useful* to the suffering masses." The route of her "escape" took her to Brussels and then to Italy where she became a key figure in the socialist movement, acting for a time as Mussolini's secretary. After 1917, she came back to Russia and served in a number of posts including Foreign Minister of the Ukraine and Secretary of the Comintern. But her ardent service to the Bolshevik regime did not prevent her from repudiating it when it failed to meet her expectations. "The deformation of the October Revolution," she wrote,

"progressed at the same rate at which the individual replaced the masses. This substitution, which was made at the outset in good faith, was bound to degenerate in time." In 1921, she resigned her positions and left Soviet Russia forever.

Kollontai was by far the most active and versatile of the Bolshevik women of this era. A member of the tiny Central Committee at the time of the overthrow, she was soon appointed Commissar of Public Welfare. During her brief tenure as Commissar, Kollontai betrayed some administrative vacillation. At first she was reluctant to use force in dealing with left-over recalcitrant civil servants of the tsarist days. Lenin chided her by asking if she thought a revolution could be made with white gloves. But when she took some rather strong public measures against the Orthodox Church, he warned her to exercise tact when dealing with religious sensibilities. But it was her marriage to the younger revolutionary sailor, Pavel Dybenko,... that undercut the confidence that the Party leaders had briefly shown in her. Her association with him and his reckless and erratic behavior brought no credit upon her political reputation. "I will not vouch for the reliability or the endurance" said Lenin a few years later "of women whose love affair is intertwined with politics." Not that her revolutionary career was over by any means. She served as Commissar for Propaganda in the Ukraine, toured the front with Dybenko on an agit-train, and headed Zhenotdel.

Kollontai's exit from Soviet politics came in 1922, in connection with her role in the dissenting Workers' Opposition Group whose leader, Shlyapnikov, was her former lover. Kollontai herself drafted the program and distributed it to Party members in 1921. It was as much a product of her longstanding faith in the creative powers of the proletariat, first enunciated in *Social Bases,* as it was a tract for the times. Against the increasing centralism, authoritarianism, and bureaucratism which had overtaken the Party during the Civil War, she proposed "the collective, creative effort of the workers themselves." Her most suggestive theme was that collective, interpersonal relations among the producers generated great productivity, and that this productivity was diminished by the alienating presence of authoritarian officials—"the bosses and the bureaucrats." Kollontai's form of syndicalism, shared by many in the Russian labor movement, was seen by Lenin and others as a menace to unity and discipline in the Party. Lenin displayed his fury at the fateful Tenth Party Congress; when Kollontai persisted in her efforts to disseminate her ideas, she was removed from her posts and sent off to Norway on a minor diplomatic mission. She was eventually promoted to Soviet ambassador to Sweden; but her career as a Bolshevik political figure was over.

As Lenin's wife, Krupskaya had been a key organizational figure of the early Bolshevik movement in emigration because of her network of correspondence with agents in Russia. But after Lenin and Krupskaya arrived in revolutionary Russia, Stasova, not she, was appointed to head up the Secretariat of the Party in the Kseshinskya Palace. Krupskaya's main work and her abiding concern both before and after Lenin's death was propaganda and education. By her own admission, high politics held little interest for her, and she was almost reprimanded by the Central Committee for failing to attend Party meetings regularly. On the other hand, she was certainly a good deal

more than "first lady of the great Russian state" (Zetkin's pious phrase). Her pedagogical and journalistic activities contributed much to the training and liberation of women. After her well-known clash with Stalin during Lenin's illness, she did emerge as a potential rallying point for oppositional elements; but by 1925, this was all over, and she had come to realize that she was far from being a political match for the wily Stalin....

ZHENOTDEL

Whenever a revolution has been preceded by a long established underground movement, the structure of that movement—just as much as its leadership and its ideology—super-imposes itself on the political life of the new society. This is why Bolshevik Russia became a land of committees, commissions, congresses, and cells. Before 1917, the Bolshevik Party had been a congeries of local committees directed from the center by a small group that communicated with its branches by means of a newspaper (for general ideas) and peripatetic agents (for specific instructions); feedback to the center came through correspondence and rare congresses and conferences. After 1917, the Bolsheviks used these devices (now amplified by railroad, telegraphy, and wireless) of political organization and communication for social mobilization of the country in the same way that they had used them to destroy its former regimes. The "novel" methods of social communication all had their counterparts in the history of the revolutionary underground. The techniques of Zhenotdel—the post-revolutionary organ responsible for women's liberation in Soviet Russia—were no exception. They were summarized long before Zhenotdel came into existence in a list of instructions given by Klavdiya Nikolaeva to women workers in May 1917: Organize Social Democratic groups in your factory; appoint a liaison to *Rabotnitsa;* arrange meetings. It was all there—organization, filtering down of leaders, responsibility to the center (an editorial board), communication back to the rank and file through liaison and newspaper, and processing the instructions at local meetings. And it had been there, in embryo, for a generation.

But would the machinery be used? And to what end? That the "proletarian women's movement" would continue after the Revolution was a tacit assumption of its leaders and was inherent in the revolutionary movement itself. Kollontai, in 1921, spoke in retrospect of the hostility to the regime nourished by the vast majority of women and of their fears that it would uproot the family, decree the "heartless" separation of children from parents, and destroy the church. In 1918, she was already aware of the danger of disillusionment among the masses of women and of the need for long-range and patient work among them. Lenin, though he had little time to voice his opinion on the matter in the first years of Soviet power, was in full agreement with Kollontai, Inessa, and the others on the need for active liberation of Russian women—in life as well as in law. Thus the formal, legislative program of emancipation (the only one usually noted by historians) had to be given meaning in a social revolution from below. This is the true historical context of the Zhenotdel. . . .

During the Civil War, Inessa used the Zhenotdel to mobilize women in support of the Red Army and the new regime. Propaganda teams, like the ones headed by Krupskaya and Kollontai, threaded their way on agit-trains and boats through the Red areas, stopping at remote villages to regale the population with poster art, song-and-dance groups, and speeches. The popular "Natasha" (K. I. Samoilova), known affectionately among Russian women as "our own mother," sailed up and down the Volga with a plea for support and a promise of liberation which she proclaimed from the decks of the *Red Star.* She died of cholera during one of her cruises. At the local level, "volunteer Saturdays" (*subbotniki*) and "days of wounded Red Army Men" were launched to recruit previously inactive women in jobs like sewing underwear, bathing soldiers, and bandaging wounds. Recruiting work grew very slowly; and the Party sometimes tended to use Zhenotdel workers exclusively in such endeavors as food distribution, child and orphan care, and the struggle against illiteracy and superstition—areas of activity that, in the context, were really the Soviet equivalents of *Küche, Kinder,* and *Kirche.* Inessa Armand drove herself to exhaustion working fourteen to sixteen hours a day. By a stroke of fate, she was ordered by the Party to the Caucasus for a rest. There, in the fall of 1920, she took cholera and died.

Kollontai was chosen to succeed her. If she had been bypassed in 1918, it was probably only because of the Party's, especially Lenin's, greater confidence in Armand's reliability and obedience. Kollontai and Inessa had helped forge the women's movement, separately before the Revolution and together after it; and they shared the same philosophy of women's liberation. Kollontai held no brief for a "feminist" movement separate from or outside the Party; she even hoped to dissolve some of the purely "female" features of Zhenotdel work (such as the "women's pages" in Party newspapers). But she was equally firm in resisting any suggestions of liquidating the Zhenotdel itself. Passivity and lack of consciousness were the hallmarks of Russian women. She told Emma Goldman (who refused her invitation to work in Zhenotdel) that women "were ignorant of the simplest principles of life, physical and otherwise, ignorant of their own functions as mothers and citizens." It was imperative, then, to raise the consciousness of these women and to deal with specifically woman-related problems, such as maternity care, in their own special way. This, she said, was not feminism.

Kollontai was right. It was not feminism, at least as the word was then understood. The feminist movement in Western Europe and America, from 1848 to 1920, had ultimately settled on the vote as the capstone of emancipation. After acquiring it, no feminist movement in the West, until recent years, made many further steps toward realizing economic or sexual liberation; even less did it engage in any mass movement for the liberation of women of the working class or minorities. Bolshevik "feminism" reversed the social timetable of Western feminism. For the latter, political emancipation was the goal; for the former, it was only the beginning.

During her manifold assignments of the Civil War period, Kollontai had always (except during a serious illness) kept in touch with Zhenotdel activities. After her appointment, she led Zhenotdel with the abundant optimism, energy, and talent which she had displayed in other realms of revolutionary work. Her two year tenure as its leader (1920–1922) also happened to be a period of deep emotional and political tribulation for her. Kollontai's most important practical accomplishment was to turn Zhenotdel's energy away from wartime auxiliary work (the War ended in 1920) toward the subtler tasks of psychological and social demobilization. More spectacular and in the long run just as important was initiating the liberation of the so-called women of the East—the Muslim, Christian, Jewish, and Buddhist women of the non-western borderlands of Caucasia, the Volga, and Central Asia who were subjected to codes of sexual behavior unknown in the rest of Russia. The most severe of these was the Muslim şeriat that in practice gave women no status and no purpose other than as pleasure-giver, servant, housekeeper, and childbearer. Their isolation and untouchability was symbolized by "the veil" in all its varieties, the most severe of which was the *paranja*, a heavy horsehair garment that hung from the nose to the floor. Aside from serious organizational work among these women, Kollontai also brought some of them to Moscow for congresses where the exotic guests would tear off their face coverings before a startled audience. Criticized by some for excessive theatricality, Kollontai told Louise Bryant that "all pioneering work is theatrical." It was not the last time that an article of women's clothing would be seen as an enslaving, sexist fetish; and the doffing of the veil became the favorite gesture of baptism into free womanhood in the Soviet East....

Provincial Zhenotdels were assigned only eight full-time people in the organizational setup. Since five of them sat in the center, this meant only one instructor or *zhenorg* for every three districts of a province. Furthermore, [Bette] Stavrakis' study indicates that Zhenotdel, like most analogous Party organizations, suffered from personnel deficiency, shortage of funds, jurisdictional overlap, and superficiality at the grass roots level. The areas of greatest resistance to its efforts were the villages and the non-Slavic borderlands. The Ukrainian organizer, Kiselëva, walked miles from *raikom* headquarters to the little village of Sripal to gather the women into a reading cabin in order to organize them. The menfolk surrounded the cabin and shouted, "We'll beat you up if you touch our wives." In Chigirin district, three Zhenotdel workers were killed in one year by "bandits." At the beginning of collectivization, women organizers in the Ukraine had to dispel the rumors which said that in the new kolkhozes the young women would be "shared" by the men and the old ones boiled down for soap. Everywhere, men (invariably called "kulaks" in the literature) fought efforts of the Zhenotdel to organize and politicize their wives.

Of vastly greater difficulty was Zhenotdel work among "eastern" women. Kollontai's congresses were only the beginning. These women could barely hint, and only after patient prying, at the kind of life they had had under the traditional order. "We were silent slaves," said one. "We had to hide in our rooms and cringe before our husbands, who were our lords." Another recalled: "Our fathers sold us at the age of ten, even younger. Our husband would beat us with a stick and whip us when he felt like it. If he wanted to freeze us, we froze. Our daughters, a joy to us and a help around the house, he sold just as we had been sold." These words were spoken to Clara Zetkin who inspected the Zhenotdel operations in the Caucasus during her recuperation there in the early 1920's. Lacking in native Bolshevik cadres, Zhenotdel sent out Russian revolutionaries and educators to take up

the work. Typical of these was Nadezhda Kolesnikova, veteran propagandist and wife of one of the fabled Twenty-Six Commissars. Another was Olga Chulkova, a librarian-teacher and Bestuzhev graduate, who worked from her Zhenotdel base in Sukhumi to organize the women of Abkhaziya. Teams were sent out into the mountain villages and women who had never left their native settlements before were brought down to Sukhumi. Some were shuttled off to Moscow to study; the rest went back to the mountains to organize day nurseries.

As Bette Stavrakis has observed, the lack of native Bolsheviks, the difficulties of language, the size of the territory, the prevalence of illiteracy, the varieties of religion, the tenuous communist control of some areas, and, most important, the ferocious hostility of the males, led the Zhenotdel leaders to adopt methods in accordance with the local situation. These included secret visits, rendezvous in bath-houses, and small groups or *artels* in the initial stages, and the "women's clubs"—social covers for political consciousness raising. In Batumi, the woman's club used male speakers at first until the first shrouded woman stood up and tore off her veil; in Baku it had thousands of members and became the school, church, and social center for women, replacing the gossipy bazaar. Zhenotdel workers appeared in places where a city person had never been seen before; in Central Asia they wandered over the steppe in makeshift transport, stopping at camp, *aul*, and oasis to lecture with the magic lantern (as the Sunday School teachers of Petersburg had done in the 1890's) or to show a motion picture featuring a Muslim heroine who refused to marry the old man who had bought her.

Men reacted to all this with savage violence. Women coming out of the club at Baku were assaulted by men with wild dogs and boiling water. A twenty-year-old Muslim girl who flaunted her liberation by appearing in a swimsuit was sliced to pieces by her father and brothers because they could not endure the social indignity. An eighteen-year-old Uzbek woman activist was mutilated and thrown into a well. Central Asia witnessed three hundred such murders during one quarter of 1929 alone. The Presidium of the Soviet Central Executive Committee, after consulting with the Zhenotdel, decided to classify such crimes as "counter-revolutionary offences." Yet, in spite of the danger, hundreds of native women volunteered as translators and assistants and eventually worked their way into administrative Zhenotdel positions. And each May Day or International Women's Day, thousands of women would assemble in the market places of "eastern" Soviet lands and defiantly tear off their chadras, paranjas, and veils. If it had accomplished nothing else, Zhenotdel would deserve a place in social history for having brought this about.

The variety of enterprises engaged in by the Zhenotdel was enormous: child and orphan care, school service and inspection, food distribution, housing supervision, preventive medicine and public health, anti-prostitution campaigns, war work, education, legislation, placement, family service, and mass propaganda for every campaign that the Party decided to undertake. Some of this resembled the kind of activity which traditional feminists had busied themselves with. But, as an arm of the Party, Zhenotdel had better resources to help it unlock the energies of the most backward and remote communities of Russia's women. In doing this, Zhenotdel served not only the cause of women's liberation but also the regime as a whole by helping to create new reserves of skilled and politically conscious labor....

A final word about Zhenotdel. There can be little doubt that it made an enormous impact on Soviet society, particularly in the cities. Its frequent mention in Soviet literature attests to its prominent place in everyday consciousness. Fictional treatment of Zhenotdel varied. Sometimes it was used merely as a backdrop; often it was a cause of domestic friction or an object of ridicule—and just as often as a problem-solver and proper haven for the newly conscious Soviet woman, but always a symbol of newness on the social landscape. The images were never far from the reality; Zhenotdel was an engine of mobilization in an environment of extreme social backwardness. Organizational and communication skills enabled it to go beyond the specific social task—the "small deed" of the nineteenth-century intelligentsia—toward the larger goal of mass socialization. As an arm of the Party, it lacked the independence and perhaps some of the imaginative initiative of prewar feminism; but, in spite of weaknesses noted above, the Zhenotdel surpassed the feminists in power and prestige. Zhenotdel represented a combination of class and sexual struggle and thus was a working out not only of Marxist notions about the female half of the labor movement, not only of the revolutionary Populist tradition of the "common cause," but also, in some ways, of the much more feminist belief, given expression by Lenin in 1919 that "the emancipation of working women is a matter for the working women themselves." The successes registered by Zhenotdel in raising the consciousness of poor and backward women were proof enough that there was something more to female emancipation than winning the suffrage. But its abolition in 1930 was also proof that without political equality, the "common cause" for which women had fought for three generations would always be defined by men.

NO

Françoise Navailh

THE SOVIET MODEL

The Russian Empire that preceded the Soviet Union was an autocracy. Although serfdom was not abolished until 1861 and the first elections were not held until 1906, the opposition quickly grew radical, and the "woman question" was incorporated into a broad revolutionary program. From the beginning large numbers of women joined the revolutionary movement, accounting for between 15 and 20 percent of the active membership of the revolutionary parties. In urban areas an independent feminist movement was especially active between 1905 and 1908. It concentrated its efforts chiefly on obtaining the right to vote, but in vain. On the eve of World War I Russian society consisted of a very small cultivated and westernized elite, a bourgeoisie still in embryo, and a backward peasantry that made up the remaining 80 percent of the population. People belonging to these different strata of society generally kept to themselves and knew little of other groups. This ignorance would prove a major impediment later on.

World War I broke out on August 1, 1914. Between 1914 and 1917 more than ten million men were mobilized, mostly peasants. Conditions in the countryside, already wretched, grew even worse. Many women were pressed into farm work, so many that women ultimately accounted for 72 percent of the rural workforce. They also replaced men in industrial jobs: the proportion of women in the workforce rose from 33 percent in 1914 to nearly 50 percent in 1917. From 1915 on, women found employment in new branches of industry and joined the government bureaucracy in large numbers. Their wages were lower than men's, however, at a time when prices were soaring. After 1916, the effort to keep food flowing to the cities and to the troops collapsed. The war, always unpopular, seemed hopeless, with no end in sight. For more than a year the country had been afflicted with bread riots and hunger strikes in which women played leading roles. Tension mounted. The regime began to crumble. The honor of initiating the revolution fell to women.

On February 23, 1917 (according to the Julian calendar, or March 8, according to our calendar), working women took their children out into the streets of Petrograd and staged a demonstration. Since the socialists had been unable to agree on a theme for the demonstration, the women improvised, calling for

From Françoise Navailh, "The Soviet Model," in Françoise Thébaud, ed., *A History of Women in the West, vol. 5: Toward a Cultural Identity in the Twentieth Century* (Belknap Press of Harvard University Press, 1994). Copyright © 1994 by the President and Fellows of Harvard College. Reprinted by permission of Harvard University Press. Notes omitted.

peace and bread. On the following day their ranks were swelled by an influx of male demonstrators, and the scope of the turmoil grew rapidly. On March 2 the czar abdicated. A provisional government was formed, and on July 20 it granted women the rights to vote and hold office (rights not granted in England until 1918 and the United States until 1920). Feminists, having achieved their goal, disappeared as an autonomous force. Liberal women lost control of events. When the Winter Palace was seized by the Bolsheviks on the night of October 25–26, it was defended by a women's contingent composed of intellectuals along with women of the bourgeoisie, aristocracy, and working class. The revolution now erupted into a bloody civil war whose outcome hung for a long time in the balance.

A DECADE OF CONTRADICTION

Though surrounded by Whites, forces of the Allied powers, and nationalists, the Bolsheviks sallied forth from Moscow and Petrograd (later Leningrad) to regain control of nearly all of the territory that had constituted the old Russian Empire. They lost no time adopting a host of new laws concerning women. A decree of December 19, 1917, stipulated that in case of mutual consent divorce was to be granted automatically by the courts or the Registry offices (ZAGS); the principle according to which one party must be assigned blame was abolished, and the divorce decree no longer had to be publicized. Russia was the first country in the world to adopt such a liberal divorce policy. A decree of December 20, 1917, abolished religious marriage and standardized and simplified the civil marriage procedure.

All children, legitimate or not, enjoyed the same legal rights. These two measures were extended by the Family Code of December 16, 1918—the most liberal in Europe at the time. The ZAGS became the chief agency for dealing with family matters. A man could no longer force his wife to accept his name, residence, or nationality. Husband and wife enjoyed absolute equality even with respect to the children. Maternity leave and workplace protection were guaranteed. The Family Code adopted a narrow definition of the family: direct ancestors and descendants together with brothers and sisters. A spouse enjoyed the same status as kin and collaterals, with no special privileges or prerogatives. The new family proved less stable than the old. Bonds between individuals were loosened: inheritance was outlawed in April 1918 (and only partially restored in 1923). Unrestricted abortion was legalized on November 20, 1920.

The Code of November 19, 1926, confirmed these earlier changes and took yet another step, abolishing all differences between marriages legally recorded by the ZAGS and de facto (common-law) marriages. Divorce could henceforth be obtained on the written request of either party: "postcard divorce" was now legal. Love was freer, but mutual obligations were more onerous owing to new alimony and child support requirements. The new Family Code was intended to liberate men, women, and children from the coercive regulations of another era. The past was to be completely effaced. People were urged to change their family names in March 1918 and their first names in 1924: suggestions for new names included Marlen (short for Marxism-Leninism), Engelsine, and Octobrine. Though intended to be an instrument of liberation, the code was also an instrument of coercion that could be used to strike at conservative segments of the society, particularly peasants and Muslims. In fact, the Communist Party, composed of a handful of urban intellectuals, deliberately ignored the views of those whom it sped along the road to a better tomorrow. Although lawmakers occasionally reversed themselves, their actions were always guided by two principles: to destroy czarism and build socialism....

Kollontai: A Reluctant Feminist

Alexandra Kollontai (1872–1952) was a pivotal figure in debates on women and the family during the first Soviet decade. She epitomizes all the contradictions of the period. Her biography is typical of her generation. Aristocratic by birth, she enjoyed a luxury-filled, dreamy childhood. After marrying at age nineteen to escape her family and milieu, she left her husband at age twenty-six and went to school in Zurich, then a Mecca for Russian intellectuals, where she became involved in politics, took increasingly radical positions, and eventually became a professional revolutionary. Her record was brilliant: as the first woman elected to the Central Committee in 1917, she voted in favor of the October insurrection. She then became the first woman to serve in the government, as people's commissar for health, and took an active part in drafting the Family Code of 1918. As an active member of the Workers' Opposition in 1920–1921, she sought to limit the vast powers of the Communist Party. In 1922 she became the first woman ambassador in the world. Her diplomatic career abroad kept her away from Moscow until 1945, yet her name is inseparable from the controversies of the 1920s, whose

passions she fueled with countless articles, pamphlets, and brochures that were widely criticized, distorted, and even caricatured. She also wrote a number of theoretical tomes (*The Social Bases of the Woman Question*, 1909; *The Family and the Communist State*, 1918; *The New Morality and the Working Class*, 1918), as well as six works of fiction, all published in 1923. Although certain aspects of her work now seem dated, much of it remains remarkably up to date.

Kollontai proposed a synthesis of Marxism with a feminism she never avowed (and in fact always combated). Marxism, combined with a touch of Fourierist utopianism, would facilitate the realization of feminist goals. Like Marx and Engels, Kollontai believed that the bourgeois family had fallen apart and that revolution would lead to the regeneration of family life. She also drew extensively on the work of Bebel, particularly his idea that oppression tends to create unity among women. But she tried to go beyond these general arguments. Aware that the revolution was merely a starting point, she argued that to change the essence of marriage required changing people's attitudes and behavior. Therein lay her originality. She stressed the reifying tendency of the masculine will and noted the alienation of women who prefer any kind of marriage to solitude and are thus driven to wager everything on love. So Kollontai taught that love could be a kind of sport: if tender erotic friendship were based on mutual respect, jealousy and the possessive instinct might be eliminated. The "new woman," one of her recurrent subjects, was energetic and self-assertive. She let men know what she wanted; she refused to be dependent either materially or emotionally; she rebelled against socioeconomic obstacles, hypocritical morals, and "amorous captivity." Autonomous and active, she was free to explore "serial monogamy." In "Make Room for Wingèd Eros," an article published in 1923, Kollontai analyzed love's many facets: friendship, passion, maternal affection, spiritual affinity, habit, and so on. "Wingless Eros," or purely physical attraction, was to make room for "wingèd Eros," wherein physical gratification was combined with a sense of collective duty, that indispensable attribute in the era of transition to socialism. Finally, once socialist society had been established, there would be room for "Eros transfigured," or marriage based on healthy, free, and natural sexual attraction. To allow couples to develop, "kitchens must be separated from homes": in other words, society must build cafeterias, day-care centers, and dispensaries in order to relieve women of certain of their traditional responsibilities. Last but not least, motherhood was cast in a new light: it was "no longer a private affair but a social duty." Women must have children for the sake of the community. Kollontai considered abortion to be a temporary evil, to be tolerated only until the consciousness of working women had been raised to the point where it was no longer necessary. She denounced the refusal to bear children as petty-bourgeois selfishness. Nevertheless, she did not advocate the collectivization of child-rearing: parents should decide whether children were to be raised in a nursery school or at home.

As a spiritual value, however, love in general—and sex—should take precedence over the maternal instinct: "The workers' state needs a new type of relation between the sexes. A mother's narrow, exclusive love for her own child must broaden to embrace all the chil-

dren of the great proletarian family. In the place of indissoluble marriage, based on the servitude of women, we look forward to the birth of free matrimony, an institution made strong by the mutual love and respect of two members of the brotherhood of Labor, equals in rights as well as obligations. In place of the individualistic, egoistic family will arise the great universal family of working people, in which everyone, men and women alike, will be first and foremost brothers and comrades." Kollontai called upon women to defend, propagate, and internalize the idea that they had value as human beings in their own right.

To be sure, Kollontai's argument was framed in terms of classical Marxism, to which the economy is primary, but she also insisted on the qualitative aspect of interpersonal relations: men and women should be attentive to each other's needs and playful toward one another. Ethics mattered to her as much as politics. Well before Wilhelm Reich, she was among the first to link sexuality with class struggle: "Why is it that we are so unforgivably indifferent to one of the essential tasks of the working class? How are we to explain the hypocritical relegation of the sexual problem to the realm of 'family affairs' not requiring collective effort? As if sexual relations and the morals governing them have not been a constant factor in social struggle throughout history."

Few people shared Kollontai's ideas in the Soviet Union of the 1920s. Her comrades looked upon her ideas as frivolous and ill-timed. Her views presupposed a yet-to-be-achieved social and economic infrastructure, and they came in for vehement criticism in a 1923 article by the Bolshevik P. Vinogradskaya, who had worked with Kollontai on Women's Department of the Central Committee Secretariat (Zhenotdel) in 1920. Vinogradskaya attacked her opponent for confusing priorities, neglecting the class struggle, and encouraging sexual anarchy in an irresponsible way, since disorder in private life could lead to counterrevolutionary agitation. The task of the moment was to protect wives and children and to champion the cause of women without attacking men. Marx and Engels had already said everything there was to be said on the question, and it was pointless to indulge in "George-Sandism."

Lenin, for his part, related everything to the economy and opted in favor of monogamous marriage, egalitarian, earnest, and devoted to the cause, like his own tranquil union with Nadezhda Krupskaya. When Ines Armand saw poetry in free love, Lenin responded that what she mistook for poetry was nothing but bourgeois immorality. He borrowed his ideal from Nikolai Chernysbevski's austere novel What Is to Be Done? (1863), which, as lie said, "bowled him over." Indeed, he thought so highly of the book that he used its title for his own theoretical work of 1902. His conversations with Clara Zetkin, which took place in 1920 but were not published until 1925, after Lenin's death, accurately reflected his rejection of lack of discipline in love and sexual matters. Lenin saw such lack of discipline as a sign of decadence and a danger to young people's health, hence to the revolution itself. He attacked the "anti-Marxist" theory according to which "in Communist society the satisfaction of sexual desires is as simple and soothing as drinking a glass of water." Lenin had nobody particular in mind. He was not attacking Kollontai, for his remarks preceded the polemic of 1923, but later Kollontai's adversaries used his wrath

against her: "Of course thirst must be satisfied! But would a normal man, under normal conditions, prostrate himself in the street to drink from a filthy puddle? Or even from a glass previously soiled by dozens of other lips?" Here, purity is restored as an absolute value, and the underlying idea is that having more than one sexual partner is in itself immoral. Lenin's credo was a negative one: "No to the monk, no to the Don Juan, and no to that supposed happy medium, the German philistine." To be sure, he denounced the slavery of housework: "Woman is stifled, strangled, stupefied, and humiliated by the trivial occupations of domestic life, which chain her to the kitchen and nursery and sap her strength for work that is as unproductive, difficult, and exhausting as one can imagine." But he said nothing about the new family.

For orthodox Marxists, children did not figure in the conjugal scheme. They were to be taken care of either by certain designated women or by all the women of the community collectively— at the outset the choice is not clear. Fathers certainly play no role in the new system of child-rearing. The community supports, envelops, permeates, and transcends the reduced couple, in which man and woman are strict equals. The woman, like her husband, is a worker; traditional femininity is disparaged as a product of old bourgeois social relations. Equality in fact means identity of the sexes. The new industrious humanity consists of male and female twins, identical insofar as both are workers. "Economically and politically, which also means physiologically, the modern proletarian woman can and must become more and more like the modern proletarian man," wrote Marxist psychoneurologist Aaron Zalkind in

1924. Sexual relations, we are told, will not be a matter of great importance for such indistinguishable twins. One can interpret this claim in two ways. If sex is merely a physiological need, then the number of partners is unimportant: this is the attitude of the youth Zhenya in Kollontai's short story, "Three Generations of Love." The other interpretation leads to Leninist asceticism. In either case love must be restrained; it is a disruptive force. All of this was merely speculative, however. During the 1920s the private sphere remained intact, and various norms of sexual behavior coexisted.

A New Russia

In order to enforce the law, achieve economic equality, bring uniformity to a very disparate country, and accelerate the integration of women into the society, the Party in 1919 created the Zhenotdel, or Women's Department of the Central Committee Secretariat, with equivalents at every echelon of the hierarchy. Five women in succession led this Department during its existence, among them Ines Armand in 1919–20 and Alexandra Kollontai from 1920 to 1922. The Zhenotdel offered advice and assistance, settled labor and domestic conflicts, proposed laws and suggested amendments to Central Committee edicts, joined in actions such as the campaigns to eradicate illiteracy and abolish prostitution, coordinated the work of various agencies, oversaw the application of quotas that favored women in hiring and admission to soviets, dealt with problems of supply, housing, and sanitation, and inspected schools and orphanages. In addition to the Zhenotdel there was also a system of female delegates: women workers and peasants elected by their colleagues to participate in year-long training and indoctrination courses, after which they spent two months working with the soviets or the courts before returning to work. This system trained women to become "Soviet citizens." More than ten million of them signed up during the 1920s. Dasha, the heroine of Fedor Gladkov's novel *Cement* (1925), is a perfect example of the liberated woman. A militant delegate, she so completely threw off her old bonds that she sacrificed her marriage, her home, and even her little daughter, who died in an orphanage. There is no doubt that the Zhenotdel, together with the delegate system, had an impact on the consciousness of women. Its political influence remained negligible, however, and all too often it served only to convey the wishes of the hierarchy to the rank and file. In 1923 it was accused of "feminist deviationism," a fatal sin....

Freedom and Disorder

... In one sense, women were granted all they could have hoped for right at the outset, without a struggle. But the most difficult part of the task remained: they had to learn how to make use of their newly won rights to forge a new way of life. But given the sociohistorical context and the gaps in the codes of 1918 and 1926, new freedoms gave rise to unintended consequences.

Two signs of the times were marital instability and a widespread reluctance to have children. The number of abortions rose, the birthrate declined precipitously, and newborn babies were frequently abandoned. Orphanages, overwhelmed by new admissions, became veritable charnel houses. Infanticide and wife-murder increased. In effect, women and children were the first victims of the new order. The condition of women clearly became more dire, especially in the cities.

Men abandoned their families, leaving their wives without resources. The availability of divorce merely on application by either party led to cynical abuses. The government allowed common-law marriages in order to protect women from seduction and abandonment (and also to protect any children that might result from fleeting affairs); men were required to provide for the women they left behind, and thus to assume a burden that the government itself was unable to bear. But women had to prove that an affair had taken place, and the law failed to specify what constituted proof. The courts improvised. Lengthy and often fruitless paternity suits poisoned relations between the sexes and became a recurrent theme of contemporary fiction. The laws governing alimony were just as vague, and the courts were obliged to fix amounts on a case-by-case basis. Often it was set at one-third or one-fourth of the man's monthly wage, which sometimes created insurmountable difficulties. How was a man to survive if ten rubles were deducted from his wage of forty rubles? How was he to support a child born out of wedlock when he already had four "legitimate" children to take care of? Few men earned enough to cover alimony, and many refused to pay up. Rulings of the court went unenforced in more than half the cases.

There were practical problems as well. Allocation of housing was a state monopoly, and waiting lists were extremely long. Divorced couples were therefore obliged in some cases to go on living together. Abram Room's film *Bed and Sofa* (1927) is a marvelous depiction of conditions under the NEP [New Economic Policy]. It offers a new perspective on the eternal triangle, portraying a husband, wife, and lover forced to share a single room. After the seduction, moreover, the two men take a nonchalant attitude toward the situation and join in a macho alliance against the woman, the wife of one and mistress of the other.

Many women who wanted children were nevertheless forced to seek abortions because of the scarcity of housing, low wages, short supplies, and/or lack of a man. In a survey conducted in Moscow in 1927, 71 percent of women seeking abortions cited "living conditions" as the reason and 22 percent mentioned unstable love lives." Only 6 percent rejected motherhood on principle.

Although intellectuals and quasi-intellectuals in the cities went on leading bohemian lives, some segments of the population resisted any change in traditional mores. In 1928, 77.8 percent of the population still consisted of peasants, compared with only 17.6 percent blue- and white-collar workers. The Code of 1926 triggered a huge controversy that illustrates the continuing influence of the peasantry. Since accurate news was hard to come by despite innumerable published articles, brochures, and meetings, peasants were liable to be affected by unsubstantiated rumors, and many were convinced that the new code was going to make the sharing of women compulsory. The most controversial provision of the law concerned the treatment of de facto marriage as completely equivalent to lawful matrimony. The Agrarian Code of 1922 reinforced the communal organization of the village, or *mir*, and retained the undivided family property, or *dvor*. If a couple sharing in the *dvor* divorced and payment "of alimony led to division of the property, the farm might cease to be viable. Wary after years of ceaseless combat (1914–1921), the peasantry, fearful of novelty, drew back and clung to its traditional values.

It was an ambiguous image of woman that emerged from all the articles, brochures, pamphlets, investigations, speeches, novels, and films of the day: sometimes she was portrayed as a member of the vanguard of the working class, wearing an earnest look, work clothes, and a red scarf; at other times she was the backward peasant with her white kerchief pulled down over her eyes; or the mannish girl of the Komsomol (Young Communists), shockingly liberated in her ways; or the pert, flirtatious typist. Woman simultaneously embodied the past and the future. Conviction vied with confusion in the minds of the masses. Novels of the late 1920s are filled with restless, confused, unhappy heroines. Urban immorality and rural conservatism were matters of concern to both rulers and ruled. Women wanted stability, men declined responsibility, and the Party wanted to keep its program on course. By 1926 it was clear that, like it or not, the family would survive. Certain sectors of light industry were sacrificed in the name of economic progress. Home and children once again became the concern of women. The woman question was held to have been resolved once and for all, and in 1929 the Zhenotdel was abolished....

A Contestable and Contested Model

By 1923 the die was cast. Although there was progress at the grass roots, there was stalemate at the top. The masses were enlisted in the struggle, but the once competent, combative, and cultivated elite was supplanted by squadrons of colorless yes-men. Strong personalities such as Alexandra Kollontai were removed or liquidated.

In the end Kollontai's fears were justified. Without a redefinition of sex roles economic emancipation proved to be a trap, for women were obliged to conform to a male model without being relieved of their burden as women. It may be that a comparable danger exists in any developing industrial society. A century of European evolution was compressed into two decades in the Soviet Union: the sexual revolution of the 1920s broke down the old family unit, while the Stalinist reaction of the 1930s reshaped the family in order to impose breakneck industrialization on a backward peasant society. The gap between the idealistic slogans and everyday reality was enormous.

The one-party state was not solely responsible for these developments, however. As in other countries, the role of women was ambiguous. Whether responding by instinct to ensure their own survival and that of their children or acting out of alienation, women accepted and internalized the rules of the Soviet game to a greater extent than men—and much to men's annoyance. Sober, long-suffering, conscientious, and disciplined, woman was one of the pillars of the regime: she did the washing, stood in line to buy food, cooked meals, took care of the children, worked in factories and offices and on collective farms, and did whatever she had to do. But to what end? Equality only added to her burden.

POSTSCRIPT

Did the Bolshevik Revolution Improve the Lives of Soviet Women?

It is one of history's ironies that, with the stroke of a pen, Soviet women were granted all the legal and political rights that women in Britain and the United States were struggling to achieve. Having won the rights to vote and hold public office, Soviet women struggled to translate those paper rights into improved lives for themselves and their children. It has been a conviction of Western feminism that legal and political equality pave the way for full emancipation of women. The Soviet case raises interesting questions about the confusion that arises when there are conflicting revolutions. Real political power belongs to those who can ensure that the goals of their revolution receive first priority. It was the socialist revolution, not women's emancipation, that the party leadership worked to achieve.

Popular accounts of the Russian Revolution may be found in John Reed's *Ten Days That Shook the World* (Penguin, 1977) and Louise Bryant's *Mirrors of Moscow* (Hyperion Press, 1973). The story of Reed and Bryant, two Americans who find themselves eyewitnesses to the Bolshevik Revolution, is captured in the film *Reds*. Another film covering the same period is *Doctor Zhivago*, which is based on the book of the same title by Boris Pasternak (1958). For Lenin's views on women, one of the best sources is his book *The Emancipation of Women* (International Publishers, 1972). *The Unknown Lenin: From the Secret Archives* edited by the eminent Russian historian Richard Pipes (Yale University Press, 1996) dips into the secret archives and brands Lenin a ruthless and manipulative leader. Robert McNeal's *Bride of the Revolution* (University of Michigan Press, 1972) focuses on the fascinating marriage and revolutionary relationship between Lenin and Bolshevik propagandist Nadezha Krupskaya. And Sheila Fitzpatrick, in *The Russian Revolution* (Oxford University Press, 1982), surveys the critical 1917–1932 period with special emphasis on the work of Zhenotdel. For essays on the lives of women during this period, students may want to see *Women in Soviet Society* edited by Gail Lapidus (University of California Press, 1978) and *Women in Russia* edited by D. Atkinson, A. Dallin, and G. Lapidus (Stanford University Press, 1977), which grew out of a 1975 conference that was held at Stanford University entitled "Women in Russia." The fascinating character Alexandra Kollontai, who died at 80, may be explored through her own writings in *Selected Writings* (W. W. Norton, 1972), *Red Love* (Hyperion Press, 1990), and *Love of Worker Bees* (Academy of Chicago Press, 1978). Books about Kollontai include *Bolshevik Feminist* by Barbara Clements (Indiana University Press, 1979).

ISSUE 19

Was German "Eliminationist Anti-Semitism" Responsible for the Holocaust?

YES: Daniel Jonah Goldhagen, from *Hitler's Willing Executioners: Ordinary Germans and the Holocaust* (Alfred A. Knopf, 1996)

NO: Christopher R. Browning, from *Ordinary Men: Reserve Police Battalion 101 and the Final Solution in Poland* (HarperPerennial, 1998)

ISSUE SUMMARY

YES: Professor of government Daniel Jonah Goldhagen states that due to the nature of German society in the twentieth century—with its endemic, virulent anti-Semitism—thousands of ordinary German citizens became willing participants in the implementation of Holocaust horrors.

NO: Holocaust scholar Christopher R. Browning argues that Goldhagen's thesis is too simplistic and that a multicausal approach must be used to determine why ordinary German citizens willingly participated in the Holocaust.

Few historical events engender stronger emotional responses than the Nazi-directed Holocaust of World War II, in which millions of Jews were systematically exterminated as part of a ghastly plan for a diabolical new world order. Since its occurrence, many scholarly works have been written in an attempt to answer the questions that this "crime against humanity" has raised: What historical factors were responsible for it? How did people and nations allow it to roll toward its final destructive consequences? What lessons did it teach us about human nature? Could something like this happen again? Who bears the ultimate responsibility for it?

Much of Holocaust scholarship has concentrated on European anti-Semitism as a major factor in the cause of the event itself and as a major reason why little was done to stop it. Some scholars have emphasized the schizophrenic nature of post–World War I politics, which they say allowed demagogic madmen to weave their magic web around an unsuspecting public. And, of course, the major blame has been placed on Adolf Hitler and his Nazi henchmen for the initiation, design, and implementation of the Holocaust.

But just how unsuspecting was this public? Most people have long dismissed (as did the Nuremberg War Crimes Tribunal) the "I was only following orders" argument that so many who actively participated in the Holocaust have used. Others who were not directly involved have cited hopelessness and fear of reprisal for their actions. But as we have been made witness to countless trials for war crimes in the last 50 years, some have wondered whether or not a larger segment of the population in those Nazi-controlled countries was involved in the Holocaust's worst aspects.

Daniel Jonah Goldhagen was not the first scholar to investigate this question, but his 1996 book *Hitler's Willing Executioners: Ordinary Germans and the Holocaust,* which is excerpted in the following selection, has raised the issue to a new level and has created a maelstrom of controversy within the historical profession. Using recently discovered sources of information and tools of analysis newly available to social scientists, Goldhagen takes a fresh look at why and how the Holocaust occurred through an analysis of three related subjects: "the perpetrators of the Holocaust, German antisemitism, and the nature of German society during the Nazi period." Goldhagen's conclusions are a stinging indictment of large numbers of ordinary Germans, who he claims willingly participated in the Holocaust's worst aspects, including police battalions, work camps, and death marches.

Goldhagen's work has received much praise, including a National Book Critics nomination for nonfiction book of the year. But it has also had its share of critics. Some have found his work to be one-sided, inflammatory, and too narrow in its focus. One of Goldhagen's most persistent critics has been Christopher R. Browning. In the second selection, Browning states that anti-Semitism may have been widespread in pre-Nazi Germany, but it was not the major ideology of all German citizens. According to Browning, there are a variety of factors that were responsible for turning "ordinary" German citizens into "willing executioners." Goldhagen is critical of Browning's conclusions and his critique can be found in "The Evil of Banality," *The New Republic* (July 13 & 20, 1992). Browning published a rejoinder to Goldhagen's critique as an afterword to the second edition of *Ordinary Men: Reserve Police Battalion 101 and the Final Solution in Poland.*

A proverbial hornet's nest has been stirred up by *Hitler's Willing Executioners,* and its reverberations are not likely to subside anytime in the near future. Regardless of opinions of the book, any future works on the Holocaust will have to at least consider the questions that it has raised.

YES
Daniel Jonah Goldhagen

RECONCEIVING CENTRAL ASPECTS OF THE HOLOCAUST

During the Holocaust, Germans extinguished the lives of six million Jews and, had Germany not been defeated, would have annihilated millions more. The Holocaust was also the defining feature of German politics and political culture during the Nazi period, the most shocking event of the twentieth century, and the most difficult event to understand in all of German history. The Germans' persecution of the Jews culminating in the Holocaust is thus the central feature of Germany during the Nazi period. It is so not because we are retrospectively shocked by the most shocking event of the century, but because of what it meant to Germans at the time and why so many of them contributed to it. It marked their departure from the community of "civilized peoples." This departure needs to be explained.

Explaining the Holocaust is the central intellectual problem for understanding Germany during the Nazi period. All the other problems combined are comparatively simple. How the Nazis came to power, how they suppressed the left, how they revived the economy, how the state was structured and functioned, how they made and waged war are all more or less ordinary, "normal" events, easily enough understood. But the Holocaust and the change in sensibilities that it involved "defies" explanation. There is no comparable event in the twentieth century, indeed in modern European history. Whatever the remaining debates, every other major event of nineteenth- and twentieth-century German history and political development is, in comparison to the Holocaust, transparently clear in its genesis. Explaining how the Holocaust happened is a daunting task empirically and even more so theoretically, so much so that some have argued, in my view erroneously, that it is "inexplicable." The theoretical difficulty is shown by its utterly new nature, by the inability of social theory (or what passed for common sense) preceding it to provide a hint not only that it would happen but also that it was even possible. Retrospective theory has not done much better, shedding but modest light in the darkness.

The overall objective of this [selection] is to explain why the Holocaust occurred, to explain how it could occur. The success of this enterprise depends upon a number of subsidiary tasks, which consist fundamentally of reconceiving three subjects: the perpetrators of the Holocaust, German anti-semitism, and the nature of German society during the Nazi period.

* * *

Foremost among the three subjects that must be reconceived are the perpetrators of the Holocaust. Few readers of this [selection] will have failed to give some thought to the question of what impelled the perpetrators of the Holocaust to kill. Few have neglected to provide for themselves an answer to the question, an answer that necessarily derives usually not from any intimate knowledge of the perpetrators and their deeds, but greatly from the individual's conception of human nature and social life. Few would probably disagree with the notion that the perpetrators should be studied.

Yet until now the perpetrators, the most important group of people responsible for the slaughter of European Jewry, excepting the Nazi leadership itself, have received little concerted attention in the literature that describes the events and purports to explain them. Surprisingly, the vast literature on the Holocaust contains little on the people who were its executors. Little is known of who the perpetrators were, the details of their actions, the circumstances of many of their deeds, let alone their motivations. A decent estimate of how many people contributed to the genocide, of how many perpetrators there were, has never been made. Certain institutions of killing and the people who manned them have been hardly treated or not at all. As a consequence of this general lack of knowledge, all kinds of misunderstandings and myths about the perpetrators abound. These misconcep-

tions, moreover, have broader implications for the way in which the Holocaust and Germany during the Nazi period are conceived and understood.

We must therefore refocus our attention, our intellectual energy, which has overwhelmingly been devoted elsewhere, onto the perpetrators, namely the men and women who in some intimate way knowingly contributed to the slaughter of Jews. We must investigate their deeds in detail and explain their actions. It is not sufficient to treat the institutions of killing collectively or singly as internally uncomplicated instruments of the Nazi leadership's will, as well-lubricated machines that the regime activated, as if by the flick of a switch, to do its bidding, whatever it might have been. The study of the men and women who collectively gave life to the inert institutional forms, who peopled the institutions of genocidal killing must be set at the focus of scholarship on the Holocaust and become as central to investigations of the genocide as they were to its commission.

These people were overwhelmingly and most importantly Germans. While members of other national groups aided the Germans in their slaughter of Jews, the commission of the Holocaust was primarily a German undertaking. Non-Germans were not essential to the perpetration of the genocide, and they did not supply the drive and initiative that pushed it forward. To be sure, had the Germans not found European (especially, eastern European) helpers, then the Holocaust would have unfolded somewhat differently, and the Germans would likely not have succeeded in killing as many Jews. Still, this was above all a German enterprise; the decisions, plans, organizational resources, and the majority of its executors were German. Comprehension and explanation of the perpetration of the Holocaust therefore requires an explanation of the *Germans'* drive to kill Jews. Because what can be said about the Germans cannot be said about any other nationality or about all of the other nationalities combined —namely no Germans, no Holocaust— the focus here is appropriately on the German perpetrators.

The first task in restoring the perpetrators to the center of our understanding of the Holocaust is to restore to them their identities, grammatically by using not the passive but the active voice in order to ensure that they, the actors, are not absent from their own deeds (as in, "five hundred Jews were killed in city X on date Y"), and by eschewing convenient, yet often inappropriate and obfuscating labels, like "Nazis" and "SS men," and calling them what they were, "Germans." The most appropriate, indeed the only appropriate *general* proper name for the Germans who perpetrated the Holocaust is "Germans." They were Germans acting in the name of Germany and its highly popular leader, Adolf Hitler. Some were "Nazis," either by reason of Nazi Party membership or according to ideological conviction; some were not. Some were SS men; some were not. The perpetrators killed and made their other genocidal contributions under the auspices of many institutions other than the SS. Their chief common denominator was that they were all Germans pursuing German national political goals—in this case, the genocidal killing of Jews. To be sure, it is sometimes appropriate to use institutional or occupational names or roles and the generic terms "perpetrators" or "killers" to describe the perpetrators, yet this must be done only in the understood context that

these men and women were Germans first, and SS men, policemen, or camp guards second.

A second and related task is to reveal something of the perpetrators' backgrounds, to convey the character and quality of their lives as genocidal killers, to bring to life their *Lebenswelt*. What *exactly* did they do when they were killing? What did they do during their time as members of institutions of killing, while they were not undertaking killing operations? Until a great deal is known about the details of their actions and lives, neither they nor the perpetration of their crimes can be understood. The unearthing of the perpetrators' lives, the presentation of a "thick," rather than the customary paper-thin, description of their actions, as important and necessary as it is for its own sake, lays the foundation for the main task of this [selection's] consideration of them, namely to explain their actions.

It is my contention that this cannot be done unless such an analysis is embedded in an understanding of German society before and during its Nazi period, particularly of the political culture that produced the perpetrators and their actions. This has been notably absent from attempts to explain the perpetrators' actions, and has doomed these attempts to providing situational explanations, ones that focus almost exclusively on institutional and immediate social psychological influences, often conceived of as irresistible pressures. The men and women who became the Holocaust's perpetrators were shaped by and operated in a particular social and historical setting. They brought with them prior elaborate conceptions of the world, ones that were common to their society, the investigation of which is necessary for explaining their actions. This entails, most fundamentally, a reexamination of the character and development of antisemitism in Germany during its Nazi period and before, which in turn requires a theoretical reconsideration of the character of antisemitism itself.

Studies of the Holocaust have been marred by a poor understanding and an under-theorizing of antisemitism. Antisemitism is a broad, typically imprecisely used term, encompassing a wide variety of phenomena. This naturally poses enormous obstacles for explaining the perpetration of the Holocaust because a central task of any such attempt is to evaluate whether and how antisemitism produced and influenced its many aspects. In my view, our understanding of antisemitism and of the relationship of antisemitism to the (mal)treatment of Jews is deficient. We must begin considering these subjects anew and develop a conceptual apparatus that is descriptively powerful and analytically useful for addressing the ideational causes of social action....

The study of the perpetrators further demands a reconsideration, indeed a reconceiving, of the character of German society during its Nazi period and before. The Holocaust was the defining aspect of Nazism, but not only of Nazism. It was also the defining feature of German society during its Nazi period. No significant aspect of German society was untouched by anti-Jewish policy; from the economy, to society, to politics, to culture, from cattle farmers, to merchants, to the organization of small towns, to lawyers, doctors, physicists, and professors. No analysis of German society, no understanding or characterization of it, can be made without placing the persecution and extermination of the Jews at its center. The program's first parts, namely the systematic exclusion of Jews from German economic and social life, were carried out in the open, under approving eyes, and with the complicity of virtually all sectors of German society, from the legal, medical, and teaching professions, to the churches, both Catholic and Protestant, to the gamut of economic, social, and cultural groups and associations. Hundreds of thousands of Germans contributed to the genocide and the still larger system of subjugation that was the vast concentration camp system. Despite the regime's half-hearted attempts to keep the genocide beyond the view of most Germans, millions knew of the mass slaughters. Hitler announced many times, emphatically, that the war would end in the extermination of the Jews. The killings met with general understanding, if not approval. No other policy (of similar or greater scope) was carried out with more persistence and zeal, and with fewer difficulties, than the genocide, except perhaps the war itself. The Holocaust defines not only the history of Jews during the middle of the twentieth century but also the history of Germans. While the Holocaust changed Jewry and Jews irrevocably, its commission was possible, I argue, because Germans had *already* been changed. The fate of the Jews may have been a direct, which does not, however, mean an inexorable, outgrowth of a worldview shared by the vast majority of the German people.

Each of these reconceivings—of the perpetrators, of German antisemitism, and of German society during the Nazi period—is complex, requires difficult theoretical work and the marshaling of considerable empirical material, and, ultimately, is deserving of a separate book in its own right. While the undertaking of each one is justifiable on its own theoretical and empirical grounds, each, in my view, is also strengthened by the others, for they are interrelated tasks. Together the three suggest that we must substantially rethink important aspects of German history, the nature of Germany during the Nazi period, and the perpetration of the Holocaust. This rethinking requires, on a number of subjects, the turning of conventional wisdom on its head, and the adoption of a new and substantially different view of essential aspects of this period, aspects which have generally been considered settled. Explaining why the Holocaust occurred requires a radical revision of what has until now been written....

This revision calls for us to acknowledge what has for so long been generally denied or obscured by academic and non-academic interpreters alike: Germans' antisemitic beliefs about Jews were the central causal agent of the Holocaust. They were the central causal agent not only of Hitler's decision to annihilate European Jewry (which is accepted by many) but also of the perpetrators' willingness to kill and to brutalize Jews. The conclusion of this [selection] is that antisemitism moved many thousands of "ordinary" Germans—and would have moved millions more, had they been appropriately positioned—to slaughter Jews. Not economic hardship, not the coercive means of a totalitarian state, not social psychological pressure, not invariable psychological propensities, but ideas about Jews that were pervasive in Germany, and had been for decades, induced ordinary Germans to kill unarmed, defenseless Jewish men, women, and children by the thousands, systematically and without pity.

* * *

For what developments would a comprehensive explanation of the Holocaust have to account? For the extermination of the Jews to occur, four principal things were necessary:

1. The Nazis—that is, the leadership, specifically Hitler—had to decide to undertake the extermination.
2. They had to gain control over the Jews, namely over the territory in which they resided.
3. They had to organize the extermination and devote to it sufficient resources.
4. They had to induce a large number of people to carry out the killings.

The vast literature on Nazism and the Holocaust treats in great depth the first three elements, as well as others, such as the origins and character of Hitler's genocidal beliefs, and the Nazis' ascendancy to power. Yet, as I have already indicated, it has treated the last element, the focus of this [selection], perfunctorily and mainly by assumption. It is therefore important to discuss here some analytical and interpretive issues that are central to studying the perpetrators.

Owing to the neglect of the perpetrators in the study of the Holocaust, it is no surprise that the existing interpretations of them have been generally produced in a near empirical vacuum. Until recently, virtually no research has been done on the perpetrators, save on the leaders of the Nazi regime. In the last few years, some publications have appeared that treat one group or another, yet the state of our knowledge about the perpetrators remains deficient. We know little about many of the institutions of killing, little about many aspects of the perpetration of the genocide, and still less about the perpetrators themselves. As a consequence, popular and scholarly myths and misconceptions about the perpetrators abound, including the following. It is commonly believed that the Germans slaughtered Jews by and large in the gas chambers, and that without gas chambers, modern means of transportation, and efficient bureaucracies, the Germans would have been unable to kill millions of Jews. The belief persists that somehow only technology made horror on this scale possible. "Assembly-line killing" is one of the stock phrases in discussions of the event. It is generally believed that gas chambers, because of their efficiency (which is itself greatly overstated), were a necessary instrument for the genocidal slaughter, and that the Germans chose to construct the gas chambers in the first place because they needed more efficient means of killing the Jews. It has been generally believed by scholars (at least until very recently) and non-scholars alike that the perpetrators were primarily, overwhelmingly SS men, the most devoted and brutal Nazis. It has been an unquestioned truism (again until recently) that had a German refused to kill Jews, then he himself would have been killed, sent to a concentration camp, or severely punished. All of these views, views that fundamentally shape people's understanding of the Holocaust, have been held unquestioningly as though they were self-evident truths. They have been virtual articles of faith (derived from sources other than historical inquiry), have substituted for knowledge, and have distorted the way in which this period is understood.

The absence of attention devoted to the perpetrators is surprising for a host of reasons, only one of which is the existence of a now over-ten-year-long debate about the genesis of the *initiation* of the Holocaust, which has come to be called by the misnomer the "intentionalist–functionalist" debate. For better or worse, this debate has become the organizing debate for much of the scholarship on the Holocaust. Although it has improved our understanding of the exact chronology of the Germans' persecution and mass murder of the Jews, it has also, because of the terms in which it has been cast, confused the analysis of the causes of the Germans' policies . . . , and it has done next to nothing to increase our knowledge of the perpetrators. Of those who defined this debate and made its central early contributions, only one saw fit to ask the question, Why, once the killing began (however it did), did those receiving the orders to kill do so? It appears that for one reason or another, all the participants in the debate assumed that executing such orders was unproblematic for the actors, and unproblematic for historians and social scientists. The limited character of our knowledge, and therefore our understanding, of this period is highlighted by the simple fact that (however the category of "perpetrator" is defined) the number of people who were perpetrators is unknown. No good estimate, virtually no estimate of any kind, exists of the number of people who knowingly contributed to the genocidal killing in some intimate way. Scholars who discuss them, inexplicably, neither attempt such an estimate nor point out that this, a topic of such great significance, is an important gap in our knowledge. If ten thousand Germans were perpetrators, then the perpetration of the Holocaust, perhaps the Holocaust itself, is a phenomenon of one kind, perhaps the deed of a select, unrepresentative group. If five hundred thousand or one million Germans were perpetrators, then it is a phenomenon of another kind, perhaps best conceived as a German national project. Depending on the number and identity of the Germans who contributed to the genocidal slaughter, different sorts of questions, inquiries, and bodies of theory might be appropriate or necessary in order to explain it.

This dearth of knowledge, not only about the perpetrators but also about the functioning of their host institutions has not stopped some interpreters from making assertions about them—although the most striking fact remains how few even bother to address the subject, let alone take it up at length. Still, from the literature a number of conjectured explanations can be distilled, even if they are not always clearly specified or elaborated upon in a sustained manner. (In fact, strands of different explanations are frequently intermingled without great coherence.) Some of them have been proposed to explain the actions of the German people generally and, by extension, they would apply to the perpetrators as well. Rather than laying out what each interpreter has posited about the perpetrators, an analytical account is provided here of the major arguments, with references to leading exemplars of each one. The most important of them can be classified into five categories:

One explanation argues for external compulsion: the perpetrators were coerced. They were left, by the threat of punishment, with no choice but to follow orders. After all, they were part of military or police-like institutions, institutions with a strict chain of command, demanding subordinate compliance to orders, which should have punished insubordination severely, perhaps with death. Put a gun to anyone's head, so goes the thinking, and he will shoot others to save himself.

A second explanation conceives of the perpetrators as having been blind followers of orders. A number of proposals have been made for the source or sources of this alleged propensity to obey: Hitler's charisma (the perpetrators were, so to speak, caught in his spell), a general human tendency to obey authority, a peculiarly German reverence for and propensity to obey authority, or a totalitarian society's blunting of the individual's moral sense and its conditioning of him or her to accept all tasks as necessary. So a common proposition exists, namely that people obey authority, with a variety of accounts of why this is so. Obviously, the notion that authority, particularly state authority, tends to elicit obedience merits consideration.

A third explanation holds the perpetrators to have been subject to tremendous social psychological pressure, placed upon each one by his comrades and/or by the expectations that accompany the institutional roles that individuals occupy. It is, so goes the argument, extremely difficult for individuals to resist pressures to conform, pressures which can lead individuals to participate in acts which they on their own would not do, indeed would abhor. And a variety of psychological mechanisms are available for such people to rationalize their actions.

A fourth explanation sees the perpetrators as having been petty bureaucrats, or soulless technocrats, who pursued their self-interest or their technocratic goals and tasks with callous disregard for the victims. It can hold for administrators in Berlin as well as for concentration camp personnel. They all had careers to make, and because of the psychological propensity among those who are but cogs in a machine to attribute responsibility to others for overall policy, they could callously pursue their own careers or their own institutional or material interests. The deadening effects of institutions upon the sense of individual responsibility, on the one hand, and the frequent willingness of people to put their interests before those of others, on the other, need hardly be belabored.

A fifth explanation asserts that because tasks were so fragmented, the perpetrators could not understand what the real nature of their actions was; they could not comprehend that their small assignments were actually part of a global extermination program. To the extent that they could, this line of thinking continues, the fragmentation of tasks allowed them to deny the importance of their own contributions and to displace responsibility for them onto others. When engaged in unpleasant or morally dubious tasks, it is well known that people have a tendency to shift blame to others.

The explanations can be reconceptualized in terms of their accounts of the actors' capacity for volition: The first explanation (namely coercion) says that the killers could not say "no." The second explanation (obedience) and the third (situational pressure) maintain that Germans were psychologically incapable of saying "no." The fourth explanation (self-interest) contends that Germans had sufficient personal incentives to kill in order not to want to say "no." The fifth explanation (bureaucratic myopia) claims that it never even occurred to the perpetrators that they were engaged in an activity that might make them responsible for saying "no."

Each of these conventional explanations may sound plausible, and some of them obviously contain some truth, so what is wrong with them? While each suffers from particular defects,... they share a number of dubious *common* assumptions and features worth mentioning here.

The conventional explanations *assume* a neutral or condemnatory attitude on the part of the perpetrators towards their actions. They therefore premise their interpretations on the assumption that it must be shown how people can be brought to commit acts to which they would not inwardly assent, acts which they would not agree are necessary or just. They either ignore, deny, or radically minimize the importance of Nazi and perhaps the perpetrators' ideology, moral values, and conception of the victims, for engendering the perpetrators' willingness to kill. Some of these conventional explanations also caricature the perpetrators, and Germans in general. The explanations treat them as if they had been people lacking a moral sense, lacking the ability to make decisions and take stances. They do not conceive of the actors as human agents, as people with wills, but as beings moved solely by external forces or by transhistorical and invariant psychological propensities, such as the slavish following of narrow "self-interest." The conventional explanations suffer from two other major conceptual failings. They do not sufficiently recognize the extraordinary nature of the deed: the mass killing of people. They *assume* and imply that inducing people to kill human beings is fundamentally no different from getting them to do any other unwanted or distasteful task. Also, none of the conventional explanations deems the *identity* of the victims to have mattered. The conventional explanations imply that the perpetrators would have treated any other group of intended victims in exactly the same way. That the victims were Jews—according to the logic of these explanations—is irrelevant.

I maintain that any explanation that fails to acknowledge the actors' capacity to know and to judge, namely to understand and to have views about the significance and the morality of their actions, that fails to hold the actors' beliefs and values as central, that fails to emphasize the autonomous motivating force of Nazi ideology, particularly its central component of antisemitism, cannot possibly succeed in telling us much about why the perpetrators acted as they did. Any explanation that ignores either the particular nature of the perpetrators' actions—the systematic, large-scale killing and brutalizing of people—or the identity of the victims is inadequate for a host of reasons. All explanations that adopt these positions, as do the conventional explanations, suffer a mirrored, double failure of recognition of the human aspect of the Holocaust: the humanity of the perpetrators, namely their capacity to judge and to choose to act inhumanely, and the humanity of the victims, that what the perpetrators did, they did to these people with their specific identities, and not to animals or things.

My explanation—which is new to the scholarly literature on the perpetrators—is that the perpetrators, "ordinary Germans," were animated by antisemitism, by a particular *type* of antisemitism that led them to conclude that the Jews *ought to die*. The perpetrators' beliefs, their particular brand of antisemitism, though obviously not the sole source, was, I maintain, a most significant and indispensable source of the perpetrators' actions and must be at the center of any explanation of them. Simply put, the perpetrators, having consulted their own convictions and

morality and having judged the mass annihilation of Jews to be right, did not *want* to say "no." ...

The perpetrators were working within institutions that prescribed roles for them and assigned them specific tasks, yet they individually and collectively had latitude to make choices regarding their actions. Adopting a perspective which acknowledges this requires that their choices, especially the patterns of their choices, be discerned, analyzed, and incorporated into any overall explanation or interpretation. Ideal data would answer the following questions:

- What did the perpetrators actually do?
- What did they do in excess of what was "necessary"?
- What did they refuse to do?
- What could they have refused to do?
- What would they not have done?
- What was the manner in which they carried out their tasks?
- How smoothly did the overall operations proceed?

In examining the pattern of the perpetrators' actions in light of the institutional role requirements and incentive structure, two directions beyond the simple act of killing must be explored. First, in their treatment of Jews (and other victims), the Germans subjected them to a wide range of acts other than the lethal blow. It is important to understand the *gamut* of their actions towards Jews, if the genocidal slaughter is to be explicated. This is discussed in more detail presently. Second, the perpetrators' actions when they were *not* engaged in genocidal activities also shed light on the killing; the insights that an analysis of their non-killing activities offers into their general character and disposition to action, as well as the general social psychological milieu in which they lived might be crucial for understanding the patterns of their genocidal actions.

All of this points to a fundamental question: Which of the gamut of perpetrators' acts constitute the universe of the perpetrators' actions that need to be explained? Typically, the interpreters of the perpetrators have focused on one facet of the Germans' actions: the killing. This tunnel-vision perspective must be broadened. Imagine that the Germans had not undertaken to exterminate the Jews but had still mistreated them in all the other ways that they did, in concentration camps, in ghettos, as slaves. Imagine if, in our society today, people perpetrated against Jews or Christians, Whites or Blacks anything approaching one one-hundredth of the brutality and cruelty that Germans, independent of the killing, inflicted on Jews. Everyone would recognize the need for an explanation. Had the Germans not perpetrated a genocide, then the degree of privation and cruelty to which the Germans subjected Jews would in itself have come into focus and have been deemed an historic outrage, aberration, perversion that requires explanation. Yet these same actions have been lost in the genocide's shadow and neglected by previous attempts to explain the significant aspects of this event.

The fixation on the mass killing to the exclusion of the other related actions of the perpetrators has led to a radical misspecification of the explanatory task. The killing should be, for all the obvious reasons, at the center of scholarly attention. Yet it is not the only aspect of the Germans' treatment of the Jews that demands systematic scrutiny and explanation. Not only the killing but also *how* the Germans killed must be explained. The "how" frequently provides great insight into the "why." A killer can endeavor to render the deaths of others—whether he thinks the killing is just or unjust—more or less painful, both physically and emotionally. The ways in which Germans, collectively and individually, sought in their actions, or merely considered, to alleviate or intensify their victims' suffering must be accounted for in any explanation. An explanation that can seemingly make sense of Germans putting Jews to death, but not of the manner in which they did it, is a faulty explanation. . . .

People must be motivated to kill others, or else they would not do so. What conditions of cognition and value made genocidal motivations plausible in this period of German history? What was the structure of beliefs and values that made a genocidal onslaught against Jews intelligible and sensible to the ordinary Germans who became perpetrators? Since any explanation must account for the actions of tens of thousands of Germans of a wide variety of backgrounds working in different types of institutions, and must also account for a wide range of actions (and not merely the killing itself), a structure common to them must be found which is adequate to explaining the compass of their actions. This structure of cognition and value was located in and integral to German culture.

NO

Christopher R. Browning

ORDINARY MEN

On several issues [Daniel Jonah] Goldenhagen [the author of *Hitler's Willing Executioners: Ordinary Germans and the Holocaust*] and I do not disagree: first, the participation of numerous "ordinary" Germans in the mass murder of Jews, and second, the high degree of voluntarism they exhibited. The bulk of the killers were not specially selected but drawn at random from a cross-section of German society, and they did not kill because they were coerced by the threat of dire punishment for refusing. However, neither of these conclusions is a new discovery in the field of Holocaust studies. It was one of the fundamental conclusions of Raul Hilberg's magisterial and pathbreaking study *The Destruction of the European Jews*, which first appeared in 1961, that the perpetrators "were not different in their moral makeup from the rest of the population. The German perpetrator was not a special kind of German." The perpetrators represented "a remarkable cross-section of the German population," and the machinery of destruction "was structurally no different from organized German society as a whole." And it was the German scholar Herbert Jäger and the German prosecutors of the 1960s who firmly established that no one could document a single case in which Germans who refused to carry out the killing of unarmed civilians suffered dire consequences. Goldhagen does credit Jäger and the German prosecutors in this regard, but he is utterly dismissive of Hilberg.

Aside from the differences in the tone that we employ in writing about the Holocaust and in the attitude that we display toward other scholars who have worked in this field of study, Goldhagen and I disagree significantly in two major areas of historical interpretation. The first is our different assessments of the role of anti-Semitism in German history, including the National Socialist era [1933–1945]. The second is our different assessments of the motivation(s) of the "ordinary" German men who became Holocaust killers. These are the two topics that I would like to discuss at some length.

In his book *Hitler's Willing Executioners*, Daniel Goldhagen asserts that anti-Semitism "more or less governed the ideational life of civil society" in pre-Nazi Germany, when the Germans "elected" [sic] Hitler to power, the

From Christopher R. Browning, *Ordinary Men: Reserve Police Battalion 101 and the Final Solution in Poland* (HarperPerennial, 1998). Copyright © 1992, 1998 by Christopher R. Browning. Reprinted by permission of HarperCollins Publishers, Inc. Notes omitted.

"centrality of antisemitism in the Party's worldview, program, and rhetoric... mirrored the sentiments of German culture." Because Hitler and the Germans were "of one mind" about the Jews, he had merely to "unshackle" or "unleash" their "pre-existing, pent-up" anti-Semitism to perpetrate the Holocaust.

To buttress his view that the Nazi regime should be seen merely as allowing or encouraging Germans to do what they wanted to do all along and not basically shaping German attitudes and behavior after 1933, Goldhagen formulates a thesis that he proclaims is "new" to the study of anti-Semitism. Anti-Semitism "does not appear, disappear, then reappear in a given society. Always present, antisemitism becomes more or less manifest." Not anti-Semitism itself, but merely its "expression," either "increases or decreases" according to changing conditions.

Then in Goldhagen's account this picture of underlying permanency and superficial fluctuation changes abruptly after 1945. The pervasive and permanent eliminationist German anti-Semitism that was the sole and sufficient motivation of the Holocaust killers suddenly disappeared. Given reeducation, a change in public conversation, a law banning anti-Semitic expression, and the lack of institutional reinforcement, a German culture dominated by anti-Semitism for centuries was suddenly transformed. Now we are told, the Germans are just like us.

That anti-Semitism was a very significant aspect of Germany's political culture before 1945 and that Germany's political culture is both profoundly different and dramatically less anti-Semitic today are two propositions that I can easily support. But if Germany's political culture in general and anti-Semitism in particular could be transformed after 1945 by changes in education, public conversation, law, and institutional reinforcements, as Goldhagen suggests, then it seems to me equally plausible that they could have been equally transformed in the three or four decades preceding 1945 and especially during the twelve years of Nazi rule.

In his introductory chapter Goldhagen provides a useful model for a three-dimensional analysis of anti-Semitism, even if he does not employ his own model in the subsequent chapters. Anti-Semitism, he argues, varies according to the alleged source or cause (for example, race, religion, culture, or environment) of the Jews' alleged negative character. It varies in degree of preoccupation or priority, or how important is anti-Semitism to the anti-Semite. And it varies in degree of threat, or how endangered the anti-Semite feels. That anti-Semitism can vary in its diagnosis of the alleged Jewish threat and along continuums of priority and intensity would suggest not only that anti-Semitism changes over time as any or all of these dimensions change, but that it can exist in infinite variety. Even for a single country like Germany, I think we should speak and think in the plural—of anti-Semitisms rather than anti-Semitism.

The actual concept Goldhagen employs, however, produces the opposite effect; it erases all differentiation and subsumes all manifestations of anti-Semitism in Germany under a single rubric. All Germans who perceived Jews as different and viewed this difference as something negative that should disappear—whether through conversion, assimilation, emigration, or extermination—are classed as "eliminationist" anti-Semites, even if by Goldhagen's prior model they differ as to cause, priority, and intensity. Such differences that do exist are analytically insignificant in any case, for, according to Goldhagen, variations on eliminationist solutions "tend to metastasize" into extermination. By using such an approach, Goldhagen moves seamlessly from a variety of anti-Semitic manifestations in Germany to a single German "eliminationist antisemitism" that, taking on the properties of organic malignancy, naturally metastasized into extermination. Thus all Germany was "of one mind" with Hitler on the justice and necessity of the Final Solution.

If one adopts the analytical model that Goldhagen proposes rather than the concept he actually uses, what then can one say about the changing variety of anti-Semitisms in German political culture and their role in the Holocaust? . . .

By the turn of the century a German anti-Semitism increasingly racial in nature had become an integral part of the conservative political platform and penetrated deeply into the universities. It had become more politicized and institutionalized than in the western democracies of France, Britain, and the United States. But this does not mean that late nineteenth-century German anti-Semitism dominated either politics or ideational life. The conservatives and single-issue anti-Semitic parties together constituted a minority. While majorities could be found in the Prussian Landtag to pass discriminatory legislation against Catholics in the 1870s and in the Reichstag against socialists in the 1880s, the emancipation of Germany's Jews, who constituted less than 1 percent of the population and were scarcely capable of defending themselves against a Germany united in hostile obsession against them, was not revoked. If the left did not exhibit a philo-Semitism comparable to the right's anti-Semitism, it was primarily because for the left anti-Semitism was a nonissue that did not fit into its own class analysis, not because of its own anti-Semitism.

Even for the openly anti-Semitic conservatives, the Jewish issue was but one among many. And to suggest that they felt more threatened by the Jews than, for example, by the Triple Entente [Great Britain, France, and Russia] abroad or Social Democracy at home would be a serious distortion. If anti-Semitism was neither the priority issue nor the greatest threat even for conservatives, how much less was this the case for the rest of German society. As Richard Levy [an associate professor who studies anti-Semitism in modern history] has noted, "One can make a convincing case that [Jews] were of very little interest to most Germans most of the time. Putting them at the center of German history in the nineteenth and twentieth centuries is a highly unproductive strategy."

For some Germans, of course, Jews were the top priority and source of greatest fear. The turn-of-the-century anti-Semitism of German conservatives fits well Gavin Langmuir's [author of *History, Religion, and Antisemitism* (University of California Press, 1993)] notion of "xenophobic" anti-Semitism—a negative stereotype comprised of various assertions that did not describe the real Jewish minority but rather symbolized various threats and menaces that anti-Semites could not and did not want to understand. Langmuir notes as well that "xenophobic" anti-Semitism provides the fertile soil for the growth of fantastic or "chimeric" anti-Semitism—or what [professor and scholar of Jewish history] Saul Friedländer has recently dubbed "redemptive" anti-Semitism. If Germany's xenophobic anti-Semitism was an important piece of the political platform of an important segment of the political spectrum, the "redemptive" anti-Semites with their chimeric accusations—from Jewish poisoning of Aryan blood to a secret Jewish world conspiracy behind the twin threats of Marxist revolution and plutocratic democracy—were still a fringe phenomenon.

The succession of traumatic experiences in Germany between 1912 and 1929 —loss of control of the Reichstag by the right, military defeat, revolution, runaway inflation, and economic collapse— transformed German politics. The right grew at the expense of the center, and within the former the radicals, or New Right, grew at the expense of the traditionalists, or Old Right. Chimeric anti-Semitism grew commensurately from a fringe phenomenon to the core idea of a movement that became Germany's largest political party in the summer of 1932 and its ruling party six months later.

That fact alone makes the history of Germany and German anti-Semitism different from that of any other country in Europe. But even this must be kept in perspective. The Nazis never gained more than 37 percent of the vote in a free election, less than the combined socialist-communist vote. Daniel Goldhagen is right to remind us "that individuals' attitudes on single issues cannot be inferred from their votes." But it is highly unlikely that he is correct in his related assertion that large numbers of Germans who voted for the Social Democratic Party for economic reasons were nonetheless of one mind with Hitler and the Nazis about Jews. While I cannot prove it, I strongly suspect far more Germans voted Nazi for reasons other

than anti-Semitism than Germans who considered anti-Semitism a priority issue but nonetheless voted for a party other than the Nazis. Neither the election returns nor any plausible spin put on them suggest that in 1932 the vast majority of Germans were "of one mind" with Hitler about the Jews or that the "centrality of antisemitism in the Party's worldview, program, and rhetoric... mirrored the sentiments of German culture."

Beginning in 1933 all the factors that Goldhagen credits with dismantling German anti-Semitism after 1945— education, public conversation, law, and institutional reinforcement—were operating in the opposite direction to intensify anti-Semitism among the Germans, and indeed in a far more concerted manner than in the post-war period. Can one seriously doubt that this had significant impact, particularly given the rising popularity of Hitler and the regime for its economic and foreign policy successes? As William Sheridan Allen [author of *The Nazi Seizure of Power: The Experience of a Single German Town (1922–1945)* (Franklin Watts, 1984)] succinctly concluded, even in a highly Nazified town like Northeim, most people "were drawn to anti-Semitism because they were drawn to Nazism, not the other way around." Moreover, the 1936 Sopade underground report to which Goldhagen repeatedly refers—"antisemitism has no doubt taken root in wide circles of the population.... The general antisemitic psychosis affects even thoughtful people, our comrades as well"—is evidence of change in German attitudes following the Nazi seizure of power in 1933, not the prior situation.

Even in the post-1933 period, however, it is best to speak in the plural of German anti-Semitisms. Within the party, there was indeed a large core of Germans for whom the Jews were a dire racial threat and central priority. The hardcore "chimeric" or "redemptive" anti-Semites of the Nazi movement differed in style and preferred response, however. At one end of the spectrum were the SA and Streicher types lusting for pogroms [an organized massacre]; at the other end were the cool and calculating, intellectual anti-Semites described by [historian] Ulrich Herbert in his new biography of [Nazi lawyer] Werner Best, who advocated a more systematic but dispassionate persecution.

What can be said of the German population at large in the 1930s? Was the bulk of the German population swept along by the Nazis' anti-Semitic tide? Only in part, according to the detailed research of historians like Ian Kershaw, Otto Dov Kulka, and David Bankier, who have reached a surprising degree of consensus on this issue. For the 1933–39 period, these three historians distinguish between a minority of party activists, for whom anti-Semitism was an urgent priority, and the bulk of the German population, for whom it was not. Apart from the activists, the vast majority of the general population did not clamor or press for anti-Semitic measures. But the majority of "ordinary Germans"—whom Saul Friedländer describes as "onlookers" in contrast to "activists"— nonetheless accepted the legal measures of the regime, which ended emancipation and drove the Jews from public positions in 1933, socially ostracized the Jews in 1935, and completed the expropriation of their property in 1938–39. Yet this majority was critical of the hooliganistic violence of party radicals toward the same German Jews whose legal persecution they approved. The boycott of 1933, the vandalistic outbreaks of 1935, and above all the *Kristallnacht* pogrom of November 1938 produced a negative response among much of the German population.

Most important, however, a gulf had opened up between the Jewish minority and the general population. The latter, while not mobilized around strident and violent anti-Semitism, were increasingly "apathetic," "passive," and "indifferent" to the fate of the former. Anti-Semitic measures—if carried out in an orderly and legal manner—were widely accepted for two main reasons: such measures sustained the hope of curbing the violence most Germans found so distasteful, and most Germans now accepted the goal of limiting, and even ending, the role of Jews in German society. This was a major accomplishment for the regime, but it still did not offer the prospect that most "ordinary Germans" would approve of, much less participate in, the mass murder of European Jewry, that the "onlookers" of 1938 would become the genocidal killers of 1941–42.

Concerning the war years, Kershaw, Kulka, and Bankier disagree on some issues but generally concur that the anti-Semitism of the "true believers" was not identical to the anti-Semitic attitudes of the general population, and that the anti-Semitic priorities and genocidal commitment of the regime were still not shared by ordinary Germans. Bankier, who in no way downplays German anti-Semitism, wrote: "Ordinary Germans knew how to distinguish between an acceptable discrimination... and the unacceptable horror of genocide.... The more the news of mass murder filtered through, the less the public wanted to be involved in the final solution of the Jewish question. Nonetheless, as Kulka put it, "a strikingly abysmal indifference to the fate of the Jews as human beings" gave "the regime the freedom of action to push for a radical 'Final Solution.'" Kershaw emphasized the same point with his memorable phrase that "the road to Auschwitz was built by hatred, but paved with indifference."...

There are two additional points on which Goldhagen and I agree. First, one must look at the attitudes and behavior of ordinary Germans not only on the home front but also in occupied eastern Europe, and second, when faced with the task of killing Jews, most ordinary Germans there became "willing" executioners. If ordinary Germans at home were indifferent and apathetic, complicitous and callous, in the east they were killers.

We differ, however, on context and motive for this murderous behavior. For Goldhagen, these ordinary Germans, "equipped with little more than the cultural notions current in Germany" before 1933 and now at last given the opportunity, simply "wanted to be genocidal executioners." In my opinion, ordinary Germans in eastern Europe brought with them a set of attitudes that included not only the different strands of anti-Semitism found in German society and fanned by the regime since 1933, but much else as well. As the Treaty of Brest-Litovsk, the *Freikorps* campaigns, and the almost universal rejection of the Versailles Treaty demonstrate, refusal to accept the verdict of World War I, imperial aspirations in eastern Europe underpinned by notions of German racial superiority, and virulent anticommunism were broadly held sentiments in German society. I would argue that they provided more common ground for the bulk of the German population and the Nazis than did anti-Semitism.

And in eastern Europe ordinary Germans were transformed even more by the events and situation of 1939–41 than they had been by their experience of the domestic dictatorship of 1933–39. Germany was now at war; moreover, this was a "race war" of imperial conquest. These ordinary Germans were stationed in the territory where the native populations were proclaimed inferior and occupying Germans were constantly exhorted to behave as the master race. And the Jews encountered in these territories were the strange and alien *Ostjuden* [Eastern Jews], not assimilated, middle-class German Jews. In 1941 two more major factors, the ideological crusade against Bolshevism and "war of destruction," were added. Is it even plausible to suggest that this wartime change in situation and context did not alter the attitudes and behavior of ordinary Germans in eastern Europe, and that only a common cognitive image of Jews predating 1933 and held by virtually all Germans accounts for their willingness, and for some even eagerness, to kill Jews?

In this regard, it is important to note that before the Final Solution was implemented (beginning on Soviet territory in the second half of 1941 and in Poland and the rest of Europe in the spring of 1942), the Nazi regime had already found willing executioners for 70,000 to 80,000 mentally and physically handicapped Germans, tens of thousands of Polish intelligentsia, tens of thousands of noncombatant victims of reprisal shootings, and more than 2 million Russian POWs. Clearly, as of September 1939, the regime was increasingly capable of legitimizing and organizing mass murder on a staggering scale that did not depend on the anti-Semitic motivation of the perpetrators and the Jewish identity of the victims....

There are, in short, a number of conceivable variables—government policy and past patterns of behavior as well as culturally induced cognitive images —that are important. Yet, in accounting for differential German behavior toward Jewish and non-Jewish victims, Goldhagen's argument does not adequately separate the variety of possible causal factors. His insistence on the German cognitive image of Jews as the "only" adequate framework is bolstered above all by his emphasis on the cruelty of the perpetrators.

However, the argument from unprecedented, singular German cruelty toward Jews is problematic on two counts. First, Goldhagen's claim of singularity is grounded on the emotional impact of his narrative rather than actual comparison. He offers numerous graphic and chilling descriptions of German cruelty toward Jews and then simply asserts to the numbed and horrified reader that such behavior is clearly unprecedented. If only that were the case. Unfortunately, accounts of Romanian and Croatian killings would readily demonstrate that these collaborators not only equaled but routinely surpassed the Germans in cruelty. And that leaves myriad possible non-Holocaust examples from Cambodia to Rwanda totally aside.

Conversely, he downplays the cruelty in the Nazi murder of other victims, particularly the German handicapped in which Germans allegedly were "coldly involved" in inflicting "painless" death without celebration. Yet the mentally handicapped were first gunned down by the firing squads of the Eimann commando before the development of the gas vans and gas chambers, and many infants were simply not fed and left to starve to death. Screaming and fleeing patients were hunted down and dragged away from asylums to the waiting buses. And at Hadamar the killers threw a party to celebrate the milestone of 10,000 victims!...

In contrast to Goldhagen, I offered a portrayal of the [Reserve Police] [B]attalion [101] that was multilayered [at the symposium at the U.S. Holocaust Memorial Museum in April 1996]. Different groups within the battalion behaved in different ways. The "eager killers" —whose numbers increased over time —sought the opportunity to kill, and celebrated their murderous deeds. The smallest group within the battalion comprised the nonshooters. With the exception of Lieutenant [Heinz] Buchmann [who verbally objected to and refused to participate in anti-Jewish actions], they did not make principled objections against the regime and its murderous policies; they did not reproach their comrades. They took advantage of [Major Wilhelm] Trapp's policy within the battalion of exempting from shooting those who "didn't feel up to it" by saying that they were took weak or that they had children.

The largest group within the battalion did whatever they were asked to do, without ever risking the onus of confronting authority or appearing weak, but they did not volunteer for or celebrate the killing. Increasingly numb and brutalized, they felt more pity for themselves because of the "unpleasant" work they had been assigned than they did for their dehumanized victims. For the most part, they did not think what they were doing was wrong or immoral, because the killing was sanctioned by legitimate authority. Indeed, for the most part they did not try to think, period. As one policeman stated: "Truthfully, I must say that at the time we didn't reflect about it at all. Only years later did any of us become truly conscious of what had happened then." Heavy drinking helped: "most of the other men drank so much solely because of the many shootings of Jews, for such a life was quite intolerable sober."

That these policemen were "willing executioners" does not mean that they "wanted to be genocidal executioners." This, in my opinion, is an important distinction that Goldhagen consistently blurs. He also repeatedly poses the interpretational dispute in the form of a false dichotomy: either the German killers must have been "of one mind" with Hitler about the demonological nature of the Jews and hence believed in the necessity and justice of the mass murder, or they must have believed that they were committing the greatest crime in history. In my view the majority of the killers could not be described by either of these polar-opposite views.

In addition to a multilayered portrayal of the battalion, I offered a multicausal explanation of motivation. I noted the importance of conformity, peer pressure, and deference to authority, and I should have emphasized more explicitly the legitimizing capacities of government. I also emphasized the "mutually intensifying effects of war and racism," as "the years of anti-Semitic propaganda . . . dove-tailed with the polarizing effects of war." I argued that "nothing helped the Nazis to wage a race war so much as the war itself," as the "dichotomy of racially superior Germans and racially inferior Jews, central to Nazi ideology, could easily merge with the image of a beleaguered Germany surrounded by enemies." Ordinary Germans did not have to be "of one mind" with Hitler's demonological view of the Jews to carry out genocide. A combination of situational factors and ideological overlap that concurred on the enemy status and dehumanization of the victims was sufficient to turn "ordinary men" into "willing executioners."

Goldhagen claims that we have "no choice but to adopt" his own explanation, because he has "irrefutably" and "resoundingly" disproved the "conventional explanations" (coercion, obedience, social-psychological observations about human behavior, self-interest, and attenuation or fragmentation of responsibility). Several problems emerge. First, these "conventional explanations" are not invoked by scholars as sole and sufficient causes of perpetrator behavior but are usually part of a multicausal approach, what Goldhagen derides as a "laundry list." Thus they do not have to meet the same high test of allegedly accounting for everything that Goldhagen sets for his own explanation. Second, to claim that one has disproved something irrefutably sets a high test that Goldhagen does not meet. And third, even a comprehensive refutation of the "conventional explanations" would not necessitate accepting Goldhagen's thesis. . . .

The same kinds of evidence and arguments that Goldhagen cites as proof of the pervasiveness of anti-Semitism inculcating hatred of Jews in Germany can also be found in support of the notion that Germany had a strong tradition of authoritarianism inculcating habits of obedience and antidemocratic attitudes. All the elements that Goldhagen himself cites as decisive for shaping political culture—education, public conversation, law, and institutional reinforcement—were at work inculcating authoritarian values in Germany long before the Nazis also used them to incessantly disseminate anti-Semitism.

Moreover, the most outspoken anti-Semites in Germany were also antidemocratic and authoritarian. To deny the importance of authoritarian traditions and values in German political culture while arguing for the pervasiveness of anti-Semitism is to insist that the glass is half-full while denying that it is half-empty. To the extent that Goldhagen's arguments about German political culture and anti-Semitism are valid, they are even more so for German political culture and obedience to authority....

It is my position... that psycho-sociological theories—based upon the assumption of inclinations and propensities common to human nature but not excluding cultural influences—provide important insights into the behavior of the perpetrators. I believe that the perpetrators not only had the capacity to choose but exercised that choice in various ways that covered the spectrum from enthusiastic participation, through dutiful, nominal, or regretful compliance, to differing degrees of evasion. Which of our two approaches, I would ask, is predicated upon the humanity and individuality of the perpetrators and allows for a moral dimension in the analysis of their choices?

Goldhagen and I agree that Reserve Police Battalion 101 was representative of "ordinary Germans," and that "ordinary Germans" randomly conscripted from all walks of life became "willing executioners." But I do not think that his portrayal of the battalion is representative. He is certainly right that there were numerous enthusiastic killers who sought the opportunity to kill, found gratification in inflicting terrible cruelties, and celebrated their deeds. All too many frightening examples of such behavior can be found in both this [selection] and his [book]. But Goldhagen minimizes or denies other layers of behavior that are important to understanding the dynamics of genocidal killing units and that cast doubt on his assertion that the battalion was uniformly pervaded by "pride" in and "principled approval" of the mass murder it perpetrated. His portrayal is skewed because he mistakes the part for the whole.

This is a flaw that appears repeatedly throughout the book. For instance, I agree that anti-Semitism was a strong ideological current in nineteenth-century Germany, but I do not accept Goldhagen's assertion that anti-Semitism "more or less governed the ideational life of civil society" in pre-Nazi Germany. I agree that by 1933 anti-Semitism had become part of the "common sense" of the German right without thereby concluding that all German society was "of one mind" with Hitler about the Jews, and that the "centrality of anti-semitism in the Party's worldview, program, and rhetoric... mirrored the sentiments of German culture." I agree that anti-Semitism—negative stereotyping, dehumanization, and hatred of the Jews—was widespread among the killers of 1942, but I do not agree that this anti-Semitism is primarily to be seen as a "pre-existing, pent-up" anti-Semitism that Hitler had merely to "unleash" and "unshackle."

In short, the fundamental problem is not to explain why ordinary Germans, as members of a people utterly different from us and shaped by a culture that permitted them to think and act in no other way than to want to be genocidal executioners, eagerly killed Jews when the opportunity offered. The fundamental problem is to explain why ordinary men—shaped by a culture that had its own particularities but was nonetheless within the mainstream of western, Christian, and Enlightenment traditions—under specific circumstances willingly carried out the most extreme genocide in human history.

Why does it matter which of our portrayals of and conclusions about Reserve Police Battalion 101 are closer to the truth? It would be very comforting if Goldhagen were correct, that very few societies have the long-term, cultural-cognitive prerequisites to commit genocide, and that regimes can only do so when the population is overwhelmingly of one mind about its priority, justice, and necessity. We would live in a safer world if he were right, but I am not so optimistic. I fear that we live in a world in which war and racism are ubiquitous, in which the powers of government mobilization and legitimization are powerful and increasing, in which a sense of personal responsibility is increasingly attenuated by specialization and bureaucratization, and in which the peer group exerts tremendous pressures on behavior and sets moral norms. In such a world, I fear, modern governments that wish to commit mass murder will seldom fail in their efforts for being unable to induce "ordinary men" to become their "willing executioners."

POSTSCRIPT

Was German "Eliminationist Anti-Semitism" Responsible for the Holocaust?

The publicity engendered by Goldhagen's book has been overwhelming, both in the United States and Germany. Criticism has been strong and so have Goldhagen's rebuttals to his critics in general (see *The New Republic*, December 23, 1996).

Needless to say, there have been many books written about the Holocaust. A few general sources that should be consulted are Raul Hilberg, *The Destruction of the European Jews* (Holmes & Meier, 1985); Yehuda Bauer, *A History of the Holocaust* (Franklin Watts, 1982); Martin Gilbert, *The Holocaust: A History of the Jews of Europe During the Second World War* (Holt, Rinehart & Winston, 1986); Michael Robert Marrus, *The Holocaust in History* (University Press of New England, 1987). Ron Rosenbaum's *Explaining Hitler: The Search for the Origins of his Evil* (Random House, 1998), provides an interesting and accessible look at Holocaust historiography, as the journalist/author interviews and writes about the world's leading scholars and their works.

In a book entitled *Hyping the Holocaust: Scholars Answer Goldhagen* (Cummings & Hathaway, 1997), 12 international scholars offer their criticisms of *Hitler's Willing Executioners*. In it, Goldhagen is rebuked for everything from intentional sensationalism and selective use of sources to faulty methodology and stereotyping at its worst. Finally, Robert R. Shandley, ed., *Unwilling Germans? The Goldhagen Debate* (University of Minnesota Press, 1998), offers a large sampling of German reaction to *Hitler's Willing Executioners: Ordinary Germans and the Holocaust,* both positive and negative.

ISSUE 20

Was Stalin Responsible for the Cold War?

YES: John Lewis Gaddis, from *We Now Know: Rethinking Cold War History* (Clarendon Press, 1997)

NO: Martin J. Sherwin, from "The Atomic Bomb and the Origins of the Cold War," in Melvyn P. Leffler and David S. Painter, eds., *Origins of the Cold War: An International History* (Routledge, 1994)

ISSUE SUMMARY

YES: Historian John Lewis Gaddis states that after more than a half a century of cold war scholarship, Joseph Stalin still deserves most of the responsibility for the onset of the cold war.

NO: Historian Martin J. Sherwin counters that the origins of the cold war can be found in the World War II diplomacy involving the use of the atomic bomb, and he places much of the blame for the cold war on the shoulders of Franklin D. Roosevelt, Harry S. Truman, and Winston Churchill.

It is hard to imagine that the cold war is over when it played such a pivotal role in world affairs for five decades. But the disintegration of the Soviet Empire has ushered in a new era in strategic diplomacy. What shape this new international relations era will take has yet to be determined, but it is unlikely that it will influence our lives in the same manner as the cold war. It is now the job of historians to compose a reassessment of the cold war, which would cover causes, effects, and responsibility.

The historiography of the cold war seemed to begin simultaneously with the onset of tensions between the free and communist worlds. In addressing the question of responsibility, the debate among historians seemed to center around two distinct groups of scholars. The first group, commonly referred to as the orthodox or traditional school, held the Soviet Union responsible for the cold war. Because some of the school's proponents were themselves participants in the events of the era, it was easy for them to see Soviet culpability in the broken promises and duplicitous actions highlighting the early cold war years. And as the Soviet Empire cast its menacing shadow over Eastern Europe, it became increasingly apparent that Joseph Stalin in particular could not be trusted. Also, the volatile nature of the postwar world—especially the vulnerability of the newly emerging nations of the postimperialist era—created a tempting morsel for the "Russian Bear." A new policy, "containment," was created to control the voracious Soviet appetite. It would last for almost half a century and would lead to many crises, wars, and conflicts, which marked the cold war.

A new school of thought was created to counteract the influence of the traditionalists. Members of this school of thought became known as the revisionists, and they began to view the cold war from an entirely different perspective. From this would come a new set of assumptions, including: (1) the postwar weakness of the Soviet Union, which prevented the Soviets from being the threat to world peace that many felt they were; (2) the obsession of free-world leaders in viewing any world problem as being Soviet-created; (3) the view that, after a careful examination of World War II diplomacy, many of the actions of the Western Allies, including the use of the atomic bomb, induced Soviet leaders to feel threatened and to react accordingly. Thus, much of the responsibility for the cold war, according to the revisionists, must be laid at the feet of the West and its leaders.

Subsequently, much of cold war historiography was dominated by this traditionalist/revisionist dichotomy. And as the historical profession became more influenced by a conflict-oriented mode rather than a consensus-centered one, the revisionists began to gain momentum in the crisis-laden 1960s and 1970s. The Vietnam War helped to trigger this response, as many began to see the mistakes of the cold war being played out again and again. There were no longer any "sacred cows" of the traditionalist variety.

The sudden decline of world communism seemed to usher in an aura of cold war justification. After all, in the eyes of many, the West had won; the enemy had been vanquished, and the end of the struggle seemed to have a ring of vindication to it. But the scars of the past were too deep, and the critical examination of cold war politics continued.

New sources of information, especially those from the formerly secret Soviet archives, were opened up in order to assist historians in their search for answers. Not so surprisingly, the results derived from these sources were not uniform. John Lewis Gaddis named this recent reexamination the "New Cold War." Having been involved in cold war historiography for most of its existence, he drew the conclusion that the Soviet Union and Stalin in particular bear most of the responsibility for the cold war.

Historians such as Gar Alperovitz, Gabriel Kolko, Martin J. Sherwin, and others continued to push the revisionist agenda, and Sherwin represents their viewpoint in his selection.

YES

John Lewis Gaddis

WE NOW KNOW: RETHINKING COLD WAR HISTORY

[Joseph] Stalin appears to have relished his role, along with [Franklin D.] Roosevelt and [Winston] Churchill, as one of the wartime Big Three. Such evidence as has surfaced from Soviet archives suggests that he received reassuring reports about Washington's intentions: "Roosevelt is more friendly to us than any other prominent American," Ambassador Litvinov commented in June 1943, "and it is quite obvious that he wishes to cooperate with us." Whoever was in the White House, Litvinov's successor Andrei Gromyko predicted a year later, the Soviet Union and the United States would "manage to find common issues for the solution of . . . problems emerging in the future and of interest to both countries." Even if Stalin's long-range thinking about security did clash with that of his Anglo-American allies, common military purposes provided the strongest possible inducements to smooth over such differences. It is worth asking why this *practice* of wartime cooperation did not become a *habit* that would extend into the postwar era.

The principal reason, it now appears, was Stalin's insistence on equating security with territory. Western diplomats had been surprised, upon arriving in Moscow soon after the German attack in the summer of 1941, to find the Soviet leader already demanding a postwar settlement that would retain what his pact with Hitler had yielded: the Baltic states, together with portions of Finland, Poland, and Romania. Stalin showed no sense of shame or even embarrassment about this, no awareness that the *methods* by which he had obtained these concessions could conceivably render them illegitimate in the eyes of anyone else. When it came to territorial aspirations, he made no distinction between adversaries and allies: what one had provided the other was expected to endorse. . . .

On the surface, this strategy succeeded. After strong initial objections, Roosevelt and Churchill did eventually acknowledge the Soviet Union's right to the expanded borders it claimed; they also made it clear that they would not oppose the installation of "friendly" governments in adjoining states. This meant accepting a Soviet sphere of influence from the Baltic to the Adriatic, a concession not easily reconciled with the Atlantic Charter. But the authors of that document saw no feasible way to avoid that outcome: military necessity required continued Soviet cooperation against the Germans. Nor were they themselves prepared to relinquish spheres of influence in Western Europe and the Mediterranean, the Middle East, Latin America, and East Asia. Self-determination was a sufficiently malleable concept that each of the Big Three could have endorsed, without sleepless nights, what the Soviet government had said about the Atlantic Charter: "practical application of these principles will necessarily adapt itself to the circumstances, needs, and historic peculiarities of particular countries."

That, though, was precisely the problem. For unlike Stalin, Roosevelt and Churchill would have to defend their decisions before domestic constituencies. The *manner* in which Soviet influence expanded was therefore, for them, of no small significance. Stalin showed little understanding of this. Having no experience himself with democratic procedures, he dismissed requests that he respect democratic proprieties. "[S]ome propaganda work should be done," he advised Roosevelt at the Tehran conference after the president had hinted that the American public would welcome a plebiscite in the Baltic States. "It is all nonsense!" Stalin complained to [Soviet Foreign Minister V. M.] Molotov. "[Roosevelt] is their military leader and commander in chief. Who would dare object to him?" When at Yalta F.D.R. stressed the need for the first Polish election to be as pure as "Caesar's wife," Stalin responded with a joke: "They said that about her, but in fact she had her sins." Molotov warned his boss, on that occasion, that the Americans' insistence on free elections elsewhere in Eastern Europe was

"going too far." "Don't worry," he recalls Stalin as replying, "work it out. We can deal with it in our own way later. The point is the correlation of forces."

The Soviet leader was, in one sense, right. Military strength would determine what happened in that part of the world, not the enunciation of lofty principles. But unilateral methods carried long-term costs Stalin did not foresee: the most significant of these was to ruin whatever prospects existed for a Soviet sphere of influence the East Europeans themselves might have accepted. This possibility was not as far-fetched as it would later seem. ... [Stalin] would, after all, approve such a compromise as the basis for a permanent settlement with Finland. He would initially allow free elections in Hungary, Czechoslovakia, and the Soviet occupation zone in Germany. He may even have *anticipated an enthusiastic response* as he took over Eastern Europe. "He was, I think, surprised and hurt," [W. Averell] Harriman [one of Roosevelt's closest advisors] recalled, "when the Red Army was not welcomed in all the neighboring countries as an army of liberation." "We still had our hopes," [Nikita] Khrushchev remembered, that "after the catastrophe of World War II, Europe too might become Soviet. Everyone would take the path from capitalism to socialism." It could be that there was another form of romanticism at work here, quite apart from Stalin's affinity for fellow authoritarians: that he was unrealistic enough to expect ideological solidarity and gratitude for liberation to override old fears of Russian expansionism as well as remaining manifestations of nationalism among the Soviet Union's neighbors, perhaps as easily as he himself had overridden the latter—or so it then appeared—within the multinational empire that was the Soviet Union itself.

If the Red Army could have been welcomed in Poland and the rest of the countries it liberated with the same enthusiasm American, British, and Free French forces encountered when they landed in Italy and France in 1943 and 1944, then some kind of Czech–Finnish compromise might have been feasible. Whatever Stalin's expectations, though, this did not happen. That non-event, in turn, removed any possibility of a division of Europe all members of the Grand Alliance could have endorsed. It ensured that an American sphere of influence would arise there largely by consent, but that its Soviet counterpart could sustain itself only by coercion. The resulting asymmetry would account, more than anything else, for the origins, escalation, and ultimate outcome of the Cold War.

* * *

... It has long been clear that, in addition to having had an authoritarian vision, Stalin also had an imperial one, which he proceeded to implement in at least as single-minded a way [as the American]. No comparably influential builder of empire came close to wielding power for so long, or with such striking results, on the Western side.

It was, of course, a matter of some awkwardness that Stalin came out of a revolutionary movement that had vowed to smash, not just tsarist imperialism, but all forms of imperialism throughout the world. The Soviet leader constructed his own logic, though, and throughout his career he devoted a surprising amount of attention to showing how a revolution and an empire might coexist....

Stalin's fusion of Marxist internationalism with tsarist imperialism could only reinforce his tendency, in place well before World War II, to equate the advance of world revolution with the expanding influence of the Soviet state. He applied that linkage quite impartially: a major benefit of the 1939 pact with Hitler had been that it regained territories lost as a result of the Bolshevik Revolution and the World War I settlement. But Stalin's conflation of imperialism with ideology also explains the importance he attached, following the German attack in 1941, to having his new Anglo-American allies confirm these arrangements. He had similar goals in East Asia when he insisted on bringing the Soviet Union back to the position Russia had occupied in Manchuria prior to the Russo-Japanese War: this he finally achieved at the 1945 Yalta Conference in return for promising to enter the war against Japan. "My task as minister of foreign affairs was to expand the borders of our Fatherland," Molotov recalled proudly many years later. "And it seems that Stalin and I coped with this task quite well." ...

* * *

From the West's standpoint, the critical question was how far Moscow's influence would extend *beyond* whatever Soviet frontiers turned out to be at the end of the war. Stalin had suggested to Milovan Djilas that the Soviet Union would impose its own social system as far as its armies could reach, but he was also very cautious. Keenly aware of the military power the United States and its allies had accumulated, Stalin was determined to do nothing that might involve the USSR in another devastating war until it had recovered sufficiently to be certain of winning it. "I do not wish to begin the Third World War over the Trieste question," he explained to disappointed Yugoslavs, whom he ordered to evacuate that territory in June 1945. Five years later, he would justify his decision not to intervene in the Korean War on the grounds that "the Second World War ended not long ago, and we are not ready for the Third World War." Just how far the expansion of Soviet influence would proceed depended, therefore, upon a careful balancing of opportunities against risks....

Who or what was it, though, that set the limits? Did Stalin have a fixed list of countries he thought it necessary to dominate? Was he prepared to stop in the face of resistance within those countries to "squeezing out the capitalist order"? Or would expansion cease only when confronted with opposition from the remaining capitalist states, so that further advances risked war at a time when the Soviet Union was ill-prepared for it?

Stalin had been very precise about where he wanted Soviet boundaries changed; he was much less so on how far Moscow's sphere of influence was to extend. He insisted on having "friendly" countries around the periphery of the USSR, but he failed to specify how many would have to meet this standard. He called during the war for dismembering Germany, but by the end of it was denying that he had ever done so: that country would be temporarily divided, he told leading German communists in June 1945, and they themselves would eventually bring about its reunification. He never gave up on the idea of an eventual world revolution, but he expected this to result—as his comments to the Germans suggested—from an expansion of influence emanating from the Soviet Union itself. "[F]or the Kremlin," a well-placed spymaster recalled, "the mission of communism was primarily to consolidate the might of the Soviet state. Only military strength and domination of the countries on our borders could ensure us a superpower role.

But Stalin provided no indication —surely because he himself did not know—of how rapidly, or under what circumstances, this process would take place. He was certainly prepared to stop in the face of resistance from the West: at no point was he willing to challenge the Americans or even the British where they made their interests clear.... He quickly backed down when confronted with Anglo-American objections to his ambitions in Iran in the spring of 1946, as he did later that year after demanding Soviet bases in the Turkish Straits. This pattern of advance followed by retreat had shown up in the purges of the 1930s, which Stalin halted when the external threat from Germany became too great to ignore, and it would reappear with the Berlin Blockade and the Korean War, both situations in which the Soviet Union would show great caution after provoking an unexpectedly strong American response.

What all of this suggests, though, is not that Stalin had limited ambitions, only that he had no timetable for achieving them. Molotov retrospectively confirmed this: "Our ideology stands for offensive operations when possible, and if not, we wait." Given this combination of appetite with aversion to risk, one cannot help but wonder what would have happened had the West tried containment earlier. To the extent that it bears partial responsibility for the coming of the Cold War, the historian Vojtech Mastny has argued, that responsibility lies in its failure to do just that....

Stalin's policy, then, was one of imperial expansion and consolidation differing from that of earlier empires only in the determination with which he pursued it, in the instruments of coercion with which he maintained it, and in the ostensibly anti-imperial justifications he put forward in support of it. It is a testimony to his skill, if not to his morality, that he was able to achieve so many of his imperial ambitions at a time when the tides of history were running against the idea of imperial domination—as colonial offices in London, Paris, Lisbon, and The Hague were finding out—and when his own country was recovering from one of the most brutal invasions in recorded history. The fact that Stalin was able to *expand* his empire when others were contracting and while the Soviet Union was as weak as it was requires explanation. Why did opposition to this process, within and outside Europe, take so long to develop?

One reason was that the colossal sacrifices the Soviet Union had made during the war against the Axis had, in effect, "purified" its reputation: the USSR and its leader had "earned" the right to throw their weight around, or so it seemed. Western governments found it difficult to switch quickly from viewing the Soviet Union as a glorious wartime ally to portraying it as a new and dangerous adversary. President Harry S. Truman and his future Secretary of State Dean Acheson—neither of them sympathetic in the slightest to communism—nonetheless tended to give the Soviet Union the benefit of the doubt well into the early postwar era....

Resistance to Stalin's imperialism also developed slowly because Marxism-Leninism at the time had such widespread appeal. It is difficult now to recapture the admiration revolutionaries outside the Soviet Union felt for that country before they came to know it well.... Because the Bolsheviks themselves had overcome one empire and had made a career of condemning others, it would take decades for people who were struggling to overthrow British, French, Dutch, or Portuguese colonialism to see that there could also be such a thing as Soviet imperialism. European communists —notably the Yugoslavs—saw this much earlier, but even to most of them it had not been apparent at the end of the war.

Still another explanation for the initial lack of resistance to Soviet expansionism was the fact that its repressive character did not become immediately apparent to all who were subjected to it....

One has the impression that Stalin and the Eastern Europeans got to know one another only gradually. The Kremlin leader was slow to recognize that Soviet authority would not be welcomed everywhere beyond Soviet borders; but as he did come to see this he became all the more determined to impose it everywhere. The Eastern Europeans were slow to recognize how confining incorporation within a Soviet sphere was going to be; but as they did come to see this they became all the more determined to resist it, even if only by withholding, in a passive but sullen manner, the consent any regime needs to establish itself by means other than coercion. Stalin's efforts to consolidate his empire therefore made it at once more repressive and less secure. Meanwhile, an alternative vision of postwar Europe was emerging from the other great empire that established itself in the wake of World War II, that of the United States, and this too gave Stalin grounds for concern....

* * *

What is there new to say about the old question of responsibility for the Cold War? Who actually started it? Could it have been averted? Here I think the "new" history is bringing us back to an old answer: that *as long as Stalin was running the Soviet Union a cold war was unavoidable.*

History is always the product of determined *and* contingent events: it is up to historians to find the proper balance between them. The Cold War could hardly have happened if there had not been a United States and a Soviet Union, if both had not emerged victorious from World War II, if they had not had conflicting visions of how to organize the postwar world. But these long-term trends did not in themselves *ensure* such a contest, because there is always room for the unexpected to undo what might appear to be inevitable. *Nothing* is ever completely predetermined, as real triceratops and other dinosaurs discovered 65 million years ago when the most recent large asteroid or comet or whatever it was hit the earth and wiped them out.

Individuals, not asteroids, more often personify contingency in history. Who can specify in advance—or unravel afterwards—the particular intersection of genetics, environment, and culture that makes each person unique? Who can foresee what weird conjunctions of design and circumstance may cause a very few individuals to rise so high as to shape great events, and so come to the attention of historians? Such people may set their sights on getting to the top, but an assassin, or a bacillus, or even a carelessly driven taxicab can always be lurking along the way. How

entire countries fall into the hands of malevolent geniuses like Hitler and Stalin remains as unfathomable in the "new" Cold War history as in the "old."

Once leaders like these do gain power, however, certain things become highly probable. It is only to be expected that in an authoritarian state the chief authoritarian's personality will weigh much more heavily than those of democratic leaders, who have to share power. And whether because of social alienation, technological innovation, or economic desperation, the first half of the twentieth century was particularly susceptible to great authoritarians and all that resulted from their ascendancy. It is hardly possible to imagine Nazi Germany or the world war it caused without Hitler. I find it increasingly difficult, given what we know now, to imagine the Soviet Union or the Cold War without Stalin.

For the more we learn, the less sense it makes to distinguish Stalin's foreign policies from his domestic practices or even his personal behavior. Scientists have shown the natural world to be filled with examples of what they call "self-similarity across scale": patterns that persist whether one views them microscopically, macroscopically, or anywhere in between. Stalin was like that: he functioned in much the same manner whether operating within the international system, within his alliances, within his country, within his party, within his personal entourage, or even within his family. The Soviet leader waged cold wars on all of these fronts. The Cold War *we* came to know was only one of many from *his* point of view.

Nor did Stalin's influence diminish as quickly as that of most dictators after their deaths. He built a *system* sufficiently durable to survive not only his own demise but his successors' fitful and half-hearted efforts at "de-Staliniza-tion." They were themselves its creatures, and they continued to work within it because they knew no other method of governing. Not until [Mikhail] Gorbachev was a Soviet leader fully prepared to dismantle Stalin's structural legacy. It tells us a lot that as it disappeared, so too did the Cold War and ultimately the Soviet Union itself.

This argument by no means absolves the United States and its allies of a considerable responsibility for how the Cold War was fought—hardly a surprising conclusion since they in fact won it. Nor is it to deny the feckless stupidity with which the Americans fell into peripheral conflicts like Vietnam, or their exorbitant expenditures on unusable weaponry: these certainly caused the Cold War to cost much more in money and lives than it otherwise might have. Nor is it to claim moral superiority for western statesmen. None was as bad as Stalin—or Mao—but the Cold War left no leader uncorrupted: the wielding of great power, even in the best of times, rarely does.

It is the case, though, that if one applies the always useful test of counter-factual history—drop a key variable and speculate as to what difference this might have made—Stalin's centrality to the origins of the Cold War becomes quite clear. For all of their importance, one could have removed Roosevelt, Churchill, Truman, Bevin, Marshall, or Acheson, and a cold war would still have probably followed the world war. If one could have eliminated Stalin, alternative paths become quite conceivable. For with the possible exception of Mao, no twentieth-century leader imprinted himself upon his country as thoroughly and with such lasting effect as Stalin did. And given his personal propensity for cold wars—a tendency firmly rooted long before he had even heard of Harry Truman—once Stalin wound up at the top in Moscow and once it was clear his state would survive the war, then it looks equally clear that there was going to be a Cold War whatever the west did. Who then was responsible? The answer, I think, is authoritarianism in general, and Stalin in particular.

NO

Martin J. Sherwin

THE ATOMIC BOMB AND THE ORIGINS OF THE COLD WAR

During the Second World War the atomic bomb was seen and valued as a potential rather than an actual instrument of policy. Responsible officials believed that its impact on diplomacy had to await its development and, perhaps, even a demonstration of its power. As Henry L. Stimson, the Secretary of War, observed in his memoirs: "The bomb as a merely probable weapon had seemed a weak reed on which to rely, but the bomb as a colossal reality was very different." That policymakers considered this difference before Hiroshima has been well documented, but whether they based wartime diplomatic policies upon an anticipated successful demonstration of the bomb's power remains a source of controversy. Two questions delineate the issues in this debate. First, did the development of the atomic bomb affect the way American policymakers conducted diplomacy with the Soviet Union? Second, did diplomatic considerations related to the Soviet Union influence the decision to use the atomic bomb against Japan?

These important questions relating the atomic bomb to American diplomacy, and ultimately to the origins of the Cold War, have been addressed almost exclusively to the formulation of policy during the early months of the Truman administration. As a result, two anterior questions of equal importance, questions with implications for those already posed, have been overlooked. Did diplomatic considerations related to Soviet postwar behavior influence the formulation of [Franklin D.] Roosevelt's atomic energy policies? What effect did the atomic legacy Truman inherited have on the diplomatic and atomic energy policies of his administration?

Although Roosevelt left no definitive statement assigning a postwar role to the atomic bomb, his expectations for its potential diplomatic value can be recalled from the existing record. An analysis of the policies he chose from among the alternatives he faced suggests that the potential diplomatic value of the bomb began to shape his atomic energy policies as early as 1943. He may have been cautious about counting on the bomb as a reality during the war, but he nevertheless consistently chose policy alternatives that would promote the postwar diplomatic potential of the bomb if the predictions of scientists

From Martin J. Sherwin, "The Atomic Bomb and the Origins of the Cold War," in Melvyn P. Leffler and David S. Painter, eds., *Origins of the Cold War: An International History* (Routledge, 1994). Copyright © 1994 by Martin J. Sherwin. Reprinted by permission of International Thomson Publishing Services. Notes omitted.

proved true. These policies were based on the assumption that the bomb could be used effectively to secure postwar diplomatic aims; and this assumption was carried over from the Roosevelt to the Truman administration.

Despite general agreement that the bomb would be an extraordinarily important diplomatic factor after the war, those closely associated with its development did not agree on how to use it most effectively as an instrument of diplomacy. Convinced that wartime atomic energy policies would have postwar diplomatic consequences, several scientists advised Roosevelt to adopt policies aimed at achieving a postwar international control system. [Winston] Churchill, on the other hand, urged the President to maintain the Anglo-American atomic monopoly as a diplomatic counter against the postwar ambitions of other nations—particularly against the Soviet Union. Roosevelt fashioned his atomic energy policies from the choices he made between these conflicting recommendations. In 1943 he rejected the counsel of his science advisers and began to consider the diplomatic component of atomic energy policy in consultation with Churchill alone. This decisionmaking procedure and Roosevelt's untimely death have left his motives ambiguous. Nevertheless it is clear that he pursued policies consistent with Churchill's monopolistic, anti-Soviet views.

The findings of this [selection] thus raise serious questions concerning generalizations historians have commonly made about Roosevelt's diplomacy: that it was consistent with his public reputation for cooperation and conciliation; that he was naive with respect to postwar Soviet behavior; that, like [Woodrow] Wilson, he believed in collective security as an effective guarantor of national safety; and that he made every possible effort to ensure that the Soviet Union and its allies would continue to function as postwar partners. Although this [selection] does not dispute the view that Roosevelt desired amicable postwar relations with the Soviet Union, or even that he worked hard to achieve them, it does suggest that historians have exaggerated his confidence in (and perhaps his commitment to) such an outcome. His most secret and among his most important long-range decisions—those responsible for prescribing a diplomatic role for the atomic bomb—reflected his lack of confidence. Finally, in light of this [selection's] conclusions, the widely held assumption that Truman's attitude toward the atomic bomb was substantially different from Roosevelt's must also be revised.

Like the grand alliance itself, the Anglo-American atomic energy partnership was forged by the war and its exigencies. The threat of a German atomic bomb precipitated a hasty marriage of convenience between British research and American resources. When scientists in Britain proposed a theory that explained how an atomic bomb might quickly be built, policymakers had to assume that German scientists were building one. "If such an explosive were made," Vannevar Bush, the director of the Office of Scientific Research and Development, told Roosevelt in July 1941, "it would be thousands of times more powerful than existing explosives, and its use might be determining." Roosevelt assumed nothing less. Even before the atomic energy project was fully organized he assigned it the highest priority.

The high stakes at issue during the war did not prevent officials in Great Britain or the United States from considering the postwar implications of their atomic energy decisions. As early as 1941, during the debate over whether to join the United States in an atomic energy partnership, members of the British government's atomic energy committee argued that the matter "was so important for the future that work should proceed in Britain." Weighing the obvious difficulties of proceeding alone against the possible advantages of working with the United States, Sir John Anderson, then Lord President of the Council and the minister responsible for atomic energy research, advocated the partnership. As he explained to Churchill, by working closely with the Americans British scientists would be able "to take up the work again [after the war], not where we left off, but where the combined effort had by then brought it."

As early as October 1942 Roosevelt's science advisers exhibited a similar concern with the potential postwar value of atomic energy. After conducting a full-scale review of the atomic energy project, James B. Conant, the president of Harvard University and Bush's deputy, recommended discontinuing the Anglo-American partnership "as far as development and manufacture is concerned." What prompted Conant's recommendations, however, was his suspicion—soon to be shared by other senior atomic energy administrators—that the British were rather more concerned with information for postwar industrial purposes than for wartime use. What right did the British have to the fruits of American labor? "We were doing nine-tenths of the work," Stimson told Roosevelt in October. Early in January 1943 the British were officially informed that the rules governing the Anglo-American atomic energy

partnership had been altered on "orders from the top."

By approving the policy of "restricted interchange" Roosevelt undermined a major incentive for British cooperation. It is not surprising, therefore, that Churchill took up the matter directly with the President and with Harry Hopkins, "Roosevelt's own, personal Foreign Office."

Conant and Bush understood the implications of Churchill's intervention and sought to counter its effect. Information on manufacturing an atomic bomb, Conant noted, was a "military secret which is in a totally different class from anything the world has ever seen if the potentialities of this project are realised." Though British and American atomic energy policies might coincide during the war, Conant and Bush expected them to conflict afterward.

The controversy over the policy of "restricted interchange" of atomic energy information shifted attention to postwar diplomatic considerations. The central issue was clearly drawn. The atomic energy policy of the United States was related to the very fabric of Anglo-American postwar relations and, as Churchill would insist, to postwar relations between each of them and the Soviet Union. The specter of Soviet postwar military power played a major role in shaping the Prime Minister's attitude toward atomic energy policies in 1943.

Churchill could cite numerous reasons for this determination to acquire an independent atomic arsenal after the war, but Great Britain's postwar military-diplomatic position with respect to the Soviet Union invariably led the list. When Bush and Stimson visited London in July, Churchill told them quite frankly that he was "vitally interested in the possession of all [atomic energy] information because this will be necessary for Britain's independence in the future as well as for success during the war." Nor was Churchill evasive about his reasoning: "It would never do to have Germany or Russia win the race for something which might be used for international blackmail," he stated bluntly and then pointed out that "Russia might be in a position to accomplish this result unless we worked together." Convinced that the British attitude toward the bomb would undermine any possibility of postwar cooperation with the Soviet Union, Bush and Conant vigorously continued to oppose any revival of the Anglo-American atomic energy partnership.

On July 20, however, Roosevelt chose to accept a recommendation from Hopkins to restore full partnership, and he ordered Bush to "renew, in an inclusive manner, the full exchange of information with the British." At the Quebec Conference, the President and the Prime Minister agreed that the British would share the atomic bomb. The Quebec Agreement revived the principle of an Anglo-American atomic energy partnership, albeit the British were reinstated as junior rather than equal partners.

The debate that preceded the Quebec Agreement is noteworthy for another reason; it led to a new relationship between Roosevelt and his atomic energy advisers. After August 1943 the President did not consult with them about the diplomatic aspects of atomic energy policy. Though he responded politely when they offered their views, he acted decisively only in consultation with Churchill. Bush and Conant appear to have lost a large measure of their influence because they had used it to oppose Churchill's position. What they did not suspect was the extent to which the President had come to share the Prime Minister's view.

Roosevelt was perfectly comfortable with the concept Churchill advocated— that military power was a prerequisite to successful postwar diplomacy. As early as August 1941, during the Atlantic Conference, Roosevelt had rejected the idea that an "effective international organization" could be relied upon to keep the peace: an Anglo-American international police force would be far more effective, he told Churchill. By the spring of 1942 the concept had broadened: the two "policemen" became four, and the idea was added that every other nation would be totally disarmed. "The Four Policemen" would have "to build up a reservoir of force so powerful that no aggressor would dare to challenge it," Roosevelt told Author Sweetser, an ardent internationalist. Violators first would be quarantined, and, if they persisted in their disruptive activities, bombed at the rate of a city a day until they agreed to behave. A year later, at the Tehran Conference, Roosevelt again discussed his idea, this time with Stalin. As Robert A. Divine has noted: "Roosevelt's concept of big power domination remained the central idea in his approach to international organization throughout World War II."

Precisely how Roosevelt expected to integrate the atomic bomb into his plans for keeping the peace in the postwar world is not clear. However, against the background of his atomic energy policy decisions of 1943 and his peacekeeping concepts, his actions in 1944 suggest that he intended to take full advantage of the bomb's potential as a postwar instrument of Anglo-American diplomacy. If Roosevelt thought the bomb could be used to create a more peaceful world order, he seems to have considered the threat of its power more effective than any opportunities it offered for international cooperation. If Roosevelt was less worried than Churchill about Soviet postwar ambitions, he was no less determined than the Prime Minister to avoid any commitments to the Soviets for the international control of atomic energy. There could still be four policemen, but only two of them would have the bomb.

The atomic energy policies Roosevelt pursued during the remainder of his life reinforce this interpretation of his ideas for the postwar period. The following three questions offer a useful framework for analyzing his intentions. Did Roosevelt make any additional agreements with Churchill that would further support the view that he intended to maintain an Anglo-American monopoly after the war? Did Roosevelt demonstrate any interest in the international control of atomic energy? Was Roosevelt aware that an effort to maintain an Anglo-American monopoly of the atomic bomb might lead to a postwar atomic arms race with the Soviet Union?

The alternatives placed before Roosevelt posed a difficult dilemma. On the one hand, he could continue to exclude the Soviet government from any official information about the development of the bomb, a policy that would probably strengthen America's postwar military-diplomatic position. But such a policy would also encourage Soviet mistrust of Anglo-American intentions and was bound to make postwar cooperation more difficult. On the other hand, Roosevelt could use the atomic bomb project as an instrument of cooperation by informing Stalin of the American government's intention of cooperating in the development of a plan for the international

control of atomic weapons, an objective that might never be achieved.

Either choice involved serious risks. Roosevelt had to balance the diplomatic advantages of being well ahead of the Soviet Union in atomic energy production after the war against the advantages of initiating wartime negotiations for postwar cooperation. The issue here, it must be emphasized, is not whether international control was likely to be successful, but rather whether Roosevelt demonstrated any serious interest in laying the groundwork for such a policy.

Roosevelt knew at this time, moreover, that the Soviets were finding out on their own about the development of the atomic bomb. Security personnel had reported an active Communist cell in the Radiation Laboratory at the University of California. Their reports indicated that at least one scientist at Berkeley was selling information to Russian agents. "They [Soviet agents] are already getting information about vital secrets and sending them to Russia," Stimson told the President on September 9, 1943. If Roosevelt was indeed worried to death about the effect the atomic bomb could have on Soviet-American postwar relations, he took no action to remove the potential danger, nor did he make any effort to explore the possibility of encouraging Soviet postwar cooperation on this problem.

Had Roosevelt avoided all postwar atomic energy commitments, his lack of support for international control could have been interpreted as an attempt to reserve his opinion on the best course to follow. But he had made commitments in 1943 supporting Churchill's monopolistic, anti-Soviet position, and he continued to make others in 1944. On June 13, for example, Roosevelt and Churchill signed an Agreement and Declaration of Trust, specifying that the United States and Great Britain would cooperate in seeking to control available supplies of uranium and thorium ore both during and after the war. This commitment, taken against the background of Roosevelt's peacekeeping ideas and his other commitments, suggests that the President's attitude toward the international control of atomic energy was similar to the Prime Minister's.

Churchill rejected the assumption that international control of atomic energy could be used as a cornerstone for constructing a peaceful world order. An atomic monopoly would be a significant diplomatic advantage in postwar diplomacy, and Churchill did not believe that anything useful could be gained by surrendering this advantage. The argument that a new weapon created a unique opportunity to refashion international affairs ignored every lesson Churchill read into history. "You can be quite sure," he would write in a memorandum less than a year later, "that any power that gets hold of the secret will try to make the article and this touches the existence of human society. This matter is out of all relation to anything else that exists in the world, and I could not think of participating in any disclosure to third or fourth parties at the present time."

When Roosevelt and Churchill met at Hyde Park in September 1944 following the second wartime conference at Quebec, they signed an *aide-mémoire* on atomic energy. The agreement bears the markings of Churchill's attitude toward the atomic bomb. It contained an explicit rejection of any wartime efforts toward international control: "The suggestion that the world should be informed regarding tube alloys [the atomic bomb], with a view to an international agree-

ment regarding its control and use, is not accepted. The matter should continue to be regarded as of the utmost secrecy." The *aide-mémoire* then revealed the full extent of Roosevelt's agreement with Churchill's point of view. "Full collaboration between the United States and the British Government in developing tube alloys for military and commercial purposes," it noted, "should continue after the defeat of Japan unless and until terminated by joint agreement." Finally the *aide-mémoire* offers some insight into Roosevelt's intentions for the military use of the weapon in the war: "When a bomb is finally available, it might perhaps, after mature consideration, be used against the Japanese, who should be warned that this bombardment will be repeated until they surrender."

Within the context of the complex problem of the origins of the Cold War the Hyde Park meeting is far more important than historians of the war generally have recognized. Overshadowed by the Second Quebec Conference on one side and by the drama of Yalta on the other, its significance often has been overlooked. But the agreements reached in September 1944 reflect a set of attitudes, aims, and assumptions that guided the relationship between the atomic bomb and American diplomacy during the Roosevelt administration and, through the transfer of its atomic legacy, during the Truman administration as well. Two alternatives had been recognized long before Roosevelt and Churchill met in 1944 at Hyde Park: the bomb could have been used to initiate a diplomatic effort to work out a system for its international control, or it could remain isolated during the war from any cooperative initiatives and held in reserve should cooperation fail. Roosevelt consistently favored the latter alternative. An insight into his reasoning is found in a memorandum Bush wrote following a conversation with Roosevelt several days after the Hyde Park meeting: "The President evidently thought he could join with Churchill in bringing about a US-UK postwar agreement on this subject [the atomic bomb] by which it would be held closely and presumably to control the peace of the world." By 1944 Roosevelt's earlier musings about the Four Policemen had faded into the background. But the idea behind it, the concept of controlling the peace of the world by amassing overwhelming military power, appears to have remained a prominent feature of his postwar plans.

* * *

Harry S. Truman inherited a set of military and diplomatic atomic energy policies that included partially formulated intentions, several commitments to Churchill, and the assumption that the bomb would be a legitimate weapon to be used against Japan. But no policy was definitely settled. According to the Quebec Agreement the President had the option of deciding the future of the commercial aspects of the atomic energy partnership according to his own estimate of what was fair. Although the policy of "utmost secrecy" had been confirmed at Hyde Park the previous September, Roosevelt had not informed his atomic energy advisers about the *aide-mémoire* he and Churchill signed. Although the assumption that the bomb would be used in the war was shared by those privy to its development, assumptions formulated early in the war were not necessarily valid at its conclusion. Yet Truman was bound to the past by his own uncertain position and by the prestige of his predecessor. Since Roosevelt had refused to open negotiations with the Soviet government for the international control of atomic energy, and since he had never expressed any objection to the wartime use of the bomb, it would have required considerable political courage and confidence for Truman to alter those policies. Moreover it would have required the encouragement of his advisers, for under the circumstances the most serious constraint of the new President's choices was his dependence upon advice. So Truman's atomic legacy, while it included several options, did not necessarily entail complete freedom to choose from among all the possible alternatives.

"I think it is very important that I should have a talk with you as soon as possible on a highly secret manner," Stimson wrote to Truman on April 24. It has "such a bearing on our present foreign relations and has such an important effect upon all my thinking in this field that I think you ought to know about it without further delay." Stimson had been preparing to brief Truman on the atomic bomb for almost ten days, but in the preceding twenty-four hours he had been seized by a sense of urgency. Relations with the Soviet Union had declined precipitously. The State Department had been urging Truman to get tough with the Russians. He had. Twenty-four hours earlier the President met with the Soviet Foreign Minister, V. M. Molotov, and "with rather brutal frankness" accused his government of breaking the Yalta Agreement. Molotov was furious. "I have never been talked to like that in my life," he told the President before leaving.

With a memorandum on the "political aspects of the S-1 [atomic bomb's] performance" in hand, Stimson went to the White House on April 25. The document he carried was the distillation of numerous decisions already taken, each one the product of attitudes that developed along with the new weapon. The Secretary of War himself was not entirely aware of how various forces had shaped these decisions: the recommendations of Bush and Conant, the policies Roosevelt had followed, the uncertainties inherent in the wartime alliance, the oppressive concern for secrecy, and his own inclination to consider long-range implications. It was a curious document. Though its language revealed Stimson's sensitivity to the historic significance of the atomic bomb, he did not question the wisdom of using it against Japan. Nor did he suggest any concrete steps for developing a postwar policy. His objective was to inform Truman of the salient problems: the possibility of an atomic arms race, the danger of atomic war, and the necessity for international control if the United Nations Organization was to work. "If the problem of the proper use of this weapon can be solved," he wrote, "we would have the opportunity to bring the world into a pattern in which the peace of the world and our civilizations can be saved." To cope with this difficult challenge Stimson suggested the "establishment of a select committee" to consider the postwar problems inherent in the development of the bomb.

What emerges from a careful reading of Stimson's diary, his memorandum of April 25 to Truman, a summary by [Major General Leslie R.] Groves of the meeting, and Truman's recollections is an argument for overall caution in American diplomatic relations with the Soviet Union: it was an argument against any showdown. Since the atomic bomb was potentially the most dangerous issue

facing the postwar world and since the most desirable resolution of the problem was some form of international control, Soviet cooperation had to be secured. It was imprudent, Stimson suggested, to pursue a policy that would preclude the possibility of international cooperation on atomic energy matters after the war ended. Truman's overall impression of Stimson's argument was that the Secretary of War was "at least as much concerned with the role of the atomic bomb in the shaping of history as in its capacity to shorten the war." These were indeed Stimson's dual concerns on April 25, and he could see no conflict between them.

Despite the profound consequences Stimson attributed to the development of the new weapon, he had not suggested that Truman reconsider its use against Japan. Nor had he thought to mention the possibility that chances of securing Soviet postwar cooperation might be diminished if Stalin did not receive a commitment to international control prior to an attack. Until the bomb's "actual certainty [was] fixed," Stimson considered any prior approach to Stalin as premature. As the uncertainties of impending peace became more apparent and worrisome, Stimson, Truman, and the Secretary of State-designate, James F. Byrnes, began to think of the bomb as something of a diplomatic panacea for their postwar problems. Byrnes had told Truman in April that the bomb "might well put us in a position to dictate our own terms at the end of the war." By June, Truman and Stimson were discussing "further *quid pro quos* which should be established in consideration for our taking them [the Soviet Union] into [atomic energy] partnership." Assuming that the bomb's impact on diplomacy would be immediate and extraordinary, they agreed on no less than "the settlement of the Polish, Rumanian, Yugoslavian, and Manchurian problems." But they also concluded that no revelation would be made "to Russia or anyone else until the first bomb had been successfully laid on Japan."

Was an implicit warning to Moscow, then, the principal reason for deciding to use the atomic bomb against Japan? In light of the ambiguity of the available evidence the question defies an unequivocal answer. What can be said with certainty is that Truman, Stimson, Byrnes, and several others involved in the decision consciously considered two effects of a combat demonstration of the bomb's power: first, the impact of the atomic attack on Japan's leaders, who might be persuaded thereby to end the war; and second, the impact of that attack on the Soviet Union's leaders, who might then prove to be more cooperative. But if the assumption that the bomb might bring the war to a rapid conclusion was the principal motive for using the atomic bomb, the expectation that its use would also inhibit Soviet diplomatic ambitions clearly discouraged any inclination to question that assumption.

Thus by the end of the war the most influential and widely accepted attitude toward the bomb was a logical extension of how the weapon was seen and valued earlier—as a potential instrument of diplomacy. Caught between the remnants of war and the uncertainties of peace, policymakers were trapped by the logic of their own unquestioned assumptions. By the summer of 1945 not only the conclusion of the war but the organization of an acceptable peace seemed to depend upon the success of the atomic attacks against Japan. When news of the successful atomic test of July 16 reached the President at the Potsdam Conference, he was visibly elated. Stimson noted that Truman "was tremendously pepped up by it and spoke to me of it again and again when I saw him. He said it gave him an entirely new feeling of confidence." The day after receiving the complete report of the test Truman altered his negotiating style. According to Churchill the President "got to the meeting after having read this report [and] he was a changed man. He told the Russians just where they got on and off and generally bossed the whole meeting." After the plenary session on July 24 Truman "casually mentioned to Stalin" that the United States had "a new weapon of unusual destructive force." In less than three weeks the new weapon's destructive potential was demonstrated to the world. Upon learning of the raid against Hiroshima Truman exclaimed: "This is the greatest thing in history."

As Stimson had expected, as a colossal reality the bomb was very different. But had American diplomacy been altered by it? Those who conducted diplomacy became more confident, more certain that through the accomplishments of American science, technology, and industry the "new world" could be made into one better than the old. But just how the atomic bomb would be used to help accomplish this ideal remained unclear. Three months and one day after Hiroshima was bombed Bush wrote that the whole matter of international relations on atomic energy "is in a thoroughly chaotic condition." The wartime relationship between atomic energy policy and diplomacy had been based upon the simple assumption that the Soviet government would surrender important geographical, political, and ideological objectives in exchange for the neutralization of the new weapon. As a result of policies based on this assumption American diplomacy and prestige suffered grievously: an opportunity to gauge the Soviet Union's response during the war to the international control of atomic energy was missed, and an atomic energy policy for dealing with the Soviet government after the war was ignored. Instead of promoting American postwar aims, wartime atomic energy policies made them more difficult to achieve. As a group of scientists at the University of Chicago's atomic energy laboratory presciently warned the government in June 1945: "It may be difficult to persuade the world that a nation which was capable of secretly preparing and suddenly releasing a weapon as indiscriminate as the [German] rocket bomb and a million times more destructive, is to be trusted in its proclaimed desire of having such weapons abolished by international agreement." This reasoning, however, flowed from alternative assumptions formulated during the closing months of the war by scientists far removed from the wartime policymaking process. Hiroshima and Nagasaki, the culmination of that process, became the symbols of a new American barbarism, reinforcing charges, with dramatic circumstantial evidence, that the policies of the United States contributed to the origins of the Cold War.

POSTSCRIPT

Was Stalin Responsible for the Cold War?

Time, place, perspective—all play a role in historical assessment, and any analysis of responsibility for the cold war must consider these factors. The cold war's first chroniclers were participants in postwar global politics, and their views were shaped by their personal experiences. Time provided distance, and the events of the coming decades nurtured a movement toward radical politics, which some have referred to as the "New Left." This paved the way for revisionist interpretations of the cold war's origins.

The use of the atomic bombs against Japan in 1945 created a cloud over cold war historiography. What course might the post–World War II era have followed if the West had sought different means to end the war? Many feel that the use of atomic weapons and the start of the cold war are inextricably connected.

Useful sources on cold war historiography begins with the authors of the two selections. Gaddis's career as a cold war scholar can be traced from his *The United States and the Origins of the War, 1941–1947* (Columbia University Press, 1972) to *We Now Know: Rethinking Cold War History* (Routledge, 1997). Sherwin has extended the scholarship of his original *American Historical Review* article, "The Atomic Bomb and the Origins of the Cold War: U.S. Atomic Energy Policy and Diplomacy 1941–1945" (October 1973) in *A World Destroyed: The Atomic Bomb and the Grand Alliance* (Alfred A. Knopf, 1975).

Other significant works written in the traditionalist vein include Louis Halle, *The Cold War as History* (Harper & Row, 1967); Herbert Feis, *From Trust to Terror: The Onset of the Cold War, 1945–1950* (W. W. Norton, 1970); and Norman Graebner, *Cold War Diplomacy: American Foreign Policy 1945–1960* (Princeton University Press, 1962). Important revisionist works on the origins of the cold war include Gar Alperovitz, *Atomic Diplomacy: Hiroshima and Potsdam* (Penguin Books, 1985) and *The Decision to Use the Bomb and the Architecture of an American Myth* (Alfred A. Knopf, 1995). The many works of George F. Kennan, considered to be containment's prime mover, provide invaluable assistance to the study of this issue, as do the works of Russian diplomats Vyacheslav Molotov and Andrei Gromyko, both of whom were "present at the creation." Two recent cold war anthologies are David Reynolds, ed., *The Origins of the Cold War in Europe: International Perspectives* (Yale University Press, 1994) and Allan Hunter, ed., *Rethinking the Cold War* (Temple University Press, 1998).

On the Internet . . .

Center for Strategic and International Studies

The Center for Strategic and International Studies is a public policy institution dedicated to analysis and policy impact. This site includes links for international news updates. *http://www.csis.org/*

United Nations System

This is the official Web site for the United Nations system of Organizations. An alphabetical index of United Nations Organizations (UNOs) is provided. Links to the home pages for some of these foundations can be found here. *http://www.unsystem.org/*

World Lecture Hall: History

At this Web site you can locate professors' lectures on topics in history. These topics include Europe in the twentieth century, the history of Western civilization, Renaissance creativity, as well as many others. *http://www.utexas.edu/world/lecture/his/*

PART 6

The Contemporary World

As the world begins a new millennium, it is difficult to predict what the new century will bring. If some of the problems facing our world today continue to grow in seriousness, it is likely that the beginning of the new millennium will not be a peaceful one.

■ Does Islamic Revivalism Challenge a Secular World Order?

■ Should Africa's Leaders Be Blamed for the Continent's Current Problems?

■ Were Ethnic Leaders Responsible for the Disintegration of Yugoslavia?

■ Will the Oslo Peace Accords Benefit Both Israelis and Palestinians?

ISSUE 21

Does Islamic Revivalism Challenge a Secular World Order?

YES: John L. Esposito, from *The Islamic Threat: Myth or Reality?* 2d ed. (Oxford University Press, 1995)

NO: Albert Hourani, from *A History of the Arab Peoples* (Belknap Press, 1991)

ISSUE SUMMARY

YES: Professor of Middle East studies John L. Esposito sees the Iranian Revolution against Western-inspired modernization and Egypt's "holy war" against Israel as examples of the Islamic quest for a more authentic society and culture, which challenges a stable world order.

NO: Albert Hourani, an emeritus fellow of St. Antony's College, Oxford, finds hope for a stable world order in modern Islam's moderate position, which blends the traditional religious commitment to social justice with a more secular strain of morality and law.

For many Westerners the adjective *Islamic* seems to be linked inexorably with either *fundamentalist* or *terrorist*. Particularly since the Islamic revolution of 1978–1979 in Iran, images of Western hostages and calls for a *jihad*, or holy war, have created a climate of fear and mistrust between the West and Islam. Are the two on a collision course, rooted in history and driven by an absolute incompatibility of beliefs and lifestyles? Or can Islam play a role in a stable world order that affirms Islam's own tradition while accommodating secularism and pluralism?

Because Islam sees itself as the fulfillment of both Judaism and Christianity —as the final word of God for human beings—it has from the beginning sought to spread its truth throughout the world. In the tradition of jihad, those who died in the attempt to bring Islam to nonbelievers were ensured a place in paradise. Early successes came during Europe's Dark Ages. Muslim learning and culture were more advanced, and it was only natural for conquering armies to assume that their religion enjoyed a comparable superiority. Unlike Christianity, Islam gained secular power within the founder Muhammad's lifetime (c. 570–632), and the rulers that followed him, known as caliphs, combined secular and religious power. There could be no conflict between church and state because the church and the state were one.

For many Muslims in the modern world, the political and military domination of the West has brought a secularism that is repugnant to all they hold sacred. They fear that Westerners—with their lack of respect for traditional authority, their emancipated and exploited women, and their shallow and materialistic values—appear to have won. Becoming modern is generally equated with embracing the consumer culture and values of the West. When the Shah of Iran Muhammad Reza Pahlavi imposed a Western revolution on his country in the 1970s, he disregarded Muslim leaders and repressed all resistance. The result was an Islamic backlash that deposed the Shah and installed in his place the Ayatollah Ruholla Khomeini, a rigid religious authority figure who demanded obedience to the teachings of the prophet Muhammad. The question seems to be whether or not Islamic countries can modernize without giving up their core values and embracing those of the West.

In the following selection, John L. Esposito notes that the clout provided by oil has brought the Islamic Middle East into the world economy and given it the power to be a significant player in either supporting or destabilizing a peaceful world order. However, the Western concept of religion as a system of belief and worship that remains separate from most of the rest of secular life is incomprehensible to traditional Muslims. Believing that Islam has superseded both Judaism and Christianity calls Muslims to impose the law of God on all the world. In the search for an authentic Islamic culture, Esposito concludes, Muslims present a strong challenge to the political and cultural values of the West.

In the second selection, Albert Hourani contends that between a total rejection of Islam in fashioning a modern state and the belief that Islamic heritage is uniquely qualified to provide the basis lies a third alternative: accepting that the prophet Muhammad received his revelation during a particular historical context might enable modern Islamic scholars to adapt religious truth to the demands of modern life. In a continuing dialogue between past and present, the Qur'an might speak to the modern world. It is this moderate position, asserts Hourani, that offers a role for Islam in a stable world order.

YES
John L. Esposito

THE ISLAMIC THREAT:
MYTH OR REALITY?

Are Islam and the West on an inevitable collision course? Are Islamic fundamentalists medieval fanatics? Are Islam and democracy incompatible? Is Islamic fundamentalism a threat to stability in the Muslim world and to American interests in the region? These are critical questions for our times that come from a history of mutual distrust and condemnation.

From the Ayatollah Khomeini to Saddam Hussein, for more than a decade the vision of Islamic fundamentalism or militant Islam as a threat to the West has gripped the imaginations of Western governments and the media. Khomeini's denunciation of America as the "Great Satan," chants of "Death to America," the condemnation of Salman Rushdie and his *Satanic Verses*, and Saddam Hussein's call for a jihad against foreign infidels have reinforced images of Islam as a militant, expansionist religion, rabidly anti-American and intent upon war with the West.

Despite many common theological roots and beliefs, throughout history Muslim-Christian relations have often been overshadowed by conflict as the armies and missionaries of Islam and Christendom have struggled for power and for souls. This confrontation has involved such events as the defeat of the early Byzantine (eastern Roman) empire by Islam in the seventh century; the fierce battles and polemics of the Crusades during the eleventh and twelfth centuries; the expulsion of the Moors from Spain and the Inquisition; the Ottoman threat to Europe; European (Christian) colonial expansion and domination in the eighteenth and nineteenth centuries; the political and cultural challenge of the superpowers (America and the Soviet Union) in the latter half of the twentieth century; the creation of the state of Israel; the competition of Christian and Muslim missionaries for converts in Africa today; and the contemporary reassertion of Islam in politics.

"Islamic fundamentalism" has often been regarded as a major threat to the regional stability of the Middle East and to Western interests in the broader Muslim world. The Iranian Revolution, attacks on Western embassies, hijackings and hostage taking, and violent acts by groups with names like the Army of God (Jund Allah), Holy War (al-Jihad), the Party of God (Hizbullah), and

From John L. Esposito, *The Islamic Threat: Myth or Reality?* 2d ed. (Oxford University Press, 1995). Copyright © 1992, 1995 by John L. Esposito. Reprinted by permission of Oxford University Press, Inc. Notes omitted.

Salvation from Hell have all signaled a militant Islam on a collision course with the West. Uprisings in the Muslim republics of the Soviet Union, in Kosovo in Yugoslavia, in Indian Kashmir, in Sinkiang in China, and on the West Bank and in Gaza, and more recently, Saddam Hussein's attempted annexation of Kuwait, have reinforced images of an expansive and potentially explosive Islam in global politics.

With the triumph of the democratization movement in Eastern Europe and the breakup of the Soviet empire, Islam constitutes the most pervasive and powerful transnational force in the world, with one billion adherents spread out across the globe. Muslims are a majority in some forty-five countries ranging from Africa to Southeast Asia, and they exist in growing and significant numbers in the United States, the Soviet Union, and Europe. For a Western world long accustomed to a global vision and foreign policy predicated upon superpower rivalry for global influence if not dominance—a U.S.–Soviet conflict often portrayed as a struggle between good and evil, capitalism and communism— it is all too tempting to identify another global ideological menace to fill the "threat vacuum" created by the demise of communism.

However diverse in reality, the existence of Islam as a worldwide religion and ideological force embracing one fifth of the world's population, and its continued vitality and power in a Muslim world stretching from Africa to Southeast Asia, will continue to raise the specter of an Islamic threat....

As Western leaders attempt to forge the New World Order, transnational Islam may increasingly come to be regarded as the new global monolithic enemy of the West: "To some Americans, searching for a new enemy against whom to test our mettle and power, after the death of communism, Islam is the preferred antagonist. But, to declare Islam an enemy of the United States is to declare a second Cold War that is unlikely to end in the same resounding victory as the first." Fear of the Green Menace (green being the color of Islam) may well replace that of the Red Menace of world communism.

Islam and Islamic movements constitute a religious and ideological alternative or challenge and in some instances a potential danger to Christianity and the West. However, distinguishing between a religious or ideological alternative or challenge and a direct political threat requires walking the fine line between myth and reality, between the unity of Islam and the diversity of its multiple and complex manifestations in the world today, between the violent actions of the few and the legitimate aspirations and policies of the many. Unfortunately, American policymakers, like the media, have too often proved surprisingly myopic, viewing the Muslim world and Islamic movements as a monolith and seeing them solely in terms of extremism and terrorism. While this is understandable in light of events in Iran and Lebanon and the Gulf crisis of 1990–91, it fails to do justice to the complex realities of the Muslim world and can undermine relations between the West and Islam....

THE ISLAMIC RESURGENCE

Islam reemerged as a potent global force in Muslim politics during the 1970s and 1980s. The scope of the Islamic resurgence has been worldwide, embracing much of the Muslim world from the Sudan to Indonesia. Heads of Muslim governments as well as opposition groups increasingly appealed to religion for legitimacy and to mobilize popular support. Islamic activists have held cabinet-level positions in Jordan, the Sudan, Iran, Malaysia, and Pakistan. Islamic organizations constitute the leading opposition parties and organizations in Egypt, Tunisia, Algeria, Morocco, the West Bank and Gaza, and Indonesia. Where permitted, they have participated in elections and served in parliament and in city government. Islam has been a significant ingredient in nationalist struggles and resistance movements in Afghanistan, the Muslim republics of the former Soviet Central Asia, and Kashmir, and in the communal politics of Lebanon, India, Thailand, China, and the Philippines.

Islamically oriented governments have been counted among America's staunchest allies (Saudi Arabia and Pakistan) and most vitriolic enemies (Libya and Iran). Islamic activist organizations have run the spectrum from those who work within the system—such as the Muslim Brotherhoods in Egypt, Jordan, and the Sudan—to radical revolutionaries like Egypt's Society of Muslims (known more popularly as Takfir wal-Hijra, Excommunication and Flight) and al-Jihad (Holy War), or Lebanon's Hizbullah (Party of God) and Islamic Jihad, which have resorted to violence in their attempts to overthrow prevailing political systems.

Yet to speak of a contemporary Islamic revival can be deceptive, if this implies that Islam had somehow disappeared or been absent from the Muslim world. It is more correct to view Islamic revivalism as having led to a higher profile of Islam in Muslim politics and society. Thus what bad previously seemed to be an increasingly marginalized force in Muslim public life reemerged in the seventies—often dramatically—as a vibrant sociopolitical

reality. Islam's resurgence in Muslim politics reflected a growing religious revivalism in both personal and public life that would sweep across much of the Muslim world and have a substantial impact on the West in world politics.

The indices of an Islamic reawakening in personal life are many: increased attention to religious observances (mosque attendance, prayer, fasting), proliferation of religious programming and publications, more emphasis upon Islamic dress and values, the revitalization of Sufism (mysticism). This broader-based renewal has also been accompanied by Islam's reassertion in public life: an increase in Islamically oriented governments, organizations, laws, banks, social welfare services, and educational institutions. Both governments and opposition movements have turned to Islam to enhance their authority and muster popular support. Governmental use of Islam has been illustrated by a great spectrum of leaders in the Middle East and Asia: Libya's Muammar Qaddafi, Sudan's Gaafar Muhammad Nimeiri, Egypt's Anwar Sadat, Iran's Ayatollah Khomeini, Pakistan's Zia ul-Haq, Bangladesh's Muhammad Ershad, Malaysia's Muhammad Mahathir. Most rulers and governments, including more secular states such as Turkey and Tunisia, becoming aware of the potential strength of Islam, have shown increased sensitivity to and anxiety about Islamic issues. The Iranian Revolution of 1978–79 focused attention on "Islamic fundamentalism" and with it the spread and vitality of political Islam in other parts of the Muslim world. However, the contemporary revival has its origins and roots in the late sixties and early seventies, when events in such disparate areas as Egypt and Libya as well as Pakistan and Malaysia contributed to experiences of crisis and failure, as well as power and success, which served as catalysts for a more visible reassertion of Islam in both public and private life.

THE EXPERIENCE OF FAILURE AND THE QUEST FOR IDENTITY

Several conflicts (e.g., the 1967 Arab–Israeli war, Chinese–Malay riots in Malaysia in 1969, the Pakistan–Bangladesh civil war of 1971, and the Lebanese civil war of the midseventies) illustrate the breadth and diversity of these turning points or catalysts for change. For many in the Arab and broader Muslim world, 1967 proved to be a year of catastrophe as well as a historic turning point. Israel's quick and decisive defeat of Arab forces in what was remembered as the Six-Day War, the Israeli capture and occupation of the Golan Heights, Sinai, Gaza, the West Bank, and East Jerusalem, constituted a devastating blow to Arab/Muslim pride, identity, and self-esteem. Most important, the loss of Jerusalem, the third holiest city of Islam, assured that Palestine and the liberation of Jerusalem would not be regarded as a regional (Arab) issue but rather as an Islamic cause throughout the Muslim world. The defense of Israel is dear to many Jews throughout the world. Likewise, for Muslims who retain a sense of membership in a transnational community of believers (the *ummah*), Palestine and the liberation of Jerusalem are strongly seen as issues of Islamic solidarity. As anyone who works in the Muslim world can attest, Israeli control of the West Bank, Gaza, and Jerusalem as well as U.S.–Israeli relations are topics of concern and bitter debate among Muslims from Nigeria and the Sudan to Pakistan and Malaysia, as well as among the Muslims of Europe and the United States.

The aftermath of the 1967 war, remembered in Arab literature as the "disaster," witnessed a sense of disillusionment and soul-searching that gripped both Western-oriented secular elites as well as the more Islamically committed, striking at their sense of pride, identity, and history. Where had they gone wrong? Both the secular and the Islamically oriented sectors of society now questioned the effectiveness of nationalist ideologies, Western models of development, and Western allies who had persisted in supporting Israel. Despite several decades of independence and modernization, Arab forces (consisting of the combined military might of Egypt, Jordan, and Syria) had proved impotent. A common critique of the military, political, and sociocultural failures of Western-oriented development and a quest for a more authentic society and culture emerged— an Arab identity less dependent upon the West and rooted more indigenously in an Arab/Islamic heritage and values. Examples from Malaysia, Pakistan, and Lebanon reflect the turmoil and soul-searching that occurred in many parts of the Muslim world....

FROM FAILURE TO SUCCESS

During the seventies Islamic politics seemed to explode on the scene, as events in the Middle East (the Egyptian–Israeli war and the Arab oil embargo of 1973, as well as the Iranian Revolution of 1978–79) shocked many into recognition of a powerful new force that threatened Western interests. Heads of state and opposition movements appealed to Islam to enhance their legitimacy and popular support; Islamic organizations and institutions proliferated.

In 1973 Egypt's Anwar Sadat initiated a "holy war" against Israel. In contrast to the 1967 Arab–Israeli war which was fought by Gamal Abdel Nasser in the name of Arab nationalism/socialism, this war was fought under the banner of Islam. Sadat generously employed Islamic symbols and history to rally his forces. Despite their loss of the war, the relative success of Egyptian forces led many Muslims to regard it as a moral victory, since most had believed that a U.S.-backed Israel could not be beaten.

Military vindication in the Middle East was accompanied by economic muscle, the power of the Arab oil boycott. For the first time since the dawn of colonialism, the West had to contend with and acknowledge, however begrudgingly, its dependence on the Middle East. For many in the Muslim world the new wealth, success, and power of the oil-rich countries seemed to indicate a return of the power of Islam to a community whose centuries-long political and cultural ascendence had been shattered by European colonialism and, despite independence, by second-class status in a superpower-dominated world. A number of factors enhanced the Islamic character of oil power. Most of the oil wealth was located in the Arab heartland, where Muhammad had received the revelation of the Quran and established the first Islamic community-state. The largest deposits were found in Saudi Arabia, a self-styled Islamic state which had asserted its role as keeper of the holy cities of Mecca and Medina, protector of the annual pilgrimage (hajj), and leader and benefactor of the Islamic world. The House of Saud used its oil wealth to establish numerous international Islamic organizations, promote the preaching and spread of Islam, support Islamic causes, and subsidize Islamic activities undertaken by Muslim governments.

No event demonstrated more dramatically the power of a resurgent Islam than the Iranian Revolution of 1978–79. For many in the West and the Muslim world, the unthinkable became a reality. The powerful, modernizing, and Western-oriented regime of the Shah came crashing down. This was an oil-rich Iran whose wealth had been used to build the best-equipped military in the Middle East (next to Israel's) and to support an ambitious modernization program, the Shah's White Revolution. Assisted by Western-trained elites and advisers, the Shah had governed a state which the United States regarded as its most stable ally in the Muslim world. The fact that a revolution against him and against the West was effectively mounted in the name of Islam, organizing disparate groups and relying upon the mullah–mosque network for support, generated euphoria among many in the Muslim world and convinced Islamic activists that these were lessons for success to be emulated. Strength and victory would belong to those who pursued change in the name of Islam, whatever the odds and however formidable the regime.

For many in the broader Muslim world, the successes of the seventies resonated with an idealized perception of early Islam, the Islamic paradigm to be found in the time of the Prophet Muhammad, the Golden Age of Islam. Muhammad's successful union of disparate tribal forces under the banner of Islam, his creation of an Islamic state and society in which social justice prevailed, and the extraordinary early expansion of Islam were primal events to be remembered and, as the example of the Iranian Revolution seemingly verified, to be successfully emulated by those who adhered to Islam. Herein lies the initial attraction of the Iranian Revolution for many Muslims, Sunni and Shii alike. Iran provided the first example of a modern Islamic revolution, a revolt against impiety, oppression, and injustice. The call of the Ayatollah Khomeini for an Islamic revolution struck a chord among many who identified with his message of anti-imperialism, his condemnation of failed, unjust, and oppressive regimes, and his vision of a morally just society.

By contrast, the West stood incredulous before this challenge to the Shah's "enlightened" development of his seemingly backward nation, and the resurrection of an anachronistic, irrational medieval force that threatened to hurtle modern Iran back to the Middle Ages. Nothing symbolized this belief more than the black-robed, bearded mullahs and the dour countenance of their leader, the Ayatollah Khomeini, who dominated the media, reinforcing in Western minds the irrational nature of the entire movement.

THE IDEOLOGICAL WORLDVIEW OF ISLAMIC REVIVALISM

At the heart of the revivalist worldview is the belief that the Muslim world is in a state of decline. Its cause is departure from the straight path of Islam; its cure, a return to Islam in personal and public life which will ensure the restoration of Islamic identity, values, and power. For Islamic political activists Islam is a total or comprehensive way of life as stipulated in the Quran, God's revelation, mirrored in the example of Muhammad and the nature of the first Muslim community-state, and embodied in the comprehensive nature of the Sharia, God's revealed law. Thus the revitalization of Muslim gov-

ernments and societies requires the reimplementation of Islamic law, the blueprint for an Islamically guided and socially just state and society.

While Westernization and secularization of society are condemned, modernization as such is not. Science and technology are accepted, but the pace, direction, and extent of change are to be subordinated to Islamic belief and values in order to guard against the penetration of Western values and excessive dependence on them.

Radical movements go beyond these principles and often operate according to two basic assumptions. They assume that Islam and the West are locked in an ongoing battle, dating back to the early days of Islam, which is heavily influenced by the legacy of the Crusades and European colonialism, and which today is the product of a Judaeo-Christian conspiracy. This conspiracy is the result of superpower neocolonialism and the power of Zionism. The West (Britain, France, and especially the United States) is blamed for its support of un-Islamic or unjust regimes (Egypt, Iran, Lebanon) and also for its biased support for Israel in the face of Palestinian displacement. Violence against such governments and their representatives as well as Western multinationals is legitimate self-defense.

Second, these radical movements assume that Islam is not simply an ideological alternative for Muslim societies but a theological and political imperative. Since Islam is God's command, implementation must be immediate, not gradual, and the obligation to do so is incumbent on all true Muslims. Therefore individuals and governments who hesitate, remain apolitical, or resist are no longer to be regarded as Muslim. They are atheists or unbelievers, enemies of

God against whom all true Muslims must wage jihad (holy war)....

As some dream of the creation of a New World Order, and many millions in North Africa, the Middle East, Central Asia, and southern and Southeast Asia aspire to greater political liberalization and democratization, the continued vitality of Islam and Islamic movements need not be a threat but a challenge. For many Muslims, Islamic revivalism is a social rather than a political movement whose goal is a more Islamically minded and oriented society, but not necessarily the creation of an Islamic state. For others, the establishment of an Islamic order requires the creation of an Islamic state. In either case, Islam and most Islamic movements are not necessarily anti-Western, anti-American, or anti-democratic. While they are a challenge to the outdated assumptions of the established order and to autocratic regimes, they do not necessarily threaten American interests. Our challenge is to better understand the history and realities of the Muslim world. Recognizing the diversity and many faces of Islam counters our image of a unified Islamic threat. It lessens the risk of creating self-fulfilling prophecies about the battle of the West against a radical Islam. Guided by our stated ideals and goals of freedom and self-determination, the West has an ideal vantage point for appreciating the aspirations of many in the Muslim world as they seek to define new paths for their future.

NO   Albert Hourani

A HISTORY OF THE ARAB PEOPLES

Among educated and reflective men and women [of Arab countries in the late 1960s], there was a growing awareness of the vast and rapid changes in their societies, and of the ways in which their own position was being affected by them. The increase of population, the growth of cities, the spread of popular education and the mass media were bringing a new voice into discussion of public affairs, a voice expressing its convictions, and its grievances and hopes, in a traditional language. This in its turn was arousing consciousness among the educated of a gap between them and the masses, and giving rise to a problem of communication: how could the educated élite speak to the masses or on their behalf? Behind this there lay another problem, that of identity: what was the moral bond between them, by virtue of which they could claim to be a society and a political community?

To a great extent, the problem of identity was expressed in terms of the relationship between the heritage of the past and the needs of the present. Should the Arab peoples tread a path marked out for them from outside, or could they find in their own inherited beliefs and culture those values which could give them a direction in the modern world? Such a question made clear the close relationship between the problem of identity and that of independence. If the values by which society was to live were brought in from outside, would not that imply a permanent dependence upon the external world, and more specifically western Europe and North America, and might not cultural dependence bring with it economic and political dependence as well? The point was forcefully made by the Egyptian economist Galal Amin (b.1935) in *Mihnat al-iqtisad wa'l-thaqafa fi Misr (The Plight of the Economy and Culture in Egypt)*, a book which tried to trace the connections between the *infitah* and a crisis of culture. The Egyptian and other Arab peoples had lost confidence in themselves, he maintained. The *infitah*, and indeed the whole movement of events since the Egyptian revolution of 1952, had rested on an unsound basis: the false values of a consumer society in economic life, the domination of a ruling élite instead of genuine patriotic loyalty. Egyptians were importing whatever foreigners persuaded them that they should want, and this made for a permanent dependence. To be healthy, their political and economic life should be derived from their own moral values, which themselves could have no basis except in religion.

In a rather similar way, another Egyptian writer, Hasan Hanafi, wrote about the relationship between the heritage and the need for renewal. Arabs like other human beings were caught up in an economic revolution, which could not be carried through unless there were a 'human revolution'. This did not involve an abandonment of the heritage of the past, for which the Arabs were no less responsible than they were for 'people and land and wealth', but rather that it should be reinterpreted 'in accordance with the needs of age', and turned into an ideology which could give rise to a political movement. Blind adherence to tradition and blind innovation were both inadequate, the former because it had no answer to the problems of the present, and the latter because it could not move the masses, being expressed in a language alien from that which they understood. What was needed was some reformation of religious thought which would give the masses of the people a new definition of themselves, and a revolutionary party which would create a national culture and so change the modes of collective behaviour.

Much of the contemporary Arab thought revolved around this dilemma of past and present, and some writers made bold attempts to resolve it. The answer given by the Syrian philosopher Sadiq Jalal al-'Azm (b. 1934) sprang from a total rejection of religious thought. It was false in itself, he claimed, and incompatible with authentic scientific thought in its view of what knowledge was and its methods of arriving at truth. There was no way of reconciling them; it was impossible to believe in the literal truth of the Qur'an, and if parts of it were discarded then the claim that it was the Word of God would have to be rejected. Religious thought was not only false, it was also dangerous. It supported the existing order of society and those who controlled it, and so prevented a genuine movement of social and political liberation. ...

At the other end of the spectrum were those who believed that the Islamic heritage by itself could provide the basis for life in the present, and that it alone could do so, because it was derived from the Word of God. This was the attitude expressed in increasingly sharp terms by some of those associated with the Muslim Brothers in Egypt and elsewhere. ...

Somewhere in the middle of the spectrum were those who continued to believe that Islam was more than a culture: it was the revealed Word of God, but it must be understood correctly, and the social morality and law derived from it could be adapted to make it the moral basis of a modern society. There were many forms of this reformist attitude. Conservatives of the Wahhabi school, in Saudi Arabia and elsewhere, believed that the existing code of law could be changed slowly and cautiously into a system adequate to the needs of modern life; some thought that only the Qur'an was sacred, and it could be freely used as the basis of a new law; some believed that the true interpretation of the Qur'an was that of the Sufis, and a private mystical devotion was compatible with the organization of society on more or less secular lines.

A few attempts were made to show how the new moral and legal system could be deduced from Qur'an and Hadith in a way which was responsible but bold. In the Sudan, Sadiq al-Mahdi

(b. 1936), the great-grandson of the religious leader of the later nineteenth century, and himself an important political leader, maintained that it was necessary to have a new kind of religious thought which would draw out of the Qur'an and Hadith a *shari'a* which was adapted to the needs of the modern world. Perhaps the most carefully reasoned attempt to state the principles of a new jurisprudence came from beyond the Arab world, from the Pakistani scholar Fazlur Rahman (1919–88). In an attempt to provide an antidote to the 'spiritual panic' of Muslims at the present time, he suggested a method of Qur'anic exegesis which would, he claimed, be true to the spirit of Islam but provide for the needs of modern life. The Qur'an was a 'divine response, through the Prophet's mind, to the moral–social situation of the Prophet's Arabia'. In order to apply its teaching to the moral and social situation of a different age, it was necessary to extract from that 'divine response' the general principle inherent in it. This could be done by studying the specific circumstances in which the response had been revealed, and doing so in the light of an understanding of the Qur'an as a unity. Once the general principle had been extracted, it should be used with an equally clear and meticulous understanding of the particular situation in regard to which guidance was needed. Thus the proper interpretation of Islam was a historical one, moving with precision from the present to the past and back again, and this demanded a new kind of religious education.

One of the signs of the new dominant position of governments in Arab societies was that they were able to appropriate to themselves the ideas which could move minds and imaginations, and extract from them a claim of legitimate authority. By this time, any Arab government which wished to survive had to be able to claim legitimacy in terms of three political languages—those of nationalism, social justice and Islam.

The first to emerge as a potent language was that of nationalism. Some of the regimes which existed at the beginning of the 1980s had come to power during the struggle for independence, or could claim to be the successors for those who had; this kind of appeal to legitimacy was particularly strong in the Maghrib, where the struggle had been bitter and memories of it were still fresh. Almost all regimes made use too of a different kind of nationalist language, that of Arab unity; they gave some kind of formal allegiance to it, and spoke of independence as if it were the first step towards closer union, if not complete unity; connected with the idea of unity was that of some concerted action in support of the Palestinians. In recent years there had taken place an extension of the idea of nationalism; regimes claimed to be legitimate in terms of economic development, or the full use of national resources, both human and natural, for common ends.

The second language, that of social justice, came into common political use in the 1950s and 1960s, the period of the Algerian revolution and the spread of Nasirism, with its idea of a specifically Arab socialism expressed in the National Charter of 1962. Such terms as socialism and social justice tended to be used with a specific meaning; they referred to reform of the system of land-tenure, extension of social services and universal education, for girls as well as boys, but in few countries was there a systematic attempt to redistribute wealth by means of high taxation of incomes.

The latest of the languages to become powerful was that of Islam. In a way, of course, it was not new. There had always existed a sense of common destiny among those who had inherited the religion of Islam—a belief, enriched by historical memories, that the Qur'an, the Traditions of the Prophet and the *shari'a* could provide the principles according to which a virtuous life in common should be organized. By the 1980s, however, Islamic language had become more prominent in political discourse than it had been a decade or two earlier. This was due to a combination of two kinds of factor. On the one hand, there was the vast and rapid extension of the area of political involvement, because of the growth of population and of cities, and the extension of the mass media. The rural migrants into the cities brought their own political culture and language with them. There had been an urbanization of the migrants, but there was also a 'ruralization' of the cities. Cut off from the ties of kinship and neighbourliness which made life possible in the villages, they were living in a society of which the external signs were strange to them; the sense of alienation could be counterbalanced by that of belonging to a universal community of Islam, in which certain moral values were implicit, and this provided a language in terms of which they could express their grievances and aspirations. Those who wished to arouse them to action had to use the same language. Islam could provide an effective language of opposition: to western power and influence, and those who could be accused of being subservient to them; to governments

regarded as corrupt and ineffective, the instruments of private interests, or devoid of morality; and to a society which seemed to have lost its unity with its moral principles and direction.

It was factors of this kind which produced such movements as the Muslim Brothers, of which the leaders were articulate and educated men, but which appealed to those who were shut out of the power and prosperity of the new societies; and it was partly in self-defense against them or in order to appeal to a wider segment of their nations that most regimes began to use the language of religion more than before. Some regimes, it is true, used the language of Islam spontaneously and continuously, in particular that of Saudi Arabia, which had been created by a movement for the reassertion of the primacy of God's Will in human societies. Others, however, appeared to have been driven into it. Even the most secularist of ruling groups, those for example of Syria, Iraq and Algeria, had taken to use using it more or less convincingly, in one way or another. They might evoke historical themes, of the Arabs as the carriers of Islam; the rulers of Iraq, caught in their struggle with Iran, appealed to a memory of the battle of Qadisiyya, when the Arabs had defeated the last Sasanian ruler and brought Islam to Iran. In most countries of mixed population, the constitution laid down that the president should be a Muslim, so linking the religion of Islam with legitimate authority. In legal codes there might be a reference to the Qurán or the *shari'a* as the basis of legislation. Most governments which took this path tended to interpret the *shari'a* in a more or less modernist way, in order to justify the innovations which were inevitable for societies living in the modern world; even in Saudi Arabia, the principles of Hanbali jurisprudence were invoked in order to justify the new laws and regulations made necessary by the new economic order. Some regimes, however, resorted to certain token applications of the strict letter of the *shar'a*: in Saudi Arabia and Kuwait, the sale of alcohol was forbidden; in the Sudan, a provision of the *shari'a* that persistent thieves should have their hands cut off was revived in the last years of Numayri's period of rule. In some countries strict observance of the fast of Ramadan, which had been spreading spontaneously, was encouraged by the government; an earlier attempt by the Tunisian government to discourage it, because it interfered with the efforts needed for economic development, had met with widespread opposition.

THE FRAGILITY OF REGIMES

... If more radical changes took place, it seemed more likely in the 1980s that they would take place in the name of an Islamic idea of the justice of God in the world than in that of a purely secular ideal. There was not one idea of Islam only, but a whole spectrum of them. The word 'Islam' did not have a single, simple meaning, but was what Muslims made of it. For 'traditional' villagers, it might mean everything they thought and did. For more concerned and reflective Muslims, it provided a norm by which they should try to shape their lives, and by which their acts could be judged, but there was more than one norm. The term 'fundamentalism', which had become fashionable, carried a variety of meanings. It could refer to the idea that Muslims should try to return to the teaching and practice of the Prophet and the first generation of his followers, or to

the idea that the Qurán alone provided the norm of human life; this could be a revolutionary idea, if Muslims claimed— as the Libyan leader Qadhafi appeared to do—that they had the right to interpret the Qur'an freely. The word could also be used of an attitude which might better be called 'conservative': the attitude of those who wished to accept and preserve what they had inherited from the past, the whole cumulative tradition of Islam as it had in fact developed, and to change it only in a cautious and responsible way. This was the attitude of the Saudi regime and its supporters, and of the Iranian revolutionary regime, although the cumulative traditions they accepted were very different from each other.

The circumstances of the different Arab countries varied greatly. An Islamic movement in one country could have a different meaning from what might appear to be the same movement in another. For example, the Muslim Brothers in Syria did not have the same role as those in Egypt; to a great extent they served as a medium for the opposition of the Sunni urban population to the domination of a regime identified with the 'Alawi community. Similarly, the fact that the Iranian revolution had taken a certain form did not mean that it would take the same form in other countries. In part at least, the revolution could be explained in terms of factors which were specific to Iran: certain powerful social classes were particularly responsive to appeals expressed in religious language, and there was a religious leadership which was able to act as a rallying point or all movements of opposition; it was relatively independent of the government, generally respected for its piety and learning, and had always acted as the spokesman of the collective consciousness.

Such a situation did not exist in the Arab countries. In Iraq, where Shi'is formed a majority, their men of learning did not have the same intimate connection with the urban masses or the same influence on the government as in Iran. Sunni 'ulama had a less independent position. Under Ottoman rule they had become state functionaries, close to the government and compromised by their relations with it; by tradition and interests they were linked with the upper bourgeoisie of the great cities. Leadership of Islamic movements therefore tended to be in the hands of laymen, converted members of the modern educated élite. Such movements did not have the sanctity conferred by leaders of inherited and recognized piety and learning; they were political parties competing with others. On the whole they did not have clear social or economic policies. It seemed likely that they would be important forces of opposition, but would not be in a position to be able to form governments.

An observer of the Arab countries, or of many other Muslim countries, in the mid-1980s might well have come to the conclusion that something similar to the Iranian path would be the path of the future, but this might have been a hasty conclusion, even so far as Iran was concerned. In a sense the rule of men of religion was a reaffirmation of tradition, but in another sense it went against tradition. The inherited wisdom of the 'ulama was that they should not link themselves too closely with the government of the world; they should keep a moral distance from it, while preserving their access to the rulers and influence upon them: it was dangerous to tie the eternal interests of Islam to the fate of a transient ruler of the world. This attitude was reflected in a certain popular suspicion of men of religion who took too prominent a part in the affairs of the world; they were as susceptible as others to the corruptions of power and wealth, and perhaps they did not make very good rulers.

It might happen too that, at a certain stage of national development, the appeal of religious ideas—at least of ideas sanctified by the cumulative tradition—would cease to have the same force as another system of ideas: a blend of social morality and law which were basically secular, but might have some relationship to general principles of social justice inherent in the Qur'an.

POSTSCRIPT

Does Islamic Revivalism Challenge a Secular World Order?

Understanding how Islam sees itself and its place in the world might make us fearful or hopeful. If Islam cannot accommodate to Western, secular values, as Esposito points out, does it challenge a stable world order? Hourani seems more hopeful that, through the process of political maturation, Islamic states may come to find in the Qur'an inspiration rather than literal law for governing their societies. In either case, the West must understand its own image in the Muslim world and not expect a commitment to secularism that would appear to Muslims as blasphemy. Whether deeper dialogue will bring Islam and the West closer together or further apart is not yet clear.

A fascinating survey of how people have perceived God from the time of Abraham to the present can be found in Karen Armstrong's *History of God* (Ballantine Books, 1993). Since Judaism exists in its own right and is the foundation for both Christianity and Islam, this "4000-year quest" provides insight into key similarities and points of difference. Any good text on religions of the world will provide an introduction to Islam; particularly accessible is Huston Smith's *Illustrated World's Religions: A Guide to Our Wisdom Traditions* (Harper-SanFrancisco, 1994), which is also available on videocassette. Students who have not read the Qur'an might like to explore these scriptures, which are available in paperback.

The dilemma of becoming modern without becoming Western is addressed by Bernard Lewis in "The West and the Middle East," *Foreign Affairs* (January/February 1997). Other books by Lewis include *Islam and the West* (Oxford University Press, 1993) and *The Middle East: A Brief History of the Last 2,000 Years* (Scribner, 1995).

Professor of history Richard Bulliet has written an account of Islam's success among people who live far from the political center, such as those in Iran. In *Islam: The View from the Edge* (Columbia University Press, 1994), Bulliet argues that the origins of today's Islamic resurgence are to be found in the eleventh century. Other books of note are *Orientalism* by Edward Said (Pantheon, 1978) and *Islam and the Cultural Accommodation to Social Change* by Bassam Tibi (Westview Press, 1991). In Francis Fukuyama's influential book *The End of History and the Last Man* (Free Press, 1992), the chapter entitled "The Worldwide Liberal Revolution" considers Islam as an alternative to liberalism and communism. Finally, *The Turban and the Crown: The Islamic Revolution in Iran* by Said Amir Arjomand (Oxford University Press, 1988) explores the conflicts between the authority structures in Shi'ite institutions and the mechanisms of the modern bureaucratic state.

ISSUE 22

Should Africa's Leaders Be Blamed for the Continent's Current Problems?

YES: George B. N. Ayittey, from *Africa Betrayed* (St. Martin's Press, 1992)

NO: Ali A. Mazrui, from *The Africans: A Triple Heritage* (Little, Brown, 1986)

ISSUE SUMMARY

YES: Economics professor George B. N. Ayittey contends that since achieving independence, many African countries' interests have been betrayed by their own incompetent, corrupt, power-hungry leaders.

NO: Political science professor Ali A. Mazrui argues that colonialism's legacy is at the root of many of the problems facing African countries today.

To say that Africa has been exploited by outsiders throughout its history is an understatement. Beginning with the East and West African slave trades and continuing through the age of imperialism, it is difficult to fathom the price that Africa has had to pay for its geographic location and richness of resources.

When European imperialists invaded Africa in the late nineteenth century, the exploitation was blatant and all-encompassing. Every conceivable reason —economic, political, social, cultural, religious—was used by Europeans to justify their actions. By the time the imperialists were finished carving up the continent, only two states, Ethiopia and Liberia, could be called free and independent nations.

The post–World War II era marked the end of worldwide imperialism. Gradually, most of the continent's nations achieved independence, some peacefully, some through armed resistance or the threat of it. As these former colonies entered nationhood, hopes were high that Africa's future would be a bright and glorious one.

One only needs to look at the continent today, almost a half-century since the demise of colonialism, to see that Africa's problems far outweigh the continent's promise. In regard to this, several questions need to be answered. One of the most important is this: Who or what is responsible for Africa's state of affairs?

It would be hard to find anyone who would state that colonialism was a positive force in the development of Africa or that its negative impact was minimal. Therefore, the standard argument is that many of the continent's problems are part and parcel of the colonial legacy. Recently, however, the focus of attention has turned to many African leaders, who some argue have betrayed their people's trust and exploited their country's wealth in the name of power and self-aggrandizement. Today, the continent seems to be filled with military dictators and political tyrants who refuse to serve anyone but themselves and their cronies and who neglect to share power with anyone, including their own people. Some feel that the fact that aid programs from Western nations often went to staunch anticommunists rather than solid, prodemocratic leaders exacerbated the problems.

The authors of the following selections—George B. N. Ayittey, a native Ghanian, and Ali A. Mazrui, born in Kenya—agree that the colonial legacy was damaging to Africa's people and their interests. Their differences lie in determining who or what is responsible for the continent's current problems. For Ayittey, the answer is simple: African leaders who have come to power since independence have betrayed their own people through usurpation of power, political corruptness, and a failure to enact democratic principles. He finds that the continent today is generally worse off than it was under colonial rule. The policies of the outside world toward Africa have not helped the situation, maintains Ayittey, but the problems that the continent faces today are more internal than external.

Mazrui argues that a "triple heritage" has influenced the development of Africa: indigenous African cultures, Western colonialism, and Islam. He sees Western colonialism as being responsible for Africa's problems because it has forced African culture to declare war against itself in order to survive. Islam, he feels, has been a positive force in the development of the continent, but its influence on African affairs seems to be declining rather than increasing. Mazrui contends that Western colonialism continues to plague Africa today because of the legacy it has bequeathed to the continent.

The question of responsibility for Africa's current problems is an important one, for these problems cannot be solved until it is understood what has caused them.

YES

George B. N. Ayittey

ALUTA CONTINUA!
(*THE STRUGGLE CONTINUES!*)

This [is an attempt] to present the true story about Africa's postcolonial experience. It is a grisly picture of one betrayal after another: economic disintegration, political chaos, inane civil wars, and infrastructural and institutional decay. These were not what Africans hoped for when they asked for their independence from colonial rule in the 1960s. It is difficult to convey their outrage and sense of indignation at the leaders who have failed them.

By the beginning of the 1990s economic and political conditions in Africa had become intolerable. African socialism has been a dismal failure, one-party rule has been a disaster, and international blindness to the nearly universal corruption of the continent's leaders has made matters immeasurably worse.

Various actors, foreign as well as domestic, participated, wittingly or not, in the devastation of Africa. It is easy for African leaders to put the blame somewhere else; for example, on Western aid donors or on an allegedly hostile international economic environment. But as the World Bank observed in its 1984 report, *Toward Sustained Development in Sub-Saharan Africa*, "genuine donor mistakes and misfortunes alone cannot explain the excessive number of 'white elephants' " (p. 24). Certainly, donor blunders and other external factors have contributed to the crisis in Africa, but in my view the internal factors have played a far greater role than the external ones.

Of the internal factors, the main culprit has been the failure of leadership. In many cases African leaders themselves created "black elephants" and state enterprises that were dictated more by considerations of prestige than by concerns for economic efficiency. Mobutu Sese Seko of Zaire once declared, "I know my people. They like grandeur. They want us to have respect abroad in the eyes of other countries" (*The Wall Street Journal*, Oct 15, 1986). Accordingly, half of Zaire's foreign debt of $6 billion went to build two big dams and the Inga-Shaba powerline, as well as a $1 billion double-decked suspension bridge over the Congo River. The upper level is for a railroad that does not exist. In many other cases elite *bazongas* (raiders of the public treasury) blatantly squandered part of the foreign aid money. Does Africa need more foreign aid?

In truth, Africa needs less—not more—foreign aid. David Karanja of Kenya wrote: "Foreign aid has done more harm to Africa than we care to admit. It has led to a situation where Africa has failed to set its own pace and direction of development free of external interference. Today, Africa's development plans are drawn thousands of miles away in the corridors of the IMF and World Bank" (New African, Jun 1992; p. 20).

Moreover, there are a number of ways that aid resources Africa desperately needs can be found in Africa itself. Maritu Wagaw wrote: "Let Africa look inside Africa for the solution of its economic problems. Solutions to our predicament should come from within not from outside" (New African, Mar 1992; p. 19). Indeed.

First, in 1989 Africa was spending $12 billion annually to import arms and to maintain the military. Second, the elites illegally transferred from Africa at least $15 billion annually during the latter part of the 1980s. Third, at least $5 billion annually could be saved if Africa could feed itself. Foreign exchange saved is foreign exchange earned. Fourth, another $5 billion could be saved from waste and inefficiencies in Africa's 3,200-odd state enterprises. This might entail selling off some of them or placing them under new management. Fifth, the civil wars raging in Africa exact a heavy toll in lost output, economic development, and destroyed property. If Angola's civil war alone cost the country $1 billion annually, $10 billion would not be an unreasonable estimate of the average annual cost of civil wars throughout the continent. Adding up these savings and the foreign exchange generated from internal sources would yield at least $47 billion annually, compared with the $12.4 billion in aid Africa received from all sources in 1990.

A bucket full of holes can only hold a certain amount of water for a certain amount of time. Pouring in more water makes little sense as it will all drain away. To the extent that there are internal leaks in Africa—corruption, senseless civil wars, wasteful military expenditures, capital flight, and government wastes—pouring in more foreign aid is futile. As a first order of priority, the leaks should be plugged to ensure that the little aid that comes in, stays. But African dictators, impervious to reason, continue to wage destructive wars.

In 1990 the OAU [Organization of African Unity] finally began to show signs of awakening from its slumber. Delegates to the OAU summit in July of that year, which Nelson Mandela addressed, observed that the summit demonstrated realism and a laudable determination to make progress in the resolution of Africa's intractable problems. Delegates realized that if Africa is to resist Western pressure for reforms and find its own solutions, it must first put its house in order. There was a genuine desire to end civil wars and disputes between neighbors, to increase regional cooperation, and to advance development.

The delegates signed a declaration, pledging to establish more democracy on the continent. According to the Washington Times, the incoming OAU chairman, President Yoweri Museveni of Uganda, averred, "Africa must find African solutions to its problems." Emphasizing that democracy could take many forms, he said that all states must have regular, free elections, a free press, and respect for human rights. In addition, the Washington Times reported that Nigerian President Ibrahim Babangida told the assembly that

Africa's leaders had failed their people. "Ever since the majority of our countries became independent in the 1960s we have conducted our lives as if the world owes us a living," he said. According to one African political analyst, the delegates realized that "unless they change they won't be coming to any other summits because they will no longer be in power" (*Washington Times*, Jul 13, 1990; p. A11). But rhetoric is one thing and action another.

While the delegates were speaking, the Babangida administration was continuing its crackdown on journalists and anyone suspected to be involved in the abortive April 22, 1990, coup attempt. In Uganda it may be recalled that journalists who put tough questions to visiting President Kaunda were arrested in spite of the free press that President Museveni called for.

If Africa is in a mess, the fault does not lie in any innate inferiority of the African people but rather in the alien, defective political systems instituted across much of the continent. It is not the charisma or the rhetoric of African leaders which makes a political system democratic and accountable. The *institutional approach...* is far superior.

Kwame Nkrumah, Julius Nyerere, Kenneth Kaunda and other nationalists were all great heroes with charisma. But they all established regimes which lacked the institutions of a free press, an independent judiciary, freedom of political association, and the most basic standards of accountability. Political systems which lack these institutions have the tendency to produce despots.... [V]irtually all African regimes have been characterized by an enormous concentration of both economic and political power in the hands of the state and, therefore, one individual.

Africa has more than its share of civilian autocrats, military dictators, and rapacious elites.... Africa's indigenous system of government produced few tyrants. The modern leadership is a far cry from the traditional. In fact, by Africa's indigenous standards the modern leadership in much of Africa has been a disgraceful failure. They refuse to learn and keep repeating not only their own mistakes but those of others as well.

In an address to the Rotary International in Accra, retired Lt. Gen. Emmanuel Erskine, former commander of the United Nations Forces in Lebanon, remarked: "The fact that some African leaders get themselves emotionally identified with their country which they consider their personal property and that they and their minority ethnic clientele should lead the country and that they should rule until death is the single major phenomenon creating serious political crisis on the continent. Not even bulldozers can dislodge some of these leaders from office" (West Africa, May 6–12, 1991; p. 722).

WHY AFRICAN DICTATORS CLING TO POWER

Recall from Chapter 6 that between 1957 and 1990, there were more than 150 African heads of state and only six relinquished power voluntarily. There are three main reasons why African heads of state refuse to step down when their people get fed up with them. First, they somehow get this absurd notion that the country belongs to them and them alone. Witness their pictures on the currency and in every nook and cranny in the country. Every monument or building of some significance is named after them: Houphouet-Boigny this, Houphouet-Boigny that, Moi National Park, and on and on. In Malawi, "President Hastings Kamuzu Banda's face is everywhere, from the buttons on Youth League uniforms to the dresses of dancers. Highways, stadiums and schools are named for him. A national holiday honors him. It is forbidden to call him by his last name; only 'Ngwazi,' meaning lion or protector, or 'the life president' are allowed (*Washington Post*, May 5, 1992; p. A22).

Second, insecure African heads of state surround themselves with loyal supporters, often drawn from their own tribes: the late Doe from the Krahn tribe, Mobutu of Zaire from the Gbande, Biya of Cameroon from the Bamileke, Moi of Kenya from the Kalenjin and Babangida of Nigeria from the Muslims. In Togoland, about 70 percent of General Eyadema's army were drawn from his own Kabye tribe (*Africa Report*, Jan–Feb 1992; p. 5).

Other supporters are simply bought: soldiers with fat paychecks and perks; urban workers with cheap rice and sardines ("essential commodities"); students with free tuition and hefty allowances; and intellectuals, opposition leaders and lawyers with big government posts and Mercedes-Benzes.

Even when the head of state is contemplating stepping down, these supporters and lackeys fiercely resist any cutbacks in government largesse or any attempt to open up the political system. This was precisely the case in The Gambia when Sir Dawda Jawara—in power since the country's independence in 1965—announced in March 1992 his intention to step down. Freeloaders and patronage junkies urged him to stay on! In Sierra Leone, Mr. Musa Gendemeh, the deputy

agriculture minister, was quite explicit. On the BBC "Focus on Africa" program (Apr 24, 1990), he declared that,

> "He won't give up his present privileged position for the sake of a multiparty system nor would one expect a policeman or soldier to give up his one bag of rice at the end of every month for the same....
>
> He warned that anyone talking about another party would be committing treason ... that ministers and MPs suspected of having something to do with the multiparty movement are now under surveillance ... and that whenever there has been trouble in the country, his people, the Mende, have suffered the most and he warned them to be careful" (*West Africa*, Jun 4–10, 1990; p. 934).

To protect their perks and benefits, these sycophants lie, deceive, and misinform the head of state. They continually praise him to the sky, even when his own tail is on fire! Kenneth Kaunda was informed that he would have "no problem" winning the October 1991 elections as he had 80 percent of the popular vote and "everything else had been taken care of." But when the actual voting took place, he was resoundingly humiliated, garnering a pitiful 25 percent of the vote. Ghanaians would recall that "party stooges" and "sycophants" also misled Nkrumah. African leaders should remember that "it is better to have wise people reprimand you than have stupid people sing you praises" (Ecclesiastes 7:5).

The third reason why African heads of state are reluctant to relinquish power is *fear*. Many of them have their hands so steeped in blood and their pockets so full of booty that they are afraid all their past gory misdeeds will be exposed. So they cling to power, regardless of the cost and consequences. But eventually they are dislodged, and only few subsequently are able to live peacefully in their own countries, much less to enjoy the loot.

Three Ways of Removing African Tyrants

In the ouster of Africa's dictators, three scenarios have emerged since 1990. By the "Doe scenario," those leaders who foolishly refused to accede to popular demands for democracy only did so at their own peril and at the destruction of their countries: Doe of Liberia, Traore of Mali, Barre of Somalia and Mengistu of Ethiopia. (Doe was killed in September 1990; Barre fled Mogadishu in a tank in January 1991; and Mengistu to Zimbabwe in February 1991.) African countries where this scenario is most likely to be repeated are Algeria, Cameroon, Djibouti, Equatorial Guinea, Libya, Malawi, Sudan, Tunisia, and Uganda.

In the "Kerekou scenario," those African leaders who wisely yielded to popular pressure managed to save not only their own lives but their countries as well: Kerekou of Benin, Kaunda of Zambia, Sassou-Nguesso of Central African Republic, and Pereira of Cape Verde Islands. Unfortunately, they are the exceptions.

The "Eyadema scenario," the third, is by far the most common. In this scenario, they yield initially after considerable domestic and international pressure but then attempt to manipulate the rules and the transition process to their advantage, believing that they could fool their people. In the end, they only fool themselves and are thrown out of office in disgrace. African countries likely to follow this route are: Angola, Burkina Faso, Burundi, Ghana, Ivory Coast, Kenya, Mozambique, Nigeria, Rwanda, Sierra Leone, Tanzania, Zaire, Zambia, and Zimbabwe. Recent events in Togo and Zaire also show that the outcome of the Eyadema scenario is highly unpredictable and its impact on economic development deleterious. Political uncertainty discourages business investment and trade. . . .

Education of Opposition Leaders

It is sad and painful to admit that the level of political sophistication and intellectual maturity of some of our opposition leaders is disgustingly low. All opposition groups and leaders must recognize that the political arena is a free marketplace and they are like merchants, peddling political ideas and solutions. If they demand the right to propagate their political philosophy, they cannot deny anyone else the right to do so. If their philosophy has any merit, the people will buy it. If not, they will reject it. It is not up to the opposition leaders to make this determination, but the people.

Furthermore, most opposition leaders define "democracy" only in terms of their right to form political parties, to hold rallies, and to criticize foolish government policies. . . . [I]nstitutions such as the rule of law, freedom of expression, and an independent judiciary are far more important.

Focus

The primary focus of all opposition groups in Africa should be on removing the tyrant in power and establishing a level political playing field. If the tyrant is crafting a dubious transition process, the focus should be on halting or changing that process. All other issues (such as who should be president, what type of ideology the country should follow, a political platform, whether the country should have a new currency or flag) are secondary.

The Covenant

Quite clearly, the opposition in Africa needs to "get its act together." One effective way of doing this is to draw up a covenant, a set of rules by which all opposition groups agree to abide. At a meeting of all opposition leaders, a covenant should be signed containing the following stipulations:

1. Politics is a competitive game, and therefore the rules of competition must be established and respected by all. The term of the president will be limited to two terms (of four years each) in office.

2. All must agree on the safeguards and the necessary structures to be adopted to ensure free and fair elections. Political maturity requires accepting electoral defeat graciously and congratulating the winner. Political violence and voter intimidation must be eschewed. Severe sanctions, such as disqualification or heavy fines, must be imposed against any political party that is guilty of murder of political opponents.

3. Ultimately, it is the African people themselves who must determine what is best for them; not what one person imposes upon them. To do this, the African people need the means and the forum as well as the freedom to participate in the decisionmaking process.

4. Each opposition leader must agree to respect and honor the OAU's Charter of People's and Human Rights. This Charter is explicit on freedom of expression, freedom from arbitrary arrests, press freedoms, and so forth.

5. No one person or party shall monopolize the means or the forum by which the people can participate. All leaders will undertake to respect the right of every African to air his opinion freely, without harassment or intimidation, even if his view diverges from that of the head of state. Tolerance of diversity of opinion is a sign of intellectual maturity.

6. The media shall be taken out of the hands of the government. Religion and foreign ideology must be kept out of government. All leaders must pledge to build on or improve Africa's indigenous institutions and culture.

7. All must agree on sanctions to be applied against any leader or political party acting in violation of this covenant. Such sanctions must be determined by the leaders themselves.

After all is said and done, it becomes apparent that it is the educated elites—the leaders and the intellectuals—who have failed Africa. The Vai of Liberia have a proverb most appropriate for this situation. If after spending their meager savings to educate a child, he returns to the village an ignoramus, Vais elders may look upon him and ruefully remark: "The moon shines brightly but it is still dark in some places." Doesn't this describe postcolonial Africa and its elites?

Common sense has probably been the scarcest commodity among the elite in postcolonial Africa. Most of the "educated" leaders lacked it, intellectuals flouted it, and the opposition, in many cases, was woefully deficient in it. The peasants may be "illiterate and backward," but at least they can use their common sense. Obviously, a *common sense revolution* is what is urgently needed in African government....

While battling current despots, Africans should be vigilant, think ahead, and formulate strategies against the next buffoon. Since the winds of democratic change began sweeping across Africa in 1990, all sorts of intellectual crackpots, corrupt former politicians, charlatans, and unsavory elements have suddenly jumped on to the "democracy bandwagon" to hijack the democratic revolution. In 1992, Kaunda, and Nyerere, for example, were all preaching multiparty democracy. Where were they back in 1985 when true democrats were laying their lives on the line to demand political pluralism? . . . The African story is one of betrayal—by one buffoon after another.

NO

Ali A. Mazrui

A CELEBRATION OF DECAY?

WESTERNISATION AND DECAY

The ancestors of Africa are angry. For those who believe the power of the ancestors, the proof of their anger is all around us. For those who do not believe in ancestors, the proof of their anger is given another name. In the words of Edmund Burke, 'People will not look forward to posterity who never look backward to their ancestors.'

But what is the proof of the curse of the ancestors? Things are not working in Africa. From Dakar to Dar es Salaam, from Marrakesh to Maputo, institutions are decaying, structures are rusting away. It is as if the ancestors had pronounced the curse of cultural sabotage. This generation of Africans is hearing the ancestral voice in no uncertain terms proclaiming,

> Warriors will fight scribes for the control of your institutions; wild bush will conquer your roads and pathways; your land will yield less and less while your offspring multiply; your houses will leak from the floods and your soil will crack from the drought; your sons will refuse to pick up the hoe and prefer to wander in the wilds; you shall learn ways of cheating and you will poison the cola nuts you serve your own friends. Yes, things will fall apart.

If this is the curse of the ancestors, what is the sin? It is the compact between Africa and the twentieth century and its terms are all wrong. They involve turning Africa's back on previous centuries—an attempt to 'modernize' without consulting cultural continuities, an attempt to start the process of 'dis-Africanizing' Africa. One consequence takes on the appearance of social turbulence, of rapid social change let loose upon a continent.

Franklin D. Roosevelt once said to Americans, when faced with the economic crisis of the 1930s, 'The only thing we have to fear is fear itself.' For my turn I am tempted to say to fellow Africans, facing a series of severe political, economic, social and cultural crises in the 1980s, 'The main thing we need to change is our own changeability.'

African states since independence have experienced a bewildering and rapid sequence of military coups and economic shifts and turns. In addition, over the last generation or two there has been a remarkable pace of cultural dis-Africanisation and Westernisation. If the Jews in the Diaspora had scrambled to change their culture as fast as Africans in their own homelands seemed to be doing until recently, the miracle of Jewish identity would not have lasted these two or three additional millennia in the wilderness. Many Africans even today seem to be undergoing faster cultural change in a single generation than the Jews underwent in the first 1000 years of dispersal.

Yet there may be hope in the very instability which Africa is experiencing in the wake of this unnatural dis-Africanisation. The fate of African culture may not yet be irrevocably sealed. With every new military coup, with every collapse of a foreign aid project, with every evidence of large-scale corruption, with every twist and turn in opportunistic foreign policy, it becomes pertinent to ask whether Western culture in Africa is little more than a nine-day wonder.

Africa is at war. It is a war of cultures. It is a war between indigenous Africa and the forces of Western civilisation. It takes the form of inefficiency, mismanagement, corruption and decay of the infrastructure. The crisis of efficiency in the continent is symptomatic of the failure of transplanted organs of the state and the economy. Indigenous African culture is putting up a fight. It is as if the indigenous ancestors have been aroused from the dead, disapproving of what seems like an informal pact between the rulers of independent Africa (the inheritors of the colonial order) and the West—a pact which allows the West to continue to dominate Africa. It is as if the ancestors are angry at the failure of Africans to consult them and to pay attention to Africa's past and usage. It is as if the apparent breakdown and decay in Africa today is a result of the curse of the ancestors. Or is it not a curse but a warning, a sign from the ancestors calling on Africans to rethink their recent past, their present and their future and calling on them to turn again to their traditions and reshape their society anew, to create a modern and a future Africa that incorporates the best of its own culture?

What is likely to be the outcome of this drama? Is the Westernisation of Africa reversible? Was the European colonial impact upon Africa deep or shallow? Was the colonial impact a cost or a benefit to Africa?

THE EPIC OF COLONIALISM

Let us take the epic school first, the insistence that these last 100 years were not a mere century but a revolution of epic proportions. The arguments for this school include a number of apparently decisive turning points.

First, there is the argument that colonialism and the accompanying capitalism effectively incorporated Africa into the world economy, for good or ill. It started with the slave trade, which dragged African labour itself into the emerging international capitalist system. This was the era of the *labour* imperative in relations between Africa and the West.

But colonialism was the era of the *territorial* imperative, as the West demanded from Africa not just labour but territory and its promise in all its dimensions. Capitalism had come knocking on the doors of the continent and enticed the host into the wider world of the international economy.

Then there was Africa's admission into the state system of the world emanating from the European Peace of Westphalia of 1648. It was that particular set of treaties which has been regarded widely as the beginnings of the modern system of sovereign states. Africa might have been dragged screaming into the world of capitalism, but it was not dragged unwillingly into the world of the sovereign state system. On the contrary, one colonial society after another framed its agitation and anti-imperialism in terms of seeking admission to the international community whose rules had grown out of European diplomatic history and statecraft. Independence for every African country was in fact a voluntary entry into the sovereign state system.

Then there is Africa's incorporation into a world culture which is still primarily Eurocentric. The major international ideologies—liberalism, capitalism, socialism, Marxism, communism and indeed fascism—have all been European-derived. To that extent, the world of ideology is in part the world of European dominance in the field of values and norms.

Another aspect of Africa's incorporation into world culture concerns the role of European languages in Africa. The significance of English, French and Portuguese especially in Africa's political life can hardly be overestimated, at least in the short run. Rulers are chosen on the basis of competence in the relevant imperial language. Nationwide political communication in the majority of African countries is almost impossible without the use of the relevant imperial medium.

Then there is Africa's incorporation into the world of international law, which is again heavily Eurocentric in origin. Many aspects of international law are named after European cities—the Geneva Convention, the Vienna Convention and the like. One looks in vain in the body of international law for conventions named after such Third World cities as

Bombay, Maiduguri or Rio de Janeiro. But nevertheless African states *seem* to be firmly and irrevocably tied to the body of legal precepts governing international diplomacy in the twentieth century.

Also part of the epic theory of the significance of colonialism is the technological variable. It is quite clear that the West has been in the lead in scientific and technological change for at least 300 years. Western colonisation of Africa could therefore be interpreted as an invitation to Africa to be incorporated into the modern technological age. At first glance this ranges from medical science to the automobile, from the tractor in African agriculture to the missile in African military establishments. Again, this would seem to be an incorporation into a global system which is basically of epic proportions and seemingly irreversible.

INFORMATION FLOWS AND THE MORAL ORDER

Next is the issue of information and data. Africa has been swallowed by the global system of dissemination of information. What Africa knows about itself, what different parts of Africa know about each other, have been profoundly influenced by the West. Even in the field of the mass media, Africa is overwhelmingly dependent on the wire services of the Western world for information about itself. What Nigerians know about Kenya, or Zambians know about Ghana, is heavily derived from the wire services of the Western world transmitting information across the globe. African newspapers and radios subscribe to these wire services and receive data for their news bulletins from Western sources.

Also apparently epic in significance was the *moral* order which had come with colonialism and Christianity. Important Western and Christian ethical factors entered the domain of African systems of restraint. Can a man have more than one wife? Is female circumcision morally legitimate? Is there such a thing as an illegitimate child if the father admits paternity and the mother acknowledges the child? How sinful was sexuality outside marriage?

All these were major moral dilemmas for Africa, *implying* a permanent change as a result of colonisation and Christianisation. How then could their impact be anything but an epic drama? How then could European influence be anything but a totally transformative force?

COLONIALISM AS AN EPISODE

Yet there is an alternative case for regarding the European impact as no more than an episode in millennia of African history.

There are two main versions of this idea. One insists that Africa could have entered the world economy and the international state system without being colonized by Europe. After all, Japan is now a major power in the world economy and has at times been a major figure in the international state system without having undergone the agonies of European colonisation and imperialism. Japan was able to acquire Western tools without succumbing to Western subjugation. But Africa was denied that option.

Related to this is the argument that modern science and technology were bound to convert the whole world into a global village. Twentieth-century science and technology had become too expansionist to have left Africa untouched. If this body of expertise could reach the Moon without colonizing it, why could

it not have reached Africa without subjugating it?

What follows from this is the conclusion that European colonisation of Africa was not the only way of Africa's entry into the global system of the twentieth century. Africa could have made such an entry without suffering either the agonies of the slave trade, or the exploitation of colonialism or the humiliation of European racism.

The second version of the episodic school asserts that the European impact on Africa has been shallow rather than deep, transitional rather than longlasting. It is not often realised how brief the colonial period was. When Jomo Kenyatta was born, Kenya was not yet a crown colony. Kenyatta lived right through the period of British rule and outlasted British rule by fifteen years. If the entire period of colonialism could be compressed into the life-span of a single individual, how deep was the impact?

The kind of capitalism which was transferred to Africa was itself shallow. Western consumption patterns were transferred more effectively than Western production techniques, Western tastes were acquired more quickly than Western skills, the profit motive was adopted without the efficient calculus of entrepreneurship, and capitalist greed was internalised sooner than capitalist discipline.

All this is quite apart from the anomaly of urbanisation without industrialisation. In the history of the Western world the growth of cities occurred partly in response to fundamental changes in production. Urbanisation followed in the wake of either an agrarian transformation or an industrial revolution. But in the history of Africa urbanisation has been under way without accompanying growth of productive capacity. In some African countries there is indeed a kind of revolution—but it is a revolution in urbanisation rather than in industrialisation, a revolution in expanding numbers of people squeezed into limited space, rather than a transformation in method and skill of economic output. It is these considerations which have made capitalism in Africa, such as it is, lopsided and basically shallow.

But alongside this phenomenon is the post-colonial state in Africa, which is also quite often in the process of decaying. The African state since independence has been subject to two competing pressures —the push towards militarisation and the pull towards privatisation. In the capitalist Western world state ownership is regarded as an alternative to or even the opposite of private ownership. The privatisation of the steel industry (its return from state nationalisation to private ownership) in England, for example, is an alternative to state ownership and state control.

In post-colonial Africa, on the other hand, the question arises whether the state in itself can be privatized or become privately owned. Is there a new echo in Africa of Louis XIV's notorious dictum, 'I am the state'?

There is an echo of a sort, but with distinctive African variations. What must be remembered is that the pressure of privatisation in Africa are accompanied by pressures towards militarisation. The pull towards privatisation is partly a legacy of greed in the tradition of Shylock, Shakespeare's creation in *The Merchant of Venice*. The push towards militarism, on the other hand, is a legacy of naked power in the tradition of Shaka, the founder of the Zulu kingdom and empire. Africa is caught between Shylock and Shaka, between greed and naked power—and the decay of the post-colonial state is one consequence of that dialectic.

In Nigeria between 1979 and 1984 the two tendencies of privatisation and militarisation appeared to be alternatives. Under civilian rule from 1979 privatisation gathered momentum. The resources of the nation were, to all intents and purposes, deemed to be the private hunting ground of those in power and of their supporters. Lucrative contracts for trade or construction were handed out on the basis of personal considerations. Foreign exchange was privately allocated and arbitrarily distributed. Millions of dollars and naira disappeared into the private accounts of key figures abroad.

This rampant unofficial and unlegislated privatisation of the state's resources seemed to have set the stage for the state's militarisation. Nigeria's armed forces— restive for a variety of reasons—found additional grounds for impatience with the civilian politicians. On 31 December 1983 the soldiers once again intervened and took over power. The push towards militarisation had triumphed over the pull towards privatisation of the Nigerian state. The soldiers justified their intervention on the basis of ending the private pillage of the country's resources. The action of the soldiers this time seemed calculated to arrest the decay of both the Nigerian economy and state....

IS THE CRESCENT ALSO DECAYING?

The first thing to note is that the most serious forms of decay seem to be occurring in the institutions inherited from the Western world, rather than those bequeathed by Islam.

But this very decomposition of the Western heritage has complex consequences for Islam in Africa. It is arguable that where Islam is already established, the decline of the West is advantageous for Islam. After all, the most important threat to Islam in Africa is not a revival of indigenous culture but the triumph of Western secularism. The materialism of Western civilisation, the superiority of Western science and technology at their home base in the West, the declining moral standards in at least certain areas of Western culture, and the glitter and temptations of Western life-styles, have all combined to pose a significant threat especially to the younger generations of the Muslim world. As these Western institutions grind to a standstill in Africa, causing new areas of poverty and deprivation, the glitter of Western civilisation begins to dim.

But while established Islam is indeed stabilised by this Western decay, Islamic expansion to new areas is probably hindered by the same decay. For example, the economic decline in West Africa has resulted in reduced traffic of Muslim traders and other migrants, many of whom have been unofficial missionaries for the Islamic faith. Also reducing the expansion of Islam are the decaying roads and railways, which reduce social and economic mobility.

To summarize the argument so far: where Islam is already established, the decay of Western civilisation is good for Islam since it helps to neutralise a major threat. On the other hand, where Islam has not yet arrived, the disintegration of African communications and the decline in commercial traffic across African borders has reduced the pace of Islamic expansion. . . .

CONCLUSION

European colonial rule in Africa was more effective in destroying indigenous African *structures* than in destroying African *culture*. The tension between new imported structures and old resilient cultures is part of the post-colonial war of cultures in the African continent. The question has therefore arisen as to whether Africa is reclaiming its own.

As we have indicated, the shallowness of the imported *economic* institutions from the West was partly due to the lopsided nature of colonial acculturation. Western consumption patterns prevailed more quickly than Western production techniques, thus promoting Western tastes without developing Western skills.

As for the shallowness of the imported *political* institutions, this was partly due to the moral contradictions of Western political tutelage. After independence these political contradictions took their toll, for the transferred institutions simply did not take root. Africa was torn between the forces of anarchy on one side, in the sense of decentralised violence, and the forces of tyranny, on the other side, in the sense of orchestrated centralised repression. The post-colonial state was in turn torn between the forces of privatisation and the forces of militarism. Privatisation puts a state outside the public sector, as it denationalises it. Militarisation, by definition, abolishes the principle of civilian supremacy.

But in the final analysis, the shallowness of the imported institutions is due to that culture gap between new structures and ancient values, between alien institutions and ancestral traditions.

Africa can never go back completely to its pre-colonial starting point but there may be a case for at least a partial retreat, a case for re-establishing contacts with familiar landmarks of yesteryear and then re-starting the journey of modernisation under indigenous impetus.

In many parts of Africa there is, as we indicated, a war between Islam and Westernism. The decay of Western civilisation is good for Islam in those parts of the continent. But the decay of the infrastructure and the decline of African economies may be bad for Islamic expansion in west Africa.

But when all is said and done, the most important cultural conflict occurring in Africa is between Western civilisation and indigenous forces. If instability in the continent is a symptom of cultures at war, perhaps Africa's identity may survive the ravages of Westernisation after all. It is still true to say that Africans in the twentieth century are becoming acculturated faster than were, for example, the Jews in the first millennium of their dispersal. But the war of cultures is by no means over in Africa. It is almost as if the indigenous ancestors have been aroused from the dead, and are fighting back to avert the demise of Africanity. In their immediate consequences decay and instability are a matter of lament. But in their longer term repercussions, they may be a matter for celebration.

But what is the way out? How can Africa's compact with the twentieth century be amended? How can the ancestors be appeased?

Two broad principles should influence and inform social reform in Africa in the coming decades. One is the imperative of looking inwards towards ancestry; the other is the imperative of looking outward towards the wider humanity. The inward imperative requires a more systematic investigation into the cultural preconditions of the success of each project, of each piece of legislation, of each system of government. Feasibility studies should be much more sensitive to the issue of 'cultural feasibility' than has been the case in the past. Africa's ancestors need to be consulted through the intermediary of consulting African usage, custom and tradition.

But since the world is becoming a village, Africa cannot just look inward to its own past. The compact with the twentieth century has to include a sensitivity to the wider world of the human race as a whole. . . .

Islam and Westernism have been part of Africa's response to the imperative of looking outward to the wider world. But Africa's own ancestors are waiting to ensure that Africa also remembers to look inward to its own past.

Before a seed germinates it must first decay. A mango tree grows out of a decaying mango seed. A new Africa may be germinating in the decay of the present one—and the ancestors are presiding over the process.

POSTSCRIPT

Should Africa's Leaders Be Blamed for the Continent's Current Problems?

Although Ayittey and Mazrui disagree on the causes of Africa's current problems, they agree on what is needed to improve conditions there—the rediscovery and promotion of the African traditions and institutions that have been misplaced or discarded since colonialism's end. The West can play a role in this process, but it must be a supportive rather than a directive role. The time has come to let Africans solve Africa's problems—using uniquely African solutions, if they are deemed necessary.

Besides the two sources from which this issue's readings were taken, there are many fine books on the subject of Africa since World War II. Robert W. July, in *An African Voice: The Role of the Humanities in African Independence* (Duke University Press, 1987), concentrates on Africa's struggles against cultural imperialism, a subject that is eloquently dealt with in Mazrui's book. Basil Davidson, Europe's most sensitive and prolific writer on African history and culture, surveys the continent's recent history in *The Black Man's Burden: Africa and the Curse of the Nation-State* (Random House, 1992). Davidson's *Search for Africa: History, Culture, Politics* (Random House, 1994) is more historical in coverage but nevertheless complementary to *Black Man's Burden*. In *Africa in Chaos* (St.Martin's Press, 1998), George B. N. Ayittey continues and extends his arguments that are first developed in *Africa Betrayed*.

For a history of the African continent and its people, see Robert W. July, *A History of the African People* (Waveland Press, 1992) and Roland Oliver, *The African Experience: Major Themes in African History from Earliest Times to the Present* (HarperCollins, 1992). Finally, two videotape series are recommended: Mazrui's *Africans: A Triple Heritage* and Davidson's *Africa: A Voyage of Discovery With Basil Davidson*.

ISSUE 23

Were Ethnic Leaders Responsible for the Disintegration of Yugoslavia?

YES: Warren Zimmermann, from *Origins of a Catastrophe* (Times Books, 1996)

NO: Steven Majstorovic, from "Ancient Hatreds or Elite Manipulation? Memory and Politics in the Former Yugoslavia," *World Affairs* (Spring 1997)

ISSUE SUMMARY

YES: Career diplomat Warren Zimmerman, the United States' last ambassador to Yugoslavia, argues that the republic's ethnic leaders, especially Slobodan Milosovic, bear primary responsibility for the nation's demise.

NO: Political science professor Steven Majstorovic contends that while manipulation by elite ethnic leaders played a role in the disintegration of Yugoslavia, the fragile ethnic divisions within the country also played an important role in the country's demise.

It is not often that the world witnesses the death of a country, but that is precisely what many say we witnessed in the 1990s with the passing of Yugoslavia. Since World War II, the creation of nations has been a common occurrence. However, what was dramatic about the situation in Yugoslavia is that we witnessed the country's disintegration on television. The nature of Balkan history has long been complicated and confusing.

The Balkans were once referred to as Europe's "powder keg." The area's history began when it was settled by the southern branch of the Slavic family tree a millennium ago. During Europe's medieval period, Serbs, Croats, and Bosnians established Balkan kingdoms, which were soon overrun and conquered by the forces of the Ottoman Empire, which maintained control over part of the area for almost 500 years. These kingdoms were eventually joined by the Austrian Hapsburgs, as the Balkans became a battleground between two rival empires, one Muslim, the other Christian. The ethnic groups were forced to make the best of an untenable situation and wait for better days.

The next major change in Balkan history would begin in 1914 with the outbreak of World War I, which began with the assassination of the heir to the Austrian Hapsburg empire by a Serbian nationalist. At the war's conclusion, the victorious Allies decided that the solution to the Balkan question was a federal republic comprising the disparate ethnic groups, many of whom had been there for 1,000 years. Thus, Serbs, Croats, Slovenes, Bosnians, Herzegovinians, Montenegrins, Muslims, Macedonians, and Albanians were asked to live together in the new nation of Yugoslavia.

The nation's initial period of establishment was brief, as World War II brought Nazi occupation to Yugoslavia. Complicating things further was the fact that while most "Yugoslavs" fought against the German occupation (Josip Broz, soon to be known as Tito, would emerge as the leader of the "Partisans"), others (Croats and Bosnian-Herzegovinians) actually collaborated with the Nazis, resulting in atrocities on both sides. The main victims of this era would be the Serbs, many of whom were massacred by the Croat Ustase puppet state. This massacre was not forgotten by the Serbs.

After the war, Yugoslavia once again became a federal republic, with separate states established in Slovenia, Croatia, Bosnia-Herzegovina, Serbia, Montenegro, and Macedonia. Tito was given the difficult job of keeping the country together, something which he was able to do until his death. He was the only European communist leader to escape Stalin's influence, and he managed to create in Yugoslavia a nonaligned communist state with a market-oriented economy. It was only after Tito's death that the republic began to disintegrate, partially caused by horrendous economic conditions. By the 1980s, Yugoslavia was a troubled area; in 1995 it had virtually disintegrated.

The problems that brought about Yugoslavia's disintegration are many. The ancient ethnic rivalries and conflicts were extremely difficult to overcome. Complicating matters were the religious differences, with Eastern Orthodoxy, Roman Catholicism, and Islam claiming the allegiance of the area's peoples. And of course there is the history—who did what to whom and when did they do it—which has influenced the myths and realities of the Balkan landscape.

Contemporary leaders of the former Yugoslavia—former communists—now represent neither ideology nor country but ethnic constituencies. To what extent are these leaders personally responsible for Yugoslavia's demise? Or, was the country eventually doomed to failure by ethno-religious-historical forces beyond control? With ethnic groups skewed within the former Yugoslavian-federated states, was the war in Bosnia-Herzegovina that occurred in the 1990s inevitable, as Croats, Serbs, Bosnian Serbs, Bosnian Croats, and Bosnian Muslims began attempts to improve their lot in Bosnia? A treaty signed in 1995 produced a tenuous peace, as the current Serbian attempt to take control of the independent province of Kosovo attests.

The answers to many questions about Yugoslavia's demise may be found in the selections by Warren Zimmerman and Steven Majstorovic. Zimmerman holds the former Yugoslavia's ethnic leaders primarily responsible for the country's disintegration. Majstorovic accepts that "elite manipulation" played a role in Yugoslavia's demise, but he states that the "ancient hatreds" that have become embedded in the Balkan psyches are difficult to ignore as factors in that process.

YES

Warren Zimmermann

ORIGINS OF A CATASTROPHE

PREFACE

This is a story with villains—villains guilty of destroying the multiethnic state of Yugoslavia, of provoking three wars, and of throwing some twenty million people into a distress unknown since the Second World War. How could this tragedy have happened to a country that by most standards was more prosperous and more open than any other in Eastern Europe? My thesis is that the Yugoslav catastrophe was not mainly the result of ancient ethnic or religious hostilities, nor of the collapse of communism at the end of the cold war, nor even of the failures of the Western countries. Those factors undeniably made things worse. But Yugoslavia's death and the violence that followed resulted from the conscious actions of nationalist leaders who coopted, intimidated, circumvented, or eliminated all opposition to their demagogic designs. Yugoslavia was destroyed from the top down.

This [selection] is primarily about those destroyers. As American ambassador between 1989 and 1992, I saw them frequently and came to know them well. Speaking with me before their faces had become familiar to Western television viewers, they hadn't yet learned the full panoply of defenses against questions from foreigners. They described their plans, sometimes honestly, sometimes deceitfully, but always passionately and with a cynical disregard for playing by any set of rules. This record of their words and actions provides evidence for a coroner's report on the death of Yugoslavia. . . .

The prime agent of Yugoslavia's destruction was Slobodan Milošević, president of Serbia. Milošević claimed to defend Yugoslavia even as he spun plans to turn it into a Serb-dominated dictatorship. His initial objective was to establish Serbian rule over the whole country. When Slovenia and Croatia blocked this aim by deciding to secede, the Serbian leader fell back on an alternative strategy. He would bring all of Yugoslavia's Serbs, who lived in five of its six republics, under the authority of Serbia, that is, of himself.

Milošević initiated this strategy in Croatia, using the Yugoslav army to seal off Serbian areas from the reach of Croatian authority. His plan in Bosnia was even bolder—to establish by force a Serbian state on two-thirds of the territory of a republic in which Serbs weren't even a plurality, much less a majority. In league with Radovan Karadžić, the Bosnian Serb leader with whom he later broke, Milošević was responsible for the deaths of tens of thousands of Bosnians and for the creation of the largest refugee population in Europe since the Second World War.

Franjo Tudjman, elected president of Croatia in 1990, also played a leading role in the destruction of Yugoslavia. A fanatic Croatian nationalist, Tudjman hated Yugoslavia and its multiethnic values. He wanted a Croatian state for Croatians, and he was unwilling to guarantee equal rights to the 12 percent of Croatia's citizens who were Serbs. Tudjman's arrogance in declaring independence without adequate provisions for minority rights gave Milošević and the Yugoslav army a pretext for their war of aggression in Croatia in 1991. And Tudjman's greed in seeking to annex Croatian areas of Bosnia prolonged the war and increased the casualties in that ill-starred republic.

Slovenian nationalism was different from the Serbian or Croatian sort. With a nearly homogeneous population and a location in the westernmost part of Yugoslavia, Slovenia was more democratically inclined and more economically developed than any other republic in Yugoslavia. The Slovenes wanted to be free of the poverty and intrigue of the rest of Yugoslavia. They particularly detested Milošević, charging him with making Yugoslavia uninhabitable for non-Serbs. Under the presidency of Milan Kučan—a conflicted figure buffeted toward secession by the winds of Slovenian politics—Slovenia unilaterally declared its independence on June 25, 1991. The predictable result, irresponsibly disregarded by Kučan and the other Slovene leaders, was to bring war closer to Croatia and Bosnia....

DECLINE...

A law graduate of Belgrade University, Milošević began his career as a communist apparatchik with an authoritarian personality already noticed by schoolmates. He was too young and too junior to have been close to [Josip Broz] Tito, but he was old enough (thirty-eight when Tito died) to have prospered in the Titoist system. I never saw in him the personal animus against Tito that many other Serbs felt. In fact, on my first visit to his office I noticed a large painting of Tito behind his desk; significantly, he took it down in 1991, the year Yugoslavia fell apart.

As he cultivated a nationalist persona, Milošević dropped the external aspects of his communist formation. He purged himself of the wooden language that makes communists the world over such hapless communicators. He dropped all references to communism. And he renamed the League of Communists of Serbia the Serbian Socialist Party.

In two ways, however, Milošević failed to break the ties. The first was his continued reliance on communist techniques of control over his party, the Serbian police, the media, and the economic sector. The second was his highly visible wife, Mirjana Marković, a Belgrade University professor and frequent author of turgid Leninist essays in glossy Serbian magazines. Marković flaunted her communism; in fact, she cofounded a communist party in 1990. She was thought to have the influence of a Lady Macbeth over her husband, particularly with regard to his frequent abrupt dismissals of hitherto trusted subordinates. Liberal Serbs described her variously as flaky, crafty, amoral, or vicious.

Whatever his real views of Tito, Milošević was nevertheless the vessel for the Serbian claim that Tito had denied Serbs the role to which destiny had entitled them. The charge may have been partly true, but it was certainly exaggerated. Serbs were a major element of Tito's partisan army during World War II, including its first two elite units, and played a prominent role in the Yugoslav army and police afterward. At his death, however, Tito left Yugoslavia so decentralized that no ethnic group—and certainly not the Serbs—could possibly dominate it. Given Serbian messianism, it became inevitable that a Serbian nationalist would rise up to redress the imagined wrongs dealt his nation. It was a tragedy for Serbia, its neighbors, and Europe as a whole that this nationalist turned out to be Slobodan Milošević. . . .

Milošević deploys his arguments with force and apparent conviction. They're always internally consistent, even when based on fallacies or delusions. "You see, Mr. Zimmermann," he would say, "only we Serbs really believe in Yugoslavia. We're not trying to secede like the Croats and Slovenes, we're not tied to a foreign country like the Albanians in Kosovo, and we're not trying to create an Islamic state like the Muslims in Bosnia. They all fought against you in World War II. We were your allies." . . .

In my view, Milošević is an opportunist rather than an ideologue, a man driven by power rather than nationalism. In the late 1980s he was a communist official in search of a legitimation less disreputable than communism, an alternative philosophy to help him consolidate his hold on Serbia, and a myth that would excite and energize Serbs behind him. He calculated that the way to achieve and maintain power in Serbia was to seize the nationalist pot that Serbian intellectuals were brewing and bring it to a boil.

I don't see Milošević as the same kind of ethnic exclusivist as Croatia's President Franjo Tudjman, who dislikes Serbs, or Bosnian Serb politician Radovan Karadžić, who hates everybody who isn't a Serb. Milošević felt no discomfort in bragging to me, no matter how fraudulently, about Serbia as a multiethnic paradise. Nor, I'm sure, did it disturb his conscience to move ruthlessly against Serbian nationalists like Karadžić when they got in his way. He has made a compact with nationalism as a way to bring him power. He can't break the compact without causing political damage to himself, but it has a utilitarian rather than an emotional value for him.

I can't recall ever seeing a cooler politician under pressure than Slobodan Milošević. In March 1991 he lunched with me and six other Western ambassadors. The meeting came during one of the most explosive crises of his political career. The week before, he had weathered the largest street demonstration ever mounted against his rule, had lost a bid to overthrow the leaderships of Slovenia and Croatia, and was in the process of trying to destroy the presidency of Yugoslavia.

He had come to our lunch from a four-hour meeting with hostile Belgrade University students. Yet he looked and acted as if nothing gave him greater pleasure than to sit down for a long conversation with us. He addressed all our questions with equanimity, asserting with good humor that the Kosovo Albanians were the most pampered minority in Europe, that street demonstrations (which had brought him to power) were wrong, and that Serbia had the freest media and the freest election system in Yugoslavia.

As I pondered the surreal quality of Milošević's remarks, I couldn't help admiring his imperturbability. I went back to the embassy and wrote a facetious cable saying that I had finally penetrated the mystery of the man. There were really two Milošević's. Milošević One was hard-line, authoritarian, belligerent, bent on chaos, and wedded to the use of force to create a Greater Serbia. Personally, he was apoplectic, he hated Westerners, and he spoke in Serbian. Milošević Two was polite, affable, cooperative, and always looking for reasonable solutions to Yugoslavia's problems. He was calm, he liked to reminisce about his banking days in New York, and he spoke good English.

I did note that Milošević One and Milošević Two had several traits in common: they disliked Albanians, they were strong in the defense of Serbian interests, and they seemed to believe that the world was ganging up against Serbia. Milošević Two, I wrote, would often be summoned to repair the horrendous damage caused to Serbia's reputation by Milošević One, who would be sent back to the locker room. There his handlers would salve his wounds and get him ready for the next round. The one sure thing, I concluded, was that Milošević One would always be back.

The strategy of this schizoid figure was based on the fact that Serbs were spread among five of Yugoslavia's six republics. Slovenia was the only exception. At the foundation of Yugoslavia after World War I, Serbia's chief interest was that all these Serbs live in a single state. Before Tito, Serbia had dominated that state. Now, after Tito, Milošević wanted to restore that dominance. His chief obstacle in the late 1980s was Slovenia, ironically the only republic without large numbers of Serbs. The Slovenes were the first to challenge the unity of Yugoslavia.

Milošević, no supporter of Yugoslav unity except as a vehicle for Serbian influence, wrapped himself in the mantle of unity as he sharpened his duel with the Slovenes. His concept of unity was Serbian nationalism buttressed by communist methods of control. It tolerated neither democracy nor power-sharing with other national groups. Because it was unacceptable to all Yugoslavs who wanted real unity or real democracy, or both, it was bound to be divisive. In fact, Milošević's pursuit of a narrow Serbian agenda made him the major wrecker of Yugoslavia....

DEPARTURES

On May 12, 1992, the State Department announced that I was being recalled to Washington in protest against the Serbian aggression in Bosnia....

The days before our departure and the weeks after gave us time for introspection about a country where we had lived six years and that had affected us deeply. How was it possible that such attractive people, on whom the gods of nature and fortune had smiled, could have plowed their way straight to hell? Shortly before we left Belgrade, I tried to answer that question in a cable entitled "Who Killed Yugoslavia?" It was intended as an analysis of the fatal elements in Yugoslavia's distant and recent past, laced with some nostalgia for what had been lost. I used as a framework the old English folk song "Who Killed Cock Robin?" a tale of murder complete with witnesses, grave-diggers, and mourners, but nobody to save the victim or bring him back to life. . . .

With the perspective of years, of the Bosnian war, and of many gross misrepresentations of Yugoslavia's collapse, it's important to eliminate some of the reasons often cited. First, Yugoslavia was not destroyed by ancient Balkan hatreds. This doesn't mean that the Balkans don't seethe with violence. The First World War was touched off by the assassination in Sarajevo of an Austrian archduke by a Bosnian Serb; the Second was for Yugoslavia not only a liberation war but a civil war with over half a million Yugoslav deaths.

But is Yugoslavia so unique? Europe, taken as a whole, has endured two civil wars in this century, involving sixty million deaths, including the genocidal annihilation of six million European Jews. Placid England suffered in the fifteenth century the Wars of the Roses, which moved Charles Dickens to remark: "When men continually fight against their own countrymen, they are always observed to be more unnaturally cruel and filled with rage than they are against any other enemy." The English lived through an even bloodier period in the seventeenth century: a king was executed and many of the people of Ireland massacred by Cromwell's forces. France had its wars of religion in the sixteenth century and its blood-drenched revolution in the eighteenth. Nor has the United States been immune from domestic conflict. More Americans died in our civil war than in any foreign war we have ever fought.

Balkan genes aren't abnormally savage. Bosnia enjoyed long periods of tranquility as a multiethnic community. Serbs and Croats, the most antagonistic of adversaries today, had never fought each other before the twentieth century. The millennium they spent as neighbors was marked more by mutual indifference than by mutual hostility. Serbs, though demonized by many as incorrigibly xenophobic, don't fit that stereotype. Milovan Djilas's son Aleksa, author of a brilliant history of nationalism in Yugoslavia, points out that, with all the manipulative tools at Milošević's disposal, it still took him four years to arouse the Serbian population and that, even then, thousands of Serbs fled the country to avoid fighting in Croatia.

The Yugoslav wars can't be explained by theories of inevitable ethnic hatreds, even when such explanations conveniently excuse outsiders from the responsibilities of intervening. There was plenty of racial and historical tinder available in Yugoslavia. But the conflagrations didn't break out through spontaneous combustion. Pyromaniacs were required.

Second, religion wasn't at the heart of Yugoslavia's demise. The Yugoslav wars were primarily ethnic, not religious, wars. The major proponents of destructive nationalism weren't driven by religious faith. Franjo Tudjman had been a communist most of his life; he converted to Catholicism when he turned to nationalist activities. Milošević, a lifelong communist, never, as far as I know, entered a Serbian Orthodox church except for blatant political purposes. I recall a visit he made for electoral reasons to a Serbian monastery on Mt. Athos in northern Greece. Not even the official photographs could disguise the disconcerted and uncomfortable look on his face. Even Bosnia was largely a secular society; a 1985 survey found that only 17 percent of its people considered themselves believers.

None of this absolves the Serbian and Croatian churches. There were many religious people in Yugoslavia, particularly among rural folk. The Serbian Orthodox Church and the Catholic Church in Croatia were willing accomplices of the political leaders in coopting their parishioners for racist designs. These two churches were national churches, in effect arms of their respective states when it came to ethnic matters. They played a disgraceful role by exacerbating racial tensions when they could have urged their faithful toward Christian healing.

With regard to Bosnia, both the Serbian and Croatian regimes felt the need to impute fanatic religiosity to the Muslims in order to satanize them. But the portrayal was false. The Bosnia I knew was probably the most secular Muslim society in the world. The growing number of Muslim adherents today is a consequence of the war, not one of its root causes.

Third, Yugoslavia was not a victim of communism or even of its demise. Yugoslavs didn't live under the Soviet yoke, unlike their neighbors in the Warsaw Pact, for whom communism was an alien and evil implant. Gorbachev's withdrawal from Eastern Europe liberated whole countries but had little direct effect on Yugoslavia, whose communism, whatever its defects, was homegrown. In Eastern Europe the fault line was between communism and Western-style democracy; in Yugoslavia it was between ethnic groups. Tito's relative liberalism within the European communist world coopted many people for the Yugoslav party who would have been Western-oriented dissidents in Czechoslovakia or Poland.

In Yugoslavia the dissidents were for the most part nationalists, not liberals, and they marched to domestic drummers beating out racist, not Western,

themes. Communists in Yugoslavia wore black hats or white hats, depending on whether they were nationalists or not. The most rabid nationalists, like Milošević or Tudjman, were or had been communists. So had many antinationalist, democratic figures, like Drnovšek, Gligorov, Tupurkovski, and many courageous journalists and human rights activists. In most of Eastern Europe, the word "communist" explained a good deal about a person; in Yugoslavia it explained next to nothing.

Fourth, Yugoslavia wasn't destroyed by foreign intervention or the lack of it. General Kadijević, in his paranoid account of the end of Yugoslavia, blames the United States, Germany, and the European Community, acting in collusion with traitors in Slovenia, Croatia, and Kosovo. Foreign countries did make serious mistakes in Yugoslavia, but they didn't destroy it. The failure to do more to support Prime Minister Marković, the lack of a forceful Western reaction to the shelling of Dubrovnik, and the European Community's premature decision to recognize the independence of Yugoslavia's republics were all mistakes, but not fatal ones. Whatever inducements or penalties the West might have devised, they wouldn't have been enough to suppress the nationalistic rage that was overwhelming the country. The war in Bosnia was another matter; there the West could have saved the situation and didn't. But the murder of Yugoslavia was a crime of domestic violence.

The victim itself had congenital defects. Yugoslavia was a state, but not a nation. Few felt much loyalty to Yugoslavia itself. Tito sought to encourage fealty by guaranteeing ethnic autonomy rather than by trying to create an ethnic melting pot. Political energy was directed more toward gaining a better position in Yugoslavia for one's ethnic group than toward preserving the viability of the state. Nobody wanted to be a member of a minority; nobody expected minorities automatically to be protected. Vladimir Gligorov, son of the wise president of Macedonia and a perceptive scholar, captured this feeling when he asked ironically, "Why should I be a minority in your state when you can be a minority in mine?"

These character traits damaged, but didn't doom, Yugoslavia. The country didn't commit suicide. As the court of history pursues its investigation of the death of Yugoslavia, I can imagine the following indictments: Slovenia for selfishness toward its fellow Yugoslavs; Tudjman's Croatia for insensitivity toward its Serbian population and greed toward its Bosnian neighbors; the Yugoslav army for ideological rigidity and arrogance, culminating in war crimes; Radovan Karadžić for attacking the principle of tolerance in Yugoslavia's most ethnically mixed republic; and—most of all—Slobodan Milošević for devising and pursuing a strategy that led directly to the breakup of the country and to the deaths of over a hundred thousand of its citizens. Nationalism was the arrow that killed Yugoslavia. Milošević was the principal bowman.

The Serbian leader made Yugoslavia intolerable for anybody who wasn't a Serb. He is hated among Albanians, Slovenes, Croats, Muslims, Macedonians, and Hungarians. And he has brought his own people into poverty and despair. The potentially prosperous and influential Serbia on which he expatiated in our last meeting in April 1992 is now an economic and civil shambles. Much of its youth and middle class—the foundation of democratic construction —has fled to the west. Milošević's dream of "all Serbs in one state" is a nightmare today; Serbs are now scattered among four states—"Yugoslavia" (Serbia and Montenegro), Bosnia, Croatia, and Macedonia. In seeking to dominate Yugoslavia, Milošević destroyed it. In seeking to tear out the pieces where Serbs lived, he wrecked, for a generation or more, the future of all Serbs.

NO

Steven Majstorovic

ANCIENT HATREDS OR ELITE MANIPULATION? MEMORY AND POLITICS IN THE FORMER YUGOSLAVIA

Any optimism generated by the Dayton peace accords in late 1995 was substantially eroded by events during the spring and summer of 1996. These events marked a protracted and tragic endgame in the former Yugoslavia. The flight from Sarajevo by Bosnian Serbs in February and March 1996 was the first indication of things to come. During the summer, refugees who tried to return to their former homes were harassed and attacked by paramilitary gangs. The early focus was on the behavior of the Bosnian Serbs, but now it is apparent that a policy of ethnic apartheid is being pursued by all sides in Bosnia....

The complexity of the Yugoslav conflict illustrates that the genesis of the war and the issues of ethnonational identity that fed the flames of conflict are far from being understood in any way that reflects some set of shared perspectives among scholars and pundits. For example, the exodus from Sarajevo by the Serbs in February and March 1996 seems to defy logic and rationality. One analytic perspective contends that the war is a product of "ancient hatreds" rooted in primordial identity and consequently any national group that falls under the political control of another is in mortal danger. The experience of some Serbs who left Sarajevo certainly reinforces this contention, as they ran a gauntlet of hostile Bosnian Muslims, supposedly bent on revenge. An opposing perspective views the war as the product of elite manipulation and fear-mongering by ethnic entrepreneurs who fanned the flames of hatred for their own purposes and who manipulated ethnonational identity issues that are themselves just a product of an "invented tradition." Analysts who adhere to the second perspective suggested that Serbs should take hold of their senses, accept the guarantees of the Bosnian-Croat Federation, ignore their leader's warnings, and stay in Sarajevo. Despite assurances, however, the Serbs who stayed in Sarajevo have been continually threatened. Bosnian Prime Minister Hasan Muratovic promised that the violence against Serbs in Sarajevo would be stopped. But unfortunately, most of the Serbs in

From Steven Majstorovic, "Ancient Hatreds or Elite Manipulation? Memory and Politics in the Former Yugoslavia," *World Affairs*, vol. 159, no. 4 (Spring 1997). Copyright © 1997 by The American Peace Society. Reprinted by permission of *World Affairs*. Notes omitted.

Sarajevo now want to leave, including many who were loyal to the Bosnian government during the war.

Clearly, the Yugoslav conflict is an almost ideal laboratory for addressing some of the central questions that scholars of nationalism and ethnicity pose. Those who espouse a primordialist conception of national identity have ample evidence to support their position, while the constructionists also have abundant data that support their contention that national identity is essentially an artificial and modern phenomenon that is often at the mercy of ambitious leaders who manipulate and instrumentalize ethnonational identity.

This [selection] argues that prevailing analyses of ethnic conflict in the former Yugoslavia that focus either on a notion of ancient, primordial hatreds rooted in centuries-old identities, or on the premise that ethnic identity in the Balkans is a modern social construction that has been instrumentalized by political elites, miss the essential nature of the ongoing struggle. Historical memory constrains the options that leaders exercise in conflict creation and in peacemaking. Ethnic identity in the former Yugoslavia, however, has also been and will continue [to] be somewhat flexible and politically adaptive but only within a framework that does not threaten the constraints imposed by myth and memory. The constraints on masses and elites imposed by historical experience and particularly applicable for the Serbs, somewhat less so for the Croats, and even less so for the Bosnian Muslims. The Balkan conflict has both premodern, primordial characteristics and modern, constructed/instrumentalized elements in which ancient antagonisms (sometimes hatreds) and modern politics have both contributed appreciably to the

tragedy, and an overemphasis on either perspective misrepresents the nature of ethnic conflict and politics in the former Yugoslavia. . . .

MEMORY AND MYTH IN SERBIAN, CROATIAN, AND BOSNIAN MUSLIM ETHNONATIONAL IDENTITY

When the term "Balkan politics" is conjured up, a mental picture that many people might have is one of incessant conflict, ethnic tinderboxes, and terrorist plots. This stereotypical view of Balkan politics is not wholly inaccurate. The Balkans have historically been a crossroads for conquest and occupation. The area that is now Yugoslavia was settled by the migration of Slavic tribes during the sixth century. Those tribes were independent until the beginning of the twelfth century, when the Croatians yielded to Hungarian political dominance, and until the beginning of the fifteenth century when the Serbians were defeated by the Ottoman Turks. External rule from Austria, Hungary, Italy, or Turkey lasted until the beginning of the twentieth century, although in a series of revolts the Serbs had formed an independent state by the middle of the nineteenth century.

In addition to being distinguished from each other by self-defined differences in tribal custom and culture, the South Slavs were further differentiated by the split in the Christian church. As a consequence, the Croats and Slovenes identified with Roman Catholicism, while the Serbs were under the jurisdiction of Byzantium and had formed by the thirteenth century an independent Serbian Orthodox Church. This division between East and West was reinforced when the Eastern Orthodox Serbs fell under Turkish rule, while the

Croats and Slovenes answered to Rome and Hungary, and eventually to the Austro-Hungarian Empire. Thus, when the South Slavs were brought into a common state in 1918, the stage for ethnonational conflict had been set by a thousand years of history.

Serbian identity can best be understood as a combination of three historical experiences: the memory of the Battle of Kosovo in 1389 and the subsequent five hundred years of servitude and resistance against the Ottoman Turks; the successful revolts against the Turks early in the nineteenth century that culminated in an independent Serbian state by the middle of the century; and the role of the Serbs as allies of the West in two World Wars.

By the fourteenth century, the Serbs under Tsar Dusan had grown into a medieval empire that spanned the Balkans from the Adriatic to Western Bulgaria and to most of Albania and some areas in northern Greece. After his death in 1355, centralized power started to ebb, and various Serb nobles started to unravel the system set up by Dusan. In 1371, however, Prince Lazar came to power and a temporary recentralization of control was established. This short period ended at Kosovo Polje (The Field of Blackbirds) on 28 June 1389.

The battle between the Serb forces of Prince Lazar and the Ottoman Turks was at the time perceived as either a pyrrhic victory for the Turks or indecisive. The Serbian state survived for another seventy years before finally succumbing to Ottoman rule. However, the cataclysmic nature of a battle in which Prince Lazar and his son were beheaded, the Turkish Sultan Murad disemboweled by the Serbian knight Milos Obilic, and in which there were

horrific losses on both sides (over 100,000 deaths in an eight-to-ten-hour battle) created a myth-making apparatus that has shaped Serbian consciousness to this day.

The battle decimated the Serb nobility and cost the Ottomans dearly. Almost immediately, Serbian poets, priests, and peasants started to propagate the notion of Christian martyrdom by the Serbian people, Prince Lazar, and Milos Oblic. The primordialization of the event had all the elements of a passion play played out in real life. Interestingly enough, the perspective of the Ottoman Turks only reinforces the Serbian myths:

> Yet this Ottoman view in some ways mirrors traditional Serbian views. Both the Ottoman and Serbian accounts emphasize the battle's cataclysmic nature. Both traditions have martyrdom as a theme.

Added to this vision shared between the Serbs and the Turks, the battle itself is routinely listed in historical surveys as one of the most important events in history. The result of all this valorization is an identity marker that is so rooted in real historical events that it is almost impossible for Serbs to escape its ubiquitous presence in Serbian identity.

Also a part of the Kosovo myth is the tale of migration by Serbs from Kosovo, the failed attempts to migrate back over a period of centuries, and the final triumphant return to Kosovo in 1912. Taken together, these events, which were kept alive by the Serbian Orthodox church in the liturgy and by traveling troubadours who annually embellished the story in an ever-growing epic poem ("The Kosovo Cycle"), suggest that even the horrible events in Bosnia may have been less destructive than the potential for catastrophe in the Serbian province of Kosovo that is today 90 percent Albanian.

The memory of an independent state that was relinquished to form the Kingdom of South Slavs is also a critical part of Serb identity. The theme of successful revolt and emancipation dominates the mythicizing of the Balkan Wars. Finally, the Serbian role in World War I and World War II completes the picture. Serbs suffered enormous losses in both wars and continually stress their part in the Allied victories, comparing their role to Croat, Bosnian Muslim, and Albanian collaboration. In particular, the role of General Draza Mihailovich and the Chetnik resistance in World War II is highlighted, as archival evidence has suggested a reassessment of [Josip Broz] Tito and the role of the partisans.

Surprisingly, Serbs do not consider the genocidal policies of the Croatian Ustasha state and their Bosnian Muslim allies during World War II as an important element of Serbian identity. Instead, the events are often used as a way to stereotype all Croatians and Muslims by both Serb masses and elites. In particular, the Ustasha- and Muslim-led genocide of Serbs in Croatia and Bosnia in World War II has been the key to understanding Bosnian Serb and Croatian Serb propaganda and military mobilization strategies against Croats and Muslims in the contemporary period. Both Rodovan Karadzic and Ratko Mladic, the Bosnian Serb military leader, have used the events of World War II to successfully demonize Croats and Muslims in the eyes of the Serbs.

Croatian identity also has a memory of a medieval kingdom, but one that peacefully gave up its sovereignty to the Hungarian crown in 1102. The project of identity primordialization by the Croats has been to present events since 1102 as evidence for the continuity of a Croatian state in waiting. The keys to this continuity are peasant uprisings, a succession of Croatian kings, advances in Croatian culture and learning that depict Croatia as a part of a Western European culture that is distinct from the Serbs, and the unbroken reality of Croatian national consciousness that goes back to the seventh century. What is often ignored by Serbs is that it was the efforts of Croat intellectuals and church leaders in the nineteenth century that first broached the idea of a single South Slav state.

Croatian identity is also tied to the Catholic church and its role in resisting Serbian dominance in the interwar period. The issue of Serbian dominance is hotly debated between Serbs and Croats. While Croats refer to Serbian dominance, Serbs refer to Croat obstructionism. The debate haś no resolution, but by 1938 Croatia did win considerable autonomy from Belgrade and was, effectively, a state within a state.

Another part of the Croatian primordialization project is to address the events of World War II by minimizing the Ustasha aspect and emphasizing the role of the Croats in the partisan resistance led by Tito. This interpretation, however, is also open for debate between Croats and Serbs, since most sources that address Tito's partisan movement make it clear that an overwhelming majority of the partisans were Serbs, and that many Croatians did not join until Tito, a Croat, offered a pardon at the end of 1943 to anyone who joined the partisans, although Tito's action did alienate many Serb partisans. It should also be noted that many Serb renegade units participated in revenge massacres against Croatian and

Muslim civilians toward the end of World War II. These killings numbered in the thousands and are remembered by Croats and Muslims who insist that the slaughter was mutual and that the world has tended to ignore Croatian and Muslim victims of World War II.

Croatian identity is also reinforced by the failure of the Croatian Republic to separate from Yugoslavia during what is called the Croatian Crises or Croatian Spring of 1968–72. The crises started out as an attempt to liberalize the economic and political system. But the movement was eventually taken over by nationalist elements who pushed for Croatian independence. An alarmed Tito brutally ended the movement and purged the Croatian party of liberals. He then did the same thing to the Serbian party to effect some semblance of ethnic symmetry. Unfortunately, many of the liberals who were purged in both the Serbian and Croatian Communist parties were the type of leaders who might have been effective in heading off the level of conflict in the Yugoslav conflict of 1991–95. But it is from the experience of 1968–72 that many Croatians today stereotype Serbs as conservative Communists while Croats see themselves as liberal democrats in the Western tradition. It was also during the period of the Croatian Crises that Franjo Tudjman became a staunch nationalist who started to write revisionist tracts about what he labeled the myth of the number of Serbian deaths in World War II.

The next element in the continual primordialization of Croatian identity will become the successful secession from Yugoslavia in 1991, Croatian suffering at the hands of the Serbs, and the German-led recognition by the world community.

Pronouncements from Zagreb seem to support this view, although it is still too early for any complete evaluation.

Until the Bosnian war and the siege of Sarajevo began in 1992, Bosnian Muslim identity was essentially a tug of war between Serbian, Croatian, and Bosnian Muslim interpretations of history. The Serb perspective is that the Muslims are Islamicized Slavs who were mostly Serbs. The Croat view is that these same Slavs were Catholic Croats. Some Bosnian Muslims, however, claim that they are descended from the Bogomils, who were a heretic Manechean sect. Moreover, many Muslim intellectuals during the nineteenth century started to claim that the Bogomils were really Turks from Anatolia and that the "only thing Slavic about the Bosnian Muslims is their language, which they absorbed from the indigenous population." There are also perspectives that contend that the Bogomils were much more than a sect and that contemporary Bosnian Serbs are not really Serbs but an offshoot of the Vlachs, a sheep-herding people related to the Rumanians.

Muslim ethnic identity got a boost in 1971 when they were officially declared a nationality by the Tito regime. He thought that this declaration might end the warring claims for Muslim identity by the Serbs and Croats. Tito's rationale was that the creation of Bosnia-Hercegovina as a republic at the end of World War II had outlived its usefulness as a buffer between the Croats and the Serbs and that some other policy was necessary.

There are many recent works that present the history of Bosnia as generally one of interethnic harmony and cooperation. But it is [Robert J.] Donia and [John V. A.] Fine's thorough research that, despite their contentions, highlights very ancient roots of the conflict in Bosnia. They present a rich chronology of Bosnian life from antiquity to the present tragedy. Their most important contribution is the thorough and impressive debunking of the incessant claims of Croatian and Serbian chauvinists. Serb nationalists produce evidence that most Bosnian Muslims are Orthodox Serbs who were forcibly converted to Islam by the Ottoman Turks, while Croat nationalists argue that Bosnian Muslims are by blood the "truest" and "purest" of Catholic Croats who were led astray by the Turks.

The conversion to Islam in Bosnia was characterized by a very complex process. Bosnian Muslims were once Slavic Christians who were neither Serbs nor Croats but had a distinct Bosnian identity and belonged to a Bosnian church that ostensibly bowed toward Rome, a fact that Croats seize upon to make their claims. But the rites of this church closely followed the Eastern Orthodox model, which Serbs contend establishes Serbian identity. But what is most evident is that the Bosnian church was never well established, there were few priests, and the Bosnian Slavic peasants maintained only a tenuous tie to Christianity. Thus, with the Ottoman penetration into Bosnia in the fifteenth century, these peasants began a gradual conversion to Islam in a pragmatic decisionmaking process that took between one and two centuries. Moreover, the contention by some modern Bosnian Muslim scholars that Muslim identity was never Christian but instead sprang from the Bogomils, a sect that rejected Christianity and its rituals, is also refuted by evidence that the Bogomils in Bosnia were very few in number and were never influential in the development of Bosnian history.

Eventually, Muslims adapted to the erosion of Ottoman hegemony, the nineteenth century influence of the Austro-Hungarian empire, the Balkan Wars and World War I, the first Yugoslavia in which Serbs predominated, World War II, the Tito period in which the Muslims finally gained official status as a nation in Bosnia, and the final degeneration into civil war. During this period, the Muslims often exhibited a predilection for compromise and pragmatism, especially after the fall of the Ottoman empire, as the Muslims formed political parties and interest groups whose purpose was to tread the narrow balance point between blatant Croat and Serb attempts to capture their loyalty. Throughout the period, the tolerant, cooperative, and multicultural nature of Bosnian society is stressed by Bosnian Muslim nationalists. But a closer examination reveals that Bosnian society was somewhat less tolerant and harmonious than some would contend.

The constructionist and instrumentalist perspectives suggest that Croat and Serb ethnic consciousness did not exist in Bosnia prior to the nineteenth century and that the often mentioned notion that the current war is based on "ancient hatreds" is false. But history presents a more complex picture. It is clear that the development of medieval Bosnia did not occur in isolation and was closely connected to events in Serbia and Croatia. Also, the Ottoman millet system identified ethnic groups by religion instead of ethnicity. Consequently, it is often mistakenly assumed that since the Turks used a non-ethnic marker to identify Croats and Serbs, a pre-nineteenth-century Croat and Bosnian ethnicity did not exist. But Serbian settlers started moving into Bosnia by the early fifteenth century to escape Ottoman expansion into Kosovo, the Serbian heartland. After some initial migration of Croats out of Bosnia, the Franciscan order successfully helped to maintain a Croat presence in the area of western Bosnia known as Hercegovina. Furthermore, the Austrians offered Serbs land to act as a military buffer against the Turks, and by the seventeenth century Serbs occupied the Krajina in Croatia and adjacent areas in Bosnia. Croat and Serb consciousness was well established and was not simply a construction of nineteenth-century nationalism.

In the social system built by the Ottomans, the Muslim converts were landowners and freeholders, and the overwhelming majority of peasants, who were taxed heavily and lived as second-class citizens, were Serbs, along with a number of Croats. The peasants, especially the Serbs, who lived in this Jim Crow system chafed at the inequities and started to revolt by the nineteenth century. Of particular interest to a contemporary understanding of ethnic frictions is that, as the Ottoman empire eroded and was forced to make concessions to subject populations, it was in Bosnia where the local Muslim landlords were the most reactionary and hostile to any changes that threatened their paramountcy.

If the above-recounted issues are not evidence of "ancient hatreds," then at least there was fertile ground in Bosnia for ancient antagonisms. When it came to manipulating public opinion, Milosevic in Serbia and Tudjman in Croatia are often cited as architects of the war in Bosnia. However, Bosnian President Alija Izetbegovic should not be left off the hook. His role in the war, his rather radical political views, and his reneging on the Lisbon Agreement of 1992 that would have maintained a multiethnic

Bosnia need to be examined closely. Still, it is clear from the evidence that despite the protestations of extremist Serbs and Croats, the reality of a Muslim national identity is undeniable. The notion of a Bosnia in multiethnic harmony before the current struggle is an insupportable myth that could be maintained only by a centralized Communist system. When Tito died and the system collapsed, history started to catch up rather quickly.

It should be apparent that at this point Muslim identity is still in the process of primordialization. The sieges of Sarajevo and Mostar and the killing fields of Srebrenica will be the building blocks as Kosovo was for the Serbs. Instead of historical records and oral history, the Bosnian Muslims will have access to videotapes, and Benedict Anderson's notion of the printing press as a vehicle for the imaging of identity has evolved to NPR and PBS. The Bosnian Muslims are quickly moving from being Yugoslavs to Bosnian Muslims, and women wearing veils have started to appear in villages and even on the streets of Sarajevo. Moreover, the flirtation with Islamic forces from the Middle East, particularly Iran, has been recently documented.

In contrast to Muslim identity, Serbian identity is rooted in a centuries-old primordialization project. Despite Milosevic's manipulation of the Serbian media and elections, the force of elite manipulation in an instrumentalist fashion is not as significant as one would think for Serbian identity today because Milosevic, or any democratic alternative to him, would be constrained by history from stepping too far outside the successful Kosovo-inspired primordialization of identity. There are even arguments that in the case of the Serbs it is the elites who have been shaped by the memories and the myths of the masses. The Serbs, more than the Croats or Muslims, are shackled by their view of history and may not be able to escape what they see as an apocalyptic destiny, a destiny that unfortunately combines national paranoia with a sense of a messianic mission to defend Christianity from the mounting forces of Islam.

The Croatian model represents an ethnic identity that is still in the process of primordialization, which is committed to reinforce the notion of a thousand-year history. This project is augmented by a heavy dose of instrumentalism as President Tudjman and his supporters on the Right try to hold onto the power and privileges that they enjoyed during the Communist era. An example of this effort is the release of the new Croatian currency during May 1994. The new currency is called the "Kuna" and refers to a forest marten. The only memory of this currency dates back to the Ustasha regime, and Jews and Serbs in Croatia have protested in vain. Croatian historians, some quite reluctantly, have scrambled to discover or perhaps imagine instances where marten skins have been used in trade within Croatia during the past thousand years. Some isolated instances have been discovered and so the process of primordialization continues.

Moreover, the Croats, as they did during the 1960s, have recently declared that Croat is a separate language from Serbian and have introduced numerous words that go back to Slavic anachronisms from the past. Differences in dialect between Serbian, Croatian, and Bosnian are probably less pronounced, according to most linguists, than between American and British English. But the process of identity differentiation through language policy is in high gear. In reaction, the Serbs and the Bosnian Muslims have also jumped on the bandwagon, and perhaps in five hundred years there will be three different languages created from the current Serbo-Croation.

The Muslims are in some sense the most free to pursue their own vision of an ethnic identity. Without a Kosovo or a thousand-year state to guide them, they are in a Big Bang period of imagining their place in the world. The process of primordialization occurs under the watchful eye of the world, and the instrumental policies of the government in Sarajevo are profoundly tied to this process. Primordialist, constructivist, and instrumentalist categories have collapsed upon each other in Sarajevo, and the Bosnian Muslims have the luxury of picking and choosing, although there is growing evidence that their role as absolute victim is starting to come under question as more recent evidence has started to point toward a more symmetrical structure of suffering in the current conflict. Choices for the Croats are more limited but still possible.

The Serbs are fanatically committed to a mythic identity that may not allow choices, even if they desire them. Moreover, the Serbs have already started to mythicize the expulsion of 250,000 civilians from the Krajina region of Croatia, an expulsion that the United States refrained from labeling "ethnic cleansing." The Serbs have also started to focus on the slaughter of Serbs in the Srebrenica area before the Bosnian Serb army atrocities of July 1995 as new fodder for their continued vision of martyrdom. If the Serbs cannot break out of a primordialization process that has exhausted itself, then the outlook for the Balkans is very bleak indeed, and the post-Dayton events of 1996 may be the harbinger of tragedy when the NATO forces leave Bosnia.

The complexity of the ethnic conflict in the former Yugoslavia has illustrated the difficulty of mono-causal analyses. Despite the penchant in postmodern analysis for stressing the decentered person who can change identities like clothing, ethnonational identity often predisposes people to dispense with rational decisionmaking and instead embrace a policy of radical ethnic altruism in which lives are sacrificed. And although the examination of elite behavior is part and parcel of the methodology of social scientists, this methodology falls short when historically rooted conflicts are examined. In the dark street of available data, it is elite behavior that is lit by the lamp at the end of the street. But it is the rest of the street in which the richness and cultural thickness of memory, myth, and shared experience lurks in shadows. The data in these shadows are often difficult to measure empirically. We must, however, seriously consider their validity lest we ignore them at great cost to future peacemaking and conflict resolution.

POSTSCRIPT

Were Ethnic Leaders Responsible for the Disintegration of Yugoslavia?

The biggest loss caused by the disintegration of Yugoslavia is to the country's people. They are the ones who have been driven from their homes, placed in "detention centers," beaten, humiliated, raped, and brutally murdered in frighteningly high numbers. The actual number of the displaced, humiliated, tortured, and dead is hard to come by, given the fluid and anarchic nature of the Yugoslavian battleground. Most chilling has been the use of the term *ethnic cleansing* to describe the "Balkan killing fields," conjuring up memories of the Nazi Holocaust. In support of such indictments, charges of genocide and "crimes against humanity" have been leveled against many former Yugoslavs, both participants in the crimes and the leaders who may have ordered or permitted them. Thus far, only some of the former have been brought to trial. Whether the latter will ever be tried remains to be seen.

It is in Bosnia-Herzegovina where many agree the suffering has been the greatest, most of it caused by forces outside the province whose actions were supposed to support their ethnic "cousins" living there. And what was the end result of all this suffering?

After years of neglect by the outside world, it is ironic that it took the disintegration of Yugoslavia to bring the country adequate attention. Many books on the subject have been written recently, and some writers have attempted to look at this crisis through the eyes of its victims, such as Roger Cohen in *Hearts Grow Brutal: Sagas of Sarajevo* (Random House, 1998). Laura Silber and Allan Little's *Yugoslavia: Death of a Nation* (Penguin Books, 1997) gives a blow-by-blow account of Yugoslavia's disintegration. It is a concise, chronological account of the last 10 years of the country's existence. Some works have examined the genocide factor; a useful anthology on this subject is Thomas Cushman and Stjepan Mestrovic, eds., *This Time We Knew: Western Responses to Genocide in Bosnia* (New York University Press, 1998). For those who need some historical background on Yugoslavia's past, see John R. Lampe's *Yugoslavia As History: Twice There Was a Country* (Cambridge University Press, 1996).

A final source recommendation is from noted writer Michael Ignatieff, who has written a small volume entitled *The Warrior's Code: Ethnic War and the Modern Conscience* (Henry Holt, 1997). The entire book is thought-provoking and well presented, but of particular value to the study of the disintegration of Yugoslavia is the chapter entitled "The Narcissism of Minor Difference," in which he attempts to take a Freudian view on the subject of human motivation and behavior as it existed in this former country.

ISSUE 24

Will the Oslo Peace Accords Benefit Both Israelis and Palestinians?

YES: Mark Perry, from *A Fire in Zion: The Israeli-Palestinian Search for Peace* (William Morrow and Company, 1994)

NO: Edward W. Said, from *Peace and Its Discontents* (Vintage Books, 1996)

ISSUE SUMMARY

YES: Journalist Mark Perry was allowed access to major participants of the Israeli and Palestinian peace process. He states that, as a result of the Oslo peace accords, Israel is returning to its borders, as well as its ideals, and that Palestine is reinvigorating the movement for national independence.

NO: Columbia University professor Edward W. Said insists that peace was not achieved by the signing of the Oslo Agreement; instead, Israel achieved all its tactical and strategic objectives at the expense of the Arab and Palestinian struggle for national independence.

The century-long struggle between Israelis and Palestinians can be traced to Jewish nationalist movement founder Theodor Herzl's call for the establishment of a Jewish state in Palestine during the First Zionist Congress in 1897. The concept was endorsed by British foreign secretary Lord Balfour in the Balfour Declaration of 1917 and codified in a League of Nations mandate, giving Britain control of the region. Hostilities erupted in the 1930s as thousands of Jews, fleeing anti-Semitism in Europe, arrived in the region. This sparked a Palestinian national revolution.

A British white paper in 1939 restricted Jewish immigration and proposed partitioning the mandate into separate Jewish and Arab states, a compromise rejected by the Arab leadership, which insisted on an all-or-nothing resolution. Following the Nazi Holocaust, world sympathy pushed the United Nations to endorse the partitioning of Palestine to create a Jewish state. Israel came into being the following year, and over the next two decades established itself as a modern democracy. During the 1967 Six-Day War, Israel conquered and took possession of the West Bank (of the Jordan River) and the Gaza Strip, which Israel continued to occupy until 1993. In 1969, Yasser Arafat assumed leadership of the Palestine Liberation Organization (PLO).

At the end of the 1991 Persian Gulf War, U.S. secretary of state James Baker began a series of trips to the Middle East, designed to persuade Arab states and Israel to attend an international peace conference. As part of the Middle

East peace process, bilateral talks between Israeli and Palestinian delegations opened in Madrid, Spain, in November 1991. These talks continued through ten rounds, concluding in June of 1993. In January of that year secret talks between Israel and the PLO began in Norway, culminating in a "declaration of Principles on Interim Self-Government Arrangements," which was initialed on August 19, 1993, and formally announced in Washington a month later.

President Bill Clinton, who had been elected the previous November, was eager to create an image of friendship, sealed by a handshake between the PLO's Arafat and Yitzhak Rabin, prime minister of Israel. It may have been Rabin's decision to seal off the occupied territories in 1993 that made the peace process possible. Many thought his own assassination two years later was inevitable. Giving away "Jewish land" was regarded by some as worthy of the death penalty.

Mark Perry sees Rabin as a realist, who recognized in 1993 that Israel was becoming a bilingual Arabic and Hebrew state and that the wave of Jewish immigrants from the Russian states after the collapse of the Soviet Union was likely to be the last. In addition, Perry asserts, Rabin was uncomfortable with Israel as an occupying army in the West Bank and Gaza and understood that to return to its founding ideals Israel would have to let go of the conquered territories. Having seen war firsthand, Rabin was unwilling to continue the inevitable bloodshed. In Perry's view, Arafat needed the peace process to maintain PLO dominance and, in addition, he was discouraged by the results of the all-or-nothing approach in 1939.

Both Israelis and Palestinians needed to revitalize their national movements and, in a unique historical moment, set aside a century-long struggle in order to begin that journey. Perry sees the peace initiative agreed to in Oslo as an ongoing process, involving both negotiation and what Itamak Rabinovich, Israeli ambassador to the United States, called "a crucial exchange of complex national narratives."

Edward W. Said disagrees with Perry. In his judgment, a weakened Arafat and untrained negotiators capitulated unnecessarily to Israeli demands. Said argues that as long as Israeli settlements in the West Bank and Gaza continue, whether or not there is an occupying army, the situation is still considered to be occupation. When his own family became refugees from Palestine in the 1948 creation of the state of Israel, Said began hoping for a Palestinian homeland. The current process, in his view, does nothing to further that hope. Indeed, Said blames a "slave mentality" for the acceptance of a harsh "pax Americana" (American peace) under which Israel controls all the crucial variables—land, water, security, and foreign policy. He sees the Oslo accords as a betrayal of the Palestinian cause as he awaits both a new vision and new leadership.

YES

Mark Perry

A FIRE IN ZION:
THE ISRAELI-PALESTINIAN
SEARCH FOR PEACE

PROLOGUE

On September 13, 1993, Israeli Prime Minister Yitzhak Rabin and Palestine Liberation Organization [PLO] Chairman Yasser Arafat took a giant step toward ending one of the world's longest and most bitter conflicts. The declaration of principles that was negotiated by a small group of Palestinian and Israeli diplomats in Oslo, Norway—and then signed by their leaders on the White House lawn that mid-September morning—stunned the world. The handshake between Rabin and Arafat began to draw down the curtain on four decades of conflict between Israel and its most intransigent enemy. The signing of the Israel-PLO declaration of principles began the slow process of reconciliation that has as its goal the end of one hundred years of unremitting strife between Jews and Arabs over control of Palestine. During that struggle, thousands of Israelis, Palestinians, Egyptians, Lebanese, Jordanians, and Syrians died in battle; hundreds of thousands were displaced; and thousands of others were taken prisoner, maimed, widowed, orphaned, or confined in fetid refugee camps.

While the White House ceremony dominated the news in the weeks that followed, no one believed that all the years of enmity and bloodshed could be forgiven by the single stroke of a pen, or that decades of misunderstanding and bitterness could be forgotten by a simple handshake. So while the airwaves and newspaper columns trumpeted the fact that Rabin had actually shaken Arafat's hand, many knew that true understanding and cooperation would be much more difficult to achieve. It was one thing for national leaders to meet at a ceremony in Washington, and quite another for Palestinians and Israelis to learn to live with one another in peace.

One of the Palestinians who knew this best was Salah Ta'mari, an exile from the village of Za'tara near Bethlehem in the occupied West Bank, a senior PLO official, and a veteran of some of its most famous battles. Ta'mari, who has lived in the United States, was invited to the ceremony but decided to watch it on television. When Arafat left his suite at a downtown Washington hotel for the ride to the White House early on the morning of September 13, Ta'mari reached out his hand to the PLO chief and wished him luck. Arafat motioned him to come along, but Ta'mari shook his head; he was unimpressed by the trappings of power and had difficulty measuring the sacrifice of the hundreds of Palestinians he had led in battles in Jordan and Lebanon against the celebratory atmosphere that greeted the news of the accord. "There has been so much death," he said, "and we have so much work to do. The conflict remains, but the form of the engagement is different."

Itamar Rabinovich had similar feelings. As the Israeli ambassador to the United States, a leading expert on Arab affairs, the former rector of Tel Aviv University, and one of Israel's best-known intellectuals, Rabinovich harbored a view of the Israeli-Palestinian search for peace that was almost mystical. He understood how much of the past both sides had to put aside and how daunting the future remained. "In many ways, our negotiations with the Palestinians have gone beyond a simple discussion of differing political positions," he once said. "We are instead learning about each other's beliefs and fundamental principles. This is much more than a negotiation. We are now engaged in a crucial exchange of complex national narratives."

Rabinovich welcomed the PLO-Israeli accord, but like Ta'mari he found it difficult to get caught up in the atmosphere of triumph that greeted news of its signing. He was subdued when he left to attend the ceremony at the White House.

Ta'mari and Rabinovich's skepticism was by no means unique. While thousands of Palestinians celebrated the Israel-PLO agreement in the streets of Jericho in the West Bank, hundreds of thousands of others in the refugee camps of Lebanon, Syria, and Jordan looked on Arafat's agreement as an admission of defeat. And while a majority of Israelis applauded Rabin's new opening to the PLO, few of them believed the agreement guaranteed a future without threats of fear. On both sides, the declaration negotiated in secret in Oslo and then signed with great fanfare in Washington was viewed as an uneasy settlement to a nearly intractable problem: It was not a perfect solution, and perhaps not even a very good one, but it was the best that could be had under the circumstances.

Ta'mari and Rabinovich are fitting symbols of the Palestinian-Israeli struggle, for while they are starkly different personalities, their views of the conflict are almost identical. For Ta'mari, the agreement was neither an end nor a beginning. "We meet our enemy on many different levels," he said after the signing, "and even when we face the Israelis across a table, the exchange is as serious as it was when we fought them on the battlefields of Jordan twenty years ago." Ta'mari's words echoed Rabinovich's view—that the exchange of "complex national narratives" is part of a continuing process. The signing of the Israel-PLO declaration of principles was a significant political event and an integral part of a long and complex discussion between two very different peoples. But the transaction has yet to be concluded.

If the ceremony and the handshake that took place on the White House lawn were so difficult to carry through, and if the two sides still had so much work to do and so much remaining enmity and mistrust to overcome, then why come to Washington at all? What motivated their leaders to begin the serious search for peace? . . .

Until the late nineteenth century, a small but distinct Jewish community was all that remained in Palestine after the Romans destroyed the temple in Jerusalem and drove the Jews into exile in A.D. 70. The native Jews who remained were farmers who lived side by side with Arabs in small communities or in villages along the Mediterranean coast.

When Jews first began to return to Palestine in large numbers, they found a land of Arab farmers and few cities; Jerusalem was no more than a medium-sized trading town and Tel Aviv was a very small village. Many of the early Zionist settlers put down roots along the Mediterranean coast and built scattered agricultural settlements among the Arab towns. The movement of Jews out of Europe increased after 1897, when Theodor Herzl called for the establishment of a Jewish state in Palestine during the First Zionist Congress. After an intense lobbying campaign during the First World War, Zionist leaders convinced the British government to support their cause. In 1917, the idea of a Jewish national home was endorsed in a declaration issued by Lord Balfour, the British foreign secretary. While there were only fifty thousand Jews in Palestine at the time, Balfour's declaration, and a League of Nations mandate giving Britain control of the region, permanently transformed the political climate of Arab society.

The first organized political opposition to the British policy came in 1922, when Palestinian Arabs closed their shops and flew black flags of mourning to protest rising Jewish immigration. For Arab farmers and merchants living under the Mandate, the arrival of European Jews armed with the new political weaponry of Zionism spelled economic and social ruin. With the approval of the British government, more and more Jewish settlements began to intrude on Arab land. The breaking point came on a summer night in 1929, when a group of Zionists from the new Jewish city of Tel Aviv planted their flag on Jerusalem's Wailing Wall, which sits at a holy site for both Jews and Muslims. The riots that followed claimed the lives of over 130 Jews. But the Arab threat to the growing Jewish community did not stem the tide of new immigrants: Pushed by growing anti-Semitism in Europe, many tens of thousands of Jews arrived in Palestine in the mid-1930s.

The growing conflict between Jews and Arabs reached a fever pitch in 1936, when hostilities broke out between the two communities. Led by Haj Amin al-Husseini, their chief religious figure, and Abd al-Qadir al-Husseini, the son of the former mayor of Jerusalem, the Arab inhabitants fought a series of brutal engagements against the British and Zionists. The Arab Revolt ravaged the Palestinian countryside for three years before the British government succeeded in imprisoning or expelling its leaders and suppressing its armed brigades. For five days, Jerusalem itself was under siege as British troops rooted out Arab guerrillas who had barricaded themselves inside the high stone houses of the Old City.

Zionist immigration sparked what Haj Amin and Abd al-Qadir could never have accomplished by themselves; it gave birth to the Palestinian national revolution. While it did not have the financial resources of Palestine's Jewish community or the modern tactics and weaponry adopted by the more adept Jewish political organizations, by the late 1930s Palestinian nationalism presented a formidable challenge to the Zionist community. The uprising of the 1930s also transformed British policies in the Mandate.

The Arab Revolt convinced British authorities that their pro-Zionist policy should be tempered to reflect Arab national aspirations. Britain retreated from the Balfour Declaration and, in 1939, issued a White Paper severely restricting Jewish immigration. Soon thereafter, various proposals began to circulate calling for the partition of the Mandate into Jewish and Arab states. The Arab leadership, however, consistently rejected these proposals, thereby setting an all-or-nothing precedent that was to be followed with disastrous consequences in the Palestinian community for the next six decades. The events that followed are well known: The United Nations endorsed the partition of Palestine in 1947, Israel was founded in 1948, and its borders were established after a short war against the Arab states.

The Jewish leaders of Israel erected a stable, economically viable, democratic state with strong ties to the world's superpower—the United States. Israel's government stood the test of time: It weathered the 1948 War of Independence, staggered the world by defeating the combined armies of its adversaries during the Six Day War in 1967, and reunited Jerusalem under its rule. But just when the nation seemed at the very height of its powers—when it was bathing in the afterglow of its most astounding military triumph—things began to go wrong.

When Israel's armies conquered the West Bank and Gaza Strip in 1967, they inherited responsibility for the lives of some one and a half million Palestinians. The new conquests presented the young state with difficult problems: While Israel claimed the lands of the West Bank as their ancestral home, they could not just "transfer" the Palestinian population to Jordan; the word itself conjured memories of the Holocaust. Nor could Israel assimilate the Palestinians, at least not if it wanted to retain its essential character as a Jewish state. The only choice left was to continue to occupy the West Bank and Gaza Strip until a political settlement resolved the conflict, or until the Palestinians of the territories left of their own accord.

Israel was founded by a group of idealists who believed they could establish a Jewish state on their ancestral lands. But the new nation was not conceived as merely a place of refuge; Zionist leaders were dedicated to creating a new Jew and repudiating a past that marked their people as perpetual victims. Freed from the ghettos of Eastern Europe, the early Zionists believed that Jewish society and culture would flourish if they were left unfettered by the destructive anti-Semitism that haunted the Jewish diaspora. Zionism demanded strong, proud, and nationalist adherents. The early socialist agricultural settlements of Palestine were built with an eye toward molding a cohesive, self-reliant community that could rebuild ancient Israel's claim to be a moral compass for the world.

The continued occupation of Arab lands after 1967 slowly undermined this view, and, inevitably perhaps, the foundations of Zionism's ideals—and its utopian exhortations—began to crumble. The very nature of military occupation and the necessities of national security pushed the Israeli government to adopt policies at variance with their movement's original ideals. Systematic economic expropriations, reliance on cheap Arab labor, and the everyday abrogation of individual rights subverted Israel's claim that it represented a new kind of society. Zionism had called the Jewish people to Palestine in order to build a new society and to repudiate the legacy of victimization. Now that dream was being undermined and, for some, Israel was becoming just another nation of victimizers.

* * *

Just as Israel's interaction with Arab society transformed Zionism, so the Arab engagement with Israel transformed the Palestinian community. The patriarchal social structure of the Mandate's Arab order was annihilated by the 1948 catastrophe and the Palestinian people were set adrift in the Arab world. For twenty years, from 1948 to 1968, Palestinian society was plunged into a state of political and social chaos. It was not until Yasser Arafat assumed the leadership of the PLO, in 1969, that Palestinians were able to begin rebuilding the national movement that had been sparked by the Arab Revolt three decades before.

Like all revolutions, the birth of Palestinian nationalism has been marked by bloody confrontations. At times, the Palestinian struggle has been more of a civil war than a single-minded national conflict against a recognized foe: In the forty-five years since the founding of Israel, more Palestinians have died at the hands of their conationalists than at the hands of the Israeli enemy. This inconvenient truth has been as difficult for Palestinians to admit as it has been for Israelis to acknowledge that their dream of a peaceful and prosperous Jewish state is still far from reality. By the end of 1987, both societies seemed locked in an endless and crippling battle.

Nevertheless, over the last seven years, key Israeli and Palestinian leaders have come to the realization that they could only reinvigorate their national movements by resolving their century-long battle. Ironically, the fears that permeated both their societies and moved their national leaders to the bargaining table were remarkably similar.

After years of hopeless struggle and sacrifice, the Palestinian leadership began to fear that by the time they had realized their dream of a national state, their movement would be drowned in a sea of hatred that would destroy their own society. The greatest anxiety among the intellectual and political elite of Israeli society, on the other hand, was *not* that they would be annihilated by their Arab enemies—Israel had never been stronger —but that they would be consumed by their own dread of those with whom they shared the land; that in their overwhelming fear for themselves, they would do unto others what had been done for over two thousand years to them, that they would lose the Zionist dream.

Individual Israelis and Palestinians have been trying to come to an understanding with each other since the founding of the Jewish state. But it has only been since 1987 that the contacts between the two sides have been matched by a serious commitment to resolve their differences....

EPILOGUE

In looking back at the Oslo channel and the Washington handshake from a distance of only a few months, American, Israeli, and Palestinian commentators were nearly unanimous in pointing out that a number of incontrovertible facts made the signing of the Israel-PLO declaration of principles inevitable. The most important of these was the fact of Israel itself. Israel had been in existence for over forty years and the nation's leadership had successfully created a stable, democratic, and economically viable nation where none had existed before. Israel was well armed and supported by the last remaining superpower.

But there were other facts.

Israel was alone. After forty years, it was not even close to becoming accepted in the Middle East, and its neighbors seemed more distant than ever. The Israeli economy was booming, but it was not part of a regional economic and trading system. And for all the talk of Israel's importance as a cog in the Western economic and strategic system, a look at the map showed otherwise. In addition to this, Israel's population was slowly being transformed. The great mass of European Jews were now being supplemented by Jews from the Middle East. Like Rabin, they had lived and worked with Arabs.

Israel's alliance with the United States meant that it could maintain a strong military; but the ties between Israel and the United States placed enormous pressures on Israeli leaders. Rabin and his top Labor strategists uniformly resented the relationship that Shamir had struck up with American Jewish groups. The friendship was starting to wear thin, and Rabin was committed to doing what was best for Israel, regardless of the views held by the diaspora [the Jews living outside Palestine]. He wanted to strengthen the relationship, but on his terms.

Israel's forty-year existence was a cause for celebration, but Yitzhak Rabin knew that the fact of the state was no guarantee of its continued existence. For Israel to prosper, it had to reaffirm its central belief—that it would remain Jewish. The greatest threat to Israel in the aftermath of the Gulf War was not an attack by its enemies, but the slow absorption of some 1.7 million Palestinians in its midst. Any traveler to Tel Aviv, Haifa, or Ashkelon could have seen this in any restaurant or office building.

Already in 1993, it was painfully clear that the Jewish state was on the road to becoming a bilingual society, where Arabic was heard as often as Hebrew—even in the heart of the business district of Tel Aviv. It took only a marginal leap of the imagination to believe that forty, fifty, or one hundred years hence, but inevitably, Israel would have become a nation of Jews and Arabs living together, with a burgeoning and possibly majority Arab population. At that point, Israel would no longer be a Jewish state, but something else entirely.

Rabin believed that Israel was facing a major domestic catastrophe of its own. Successive aliyahs, the taking in (or, literally, "going up" to Israel) had built the Jewish state, but the constant, historical taking in of the world's diaspora Jews had ended. Rabin must have realized that the last aliyah, of Russian Jews, was the final aliyah. Israel could no longer count on other regimes to inadvertently build its population. The fear now was that there would be a massive movement of Israeli citizens leaving the country—a *yerida.*

"How much can you sacrifice before you become tired?" the Israeli woman Alya asked on her return trip to the adopted land that she loved, but was leaving. "How many years can you go on and on before you need some peace?"

No country—let alone Israel—can afford to allow such questions to remain unanswered.

While Palestinians and Israelis alike focused on Rabin's dramatic call for peace in his first speech to the Knesset on becoming prime minister in July 1992, Rabin himself returned to the theme of building a nation where people would want to live. "We want the new immigrants and our sons and daughters to find work, a livelihood, and a future in this country. We don't want Israel's main export to be our children," he said, then, later, repeated his special plea. "The homeless, families living in overcrowded conditions, and others overburdened by their mortgages will come first in our order of priorities. Israel will be not just a state; it will also be a home."

Few realized what Rabin was saying in July 1992, but in September of 1993, his vision for Israel became a reality; he wanted a Jewish state that was more than a refuge for the world's dispossessed and hunted Jewish population. He settled Israel's future course, finally, when he ordered the closing of the West Bank and Gaza. "Let them stay there," he said of the Palestinians. On September 13, he confirmed his belief by returning Israel, not just to its borders, but also to the ideals that had founded it.

Yitzhak Rabin's actions set aright the words of the prophet Jeremiah, the reputed author of the book of Lamentations, a series of dirges in the Hebrew Bible that tells of the destruction of Jerusalem by its enemies. The elegy is for a people in agony who, the author implies, had lost their land through the "iniquities" of its leaders. Seeing this, "the Lord gave full vent to his wrath, he poured out his hot anger; and he kindled a fire in Zion, which consumed its foundations."

Yitzhak Rabin would surely agree with Benny Begin's cry: "We are not a nation of victims." But he would also expand the thought: "We are not a nation of victims —nor are we a nation of oppressors."

The Palestinians were facing their own set of facts. The PLO was bankrupt and divided. Yasser Arafat was under fire from his top aides, and criticism of his leadership was mounting in every part of the Palestinian community. Hamas [an Islamic guerrilla group that was formed over 40 years ago] was gaining strength and, while it was evident that it could never totally control the political environment of the occupied territories, its growing credibility provided a daunting challenge to Palestinian moderates.

Arafat needed to maintain PLO dominance in an uncertain political environment, but he couldn't. The PLO was failing. Knowing that the leadership of the territories was incapable of reaching an agreement with Israel and that Hamas was unwilling, Arafat acted on their behalf. He was convinced that if he didn't, the PLO would die. With it would go the dream of a Palestinian state. He had no choice but to negotiate with Israel.

Arafat, like Rabin, was being pushed to extremes by his own diaspora community. When the PLO chairman journeyed to Washington, Palestinian leaders in Syria and Lebanon condemned the agreement and vowed to overturn it. Just as a small group of conservatives in pro-Israel organizations in America condemned Rabin for being naive, so Arafat's opposition denounced him for selling out to "the Zionists." There was a curious dynamic at work in both cases, a kind of "diaspora mentality" that placed Jews and Palestinians not living in the lands of the former Mandate in an uncomfortable association.

Jews and Palestinians who oppose the agreement indignantly resent the notion that they have anything in common with each other. But a look at the position they share shows otherwise. The salient feature of the "diaspora mentality" is that it rejects compromise in favor of continued confrontation, and advocates the realization of maximalist dreams: a fight to the death for Eretz Yisra'el; all of Palestine or nothing for the Palestinians. The only requirement is that someone else do the fighting.

Neither Rabin nor Arafat was so removed from the harsh realities of war that he could afford to choose this extreme position. Rabin had seen men die in battle and he was thoroughly sick of it, while Arafat had had more than twenty years of "nothing at all." Both realities led to Oslo, and then to Washington.

Will it work? Will the one-hundred-year war for the land of Palestine end? Will Israelis and Palestinians learn to live together? There is no certain answer to the question, and no way to predict the future. But there is a hint, and a clue on how the two sides might cast their lot together.

Not so long ago the Soviet empire crumbled and washed away. The collapse set loose the stored creative energies of millions of people in the former lands of the USSR and in Eastern Europe. One of them, the writer Milan Kundera, reflected on a generation of men and women who had lost their past. The simple act of remembering the past, investigating and researching it, and writing its true history, he suggested, is a political act of liberation. "The struggle of man against power," he wrote, "is the struggle of memory against forgetting."

The Palestinians and Israelis have a different problem. If they are to get along in the future, they have to go on without looking back. Ideas must triumph over beliefs. The struggle of man against hatred is the struggle for the future against remembering. The Eastern Europeans have to retrieve the past, but the Palestinians and the Israelis have to forget it.

NO

Edward W. Said

PEACE AND ITS DISCONTENTS

INTRODUCTION

... In the past I spoke out for peace *and* Palestinian rights *and* against Israeli practices. All of a sudden the major Palestinian leader, Yasir Arafat, signed an agreement with Israel (under United States sponsorship), and I found myself criticizing the so-called peace, as well as the PLO and its titular head. Besides, there was no ready constituency in either the West or the Arab world for views that questioned and steadily went counter to the ready mood of relief and supposed peace. In time, however, more and more readers were won over, and now, in the general despair and disrepair, people have at last begun to ask questions, express opposition, challenge the clammy embrace of Arafat, [Israeli Prime Minister Yitzhak] Rabin, and their apparatchiks, enforcers, and sophists.

My contention in this [selection] is that from the secret negotiations in Oslo between the PLO and Israel to the Israeli-Jordanian agreement proclaimed in Washington, and after, there has run a clear and, to me, unnecessary line of Arab capitulation by which Israel has achieved all of its tactical and strategic objectives at the expense of nearly every proclaimed principle of Arab and Palestinian nationalism and struggle. Thus Israel has gained recognition, legitimacy, acceptance from the Arabs without in effect conceding sovereignty over the Arab land, including annexed East Jerusalem, captured illegally by war. Without declared international boundaries, Israel is now the only state in the world to be recognized as "legitimate and secure" by its neighbors: the formula is unprecedented. Always disunited and dithering, the Arabs have simply lost the will to resist. They now hope to gain acceptance from the United States and Israel by negotiations begun through an act of abjection that betrayed both the cause of liberation and the people—Arabs, Jews, and others—who sacrificed their lives on its behalf.

Though I live and write in New York, at a great distance from the Middle East, I have never been far away from the Arab world in which I was born and grew up. In 1948 my entire family became refugees from Palestine. We lived variously in Egypt (where I spent my youth), Lebanon, Jordan, and the United

States. Whether I wanted it or not, the fate of the exiled and dispossessed Palestinian people has been my fate too, although my circumstances have been very fortunate in comparison with those who are still stateless and under military occupation. On the other hand, I think it is also true that distance gives one a perspective and a certain freedom by which to see and judge matters that might be imperceptible or difficult to assess by those who live in the midst of rapidly unfolding events. I have always believed that there could not be a military solution to the Arab-Israeli, and in particular the Palestinian-Zionist, conflict. I sincerely believe in reconciliation between peoples and cultures in collision, and have made it my life's work to try to further that end. But true reconciliation that can bring real peace can only occur between equals, between partners whose independence, strength of purpose, and inner cohesion allows them fully to understand and share with the other.

In the present situation Israel has managed to convince the Arabs, and in particular the exhausted Palestinian leadership, that equality is impossible, that only peace on Israeli terms and those dictated by the United States is possible. Years of unsuccessful wars, empty bellicosity, unmobilized populations, and incompetence and corruption at every level bled the life out of our societies, already crippled by an almost total absence of participatory democracy and the hope that goes with it. We must all take the blame for this colossal failure. Blessed with enormous human and natural resources, the Arab world has declined in production in nearly every sphere: during the last decade the gross national product has shrunk, agricultural output has grown smaller, reserves of money and resources have dwindled, and a whole series of civil wars (Lebanon, the Gulf, Yemen, Sudan, Algeria) have sapped much of the vitality of our societies. Contemporary Arab contributions to the advancement of science and research are practically nonexistent, as they are to international discourse in the humanities and social sciences. Our best writers, intellectuals, and artists are either silenced and tamed or imprisoned and in exile. Arab journalism is at an all-time low. Unpopular opinions are rarely expressed, and in nearly every society the media exist basically to further the regime's own version of reality. Yet no countries on earth possess more durable systems of government and power; they have resisted major changes for almost two generations. Little of this can be blamed on imperialism or Zionism. The big question for all of us to answer is, Why have we tolerated such an unacceptable state of affairs for so long?

Not surprisingly then, Arab ruling elites, the Palestinians' included, have succumbed not so much to America but to the myth of America. I have often been shocked and amused to note how little "America" is really known in the Arab world at the same time that reams of attacks and analyses of America and the West provide Arab readers with large amounts of disinformation and crude misrepresentation. These have increased since the end of the Cold War. Moreover, it is assumed that since the United States is the only remaining superpower, we must accept its edicts and follow it pronouncements literally. Along with this there often goes a paradoxically blind hostility to the United States, as if America and Americans are reducible to extremely simple stereotypes. Regrettably, a slave mentality prevails among Arab leaders, for whom a favorable reception in Washington is the summit of their political lives. Little note is taken of how American politics and society actually functions; even less is known about America's dealings with the Third World —where its record is positively disgraceful—or how its internal crises have a bearing on foreign policy. Thus the pax Americana envisaged by the Middle East "peace process" has been supinely accepted by the Arabs, without adequate coordination between them or real preparation for the details and outcome of the process.

It it amazing to me that what little is known about the United States rests on several invalid and finally inadequate assumptions. The main one is the U.S. policy is beneficial to the Arab people. Yasir Arafat, for example, persists in speaking of his "friend" Bill Clinton, even as (like all his recent predecessors) that "friend" supports Israel unconditionally, has refused to condemn Israeli settler violence, and has not lifted a finger in favor of Palestinian (to say nothing of the PLO's) well-being. From late 1993 to early 1994, when Israeli troops partly evacuated and partly redeployed in Gaza, Congress voted $180 million to assist Israel in those moves, in addition to the nearly $5 billion given annually. Not only does America still officially consider the PLO a terrorist organization but it opposes Palestinian statehood and under Clinton has changed its policy to accommodate Israel's annexation of Jerusalem and the expansion of its over 200 illegal settlements. Official PLO assessments of Israel—whose prime minister is given endless certificates of confidence by the ever-pliant Arafat— are just as foolish and ill-founded. Yet there has never been a coordinated Arab information and cultural policy aimed at addressing the American people, many of whom oppose their government's Middle East policy.

Nowhere have such incongruities been more in evidence than in Palestine, whose cause I served as a member of the Palestine National Council beginning in 1977. In 1991 I resigned from its ranks: I had just been diagnosed with a serious illness, but I had also felt that the terms we accepted for going to Madrid were disastrous. I had voted for the two-state solution at our 1988 Algiers meeting. I could see in 1991, however, not only that the gains of the *intifada* were about to be squandered but that Arafat and a few of his closest advisers had already decided on their own to accept anything that the United States and Israel might throw their way, just in order to survive as part of the "peace process." The major losses incurred by the misguided policies of the PLO leadership during the Gulf crisis, and by the constant mismanagement of funds and assets that were never accounted for, caused the PLO leadership in a panic to concede every single national aim and legal principle to the so-called interim solution proposed by Yitzhak Shamir and seconded by George Bush and James Baker. We received no acknowledgment of self-determination, no certainty of future sovereignty, no right of representation, no mention of reparations (and this from a state which received billions of dollars from Germany for the Nazi Holocaust).

And if that was not bad enough, the Oslo Declaration of Principles celebrated on the White House lawn on September 13, 1993, was actually a good deal worse. For the first time in our history, our leadership had simply given up on self-determination, Jerusalem, and the refugees, allowing them to become part of an undetermined set of "final status negotiations." For the first time in our recent past, we accepted the division of our people—whose unity we had fought for as a national movement since 1948 —into residents of the Occupied Territories and all the others, who happen today to constitute over 55 percent of the Palestinian population; they exist in another, lesser category not covered by the peace process. For the first time in the twentieth century, an anticolonial liberation movement had not only discarded its own considerable achievements but made an agreement to cooperate with a military occupation before that occupation had ended, and before even the government of Israel had admitted that it was in effect a government of military occupation. (To this day Israel has refused to concede that it is an occupying power.) We now also know that the Palestinian side had no legal consultants to help it conclude a binding international agreement, that its tiny handful of secret negotiators were untrained, poorly educated, and unmandated "guerrilla" leaders who ignored Palestine National Council resolutions as they set about dismantling the whole structure of Palestinian resistance without a decent map, without any real command of the facts and figures, without any serious attention to what Israel was all about and what the Palestinian people's interest dictated.

Subsequent events and agreements have proved my views correct, although I wish that I had been wrong. When it was announced, I considered the Oslo Declaration to be an instrument of capitulation, and when I was invited by President Clinton's office to attend the White House ceremony, I refused, saying

that for all Palestinians September 13 ought to be a day of mourning. Since that signing, the record speaks for itself. Of course we have failed as a people in our struggle to restore our rights. Israel has maintained its settlement and very partially redeployed its army. It controls land, water, security, and foreign policy for the Palestinian "self-rule" authority. But what made the American peace process and its celebrations so vulgar and distasteful was that all along the Palestinian leadership has pretended that it won a great victory, and that its deal with Israel gave us real independence. When Israel still has the right to control exits and entrances to Gaza and Jericho, when it must approve all laws passed and appointments made, we can hardly speak of independence. How much more dignified and admirable it would have been to admit defeat and ask the Palestinian people to rally in order to try to rebuild from the ruins.

In all this one imperative kept me at my desk: the need to tell the truth and not to let the language of hypocrisy, flattery, and self-delusion rule. Most Palestinians, I am convinced, feel the utter indignity of our situation. Israeli soldiers prevent our people from traveling on what is supposed to be our territory, kill innocent civilians, torture prisoners to death, steal their land, imprison them, and destroy their houses and vineyards while Yitzhak Rabin and Shimon Peres flaunt their new victories as successes of peace and humanity. But what has seemed to me most troubling is the absence of a language that is critical and responsible at the same time. Why do PLO representatives say one thing in private (for example, that Arafat is a megalomaniac) and its exact opposite on television? Why don't our intellectuals feel it their duty to tell the truth about the pitfalls of Gaza–Jericho and to say that we have signed an agreement that gives Israel control over our affairs with *our cooperation?* Perhaps too many of us have internalized the norms prevailing in most of the Arab world, that you must always serve a master, that you must defend your patron and attack his enemy, and that you must be careful not to harm your chances of a good career and a handsome reward. Language has been degraded into slogans and clichés.

To some extent, this insecurity is the result of the moral and intellectual penetration of our ranks by Israel and the United States, so that it becomes the goal of an Arab or Palestinian intellectual not so much to struggle for the independence of his or her people but to be accepted by Israeli politicians and academics, or to get a grant from the European community, or to be invited to a conference in Paris or New York. What one misses in current Arab and Palestinian culture is a moral and intellectual standard by which truth and falsehood can be distinguished and according to which intellectuals act regardless of profit or patronage. Perhaps the Islamic resurgence with which I am not in sympathy speaks to that lack.

The omens for the future are not good. Shortly after Yasir Arafat entered Gaza in early July 1994, it was reliably reported that five, or six, or maybe even seven intelligence services (many of them affiliated with the Shin Bet and Mossad) were reporting to him; since that time the number has increased to *nine!* People have been tortured to death. Newspapers have been closed. His opponents are being rounded up. And still he rules, and most of his people either endure that rule silently or try to get a position in it. His appointments have been an in-sult not just to the present but also to the past. He appoints his former ambassador to Tunis, a man whose office was penetrated by the Mossad in 1992, as overall coordinator of intelligence and security. The military commander of Jericho is the very man accused in 1982 for desertion and cowardice in South Lebanon. Reports of large-scale corruption involving various international crooks emanate from PLO headquarters. And, despite having himself signed every agreement he made with Israel, Arafat declares to the world that he is "frustrated" and "humiliated" by Israel. What did he expect when he signed an agreement with his people's oppressor, and when he canceled that people's past and its future rights, as well as its present hopes?

Well-meaning critics have suggested to me that I have made my critique of the Palestinian scene too personal, and that I have unfairly concentrated on the personality and indeed the person of Yasir Arafat. Partly because of our history of being colonized, our tragedy as a people and as a movement is that we have few institutions, no civil society, no properly constituted process of accountability and redress. What we have instead is an all-powerful ruler who survives despite a seemingly unending record of failure. The major benefits of the Gaza–Jericho agreement is that it restored Arafat and a small band of cronies to relative power and authority; this may serve the peculiar purposes of the "peace process," but it does not serve Palestinian interests.

There are chaos and desperation in Gaza and Jericho today. Surely the Israelis are glad to be rid of Gaza (Rabin openly said that he wished Gaza would sink into the sea, so great were its problems, so unruly its people), crowing as they watch an ill-equipped, understaffed, woefully incompetent Palestine National Authority struggling unsuccessfully to keep hospitals open and supplied, pay teachers' salaries, pick up garbage, and so on. And all this with the same aging former *feda'i* totally in charge, unwilling to delegate authority, postponing elections, ranting and railing at the absence of money, leading to the demand that he safeguard Israel's security, crush his opponents, act as Gaza's new military governor.

I remain convinced that reforming Yasir Arafat is impossible. He fulfilled his functions as Palestinian leader until the September 13 signing, which is entirely his achievement and responsibility. There is no doubt that today Israel, the United States, the Europeans, and the Arabs need him: his presence in Gaza testifies to the durability of an agreement that ensures Palestinian dependence and subservience. That is why it has so much international support. Gaza may slowly acquire a successful separate independence, although in April 1995 Arafat turned down Shimon Peres's suggestion that it be made an independent state. But now that Jordan has signed its own agreement with Israel, we can be certain that a tiny West Bank Palestinian protectorate or Bantustan, sandwiched between the two new allies, will be ground further and further down. Poverty and the absence of any sort of real independence will be its continued fate, although ironically of course the Israelis hold Arafat responsible for enforcing the peace and for assuring the "security" of over 300,000 Israeli settlers (including those in East Jerusalem), many of them violent and abetted by the army in their crimes. In the meantime, according to Israeli figures, 20,000 more acres of Palestinian land have been expropriated or designated "security" areas since September 1993.

Other than that it seems obvious that the leadership that signed an agreement with the Israeli occupation really must remove itself, or be removed by some sort of election procedure. I believe it is impossible to argue or act on the flawed premise that these peace agreements with Israel represent a beginning on which we can build for the future. How can such agreements as the May 4 Cairo treaty succeed except in *further* legalizing Israeli control over the Occupied Territories? I agree that these agreements constitute a new reality, but what we now need is an open debate by all Palestinians and concerned Arabs on the future of our region. I should think that non-Israeli and Israeli Jews, as well as Americans and Europeans with a commitment to real peace in the Middle East, ought to feel a part of that debate. We Palestinians must still reconcile ourselves with our history, and with the perhaps futile sacrifices of the past century. And we must restore Palestine to its place not simply as a small piece of territory between the Mediterranean Sea and the Jordan River but as *an idea* that for years galvanized the Arab world into thinking about and fighting for social justice, democracy, and a different kind of future than the one that has been imposed on it by force and by an absence of Arab will.

In a very modest way, therefore, this [selection] is meant to stir up debate and to open up discussion. I am neither a political scientist nor a prophet with a new vision. I would like, however, to try to say things that need to be said but have not been, and to ask questions that others, living close to the tumultuous events of the past two years, have been perhaps unable to raise.

I believe we need to connect, rather than forget, the years of sacrifice and struggle with both the present and future. I should also like here to suggest that no society can go forward without ideas and values to guide it. It is simply not enough to say that we live in the New World Order, which requires "pragmatism" and "realism," and that we must shed the old ideas of nationalism and liberation. That is pure nonsense. No outside power like Israel or the United States can unilaterally decree what reality is, any more than a tiny handful of local leaders can say, Yes, those are our new ideas and we shall go along with them obediently. These are matters for intellectuals, concerned citizens, and partisans from within our society to contribute to, and if I have any hopes for this [selection] they are, first, that it will supply a truthful record of what the great changes in our area have wrought and, second, that it might serve as a starting point for a debate on our collective future.

Certainly the shape of that future is formed by American and Israeli power. The peace process will grant Israel what it has wanted from the Arabs, an unequivocal legitimacy as a state built on the ruins of an Arab society and, perhaps more important, an opportunity, with the United States, to enter and benefit from a vast new Arab market. There is much talk of a Middle East common market; of cooperation in joint ventures between Western capital, Israeli know-how, and Arab labor and consumer appetites. Trade and tourism are touted as eradicators of barriers. Harmony and friendship, perhaps even a bit of democracy for the oppressed and downtrodden, are projected for the future. How all this is supposed to occur in a region where the wounds of war and conflict still fester, where refugees stagnate in camps, where millions are denied the right to vote in meaningful elections, where women, the poor, minorities, and the gifted are still treated as lesser human beings, and where the governments offer little inkling of how it is they are going to convert a culture of hostility and belligerence into one of peace and openness: all this is not talked about or debated.

As for Israel and the Palestinians, we can speculate as to whether their agreement can survive in its current form. Will Palestinians in the Occupied Territories long endure the servility and incompetence of their leaders as well as the continued unfairness of an occupation regime and its vast web of colonial settlements? Can Arafat last in his people's eyes as simply another Arab despot, albeit one working hand in glove with the very state that destroyed his people's society and has enslaved and persecuted their survivors? Will the Gaza–Jericho enclaves collapse under the pressures of poverty and hopelessness? Will a new vision, a new leadership rise from Palestinian ranks to project renewed hope and determination? These are questions no one can answer now. But what we can say is that no scheme, no plan, no deal, no imposed "peace process," no matter how powerful, can completely destroy our alternatives. I feel that as Palestinians we must have faith in ourselves as a people with important resources of hope. And as Palestinians and Arabs we must remember that our desire to coexist in peace with each other and with our neighbors is sustained not by blind loyalty to one or two personalities and their rhetoric, but by an abiding faith in real justice and real self-determination.

POSTSCRIPT

Will the Oslo Peace Accords Benefit Both Israelis and Palestinians?

Peace in the Middle East remains fragile. Both Israeli and Palestinian leaders are pushed toward extremes by scattered diaspora communities of true believers, who tend to reject compromise and prefer confrontation as a way to achieve goals. After Rabin's assassination, the new Israeli prime minister, Benjamin Netanyahu, faced strong challenges. Arafat remains titular head of the PLO, but he has had difficulty controlling the actions of the more radical Hamas group. Israel was carved out of land that in recent history belonged to Arabs; and, for Jews, the creation of the state of Israel was the fulfillment of God's gift of the promised land. With such ancient and historical contentions, the making of peace cannot be expected to run smoothly. Perhaps the strongest challenge and the greatest necessity is for people on both sides to forget the past in order to craft a habitable present.

For historical context, David Fromkin's *A Peace to End All Peace: The Fall of the Ottoman Empire and the Creation of the Modern Middle East* (Avon Books, 1989) provides excellent background on this issue. In *Palestinians: The Making of a People* (Harvard University Press, 1994), Baruch Kimmerling of the Hebrew University of Jerusalem and Joel S. Migdal of the University of Washington contend that the concept of the "Palestinian People" arose in response to pressures exerted by Zionism. The key challenge is knitting this group of people into a functioning, politically unified society. Further amplification of Said's thesis that without political independence there can be neither sovereignty nor real political freedom for the Palestinian people may be found in his *The Politics of Dispossession: The Struggle for Palestinian Self-Determination, 1969–1993* (Pantheon Books, 1994).

In the Land of Israel by Amos Oz (Harcourt Brace, 1983) is based on interviews with people who live in Jerusalem and in the surrounding mountainous regions. Oz was born in Jerusalem in 1939 and currently lives in Israel's Negev desert. He calls the conflict "a clash between right and right, between one very strong case and another." As a veteran of the 1967 and 1973 wars, Oz is encouraged that the struggle is no longer cast in theological or racial terms but is instead recognized as a dispute over real estate. Broadcast journalist David Dolan disagrees. In *Israel at the Crossroads: Fifty Years and Counting* (Fleming H. Revell, 1998), originally published as *Holy War for the Promised Land,* Dolan, a Christian who has lived in Israel since 1980, blames Islam for fueling the conflict.

CONTRIBUTORS
TO THIS VOLUME

EDITORS

JOSEPH R. MITCHELL is a history instructor at Howard Community College in Columbia, Maryland. He also teaches for the Evergreen Society, a branch of the Johns Hopkins University's Continuing Studies Program. He received an M.A. in history from Loyola College in Maryland and an M.A. in African American History from Morgan State University, also in Maryland.

HELEN BUSS MITCHELL is a professor of philosophy and director of the women's studies program at Howard Community College in Columbia, Maryland. She is the author of *Roots of Wisdom: Speaking the Language of Philosophy* and *Roots of World Wisdom: A Multicultural Reader*. Both books were published by Wadsworth Publishing Company and are now in their second editions. She has also created, scripted, and hosted a philosophy telecourse, *For the Love of Wisdom,* which has been distributed throughout the country by PBS. She has received numerous degrees, including a Ph.D. in women's history from the University of Maryland.

AUTHORS

RICHARD E. W. ADAMS is a professor of anthropology at the University of Texas at San Antonio. He is also director of the Rio Azul Archeological Project.

KAREN ARMSTRONG teaches at the Leo Baeck College for the Study of Judaism and the Training of Rabbis and Teachers in London, England. An honorary member of the Association of Muslim Social Sciences, her published works include *Beginning the World* (St. Martin's Press, 1983) and *Holy War* (Macmillan, 1988).

GEORGE B. N. AYITTEY is a professor of economics at the American University in Washington, D.C. He is the author of *African Institutions* (Transnational, 1991) and *Africa in Chaos* (St. Martin's Press, 1998).

KATHRYN A. BARD is an assistant professor of archaeology at Boston University. She received her Ph.D. in Egyptian archaeology from the University of Toronto.

ANNE LLEWELLYN BARSTOW is professor of history, retired, at the State University of New York at Old Westbury, New York. She is the author of *Joan of Arc: Heretic, Mystic, Shaman* (Edwin Mellen Press, 1986).

MARY R. BEARD (1876–1958), the founder of the World Center for Women Archives, was a leading suffragist and participant in the labor movement. She coauthored with her husband Charles many works in American history, and she is the author of *A Short History of the American Labor Movement* (Greenwood Press, 1924).

RUTH BENEDICT (1887–1948) was one of the twentieth century's leading anthropologists. Her major work, *Patterns of Culture* (Houghton Mifflin, 1934), has become a classic in the field.

JOHN BOSWELL (1947–1994) was A. Whitney Griswold professor of history at Yale University. He is the author of *The Kindness of Strangers: The Abandonment of Children in Western Europe from Late Antiquity to the Renaissance* (Pantheon Books, 1988).

ROBIN BRIGGS is a senior research fellow of All Souls College and a university lecturer in modern history.

CHRISTOPHER R. BROWNING is professor of history at Pacific Lutheran University. He is the author of three books and numerous articles on the subject of Holocaust studies, as well as a contributor to Yad Vashem's official twenty-four volume history of the Holocaust.

RACHEL CASPARI is a teacher and researcher at the University of Michigan. She coauthored with Milford Wolpoff *Race and Human Evolution: A Fatal Attraction* (Simon & Schuster, 1997).

GEORGE L. COWGILL is a professor of anthropology at the University of Arizona. He is coeditor, with Norman Yoffee, of *The Collapse of Ancient States and Civilizations* (University of Arizona Press, 1988).

CLINTON CRAWFORD is an assistant professor in the Department of Literature, Communication and Philosophy at Medgar Evers College, City University of New York. His field of specialization is African arts and languages as communication systems.

JOHN L. ESPOSITO is a professor of religion and international affairs at Georgetown University in Washington, D.C., and director of the Center for Muslim-Christian Understanding at Georgetown University's Edmund A. Walsh School of Foreign Service. His publications include *Islam and Democracy* (Oxford University Press, 1996).

JOHN KING FAIRBANK (1901–1991) taught modern Chinese history at Harvard University from 1936 to 1977. He was recognized as one of the nation's leading scholars on Chinese history.

STEVEN FEIERMAN is a professor in and chair of the department of the history and sociology of science at the University of Pennsylvania in Philadelphia. He is the author of many works, including *Peasant Intellectuals* (University of Wisconsin Press, 1990) and *The Social Basis of Health and Healing in Africa* (University of California Press, 1991).

FELIPE FERNÁNDEZ-ARMESTO is a writer who specializes in works on the Age of Exploration. His works include *Before Columbus* (University of Pennsylvania Press, 1987) and *The Spanish Armada* (Oxford University Press, 1988).

RONALD C. FINUCANE is professor of history at Oakland University in Rochester, Michigan. He is the author of *Soldiers of the Faith: Crusaders and Moslems at War* (St. Martin's Press, 1984).

JOHN LEWIS GADDIS is Robert Lovett Professor of History at Yale University. He has contributed extensively to cold war historiography and has authored at least six major works on the subject.

DANIEL JONAH GOLDHAGEN is a professor of government and social studies at Harvard University. He is the author of *Hitler's Willing Executioners: Ordinary Germans and the Holocaust* (Alfred A. Knopf, 1996), for which he was awarded the Democracy Prize by Germany's *Journal for German and International Politics*.

N. G. L. HAMMOND is professor emeritus of Greek at Bristol University in England and an honorary fellow of Clare College at Cambridge University. He is the author of *Alexander the Great: King, Commander, and Statesman* (Noyes Press, 1981).

CHARLES HOMER HASKINS (1870–1937) was a history professor and dean of the Graduate School of Arts and Sciences at Harvard University. He is the author of *Studies in the History of Mediaeval Science* (Harvard University Press, 1927).

ALBERT HOURANI is an emeritus fellow of St. Antony's College at the University of Oxford. His publications include *The Emergence of the Modern Middle East* (University of California Press, 1981) and *Islam in European Thought* (Cambridge University Press, 1991).

THOMAS M. HUBER is a historian for the United States Army. He is the author of *Strategic Economy in Japan* (Westview Press, 1994).

DENIS JUDD is professor of history at the University of North London and is a fellow of the Royal Historical Society. He is the author of *Evolution of the Modern Commonwealth* (Macmillan, 1982).

JOAN KELLY-GADOL (1928–1982) was a Renaissance scholar and theorist in women's history. Her works include *Leon Battista Alberti: Universal Man of the Early Renaissance* (University of Chicago Press, 1969).

PETER KROPOTKIN (1842–1921) was a Russian revolutionary who wrote his autobiography *Memoirs of a Revolutionist* in 1899.

STEVEN MAJSTOROVIC is an assistant professor of political science at Duquesne University in Pittsburgh, Pennsylvania.

HANS EBERHARD MAYER is professor of medieval and modern history at the University of Kiel, Germany.

ALI A. MAZRUI is director of the Institute of Global Cultural Studies at the State University of New York at Binghamton, as well as the Ibn Khaldun Professor-at-Large at the School of Islamic and Social Sciences in Leesburg, Virginia. His books include *Cultural Forces in World Politics* (Heinemann, 1990).

ROBIN McKIE is science editor of the *London Observer*.

WILLIAM H. McNEILL taught history at the University of Chicago from 1947 to 1987. He served as president of the American Historical Association in 1981 and received the Erasmus Prize from the Dutch government in 1996.

MEHDI NAKOSTEEN is a contributor to *Encyclopedia Britannica* and a former professor of history and philosophy of education at the University of Colorado. He received his Ph.D. from Cornell University. He has written several books and articles on education, including *The History and Philosophy of Education* (Ronald Press, 1965).

FRANÇOISE NAVAILH is a Russian film historian at the University of Paris. She teaches Russian language and is a specialist in Russian cinema.

MARK PERRY is a journalist who has written for many journals, magazines, and newspapers.

PHILIP LYNDON REYNOLDS is director of the Aquinas Center of Theology at Emory University. He is the author of *Marriage in the Western Church: The Christianization of Marriage During the Patristic and Early Medieval Periods* (Brill Academic Publishers, 1994).

E. E. RICE is senior research fellow at Wolfson College at Oxford and lecturer in classical archaeology at Herford College at Oxford. She is a specialist in military history, topography, and the social history of the Greek world in the Hellenistic period.

EDWARD W. SAID is one of the Arab world's leading intellectuals and scholars, having written more than a dozen books. His works include *Orientalism* (Pantheon Books, 1978) and *Culture and Imperialism* (Alfred A. Knopf, 1993).

KIRKPATRICK SALE is a writer for *The Nation* and the author of many books. He is also a founder of the Green Party.

SIMON SCHAMA is a professor of art and art history at Columbia University. He is the author of *The Embarrassement of Riches: An Interpretation of Dutch Culture During the Golden Age* (Alfred A. Knopf, 1987) and *Landscape and Memory* (Alfred A. Knopf, 1995).

JOAN W. SCOTT is a professor of social science at Princeton University's Institute for Advanced Study. She is the author of *Gender and the Politics of History* (Columbia University Press, 1988).

MARTIN J. SHERWIN is Walter S. Dickson Professor of History at Tufts University and the director of the University's Nuclear Age History and Humanities Center. He is the author of *A World Destroyed: The Atomic Bomb and the Grand Alliance* (Random House, 1977).

EDWARD SHORTER directs the history of medicine program at the University of Toronto. He is the author of *From the Mind into the Body* (Free Press, 1996) and *Psychiatry: From the Era of the Asylum to the Age of Prozac* (John Wiley & Sons, 1997).

JONATHAN D. SPENCE is the George Burton Adams Professor of History at Yale University. His published works include *God's Chinese Son* (W. W. Norton, 1996) and *The Chan's Great Continent: China in Western Minds* (W. W. Norton, 1998).

RICHARD STITES is a professor of history at Georgetown University. He is the author of *Revolutionary Dreams* (Oxford University Press, 1989) and *Russian Popular Culture* (Cambridge University Press, 1992).

CHRISTOPHER STRINGER is a principal researcher at London's Natural History Museum.

LOUISE A. TILLY is an assistant professor of history and director of the women's studies program at the University of Michigan. She is the author of numerous articles on social history.

KAREN JO TORJESEN is the Margo L. Goldsmith Chair of Women's Studies and Religion at Claremont Graduate School in California. She is also an associate of the Institute for Antiquity and Christianity.

LUISE WHITE wrote her doctoral dissertation for Cambridge University on the history of prostitution in Nairobi, Kenya. She currently teaches African history at Rice University in Houston, Texas.

MILFORD WOLPOFF is a professor of anthropology at the University of Michigan at Ann Arbor. He coauthored with Rachel Casperi *Race and Human Evolution: A Fatal Attraction* (Simon & Schuster, 1997).

WARREN ZIMMERMANN served as the last United States Ambassador to Yugoslavia and is retired from the Foreign Service. Currently, he is a professor of international diplomacy at Columbia University.

INDEX